ANCIENT GREECE

This sourcebook presents a wide range of documents on Greek social and political history from 800 BC to 399 BC, from all over the Greek world. Evidence for developments within Greece during this period is taken not only from historical sources, but from inscriptions, graffiti, law codes, epitaphs, decrees, drama and poetry. Each section covers sources not only from the Greek mainland, but also from Greek settlements as far apart as Sicily and Italy, Cyrene, Egypt, Thrace, Asia Minor and the Black Sea. The book is arranged thematically, and includes sections devoted to Sparta, tyranny, the position of women, slavery, colonization, the city-state and religion.

The documents have been clearly and accurately translated. Each is accompanied by detailed and succinct comments explaining the social and historical context and providing relevant, up-to-date bibliographies. Many passages appear here translated for the first time into English or any modern language.

Ancient Greece provides a lively and innovative look at the Greek world as a whole, with its emphasis on a wide range of evidence for Greek culture clearly proving that Ancient Greece consisted of far more than just Athens and Sparta.

Matthew Dillon and **Lynda Garland** are both lecturers at the University of New England, New South Wales.

ANCIENT GREECE

Social and Historical Documents
from Archaic Times to the Death of Socrates
(c. 800 – 399 BC)

Matthew Dillon

and

Lynda Garland

London and New York

First published 1994
by Routledge
11 New Fetter Lane, London EC4P 4EE

Simultaneously published in the USA and Canada
by Routledge
29 West 35th Street, New York, NY 10001

Printed and bound in Great Britain by
T.J. Press (Padstow) Ltd, Padstow, Cornwall

British Library Cataloguing in Publication Data
A catalogue record for this book is available from the British Library

Library of Congress Cataloging in Publication Data
A catalogue record for this book has been requested

ISBN 0–415–11366–0 (hbk)
ISBN 0–415–11367–9 (pbk)

For all our students —

past, present and future.

Contents

Preface

This work was originally intended as a sourcebook for use with the first unit of Ancient History offered by the Open Learning Agency of Australia, Ancient Greece: Early History, which we wrote in 1993. But in the event it has developed into a sourcebook aimed at undergraduate students of Greek history at all levels, with some uses also as a research tool for the reader interested in further study. The period covered is that of the Greek world from the archaic period to the end of the fifth century and the documents have been carefully chosen to reflect contemporary views of the main issues of political and social history within that period. Any sourcebook is naturally open to criticisms regarding the selection of material: the authors have attempted impartiality in their choice of topics and documents but inevitably some imbalance of emphasis has probably occurred. Nevertheless the main areas of Greek social and political history have been covered in depth, with especial focus on the manifestations in the archaic period of colonization and tyranny throughout the Greek world and Athenian politics in the sixth century. The history of the classical period *per se* is represented by sections on the Persian Wars, the Delian League and Pentekontaetia and the Peloponnesian War, and Sparta's history and society in both archaic and classical times is covered by a separate section. These chapters, however, are also intended to be supplemented by the material in the so-called 'social' sections of this book. In these chapters on social history, we present a view of the realities of life in ancient Greece, with particular emphasis on the city-state and its relevance to Greek life and politics, labour, and the extent to which slaves, metics, serfs and citizens competed in the labour market, religion in all its manifestations, and women and sexual relationships in Greek society. The aim has been to give a wide range of material from contemporary sources, which will, if the authors' aim is achieved, be more than sufficient for study at an undergraduate level.

Since this book is intended to give a view of the Greek world as a whole, where possible documents have been chosen not relating simply to Athens and Sparta but to the lesser known centres of Greek civilization and culture and the aim has been to keep the reader continually in mind of the geographical and chronological scope of Greek history and civilization. A book covering so broad a subject must inevitably suffer from incompleteness in some areas, and we have had to limit not merely the topics covered, but the number of texts illustrating each section. We can only hope that our choice of material does not appear too arbitrary, and have tried to ensure that we have given references throughout to other useful passages which will direct the student to further documents of relevance in the area. We have also given suggestions for further reading on particular points of importance and envisage that the chapter bibliographies will enable students to pursue detailed research on particular topics.

In our translations we have followed the Greek as closely as possible, even to punctuation where this does not involve confusion, and poetry is as far as possible translated in lines following those of the original text. Present in our minds has been the thought that this would be a suitable text for use in a unit on 'Greek for historians', and to that end we have made comparisons of the translations with the original sources as easy as possible. For this reason we have carefully inserted all chapter and section numbers of the original sources in the text of our translations. For those students who do not as yet have Greek, we can perhaps hope that this study of some of the more important documents of Greek history will inspire them to attempt to acquire the language. Titles of ancient sources are given in English, but references to the texts used in our translations can be found in the index of ancient sources. There is probably no way to avoid the pitfalls inherent in the transliteration of Greek names and terms into English. Where possible a literal transliteration has been preferred, except where the names and terms might be thought to be better known to the reader in an anglicised form. This naturally has involved some arbitrary judgements and appearance of inconsistency, of which the authors are aware.

Our thanks are particularly due to two of our colleagues for their help and support: Professor Trevor Bryce, now Deputy Vice-Chancellor of Lincoln University in New Zealand, and Mrs. Annette Ince, who has given us invaluable assistance with the formatting and presentation of this book. Our thanks are also due to Dixson Library, University of New England.

Armidale, NSW
June 1994

List of Tables and Maps

GENEALOGICAL TABLES

MAPS

Glossary

acropolis: citadel, highest part of a city
agoge: the Spartan system of education
agora: the market square, civic centre of a city state
agoranomoi: market magistrates at Athens
aisymnetes: an elected tyrant
Amphictyonic Council: representatives of the 12 states responsible for the upkeep and welfare of the sanctuary and games at Delphi
apoikia: a colony or settlement (plural: apoikiai)
architheoros: leader of a sacred embassy
archon: magistrate; the most important archonship in Athens was the eponymous archonship (the holder gave his name to the year)
Areiopagos: a hill west of the acropolis; the council of the Areiopagos which was composed of ex-archons met here
atimia: loss of citizen rights (adjective: atimos, plural: atimoi)
boule: the council of a city; the bouleteurion (council chamber) was its meeting place
choregos: a wealthy citizen who financed a dramatic chorus for a festival
demagogue: a popular leader or speaker (a fourth century term)
deme: a village; Kleisthenes divided Attica into 140 units called demes
demos: the people of a city, the citizens; sometimes the assembly
dikasterion: jury-court (plural: dikasteria)
dokimasia: scrutiny of a person's qualifications for office or citizenship
ekklesia: the assembly of adult male citizens
the Eleven: the police-commissioners at Athens
emporion: a trading station (plural: emporia)
ephor: a Spartan magistrate; 5 were elected annually
epimetelai: supervisors
epoptes: the highest grade of initiate at Eleusis (plural: epoptai)
eunomia: good order
eupatridai: nobles, aristocrats
euthyna: examination of an official's conduct or accounts at the end of his term (plural: euthynai)
genos: clan, group of families (plural: gene)
gerousia: council of 28 elders (gerontes) in Sparta plus the 2 kings
gnorimoi: the notables, wealthy
heliaia: a court (generally of appeal) at Athens
helot: Spartan serf
hetaira: courtesan, higher-class prostitute
hetaireia: club, association of citizens (plural: hetaireiai)
hieropoioi: sacred officials, temple overseers
hippeis: cavalry, the second of Solon's four property-classes

homoioi: 'equals': a term used in Sparta for full citizens
hoplite: heavy-armed infantryman
isonomia: equality of rights
kolakretai: Athenian financial officials
Lakedaimon: Sparta; the Spartans were known as Lakedaimonians
Lakonia: Sparta's immediate countryside; 'Lakonian' often means Spartan
liturgy: public duty imposed on wealthy citizens, such as financing a dramatic chorus or paying for the maintenance of a trireme for a year
medize: to support or collaborate with the Persians
metic: immigrant, foreign resident
mystagogos: someone who introduces others to the Eleusinian Mysteries
mystes: an initiate, especially at the Eleusinian Mysteries (plural: mystai)
oikistes: the founder of a colony (plural: oikistai)
oikos: a household (plural: oikoi)
Olympiad: the four-year period between one Olympic Games and the next
penestai: Thessalian serfs
pentakosiomedimnoi: the 500 bushel-class, the first of Solon's four property-classes
perioikoi: neighbours; peoples subject to Sparta in the Peloponnese
phoros: tribute contribution
phratry: brotherhood with social and religious associations
phyle: tribe; Kleisthenes organised the Athenians into 10 tribes (phylai)
polemarch: war leader, one of the archons in Athens
polis: city-state (plural: poleis)
politeia: constitution; or (by extension) citizenship
poletai: Athenian financial officials
prostates: champion, leader of a political party
prytany: one-tenth of the Athenian administrative year, during which the representatives of one of the ten tribes (the 50 prytaneis) presided in the boule and assembly; the prytaneion was the town hall
Pythia: the priestess at Delphi
rhapsode: a bard, minstrel
skolion: a drinking song (plural: skolia)
Spartiate: a full Spartan citizen
stasis: civil dissension, factional disturbance; a party or faction
stele: a slab; an inscription, such as a grave-stone or decree (plural: stelai)
strategos: general (plural: strategoi); strategia is the command
synoecism: the union of several towns to form a single state
syssitia: public messes at Sparta
theoria: sacred embassy
theoroi: sacred envoys
thetes: the lowest of Solon's four property-classes
the Thirty: the oligarchs who ruled Athens 404/3
tholos: round house; the headquarters of the prytaneis
trireme: a warship
trierarch: commander of a trireme
trittys: regional division of Attica (plural: trittyes)
tyrant: ruler with no hereditary right to rule
tyrannos: a tyrant (plural: tyrannoi)
zeugitai: the third of Solon's four property-classes

Some Useful Definitions

Athenian Months:

Hekatombaion (June/July)
Metageitnion (July/August)
Boedromion (August/Sept.)
Pyanopsion (Sept./Oct.)
Maimakterion (Oct./Nov.)
Posideion (Nov./Dec.)
Gamelion (Dec./Jan.)
Anthesterion (Jan./Feb.)
Elaphebolion (Feb./March)
Mounichion (March/April)
Thargelion (April/May)
Skirophorion (May/June)

The 10 Athenian Tribes in their Official Order:

Erechtheis (I)
Aigeis (II)
Pandionis (III)
Leontis (IV)
Akamantis (V)
Oineis (VI)
Kekropis (VII)
Hippothontis (VIII)
Aiantis (IX)
Antiochis (X)

Attic coinage:

6 obols (ob.) = 1 drachma (dr.)
100 dr. = 1 mina
2 minas = 1 stater
60 minas = 1 talent (T.)

Measurements of Capacity:

1 kotyle (jug) = 285cc
12 kotylai = 1 chous (3.4 litres)
12 choes = 1 metretes (41 litres)
192 kotylai = 1 medimnos (55 dry litres)

Measurements of Distance:

1 daktylos (finger) = approx. $^{7}/_{10}$ in; 1.9 cm.
24 daktyloi = 1 cubit (approx. 1 ft 5 in; 45 cm.)
1 orguia = 1 fathom (approx. 6 ft; 1.80 metres)
100 orguiai = 1 stade (approx. 606 ft; 180 metres)

Symbols Used in Documents:

( )	explanatory addition to text
[ ]	letters or words in inscriptions restored by modern scholars
[[ ]]	enclosed letters or words deliberately erased
< >	letters thought to have been accidentally omitted
v	vacant space for one letter in the original document
vv	vacant space for two or more letters in the original document
vacat	an entire line or space between entire lines left vacant
lacuna	portion of document missing
† †	dubious reading
F	fragment

1

Colonization

Greek history begins with the Mycenaean world, which comprised a chain of city states across mainland Greece inhabited by the historical originals of Homer's warlords. Shortly after the capture of Troy — if that was indeed a historical event — Greece was to enter a Dark Age until the eighth century and the dawn of the history of archaic Greece. But even in Mycenaean times, Greek states were not confined to the mainland. As early as the fifteenth century BC, there are records of Greeks in Western Anatolia (Asia Minor), and archaeology makes clear the fact that Greek expansion had already taken place, with evidence for settlements and trading centres along the Asia Minor coastline. From c. 1200 to 1000 a major wave of migration took place from mainland Greece to Asia Minor. Greece always comprised far more than just the well-known cities of the Greek mainland and from the eighth to the sixth century, sometimes known as the 'Age of Colonization', the Greeks of Asia Minor and the Greek mainland sent out large numbers of colonies, both east and west of their homeland. This, however, was not the only period during which colonies were settled, and Greek cities founded several important colonies in the fifth century and later. In this way, Sicily and Southern Italy, the Black Sea area, Africa, and even France and Spain, provided sites for new Greek cities.

The reasons behind colonization are frequently debated, but it appears that 'land-hunger', trading considerations, drought, and political problems at home were the primary social and economic factors that impelled cities to send out settlements elsewhere. Certainly many of the colonies in the west were inspired by the availability of agricultural land (doc. 1.10). While the specific choice of location for individual colonies, such as Pithekoussai (doc. 1.9), can still be the subject of much debate, good agricultural land in the vicinity would always have been an incentive, for colonists would have needed to be self-sufficient in food. Most colonies probably resulted from mixed motives; when the Phokaians established colonies in the far west, like the Teians in Thrace (doc. 1.11) they did so because they were fleeing from Persian domination. This provides a political explanation for their settlements, but it is also clear that the Phokaians both in Corsica and in Sicily made the most of opportunities for trading and for piracy. The Spartans founded Taras in south-east Italy in the late eighth century to solve the pressing political problem of the partheniai, who were clearly Spartan in origin but without political rights (doc. 1.18), but Dorieus' attempt to colonize Africa and Italy was in essence a private venture, for he left Sparta because his half-brother Kleomenes was made king (doc. 1.17). Later colonies, such as Herakleia in Trachis settled by Sparta in the fifth century, could have a partial political and strategic motive, for Herakleia was ideally suited as a base from which to attack Euboea (doc. 1.19; cf. 8.27). Nevertheless, it is important to realise how significant population size could be in Greek cities throughout this period: the people of Thera, when due to severe drought they drafted their colonists to settle Cyrene, cursed any of those who might attempt to return, and when they later did so attacked them and drove them away (docs. 1.24–25).

The Greeks, naturally, took their way of life with them, and founded cities which were similar to the cities which they had left. Colonists apparently took with them fire from their mother-city (metropolis) and thus established continuity with their homeland (doc. 1.3). Relationships in general remained strong between mother-cities and colonies, and even a colony of a colony could claim aid from the original mother-city, as Epidamnos did from Corinth, and mother-cities expected that their colonies would maintain links with them. Each city had an oikistes, a 'founder' (plural: oikistai), and sometimes more than one, whose role was to act as leader while the colony was being established. The tie of a colony with its mother-city was so important that when the colonies themselves sent out colonies, the oikistai for these were chosen from the original mother-city, as in the case of Epidamnos (doc. 1.7). When they founded colonies, the Greeks often had to fight the native inhabitants for the land which they desired (docs. 1.21–22, 25). But it is also clear that on other occasions the Greeks would compete against each other for sites, as the Athenians and Mytilenaeans did at Sigeion (doc. 1.15). There was often no feeling of mutual solidarity between Greek colonies even in areas where the locals were hostile, as in Sicily, and on the Black Sea coast Greeks dispossessed by later Greek settlers joined Scythian tribes, forming a Hellenic-Scythian culture (docs. 1.29–30). Yet in many cases it is apparent that the natives became partially hellenised, and that there was interaction between Greeks and natives (docs. 1.31–32).

Socrates' opinion of the Greek world is a significant one for any understanding of Greek civilisation. He is recorded by Plato as thinking of the Greeks as living around the shores of the Mediterranean and Black Sea like 'ants or frogs around a pond' (doc. 1.33). The Greeks inhabited a world which was not restricted to the Greek mainland and coastline of Asia Minor but which reached from Spain to the far end of the Black Sea. Colonization was an intrinsic part of Greek history from the eighth century, and one that had significant implications for the social, economic and military history of the Greek world.

For a list of important colonies with the dates which Eusebius gives for their foundation, see Cook (1946) 77; for a list of colonies and literary foundation dates and the date of the first archaeological evidence for Greek presence, see also Graham (1982a) 160–62 (and (1982b) 88, 96, and 114 for maps); Malkin (1987) xiv–xv (less detailed maps); for a list of the most important colonies in Italy and Sicily grouped according to founding cities, see Boardman (1980) 165; and note Forrest (1966) 72–73 for a map showing some of the main colonies and colonisers.

1.1 Ancient Foundation Stories of Cities

Xenophanes of Kolophon A1 (Diogenes Laertius 9.18, 20)

Numerous accounts of the foundation of colonies and other cities were written by ancient authors. Polybios wrote that his history would not appeal to those interested in colonies (apoikiai, singular: apoikia) or the foundations of cities (ktiseis, sing: ktisis), accounts of which could be found in the writings of Ephoros (Polyb. IX.1.4). Xenophanes wrote a ktisis for Kolophon, his native city, an Ionian city of Asia Minor founded c. 1200–1000, in a previous colonizing wave; Elea was a Phokaian colony in Italy settled c. 540.

9.18 He wrote both poems in epic verse and works in elegiacs and iambics against Hesiod and Homer, censuring the things they say about the gods .... **9.20** He also composed a poem called *The Foundation of Kolophon* and *The Settlement of the Colony of Elea in Italy*, comprising two thousand lines.

THE DELPHIC ORACLE

1.2 Delphi and Colonization

Lucian *Astrology* 23

Cf. Cicero *De Divinatione* I.3. Delphi played an important role in Greek colonization, but the view that Delphi was in any sense a 'think-tank', a repository of information about possible sites for colonies (as advocated by Pease (1917) 16–17, Forrest (1957) 174), is false and most mother-cities would have known their destination in advance. While it was important, by the fifth century, to ensure that the colony had the backing of Apollo at Delphi, there are no recorded foundation oracles for several colonies of the eighth and early seventh centuries. Pease argues (1917) 1–21, esp. 18–20, that when it later became normal for Delphi to be consulted about founding colonies, numerous oracles were forged by colonies to support their credentials. As Forrest (1957) 171–73 states, Delphi's role in early colonization was limited because the oracle did not take on a Panhellenic nature until later; in the eighth century only a few cities close to Delphi — Corinth and Chalkis — consulted the oracle. For Delphi's role in Greek colonization, see Pease (1917) 1–20; Parke & Wormell (1956) 49–81 (less useful); Forrest (1957) 160–75; Fontenrose (1978) 137–44, esp. 142–44; Malkin (1987) 17–29; Morgan (1990) 172–78.

The men of former times were very much given to divination and considered it by no means incidental, but would not found cities, or surround themselves with walls, or kill anyone, or get married, before they had learnt all the details from the seers.

1.3 The Sacred Fire

EM 694.28–31: s.v. Prytaneia

There is no explicit evidence from the classical period about the transfer of sacred fire from the mother-city to a colony, although this is generally accepted as having occurred. The evidence is late, such as this entry from the *Etymologicum Magnum* (*EM*). Malkin (1987) 114–34, however, discusses the available evidence, and reasonably concludes that the transfer of sacred fire from mother-city (metropolis) to colony was customary. The prytaneion (plural: prytaneia) was the town hall.

Prytaneia: The sacred fire is kept there; and those who are at any time setting out to a colony, from there light a fire from the hearth, that is they 'kindle it'.

THE OIKISTES

The oikistes or founder was the leader of the colonists in their enterprise; there could be more than one oikistes for each colony. In the eighth to sixth centuries the oikistes will presumably have remained in the colony; there are two fifth century examples, however, in which the oikistes set up the colony and then returned to the mother-city; see docs. 1.6, 1.19. For a discussion of the role of the oikistai, see Graham (1983) 29–39; for the consultation of the Delphic oracle by oikistai, see Morgan (1990) 173–75.

1.4 The Duties of an Oikistes

Homer *Odyssey* VI.1–12

This passage, despite its mythical setting, describes the main duties of the founder of a colony, the oikistes; it is discussed by Malkin (1987) 138. On land put aside for sanctuaries for the gods in colonies, see Malkin, 135–86; doc. 1.26. There is evidence, acquired through aerial photography, for the division of land into farms at Metapontum in Italy (the literary foundation date is 733, with the earliest archaeological evidence from c. 650); see Adamesteanu (1967) esp. 26–27; Graham (1971) 36, (1982b) 184–85.

So the much-enduring godlike Odysseus lay there asleep,
Worn out by sleep and toil; but Athena
Went to the land and city of the Phaeacian people,
Who long ago used to dwell in spacious Hypereia,
Near the Cyclopes an overbearing people,
Who used to plunder them, and were stronger than they.
Godlike Nausithoos removed them from there and led
And settled them in Scheria, far from hard-working men,
And he drew a wall around the city, and built houses,
And made temples to the gods, and divided up the corn-lands.
But already overpowered by fate he had gone to Hades,
And Alkinoos now ruled, who had counsel from the gods.

1.5 A Dedication to an Oikistes

Graham (1983) 21–22n.7

This inscription on a fragment of a fifth-century Attic kylix (wine-cup) found at Gela in Sicily indicates that the kylix was dedicated to Antiphemos (Antiphamos is the Doric form) of Rhodes, who founded Gela in 688. He did so in conjunction with the oikistes Entimos of Crete, ie there was an oikistes for each group involved in founding the city (Thuc. VI.4.3; Hdt. VII.153.1 mentions only Antiphemos). As Malkin (1987) 194–95 notes (cf. 259), the dedication indicates that the cult of an oikistes could survive in the colony well after his death; for a photo, see Malkin, frontispiece; note esp. Graham (1983) 21–22n.7. Miltiades the Elder was honoured with an annual festival after his death by the Greeks of the Chersonese (Hdt. VI.38.1); for other annual foundation ceremonies, see Athen. 149d (Naukratis); Callim. *Aetia* II F43, lines 50–64, 72–83; cf. doc. 1.26.

'Mnasithales dedicated (this) to Antiphamos.'

1.6 Oikistai at Amphipolis: Hagnon and Brasidas

Thucydides V.11.1

There were several attempts to settle the site of Amphipolis in Thrace. Aristagoras of Miletos, fleeing from Darius, attempted to settle there but was driven out by the Edonians. The Athenians, thirty-two years after this, sent out 10,000 colonists to 'Nine Ways' (Ennea Hodoi), as Amphipolis was then known, who drove out the Edonians, but who were destroyed by the Thracians at Drabeskos. Twenty-nine years later the Athenians made another attempt, this time successful, with Hagnon as oikistes (Thuc. I.100.3, IV.102; Diod. XII.68.2; Polyaen. *Strat.* VI.53; Schol. Aisch. II.31; cf. docs. 8.7, 8.27). This apoikia dates to 437/6 (Diod. XII.32.3), and the advantages of the site included its command of trade routes and an important crossing of the Strymon river; the district was also rich in timber, which Athens needed for her fleet, and in silver; see Meiggs (1972) 195–96; doc. 10.43. *IG* I^3 47 may represent the foundation decree for Amphipolis.

For Hagnon, who was one of the ten probouloi chosen after the disaster in Sicily (Lys. XII.65; doc. 9.24), and father of Theramenes (Thuc. VIII.68.4), see Graham (1983) 37–38; Pesely (1989) 191–209; Hagnon had returned to Athens by 430/29, and thus did not stay in the colony he had established. When the Amphipolitans surrendered their city to the Spartan Brasidas, who died in the battle with the Athenians outside the city in 422 (in which Socrates took part: Plat. *Apol.* 28e), the city felt that Hagnon would no longer benefit them as their oikistes. See Lewis (1992) 13, 145 for the foundation and site of the city; for Hagnon and Brasidas as oikistai, see Malkin (1987) 228–32.

V.11.1 After this all the allies with their weapons publicly attended and buried Brasidas in the city in front of what is now the agora; henceforward the Amphipolitans, after enclosing his tomb, sacrificed to him as a hero and gave him the honour of games and yearly sacrifices, and attributed the colony to him as founder, pulling down the buildings of Hagnon and getting rid of anything which might still survive as a reminder of his settlement. They considered that Brasidas had been their saviour (at the same time, they were at that point fostering the alliance with the Spartans through fear of the Athenians), and moreover that because they were at war with the Athenians Hagnon could no longer be honoured with similar benefit or contentment.

MOTHER-CITIES AND THEIR COLONIES

1.7 Corinth and her Colony Corcyra

Thucydides I.24.1–26.2

Corinth colonized Corcyra in the late eighth century and Corcyra had in turn colonized Epidamnos in 627, but the oikistes for this had come, as was customary, from Corcyra's own mother-city, Corinth. The passage clearly exemplifies the normal relationship between mother-city and colonies. **I.25.1**: Even the colony of a colony could claim aid from the original mother-city. **I.25.4**: Note the honours which a mother-city might expect (see also Thuc. I.38.3). For an earlier dispute between Corinth and Corcyra over a colony, see Plut. *Them.* 24.1; cf. Thuc. I.55.1. While some scholars have argued that colonies remained part of the mother-city in terms of citizenship, this view ought to be rejected: see Graham (1962) 246–52. **I.26.1**: Ambracia and Leukas were both Corinthian colonies established by the tyrant Kypselos; see Strab. X.2.8 (452), cf. VII.7.6 (325); Salmon (1984) 209–17; Syracuse was also a Corinthian foundation c. 733 (Thuc. VI.3.2).

I.24.1 Epidamnos is a city on the right as one sails into the Ionian gulf; Taulantian barbarians, an Illyrian race, dwell nearby. **I.24.2** The Corcyraeans colonized it, and its founder was Phalios, son of Eratokleides, a Corinthian from the family of the Herakleidai, who had been invited from the mother-city according to ancestral custom. Some Corinthians and others of the Dorian race joined in colonizing it. **I.24.3** As time passed, the Epidamnians' power became great and populous; **I.24.4** but they were split by factional strife amongst themselves for many years, as it is said, because they had been ruined and deprived of most of their power through a war with the neighbouring barbarians. **I.24.5** Finally, before the (Peloponnesian) war, the people expelled those of influence and power, and so these attacked with the barbarians and plundered the inhabitants of the city by both land and sea. **I.24.6** Since the people in the city were hard-pressed, as they were Epidamnians they sent envoys to Corcyra, since it was their mother-city, begging that it would not suffer them to be destroyed, but would reconcile them with their exiles and put an end to the war with the barbarians. **I.24.7** They sat as suppliants in the Heraion and made this request. But the Corcyraeans did not accept their plea, sending them away unsuccessful. **I.25.1** When the Epidamnians realised that they were going to get no assistance from Corcyra, they were at a loss as to what they could do, and so they sent to Delphi and consulted the god as to whether they should hand over the city to the Corinthians as their founders and try to obtain some assistance from them. He replied that they should hand it over and make the Corinthians their leaders. **I.25.2** The Epidamnians went to Corinth and handed over the colony in accordance with the oracle, pointing out that their founder was from Corinth and making known the oracle's response, and begged that they would not suffer them to be destroyed, but come to their aid. **I.25.3** The Corinthians promised their assistance, feeling they had a right to do so, as they considered that the colony was no less theirs than the Corcyraeans, and motivated at the same time by the fact that they hated the Corcyraeans, in as much as they disregarded them though they were their colonists; **I.25.4** for they neither gave the Corinthians the customary honours in their common festivals, nor served Corinthians with the first portion of the sacrifices, as the other colonies did. Instead they despised the Corinthians because they themselves were both equal to the richest of the Greeks at that time in monetary power and more powerful in military resources, and boasted that they were far superior in their fleet .... **I.26.1** So, having all these complaints against the Corcyraeans, the Corinthians were glad to send help to Epidamnos, bidding anyone who wished to go as a colonist, as well as guards of Ambraciots, Leukadians and their own citizens. **I.26.2** And they went by land to Apollonia, a Corinthian colony, for fear that they might be hindered by the Corcyraeans if they crossed by sea.

1.8 Athenian Interference with Potidaea

Thucydides I.56.1–57.1

It is clear that there were strong bonds between some mother-cities and their colonies, and that the mother-city expected that the colonies would 'follow her lead'. Potidaea, founded by Corinth c. 625–585, was still receiving annual magistrates from Corinth in 432. It must not be concluded that all colonies, not even all those of Corinth, received such officials; see Graham (1983) 136–37, but cf. doc. 1.19 where Herakleia Trachinia has magistrates sent from Sparta. Potidaea is situated in the Chalkidike, where there were numerous colonies, mostly sent out by Chalkis (hence 'Chalkidike' as the name of the three-pronged peninsula), and some by the island of Andros. See Bradeen (1952) 356–80 for the Chalkidians. The context is, like doc. 1.7, the outbreak of the Peloponnesian War.

I.56.1 Immediately after this the following differences also occurred between the Athenians and Peloponnesians which led to war. **I.56.2** For since the Corinthians were planning how to revenge themselves on the Athenians, they, suspecting their enmity, gave instructions to the Potidaeans, colonists of Corinth and their own tributary allies who live on the isthmus of Pallene, to demolish their wall on the side towards Pallene, give hostages, and expel the magistrates (epidemiourgoi) sent them by Corinth and not in future receive those sent every year. For the Athenians were afraid that the Potidaeans might revolt under the persuasion of Perdikkas and the Corinthians, and might draw into the revolt with them Athens' other allies in Thrace. **I.57.1** The Athenians took these precautions regarding Potidaea immediately after the sea-battle at Corcyra.

THE COLONIZATION OF THE WEST: ITALY AND SICILY

Dunbabin (1948) 1–47; Woodhead (1962) 31–71; Graham (1982a) 94–113, (1982b) 163–75, provide a sound overview of Greek colonization in the west, and, for the expansion of these colonies, see Dunbabin 95–145 (Sicily), 146–170 (Italy); Graham (1982b) 175–86 (Sicily and Italy). Wilson (1988) 179–201 has photographs and useful discussion of the art and architecture of the Western Greeks; see also docs. 1.18, 1.31–32. The colonies in Sicily were spectacularly successful; the whole area was later known as Magna Graecia, 'Greater Greece'. For a detailed account of colonization in Sicily, see Thuc. VI.3.1–5.3. Foundation dates for the some of the cities he mentions are as follows: Akrai 663; Camarina 598; Catana 729; Gela 688; Himera c. 648; Kasmenai 643; Leontinoi 729; Naxos 734; Rhegium c. 730–20; Selinous 628; Syracuse 733; Zankle c. 730–20; for the dates of the Sicilian colonies, see the detailed treatment of Miller (1970), especially 42 for a comparison of Thucydides and Eusebius' dates. For the Greek colonization of Sicily, see Finley (1979) 15–25; Graham (1992) 103–09; Boardman (1980) 161–89, and for their relations with the native peoples, Boardman 189–92.

1.9 'Nestor's Cup' from Pithekoussai

Meiggs & Lewis 1

Hansen 454. Pithekoussai was the earliest Greek colony in the west, founded by the Euboean cities of Chalkis and Eretria (Strab. V.4.9 (247)), probably c. 750–25, on the island of Ischia (opposite the west coast of Italy). Chalkis also founded in the area Cumae (with Eretria), Sicilian Naxos, Catana, Leontinoi, Zankle and Rhegium; Zankle and Rhegium guarded the straits of Sicily. 'Nestor's Cup' (a 'kotyle', drinking cup) has the longest eighth century inscription in Greek, and it is a written in continuous retrograde, with each of the three lines being read from right to left (c. 720–710). This inscription is particularly important as Pithekoussai's neighbour colony Cumae on the mainland opposite (founded c. 725–700) was the first Greek city with which the Etruscans came into contact; the Chalkidic alphabet (ie the alphabet from Chalkis) used by Cumae, of which the inscription on the cup from Pithekoussai is an example, was the alphabet to be adopted by the Etruscans, from whom the Romans adopted their alphabet, and from which our own alphabet derives (see ML p.1; Fine (1983) 70; Millar (1983) 93–94; Ridgway (1992) 57; cf. *LSAG* 235–36). See a sketch of the cup and transcription of the inscription in *LSAG* 239n.1; Boardman (1980) 167, fig. 205; Graham (1982a) 100, fig. 16; Ridgway (1992) 55–56, figs. 8–9. The lines refer to Nestor's cup: see Homer *Iliad* XI.632–37.

Pithekoussai and Cumae were the earliest Greek colonies in the west, and yet were the colonies in Italy furthest from Greece. The discovery that iron was smelted at Pithekoussai has been taken to mean that it was this metal which brought the colonists here. Graham (1971) 43–45, (1982a) 102–03 argues that there was no need for the Euboeans to travel so far for iron for trading purposes, as they had sources on their own island. Rather the fertility of the soil, and iron for their own use, explains their presence; cf. Cook (1962) 113–14. Ridgway (1973) 17–19 defended the iron thesis, but at (1992) 107–09 his views are towards a compromise and not for the site as an emporion rather than an agriculturally orientated colony; cf. Boardman (1980) 168; Fine (1983) 69–70; Cunliffe (1988) 13. For Greeks in the Adriatic region, see Beaumont (1936) 159–204; for the Greek harbour at Cumae, see Paget (1968) 148–59.

Nestor's cu[p] was good to drin[k from],
But whoev[er] dr[in]ks from this cu[p] will immediately
[Be sei]zed with desi[re] for beautifully-cro[wn]ed Aphrodite.

1.10 Land Hunger as a Motive for Colonization

Ephoros *FGH* 70 F137 (Strabo VI.2.2 (267))

Although the motive for colonization is sometimes debated, as in the case of Pithekoussai (doc. 1.9) or Sinope (doc. 1.14), in the following case, in Sicily, land hunger was clearly the motivating force.

The cities along the side which forms the strait are first Messene, then Tauromenion, Catana and Syracuse; but those between Catana and Syracuse, that is Naxos and Megara, have been deserted. This is also the location of the outlets of the river Symaithos and all the others that flow down from Aetna into well-harboured mouths; here too is the promontory of Xiphonia. Ephoros says that these were the first Greek cities to be founded in Sicily, in the tenth generation after the Trojan War; for men before that were so afraid of the bands of Etruscan pirates and the savagery of the barbarians there that they would not even sail there for trade. But Theokles, an Athenian, who had been carried away by the winds to Sicily, observed the worthlessness of the people and the excellence of the land, and as he was unable on his return to persuade the Athenians, he took with him when he sailed many Chalkidians from Euboea and some of the Ionians, and also Dorians, most of whom were Megarians; accordingly the Chalkidians founded Naxos, while the Dorians founded Megara, which was previously called Hybla. Though the cities are no longer in existence, the name of Hybla continues to last because of the excellence of the Hyblaian honey.

1.11 The Peoples of Phokaia and Teos Flee the Persians

Herodotos I.163.1–169.1

The Phokaians fled the Persians, c. 545, but half returned to their city. The remainder went to their colony Alalia, on Corsica, established c. 565, and settled themselves as pirates; the battle of Alalia against the coalition of the Carthaginians and Etruscans took place c. 537. The Teians also abandoned their city c. 545, amongst them Anacreon; cf. Strab. XIV.1.30 (644). They honoured as a hero Timesios of Klazomenai, who had failed to establish a colony at Abdera in 654. Pind. *Paian* 2.38–44 honours the Abderans and mentions their conflict with the barbarians (see Graham (1992) 49). In the fifth and fourth centuries Abdera enjoyed peaceful relations with the Thracians (Graham (1992) 66–67) and many of the Greek cities in the vicinity seem to have hired Thracian peltasts for their armies; see Best (1969) 12–15. For Hdt. I.168 on Abdera, see esp. Graham (1992) 48–53; on Abdera: Danov (1990) 151–54. **I.165.1**: the Chians' reluctance to let them settle nearby shows the importance of trade at this stage; for Phokaian trade, see Graham (1984) 3–6; for the Phokaians as pirates, see Rihll (1993) 93–94.

I.163.1 These Phokaians were the first of the Greeks to make long sea voyages, and they were the ones who discovered the Adriatic, Etruria, Iberia and Tartessos. **I.163.2** They sailed not in merchant ships but in pentekonters. (*Arganthonios, tyrant of Tartessos, failed to persuade them to settle in his country, but gave them money to build a wall around their city.*) **I.164.1** So the Phokaians' wall was constructed in this way, and Harpagos, who led the army against them and was besieging them, made the proposal that he would be satisfied if the Phokaians wished to pull down one battlement of the wall and to sacrifice one house. **I.164.2** The Phokaians, though aggrieved at slavery, said that they wished to consider for one day and then answer; and while they were deliberating they told him to lead his army away from the wall. Harpagos said that he knew well what they were planning to do, but that even so he would allow them to deliberate. **I.164.3** And while Harpagos was leading his army away from the wall, the Phokaians in the meantime hauled their pentekonters down to the sea, put their children and women and all their belongings aboard, as well as the statues from their temples and the other votive offerings, except what was of bronze or stone or paintings, and, after putting everything else aboard, embarked themselves and sailed towards Chios; and the Persians possessed Phokaia without its people. **I.165.1** As the Chians chose not to sell them the islands called the Oinousai when they offered to buy them, being afraid that they would became a trading centre, and their island might be excluded because of this, accordingly the Phokaians set out for Corsica (Kyrnos). For they had built themselves a city on Corsica on the advice of an oracle twenty years before these events, the name of which was Alalia. **I.165.2** At that point Arganthonios had already died. When they set out for Corsica, they first sailed back to Phokaia, killed the Persian guard who had taken the city over from Harpagos, and afterwards, so that this should be incumbent on them all, laid heavy curses on anyone of their number who should fail to accompany the fleet. **I.165.3** In addition to this, they dropped a lump of iron into the sea and swore they would never return to Phokaia until this reappeared. But while they were on their way to Corsica, half of the citizens were gripped by longing and regret for their city and their country's customs, and they made perjurers of themselves by sailing back to Phokaia. Those who kept their oath set out from the Oinousai and continued their voyage. **I.166.1** When they reached Corsica, they lived there for five years in common with those who had previously arrived there and erected temples. They continually plundered all their neighbours to such an extent that the Etruscans and Carthaginians came to an agreement and made an expedition against them each with sixty ships. **I.166.2** The Phokaians too manned their ships, which were sixty in number, and met them in what is called the Sardinian Sea. In the sea battle which followed their encounter, the Phokaians gained a sort of Kadmeian victory (where more was lost than gained). Forty of their ships had been destroyed, and the twenty surviving ones were useless; for their rams were bent back. **I.166.3** They sailed back to Alalia, took with them their children and wives and as much of their property as the ships were able to carry, and then left Corsica and sailed to Rhegium. **I.167.1** The Carthaginians and Etruscans drew lots for the men from the ships which were destroyed, and of the Etruscans the Agyllaioi obtained by far the largest share, and these they led out and stoned.[1] .... **I.167.3** This group of Phokaians suffered this fate, while those who escaped to Rhegium used it as a base of operations from which they established a city in Oinotria, which is now called Elea .... **I.168.1** The Teians' history closely resembles theirs; for when Harpagos captured their wall with his mound, they all embarked in their ships and sailed to Thrace and there they founded the city Abdera, which before them Timesios of Klazomenai founded but had no joy of, but was driven out by the Thracians and is now honoured as a hero by the Teians in Abdera. **I.169.1** These were the only Ionians who abandoned their native lands because they were unable to endure slavery; the other Ionians, except the Milesians, engaged Harpagos in battle, like those who left, and behaved valiantly, each fighting on behalf of his own home; but they were defeated and conquered and all remained in their countries and submitted to the orders given them.

[1] There is a lacuna here and the text is that suggested by Stein.

THE BLACK SEA AND PROPONTIS

The reasons for colonization in the Black Sea area are debated: Noonan (1973) 231–42 argues that exports of grain did not begin from the Black Sea colonies until the end of the sixth century, when the colonies purchased the grain from the native inhabitants (Hdt. IV.17.2). Certainly by the fifth century, the colonies of the Black Sea were trading grain with the older cities: see doc. 10.38. Greek colonization of the Black Sea area probably started to relieve the mother-cities of surplus population. Hdt. IV.24 writes of emporia on the Black Sea, but this reflects fifth century conditions. The view that colonization in the area did not commence until c. 680 and the invention of the pentekonter has been refuted; see Labaree (1957) 29–33 and Graham (1958) 27–31 who conclude that the ordinary

Greek merchantman negotiated the straits at appropriate times of the year. But while Greek colonization of the Black Sea began in the eighth century, it mostly took place in the seventh century.

1.12 Chalkedon: a City Founded by the 'Blind'

Herodotos IV.144.1–2

Byzantium was on the European side of the Hellespont, while Chalkedon was on the Asiatic side. Chalkedon was founded first, and the ancient view was one of surprise that the site of Chalkedon was founded before that of Byzantium which was better placed for controlling trade in and out of the Black Sea (Strab. VII.6.2 (320); Tac. *Ann.* 12.63; see Polyb. IV.38.1–44.11). It would appear that the colonists at Chalkedon were primarily interested in land; see Boardman (1980) 241; Graham (1971) 39 suggests that the hostility of the natives could explain why Byzantium was not settled until seventeen years after Chalkedon (for serfs in Asia Minor, see doc. 11.32). Both cities were founded by Megara, according to the literary evidence, in the early seventh century. For Megara's colonization, see Legon (1981) 71–85.

IV.144.1 This same Megabazos made the following remark and left an undying remembrance of himself amongst the people on the Hellespont; **IV.144.2** for when he was in Byzantium he learnt that the Chalkedonians had settled there seventeen years earlier than the men of Byzantium, and when he learnt this he said that the Chalkedonians must have been blind at the time; for with a finer one at hand they would never have chosen to settle on the worse site, if they had not been blind.

1.13 Miletos' Impact as Coloniser

Anaximenes *FGH* 72 F26 (Strabo XIV.1.6 (635))

Miletos was one of the most powerful cities in Asia Minor, and founded many colonies between the eighth and sixth centuries. As well as Sinope (doc. 1.14), in the Black Sea area Miletos also established Amisos (with Phokaia), Apollonia Pontika, Berezan (see doc. 10.37), Kepoi, Istros, Odessos, Olbia, Phasis, Theodosia, Tieion, Tomis, Tyros, and possibly Myrmekion, Hermonassa and Nymphaion. According to Plin. *Nat. Hist.* V.31.112 Miletos sent out more than ninety colonies; for a general overview of the history of Miletos, see Freeman (1950) 129–67.

This city (Miletos) is responsible for many achievements, but the greatest is the number of its colonies; for all the Black Sea has been colonized by the Milesians as well as the Propontis and many other places. At any rate, Anaximenes of Lampsakos says that the Milesians colonized the island Ikaros, and Leros, and near the Hellespont Limnai in the Chersonese, and Abydos, Arisba and Paisos in Asia; and Artake and Cyzicus on the island of Kyzikenai; and Skepsis in the Troad's interior.

1.14 Exiles from Miletos Refound Sinope

Pseudo-Skymnos *Geographical Description* 986–97

Sinope, on the shore of the Black Sea, was founded in the mid-eighth century by Habrondas (here called Abron), from Miletos, but he was killed by the Cimmerians, who overran the area from about 700–650 (Hdt. IV.12.2 notes that the Cimmerians built on the site of Sinope). The Greek settlement had to be re-established by Milesian exiles in 631 (see Graham (1958) 34, (1971) 39; and, for Sinope's site, 32–33). See Drews (1976) 22 who criticizes this reconstruction of Sinope's history, and Cook (1946) 72, but there is no reason to doubt Pseudo-Skymnos' account. Sinope established other colonies in the area, Kerasous, Kotyora, and Trapezous, taking land from barbarians for this purpose, and the colonies paid Sinope tribute in return (Xen. *Anab.* V.5.10; cf. Graham (1983) 201–03). Drews (1976) 26–31 (cf. Roebuck (1959) 47, Graham (1982a) 122) argues that Sinope was founded for the metals in the region rather than for fish, though no doubt this could have been an additional inducement. For Sinope, see also Polyb. IV.56.5–9; Boardman (1980) 254–55; Graham (1982a) 123. Pseudo-Skymnos was writing at some time between 138 and 75/4, his aim being to describe the whole accessible world, especially the foundation of cities and colonies; see Graham (1982a) 87

Then Sinope a city named for one of
The Amazons, who dwell nearby,
Which once noble Syrians inhabited,
And after these, they say, all those of the Greeks
Who crossed over in the time of the Amazons, Autolykos
And Phlogios, with Deileon, who were Thessalians,
And then Abron, a Milesian by race;
He is thought to have been killed by Cimmerians;
After the Cimmerians, Koos, and again Kretines,
Who were exiles from the Milesians;
These together settled it, when
The Cimmerian army overran Asia.

1.15 Mytilenaean and Athenian Conflict over Sigeion

Herodotos V.94.1–95.2

Athens did not send out large numbers of colonists, her most important colonial foundation being at Sigeion, in the late seventh century, on the Asian shore of the Hellespont. Athens' control of this site was contested by Mytilene, in a battle in 607/6 in which the Athenian general Phrynon was killed in single combat with Pittakos (Plut. *Mor.* 858a–b; Diog. Laert. 1.74; Polyaen. *Strat.* I.25; see Page (1955) 158n.1 for the date). The dispute was referred to the arbitration of Periander, tyrant of Corinth, who awarded Sigeion to Athens (Diog. 1.74). When Hippias was expelled from Athens, he went to Sigeion, and that is the context of Herodotos' account. For the lead-up to this passage (the Corinthian Sokles' speech against tyranny), see doc. 2.9. The Chersonese, the peninsula to the north, came under Athenian domination during Peisistratos' tyranny. The story of how Miltiades the Elder become tyrant is recorded in Hdt. VI.34.1–2. Miltiades' nephew and successor, Miltiades the Younger, who kept a force of 500 mercenaries and married a daughter of the Thracian king Oloros, fled the Chersonese in advance of Darius' attack (see Hdt. VI.34.1–41.4; Carawan (1987) 192–94; Table III). Perikles sent out 1,000 colonists to the Chersonese as part of a series of colonial ventures (Plut. *Per.* 11.5; doc. 8.21).

V.94.1 This put an end to the matter, and as Hippias was departing Amyntas the Macedonian gave him Anthemous and the Thessalians gave him Iolkos. He took neither of these offers, and went back to Sigeion, which Peisistratos had taken in battle from the Mytilenaeans, and after conquering it had set up his own illegitimate son Hegesistratos as tyrant, whom he had by an Argive wife. Hegesistratos kept control of what he had received from Peisistratos, but not without a fight. **V.94.2** For from their bases of Achilleion and Sigeion the Mytilenaeans and Athenians kept issuing out to do battle over a long period of time, the Mytilenaeans demanding the site, and the Athenians not recognising their claim and pointing out that the Aeolians had no more right to a share of the Trojan country than they or any of the other Greeks who assisted Menelaos in avenging the abduction of Helen. **V.95.1** While they were waging war all sorts of things occurred in the battles, including an incident in which the poet Alcaeus, when the engagement took place and the Athenians were victorious, escaped by running away, and the Athenians kept his arms and hung them up in the Athenaion at Sigeion. **V.95.2** Alcaeus put this in a poem which he sent to Melanippos, a friend of his, at Mytilene recounting his accident. Periander son of Kypselos reconciled the Mytilenaeans and Athenians; they referred the matter to him as arbitrator; and he settled it thus, that each should keep what they possessed. Sigeion thus came under Athenian control.

1.16 The Poet Alcaeus Runs Away

Alcaeus 428

This incident took place when Pittakos of Mytilene was challenging Athenian control of Sigeion; cf. Strab. XIII.1.38 (599); doc. 1.15. Athena is frequently known in the Homeric poems as 'glaukopis' (with grey-blue eyes). Burnett (1983) 143–44 considers that Alcaeus is here adapting Archilochos' famous poem (doc. 1.21).

Alcaeus is safe but †the shield that protected him†
The Athenians hung up in the temple of the grey-eyed goddess.

SPARTAN COLONIZATION

1.17 Dorieus Fails to Colonize Africa and Sicily

Herodotos V.42.2–45.1

Dorieus' venture, although with the state's consent, was more like a private than a public venture. His failure in Africa underlines the uniqueness of Cyrene and its settlements as the only Greek centre on the African coast; the Phoenicians were too dominant along the Gulf of Syrtis to the west of Cyrene (Graham (1982a) 138). For Dorieus, see Dunbabin (1948) 348–52; Asheri (1988) 751–52; one of Dorieus' companions, Euryleon, set up a brief tyranny at Selinous in 507/6 (Hdt. V.46). Taras was Sparta's only official foundation in the 'colonization period', though Sparta traditionally founded Thera (doc. 1.26). For Delphi and Sparta, see Morgan (1990) 168–71.

V.42.2 When Anaxandridas died and the Spartans according to custom made Kleomenes, the eldest, king, Dorieus took this badly and not consenting to being ruled by Kleomenes asked the Spartiates for a body of men and took them off to found a colony, though he neither consulted the oracle at Delphi about which country he should go to for his settlement, nor followed any of the customary usages. Feeling very angry about the whole affair he went off with his ships to Libya; men from Thera guided him there. **V.42.3** Arriving there, he settled at Kinyps, a lovely spot belonging to the Libyans beside a river. In the third year he was driven out from there by the Makai, Libyans and Carthaginians and returned to the Peloponnese. **V.43.1** There Antichares, a man from Eleon, advised him in accordance with Laios' oracles to found Herakleia in Sicily, saying that all the country of Eryx belonged to the Herakleidai as Herakles himself had conquered it. After hearing this Dorieus went to Delphi to consult the oracle, to ask whether he would obtain the land for which he was setting out; the Pythia responded that he would obtain it. Dorieus took the expedition which he had led to Libya and travelled along the Italian coast. **V.44.1** At this time, according to the people of Sybaris, they and their king Telys were preparing to make war on Croton, and the Crotoniates in great fear begged Dorieus to help them, and obtained their request; Dorieus joined forces with them against Sybaris and helped them to capture it .... **V.45.1** Each of them points out these proofs, the Sybarites a precinct and temple beside the dry river Krathis which they say Dorieus dedicated to Athena Krathias after helping to take the city, and the death of Dorieus himself they consider as the greatest proof, because he was killed for transgressing the instructions of the oracle; for if he had not gone beyond these instructions, and done what he had been sent to do, he would have taken the country of Eryx and held it, and neither he nor his army would have been destroyed.

1.18 The Spartan Partheniai found Taras in Italy

Antiochos *FGH* 555 F13; Ephoros *FGH* 70 F216 (Strabo VI.3.2–3 (278–280))

Taras (Tarentum), in south-east Italy was founded by Spartans who were not full citizens. The story of the partheniai may contain some semi-mythical elements, but it is clear that there were political differences of some sort between the Spartans and the partheniai, who were clearly of Spartan background but without full citizen rights, that Delphi was said to have been consulted, and that the city was Dorian in character and retained its links with Sparta. This was the only official colony of the Spartans during the 'Age of Colonization', though there were the unofficial attempts of Dorieus: the Spartans conquered Messenia as a means of extending their territory. From the fourth century Taras became the most prominent of the Greek cities in southern Italy.

According to Eusebius, Taras was founded in 706, and the earliest pottery on the site dates to the last quarter of the eighth century (see Graham (1982a) 112). For the oracle (and another on the same topic), see Parke & Wormell (1956) I.72, II.20–21 Responses 46–47; Fontenrose (1978) 140, 280, Responses Q34–35. For the partheniai, see also Arist. *Pol.* 1306b 29–31; Diod. VIII.21; Paus. X.10.6; Theopompos *FGH* 115 F171; Dunbabin (1948) 29–31; Michell (1952) 85–88; Huxley (1962) 37–38; Jones (1967) 11–12; Jeffery (1976) 115; Cartledge (1979) 123–24; Graham (1982a) 112; Vidal-Nacquet (1986) 212–14; Brauer (1986) 3–10; Parker (1991) 28–31.

VI.3.2 When speaking about the foundation of Taras, Antiochos says that when the Messenian War took place those Spartans who did not take part in the campaign were adjudged slaves and named helots, and all children born during the campaign they called partheniai and decided that they should not have citizen rights; the partheniai did not tolerate this (for there were many of them) and plotted against the citizens .... (*The plot is betrayed by Phalanthos.*) Telling the conspirators not to worry, the Spartans gave them into custody and sent Phalanthos to the god to ask about a colony. The response was:

'I have given you Satyrion, and the rich land of Taras
To dwell in and become a bane to the Iapygians.'

So the partheniai went with Phalanthos, and both the barbarians and the Cretans who previously occupied the site welcomed them .... **VI.3.3.** But Ephoros' account of its foundation is as follows: the Spartans were at war with the Messenians because they had killed their king Teleklos when he went to Messene to sacrifice, and they had sworn not to return home before either they had captured Messene or all been killed .... (*In the tenth year, the Spartans sent home their youngest men to cohabit with the maidens; the children thus born were called partheniai, who on being denied citizen rights after the end of the war leagued with the helots, but were betrayed.*) The conspirators on learning that the deed had been disclosed held back, and the Spartans persuaded them through their fathers to leave and found a colony; and if they got possession of a satisfactory site they were to stay there, and if not, they were to be assigned on their return the fifth part of Messenia. They were sent out, finding on their arrival the Achaeans waging war with the barbarians, and, after sharing their dangers, founded Taras.

1.19 Herakleia: A Fifth Century Spartan Colony

Thucydides III.92.1–93.2

Following the great age of colonization, there were colonial enterprises in the fifth century, notably by Athens and even Sparta. Athens had not participated to a great extent in the colonization movement, except for Sigeion and the Chersonese. For other fifth century colonies, see for Thurioi, Ehrenberg (1948) 149–70; Parker (1985) 307; doc. 8.21; for Brea, see doc. 8.27; Woodhead (1952) 57–62 for its site. In 426 the Spartans established Herakleia in Trachis (Herakleia Trachinia), consulting Delphi after making the decision; see Parker (1985) 307; Cawkwell (1992) 292; cf. Parke & Wormell (1956) I.191, 199–200; II.70, Response 159 and Fontenrose (1978) 246, Response H6. None of the three oikistai involved seem to have remained long in the colony: Graham (1983) 38–39; Cartledge (1987) 145 (for Leon). For Herakleia, obviously a colony founded with a specific strategic and political motive, see Hornblower (1991) 501–08.

III.92.1 It was at about this time that the Spartans established their colony Herakleia in Trachis for the following reason. **III.92.2** The Malians are comprised of three groups, the Paralians, Irieans and Trachinians; and of these the Trachinians had suffered badly in a war at the hands of their neighbours the Oitaians, and at first were going to ally themselves with the Athenians. Fearing, however, that they might not be reliable, they sent to Sparta, after choosing Teisamenos as their envoy. **III.92.3** The people of Doris, the Spartans' mother-city, joined in the embassy with the same request; for they too were suffering at the hands of the Oitaians. **III.92.4** When the Spartans heard this, they resolved to send out a colony, wishing to assist both the Trachinians and the Dorians. And at the same time the city appeared to them to be well situated for the war against the Athenians, for a fleet could be prepared there against Euboea, with the result that the crossing would be short, and would also be useful for the route to Thrace. So all things considered they were eager to found the place. **III.92.5** First of all, therefore, they consulted the god at Delphi, and at his bidding they sent out the colonists from both Sparta and their neighbours, and invited any of the other Greeks who wished to join them, except the Ionians and Achaeans and some other races. Three Spartans led them as their oikistai, Leon, Alkidas and Damagon. **III.92.6** And they established and fortified the city from scratch, which is now called Herakleia and is approximately four hundred stades from Thermopylai and twenty from the sea. They also started constructing dockyards and secured the side facing Thermopylai by building across the pass itself, so they might be well-protected. **III.93.1** The Athenians, while this city was being settled, were at first afraid and thought that it was particularly aimed at Euboea, because it is only a short crossing to Kenaion in Euboea. However, things turned out quite contrary to their expectation; for no harm came of it. **III.93.2** The reason was that the Thessalians, who were dominant in those regions and whose land was being threatened by the settlement, were afraid that they would have very powerful neighbours and so kept causing destruction and continually waging war on the new settlers until they had worn down what had at first been a very large population — for everyone had gone with confidence, thinking that the city would be safe because it was being founded by Spartans. Not least, however, it was the magistrates sent out by the Spartans themselves whose arrival ruined matters and aided the decline in population, by frightening away the majority through their harsh and often unjust government, so that it was all the easier for their neighbours to prevail over them.

THE COLONIZATION OF THASOS BY PAROS

An early Phoenician presence on Thasos is attested by Hdt. II.44.3–4, VI.47.1–2 (see Graham (1978) 61, (1982) 116). The island was rich in gold, and this attracted the Phoenicians, as it did the Greeks of the island of Paros in the seventh century, and valleys on the island were suitable for agriculture; most scholars now prefer c. 680 as the foundation date, but Graham (1978) 72–87 argues for c. 650. For the relationship between Paros, the mother-city, and her colony Thasos, see Graham (1983) 72–80 (esp. 74–75, with a discussion of Akeratos, who held office in both Paros and Thasos at the end of the sixth century). Thuc. IV.104.4 and Strab. X.5.7 (487) mention Thasos as a Parian colony. Thasos sent out its own colonists to the Thracian mainland opposite; for these colonies, see Graham (1983) 81–90; doc. 9.28. For a detailed discussion of Thasos, see Boardman (1980) 229–32; Graham (1978) 61–98; see Graham (1982a) 115–17 for a good overview on Archilochos and Thasos, and, less usefully, Forrest (1982) 255–56; Rihll (1993) 97–100; for Archilochos and his poetry, see Burnett (1983) 15–104. When Thasos unsuccessfully rebelled against Athenian control probably in 465, it lost its control of the mainland and the mines (Thuc. I.100.2–101.3; doc. 8.7); see Hdt. VI.46.2–47.2 for the revenues from these.

1.20 The Foundation of Thasos

Stephen of Byzantium, *Lexicon* s.v. Thasos

The oracle is also found at Euseb. *Praep. Evang*. VI. 6.256b; for a detailed discussion, see Graham (1978) 75–80. Parke & Wormell (1956) I.66, II.94–95, Response 230 point out that, like most 'foundation oracles', this one will presumably have been given to Telesikles when he went to Delphi to seek approval of the colonization of Thasos; Fontenrose (1978) 286, Response Q55, however, rejects the oracle as not genuine.

That Thasos is very high is clear from the oracle that was given to Archilochos' father:

> 'Report to the Parians, Telesikles, that I bid you
> Found a far-seen city on a lofty island.'

1.21 Archilochos Throws away his Shield

Archilochos 5

Archilochos was himself involved in fighting against the Saians, a group of Thracians on the mainland. Archilochos' attitude here is contradicted by his supposed epitaph (Archilochos 1) when he boasts of his achievements first as a warrior and only secondly as a poet, 'I am a servant of Lord Enyalios, / And yet skilled in the lovely gift of the Muses'; for Enyalios, see docs. 4.40, 12.29. Kritias also blamed Archilochos for writing about this incident (F44 (Diels II)). This passage is from Plut. *Mor*. 239b.

When Archilochos the poet went to Sparta, they immediately drove him out because they discovered that he had written in a poem that it was better to throw away your weapons than be killed:

> 'One of the Saians rejoices in my shield, which, beside a bush,
> I unwillingly abandoned, though it was not at fault;
> At least I saved myself. Why should I care about that shield?
> Hang it! I'll get another one just as good.'

1.22 Archilochos' Opinion of Thasos

Archilochos 20–21, 102

Archilochos found little to admire on Thasos; cf. Archilochos 22, where he compares Thasos to Siris in Southern Italy, to Thasos' disadvantage: 'For there is no spot as beautiful or desirable or lovely as the banks of the Siris.' His dislike of Thasos has obviously become a commonplace in later writers. In (i) the troubles of the Magnesians, attacked by the Cimmerians (cf. doc. 1.14), may have been bad, but Archilochos thinks those of Thasos worse. Elsewhere (93a) he complains of the misfortunes which the quest for gold has caused; see Graham (1978) 85, (1982) 116, referring to the inscription from Paros which preserves details of the poet's life: *FGH* 502; translated by Edmonds (1931) 161–75.

(i) Archilochos 20

'I lament the misfortunes of the people of Thasos, not those of the Magnesians.'

(ii) Archilochos 21 (Plut. *Mor.* 604c)

But we (see only one aspect of exile), like Archilochos, who disregards the fruitful lands and vineyards of Thasos and blames it for being rugged and mountainous, and who says:

'But it stands like an ass's backbone,
Crowned with wild forest.'

(iii) Archilochos 102

The misery of all the Greeks has gathered on Thasos!

1.23 Al Mina, an Emporion in the Levant, c. 825–301

Archaeological Evidence

Al Mina is located in Northern Syria, at the outlet of the Orontes river on the coast. The site was settled by the Greeks about 825, or perhaps even earlier; it is commonly thought to have been a trading depot, emporion, rather than an enoikismos, a settlement of Greeks living amongst the local people, or a colony. The Euboean element is dominant in the archaeological finds until c. 700, possibly corresponding to the destruction of the site at that date; after c. 700 Corinthian ware takes over, suggesting a change in the composition of the community. The Greeks by this settlement will have resumed the trade which the Mycenaeans had conducted with the Levant until the eleventh century. The site prospered until Seleukia, Antioch's port, replaced it in 301. The remains of numerous warehouses have been uncovered at Al Mina, especially after c. 700; the site was exclusively commercial. Another Greek emporion seems to have been established 70 kilometres to the south, at Tell Sukas, with a shorter history, c. 850–500.

Boardman (1990) 169–86 discusses the role played by Al Mina in the Greek traffic with Northern Syria which resulted in the orientalizing revolution on the Greek mainland and the dissemination of cultural influences westwards in the areas of religion, myth, literature, science and perhaps law (Boardman (1990) 185–86); for a Greek inscription found there, probably part of a proper name with the letters 'nabeo', see Boardman (1982) 365–67. It is suggested that the main item the Euboeans and the later Greek traders at Al Mina and the other sites would have sought was copper, as well as manufactured goods such as dyed Phoenician cloth, worked gold and silver, ivories and bronzes (Braun 13–14; cf Boardman (1990) 179–82). Greek, specifically Ionian, piracy in the area is mentioned in an Assyrian text of c. 735; see Boardman (1980) 45; Braun 15; Brinkman (1989) 55 (cf. 53–61 for a linguistic and historical discussion of Ionians in Akkadian documents, 735–521 BC). For Al Mina, see in particular the excavation report of Woolley (1938) 1–30, with reconstructions of the warehouses, 14–15, figs. 3–4; cf. Boardman (1965) 12–14, (1980) 38–54; Braun 9–11. Braun (1982a) 10, criticizes the attempt of Woolley, the excavator, to identify Al Mina as the Posideion (Posideum) of Hdt. III.91.1, which is identified by Strab. XVI.2.8 (751) as being 24 kilometres further south (Boardman (1980) 44–45; Braun 10).

THE GREEKS AT CYRENE

Thera (Santorini), a small volcanic island, sent out a small number of men to Libya, who eventually founded Cyrene on the African coast. Various other settlements sprang up on the nearby coast to create a series of Greek towns in the area (known as Cyrenaica); see Boardman (1966) 149–56. The colonists set out in 637, settling at Cyrene in 631. Cyrene, Naukratis and the mercenary settlements in Egypt were the only Greek colonies in Africa. Later, as Cyrene expanded, there were conflicts with the Libyans; see Laronde (1990) 169–80. The colonists married local women when they settled in Libya; see Pind. *Pyth.* 9.105–25 for a myth of how Alexidamas won a Libyan bride by swift running; cf. Callim. *Hymn* 2.85–92. For women and Greek colonization, see Rougé (1970) 307–17; Graham (1980–81) 293–314, (1982a) 148; Cawkwell (1992) 291. Cawkwell argues that the case of Thera undermines the argument that the main reason for colonization was over-population, believing that it was widespread drought and crop-failure that caused the sending out of colonies. However, he can provide only one example of crop failure leading to colonization (Strab. VI.1.6 (257); Antiochos *FGH* 555 F9) where colonists leave Chalkis for Rhegium; cf. Diod. VIII.23.1–2; Malkin (1987) 31–41. For Cyrene, see Freeman (1950) 183–94; Graham (1982a) 135–38; Forrest (1982) 256–57 (with a literal acceptance of Herodotos); Boardman (1980) 153–59; Cawkwell (1992) 290–92; for a discussion of other foundation decrees, Graham (1983) 40–68.

1.24 The Foundation Decree of Cyrene is Reaffirmed

Meiggs & Lewis 5 (*SEG* 9.3)

This inscription of the fourth century BC concerns the rights of a new group of colonists who have arrived from Thera and embodies what purports to be the foundation decree for the colony. Scholars debate whether this decree is genuinely seventh century, or whether it is a forgery of the fourth century; authentic: Graham (1960) 94–111; Jeffery (1961) 139–47; ML 5; a forgery: Dušanić (1978) 55–76; all have further bibliographical references to the debate. It is quite possible that the decree is authentic. The decree claims to quote (lines 23–51) the oath sworn when the colonists left Thera for Libya in the seventh century. The Cyrenaean account that Battos received the oracle is given in the inscription; the Therans had a version that the oracle was given to Grinnos. Herodotos gives both, and such discrepancies mean that his accounts can be accepted in its broadest outlines only. That the response of the oracle was spontaneous is improbable and it could be argued that all the oracles associated with Cyrene can be rejected as non-genuine, and probably invented in the sixth century, as believed by Parke & Wormell (1956) II.17–19, Responses 37–42; Fontenrose (1978) 120–23, 283–85, Responses Q45–51.

According to the inscription, the colonists were only taken from families where there was more than one son; the account here is similar to that of Hdt. IV.153. The decree gave the colonists five years to establish the colony, and then they could return; in Herodotos, the colonists returning home prematurely had things thrown at them (IV.156.3). Cawkwell (1992) 292 suggests that the seven year drought was considered to be a divine punishment for some unknown sin, and that the colonists were seen as 'scapegoats' to avert divine wrath. The seriousness of the oaths taken is reflected in the burning of wax-images and clearly the colonists were not volunteers; for this oath and parallels in Near Eastern oath ceremonies, see Faraone (1993) 60–80; cf. the curses laid on any of the Phokaians who returned to Phokaia (doc. 1.11). While the stele is now lost, the restorations are few and fairly certain, and are not marked.

(1) God. Good Fortune. (2) Damis son of Bathykles proposed the motion: concerning the matters raised by the Therans (through their spokesman) Kleudamas son of Euthykles, so that the city may prosper and the people of Cyrene be fortunate, we grant the Therans (5) citizenship according to ancestral custom, which our forefathers instituted, both those who founded Cyrene from Thera and those who stayed in Thera, just as Apollo gave to Battos and to the Therans who founded Cyrene good fortune if they abided by the sworn agreement which our forefathers concluded with them when (10) they sent out the colony in accordance with the injunction of Apollo the Founder (Archagetas). With good fortune. It has been resolved by the people that the Therans should continue to have equal citizenship in Cyrene according to the same conditions; and that all Therans who dwell in Cyrene should take the same oath as the others once (15) swore and shall be assigned to a tribe and phratry and nine hetaireiai. This decree shall be inscribed on a white marble stele and the stele be placed in the ancestral temple of Pythian Apollo, and the sworn agreement, which the colonists made when they sailed to Libya with (20) Battos from Thera to Cyrene, shall also be inscribed on the stele. As to the expenditure which is necessary for the stone or inscription, let the superintendents of the accounts provide it from Apollo's revenues.

The sworn agreement of the settlers. It has been resolved by the assembly; since Apollo spontaneously told Battos (25) and the Therans to colonize Libya, it has been decided by the Therans to send Battos to Libya as founder (archagetas) and as king, and for the Therans to sail as his companions; they are to sail on equal and similar terms according to family, and one son is to be enlisted [....] the adults and of the other (30) Therans the free-born [....] are to sail. And if the colonists establish the settlement, any of their relatives who sail afterwards to Libya are to share in citizenship and magistracies and be allotted portions of the unowned land. But if they do not establish the settlement and the Therans are unable to assist it, (35) and they are oppressed by hardship for five years, they shall depart without fear to Thera from that land to their own property and be citizens. Whoever refuses to go when the city sends him shall be liable to the death-penalty and his property shall be confiscated. And the man who harbours or hides him, whether a father his son or a brother his brother (40) is to suffer the same as he who refuses to sail. On these conditions those who were to remain there and those who were to sail to found the settlement concluded a sworn agreement and cursed those who should transgress it and not abide by it, whether those settling in Libya or remaining there. They made wax images and burnt them, calling down this curse, (45) after everyone had gathered together, men and women, boys and girls: 'he who does not abide by this sworn agreement but transgresses it shall melt away and dissolve just like the images, both himself and his descendants and his property, but those who abide by the sworn agreement, both those (50) who sail to Libya and those who stay in Thera, shall have abundant good things, both themselves and their descendants.'

1.25 Herodotos' Account of the Foundation of Cyrene

Herodotos IV.150.2–159.4

IV.156.2: The Therans founded the colony at Cyrene with two pentekonters of men. A pentekonter has fifty rowers, and other crew, and Hdt. VII.184.3 has eighty men per pentekonter when used as warships. At Hdt. IV.153, after the word men, scholars, reasoning that a number must originally have been written after this word, have restored a sigma, σ´, the Greek number for two hundred. This, however, is unnecessary, as Cawkwell (1992) 290–91 notes; cf. Oliver (1966) 25–29. What is clear is that the number of colonists to be sent out was small, but enough to reduce the number of Therans to a level which the drought stricken island could support.

Cyrene flourished as the exporter of the plant silphion, the sap of which was highly regarded as a medicament throughout Greece; the plant appeared on Cyrene's coinage (see Boardman (1980) 157, fig. 198; Graham (1982a) 138, fig. 25). For the plant, see Hdt. IV.169; Theophrastos, *Inquiry into Plants* VI.3.1–7; Plin. *Nat. Hist.* XIX.15.41–45. A famous Spartan cup depicts King Arkesilas II of Cyrene, of the mid-sixth century supervising weighing (see the plate at Boardman (1980) 149, fig. 185); the product is often taken to be wool (Boardman 149), but could be silphion (see Graham (1982a) 138). **IV.155.1**: Herodotos mentions the story that Battos was so-called because he stammered; cf. Pind. *Pyth.* 5.57–59 (doc. 1.26) and Paus. X.15.7 who state that he was cured of this by his terror at meeting a lion near Cyrene. **IV.158.3**: The sky with the holes refers to rainfall, which will have contributed to Cyrene's prosperity. Kings descended from Battos, the Battiad dynasty, ruled Cyrene until a democracy took over c. 440. The colony remained small, but, in the reign of the third king c. 580, Greeks in general were invited to come as colonists and receive land grants, which provoked the Libyans, with whom previously there seem to have been good relations. The defeat of the Egyptian force sent by Apries to aid the Libyans had repercussions in Egypt (see doc. 1.27). Herodotos gives further details of Cyrene's history and Cyrene's relations with Persia, at IV.160.1–167.2, IV.199.1–205. Cyrene surrendered to Cambyses when he captured Egypt (Hdt. III.13.3–4, cf. IV.165.2) and was included in the province of Egypt (Hdt. III.91.2). For Cyrene's relations with Persia, see Mitchell (1966) 99–113.

IV.150.2 Grinnos son of Aisanias, who was a descendant of Theras and king of the island of Thera, arrived at Delphi with a hundred victims for sacrifice (a hecatomb) from his city; other citizens were with him including Battos son of Polymnestos, one of the Euphemidai of the race of the Minyans. **IV.150.3** And while Grinnos the king of the Therans was consulting the oracle about other matters, the Pythia gave the response that he should found a city in Libya. In reply he said, 'I, Lord, am already too old and inactive to set out; you should bid one of these younger men to do this.' As he spoke he pointed at Battos. **IV.150.4** This is all that happened at that point, and they then went away and forgot about the oracle, neither knowing where on earth Libya was, nor daring to send out a colony to an uncertain destination. **IV.151.1** For the next seven years there was no rain on Thera, during which all the trees on the island died of drought except one. And when the Therans consulted the oracle, the Pythia proposed sending the colony to Libya. (**IV.151.2–152.5:** *A purple-fisherman called Korobios from Crete guided them to the island of Platea, and the Therans returned home with this news.*) **IV.153.1** When the Therans who had left Korobios on the island arrived at Thera, they reported that they had established a settlement on an island off the coast of Libya. The Therans decided to send a party with brother drawing lots with brother and including men from all the seven villages, with Battos as their leader and king. And thus they sent two pentekonters to Platea .... **IV.155.1** This is what the people of Thera and Cyrene say, but my opinion is different: **IV.155.2** it is that he took the name of Battos when he reached Libya, choosing the name both as a consequence of the oracle's response at Delphi and because of the honour he had there; for to the Libyans 'battos' means 'king', and because of this I think that the Pythia when she was prophesying spoke to him in Libyan, knowing that he would be a king in Libya. **IV.155.3** For when he reached manhood, he went to Delphi to ask about his speech; and when he made his inquiry the Pythia spoke to him thus:

'*Battos*, you have come regarding your speech; but Lord Phoibos Apollo
Sends you to found a city in Libya, feeder of sheep,'

as if she had said in Greek, '*King*, you have come regarding your speech.' **IV.155.4** And he replied thus: 'Lord, I came to you to inquire about my speech, but you proclaim to me other things which are impossible, bidding me to found a colony in Libya — with what means, with what men?' But as she started to prophesy to him in the same way as before, Battos left in the middle of what she was saying and went to Thera. **IV.156.1** But afterwards things continued to go badly for both him and the other Therans. Not knowing what was wrong the Therans sent to Delphi concerning their current troubles. **IV.156.2** And the Pythia told them that if they joined with Battos in founding Cyrene in Libya they would fare better. After this the Therans sent off Battos with two pentekonters. When these had sailed to Libya, they could not decide what to do next, so they returned to Thera; **IV.156.3** but the Therans threw things at them as they were putting ashore and did not allow them to land, but told them to sail back again. Thus compelled, they sailed back again and settled on an island lying off the coast of Libya, the name of which, as mentioned previously, was Platea. The island is said to be the same size as the city of Cyrene is now. **IV.157.1** They lived there for two years, but nothing went well for them, so they left one of their number behind and all sailed to Delphi, and arriving at the oracle they inquired of it, saying that they had settled in Libya, and though they were living there they were no better off. **IV.157.2** In reply the Pythia proclaimed this:

'If you know Libya, feeder of sheep, better than I,
I who have been there, though you have not, I much admire your wisdom.'

When they heard this, Battos and his men sailed back again; for the god was not going to let them off from the colony before they had reached Libya. **IV.157.3** When they arrived at the island and picked up the man they had left there, they settled a site in Libya itself opposite the island called Aziris, which is shut in on both sides by beautiful valleys with a river running past on one side. **IV.158.1** They inhabited this spot for six years; but in the seventh year the Libyans offered to lead them to a better site and persuaded them to leave. **IV.158.2** And the Libyans took them from there and removed them towards the west, and, so that the Greeks did not see the best of the sites as they passed through, they calculated the time of day so they passed by it during the night. The name of this site is Irasa. **IV.158.3** And they took the Greeks to a spring said to be sacred to Apollo and said, 'Men of

Greece, here is a fitting place for you to settle; for here the sky has holes in it.' **IV.159.1** During the lifetime of Battos the founder, who ruled for forty years, and that of his son Arkesilas, who ruled for sixteen, the Cyrenaeans who lived there were the same number as had originally been sent to the colony; **IV.159.2** but under the third king, called Battos the Fortunate, the Pythia in a proclamation encouraged all Greeks to sail to settle Libya with the Cyrenaeans; for the Cyrenaeans were inviting others to an apportionment of the land. **IV.159.3** The words of the oracle were:

'Whoever comes to lovely Libya after
The land has been apportioned, I say will later regret it.'

IV.159.4 A large crowd of people collected at Cyrene and the neighbouring Libyans, who were being deprived of a large amount of land, and their king, whose name was Adikran, because of their loss of land and insulting treatment from the Cyrenaeans, sent to Egypt and handed themselves over to the protection of Apries, the king of Egypt.

1.26 Pindar Honours Battos' Descendant Arkesilas IV

Pindar *Pythian* 5, lines 55–62, 72–97

Pindar wrote three odes for victors at Delphi who came from Cyrene, one, *Pyth.* 9, for Telesikrates, winner of the foot-race in full armour in 474, and two, *Pyth.* 4 & 5, for Arkesilas IV who won the four-horsed chariot race in 462. Arkesilas' race was noted for the fact that forty of the chariots crashed; this ode was sung at Cyrene on the return of the horses and charioteer, Arkesilas' brother-in-law Karrhotos (ll. 23–53); ll. 72–76 refer to the foundation of Thera, Cyrene's mother-city, by the Spartans: the Karneia, an important Spartan national festival, was inherited by Thera and then by Cyrene; prior to the arrival of the Therans, the local heroes of Cyrene were supposedly Trojans (ll. 82–84). For this and other poetic accounts of Cyrene's foundation, see Calame (1990) 277–341.

Yet after one thing and another, Battos' ancient prosperity still attends us,
A tower of the city and brightest light
To strangers. From him even loud-roaring
Lions fled in fear,
When he let loose on them his speech from overseas;
And Apollo Archagetas gave
The wild beasts to dread fear,
So his oracles for Cyrene's lord should not be unfulfilled ....

And he (Apollo) celebrates in song my
Well-loved glory that comes from Sparta;
From there sprang
The Aigeidai who came to Thera,
My forefathers, not without the gods, but some destiny led them;
The feast abounding in sacrifices
We received from there,
Karneian Apollo, and
In your banquet we honour
The well-built city of Cyrene,
Which is held by bronze-armoured strangers

Trojans, the sons of Antenor. For they came with Helen,
When they saw their fatherland in smoke
In war. With kindness that chariot-driving nation
Was welcomed with sacrifices by men who came with gifts,
Whom Aristoteles (Battos) led, in swift ships
Opening a deep path in the sea.
He built greater groves for the gods,
Made a straight-cut level path for Apollo's
Processions, which shield men from ill,
Sounding with the tramp of horses,
A paved road, where now apart at the far end of the agora
he lies in death.
He was blessed amongst men
While he lived, and afterwards a hero worshipped by the people.
And apart, before the palace, lie others who have found death
Holy kings ....

THE GREEKS IN EGYPT: TRADERS AND MERCENARIES

The Greeks had had trading connections with Egypt in the Mycenaean period, and these were renewed in archaic times. The Greeks sold wine to Egypt, and bought corn (Bacchyl. F20B, 14–16, 'and wheat-bearing ships across the gleaming sea bring immense wealth from Egypt'), as well as importing Egyptian art, which had a profound influence on the development of Greek art; see Braun (1982b) 53–56. The mercenaries employed by the kings, and many of the traders at Naukratis, settled permanently in Egypt. For Greeks in later Egypt, see Lewis (1986).

1.27 Greek Settlers in Egypt

Herodotos II.152.3–154.5, 178.1–181.2

The Egyptian king Psammetichos I (664–10), of Libyan origin, employed Carian and Ionian Greeks to establish him in power. These mercenaries settled down permanently in Egypt, being colonists of a specialized type, and Greek mercenaries may have been employed by Necho II (610–594) in his Syrian campaign of 608 (Hdt. II.159); see Parke (1933) 4–6; Austin (1970) 16–22; Boardman (1980) 114–17. Herodotos III.26.1 mentions a group of Samians at an oasis seven days' journey across the desert from Thebes, who may have been retired mercenaries. After Apries (589–70) sent an unsuccessful expedition against Cyrene (Hdt. II.161.4), the Egyptians rose in rebellion, and Amasis (570–26) led a force against Apries, who despite having 30,000 Carian and Greek mercenaries was defeated (Hdt. II.163.1, 169.1). It is clear that Naukratis was settled not by Amasis but during the reign of Psammetichos I, as Greek pottery is found there in quantity from his time on: Cook (1937) 227–37; Roebuck (1951) 213–14; Austin (1970) 23–24; Boardman (1980) 121; Snodgrass (1983) 144; Fine (1983) 84; cf. Strab. XVII.1.18 (801). For Naukratis, see Roebuck (1951) 212–20; Austin (1970) 22–33; Boardman (1980) 118–33; Braun (1982b) 37–43; cf. Gardiner (1961) 362. According to Herodotos, Amasis was also involved with Greek sanctuaries and married a Greek wife from Cyrene: see II.181.2–5. Note his dedications at Rhodes: Hdt. II.182.2, III.47.3; *FGH* 532 F29.

II.152.3 Psammetichos sent to the city Buto, where the Egyptians' most truthful oracle is, and received the response that revenge would come in the form of bronze men appearing from the sea. **II.152.4** Psammetichos was totally disinclined to believe that bronze men would come to his assistance; but not long afterwards necessity overtook men from Ionia and Caria who had sailed out in search of plunder and they were carried off course to Egypt; they disembarked and armed themselves in bronze and one of the Egyptians, who had not seen men armed in bronze before, arrived at the marshes and reported to Psammetichos that bronze men had come from the sea and were plundering the plain. **II.152.5** On learning that the oracle had been fulfilled, he made friends with the Ionians and Carians, promised them great rewards and persuaded them to be on his side; having persuaded them, with the help of his own Egyptian supporters and his mercenaries, he deposed the kings .... **II.154.1** To the Ionians and Carians who assisted him Psammetichos gave sites to dwell in opposite each other, with the Nile in the middle, which were called the Camps. He gave them these sites as well as all the other things he had promised them. **II.154.2** Moreover he entrusted to them Egyptian boys to be taught the Greek language, and it is from these who were trained in the language that the current interpreters in Egypt are descended. **II.154.3** Both the Ionians and the Carians inhabited these sites for a long time; these sites are in the direction of the sea a little below the city of Boubastis on what is called the Pelousian mouth of the Nile. Some time afterwards King Amasis removed them from there and established them in Memphis as protection for himself against the Egyptians. **II.154.4** Once these had settled in Egypt we Greeks from our dealings with them have known with certainty all that has happened in Egypt from the time of King Psammetichos onwards; they were the first non-native speakers to be settled in Egypt. **II.154.5** In the places from which they were expelled the hauling-engines of their ships and the ruins of their houses still existed up till my time .... **II.178.1** Amasis was well-disposed towards the Greeks and, as well as the other favours he granted to some of them, he moreover gave to those who came to Egypt Naukratis as a city to settle in, while to those who sailed there but did not choose to live there he gave sites where they could set up altars and precincts to their gods. **II.178.2** The greatest of these precincts, which is also the best known and most frequented, is called the Hellenion, and these are the cities which jointly dedicated it: of the Ionians Chios, Teos, Phokaia and Klazomenai, and of the Dorians Rhodes, Knidos, Halikarnassos and Phaselis, and of the Aeolians only the Mytilenaeans. **II.178.3** The precinct belongs to these, and these cities provide the men in charge of the trading-station (emporion); as many other cities as lay claim to a share of it do so without justification. The Aeginetans independently dedicated a precinct to Zeus on their own, and the Samians another one to Hera and the Milesians one to Apollo. **II.179.1** In former times Naukratis was the only trading-station and there was no other in Egypt. And if anyone arrived at any of the other mouths of the Nile, he had to swear that he had not come there deliberately, and after denying this on oath sail ship and all to the Canopic mouth; or if it was impossible to sail against opposing winds he had to take his cargo round the Delta in flat-bottomed boats, until he reached Naukratis. This was the unique position held by Naukratis.

1.28 Greek Mercenaries as Sightseers in Nubia

Meiggs & Lewis 7

Hdt. II.161.1 mentions the expedition of Psammetichos II (594–89) to Ethiopia (calling him Psammis), in 591 BC. His Greek (and Carian) mercenaries carved inscriptions on the legs of the colossi of Ramesses II at Abu Simbel in Nubia, which indicate the mercenaries' origins; it has been suggested that the Greeks without ethnics (places of origin) were born in Egypt (see ML p.13); the others may have been as well, but were simply more conservative in retaining their fathers' ethnics. In (a), Peleqos son of Eudamos (line 5), is literally, 'axe, son of nobody', ie the implement with which the inscription was written: this must be one of the earliest examples of Greek humour in an inscription; for a line drawing of (a), see Boardman (1980) 116; this is in continuous retrograde (cf. doc. 1.9).

(a) When King Psammetichos came to Elephantine,
This was written by those who, with Psammetichos son of Theokles,
Sailed and came above Kerkis, as far as the river permitted;
Potasimto commanded the non-native speakers, and Amasis the Egyptians;
Archon son of Amoibichos wrote us and Axe son of Nobody.

(b) Helesibios the Teian.

(c) Telephos the Ialysa[n] wrote me.

(d) Python son of Amoibichos.

(e) [....] and Krithis wro<t>e m[e].

(f) Pabis the Kolophonian with Psammates.

(g) Anaxanor [....] the Ialysan when King
Psammetichos [....] marched his army the first time.

GREEKS AND NATIVE POPULATIONS

There was often conflict between the Greeks and the local populations, who were sometimes displaced by the Greek colonists. There is also evidence, however, for cross-cultural influence and commercial interchanges between Greeks and natives: Graham (1984) 3–10; Rihll (1993) 100–05. Clearly along the shores of the Black Sea in the Scythian area there was even intermarriage amongst Greeks and Scythians, though Skyles, the Scythian king, with a Greek mother, was said to have lost his throne because of his addiction to Greek culture (Hdt. IV.78.3–80.5). For Greek-native troubles at Parion in the Propontis region, see Plut. *Mor.* 255a–e.

1.29 Graeco-Scythians in the Black Sea Region

Herodotos IV.16.1–17.1

Herodotos here writes of 'Greek Scythians', who lived west of the Borysthenes river on the Black Sea. Olbia, the best known colony in the region, was of Milesian origin, and situated on the Borysthenes; for Olbia, see Graham (1982a) 125–29, cf. (1984) 6–7. The Kallippidai might have been dispossessed Greeks who had 'gone native' or an originally Scythian tribe which became partially hellenised.

IV.16.1 Concerning this area which is now under discussion, no one knows accurately what is beyond it; for I have not been able to learn from anyone who says that he knows it at first-hand .... **IV.16.2** But as much as I was able precisely to learn by hearsay at a distance will all be recounted. **IV.17.1** From the trading-centre at the mouth of the Borysthenes (for this is the midmost point of the whole Scythian coastline), from here the first inhabitants are the Kallippidai who are Scythian Greeks, and beyond them is another race called the Alizones. Both these and the Kallippidai have a way of life like that of the Scythians in other respects, but they also sow and eat grain, and onions, garlic, lentils and millet.

1.30 Greek Settlers Go Native in Scythia

Herodotos IV.108.1–109.1

The Gelonoi were originally Greeks, but had been driven out of the emporia, presumably by other Greeks who came along later, and settled amongst the Boudinoi, a group of Scythians. Graham (1982a) 127 also points out that an inscription from the Black Sea area, *SIG*[3] 495.114, speaks of 'Mixellenes' ie: 'Mixed Greeks'; see Coja (1990) 157–68 for the peaceful co-existence of Greeks and the native population, the Getai, on the western Black Sea. The word phtheir (louse) can have a secondary meaning of 'pine-nut', and Herodotos has possibly misunderstood his informant.

IV.108.1 The Boudinoi, a populous and powerful nation, all have the very marked characteristics of grey eyes and red hair. In their territory there is a city built of wood, and the name of this city is Gelonos; each side of its wall has a length of thirty stades, being high and made of wood throughout, and their houses and temples are also made of wood. **IV.108.2** There are temples of Greek gods there decorated in the Greek manner with statues, altars and shrines all of wood, and they celebrate a festival in honour of Dionysos with Bacchic rites every two years. For the Gelonoi were originally Greeks, who were expelled from the trading-stations and settled among the Boudinoi; and in language they speak half-Scythian and half-Greek. **IV.109.1** The Boudinoi do not have the same language as the Gelonoi, nor is their way of life the same; for the Boudinoi are natives and nomads and have the unusual practice of eating lice, and the Gelonoi work the land and eat grain and keep gardens, and resemble them in neither appearance or colouring.

1.31 Naples: a Mixed Greek and Campanian Population

Strabo V.4.7 (246)

The city of Naples or Neapolis (which is the Greek for 'New City'), founded before 650, long retained its Greek character. Augustus himself attended the contests, while the emperor Nero performed here and addressed the crowd in Greek (Suet. *Aug*. 98.5, *Nero* 20.2–3). Note the difficulties which the colony experienced with its neighbours, here solved by a compromise.

After Dikaiarchia there is Neapolis of the Cumaeans; later the Chalkidians settled a colony there with some of the Pithekoussaians and Athenians, with the result that it was called Neapolis for this reason. A monument of one of the sirens, Parthenope, is pointed out there, and an athletic contest is celebrated in accordance with an oracle. But later on, after some dissension, they accepted some of the Campanians as fellow-settlers and were forced to treat their worst enemies as their closest friends, since their closest friends were now alienated. The names of their chief magistrates (demarchs) reveal this, the first being Greek, and the later ones Campanian mixed with Greek. Many traces of the Greek way of life are preserved there, gymnasia, and courts for wrestling (ephebeia) and phratries and Greek names, although the people are Romans. And at the present time a sacred contest is celebrated by them every four years both in music and athletics lasting for several days, which is equal to the most famous of those held in Greece.

1.32 Emporion in Spain

Strabo III.4.8 (160)

See also Livy 34.9.1–3. For Emporion, literally 'trading-centre', situated on the Spanish coast and founded between 600 and 575, south-west of its mother-city Massalia (modern Marseilles), see Cunliffe (1988) 17 (map at 14); 15–19 for Phokaian colonization; and Graham (1971) 37. Massalia was a Phokaian colony, founded c. 600, and the Massalians were well known for their treasury at Delphi (dated to 525). The city had good relations with the Celts of the interior and their oikistes Euxenos married a local princess, the daughter of the king Nanos: Arist. F549; Cunliffe (1988) 19–23; Rihll (1993) 101–02.

Formerly the Emporitans used to live on a small off-shore island, now called Old City, but now they live on the mainland. They have a double city, for it has been divided into two by a wall, since in earlier times it had as neighbours some Indiketans, who, although having their own government, wanted to have a wall shared with the Greeks encircling them for the sake of security; so the enclosed area was in two parts, divided by a wall in the middle. But in time they united in the same constitution which combined barbarian and Greek usages, as has happened in many other cases.

1.33 Socrates' View of the Greek World

Plato *Phaedo* 109a–b

Phasis was the most easterly of the Greek colonies, situated at the extreme eastern end of the Black Sea; the Pillars of Herakles are the Straits of Gibraltar.

'And then', said Socrates, 'I believe that the earth is extremely large, and that we who live between the pillars of Herakles and Phasis inhabit some small part of it around the sea, just like ants or frogs around a pond.'

2

Tyrants and Tyranny

Tyranny in ancient Greece was not confined to a particular period, and tyrants are found ruling Greek cities from the seventh until the second century BC, the time of the Roman conquest of Greece. However, the seventh and sixth centuries were a period when numerous tyrannies arose, particularly in the Peloponnese, and this is accordingly sometimes referred to as the 'Age of Tyrants'. This ended on the Greek mainland with the expulsion of the tyranny of the Peisistratidai from Athens in 511/0. Tyranny had a longer history in Sicily, and the tyrannies there, in the absence of Spartan interference, lasted until 467, the death of Hieron. A new age of tyranny developed in Sicily with the accession of Dionysios I of Syracuse (405–367), and this period is often referred to as the time of the later tyrants, while in Asia Minor, tyranny survived the Persian conquest. The first appearance of the word 'tyrannis', tyranny, is in the poetry of Archilochos (doc. 2.1), who uses it to describe the reign of Gyges, the usurper of the Lydian throne, and tyrants in Greece resemble Gyges in as much as they usurped power. Many of them were ostentatious figures, and, just as Gyges was wealthy, it is possible that this was one of the connotations of the word for the Greeks. The first time the word 'tyrannos', tyrant, is applied to a specific Greek ruler in our surviving sources is in the work of another poet, Alcaeus, and is used of Pittakos of Mytilene (doc. 2.24). The main character of tyranny was the usurpation of power, because the tyrants overthrew the existing political system and replaced it with one-man rule.

Tyrannies arose in the Greek cities for a variety of reasons. They rarely lasted beyond two or three generations (doc. 2.45), often but not always because of Spartan interference in the sixth century. The Spartans not only had a policy of putting down tyrannies on the Greek mainland, but in fact sent an expedition to Samos in an unsuccessful attempt to overthrow the island tyranny of Polykrates of Samos, and succeeded in deposing Lygdamis of Naxos (docs. 2.5, 2.28, 41–42). According to Thucydides, tyrannies arose at a time when the nature of Greek society was changing with the creation of new wealth (doc. 2.43). While the growth of tyrannies was part of the breakdown of the traditional aristocratic government, most of the tyrants came from an aristocratic background, and seized power as part of a power-struggle with their peers. The support of the people was often important for the tyrants (doc. 2.44), but they themselves were not from the lower socio-economic class of society, though they were sometimes accused of having been of low birth (doc. 2.24).

Solon's attempts to defuse Athens' socio-political crisis centred around relieving the poor from economic oppression. His reforms were significant, but not enough to relieve the poor of all of their grievances, and they found a leader in the aristocrat Peisistratos, who became tyrant, while Theagenes of Megara also seems to have come to power by attacking the wealthy (doc. 2.15; cf. 2.8, 4.2, 4.11). At Athens, possibly as elsewhere, tyranny arose out of dissension within the state, not just between rich and poor, but also between rival aristocratic leaders.

There are numerous reasons for the development of tyrannies in the seventh and sixth centuries, and various theories have been put forward to account for the rise of tyranny. Ambition was clearly a factor, doubtless connected with this acquisition of new wealth, for many tyrants, such as Polykrates, enriched themselves and enjoyed a luxurious lifestyle (docs. 2.30–31, cf. 2.4). Kylon attempted to seize Athens, probably in the 630s, apparently simply because he wanted to be tyrant: there is no evidence of aristocratic rivalry or championing of the poor (docs. 2.17–18). Kypselos of Corinth and Orthagoras of Sicyon had shown that one-man rule was in fact a possibility. Yet if ambition was one factor, the political climate in which it was possible to entertain the idea of seizing power must have been favourable. Military power, or its equivalent, was clearly important in the usurpation of power by tyrants. Both Orthagoras and Kypselos were polemarchs in their cities (docs. 2.3, 2.8); Gelon was commander of the cavalry (doc. 2.33); Theagenes of Megara (doc. 2.15) and Peisistratos at Athens, in his first attempt at tyranny (docs. 4.3–4), used the services of a bodyguard to obtain power; Theron used slaves (doc. 2.32); and Kylon had a force of men from his father-in-law Theagenes in his attempted coup at Athens (doc. 2.18). Kylon's failed coup hints at the conditions necessary for the establishment of a tyranny, for the Athenian people united against Kylon's bid for power. Similarly, Peisistratos' first tyranny was aborted when two rival groups, those of Lykourgos and Megakles, joined forces. Presumably, when Kypselos and Orthagoras took over at Corinth and Sicyon, they could do so because there was no group strong enough to oppose them.

Despite the fact that by the fifth century and perhaps earlier the word tyrant had acquired a pejorative meaning, many of the tyrants were clearly no worse rulers than the aristocrats who had held power before them, and some were obviously better. The worst ones no doubt helped to give tyranny a bad name. But even in democratic Athens, Peisistratos' tyranny could be looked upon as the Age of Kronos, the mythical utopian age (doc. 4.16). Tyranny under the social conditions prevailing in the seventh and sixth centuries was not necessarily seen as a political evil at the time, and it was only later that tyranny came to have unacceptable connotations for Greek society as a whole.

2.1 The First Use of the Word Tyrannis (Tyranny)

Archilochos 19

The poet Archilochos is the first Greek to refer to tyranny (as noted by Hippias *FGH* 6 F6). In the following passage concerning Gyges of Lydia, who reigned c. 680–40, the word tyranny presumably refers to absolute rule: see White (1955) 2; cf. Arist. *Rhet.* 1418b 27–31; Hdt. I.12.2. Gyges was himself a usurper (Hdt. I.8.1–12.2), and the word in subsequent history is used in the sense of an individual who seized power for himself. Tyrannos, tyrant, is a loan word from Lydian (see White 2; Graf (1985) 80, 107n.6). When the term tyranny became derogatory is debated. Sealey (1976) 39 sees it first in the Athenian drinking-songs in honour of the tyrannicides (docs. 4.43–46); White 2 and Fine (1983) 105 view it as already present in Alcaeus as a term of abuse. Certainly Solon (see docs. 3.37–8) associates tyranny with force, and considers it something which would tarnish his name if he took it, while Herodotos uses the word in a pejorative sense (Ferril (1978) 385–98). As Gyges was wealthy, it is also possible that this was one of the connotations of the word for the Greeks (Sealey (1976) 38–39; cf. doc. 8.22 for Kimon).

To me the possessions of Gyges rich in gold are of no concern;
Envy has not seized me, and I do not look with jealousy
On the works of the gods, nor do I passionately desire great tyranny;
Such things are far from my eyes.

2.2 Pheidon of Argos

Ephoros *FGH* 70 F115 (Strabo VIII.3.33 (358))

Pheidon of Argos, ruling in the first half of the seventh century, is mentioned by Herodotos as introducing a system of weights and measures for the Peloponnesians, and as assuming control of the Olympic games; he also calls him a tyrannos (Hdt. VI.127.3; cf. doc. 3.24). Despite the fact that Herodotos has a Leokedes, son of Pheidon of Argos, as a suitor of the daughter of Kleisthenes of Sicyon, there is a sound argument for dating Pheidon to the second quarter of the seventh century in Andrewes (1949) 74–77, accepted by Hammond (1982) 325, but Kelly (1976) 113–29 argues for Herodotos' dating (which is too late), while Huxley (1958) 588–601, (1962) 28–31, opts for the eighth century. There were no coins in Athens until after Solon (see doc. 3.24), and certainly none in Greece in Pheidon's time. For an overview of Pheidon, see Jeffery (1976) 133–44.

The Argives defeated Sparta in 669/8 at Hysiai (Paus. II.24.7), and Ephoros here states that Pheidon deprived the Spartans of their hegemony over the Peloponnese. Pheidon's seizure of the Olympic festival and transfer of control to the Pisatans, who were long Elis' rivals for this position (Hammond (1982) 325, 338), was temporary, and the Eleians were soon in control again. Pheidon's intervention can be dated to 668/7. Aristotle (doc. 2.44) states that Pheidon's tyranny developed from an existing kingship; Sealey (1976) 45 suggests that his display of power may have reminded those of either his own time or later of the reign of Gyges, the first to be described by the Greeks as a tyranny (tyrannis); this would explain why the term tyrant is used for Pheidon, who was a hereditary ruler.

Pheidon the Argive, who was tenth in descent from Temenos, and who surpassed all the men of his time in power, through which he both recovered the whole inheritance of Temenos which had been broken up into many parts, and invented the measures which are called 'Pheidonian' as well as weights and stamped coinage from both other metals and silver, in addition to this attacked the cities that had been captured by Herakles and claimed for himself the right to hold the contests which Herakles had established, the Olympian Games being one of these; and he attacked and forcibly celebrated the games himself, as the Eleians did not have weapons with which to prevent him, because of the peace, and all the rest were under his sovereignty; however, the Eleians did not publicly record this celebration, but because of this obtained weapons and began to defend themselves; and the Spartans also joined in with them, either because they had been jealous of their prosperity on account of the peace, or because they thought they would have their help in deposing Pheidon, who had deprived them of the hegemony over the Peloponnesians which they had previously possessed; and the Eleians did help to depose Pheidon; and the Spartans helped the Eleians establish power in Pisatis and Triphylia.

TYRANNY AT SICYON: THE ORTHAGORIDS 656/5?–556/5?

Diod. VIII.24 records that the Sicyonians at Delphi received an oracle that they would be 'governed by the scourge' for 100 years. Aristotle in doc. 2.45 also states that the tyranny lasted 100 years and was the longest Greek tyranny. That the tyranny lasted this long seems possible, but the figure is not necessarily precise. The genealogy of the family is complicated; see the discussions in Hammond (1956) 45–53, esp. the family tree on 47; Wade-Gery (1925) 570; Sealey (1976) 60–65; Griffin (1982) 40–43; Parker (1992) 165–66. Hammond suggests that Orthagoras, as the son of Andreas, was the first tyrant, followed by his brother Myron I, then by Orthagoras' sons Myron II and Isodamos, and then by Kleisthenes, whose son Aischines was expelled by the Spartans. Most of our information comes from Herodotos on Kleisthenes, while *FGH* 105 F2 preserves an account of how Orthagoras rose to power on the basis of his military reputation and position as polemarch. For the 'hoplite theory', see White (1955) 5–7; cf. Snodgrass (1965) 110–22, noting, at 122, that the early tyrants did not aid the political rise of this group. Military power, however, or armed force, was clearly important in the usurpation of power by tyrants, as is argued by Drews (1972) 127–44.

2.3 Kleisthenes' Anti-Argive Policy

Herodotos V.67.1–68.2

It is usually assumed that Kleisthenes' tyranny was an anti-Dorian one, with the tyrant championing that element of Sicyon's population which was pre-Dorian; see Andrewes (1956) 59; Sealey (1976) 47. The main thrust of many of his policies was, however, anti-Argive and the only trace of internal tensions here are the insulting names given to the Dorian tribes of Sicyon. The other main event of Kleisthenes' career was his participation in the 'First Sacred War', c. 595–91. The city of Cirrha was destroyed in the conflict, in which the fleet provided by Kleisthenes played a role; one of the causes of the war was Cirrha's exploitation of pilgrims to Delphi. As a result of the war the sanctuary was placed under the authority of the Amphictyonic Council. Robertson (1978) 38–73 doubts that there was such a war; but see Lehmann (1980) 242–46; Griffin (1982) 52–53; Tausend (1986) 49–66. **V.67.1**: Adrastos was a mythological figure, one of the heroes of the ancient epic the *Thebaid*, now lost, and of the *Seven against Thebes* of Aeschylus; Melanippos was one of the Theban champions opposed to the Seven, who defeated them. **V.67.2**: Parke & Wormell (1956) I.121–22, II.12, Response 24 accept the validity of this response of the Pythia, which Fontenrose (1978) 292–93, Response Q 74 rejects.

The implication of the term 'stone-thrower' is uncertain. Kleisthenes planned to introduce Melanippos by building him a shrine.

V.67.1 Kleisthenes, after making war against the Argives, stopped the rhapsodes from competing at Sicyon in their recitations of the Homeric epics because the Argives and Argos are highly commended throughout them; and there was, and still is, in the agora at Sicyon a shrine of Adrastos son of Talaos, whom as he was an Argive Kleisthenes desired to expel from the country. **V.67.2** So he went to Delphi and asked the oracle if he should expel Adrastos; but the Pythia's response was that Adrastos was King of the Sicyonians while he was merely a stone-thrower. Since the god did not allow this he returned home and considered a scheme which would bring about Adrastos' departure. When he thought he had found one he sent to Boeotian Thebes, saying that he wanted to introduce Melanippos son of Astakos (to Sicyon); and the Thebans gave permission. **V.67.3** Kleisthenes therefore introduced Melanippos and assigned him a precinct in the town hall (prytaneion) itself and settled him there in the greatest possible security. Kleisthenes introduced Melanippos (for this should be explained) as being Adrastos' greatest enemy, as he had killed Adrastos' brother Mekisteus and his son-in-law Tydeus. **V.67.4** When he had assigned him the precinct, he took away the sacrifices and festivals of Adrastos and gave them to Melanippos .... **V.68.1** He also changed the names of the Dorian tribes, so the Sicyonians and Argives should not be called the same. As a result he had a very good laugh at the Sicyonians; for he gave them names derived from the words pig and donkey and piglet, just changing the endings, except for his own tribe; this he named from his own sovereignty. These were called Rulers of the People (Archelaoi), and the others Pig-men (Hyatai), Donkey-men (Oneatai), and Piglet-men (Choireatai). **V.68.2** The Sicyonians used these names of the tribes while Kleisthenes was in power and for another sixty years after his death.

2.4 The Marriage of Kleisthenes' Daughter Agariste

Herodotos VI.126.1–131.1

The suitors for Agariste came from throughout the Greek world (though none from Ionia), indicating Kleisthenes' importance. Megakles, leader of the coastal party and opponent of Peisistratos, was the successful suitor; their son Kleisthenes was archon in Athens in 525/4 (see doc. 5.1); their great-great-grandson was Perikles (see Table I). It is perhaps significant that Kleisthenes approved of Hippokleides because of his connection with the Kypselids. Such alliances between tyrants could be of great importance: see docs. 4.34, 2.18; Hdt. III.50.2 (Periander and the daughter of Prokles of Epidauros). **VI.126.1**: Herodotos omits Orthagoras, the brother of Myron, because he was not part of the direct line of Kleisthenes' descent. Parker (1992) 167 with n.15 dates this marriage to c. 575; Kleisthenes won the four-horse chariot race at the Pythian games in 582/1 (Paus. X.7.6), and his victory at Olympia can be dated to 580, 576 or 572.

VI.126.1 Later, in the next generation, Kleisthenes tyrant of Sicyon raised the family (of the Alkmeonidai) so it became far more renowned in Greece than it had been before. Kleisthenes, son of Aristonymos, grandson of Myron, and great-grandson of Andreas, had a daughter whose name was Agariste. He wanted to find the best of all the Greeks and give her to him in marriage. **VI.126.2** So during the Olympian Games, when he had won the four-horse chariot race there, Kleisthenes had it proclaimed that any Greek who thought himself worthy of being Kleisthenes' son-in-law should come on the sixtieth day or before to Sicyon, as Kleisthenes would celebrate the marriage within the year following that sixtieth day. **VI.126.3** Then all the Greeks who were proud of themselves or their descent came along as suitors; Kleisthenes had had a race-track and wrestling-ring made for them for this purpose. (**VI.127.1–4:** *the suitors come from Italy, the Ionian Gulf, Aetolia, the Peloponnese, and Arcadia, and include Leokedes, son of Pheidon of Argos, and Megakles and Hippokleides of Athens.*) **VI.128.1** When they had all arrived on the appointed day Kleisthenes first inquired about the descent and family of each of them, and then kept them for a year and made trial of their bravery, temper, education and manners, conversing with them individually and all together; he took all the younger ones to the gymnasia, but the most important thing was his trial of their behaviour in company[1] and, for as long as they were his guests, he kept up his investigations and simultaneously entertained them magnificently. **VI.128.2** Of the suitors he was especially pleased with those who came from Athens, and of these in particular Hippokleides son of Teisander, preferring him for his bravery and because he was connected by descent with the Kypselids in Corinth. **VI.129.1** On the day appointed for the celebration of the marriage and Kleisthenes' decision as to whom he chose of them all, Kleisthenes sacrificed a hundred oxen and sumptuously entertained the suitors and all the Sicyonians. (**VI.129.2–4:** *Hippokleides, however, danced on a table and disgusted his host.*) **VI.130.1** Kleisthenes called for silence and spoke to the company as follows: 'Suitors of my daughter, I commend you all and, were it possible, I would gratify you all, not choosing one of you as exceptional or rejecting the rest; but as I only have one daughter I cannot deal with you all as you would wish, so to those of you who are rejected for this marriage I give a present of a talent of silver for wanting to marry into my family and to compensate for your absence from home, while I betroth my child Agariste to Megakles son of Alkmeon according to Athenian customs.' When Megakles said that he accepted the betrothal the marriage was formalised by Kleisthenes. **VI.131.1** This was what happened in the trial of the suitors and in this way the Alkmeonidai became celebrated throughout Greece.

[1] This is often translated as 'at the dinner-table' but it has a wider connotation; see *LSJ*[9] 1712.

2.5 The Overthrow of the Orthagorid Tyranny

FGH 105 F1 (Rylands Papyrus 18)

The Rylands Papyrus 18 claims that Aischines of Sicyon (the scholiast on Aisch. II.77 states that he was an Orthagorid) was deposed in the ephorate of the Spartan Chilon, which Diog. Laert. 1.68 dates to the 55th Olympiad, ie 556/5–553/2 (ἐφορεύσας in the fragment must mean while Chilon was ephor, rather than having been ephor, and the ephorate could date to any year in the Olympiad); if the overthrow of the tyranny was in 556/5 this could give 656/5–556/5 (counting inclusively) as a full century, but this relies on the accuracy of the figure of 100 years for this dynasty. This 'traditional' dating is supported by Leahy (1956) 406–35 and Hammond (1956) 45–53. White (1958) 2–14, however, argued that the tyranny of the Orthagorids is to be dated from 615–610 to 515–510. Leahy replied (1959) 31–37, and see also (1968) 1–23; cf. Andrewes (1956) 57, 61. For a recent attempt to down-date the dynasty to c. 620/10 – c. 520/10, see Parker (1992) 165–75. The main problem is caused by the papyrus, which has the depositions of Aischines and Hippias (which took place in 510) in close chronological proximity. The problem of the papyrus is intractable, and it is almost certainly inaccurate, and should be set aside as evidence (Griffin (1982) 45n.8), except for providing a confused confirmation of the Spartan policy of putting down tyrannies. The restorations are fairly certain and are not shown below.

Chilon the Spartan | as ephor and Anaxandridas as gener|al put down the tyrannies amongst the Greeks; | Aischines in | Sicyon, in Athens Hippias (son of) Peisistrat(os) .....

TYRANNY AT CORINTH: THE KYPSELIDS c. 658 – c. 585

2.6 The Bakchiadai

Strabo VIII.6.20 (378)

The family of the Bakchiadai dominated Corinth for nearly two hundred years, according to Strabo, although it is incorrect for him to call them tyrants; Hdt. V.92b.1 describes them as an oligarchy; for this dynasty, see Forrest (1966) 98–122; Oost (1972) 10–30. For the statue, see Plat. *Phaedr.* 236b; Agaklytos *FGH* 411 F1; Strab. VIII.3.30 (353).

The Bakchiadai, who became tyrants (of Corinth), were wealthy and numerous and of distinguished family, and held power for nearly two hundred years and enjoyed in security the profits from this trade; and when Kypselos overthrew them he became tyrant and his house lasted for three generations. Evidence for the wealth of this house is Kypselos' dedication at Olympia, an immense statue of hammered gold.

2.7 The Oracles Regarding Kypselos' Birth

Herodotos V.92b.1–92f.1

The first of the dynasty of tyrants at Corinth, Kypselos came to power in the 650s (Diod. VII.9.3: 655 BC; Eusebius: 657; Diog. Laert. 1.95 has Periander dying in 585, yielding a date of 658 for Kypselos' coup). The low chronology for the tyranny (Kypselos reigning from 620) first advanced by Beloch (1913) 274–84 is not generally accepted; see Oost (1972) 10–30; Salmon (1984) 186n.1. There is no reason to accept the oracles surrounding Kypselos' birth as genuine (*contra* Salmon (1984) 186–87; cf. Fontenrose (1978) 287–88, Response Q 59–60 (not genuine)) and they are presumably *post eventum* fabrications, as they portray the Bakchiadai in a hostile light; for the Kypselid oracles, see Morgan (1990) 178–83. Note the character of Kypselos' reign according to Hdt. V.92e.2–f.1 (doc. 2.9, which continues on from this passage).

V.92b.1 The Corinthian political system was as follows: it was an oligarchy, and the family called the Bakchiadai ruled the city, who married only amongst themselves. Amphion, one of them, had a daughter who was lame; her name was Labda. None of the Bakchiadai wanted to marry her, so Eetion son of Ekhekrates, a man from the village of Petra but in descent one of the Lapithai and Kaineidai, married her. **V.92b.2** He had no children by this wife or any other woman, so he set out to Delphi to inquire about a heir. As he entered, the Pythia immediately addressed him in these words:

'Eetion, no one honours you, who are worthy of high honour.
Labda is pregnant, and she will bear a boulder; it will fall upon
Men who rule on their own (monarchoi) and will bring justice to Corinth.'

V.92b.3 These prophecies made to Eetion were betrayed to the Bakchiadai, to whom an earlier oracle about Corinth had been meaningless, but which bore on the same thing as that of Eetion, and which said this:

'An eagle (aetios) in the rocks is pregnant, and will bear a lion,
A powerful eater of raw flesh; he will loose the knees of many.
Now ponder these things well, people of Corinth, you who live
Around beautiful Peirene and Corinth on the steep rock.'

V.92c.1 This earlier oracle had baffled the Bakchiadai, but then, when they heard the one given to Eetion, they immediately realised that it was in accordance with that one. Now they knew this, they kept quiet, intending to kill the child to be born to Eetion. As soon as Labda had given birth, they sent ten of their number to the village in which Eetion lived to kill the child .... (**V.92c.2–e.1:** *The assassins were unable to kill the baby as when they picked it up it smiled at them. They later returned, but Labda had overheard their plan and hidden the baby in a chest.*)
V.92e.1 Eetion's son grew up and as he had escaped this danger by means of the chest (kypsele) they gave him the name Kypselos. After Kypselos had reached manhood, he consulted the oracle at Delphi where he received an ambiguous answer, relying on which he made a successful attempt to seize power in Corinth. **V.92e.2** The prophecy was as follows:

'Fortunate is this man who goes down into my house,
Kypselos son of Eetion, king of famous Corinth,
He and his sons, but not his sons' sons.'

This was the prophecy, and Kypselos became tyrant and behaved like this: he exiled many Corinthians and deprived many of their property, and a lot more by far of their lives. **V.92f.1** After ruling for thirty years he finished his life in prosperity, and his son Periander succeeded him in the tyranny.

2.8 Kypselos Seizes Power

Nicholas of Damascus *FGH* 90 F57.4–6 (Exc. De Insid. p. 20, 6)

In this account Kypselos has been sent from Corinth to Olympia for safety as a child. Nicholas' reference to Kypselos as a king is his way of expressing the term tyrant; it probably does not go back to Hdt. V.92e.2 (doc. 2.7). For Nicholas, who was tutor to the children of Anthony and Cleopatra, see Toher (1989) 159–72. For Kypselos' treasury at Delphi, see Hdt. I.14.1–2; Plut. *Mor.* 400d–e.

4 In the course of time Kypselos wanted to return to Corinth and consulted the oracle at Delphi. He received a favourable response and without delay went to Corinth and was soon especially admired by the citizens, as he was brave and sensible and seemed to have the popular interest at heart when compared to the other Bakchiadai, who were arrogant and violent. **5** He became polemarch and was even more greatly loved, being the best by far of those who had ever held office there. For he did everything rightly, including the following: the Corinthians had a law that those who had been convicted in court should be taken before the polemarch and be imprisoned because of the damages assessed, of which he also took a share. But he neither imprisoned nor put any citizen in chains, but accepted the guarantors of some and let them go, and became the guarantor of others himself, and to them all gave up his own share; because of this he was particularly liked by the populace. **6** Seeing that the Corinthians were hostilely disposed towards the Bakchiadai, and that they did not have a champion, whom they might employ to overthrow the Bakchiadai, he offered himself and conciliated the populace, telling them the oracle that it was fated that the Bakchiadai would be overthrown by him, for which reason in the past they had hastened to do away with him and now were plotting against him; but they would not be able to avert their doom. The people gladly believed his words, being inimical to the Bakchiadai and well-disposed to him and considering that the deed would surely be accomplished because of his bravery. Finally having formed a party (hetairikon) he killed the ruler Hippokleides[1] who was lawless and oppressive. And the people quickly set him up as king in his stead.

[1] Here reading Hippokleides (for Patrokleides) as suggested by Jacoby (app. crit.).

2.9 Periander and Thrasyboulos

Herodotos V.92f.1–92g.1

While it cannot be said that the tradition concerning Kypselos was 'generally favourable' (*contra* Salmon (1984) 197), his son Periander had a much more colourful career: for the anecdote of his murdered wife's ghost and his necrophilia with her corpse, see Hdt. V.92g.2–4; cf. Strab. VIII.3.20 (347). But the tradition is not universally condemnatory: he had a favourable taxation policy (doc. 2.12) and according to Diog. Laert. 1.98 was one of the seven sages. However, Diogenes states that others, including Herakleides (F145 Wehrli), recorded that there were two different Perianders, and Plat. *Prot.* 343a excludes him from the list. Herodotos and Diog. Laert. 1.100 have Thrasyboulos giving the advice to Periander; Arist. *Pol.* 1311a 20–22 reverses this (cf. *Pol.* 1313a 34–1313b 16). The Spartans were generally the opponents of tyranny, but this passage, which follows doc. 2.7, is part of Sokles' speech against their plan to restore Hippias.

V.92f.1 Periander was initially milder than his father, but he then had contact through messengers with Thrasyboulos, tyrant of Miletos, after which he became much more bloodthirsty than Kypselos. **V.92f.2** For he had sent a herald to Thrasyboulos to learn what was the safest way to ensure control of affairs and best govern the city. Thrasyboulos took the man who had come from Periander outside the city and entered a field of arable land. As he passed through the crop questioning and cross-examining the herald about why he had come from Corinth, he kept cutting off any of the ears of corn he saw which stood above the others, and threw them away, until in this way he had destroyed the best and most abundant of the crop. **V.92f.3** After he had gone through the field in this way and uttered no word of advice he sent the herald away. When the herald returned to Corinth Periander was eager to learn his advice. But the herald said that Thrasyboulos had given no advice and that he was surprised at being sent to such a man, who was mad and who ruined his own property, describing what he had seen Thrasyboulos do. **V.92g.1** Periander understood what was meant and, realising that Thrasyboulos had advised him to murder the pre-eminent citizens, from then on displayed his evil side to the citizens. Whatever Kypselos had omitted in the way of murder or banishment Periander accomplished for him.

2.10 Periander and the Three Hundred Boys

Herodotos III.48.2–4

In this incident Periander attempted revenge on the Corcyraeans for their murder of his son. Periander had killed his wife Melissa, daughter of Prokles, tyrant of Epidauros, and thus became estranged from his younger son, Lykophron, who was sent to Corcyra. Periander towards the end of his life wanted Lykophron to succeed him. But when the Corcyraeans learnt of this, they murdered Lykophron to prevent Periander coming to Corcyra (Hdt. III.49.2–53.7; see also Herakl. F144 Wehrli). For the connection between Periander, Thrasyboulos and Alyattes, see Hdt. I.20–22.1; see also Diog. Laert. 1.95; Nich. Dam. *FGH* 90 F59.1–3. The 300 boys were perhaps to be sold as slaves; but they might well have been a gift (cf. Salmon (1984) 225).

III.48.2 Periander, son of Kypselos, had sent three hundred boys, the sons of the leading men in Corcyra, to Alyattes at Sardis to have them made eunuchs; the Corinthians conveying the boys put in at Samos, and when the Samians learnt the reason why they were being taken to Sardis, they first told the boys to take sanctuary in the temple of Artemis, **III.48.3** and then did not allow the Corinthians to drag the suppliants from the temple. When the Corinthians shut them up without food, the Samians instituted a festival, which they still keep even today in the same way; after nightfall, for the whole period that the boys were in sanctuary, they organized dances of maidens and youths, and, when organizing the dances, they made it a custom to carry sweetmeats of sesame and honey, so that the Corcyraean boys could snatch these and obtain food. **III.48.4** This continued until the boys' Corinthian guards left and went home; and the Samians then took the boys back to Corcyra.

2.11 Further Evidence for Periander's Methods of Rule

Nicholas of Damascus *FGH* 90 F58.1 (Exc. De Virtut. I p. 342, 22)

Other sources relate that Periander did not allow those who wished to do so to live in the city (Ephoros *FGH* 70 F179; Arist. F516). It has been suggested that this policy was similar to that adopted by Peisistratos (Jones (1980) 190–91; doc. 4.16). According to Diog. Laert. 1.98, Periander was the first tyrant to have a bodyguard; both Diogenes and

Nicholas saw this as changing the nature of his rule (though, once again, Nicholas incorrectly describes the tyrants as kings).

Periander, son of Kypselos, King of Corinth, took over the kingship from his father by right of inheritance and through his savagery and violence turned it into a tyranny and had a bodyguard of three hundred men. He prevented the citizens from acquiring slaves or having leisure-time, always inventing jobs for them. And if anyone should be sat down in the agora, he used to fine him, fearing that he might be plotting something against him.

2.12 Periander's Attacks on Corruption and Luxury

Aristotle F611.20

Despite his attacks on luxury, Periander was a patron of the arts, and Arion, the best cithara-player of that time, lived at his court before departing for Sicily and Italy (Hdt. I.23–24.1); for the episode of Arion and dolphin, see Hdt. I.23.1–24.8.

Periander first established his government by having a bodyguard of spear-bearers and not allowing people to live in the city, completely putting a stop to the acquisition of slaves and a luxurious way of life. He was moderate in other respects, in exacting no other tax and in being satisfied with those from the agora and harbours. He was also neither unjust nor arrogant, but a hater of corruption, and threw in the sea all the brothel madams. Finally[1] he set up a council, which did not permit the expenditure to exceed the revenues.

[1] See Salmon (1984) 199 n.55 for other possible translations of this expression.

2.13 Kypselid Military Activities in Euboea

Theognis 891–94

Even if these lines were not actually written by Theognis as West I.173 suggests, they must at least date to the period of Kypselid activity. Kyrinthos was a city in Euboea, and Lelantos is a reference to the Lelantine Plain; for the Lelantine war in the late eighth century, see Thuc. I.15.3; Jeffery (1976) 64–67. Nothing is known of Kypselid military activities in the region; see Figueira (1985) 288–91, who suggests a date of c. 600–581.

891 Alas for weakness! Kyrinthos has been destroyed,
The good vineyard of Lelantos is cut down;
The noble are in exile, the base manage the city.
If only Zeus would destroy the race of the Kypselids!

2.14 The Overthrow of Tyranny at Corinth

Nicholas of Damascus *FGH* 90 F60.1 (Exc. de Insid. p. 22, 4)

The Kypselid tyranny lasted into a third generation. Aristotle calls the nephew Psammitichos, but as Salmon (1984) 229n.168 observes Nich. Dam. (*FGH* 90 F59.4–60) calls him Psammitichos as ruler of Corcyra, but Kypselos as tyrant at Corinth. For the throwing out of the bones of enemies, cf. doc. 2.18. For Periander's family in later times: see doc. 13.31, the epitaph of his great-great-grand-daughter.

Periander left Kypselos the son of his brother Gorgos as successor to the kingship. When he arrived from Corcyra, he ruled Corinth as tyrant until some of the Corinthians rose up and killed him, after he had held the tyranny for a short time, and liberated the city. The people razed the houses of the tyrants to the ground and made their belongings public property, and exposed Kypselos unburied and dug up the tombs of his ancestors and threw out the bones.

THEAGENES AND TYRANNY IN MEGARA, c. 640

According to Aristotle (*Pol.* 1305a 24–27), Theagenes seized power after attacking the flocks of the wealthy, presumably flocks of sheep. Legon (1981) 88 suggests that Megara was moving into the wool trade at this time; possibly an aristocracy or a new class was exploiting this form of wealth (Sealey (1976) 56; cf. Legon 88; both toning down Ure's view, (1922) 266–67, of these wealthy owners as a new 'class of capitalists'); the lifestyle of the poor may have been threatened because of competition for grazing land. Involvement with Kylon places Theagenes in the second half of the seventh century. Arguments which seek to down-date him because of the poet Theognis are fruitless, as this poet is certainly seventh century. Plut. *Mor.* 295c–d states that Theagenes was overthrown; perhaps this occurred in the wake of Kylon's attempt at tyranny in Athens (see doc. 2.18).

2.15 Theognis on Tyranny and Social Discord

Theognis 39–52

Theognis of Megara flourished c. 640–600 according to West I.172–73. Many of his poems are addressed to Kyrnos, son of Polypais. Clearly in Megara the traditional social hierarchy was undergoing change, as at Athens where the rich and poor were in conflict; certainly Theagenes was said to have achieved power through use of an armed bodyguard (Arist. *Rhet.* 1357b 31–33). The term 'monarchos' (mounarchos in Ionic) means monarch or sole ruler, and can be used of both kings and tyrants; this is the first time that it is recorded as appearing in Greek (*LSJ*[9] 1143). Lines 41–42 are again repeated as lines 1081–1082b; for this passage, see Nagy (1985) 41–44.

Kyrnos, this city is pregnant, and I fear that she may bear a man
Who will correct our wicked presumption (hybris).
For even if her citizens are still prudent, her leaders
Have descended to great wickedness.

Good men, Kyrnos, have not yet destroyed a city;
But when it pleases the base to be insolent,
And they corrupt the people and give judgement in favour of the unjust
For the sake of their own gains and advancement,
Do not hope that that city will remain long untroubled,
Not even if it now lies in great tranquillity,
When these things become dear to base men,
Gains which bring with them public misfortune.

For from such come discords and kindred murders
And sole rulers (mounarchoi); may they never be pleasing to this city!

2.16 The Fountainhouse of Theagenes

Pausanias I.40.1

Theagenes built a 'fountainhouse', with two reservoirs, 14 by 21 metres in size. It will have been an important part of Megara's water supply, and the fact that it was remembered as a work of Theagenes indicates that the tyrants were known for their public buildings. For a photograph, see Legon (1981) 151, with discussion at 150; cf. Paus. I.41.2; doc. 4.28.

In the city there is a fountain, which Theagenes built for them, who as I mentioned before married his daughter to Kylon the Athenian. When Theagenes became tyrant, he built the fountain which is remarkable for its size, beauty and number of pillars; and the water which flows into it is called the water of the Sithnid nymphs. The Megarians say that these nymphs belong to that region and that Zeus had intercourse with one of them.

KYLON'S ATTEMPTED TYRANNY AT ATHENS

Kylon attempted to become tyrant some time after he won an Olympic victory in the foot-race, diaulos, (Paus. I.28.1) in 640 BC (Lévy's suggestion (1978) 513–21 dating Kylon's Olympic victory to 598/7 and the coup a year or two after has not gained acceptance). He made his attempt in a subsequent Olympic year (ie in either 636, 632, 628 or 624), but before Drakon's legislation in 621/0 ([Arist.] *Ath. Pol.* 4.1). The date 632 or a little later is usually preferred (Andrewes (1956) 84; Sealey (1976) 98–99), on the hypothesis that when Kylon won his victory he will have been relatively young (and thus still too young in 636), but that he would not have waited too long lest his Olympic reputation fade; cf. Rhodes 79–82. For the status gained by athletic success, see Morgan (1990) 211–12. Kylon's failed coup seems to be the first instance of stasis, civil strife, which was to be the dominant feature in Athenian politics until Peisistratos' third attempt to become tyrant. The way in which the Athenians rallied together tends to suggest that the socio-economic divisions which were to appear later on were not yet evident or, at least, not yet extreme and Kylon's case does not prove that regionalism and disaffected aristocrats were features of pre-Solonian Athens (*contra* Sealey (1960) 167–68), nor is it evidence for clan rivalry (*contra* Ellis & Stanton (1968) 95–97); while Plutarch (*Sol.* 13.1–2, *Mor.* 763d, 805d) places the regional squabbles prior to Solon, Herodotos and the *Ath. Pol.* clearly date them to after Solon (docs. 4.1–2). For Kylon, see also Plut. *Sol.* 12.1–2 and the scholiast on Ar. *Knights* 445. Neither Herodotos nor Thucydides mentions Megakles the Alkmeonid, whom Plut. *Sol.* 12.1 states was eponymous archon; see Cadoux (1948) 91.

2.17 Why the Alkmeonidai were 'Accursed'

Herodotos V.71.1–2

There are significant differences between the accounts of Herodotos and Thucydides: Herodotos does not mention Theagenes, the oracle, the festival, or the escape of Kylon and his brother. Lang (1967) 243–49 points out these differences and argues that

Thucydides' narrative has accretions which should be rejected; however, many of the differences occur because Herodotos' account is short, whereas Thucydides' is detailed, both, however, being digressions from the main narrative. For the naukraroi, see doc. 3.18; Hignett (1952) 67–74; Jordan (1970) 153–75; Billigmeier & Dusing (1981) 11–16.

V.71.1 The 'accursed' Athenians were so named for the following reason: Kylon was an Athenian who had won a victory at the Olympic games. He aimed at becoming tyrant, so he collected a hetaireia of men of his own age and attempted to seize the acropolis. However, he was unable to hold it and sat as a suppliant at the statue there. **V.71.2** The chief administrative officials (the prytanies of the naukraroi), who then governed Athens, persuaded them to leave by promising to spare their lives; but they were murdered and the Alkmeonidai are said to have been responsible. All this happened before the time of Peisistratos.

2.18 The Reasons for the Failure of Kylon's Attempt

Thucydides I.126.3–12

Thucydides' account is in the context of the Spartan demand, prior to the outbreak of the Peloponnesian War, that the Athenians 'drive out the curse', and Thucydides explains that the curse had arisen because of the way in which Kylon's attempted tyranny had been put down. Perikles was the great-great-great grandson of Megakles, who brought the curse upon the Alkmeonidai (Thuc. I.127.1; Table I). While Herodotos gives charge of the affair to the prytanies of the naukraroi, Thucydides states that the nine archons took over the siege, apparently correcting Herodotos' account; see Lambert (1986) 105–12 for the suggestion that the archons were away at the Olympic festival, acting as theoroi. Theoroi, however, tended to be specifically chosen for this religious task. Jameson (1965) 167–72 argues that Kylon's attempt took place during the Diasia but this contradicts the passage. For Thucydides' attitudes towards oracles, see Marinatos (1981) 138–40; contrast Hornblower (1992) 169–97 who incorrectly argues that Thucydides neglects religious factors in his history; cf. doc. 8.17.

I.126.3 In former times there was an Athenian, Kylon, an Olympic victor, of noble family and powerful, who had married the daughter of Theagenes a Megarian, who at that time was tyrant of Megara. **I.126.4** When Kylon consulted the oracle at Delphi the god ordered him to seize the Athenian acropolis during 'the greatest festival of Zeus'. **I.126.5** He obtained troops from Theagenes and persuaded his friends to help, and when it was time for the Olympic festival in the Peloponnese, seized the acropolis with the idea of setting himself up as tyrant, thinking that that was 'the greatest festival of Zeus' and that it was an appropriate time for himself as he was a past Olympic victor. **I.126.6** That the 'greatest festival' which was spoken of might be in Attica or somewhere else, he did not consider nor did the oracle make clear (in fact the Athenians celebrate the Diasia, which is called the greatest festival of Zeus the Protector (Meilichios) and this takes place outside of the city, and all the people make many sacrifices, though not of victims but offerings from the countryside). But Kylon considered that his view was right and went ahead with his attempt at power. **I.126.7** When the Athenians realised what had happened they all came in from the country to oppose them and settled down and besieged them. **I.126.8** As time went by, the Athenians grew tired of the blockade and the majority withdrew, leaving the nine archons in charge of the siege with the power to manage everything on their authority, however they thought best; at that time the nine archons handled most political matters. **I.126.9** Kylon and his associates who were under siege were badly off through lack of food and water. **I.126.10** So Kylon and his brother succeeded in making a run for it; the others, as they were in such a bad way, some even dying of hunger, sat as suppliants at the altar on the acropolis. **I.126.11** When those Athenians who were in charge of the guard saw them dying in the temple they got them to leave, promising that they would suffer no harm, but killed them as they conducted them out; they even killed some who sat down at the altars of the august goddesses (the Erinyes) as they passed by. Because of this they and their descendants were called accursed and offenders against the goddess. **I.126.12** So the Athenians drove out these accursed men, as did Kleomenes the Spartan later on with his Athenian supporters, driving out the living and taking up and throwing out the bones of those who died there; afterwards however they returned from exile and their family is still in the city.

2.19 Epimenides Purifies the City

[Aristotle] *Athenaion Politeia* 1

1 .....With Myron as prosecutor a court, chosen by birth, was sworn in upon the sacrifices. The verdict was that sacrilege had been committed, and the offenders were thrown out of the tombs, while their descendants went into permanent exile. On account of these events Epimenides the Cretan purified the city.

TYRANNY AT MYTILENE

There is a general discussion in Andrewes (1956) 92–99; see Page (1955) 149–243 for the political nature of Alcaeus' poetry and Mytilenaean tyranny. The text, translation and notes on the fragments of Alcaeus in Campbell (1982) I.206–455 are also useful. The Penthilidai, because of their habit of striking people with clubs, implying a repressive form of government, had been overthrown at Mytilene, by one Megakles and his associates; but later another of the family had to be killed, indicating further troubles (Arist. *Pol.* 1311b 26–30). These incidents occurred some time in the seventh century, and seem to have ushered in a period of unrest in the city. Pittakos, with the brothers of Alcaeus, overthrew the tyrant Melanchros (Diog. Laert. 1.74). Alcaeus may have been too young to participate (cf. Alcaeus 75) and this took place in the 42nd Olympiad, ie 612–09 BC. Strab. XIII.2.3 (617) notes that there were several tyrants at Mytilene: Melanchros, Pittakos, Myrsilos, and others, and that Alcaeus reviled them all; see Burnett (1983) 107–20. Alcaeus was an aristocrat and lyric poet, and many of his poems were against Myrsilos and Pittakos. Strabo (*loc. cit.*) suggests that Alcaeus may himself have aimed at tyrannical power, but it is more likely that Alcaeus and his brothers were fighting against tyranny with the aim of preserving the power of the aristocracy to which they belonged.

2.20 Pittakos' Betrayal of Alcaeus and his Associates

Alcaeus 70, lines 6–13

After the overthrow of Melanchros, another tyrant had arisen, Myrsilos, and Alcaeus may have fled to Pyrrha on Lesbos (according to the Schol. on Alcaeus 113, quoted by Page (1955) 179); Burnett (1983) 175 considers that Pittakos was now moving towards his final assertion of power, and the faction Alcaeus belonged to was still in the city; Pittakos had became associated with Myrsilos, and, moreover, he had married into the Penthilidai, who claimed descent from Atreus, the father of Agamemnon.

Now a kinsman by marriage of the Atreidai,
Let that man (Pittakos) devour the city just as he did with Myrsilos,
Until Ares wishes to turn us to arms,
May we completely forget this anger;
Let us have a remission from heart-gnawing sedition
And internecine fighting, which one of the Olympians
Has inspired, leading the people to ruin
But giving Pittakos the glory which he loves.

2.21 Alcaeus in Exile

Alcaeus 130, lines 16–27

This poem belongs to one of Alcaeus' periods of exile on Lesbos, after the failure of a conspiracy against Myrsilos; see Page (1955) 197–98; Burnett (1983) 176–81.

.... I poor wretch,
Live a rustic life
Desiring to hear the assembly
Being summoned, Agesilaidas,
And boule; what my father and father's father
Have grown old possessing, amongst
These citizens who wrong each other,
From this I have been driven out
An exile at the world's end, and, like Onymakles,
I dwelt alone among wolf-thickets
..... war; for it is not good to renounce
Strife (stasis) against .....

2.22 When Myrsilos Died, Alcaeus Celebrated

Alcaeus 332

This song dates to Alcaeus' return from his first exile. For Alcaeus' audience of relatives and friends, his hetaireia, who dined together as frequently as possible and whose kinship was outwardly displayed in common military action, see Burnett (1983) 121–55, 166.

Now everyone should be drunk and with all their might
Drink, since Myrsilos has died.

2.23 The Lydians Finance Alcaeus' Attempt to Return

Alcaeus 69

It is generally assumed that Alcaeus, his brother Antimenidas, and Sappho were exiled from Lesbos at some stage (for example Andrewes (1956) 93; cf. Page (1955) 223), for Alcaeus visited Egypt (Alcaeus 432), Antimenidas fought with the Babylonians (Alcaeus 350) and Sappho is said to have gone to Sicily (but the Marmor Parium *FGH* 239.36 dates this much earlier). It may have been during this exile that Alcaeus and others attempted to gain control of Mytilene with the aid of the Lydians, who provided two thousand staters in assistance. Pittakos' election as tyrant 'against the exiles' (Arist. *Pol.* 1285a 29–b 1), is generally linked with this (Andrewes 93); see, for the difficulties in interpreting the poem, Page (1955) 228–33 and Burnett (1983) 163–66, who considers that the city does not refer to Mytilene, but that Pittakos has tried to trick Alcaeus and his fellow-conspirators into going to mend their fortunes as mercenaries in Lydia, by magnifying the amount of remuneration involved.

Father Zeus, the Lydians, indignant at our misfortunes, gave us two thousand staters, if we could enter the holy city,
Though they had had nothing good from us nor are acquainted with us; but he (?Pittakos), like a wily fox, predicted easy things, and hoped to escape notice.

2.24 Pittakos Elected as Tyrant

Aristotle *Politics* 1285a 29–b 3 (III, xiv) (Alcaeus 348)

Pittakos, as the following passage indicates, was an aisymnetes, an elected tyrant, whom the Mytilenaeans chose as their leader 'against the exiles' Antimenidas and Alcaeus. Alcaeus, in this fragment quoted by Aristotle, refers to Pittakos as a tyrant (tyrannos) and this is the first occurrence of the word used to refer to a specific Greek ruler. Alcaeus, as an aristocrat, objected to Pittakos as low-born (kakopatrides). Page (1955) 169–73 argues that Pittakos was not in any sense a 'plebeian' and that the adjective refers to Pittakos' Thracian paternity: Duris *FGH* 76 F75; this was enough for Alcaeus to be able to impugn the birth of his rival. For the 'two kinds of monarchy', kingship and tyranny, see Arist. *Pol.* 1285a 25–29.

1285a 29 So these are the two kinds of monarchy, and there is a third called 'aisymnetes' which existed among the Greeks of ancient times. This can be described in simple terms as an elective tyranny, which differs from the barbarian type of kingship not by being in opposition to the law, but only in not being ancestral. Some of these rulers kept their power throughout their lives, others until certain stated times or events. It was in this way that the Mytilenaeans chose Pittakos against the exiles who were led by Antimenidas and the poet Alcaeus. Alcaeus makes clear that they chose Pittakos as tyrant in one of his drinking-songs; for he makes the complaint that 'with great praises of the low-born Pittakos the masses set him up as tyrant of their easy-going and ill-fated city.' **1285b 1** This type of rule is and was like that of tyranny in being despotic, but royal in being chosen and over willing subjects.

2.25 Alcaeus' Judgement of Pittakos

Alcaeus 429

Pittakos was aisymnetes for ten years, organized the affairs of Mytilene, and then relinquished the office, living for another ten years, and dying in 570. His election is therefore to be dated to 590 (Diog. Laert. 1.75, 79; Strab. XIII.2.3 (617)). The only specific law that is attributed to him was that offences committed while drunk incurred a double penalty (Arist. *Pol.* 1274b 18–23; Diog. Laert. 1.76). After relinquishing office he was given a grant of land, and he was numbered amongst the Seven Sages (Diog. Laert. 1.56–80). Clearly Alcaeus' insults must be set against the favourable tradition concerning this tyrant.

Alcaeus calls him (Pittakos) 'splay-footed' and 'splay-feet' (because he had flat feet and trailed his feet), 'chapped-feet' (because of the cracks in his feet, which they call chaps), 'braggart' (because he pranced around at random), 'pot-belly' and 'fat-belly' (because he was overweight), 'diner in the dark' (because he did not use a light) and 'swept and garnished' (since he was slovenly and filthy).

POLYKRATES OF SAMOS

The aristocrats, geomoroi, of Samos were overthrown c. 600 BC by the generals (Plut. *Mor.* 303e–304c). In 532 Polykrates disposed of one brother and exiled another, Syloson, before assuming sole rule, suggesting that the brothers had a hereditary power, devolving to them from their father; see White (1954) 37–43. (Polykrates' father, Aiakes, is not, however, the dedicant of ML 16.) Syloson, the exiled brother, later became tyrant after Polykrates' death. Barron (1964) 210–29 incorrectly argues that there were in fact two tyrants called Polykrates, father and son, at Samos and that Herodotos deals with the life and death of Polykrates II; this has not been generally accepted (see esp. West (1970) 208), but for the view that tyranny began at Samos c. 590, see Mitchell (1975) 75–91; Shipley (1987) 68–73.

2.26 Polykrates Comes to Power

Herodotos III.39.1–4

The date of Polykrates' accession to power is given by Eusebius as taking place in 532 BC, which is generally accepted as his activities coincided with the reign of Cambyses (Hdt. III.39.1; Thuc. I.13.6, doc. 2.27) who reigned from 530–522. Some scholars date Polykrates' tyranny, however, to c. 540 (see White (1954) 36 with nn.8–9; Mitchell (1975) 81–85; note Berve (1967) II.583). According to Polyaenus (*Strat.* I.23.2) Polykrates had his brothers kill those of the Samians who had put aside their armour at a festival (cf. docs. 4.13, 4.30) and then welcomed those who were fleeing from the slaughter which his brothers had carried out. He received assistance from Lygdamis, who had been made tyrant of Naxos by Peisistratos (Hdt. I.64.2).

III.39.1 While Cambyses was making war on Egypt, the Spartans made an expedition against Samos and Polykrates son of Aiakes, who had risen up and taken control of Samos. **III.39.2** Initially he divided control of the city into three parts and shared it with his brothers Pantagnotos and Syloson, but later on he killed the former and banished Syloson, the younger of the two, and controlled all Samos. He then made a treaty of friendship with Amasis, King of Egypt, sending him gifts and receiving others in exchange. **III.39.3** In a short time Polykrates' power quickly increased and he was celebrated throughout Ionia and the rest of Greece. Wherever he chose to wage war, everything turned out successfully for him. He possessed a hundred pentekonters and a thousand archers. **III.39.4** He used to rob and plunder everyone indiscriminately; for he said that he would oblige a friend more by giving back the things he had taken from him than if he had not taken them to begin with. He had captured many of the islands and also many of the cities of the mainland. He even captured the Lesbians who had come to the help of the Milesians with all their forces after conquering them in a sea-battle, and it was they who, in chains, dug the whole moat which surrounds Samos' wall.

2.27 The Thalassocracy of Polykrates

Thucydides I.13.6, III.104.2

Polykrates had a large and powerful navy, with which he established control over several islands. He was clearly the most important ruler in the Aegean, and also engaged in piracy (doc. 2.26); Shipley (1987) 94–95. His conquest of Delos may have been provoked by Peisistratos' purification (doc. 4.17); Parke (1946) 105–08. Anacreon 349 is also a possible indication that the city of Ialysos on Rhodes was part of Polykrates' empire.

I.13.6 And afterwards the Ionians had a large fleet in the time of Cyrus (559–546), first king of the Persians and of Cambyses his son, and when they were fighting against Cyrus they had control of the sea in their region for some time. Polykrates, the tyrant of Samos in the time of Cambyses, also had a powerful navy; he made a number of the islands subject to himself, including Rheneia which he took and dedicatedto Delian Apollo .... **III.104.2** Rheneia is so little distance from Delos that Polykrates, the tyrant of Samos, during the time of his naval supremacy, not only ruled the rest of the islands, but, when he took Rheneia, dedicated it to Delian Apollo by attaching it to Delos by a chain.

2.28 The Spartans Attempt to Overthrow Polykrates

Herodotos III.44.1–47.3, 54.1–2, 56.1–2

The Spartans in 525/4 attempted to overthrow the tyranny of Polykrates, encouraged by Samian exiles, potential rebels whom Polykrates had sent to Cambyses to aid in the conquest of Egypt. At Sparta the exiles encountered the famous Spartan taciturnity. The Spartans claimed not to be able to understand long speeches — criticizing the Samians for using three words (in the Greek) when two would have sufficed (cf. Plut. *Mor.* 232b). Polykrates had been in alliance with Amasis of Egypt (570–26), and Herodotos has Amasis renounce the alliance (III.43.1–2). But Polykrates' support of Cambyses has the appearance of a calculated decision to side with the Persians, who did conquer Egypt: see Austin (1990) 293. For the story of Polykrates and the ring, see Hdt. III.40.1–43.2, III.125.4; Walcot (1978) 28, 38; Fisher (1992) 361–64; van der Veen (1993) 434–57. Doc. 2.26 mentions pentekonters, but Polykrates (III.44.2) sends the untrustworthy Samians to Cambyses in forty triremes. Thuc. I.13.2 (doc. 10.35) states that the

Corinthians developed the trireme c. 700 BC; Polykrates may have been instrumental in the switch from pentekonters to triremes (Davison (1947) 18–24; Cook (1982) 218).

III.44.1 So the Spartans made an expedition against the all-successful Polykrates. They had been called in by the Samians, who afterwards built Kydonia on Crete. Polykrates had sent a herald without the knowledge of the Samians to Cambyses, son of Cyrus, who was raising an army against Egypt, requesting that Cambyses should send to Polykrates at Samos as well and ask for an army. **III.44.2** When Cambyses heard this he gladly sent to Samos to ask Polykrates to send a naval force against Egypt alongside his own. Polykrates then picked out those of the citizens whom he suspected in particular of rebellious tendencies and sent them off in forty triremes, instructing Cambyses not to send them back. **III.45.1** Some say that those Samians who were sent off never arrived in Egypt, but when they had sailed as far as Karpathos deliberated and preferred not to sail any further; others say that they arrived at Egypt where they were guarded but escaped from there. **III.45.2** As they were sailing home, Polykrates encountered them with his ships and engaged battle; the Samian exiles won and landed on the island, but in a battle on land they were defeated and accordingly sailed to Sparta. **III.45.3.** Some say that the men from Egypt defeated Polykrates, but in saying so they seem to be wrong. For they had no need to call in the Spartans, if they were themselves able to bring Polykrates to terms. Moreover it is unreasonable to suppose that a man who had a large force of hired mercenaries and his own archers would be defeated by the small number of returning Samians. **III.45.4** Polykrates shut up in the boat-sheds the children and wives of the citizens under his control and had them ready to burn, boat-sheds and all, should the citizens betray him to the Samian exiles. **III.46.1** When the Samians who had been driven out by Polykrates reached Sparta, they went before the magistrates and spoke at length like men in great need. But at this first presentation of their case the Spartans replied that they had forgotten what had been said to begin with, and not understood the rest. **III.46.2** Later on, when the Samians came before them for the second time carrying a sack, they said nothing else but 'The sack needs meal.' The Spartans replied that the word 'sack' was unnecessary; but they decided to help them .... **III.54.1** The Spartans arrived with a large fleet and besieged Samos. They made an attack against the wall and set foot on the tower standing near the sea on the suburban side of the city, but then, when Polykrates came to the rescue with a large force, they were driven off. **III.54.2** The mercenaries and many of the Samians themselves sallied out near the upper tower which stands on the ridge of the hill and held the Spartans for a short time before retreating; but the Spartans followed and killed them .... **III.56.1** When the Spartans had been besieging Samos for forty days and had made no progress, they went back to the Peloponnese. **III.56.1** A foolish report exists that Polykrates coined a large amount of native coinage in lead which he gilded and gave to them, and they took it and it was for that reason they departed.

2.29 The Murder of Polykrates

Herodotos III.120.1–125.1

Hdt. III.120.1 dates Polykrates' murder to the time of Cambyses' (last) illness in 522. His death ushered in a period of Persian domination of Samos and represented further Persian expansion against the Greeks. For the dream of Polykrates' daughter foretelling her father's fate and his refusal to listen to her warning, see Hdt. III.124, 125.4; for Polykrates' successors, Maiandrios and Syloson, see Hdt. III.139.1–149; cf. Graf (1985) 79–123; Austin (1990) 289–306.

III.120.1 At about the time of Cambyses' illness the following events occurred. A Persian, Oroites, had been appointed viceroy (hyparchos) of Sardis by Cyrus. He became possessed of an unlawful desire; for although he had not suffered any wrong or heard any rash word from Polykrates of Samos, and had not even previously seen him, he desired to capture and kill him .... **III.122.1** Oroites was then in Magnesia, which lies above the Maiander river, and sent Myrsos son of Gyges, a Lydian, to Samos with a message, having learnt Polykrates' intention. **III.122.2** For Polykrates was the first of the Greeks we know of who planned to dominate the sea, except for Minos of Knossos and anyone else who may have ruled the sea before him. In what is called the historical age Polykrates was the first, and he had many hopes of ruling over Ionia and the islands. **III.122.3** Oroites learnt that he was planning this and sent him the following message: 'Oroites says this to Polykrates: I hear that you are planning great things, but that you do not have enough money for your designs. If you do as I suggest, you will ensure your own success and save me; for King Cambyses plans my death and this has been plainly reported to me. **III.122.4** If you now get me and my money away, you can have some of it for yourself and leave me the rest; and through this money you will rule all Greece.'.... **III.125.1** Polykrates paid no regard to any advice, but sailed to Oroites, taking with him a large number of companions, among whom was Demokedes, son of Kalliphon, from Croton, who was a doctor and the most skilful practitioner of his time. When Polykrates arrived at Magnesia, he was cruelly murdered, which neither he nor his designs had deserved; for except for the tyrants of Syracuse there is no other Greek tyrant worthy to be compared to Polykrates for magnificence. After killing him (in a manner not fit to be narrated) Oroites had him crucified; all of those with him who were Samians Oroites let go, telling them to be grateful to him for their freedom; those who were not Samians or were slaves of Polykrates' companions he kept, considering them as prisoners of war.

POLYKRATES' PATRONAGE OF THE ARTS

Several poets are heard of at the court of Polykrates. Anacreon of Teos is mentioned several times; in addition to Hdt. III.121.1, see also Strab. XIV.1.16 (637–38) 'the poet Anacreon lived together with Polykrates and indeed all his poetry is full of references to him'; Aelian *VH* 9.4 (Anacreon is said to have been brought to Samos by Polykrates' father: Anacreon 491). Most of Anacreon's poems are concerned with love and wine, and were written for drinking-parties, symposia. Anacreon was born on Teos but helped found

Abdera, and went to Athens after Polykrates' death at the invitation of Hipparchos (see docs. 1.11, 4.22–23; cf. 2.12). Pythagoras, too, left Samos, c. 531 (during Polykrates' tyranny), for Croton. Polykrates' court had a luxurious lifestyle: Hdt. III.123.1 states of Maiandrios, 'it was he who not long afterwards (ie after Polykrates' death) sent as an offering all the remarkable adornment of Polykrates' men's apartments to the Heraion.'

2.30 Luxury Goods on Samos

Alexis *FGH* 539 F2 (Athenaeus *Deipnosophistae* 540d–e)

For a similar list of imported animals, see Klytos *FGH* 490 F2; for the *Samainai*, see also Plut. *Per.* 26.4; Berve (1967) II.584. Polykrates also attracted Demokedes the well-known medical practitioner from Athens by offering him a salary of two talents; Demokedes had previously held a state appointment in Aegina where he was paid one talent per annum, and his salary in Athens under Peisistratos was 100 minas (doc. 2.29; Hdt. III.131.2; de Ste. Croix (1981) 271). Obviously tyrants were willing to pay to acquire the best professional services from doctors as well as poets.

Alexis in the third book of his *Samian Annals* says that Samos was embellished from many cities by Polykrates, who imported Molossian and Lakonian hounds, goats from Skyros and Naxos, and sheep from Miletos and Attica. He says that he also summoned craftsmen at very high wages. Before he became tyrant he had extravagant carpets and cups and used to allow them to be used by those celebrating a marriage or the larger sort of receptions. From all of this it is worthy of remark that the tyrant is nowhere recorded as having sent for women or boys, although he was passionately excited by the society of males, so that he was even a rival in love to Anacreon the poet, when, in a rage, he cut off the hair of his beloved boy. Polykrates was the first to construct certain ships called Samainai, after his country.

2.31 Polykrates Honoured in Song

Ibycus 282, lines 10–22, 40–48

Ibycus was possibly born at Rhegium, and there is a later story that he might have been tyrant but preferred to leave (Diog. Laert. 2.71). He went to Samos, possibly in the reign of Polykrates' father, who may thus have been the first 'tyrant patron' of court poets. Ibycus is believed to have arrived there c. 547/6 or perhaps before, and may have left, as Anacreon did for Athens, at the murder of Polykrates in 522. He may have been the earliest composer of victory odes, epinicians (ie before Simonides), though his works generally feature either mythological or erotic themes. That Ibycus went to Samos in the reign of Polykrates' father is also partly inferred from this poem where Polykrates' fame seems to be due to his beauty, in which case he was a youth and not yet tyrant (Campbell (1991) III.6), but this is not necessarily the case; cf. Barron (1964) 210–29, (1969) 119–49; West (1970) 206–08. The mythical references in the poem relate to the Trojan war: Cassandra and Troilos were children of the Trojan king Priam.

10 Now it is not my desire to sing of Paris, who deceived his host, or slender-ankled Cassandra or the other children of Priam,
14 Or the inglorious day when high-gated Troy was captured; nor yet of the proud courage of the heroes whom the hollow

18 Many-nailed ships brought to be an evil for Troy, noble heroes; Lord Agamemnon commanded them, of the house of the Pleisthenidai, a king, chief of men, the son born of noble Atreus....

40 .... he whom golden-haired Hyllis bore, to him, like already thrice refined gold to mountain copper,

44 The Trojans and Greeks (Danaoi) compared Troilos of similar and lovely form. They will always have beauty hereafter and you Polykrates will have undying renown, just as I too shall have renown through my song.

THE SICILIAN TYRANTS

2.32 Theron of Selinous

Polyaenus *Strategemata* I.28.2

The precise date of Theron's attempt to become tyrant of Selinous, in western Sicily, cannot be determined, but it took place towards the end of the sixth century. The use of slaves is unusual, but falls into a typical pattern of tyrants having armed supporters. The slaves were presumably rewarded with their freedom and possibly citizenship, given the number of citizens killed in the *coup*; see Berger (1992) 30–31. The Spartan Euryleon later unsuccessfully attempted a tyranny at Selinous (Hdt. V.46). The Greeks shared the island with the native Sicels and Carthaginians; for sixth century clashes between Greeks and Carthaginians, see Asheri (1988) 748–53 and, for Selinous, *ibid.* 754–57.

After the people of Selinous had done battle against the Carthaginians, many of the fallen lay unburied and they were not sufficiently bold to bury the corpses of their enemies which lay there. However, they were unable to endure leaving them unburied and debated what they ought to do. Theron promised that if he could take three hundred slaves, who would be able to fell timber, he would go with them and both burn the bodies and erect a communal tomb; and if the enemy should get the better of them, there would be no great danger to the city, for it would only lose one citizen and the value of three hundred slaves. The people of Selinous praised this proposal and allowed him to take his choice of slaves. He picked out those who were robust and in their prime and led them out equipped with scythes and axes, as if they were going to fell timber to make a funeral pyre for so many corpses. When they had left the city, Theron persuaded them to attack their masters and returned to the city late in the evening. The guards on the walls recognized them and let them in. After Theron slew these guards and killed the majority of the citizens while they were asleep, he took the city and became tyrant of Selinous.

2.33 Gelon Refuses to Help the Greeks

Herodotos VII.165–166

Gelon, a commander (hipparchos) of the cavalry (Hdt. VII.154.2), made himself tyrant c. 491, and in 485 moved his base of operations to Syracuse, where he carried out a synoecism (Hdt. VII.153.1–156.3); see Demand (1990) 46–50; for Sicilian tyrants, see Dunbabin (1948) 376–434; Asheri (1988) 757–66. Prior to Xerxes' invasion Herodotos states (VII.158.4–5) that Gelon agreed to come to the aid of the Greeks — with 200 ships, 20,000 infantry, 2,000 cavalry, 2,000 archers, 2,000 slingers, and 2,000 light horsemen — and to feed the entire Greek army, if he were made strategos and hegemon, leader, of the Greek forces, but the condition was rejected. Hdt. VII.163.2 also records that if the Persians were victorious, Gelon was prepared to surrender to them, presumably as a client-tyrant, and that he sent an envoy with a large sum of money to Delphi to be given to Xerxes, if he defeated the Greeks. But the Sicilians were later able to claim that Gelon would have fought under the Spartans, if the Carthaginians had not kept him occupied in Sicily at the Battle of Himera in 480; see Dunbabin (1948) 421–23.

VII.165 It is said by the inhabitants of Sicily that Gelon, even if he had to serve under the Spartans, would still have helped the Greeks, if Terillos, son of Krinippos and tyrant of Himera, had not been expelled by Theron son of Ainesidemos, ruler (mounarchos) of Akragas. At about this time Terillos brought with him three hundred thousand Phoenicians, Libyans, Iberians, Ligurians, Elisykans, Sardinians and Corsicans with Hamilcar son of Hanno, himself a Carthaginian king, as their general .... In this situation, as it was not possible for Gelon to help the Greeks, he sent the money to Delphi. **VII.166** They also say that it happened that Gelon in Sicily conquered Theron and Hamilcar the Carthaginian on the same day that the Greeks conquered the Persians at Salamis.

2.34 A Dedication in Honour of Sicilian Victory

Simonides 34

The poet Simonides was born on Keos and c.556–c.468 are generally accepted as his dates. Like Anacreon and Lasos he was in Athens in the time of Hipparchos (527–14), after which he seems to have gone to Thessaly. He spent his last years in Sicily where he was a friend of Hieron. This fragment purports to be a Delphic inscription written by him, but it is probably not genuine: see Page 247–50. The second couplet is almost certainly a Hellenistic addition. Gelon had dedicated a limestone tripod base at Delphi for his victory at Himera, see ML 28 (*SIG*[3] 34a–b).

I say that Gelon, Hieron, Polyzelos and Thrasyboulos,
The sons of Deinomenes, set up these tripods,
After defeating barbarian nations, and provided a great
Hand as allies to the Greeks in regard to liberty.

2.35 Hieron Defeats the Etruscans

Meiggs & Lewis 29 (*SIG*[3] 35 B, a)

This inscription is on a captured Etruscan helmet, sent to Olympia as a dedication; see *SEG* 23.253 & 33.328 for two other helmets dedicated by Hieron at Olympia. For a line drawing of the helmet, now in the British Museum, with inscription, see Asheri (1992) 152, fig. 6. Spoils destined for Delphi were lost at sea (if Simonides 76 is to be associated with Cumae; see Athen. 231f–232d; Bacchyl. 3.17–21). Hieron defeated the Etruscans off Cumae, which they were attacking, in 474/3 (Diod. XI.51).

Hieron son of Deinomenes
And the Syracusans (dedicated these)
Etruscan spoils from Cumae to Zeus.

2.36 The End of the Deinomenids' Tyranny

Aristotle *Politics* 1312b 9–16 (V, x)

Hieron took over the tyranny from Gelon in 478 and died in 467. Thrasyboulos was overthrown in 466. The tyranny collapsed as two factions in the Deinomenids struggled for power and the Syracusan epicracy fell apart; see Asheri (1992) 156–57.

Another way (to destroy a tyranny) is from within, when there is dissension among those who have a share in it, as with the tyranny of Gelon and in our day that of Dionysios. In Gelon's case, Thrasyboulos, Hieron's brother, won the support of Gelon's son and impelled him towards the enjoyment of pleasures, so he might rule. The family united to make sure that Thrasyboulos but not the tyranny itself was put down, but their fellow conspirators, having the opportunity, expelled them all.

TYRANTS AND THE PANHELLENIC GAMES

The Sicilian tyrants sent chariots to compete at the Panhellenic festivals, not attending themselves, but sending representatives. They thus maintained links with the 'motherland', which was clearly important to them, and publicized their own wealth and importance. The following passages are examples of eulogy written for tyrants by court poets to celebrate such victories, and are evidence for patronage of the arts by Hieron.

2.37 Hieron's Victory in 468 at the Olympic Games

Bacchylides 3, lines 1–14, 93–98

Hieron had also been victorious in the Olympic chariot races in 476 (commemorated in Bacchyl. 5) and in 472. Bacchylides of Keos, the nephew of Simonides, wrote for patrons all over Greece, including Athens, Sparta, Thessaly, Macedon and the West. His most important patron was Hieron for whom he composed epinicians 5, 4 and 3 in 476, 470 and 468. Lines 9–12 bear out the power and influence of Sicilian tyrants.

1 Sing of Demeter, the lady of fair fruited Sicily, and of violet-garlanded Persephone, Clio of sweet gifts, and of the swift horses of Hieron which ran at the Olympic Games.

5 For they sped with prominent Victory and Glory beside the wide-eddying Alpheios, and there made the son of Deinomenes prosperous in the successful attaining of garlands;

9 And the people cried aloud. Ah, thrice-happy man, who obtained from Zeus the honour of holding widest sway over Greeks and who does not know how to hide his towering wealth in gloom-shrouded darkness ....

93 Hieron, you have displayed to mortal men the most beautiful flowers of worldly happiness; to a man who has done well silence does not bring ornament; and with the truth of your success someone will also celebrate the grace of the honey-tongued Kean nightingale (ie Bacchylides of Keos himself).

2.38 Hieron's Victory in 470 at the Pythian Games

Pindar *Pythian* I, lines 56–60b, 92–100b

This victory of Hieron was also celebrated in Bacchyl. 4; Hieron had also won the chariot-race at Delphi in 482 and 478. Deinomenes was Hieron's son; for the refoundation of Aetna, on which Aeschylus wrote a play (*The Women of Aetna*), see Herington (1967) 76; Demand (1990) 51–52. Aeschylus visited Sicily on more than one occasion and died there (doc. 7.10). Hieron is here compared to the wealthy and hospitable Croesus, king of Lydia, and contrasted with Phalaris of Akragas (see Diod. IX.18–19 for the bull).

56 Thus may god be Hieron's preserver in the coming time,
Giving him due measure of his desires.
Muse, obey me and sing in the house of Deinomenes
The reward for his four-horse chariot;
59b His father's victory is a source of joy which belongs to no one else.
60 Come then for the king of Aetna
60b Let us invent a loving song ....

92 The glory of renown that lives after men
Is what reveals the way of life of the departed
Both in words and songs. The friendly virtue of Croesus does not fade.
95 But that ruthless mind, who burned victims in a brazen bull,
Phalaris, is everywhere the subject of hostile talk.
No lyres in the house welcome him
Mingling his name softly with the songs of boys.
99 To be fortunate is the first of prizes;
99b The next most fortunate destiny is to be well spoken of; the man
100 Who has met with both and keeps them
Has won the highest crown.

TYRANTS AND PUBLIC WORKS

In addition to the public works at Samos, Athens and Megara, note also the diolkos, the six kilometre stone carriageway built by Periander, which enabled ships and cargo to be transported across the Isthmus; see Cook (1979) 152–54; Salmon (1984) 136–39; Drijvers (1992) 75–78; line drawing at Hammond (1982) 349, fig. 52; cf. doc. 10.35; and for the Corinthian tyrants' attention to the water supply, see Salmon (1984) 201.

2.39 Construction Work on Samos

Herodotos III.60.1–4

It is commonly supposed that the three works mentioned in the following passage of Herodotos are to be dated to Polykrates' reign, though Herodotos does not actually state this; see White (1954) 40–42; Cook (1982) 219; Shipley (1987) 75–79; with a plan of the city showing the tunnel, which safeguarded the water supply, at Boardman (1982) 444, fig. 55; White 41 is incorrect, however, in stating that the tunnel used by Maiandrios to escape from Samos was Eupalinos' work: see Hdt. III.146.2. The older Heraion was destroyed by fire in Polykrates' reign soon after completion, possibly during the Spartan attack of 525; Polykrates began rebuilding, but it was not completed until Hellenistic and Roman times.

III.60.1 I have written somewhat at length concerning the Samians, because they have the three greatest constructions of all the Greeks: first a channel with two mouths dug beneath a mountain a hundred and fifty fathoms high. **III.60.2** The length of the channel is seven stades, the height and breadth each eight feet. Through its whole length another channel is dug twenty cubits in depth, and three feet in breadth, through which the water coming from an abundant spring is carried through pipes to the city. **III.60.3** The architect of this channel was a Megarian, Eupalinos son of Naustrophos. This is one of the three, and the second is a breakwater in the sea around the harbour, twenty fathoms in depth, while the length of the breakwater is more than two stades. **III.60.4** Their third construction is the greatest of all known temples, of which the first master-builder was Rhoikos son of Phileus, a Samian. It is because of these that I have written at length about the Samians.

2.40 Public Works as a Method of Good Government

Aristotle *Politics* 1313b 18–32 (V, xi)

In this passage, Aristotle claims that tyrants' public works played a role in keeping their subjects busy, though the examples do not prove this. The temple of Zeus was not completed until the reign of Hadrian; and even if Polykrates is credited with all the works on Samos, it is doubtful how much employment this would have provided (and he used slaves captured in war for the moat around Samos: doc. 2.26). The pyramids are also incorrectly interpreted: they were built for religious reasons. For Dionysios, see Caven (1990) 160–66, esp. 161, and for the Kypselid treasury at Delphi, Hdt. I.14.1–2.

It is in a tyrant's interests to impoverish those he governs, so that he can afford to keep his bodyguard and so that the people are so busy with their daily lives that they have no time for plotting. An example is the pyramids of Egypt and the dedications of the Kypselids and the construction of the temple of Olympian Zeus by the Peisistratidai, and the works on Samos owed to Polykrates (for all these achieved the same, the lack of leisure and impoverishment of their subjects); another method is the payment of taxes, as at Syracuse (for in five years under Dionysios the whole value of property there was paid in). The tyrant is also an instigator of wars, as this keeps his subjects busy and continuously in need of a leader. And while kingship is preserved through friends, the policy of a tyrant is especially to distrust friends, as, what all men want, these in particular have the ability to put into practice.

THE SPARTAN OPPOSITION TO TYRANNY

2.41 The Spartans as Liberators

Thucydides I.18.1

In the sixth century the Spartans pursued a policy of putting down tyranny. In the case of Athens, they needed some persuasion to do so, and later, according to Herodotos, proposed to restore Hippias (doc. 6.37). The phrase 'only a few years afterwards' in fact covers a period of 20 years from 511/0 to 490; cf. Scanlon (1987) 291.

I.18.1 Finally, the Spartans expelled the tyrants from Athens and, excepting those in Sicily, from the rest of Greece as well, which for the most part had been ruled by tyrants for even longer than Athens. Sparta, from the time when the Dorians who now inhabit it first settled there, suffered from political discord for most of its history, even though from a very early date it has had good laws and never been ruled by tyrants. It is about four hundred years and rather longer to the end of this last war (the Peloponnesian War) that the Spartans have had the same constitution, and because of this they have been strong themselves and intervened in the affairs of other cities. And after the tyrants in Greece had been put down, it was only a few years before the battle at Marathon took place between the Persians and Athenians.

2.42 Plutarch Defends Spartan Motives

Plutarch *Moralia* 859b–e (*On the Malignity of Herodotos* 21)

In response to Herodotos' story (III.47.1) that the Spartans wanted to depose Polykrates because the Samians had seized a mixing bowl which the Spartans were sending to Persia, Plutarch lists the tyrannies which the Spartans had been instrumental in putting down. 'On the Malignity of Herodotos' points out a number of incredible and contradictory stories, but sometimes misinterprets Herodotos; for a commentary, see Bowen (1992) 105–47; cf. Hershbell (1993) 143–63.

859b In his third book, when Herodotos recounts the Spartan expedition against the tyrant Polykrates, he says that the Samians themselves think and say **859c** that the Spartans went to war for the sake of repaying them for their help against Messene, restoring those citizens who were in exile and making war against the tyrant; but he says that the Spartans deny this to be the reason and say that they were neither helping nor liberating the Samians, but went to war to punish them, since they had misappropriated a mixing-bowl (krater) the Spartans had sent to Croesus and also a breastplate that was being brought to them from Amasis. And yet we know that no city in those times so loved honour or hated tyranny as that of the Spartans. **859d** For the sake of what breastplate or mixing-bowl did they expel the Kypselids from Corinth and Ambracia? Lygdamis from Naxos? The sons of Peisistratos from Athens? Aischines from Sicyon? Symmachos from Thasos? Aulis from Phokis? Aristogenes from Miletos? And put an end to the dynasty in Thessaly after King Leotychidas deposed Aristomedes and Agelaos? These events have been more accurately narrated by others; but according to Herodotos the Spartans went to an extreme of both cowardice and fatuity, if they denied the best and most righteous reason for their expedition **859e** and admitted that they attacked wretched and unfortunate people because of malice and pettiness.

THUCYDIDES AND ARISTOTLE ON TYRANNY

2.43 Tyranny and the Achievements of Tyrants

Thucydides I.13.1, 17.1

In this passage, Thucydides relates the development of trade and a growing economy to the emergence of tyranny. He notes that tyrannies were widespread, and in the seventh and sixth centuries they do in fact seem to have been one of the most common forms of government. Thucydides seems to equate successful tyranny with the military achievements of the states over which the tyrants ruled, seeing combinations of cities as dynamic, and will no doubt have been influenced in this by the achievements of the Athenians as the head of the Delian League.

I.13.1 As Greece became more powerful and the acquisition of money still more important than before, tyrannies were established for the most part in the cities, and as the revenues were increasing (previously there were hereditary kingships based on established prerogatives), Greece began to build her navies and turned even more to the sea .... **I.17.1** In the Greek cities governed by tyrants, the tyrants' only concern was for themselves, that is for their physical safety and increasing the power of their family. As a result they governed their cities as far as possible with a view to security. So no deed worthy of note was done by them, except in relation to their own immediate neighbours, which allowed the Sicilian tyrants to rise to great power. Thus the situation everywhere in Greece was such that nothing remarkable was being achieved by joint action and even the individual cities were lacking in enterprise.

2.44 The Origins of Tyranny

Aristotle *Politics* 1310b 14–31 (V, x)

At *Pol.* 1305a 7–27 Aristotle notes that the champions of the people, like Peisistratos and Theagenes, aimed at tyranny with the people's support; see doc. 3.38, cf. 3.11 for Solon's awareness that he could have become tyrant. But some tyrants were clearly aristocrats who then had to take action against their fellow aristocrats in order to maintain power. Panaitios was ruler of Leontinoi in the early sixth century: see Graham (1982) 190; Polyaen. *Strat.* V.47; for the Ionian tyrants, see Graf (1985) 79–123. Kypselos had been polemarch, and Dionysios strategos autokrator, general with absolute powers, in 406/5: Diod. XIII.94.5; Caven (1990) 50–58. Cf. *Pol.* 1285a 25–29, *Rhet.* 1357b 30–36 for tyrants and their need for bodyguards.

Nearly all tyrants started out as popular leaders (demagogoi), it is fair to say, who were trusted because they spoke against the distinguished. Some tyrannies were established in this way, when cities had increased in size, while some, before these, were kingships which deviated from ancestral practices and grasped at more despotic powers; some again were from elected officials who then aimed at authoritarian rule (for in old times the populace used to set up long-term offices (demiourgiai) and embassies to religious sites (theoriai)), and others from oligarchies choosing one person as supreme over the highest positions. In all these ways achieving the object was easy, and only needed to be desired, because of the power existing either in the kingship or in the magistracy. For example Pheidon of Argos was one of several tyrants who set up tyrannies from an existing kingship; a number of Ionian tyrants and Phalaris did so from magistracies; and Panaitios in Leontinoi, Kypselos in Corinth, Peisistratos in Athens, and Dionysios in Syracuse, as well as others in the same way, got their start from being popular leaders.

2.45 The Short-lived Nature of Tyranny

Aristotle *Politics* 1315b 11–18, 21–39 (V, xii)

Few of the Greek tyrannies lasted for long. Clearly the conditions that favoured the seizing of power did not recur, with the exception of Sicily, where the first tyrannies ended in 466 but tyranny re-emerged with Dionysios I. For the ways in which tyrants maintained their power, such as Hieron's use of eavesdroppers, see *Pol.* 1313a 34–1313b 16; and cf. Polyaen. *Strat.* V.2.13 for Dionysios' use of singing girls (mousouroi) and hetairai to report to him about the views of his opponents (Caven (1990) 166–67).

Of all constitutions, however, oligarchy and tyranny are the shortest-lived. The tyranny at Sicyon, that of Orthagoras and his sons, was the longest; it lasted a hundred years. The reason for this was that they treated their subjects moderately and in many respects observed the laws .... Secondly we have the tyranny of the Kypselids in Corinth, which lasted seventy-three years and six months, with Kypselos as tyrant for thirty years, Periander for forty and a half, and Psammitichos, son of Gorgos, for three. There are the same reasons for this; Kypselos was a popular leader and continued throughout his reign without a bodyguard, while Periander was more tyrant-like, but warlike too. The third was that of the Peisistratidai at Athens, though this was not continuous, for Peisistratos twice as tyrant went into exile. As a result he was tyrant for seventeen years out of thirty-three, and his children for eighteen, which makes the total thirty-five years. Of the rest there was the tyranny of Hieron and Gelon in Syracuse, though even this did not last many years, only amounting to eighteen. Gelon was tyrant for seven years and died in the eighth, Hieron for ten, and Thrasyboulos was expelled in the eleventh month. But the majority of tyrannies are all extremely short-lived.

3

The Law-Givers: Drakon and Solon

Despite the fact that colonization and tyranny were common phenomena in Greece in the eighth and seventh centuries, these were developments which largely passed Athens by in that period. When Kylon attempted to set up a tyranny at Athens with the support of his father-in-law Theagenes the tyrant of Megara, the attempt failed miserably (docs. 2.17–19). But it did have an important long-term political repercussion, the curse which lay upon the Alkmeonidai for their role in killing Kylon's supporters. It is also possible that Drakon was appointed to codify the laws in 621/0 as a result of the Kylonian conspiracy, to prevent blood feuds and clan killing that might have taken place as a consequence. Little is known of Drakon's laws because they were superseded by those of Solon (doc. 3.15), except for the law on homicide, which remained in force and was in fact republished in the year 409/8 (doc. 3.3). There was a later tradition that Drakon's laws were harsh (doc. 3.4), but such a tradition can be discounted, as the law on involuntary homicide seems humane; it may have simply arisen out of a feeling that any older set of laws was bound to be harsher than the present code. Drakon was not archon when he was lawgiver, and in this sense differed from Solon, who carried out his reforms as archon. Drakon's law-code was not unique in the Greek world in the seventh century: at Dreros a law was passed c. 650–600 about the holding of office (doc. 10.23), and Zaleukos of Locri in southern Italy, who was known as the first law-giver, also belongs to this period.

By the 590s, Attica was engulfed in a struggle between the rich and the poor, with Athenians being sold into slavery for failing to meet their obligations to wealthy landowners. The poor also had a political grievance: not being allowed political rights exacerbated their downtrodden economic status and for the *Athenaion Politeia* both the political and economic problems were to be viewed in terms of a struggle between the rich and the poor (doc. 3.7, cf. 3.9). In 594/3, the Athenians chose Solon as archon to resolve the crisis facing Attica. Prior to this he had been active in the prosecution of the war against Megara for control of the island of Salamis, though his self-appointed role as public critic, as evidenced in his poems (docs. 3.5–6, 8–9, 12, 20), seems more likely to have been responsible for his election. Like poets such as Archilochos, Alcaeus, Theognis and Hesiod, Solon used poetry to convey his ideas and feelings about the current political situation and his poems provide a first hand account of his reforms, though they do not give a detailed analysis of their contents, which helps to explain why there is debate about their actual nature. Moreover, the fourth century tendency to attribute all ancestral laws to Solon, regardless of their true origin, means that many laws attributed to Solon may not have been his. Solon as archon, lawgiver and mediator, attempted to address the various problems facing Attica, and carried out a significant series of reforms, both economic and political, though it is better not to divide them into two distinct categories, as his economic reforms benefited the poor by freeing them from the fear of enslavement and thus defused the worst of the political agitation. The poor had the status of pelatai and hektemoroi, and the *Ath. Pol.* describes the status of the hektemoroi, but not of the pelatai, so that their precise standing is not known: perhaps the pelatai were clients partially or completely dependent on a wealthy landowner. The hektemoroi paid one-sixth of the produce of their land over to the wealthy landowners and slavery resulted if this were not paid. Why the oppression of the poor by the rich had reached the stage where the poor were being enslaved is not quite clear. Solon's main reforms were the seisachtheia (docs. 3.11–13), the classification of political privilege according to wealth (doc. 3.16), the creation of a council of 400 (doc. 3.19) and a system of appeal against decisions of the magistrates (docs. 3.22–23). The seisachtheia, the 'shaking off of burdens', cancelled debts and entailed drawing out from the 'black earth' the horoi (boundary-markers) which enslaved her. There were now no pelatai and hektemoroi, and the farmers could work their land free of the fear of enslavement; a class of independent farmers with small plots of land was thus established (this may have been a re-establishment of the situation before the status of hektemoros was created). Solon did not redistribute the land, as demanded by some Athenians (doc. 3.12), but he did 'free' it: clearly the land had belonged to the hektemoroi but was encumbered by obligation to the landlord.

Prior to Solon, Athenian society had been controlled by the aristocrats, the eupatridai or 'well-born', a group closely-knit by intermarriage and kinship ties, who dominated Athens after the downfall of the monarchy, and ruled the state, formally, through the archonship and the Areiopagos. The Kylonian conspiracy was the result of one man's ambition for tyranny, not the work of a dissatisfied group of aristocrats, and Solon's own poems are primarily concerned not with feuding aristocrats but with the fact that the wealthy, as a group, were oppressing the poor. In Solon's time the wealthy seem to have closed ranks against the poor; there is no indication under Solon that the eupatridai felt that one of their number would rally the poor, and the aftermath of Solon's reforms show that the eupatridai were not looking for a protector against one of their own number as champion of the masses. In the political struggles following Solon, Megakles and Lykourgos ignored the people as a group, and while Peisistratos attached them to his own following the people, though Peisistratos' loyal supporters, were never strong enough in their own right for Peisistratos' rule as tyrant to be based simply on their support. If the eupatridai feared one of their number rallying the poor, their fears (with the benefit of hindsight) were groundless. Solon himself thought he gave the people 'as much privilege as was appropriate' (doc. 3.20). His reforms meant that each of the four property classes had specific rights and privileges: the magistrates were drawn from the wealthy, but the people chose them; there was also appeal against the decision of magistrates to the people. This was not a democratic system but a timocratic one, but the potential for extending this system into a democratic one was to be realised, and in less than a century Athens was a democracy. Solon is often said to have been 'a failure' as the strife within Attica continued after his archonship in 594/3. However, he had largely defused the struggle between the rich and the poor and while post-Solonian Attica had political troubles, with open rivalries amongst the wealthy becoming evident, there was no more enslavement for agricultural debt, resulting in a more stable society. Solon had refused to become a tyrant (doc. 3.38), and clearly hated tyranny as a form of government. Within decades, however, Peisistratos set up a tyranny; in this sense, Solon had not been successful. But it is important that Solon's laws remained more or less in force, and that by the time the tyranny ended in 511/0 Attica had been under Solonian laws for more than eight decades.

DRAKON THE LAW-GIVER

3.1 The Council of the Areiopagos before Drakon

[Aristotle] *Athenaion Politeia* 3.6

The *Ath. Pol.* here describes the functions of the Areiopagos prior to Drakon; see also doc. 3.2. The nine archons of any one year automatically joined the Areiopagos, though Solon was to change the criterion of election of the archons, from birth to wealth (doc. 3.16); at *Ath. Pol.* 8.2 the Areiopagos is said to have made the appointments before Solon. The pre-Solonian Areiopagos, chosen by birth, was purely an aristocratic body, which ruled Athens; all other offices were held for a period of one year. There was a view that Solon instituted the Areiopagos, but Plutarch argues that this was not the case: Plut. *Sol.* 19; see also *Ath. Pol.* 4.4; 8.4. The general view is that the Areiopagos began as a council that advised the kings of Athens and continued after the downfall of the monarchy (in 682 according to the archon list); see Laix (1973) 7–8; MacDowell (1978) 27; Rhodes 106–07; cf. Wallace (1985) 32–47. See Hignett (1952) 321–26 for the view that the archons were directly elected by the assembly both before and after Solon's reforms.

3.6 The council of the Areiopagos had the task of keeping watch over the laws, and it controlled the majority and the most important of the city's affairs, having full authority to punish and fine all the disorderly. For the selection of the archons was by birth and wealth, and the Areiopagos was made up of these; for this reason this is the only office to have remained until this day one held for life.

3.2 The Constitution of Drakon

[Aristotle] *Athenaion Politeia* 4.1–5

The *Ath. Pol.* 7.1 (doc. 3.15) states that Solon's constitution did away with Drakon's laws apart from that on homicide, which therefore remained in force for only 27 years (621/0 to 594/3; Stroud (1978) 23). Only one axon of Drakon's laws has survived (doc.

3.3); it deals with involuntary homicide, so presumably there was at least one other axon dealing with intentional homicide (see Stroud (1968) 32–37). The law was still in force in 409/8 when it was re-inscribed. Drakon's laws belong the archonship of Aristaichmos (*Ath. Pol.* 4.1) which can be dated to 621/0; see Cadoux (1948) 92; Stroud (1968) 66–70; Samuel (1972) 200; Rhodes 109; Chambers (1986) in the Teubner edition prefers to place a question mark after this date. The constitution of Drakon here contains anachronisms: there was no coinage in Attica at the time and three decades later, Solon still defined the classes in terms of produce not money; a council of 401 members, chosen by lot, is unlikely in a period dominated by the aristocrats (see Fuks (1953) 84–101; von Fritz (1954) 74–93; Rhodes 84–87; Moore (1983) 213; Ober (1989) 57n.11); and the emphasis on the importance of strategoi is clearly anachronistic, belonging to the fifth century, when the strategia overshadowed the archonship (see doc. 5.8). Not only does the constitution as follows seem to be not authentic, it also appears that it is an insertion into the text of the *Ath. Pol.* (ie not by the author of the *Ath. Pol.* himself), though Rhodes (1981) 86–87 argues that 4.1 can stand as an original part of the *Ath. Pol.*

4.1 So this is the outline of the first constitution. After this only a short time passed before Drakon enacted his ordinances in the archonship of Aristaichmos (621/0); his political organization had the following form. **4.2** A share in the constitution had been given to those who supplied their own arms. They chose the nine archons and the treasurers from those who had an unencumbered property of not less than ten minas, the other lesser officials from those who supplied their own arms, and the generals and cavalry commanders (hipparchoi) from those who could declare an unencumbered property of not less than one hundred minas and had legitimate sons over ten years of age from a wedded wife; the prytaneis had to take security from these and from the generals and cavalry commanders of the previous year until they had been publicly examined, accepting as guarantors four men of the same class as the generals and cavalry commanders. **4.3** There was to be a council of four hundred and one members appointed by lot from those who had citizenship. The men over thirty were to draw lots for this and the other magistracies, and the same man could not hold office twice before everyone had been in office; then they were again appointed by lot from the beginning. If any of the council members was absent from a meeting when a session of the council or assembly was being held, he was fined three drachmas if he was one of the pentakosiomedimnoi, two if one of the hippeis, and one if one of the zeugitai. **4.4** The council of the Areiopagos was the guardian of the laws and supervised the officials to make sure that they ruled in accordance with the laws. Anyone who had been wronged was able to lay information before the council of the Areiopagites declaring the law under which he was wronged. **4.5** Loans were made on the security of the person, as has already been said, and the country was in the hands of a few.

3.3 Republication of Drakon's Law of Homicide, 409/8

IG I^3 104 (Meiggs & Lewis 86)

A revision of the laws of Solon took place after the fall of the Four Hundred, and Drakon's law on homicide was republished as part of this; this revision of the laws is also evidenced by *IG* I^3 105 (*IG* I^2 114) and other fragmentary laws; see Robertson (1990) 43–75; Rhodes (1991) 87–100. The person guilty of involuntary homicide was to be exiled (not killed) but could be pardoned if the relatives of the victim permitted (father, brothers or sons are listed), but not if one of them opposed the pardon. Provisions were also made if there were no relatives. The legislation was to be retrospective, binding previous killers. If the murderer was killed while keeping away from the frontier agora, games and Amphictyonic rites (ie correctly observing exile by avoiding contact with Athenians at the border, and religious ceremonies), then the killer of the murderer was to be tried. Killers found within Attica (violating the terms of the exile) could be killed and killing in self-defence was permissible. There are detailed discussions of the provisions in Stroud (1968) 19–64; Gagarin (1981); see also Gagarin (1986) 86–89, 109, 112–15. A connection between this code and the Kylonian affair is usually assumed: Stroud (1968) 70–74, Andrewes (1982) 370; Gagarin (1986) 137; cf. Hignett (1952) 87; Sealey (1983) 120–22; Ober (1989) 58–59. The inscription can be restored with the aid of Dem. XXIII.37, LXIII.57. The re-inscribed law was to be exhibited in front of the stoa basileios, the stoa of the basileus archon, in the agora; see Thompson & Wycherley (1972) 83–90; Thompson (1976) 82–87; Wycherley (1978) 30–32; Camp (1986) 53–57, 100–04; for testimonia, see Wycherley (1957) 21–25. *Ath. Pol.* 7.1 (doc. 3.15) points out that Solon's laws were also displayed there; cf. Andok. I.82, 85. The duties of the basileus archon included presiding over cases concerned with impiety like that involving Socrates: see *Ath. Pol.* 57. For the anagrapheis, recorders, see MacDowell (1978) 46. The poletai let out state contracts, and sold confiscated property; the hellenotamiai were the 'Hellenic Treasurers'; the nature of the ephetai remains obscure.

Diogn[e]tos of Phrearrhioi was secreta[ry]; Diokles was archon. It was resolved by the boule and the people; (the tribe) Aka[m]antis held the p[r]ytany, [D]io[g]netos was secretary, Euthydikos [p]resided, [..]e[..ph]anes proposed the motion: let the anagrapheis reco[r]d th[e] law of Drakon concerning hom[ic]ide, when they have received it from the bas[i]le[us] archon [toge]the[r with the secre]tary of the council, on a stone stele and se[t it up in fro]nt of the stoa basileios; let the poletai put this [out to cont]ra[ct in accordance with the l]aw; let the hellenotamiai provide the mo[n]e[y].

First Axon. Even if without [p]remedit[at]ion [someone k]i[lls someone, he is to go into exi]l[e;] the basileis are to pass [j]udgement on him as guilt[y] of homicid[e] either [....] or he [who pl]anned it; the ephetai are to gi[v]e the verdict. [He may be pardoned if the fath]er is alive or brothe[rs] or sons, al[l] of them, otherwise the one op[posing it is to prevail; if] these are [not] alive, then (by the male relatives) as far as the co[usi]n's son and [cousin, if all] are willing to [par]don, the op[po]ser to [p]rev[ail; and if not even one of these is alive and the ki]lling was involun[tary] and it is judged by the [F]i[fty-One, the ephetai, that it was involun]tary homicide, let t[he ph]ratry [members] adm[i]t him into the country, [if ten are willing; these] the Fif[t]y-One [are to chose] according to their m[e]r[it]. [And those who be]fore this were [also] k[i]lle[rs let them be bound by] th[is ordinance. Let proclamation be made] against the kill[er in the a]gor[a (by the male relatives) as far as the degree of cousin's son and cousin; and let the prosec]ution be made jointly by cous[ins and sons of cousins and sons-in-law and fathers-in-la]w and phr[a]tr[y members ....] guilty of homic[ide .... the Fift]y-One [....] convicte[d] of homicide [.... If a]nyone [kills] th[e mu]rd[erer or is responsible for his death, when he has kept away from the agor]a on the fron[t]ier a[n]d [the games and the Amphictyonic rites, let him be treated the same as one who] has k[ill]e[d an

Athen]ian; [the] e[ph]eta[i are to judge the case .... (33)] the ag[gressor ....] (34) kil[ls] the aggressor .... (35) the e[phe]tai [are to give the verdict ....] is a fr[e]e man. An[d if a man immediately] defends himself [against someone who is unjustly plundering him by force] and kil[l]s him, [that man shall die without a penalty being paid ....] (56) Second Axon ....

3.4 Laws Written in Blood

Plutarch *Solon* 17.1–3

Drakon's laws were renowned in antiquity for their severity: hence the term 'draconian'. Scholars, however, have argued that this tradition is incorrect, and the law about unintentional homicide shows the lawgiver in a humane light (Gagarin (1981) 116–21, bibliography at 116n.16, cf. (1986) 66–67). Plutarch's examples can therefore be taken as unreliable accretions. For Solon's law on idleness, see doc. 3.25.

17.1 So first of all Solon repealed all Drakon's laws, except those concerning homicide, because of their harshness and the magnitude of their penalties. **17.2** For one punishment, death, was laid down for nearly all offenders, with the result that even those convicted of idleness were put to death and those who stole vegetables or fruit were punished just like those who committed sacrilege or murder. **17.3** That is why Demades was later on well known for his remark that Drakon wrote his laws in blood, not ink.

POVERTY AND INEQUALITY IN ATTICA BEFORE SOLON

It has sometimes been argued that over-population, over-cropping, and the importation of foreign grain had led to an agricultural crisis by Solon's time; see French (1956) 11–25, cf. (1964) 11–12, Ehrenberg (1973) 60. This theory, however, rests on Thuc. I.2.6, which refers to the period before the Ionian colonization of Asia Minor and the islands, and over-population in archaic Attica is not attested. Sigeion and the Chersonese (see doc. 1.15) did not provide an outlet for surplus population. Snodgrass (1980) 22–24 argues for a dramatic population increase in Attica, 750–700, but more care is needed in deriving statistics from the incidence of graves; Camp (1979) 397–411 adopts an opposing view, also unconvincing, based on the hypothesis of drought in the eighth century. Forrest (1966) 151 overstates the extent to which deforestation had taken place in the archaic period, and, while Plato (*Krit.* 111 a–d) can complain of the ill-effects of wood clearing on water sources, French (1956) 14 is anachronistic in giving this an archaic context. It is not clear whether the average Athenian farmer was a subsistence farmer or exchanged his crop for other goods, but archaic Athens seems a little early for a 'cash-crop' system on a large scale, so the argument (French 15–16) that imported grain ruined the small farmer is not likely. There appears to have been a general absence of trade with Attica at this time (see doc. 3.27). In short, while the ecology of a particular state will naturally have a bearing on its history, the environmental models described above are not applicable to Attica.

Doc. 3.7 (*Ath. Pol.* 2.1) is essentially a description of a typical class struggle between rich and poor. Hignett (1952) 87–89 sees the Solonian reforms as aimed at the poor, but also with Solon supported by families from the outer regions of Attica who were excluded from power (102–06), but this view is unconvincing. Kylon's case (docs. 2.17–19) does not prove that regionalism and disaffected aristocrats were a feature of pre-

Solonian Athens: it was rather the attempt of one individual to imitate the tyrants of other states. The crisis which Solon attempted to solve in 594/3 was one between exploiters and exploited, rich against poor. Plut. *Sol.* 13.1–2 (cf. 29.1) is not to be taken seriously in stating that there were regional groups in Attica prior to Solon, as this contradicts Herodotos I.59.3 and *Ath. Pol.* 13.4–5 (docs. 4.2–3), which date the emergence of three distinct groups, largely based on regional centres, after Solon. Regional tendencies in archaic Attica accordingly emerged *after* Solon, and political trouble before this was not along these or factional or clan lines (*contra* Sealey (1960) 167–68; Ellis & Stanton (1968) 95–110; while Lewis (1963) 22–23 correctly dates the regionalism to the 560s). Both sides chose Solon as the mediator in the class strife (doc. 3.9); the poor to gain redress, the rich so that the people would be restrained (*Ath. Pol.* 12.4, doc. 3.12). de Ste. Croix (1981) 281–82 sees the situation in 594/3 as one of 'severe class strife' (282); Ober (1989) 62–65 stresses that the poor gained security from enslavement, which certainly was one of their main concerns.

3.5 Social Disorder in Attica

Solon 4, lines 1–10, 17–39

In addition to his poems urging the Athenians to action over Salamis (doc. 3.8), Solon produced many verses about the state of affairs in Attica, attempting to point out the various problems of his time. It was presumably because of his prominence as a critic that he was appointed as mediator and archon (*Ath. Pol.* 5.1; doc. 3.9). Adkins (1972) 46–51 discusses eunomia in Solon's poetry; for Solon as poet, see Knox (1978) 44–46.

Our city will never perish in accordance with the decree of Zeus
And the will of the blessed immortal gods;
For such a great-hearted guardian, daughter of a mighty father,
Pallas Athena holds her hands over us;
But to destroy a great city by their thoughtlessness
Is the wish of the citizens, won over by money,
And unrighteous is the mind of the people's leaders, who are about
To suffer many pains from their great presumption (hybris);
For they know not how to restrain excess or
Arrange in peace the present good cheer of the feast ....
This is an inescapable wound which comes to every city,
And swiftly brings it to wretched slavery,
Arousing civil discord and sleeping war,
Which has destroyed the lovely prime of many;
For by men of ill-will a much-loved city is swiftly
Consumed in the gatherings of those who harm their friends.
These evils are at large amongst the people; and of the poor
Many arrive at a foreign land
Sold for export and bound in unseemly chains [....]
Thus the public evil comes to each at home,
And house doors can no longer keep it out,
It has leapt over high fences, found people in all ways,
Even one who runs and hides in his chamber's recess.
This my spirit bids me tell the Athenians,
That most evils are brought to a city by bad order (dysnomia);
But good order (eunomia) makes all things well-run and perfect,

And frequently puts fetters on the unrighteous;
She smooths the rough, stops excess, obscures presumption (hybris),
Withers the growing flowers of ruin,
Straightens crooked judgements, proud deeds
She softens; she stops the works of sedition,
Ends the wrath of painful strife, and by her
All is made perfect and prudent amongst mankind.

3.6 Greed and Injustice in Attica

Solon 13, lines 1–25, 71–76

Solon praises wealth, but only if gained legitimately. He appears to be criticizing 'new' wealth, gained unjustly, perhaps referring to extortionate methods of dealing with dependants. For the ethos of wanting to harm enemies, see Adkins (1972) 55–56. The simile in lines 17–25 is typically Homeric and shows Solon's debt to traditional poetry.

Glorious children of Memory and Olympian Zeus,
Pierian Muses, listen to my prayer;
Give me prosperity at the hands of the blessed gods, and
At the hands of all men let me have always good repute;
Make me very dear to my friends, and bitter to my enemies,
Reverenced by those, and to these dreadful to behold.
I desire to possess money, but to have acquired it unjustly
I do not choose; for justice always comes afterwards.
Wealth which the gods give stays with a man
Lastingly from the lowest foundation to the peak;
While that which man values from presumption (hybris), comes not
By right, but, persuaded by unjust deeds,
Follows unwillingly, and soon is mixed with ruin;
Which from a small beginning grows like fire,
Trivial at first, but grievous in the end;
For the presumptuous deeds done by mortals do not last,
But Zeus watches over the end of everything, and suddenly,
Just as a wind has quickly scattered clouds
In spring, and has stirred the unharvested many-waved ocean
To its depths, and throughout the wheat-bearing land
Laid waste the good lands, reaching the high seat of the gods,
Heaven, and again has made the aether clear to view,
And the strength of the sun shines down on land rich and
Fair, but not a single cloud is still to be seen —
Such is the vengeance of Zeus; ....
For men there is no limit apparently laid down as to wealth;
For those of us who now have greatest means,
Are eager for twice as much; who could satisfy everyone?
The immortals have granted men gains,
But these produce ruin, which when sent by Zeus
As retribution, is possessed now by this man and then that one.

3.7 The Enslavement of the Masses

[Aristotle] *Athenaion Politeia* 2.1–3

Gallant (1982) 111–24 incorrectly argues that land previously 'uncultivated and unoccupied' was at the centre of the dispute, and revives (123–24, cf. 113) in a new guise the idea that the hektemoroi paid five-sixths of their produce to the wealthy, with this five-sixths of produce coming from farming the land of the wealthy, the hektemoroi fulfilling their obligations by working the land of 'the larger landholder' and receiving one sixth of the produce, in addition to working their own land. Rihll (1991) 101–27 suggests that the land marked by horoi and worked by the hektemoroi was public land. But the *Ath. Pol.* is clear: the hektemoroi paid one-sixth of their produce to the wealthy. Solon writes that he freed the land by removing the horoi, thus abolishing hektemoros status. For the term 'pelates', in the sense of 'one who approaches another for protection', see Millett (1989) 21.

2.1 After this there was a long period of strife between the notables (gnorimoi) and the populace. **2.2** For not only was their state oligarchic in all other respects, but the poor were also slaves of the rich, both themselves, their children and their wives. They were called dependants (pelatai) and sixth-parters (hektemoroi), as it was for this rent (of one-sixth of their produce) that they were working the fields of the rich. All the land was in the hands of a few; and if they did not pay the rents, both they and their children were liable to seizure. Also all loans were made on the security of the person until Solon's time; he was the first champion of the people. **2.3** For the masses the harshest and most unbearable aspect of the constitution was their enslavement, though they were discontented on other grounds as well; for they had, so to speak, no share in anything.

SOLON AND HIS BACKGROUND

3.8 Solon: 'A Herald from Lovely Salamis'

Solon 1–3

These fragments are from the 'Salamis' a 100 line poem justifying Athens' conflict with Megara; after a long struggle the Athenians had decreed that the matter was no longer open for discussion; Solon evaded this by pretending madness and reciting these verses exhorting the Athenians to action. The Athenians recaptured Salamis, and eventually both sides agreed to have the Spartans arbitrate the matter; they awarded the island to Athens; see Plut. *Sol.* 8–10. At about the same time the Athenians were also fighting against the Mytilenaeans for control of Sigeion; see doc. 1.15; cf. Plut. *Sol.* 11 for Solon's role in the First Sacred War. See Linforth (1919) 249–64; French (1957) 238–46; Legon (1981) 122–31, 136–39 (with source references).

1. I have come as a herald from lovely Salamis,
   And have composed a song, an ornament of words, instead of speech.

2. May I be then a man of Pholegandros or Sikinos
   Instead of an Athenian, after changing my native land;

For this would shortly be men's common talk:
'This man is an Athenian, one of the family that let Salamis go'
(one of the family of the 'Salaminaphetai').

3. Let us go to Salamis, to fight for an island
That is lovely, and repel grievous shame.

3.9 Solon as Mediator and Archon

[Aristotle] *Athenaion Politeia* 5.1–2 (Solon 4a)

The *Ath. Pol.* gives Solon's background as one of moderate position but high birth (doc. 3.10). In 4c Solon upbraids the rich for their greed, but the *Ath. Pol.* also points out that he took the part of both sides. As at *Ath. Pol.* 2 (doc. 3.7), the crisis is here viewed in socio-economic terms and *Ath. Pol.* 2.1 indicates that the dissension seems to have started some time after Kylon's coup, and lasted until Solon's time.

5.1 So with the constitution organized in this way, and the many enslaved to the few, the people rose up against the notables (gnorimoi). **5.2** As the dissension (stasis) was fierce and they remained opposed to each other for a long time, both sides agreed to choose Solon as mediator and archon and they entrusted the state to him, after he had composed the elegy of which this is the beginning (F4a):

'I look on, and pains lie within my breast,
As I behold Ionia's eldest land
Being slain'.

In this he fights with each side on behalf of the other and debates the points at issue, afterwards exhorting them to join together and put an end to their contention.

3.10 Solon's Views of the Wealthy

[Aristotle] *Athenaion Politeia* 5.3 (Solon 4c)

The *Ath. Pol.* describes Solon as well-born but not especially wealthy. As to the common view that he belonged to the 'middle class' and engaged in trading, de Ste. Croix (1981) 129–31 makes it clear that Solon left Athens mainly to avoid being consulted about his laws, and to 'see the world' (Hdt. I.29.1–30.1; doc. 3.31); while the *Ath. Pol.* 11.1 (doc. 3.35; cf. 3.34) states that Solon 'went abroad for trade and to see Egypt', Solon may have done little more than carry a cargo to help pay for expenses. Certainly Solon himself described the trader's occupation (amongst others) as something one is forced to engage in through penury (F9, 41–46; doc. 11.34); but see doc. 3.39 for his love of travelling.

5.3 By both birth and reputation Solon was one of the leading men, but in wealth and occupation he was middle class, as other evidence confirms and as he himself admits in his poems, when he advises the rich not to be grasping (F4c);

'But calm your mighty hearts in your breasts,
You who have pushed on to surfeit yourselves with many good things,
Set your ambitious mind within limits; for
We will not allow you, nor will all this turn out according to your wishes.'

On the whole he always lays the responsibility for the dissension on the rich; accordingly even at the beginning of his elegy he says that he fears 'their avarice and their arrogance', implying that these had been the cause behind the ill-feeling.

THE SEISACHTHEIA

The seisachtheia or 'shaking off of burdens', was a cancellation of debts, but the extent and nature of the cancellation is debated. It must at least have encompassed the obligation of the hektemoroi, for the horoi on their land were uprooted; certainly the *Ath. Pol.* 12.4 refers primarily to agricultural obligation. The charge of corruption made against Solon also raises the notion of the inalienability of land, which seems to have been the case until at least the reforms of Solon. Fine (1951) 177–80, cf. 183, has argued that as the security of the farmer's person, rather than his land, was the collateral on which credit was raised prior to Solon's reforms of 594 a farmer's land could not be alienated. Hammond (1961) 76–98 supports Fine; cf. Woodhouse (1938) 81; French (1963) 242–47; on the question of alienability of land in general in Greece, see Finley (1968) 25–32; doc. 3.14.

Before Solon's archonship, the enslaved were those who could not meet their obligations, for which their persons, prior to Solon, were the security. The enslaved may have been hektemoroi who had failed to meet their obligations of one-sixth to the wealthy, or farmers who were not hektemoroi, or hektemoroi who were in debt through borrowing. The mechanics by which those Athenians who had been sold into slavery were freed by Solon are unknown, but his poetry indicates that a serious attempt was made to free such slaves. As part of Solon's reforms, loans could no longer be made on the security of the person (see de Ste. Croix (1981) 137, 164, 282). Athenian citizens could no longer be enslaved for agricultural debt, though some possibility of debt slavery remained (Rhodes 126), and it was still a possibility elsewhere in the Greek world (see doc. 11.16; de Ste. Croix (1981) 162–63). The *Ath. Pol.* interprets Solon 36 (doc. 3.12) as the seisachtheia: the uprooting of the horoi, which freed the enslaved earth, and the freeing of those who had been enslaved. It is usually suggested that Solon's prohibition may also have made the obtaining of credit more difficult for farmers (Rhodes 127; Ober (1989) 62); creditors who had lent on the security of the borrower's person would now have had less security for their credit. But the accepted view, that Solon's 'shaking off of burdens' harmed farmers in that it would now be difficult for them to find anyone to give them financial assistance, overlooks the nature of hektemoros status: the landlords did not give them assistance; rather the hektemoroi gave a proportion of their produce to the land-lords. Hektemoroi may *also* have borrowed from the landlord, but this is a separate issue. The main sources for the seisachtheia are: *Ath. Pol.* 6.1–4 below; 12.4 (doc. 3.12); Androtion *FGH* 324 F34 (doc. 3.13); Philochoros *FGH* 328 F114. For general discussions, see Linforth (1919) 269–74; Freeman (1926) 85–89; Forrest (1966) 147–56; de Ste. Croix (1981) 137, 164, 215, 281–82.

3.11 The 'Shaking off of Burdens'

[Aristotle] *Athenaion Politeia* 6.1–4

The charge of corruption levelled against Solon is clearly anachronistic; it is also found in Plut. *Sol.* 15.7–9, *Mor.* 807d–e; cf. doc. 3.13. In Solonian Athens there would not have been huge estates up for sale, and the wherewithal to purchase them through borrowing would not have been available at such short notice (there was also no coinage; doc. 3.24). The story is not intended so much to discredit Solon, and those who profited, but the descendants of those named at Plut. *Sol.* 15.7, especially Konon, Alkibiades and Kallias, all important in the later phases of the Peloponnesian war: the slander is clearly fifth century in origin (Davies (1971) 12, 255, 403, 506; Rhodes 128–29 with bibliography).

6.1 When Solon gained control of affairs, he liberated the people both immediately and for the future, by preventing loans on the security of the person, and enacted laws and brought about a cancellation of debts both private and public, which they call the 'shaking off of burdens' (seisachtheia), since they shook off their load. **6.2** Some people in this try to discredit Solon; for when he was about to bring in the seisachtheia he first spoke of it to some of the notables, and then, according to the popular party, he was outmanoeuvred by his friends, or as those wishing to slander him say, he joined in it. For these men borrowed money and bought up large amounts of land, and not long after became rich through the cancellation of debts; in this way men who were later thought to be of ancient wealth are said to have become rich. **6.3** But the popular version is certainly the more probable; for it is not likely that he, who was so moderate and impartial in other respects, and who could have subordinated the rest of the people to himself and become tyrant of the city, but chose to be hated by both sides and considered right and the safety of the city of more importance than his own aggrandisement, should sully himself with such petty and easily detectable matters. **6.4** That he had this power is made clear by the unhealthy state of affairs, and he refers to it in many places in his poems and everyone else agrees with him. This charge must therefore be considered to be false.

3.12 Solon's View of his Achievements

[Aristotle] *Athenaion Politeia* 12.3–5 (Solon 34, 36, 37)

Despite the arguments of Rosivach (1992) 153–57, who interprets Solon 34 as meaning that some of Solon's supporters expected him to seize the property of his opponents and give it to them, the *Ath. Pol.* is certainly correct in interpreting Solon 34 as a reference to calls for redistribution of the land. The call could have come from the hektemoroi, who had their own land but might have wished to increase their holdings by a distribution of the land of the wealthy, or from a group of landless poor, or perhaps both groups; cf. *Ath. Pol.* 11.2 (doc. 3.35); Plut. *Sol.* 16.1. In the classical period, there was a distinct Athenian distaste for notions of land redistribution: *Ath. Pol.* 56.2; Dem. XXIV.149; cf. Harding (1974) 286; Rosivach (1992) 154; de Ste. Croix (1981) 298; cf. doc. 3.14.

12.3 Again he speaks elsewhere concerning those who wanted the land to be redistributed (F34):

'Those who came for plunder had rich hope,
Each of them expecting to find great prosperity,
And that, despite smooth words, I would show an intransigent mind.
Then they contrived vainly, and angry with me
All looked at me askance as at an enemy.
It is not right. For what I said, I achieved with the gods' help,
But did nothing in vain, nor with the force of tyranny
Did I choose to act, nor that the rich earth
Of our native land should equally be shared by base and good.'

12.4 Again regarding the cancellation of debts and liberation of those previously enslaved through the seisachtheia, he says (F36):

'Of those things for the sake of which I gathered together
The people, which did I abandon unaccomplished?
May she bear witness to these things in the tribunal of time
The greatest mother of the Olympian gods
And the best, black Earth, from whom I once
Removed markers (horoi) fixed in many places,
She who before was enslaved, and now is free.
To Athens, their god-built native land, many
I brought back who had been sold, some unjustly,
Some justly, and some who constrained by debt
Had gone into exile, who no longer spoke the Attic tongue,
So widely had they wandered;
And some who here suffered shameful slavery
Trembling before their masters' ways,
I made free. And these things by the power
Of law, by a combination of force and justice,
I accomplished, and completed them as I promised.
Ordinances for bad and good alike,
Setting up straight justice for each man,
I wrote. Another man taking up the goad like I,
A foolish and greedy man,
Would not have restrained the people; for if I had been willing to do
What then pleased their opponents,
Or again what the other side contrived for them,
This city would have been bereft of many men.
For this reason making a defence on every side,
I turned about like a wolf among many hounds.'

12.5 And again, reproaching both sides for their later fault-finding (F37.1–5):

'If it were right to reproach the people openly,
What they have now, they would never with their eyes
Have seen even in their sleep.
While all those who are greater and more powerful
Should praise me and should make me their friend;' for if another man, he says, had achieved this position (F37.7–10):

'He would not have restrained the people or stopped,
Before he had stirred up the milk and taken off the cream.
But I between them on neutral ground
Stood like a marker.'

3.13 A Fourth Century View of the Seisachtheia

Androtion *FGH* 324 F34 (Plutarch *Solon* 15.2–4)

Androtion's interpretation of the seisachtheia was that it was only a partial reduction of debt. Plut. *Sol.* 15.5–6 points out that most writers took it to be a cancellation of debts and that Solon's poetry confirms this. Jacoby *FGH* 3b Suppl. 1.145 (cf. Harding (1974) 282–89) argued that Androtion's view was due to a desire to downplay the radical nature of

Solon's reforms, so that he would not provide inspiration for radical reform in fourth century Athens. The devaluation referred to at 15.4 should therefore be ignored.

15.2 For this was the first measure that Solon instituted, decreeing that existing debts should be cancelled, and that for the future no one could lend money on the security of the person. **15.3** And yet some people have written, of whom Androtion is one, that the poor were so pleased at being relieved not by a cancellation of debts, but by a reduction of interest rates, that they gave the name of 'seisachtheia' to this philanthropic act, as well as to the increase of measures and rise in value of the coinage which took place at the same time. **15.4** For he made the mina a hundred drachmas, it having previously been seventy-three, with the result that people paid back an equal amount numerically speaking, but less in value, and greatly benefited those paying off debts, while not disadvantaging those who recovered their money.

3.14 Land as the Source of Political Power

Aristotle *Politics* 1266b 14–24 (II, vii)

According to Aristotle, Solon realised that equality of property was an issue of political significance; Aristotle is presumably referring to the seisachtheia and the uprooting of the horoi. Solon's reforms meant that there was from that point on a freehold peasantry in Attica. For Aristotle on property in Sparta, see doc. 13.18.

Accordingly the equality of property has some effect on the political community, and some men of former times seem to have discerned this, such as Solon in his legislation, while other places have a law which prevents people obtaining as much land as they wish, and similarly laws prevent the sale of property, like that at Locri forbidding you to sell property unless you can show that an obvious misfortune has taken place, as well as those which preserve ancient estates (this was repealed at Leukas and made their constitution over democratic; for it was no longer possible to appoint officials from the specified property-classes).

SOLON'S CONSTITUTIONAL REFORMS

In 411, in the aftermath of the disastrous Sicilian expedition, Kleitophon recommended a return to Kleisthenes' constitution: *Ath. Pol.* 29.3, cf. 34.3; for Kleitophon, see Fuks (1953) 1–32. By contrast, the shift towards Solon's constitution was a fourth century phenomenon, and by fourth century politicians Solon was viewed as the founder of the Athenian democracy; see Hansen (1989) 71–99. Solon's constitution could be seen as 'democratic' and as ancestral (a 'patrios politeia'), but nevertheless, for the conservative element, preferable to Kleisthenes' or Ephialtes' democracy (Jacoby (1949) 77, 153–55; Wallace (1985) 51–52). The question as to whether Solon's laws, nomoi (in his poetry referred to as thesmoi), constituted a politeia, or constitution, is answered in the affirmative by: Finley (1971) 37–38; Wallace (1985) 49–52; in the negative by: Ruschenbusch (1958) 401–08, (1966) 25–26; Sealey (1960) 160–62; Day & Chambers (1962) 71–75, 79–89; see Hignett (1952) 26–27. Many of his nomoi were political in nature and altered the political 'system', with changes in the competency of the various organs of government, and in this sense Solon changed the political structure of Attica.

3.15 Drakon's Laws Superseded

[Aristotle] *Athenaion Politeia* 7.1

Solon's legislation superseded that of Drakon, except for the law on homicide (doc. 3.3). All the Athenians may have sworn to observe the laws as the *Ath. Pol.* states: see Rhodes 135, with references. For the oath taken by the archons, cf. Plut. *Sol.* 25.3. This became a traditional procedure: *Ath. Pol.* 55.5; Pollux 8.86; and, for *Ath. Pol.* 7.1, Wycherley (1957) 22–23, no. 9, with references. The stone mentioned here has been identified with the large limestone block discovered outside the stoa basileios, see Thompson (1976) 85; Camp (1986) 101 (with ph. at fig. 75); for the kyrbeis, see doc. 3.33.

7.1 Solon established a constitution and made other laws, and they stopped using the ordinances of Drakon except those concerning homicide. They inscribed the laws on the tablets (kyrbeis) and set them up in the stoa of the basileus archon and everyone swore they would observe them. The nine archons used to swear their oath at the stone and declare that they would dedicate a golden statue, if they transgressed any of the laws; and even today they continue to swear in the same manner.

3.16 The Four Classes

[Aristotle] *Athenaion Politeia* 7.3–4

The four property classes apparently already existed according to the *Ath. Pol.*, and what was new was that Solon made these classes the basis of political privilege. They were organized on the criterion of wealth, measured in terms of annual agricultural produce. This new system was timocratic in nature. Solon allowed the top two classes, the pentakosiomedimnoi ('five hundred bushel men') and the hippeis ('cavalry', 'knights'), to stand for election to the archonship (see Hignett (1952) 101–02); in 458/7 the zeugitai ('able to keep a team of oxen' or 'rankers') were also to be admitted (*Ath. Pol.* 26.2). The thetes, the lowest property qualification, were ineligible for any of the magistracies. For the law-courts, see the discussion at *Ath. Pol.* 9.1–2 (doc. 3.23). Aristotle's listing (doc. 3.22) of the second and third classes reverses that given here. Hignett (1952) 100–03 has pointed out that the reform involving the four classes presupposes more than conflict between the rich and the poor. The classification of offices by wealth and not birth suggests that there was a group of wealthy non-eupatridai in Attica, and that Solon thought that the extension of political power to this group would be of benefit to Attica. Solon may have given the wealthy non-eupatridai political power to offset that of the eupatridai; see Finley (1951) 58–59 for a discussion of the landholdings needed for each of Solon's classes (perhaps 75–145 acres of grain-producing land, or 20–25 acres of vineyards and olive orchards, for the pentakosiomedimnoi). Upward social mobility is testified by the example of Anthemion son of Diphilos (*DAA* 205–07); the statue could not have been of Diphilos as it has to be an equestrian statue of Anthemion, signifying his social mobility from the rank of thes to hippeus (Rhodes 143–45; cf. Ober (1989) 61n.22).

7.3 By a property assessment he divided everyone into four classes, as they had been divided before: pentakosiomedimnoi, hippeis, zeugitai and thetes. The magistracies he assigned to the pentakosiomedimnoi, hippeis and zeugitai, that is the nine archons, the treasurers, the poletai (sellers), the Eleven and the kolakretai (financial officials), allocating the magistracies to each class according to the size of their property assessment. But to those registered in the class of thetes he only gave a share in the assembly and law-courts. **7.4** Whoever made five hundred measures of dry and liquid goods both together from his property was to belong to the pentakosiomedimnoi, while those who made three hundred belonged to the hippeis, though some people describe them as those who were able to keep horses. They mention the name of the class as proof, and as confirming the fact, as well as the dedications of former times; for dedicated on the acropolis there is a statue of Diphilos, on which this has been inscribed:

'Anthemion son of Diphilos dedicated this to the gods,
After exchanging the labourers' class for the hippeis.'

And a horse stands beside him as witness that this is what the hippeis class means. Nevertheless it is more reasonable that this class should have been differentiated by measures like the pentakosiomedimnoi. Those who made two hundred measures both together belonged to the zeugitai; and the others belonged to the thetes and had no share in the magistracies. Accordingly when anyone who is about to draw lots for a magistracy is asked what class he belongs to, he would never say the thetes.

3.17 The Election of the Archons

[Aristotle] *Athenaion Politeia* 8.1–2

The *Ath. Pol.* here on the election of archons (preliminary direct election of candidates and then the archons chosen from these by lot) is often taken to contradict the account of Aristotle (see doc. 3.22). Staveley (1972) 34 argues that there is no contradiction, as Aristotle's use of the word 'election' does not rule out the method the *Ath. Pol.* describes, and that choice partly using the lot need not be anachronistic, even if there is evidence that the archons were directly elected (with no partial use of the vote) during the tyranny and for a while after it; it need not after all be assumed that the constitution progressively continued to evolve towards democracy, with no regressive changes; see also Develin (1979) 455–68; Hignett (1952) 321–26; Rhodes 146–48. The attacks on the use of mixed sortition and election centre on the question of the *Ath. Pol.*'s sources, and the fact that he may be anachronistically describing fourth century practices in a sixth century context, perhaps motivated by the fourth-century idea that Solon was the 'father of democracy' (see Hignett (1952) 321–26; Day & Chambers (1962) 71–89, esp. 81–84).

Ath. Pol. 8.2 states that the Areiopagos had previously 'judged the suitability of candidates for office', ie conducted the 'dokimasia' of would-be officials, and apportioned the archonships amongst those chosen, not choosing the archons, but assigning to them their various duties (Develin (1979) 460–61). Forrest and Stockton (1987) 235–40 argue that individuals could have held more than one type of archonship in the course of their life: if so there would have been fewer members of the Areiopagos, and the body would have been even more elite in nature in the seventh and sixth centuries than is usually thought. They also challenge the view that archons became members of the Areiopagos only after their term of office expired, and it is difficult to see how the archons of this period could effectively have functioned without regular interaction with the Areiopagos.

8.1 He laid down that the magistrates were to be appointed by lot from a preliminary list of candidates, whom each of the tribes had pre-selected. Each tribe chose ten candidates for the nine archons, and they appointed by lot from these; from which the practice still continues that each of the tribes selects ten men by lot, and then they choose by lot from them. Proof that he made (the offices) appointed by lot from the propertied classes is the law concerning the treasurers, which is still in force even today; for it says that the treasurers should be chosen by lot from the pentakosiomedimnoi. **8.2** So, this was how Solon legislated regarding the nine archons. In former times the Council of the Areiopagos according to its own judgement summoned people and appointed the most suitable person to each of the magistracies for the year.

3.18 The Four Tribes and the Naukraroi

[Aristotle] *Athenaion Politeia* 8.3

This passage describes some features of the Solonian constitution; little is known of the phylobasileis. There were four tribes, the typical Ionian ones, at Athens (see Hignett (1952) 50–55); in 508/7 Kleisthenes changed these to ten (doc. 5.7).

8.3 There were four tribes as before and four heads of tribes (phylobasileis). Each tribe was divided into three thirds (trittyes) and there were twelve naukrariai in each (tribe). There were officials, the naukraroi, in charge of the naukrariai, who were responsible for income and expenditure; accordingly in Solon's laws, which are no longer in force, there is often written, 'the naukraroi shall exact' and 'expend from the naukraric fund'.

3.19 Solon's Council of 400 and the Areiopagos

[Aristotle] *Athenaion Politeia* 8.4

The Areiopagos had clear functions under Solon, in particular the general oversight of the state. The council of 400 was the boule, and when Kleisthenes re-organized the Athenians into ten tribes its number was increased to 500. Hignett (1952) 92–96 argues that Solon did not introduce a council of 400; cf. Ehrenberg (1973) 68–69. The existence of a Solonian boule of 400 is accepted by Forrest (1966) 164, 166; Laix (1973) 13–17; Rhodes (1972) 208–09 (bibliography at 208n.2); cf. Rhodes (1981) 153; Ober (1989) 64; Starr (1990) 8–9. The *Ath. Pol.* 8.4 and Plut. *Sol.* 19.1 both mention this Solonian boule. A council would have been needed to organize the agenda for the ekklesia; the boule thus had a 'probouleutic' function (cf. Arist. *Pol.* 1322b 12–17; Plut. *Sol.* 19.1; Hansen (1989) 98). Solon may have thought that the Areiopagos, dominated by the aristocrats and likely to remain so for some time (because members were chosen for life), was unsuitable for this purpose. The council which Kleomenes attempted to depose will presumably not have been the Areiopagos but the boule (see doc. 5.3).

Because of the aristocratic nature of the Areiopagos in 594, another council, with a wider basis for election and membership changing annually, would have been part of Solon's policy of broadening the basis of political participation. For two councils in Chios in the mid-sixth century, see ML 8 (doc. 10.24), which provides a parallel to two councils at Athens (Hignett's contention (95) that the Ionians of Asia Minor were more politically advanced than the Athenians will not stand as an argument against Athens having two councils). Hignett, however, notes that the restoration of a reference to the boule in *IG* I^3 1.12 (ML 14), as well as the date, is far from certain. For the boule, see Rhodes (1972); the summary of Hansen (1991) 246–65 (mainly from fourth century evidence) is useful.

8.4 He created a boule of four hundred, a hundred men from each tribe, and assigned that of the Areiopagites to guard the laws, just as previously it had been guardian of the constitution. It used to watch over the majority and the greatest of the city's affairs and chastise wrongdoers, having full power to impose fines and punishments, and it deposited the fines on the acropolis, without recording the reason for the fine, and judged those who had conspired to put down the democracy, Solon having made a law of impeachment for such cases.

3.20 Solon's View of the People

[Aristotle] *Athenaion Politeia* 12.1–2 (Solon 5, 6)

Solon criticized the excesses of the wealthy, but nevertheless created a political system where wealth was the prerequisite for office, while the poor had power in the ekklesia and heliaia. Solon thought that the people had a specific place in society, and that they ought not to exceed their 'station in life'. He saw himself as standing between the two opposing groups, the wealthy and the 'ordinary' people, and his legislation, which enshrined the right of the wealthy to rule but protected the people by giving them specific rights, is reflected in his poetry; cf. doc. 2.15 for Theognis on social discord.

12.1 Everyone agrees that this is what he did and he himself refers to it in his poetry in the following lines (F5):

'To the people I gave as much privilege as was appropriate,
Neither taking from their honour nor reaching out to do so; [1]
And those that had power and were admired for their possessions,
I also made sure that they should suffer nothing unseemly.
I stood firm holding my strong shield in defence of both,
And did not allow either to conquer unjustly.'

12.2 And again he makes clear how to deal with the populace (F6):

'In this way the people will best follow their leaders,
If they are neither left too free nor restrained too much.
For surfeit breeds presumption (hybris), when too much prosperity comes
To men whose mind is not sound.'

[1] Here adopting the suggestion of Rhodes 172 as against *LSJ*[9] 676 'enhancing it'.

3.21 Solon's Law against Political Apathy

[Aristotle] *Athenaion Politeia* 8.5

This law against political apathy is also given at Plut. *Sol.* 20.1 (cf. Plut. *Mor.* 550c). If genuine, it seems to have been a response to the civil disorder of his period and could have stemmed from a belief that if everyone became politically involved there would be more stability in society. The notion of participation in public affairs was also a theme in Perikles' 'funeral oration' (see doc. 10.9): what was law under Solon had become ideology by the 430s, and participation in public affairs was seen as the sign of a healthy polis. The deprivation of citizen rights was atimia, the person so punished was an atimos; see Manville (1980) 213–21, esp. 217–19, who discusses atimia in archaic Athens. Lysias XXXI is the main basis for all discussion regarding the historicity of this law: see Hignett (1952) 26–27; Ruschenbusch (1966) 82–83; Goldstein (1972) 538–45; Bers (1975) 493–98; Develin (1977) 507–08; Sealey (1983) 100–06. David (1984) 129–38 dismisses the law as non-genuine, suggesting that Solon's 'boast of impartiality' (he cites F5.5–6; 37.9–10; docs. 3.12, 20) contradicts a law against apathy (131). However, it is clear that Solon was not a 'neutral' figure: he saw the rights and wrongs of the situation and acted accordingly. The similarity between the law and Solon 4, lines 19, 26–29 (doc. 3.5) is often noted.

8.5 Seeing that, although the city was often in dissension (stasis), some of the citizens through reluctance to take action were happy to accept whatever happened, he made a particular law with them in mind, that whoever did not stack arms at the service of one side or the other when the city was in dissension would be deprived of civic rights and have no share in the life of the city.

3.22 Solon as the 'Founder of Athenian Democracy'

Aristotle *Politics* 1273b 35–1274a 21 (II, xii)

Aristotle views the Solonian constitution as a mixed one, with oligarchic, aristocratic and democratic features. Similarly, he sees the Spartan constitution as mixed (doc. 6.19). Aristotle notes that Solon did not intend his constitution to become a democracy, as Solon gave 'the people just the power that was absolutely necessary', and this theme is found in Solon's poems (doc. 3.20). Aristotle's 'elective magistracies' here do not necessarily contradict *Ath. Pol.* 8.1, where the method described is that of election and sortition (see note at doc. 3.17). Ostwald (1986) 5–15 discusses the importance which Aristotle places on popular control of the dikasteria, law-courts (see also the *Ath. Pol.*, doc. 3.23). The power of examining the conduct of officials after their term of office, the 'euthyna' (plural: euthynai), meant that officials were fully accountable to the people; but this is an anachronism as the Areiopagos held these powers prior to Ephialtes' reforms. The order of the four classes given here differs from that of the *Ath. Pol.* (doc. 3.16).

1273b 35 Some people think that Solon was an excellent law-giver, for he put an end to the oligarchy that was too elitist, and he stopped the people being enslaved, and he established the traditional democracy by a good constitutional mixture; for the Council of the Areiopagos is oligarchic, the elective magistracies aristocratic, and the law-courts democratic. But it seems probable that Solon merely did not abolish the first two which were already in existence, **1274a 1** that is the council and the election of magistrates, but that he did establish the democracy by having the law-courts drawn from everybody. Accordingly some people blame him, in that he undid his other reforms by making the law-court, which is chosen by lot, supreme over everything. For when this became powerful, they changed the constitution into the present democracy to please the people, just as if it were a tyrant; and Ephialtes curtailed the power of Council of the Areiopagos as did Perikles, while Perikles instituted payment for the law-courts, and in this way each of the popular leaders (demagogoi) enlarged and promoted it into the democracy we have now. But it appears that this happened not according to a plan of Solon's, but rather by chance (for, as the people were responsible for naval supremacy in the Persian wars, they became presumptuous and chose inferior men as popular leaders when reasonable men pursued opposing policies), since Solon seems to have given the people just the power that was absolutely necessary, that of electing officials and of examining their conduct (for if the people were not supreme in this they would have had the status of slaves or enemies), and he ensured that all the magistracies would be filled by the notables and wealthy, that is the pentakosiomedimnoi and zeugitai and the third class called that of the hippeis; the fourth class were the thetes who had no share in office.

SOLON'S SOCIAL LEGISLATION

3.23 Solon's Judicial Reforms

[Aristotle] *Athenaion Politeia* 9.1–2

The *Ath. Pol.* defines three features of Solon's reforms as particularly 'democratic', though Solon will not have intended them to be so; the laws would certainly not have been deliberately obscure, and are only so from a fifth and fourth century perspective, probably relating to the archaic vocabulary employed by Solon (cf. Lysias X, XI). In addition to the judicial powers of the Areiopagos, *Ath. Pol.* 9 records that Solon gave anyone who wished the right to seek redress on behalf of another citizen, which indicates that anyone could enforce the laws of Solon (Ostwald (1986) 15), and every citizen had the right of appeal (ephesis) from a decision of a magistrate to a law-court (the third 'democratic feature'). While the *Ath. Pol.* uses the term dikasterion, Solon used the term heliaia (for the correct transliteration (smooth breathing), see Ostwald 10n.27 for references; MacDowell (1978) 30), as indicated by quotations of his laws in Lys. X.16 & Dem. XXIV.104 (cf. 114). As MacDowell (1978) 29 notes, this was the first time that the ordinary people of Athens had been given any judicial competence. That Athenians could now appeal against decisions of the magistrates was meant to be a curb on the power of the wealthy, and is a further indication that the main thrust of Solon's reforms was the protection of the poor against the wealthy. The heliaia is usually thought to have been the ekklesia sitting in judgement in a legal capacity (MacDowell 30). Hansen (1975) 51–52, (1978) 127–46, (1981–82) 9–47, has argued that the heliaia which Solon instituted was divided into separate courts along the lines of the dikasteria known from fourth century Athens, but cf. Rhodes (1979) 104; Ostwald 10–11; Starr (1990) 9, 66n.15; see also Sealey (1987) 60–70. The exact nature of appeal is debated, but Plut. *Sol.* 18.3 makes clear that Solon allowed anyone to appeal from a decision of a magistrate to the heliaia (see esp. MacDowell (1978) 30–31; Ostwald 12–13, with 12n.31 for bibliography). This would mean that anyone judged by a magistrate could appeal to the heliaia if he was dissatisfied with the verdict given.

9.1 So this was what he did with regard to the magistracies. In Solon's constitution these three features seem to be the most democratic: first and greatest was not allowing loans on the security of the person, the next was that it was possible for anyone who wished to seek vengeance on behalf of those who were being wronged, and the third, the one by which they say the populace became especially powerful, was the right of appeal to the law-court (dikasterion); for when the people have control of the vote they come to have control of the state. **9.2** Furthermore, because the laws were not written simply and clearly, but were like the one concerning legacies and heiresses, there was need for many disputes and for the court to decide on all matters both public and private. So some people think that he made his laws obscure on purpose, so that the people would be in control of the decisions. Nevertheless this is not likely, but rather that he was unable to formulate what was best in general terms; for it is not right to judge his intention from present-day occurrences, but from the rest of his constitution.

3.24 Solon's Reform of Athenian Weights and Measures

[Aristotle] *Athenaion Politeia* 10.1–2

There was no coinage in Athens in Solon's time and the *Ath. Pol.* is incorrect in attributing a reform of Athenian currency to Solon; the system used before the invention of coins would have been iron spits (originally known as 'obols'). It is clear that coinage was not introduced at Athens until at least 560 on the earliest dating now advocated by numismatists: Kraay (1988) 438. Kroll & Waggoner (1984) 325–40 argue that there was no coinage at Athens prior to 550, refuting Kagan (1982) 343–60, who has implausibly argued for a return to a seventh century dating for coinage at Aegina, Corinth and Athens; for a mid-sixth century date, see also Holloway (1984) 5–18; Vickers (1985) 1–44 (full bibliography). Kroll & Waggoner point out that Athenian coinage 'began with a drachma of "Euboic-Attic" weight of about 4.3g.[rams], and this standard remained in effect down through the Hellenistic period....' (327), that is, there is no evidence in the numismatic record for changes in the weights of Athenian coins, as is claimed for Solon by Androtion (doc. 3.13) and the *Ath. Pol.* Even the hypothesis that prior to minting its own coinage, Athens made use of Aeginetan coins, which were heavier that Athenian coins by a ratio of 7:10 (which is the ratio mentioned in the sources) and that Solon replaced these with Athenian coins which were lighter, is not possible because the dates of the earliest Athenian coins are still too late (Kroll & Waggoner 327–333), as are the Aeginetan, which date to the later sixth century (335–39). For a detailed discussion of the earliest Athenian coins, the Wappenmünzen, see Hopper (1968) 16–39, with pls. 2–5 for photographs; Kraay (1976) 56–60; Kroll (1981) 1–32 (pls. 1–2); Kroll & Waggoner (1984) 327–28, 334.

Pheidon was credited with the invention of coinage: Strab. VIII.3.33 (358); Ephoros *FGH* 70 F176 (Strab. VIII.6.16 (376)), and Ephoros says that he minted the first coins on Aegina. But Pheidon, ruling in the second quarter of the seventh century (see discussion at doc. 2.2) reigned too early for any Greek coinage, and may never in fact have ruled Aegina; see Kroll & Waggoner 335–36; Kraay (1988) 432–33; but cf. Kagan (1960) 121–36. Herodotos VI.127.3, while crediting Pheidon with the invention of Peloponnesian weights and measures, does not mention coinage. If, however, Solon and Pheidon reformed a system of weights and measures, this could have led fourth century writers to credit them with the invention of coinage. On *Ath. Pol.* 10, see Kraay (1968) 1–9; Chambers (1973) 1–16; for the introduction of coinage to the Greek world, Kraay (1988) 431–45; on the origin of coinage, Cook (1958) 257–62; Kraay (1964) 76–91.

10.1 So these seem to be the democratic aspects of Solon's laws, but even before his legislation he had brought in the cancellation of debts and afterwards the increase in measures and weights and in the coinage. **10.2** For it was under Solon that the measures became greater than those of Pheidon, and the mina which had previously had a weight of seventy drachmas was made up to a hundred. The old standard coin was the two drachma piece. He made the weights in respect of the coinage sixty-three minas to a talent, and the three extra minas were apportioned to the stater and the other weights.

3.25 Solon's Law on Idleness

Herodotos II.177.1–2

This law is against idleness; Drakon was said to have enacted a similar nomos argias (doc. 3.4). Plutarch records that Theophrastos thought that Peisistratos was responsible for the provision, not Solon (Plut. *Sol.* 31.5; Theophrastos F99 Wehrli; cf. Hignett (1952) 320). The law was still in force in the fourth century, see Wallace (1985) 244n.60 (to his collection here of evidence for measures against idleness in ancient Greece, add doc. 2.11). The Solonian equivalent of the Egyptian law was not so harsh as the Egyptian; Plut. *Sol.* 22.3 states that Solon provided that the Council of the Areiopagos look into livelihoods and punish the idle. It is chronologically implausible (see note at doc. 3.31) that Solon obtained the law from Amasis, for it would mean that Solon's nomothesia took place after his visit to Egypt and Amasis as recorded, almost certainly incorrectly, by Herodotos. In fact, it seems likely that the law was indeed originally Drakon's and Solon adapted the law of his predecessor. See Wallace (1985) 62–64, putting the law in the context of Solon's social legislation with its emphasis on the Areiopagos' role as guardian of 'behaviour and morality'; docs. 3.17, 3.19; Isager & Skydsgaard (1992) 145.

II.177.1 It is said that under King Amasis Egypt was particularly prosperous both in what the river gave the land and what the land gave the people, and the total number of its inhabited cities was twenty thousand. **II.177.2** Amasis was the one who established this law for the Egyptians, that every year each of the Egyptians should inform the governor (nomarch) of his source of livelihood; if he did not do this or was unable to show that his way of life was honest he was condemned to death. Solon the Athenian copied this law from Egypt and put it into force in Athens; it is still in use, being an excellent law.

3.26 Canine Control in Sixth Century Athens

Plutarch *Solon* 24.3

For similar canine control measures, see Plut. *Fab. Max.* 20.4; Xen. *Hell.* II.4.41; Eur. *Cyc.* 234–35; doc. 10.17; for pictures of domestic dogs in Athens, see Ducrey (1986) 206, 264 pls. 140, 179; Bérard et al (1989) figs. 61, 68, 80; cf. doc. 7.32.

24.3 He also composed a law concerning injury from animals, in which he said that a dog who had bitten anyone had to be tied up with a wooden dog-collar and pole three cubits (four and a half feet) long and be delivered up (to the victim); this clever device was for safety.

SOLON ON TRADE AND AGRICULTURE

The evidence of Solon's poetry is that he was very much concerned with the exploitation of the poor by the rich, and with the plight of the farmer. However, the fact that information on trade and agricultural legislation is only given by Plutarch perhaps means that it should be viewed with some caution. Athenian trade was relatively backward in the seventh century, which can be ascribed to her lack of colonies; compare Corinth's flourishing commercial life: docs. 2.6, 10.35. Solon encouraged manufacturing, according to Plutarch, and there is a distinct increase in the distribution of Athenian pottery in the sixth century, but that Athens was becoming a manufacturing centre is now (correctly) being disputed: Garnsey (1988) 110; Morris (1991) 34–35, esp. against Starr (1977) 104–05 (whose estimate of 'not more than 6000 (individuals) for the industrial and commercial sectors of sixth-century Athens' must be far too high). Solon was more concerned with agriculture than manufacturing; Peisistratos' main 'economic' concern was also with farmers (doc. 4.16). Attica was always primarily a land of farmers: Thuc. II.14 (doc. 9.4), II.16; cf. Morris (1991) 35n.1. Solon may have encouraged craftsmen in limited numbers to come to Attica, but this cannot be taken as the beginning of an upsurge in manufacturing; for Solon's attitude to various occupations, cf. doc. 11.34.

3.27 Solon Encourages Trade

Plutarch *Solon* 22.1

It has long been assumed that Plutarch's picture of Solon encouraging crafts finds confirmation in the archaeological record. The Corinthianising of Attic pottery has been taken to suggest that Corinthian potters made their way to Attica and that Solon did aim to encourage trade; see Bailey (1940) 60–70, esp. 64; Dunbabin (1948) 241–42, 480–82; Waters (1960) 184, 188–90; French (1964) 25; Andrewes (1982) 384; cf. Finley (1985) 132. However, Plutarch's colourful account of Greeks pouring into Attica can be discounted. The evidence for the numbers of potters, possibly 100 with about half seeming to be foreign in origin, in the sixth and fifth centuries (Starr (1982) 430) seems against this, and certainly Plut. *Sol.* 24.4 (doc. 3.28) points to restrictions on grants of citizenship. The spread of Attic black-figure ware throughout the Greek world from the early sixth century on cannot be taken to reflect (as it often is) an 'industrialisation' of Athens, because this is only one 'industry', which was carried out by small numbers. The pots as containers suggest a good trade, probably in olive oil, but for the debate on whether fine pots were important independent items of trade, see Gill (1991) 29–47.

22.1 Seeing that the city was filling up with men who kept pouring into Attica from every side on account of its secure conditions, but that most of the country was poor and undeveloped, and that those who sail the seas are unaccustomed to send their goods to those who have nothing to give in exchange, he encouraged the citizens to turn to manufacture and made a law that there was no compulsion for a son to maintain his father if he had not had him taught a trade.

3.28 Solon's Restrictions on Immigrants

Plutarch *Solon* 24.4

Access to citizenship was always restricted, and non-Athenians coming to Attica could not usually hope for citizenship. Solon granted citizenship to some, especially those with a trade, the tyrants guaranteed this grant of citizenship, and Kleisthenes re-enfranchized those who lost their citizenship with the downfall of the tyranny (docs. 4.2, 5.15); see Sealey (1983) 111–15.

24.4 The law concerning new citizens is a puzzling one, because it only granted citizenship to those who had been exiled for good from their country or those who emigrated to Athens with their entire families to practise a trade. They say that he did this not so much to exclude other people as to invite these to Athens with the certainty of becoming citizens, at the same time considering that those who had been forcibly expelled from their own countries and those who had left there for a specific purpose would be loyal.

3.29 Legislation against Exports

Plutarch *Solon* 24.1–2

While Sealey (1960) 157 thinks that this law is probably not genuine, rejection or acceptance of many of Solon's laws is often a case of simple faith. The following is his most famous law; Plutarch gives as his authority the first axon, which seems to imply that it is genuine. For the cultivation of olives, see Sallares (1991) 304–08; Isager & Skydsgaard (1992) 33–40. Garnsey (1988) 110 (cf. Jameson (1983) 11) points out that Plutarch does not actually state that Solon encouraged oleoculture; rather the law, as its primary objective, provided for the prohibition of the export of agricultural products, esp. grain (cf. doc. 10.39 for Teos). He like others sees this prohibition as a temporary measure in the context of a food crisis (74–75, 110); while there is no evidence for such a food crisis, it is possible that large landowners were selling grain abroad in a time of shortage for higher returns than they could receive in Attica. With the prohibition on grain exports, olives may have come to be cultivated more extensively and/or intensively and the leap in Attic pottery exports might be thus explained (see discussion at doc. 3.27; cf. Starr (1977) 175, 184). For the sacred olive trees, see esp. Lysias VII; *Ath. Pol.* 60.2; Rhodes 673–74; Wallace (1985) 107; Isager & Skydsgaard (1992) 203–05.

24.1 He allowed the sale of products to foreigners only in the case of olive oil, and prohibited their export, and he ordered the archon to lay curses against those who exported them, or else pay a fine of hundred drachmas to the public treasury; **24.2** the first tablet (axon) is that which contains this law. So one should not consider entirely improbable those who say that even the export of figs (syka: singular: sykon) was forbidden in former times, and that anyone informing against the exporters was called a 'sycophant' or 'fig-declarer'.

3.30 Solon's Agricultural Legislation

Plutarch *Solon* 23.7–8

The precise details given here might argue against the authenticity of these measures. They may, however, preserve the tradition of Solon's very real concern with day-to-day aspects of agriculture (Andrewes (1982) 384).

23.7 He also laid down rules about distances for planting with great expertise, stating that anything planted in a field had to be five feet away from the neighbour's property, and nine feet away, if a fig or an olive tree; for these reach further with their roots and can not be placed next to all plants without harm, because they deprive them of nutriment and give off an emanation, which is harmful to some. **23.8** He stated that anyone who wished to dig pits or trenches had to do so the equivalent of their depth away from someone else's property, and anyone positioning beehives had to keep them three hundred feet away from any previously put in position by someone else.

SOLON'S 'APODEMIA' AND THE DATING OF HIS REFORMS

After instituting his reforms in 594/3, Solon left Athens. This journey abroad, apodemia, is central to the attempt to down-date Solon's reforms. Herodotos (I.30.1) has Solon leaving Athens for ten years and visiting Croesus (reigned 560–546) and Amasis (reigned 570–26); cf. Hdt. II.177.2 (doc. 3.25). The *Ath. Pol.* 11.1 and Plut. *Sol.* 25.6 also state that after Solon enacted his laws he travelled for ten years. Solon himself, F28 (doc. 3.34), writes of his visit to Egypt (cf. *Ath. Pol.* 11.1; Plut. *Sol.* 26.1; Plat. *Tim.* 21c). Herodotos' account presents chronological problems. Solon as archon and law-giver in 594/3 cannot have visited Croesus and Amasis in a trip beginning soon after this date. It has been argued that Solon did not enact his reforms while archon, but sometime in the 570s, on the basis that he did visit both Amasis and Croesus. However, Solon's archonship and his reforms are linked by numerous sources, and he must have been archon and lawgiver in 594/3. See Miller (1969) for the view (not generally accepted) that Solon was not archon in 594/3 but in 573/2. Hammond's view, (1940) 71–83, adopted to overcome discrepancies between *Ath. Pol.* 13.1 and 14.1, that the seisachtheia was enacted in 594/3, but that his nomothesia (law-giving) took place in 592/1, has also not found acceptance (note esp. Cadoux (1948) 96–99) and it is better either to emend the text of 14.1 or to assume that the *Ath. Pol.* made a mistake, than to assume that Solon was reforming in two different years; see also Hignett (1952) 316–17; Sumner (1961) 50–54. Although Solon's reforms were wide-ranging, they could easily have been promulgated in the course of a single year. Plut. *Sol.* 16.4–5 does not mean that they took more than a year (Wallace (1983) 82–83).

Hignett (1952) 318–21 was the first to argue in detail that Solon's reforms should be down-dated radically, accepting that Solon was archon in 594/3, but dating the reforms to the late 570s on the evidence of Herodotos. He also argues that 594 is too early from the point of view of the seizing of power by Peisistratos (ie thirty years is too long a period for civil dissension before the tyranny was first established); but while the poor were among Peisistratos' supporters, he seized power with a bodyguard in the first instance (docs. 4.3–5), held power in conjunction with Megakles in the second (docs. 4.6–7), and won power by force with outside assistance in the third (docs. 4.9–11): it cannot be argued that Solon's reforms and Peisistratos' first coup must be brought into closer chronological proximity simply on the basis that the poor did not gain relief from Solon's reforms and so quickly turned to another advocate of their rights. Markianos (1974) 1–20, on the basis of the Herodotean chronology, argues that for the ten year trip to coincide with both Amasis' and Croesus' reign, Solon must have carried out his reforms in the 570s. One problem with this (as Markianos 7–8 notes) lies with the law on idleness: if Solon visited Amasis during his apodemia, he could hardly have taken the law and put it into his legislation (but, clearly, the nomos argias does not have an Egyptian origin). However, the main discrepancy remains: Amasis ruled 570–526, Croesus 560–546, and Herodotos has Solon visiting these men during his apodemia. It has been suggested that Solon could well have visited Croesus and Amasis, not as part of his original apodemia, but during a subsequent trip (cf. Rhodes 170; doc. 3.39 for his love of travel), but this is not what Herodotos states. Most recently, Wallace (1983) 81–95 argues against the down-dating of the reforms (with a useful list of scholars accepting the down-dating at 90n.1), pointing out (83) that all sources, bar one, assign the nomothesia to the archon year (*Ath. Pol.* 5.2; Plut. *Sol.* 14.3; Diog. Laert. 1.62; Aelian *VH* 8.10; Schol. Dem. XXIV.210; cf. Diod. IX.17; Eusebius-Jerome 99b (Helms). Aulus Gellius XVII.21.4 alone yields a different date).

Wallace notes that the visits during Solon's travels fall into a standard literary topos: the wise man visiting the powerful (87–89), and could well be fictitious or partly so. Solon's attested visit to Egypt means that the temptation to link him with Amasis will have been irresistible. The visit to Soloi in Cilicia is also doubted by Wallace 87, who points out that Soloi was already known as Sillu in seventh-century Assyrian texts;

Solon's visit to Cyprus and Soloi's ruler (Hdt. V.113.2; Plut. *Sol.* 26.2–4; cf. Solon F19), Philokypros, is an 'obvious aetiological invention' to explain the name 'Soloi'. Markianos (9) who accepts the incident nevertheless notes that the visit to Philokypros could have taken place as early as 587/6, so this does not help to down-date Solon's reforms. The chronology of Herodotos can be dismissed when the nature of his portrayal of Solon is noted. He is not interested in Solon the reformer, but in Solon the Sage. Chiasson (1986) 249–62 argues that Herodotos' Solon is a composite picture derived from Solon's poetry and from Herodotos' outlook on life; the Croesus-Solon incident (Hdt. I.30.1–33, I.86.1–87.2) has thus been modified to express Herodotos' own views on wealth and happiness; cf. Herodotos' account of Alkmeon's visit to Croesus (VI.125.2–5). Herodotos says nothing in detail about Solon's reforms except for the nomos argias, and for him Kleisthenes was the founder of Athenian democracy (Hdt. VI.131.1). The ancient tradition was that Solon was archon and lawgiver in 594/3; and while Herodotos' account of Solon's visits would date his nomothesia to the 570s, it is not historical but literary. Solon's archonship and his reforms belong firmly in 594/3.

3.31 Solon Leaves Athens for Ten Years

Herodotos I.29.1–30.1

I.29.1 With these (peoples) subdued and added by Croesus to the Lydian kingdom all the wise men of that time from Greece, one after another, came to Sardis, which was now at the height of her wealth, including Solon the Athenian, who made laws for the Athenians at their request and then went abroad for ten years, sailing away on the pretence of seeing the world, but really in order not to be compelled to repeal any of the laws he had made. **I.29.2** For the Athenians were unable to do this, as they had constrained themselves by solemn oaths to keep the laws Solon had made for them for ten years. **I.30.1** For this reason and in order to travel Solon went abroad and visited Amasis in Egypt and, furthermore, Croesus in Sardis.

3.32 The Observance of Solon's Laws for 100 Years

[Aristotle] *Athenaion Politeia* 7.2

Herodotos (doc. 3.31) says the Athenians swore to observe the laws for 10 years (Plut. *Sol.* 25.1 has 100 years). 10 years might seem more likely, as individuals could hardly swear to observe the laws for 100 years, but the tyrants are said not to have changed Solon's laws (doc. 4.21), and they were still in use under the classical democracy, though the tendency to ascribe many old laws to Solon needs to be noted (Hignett (1952) 89).

7.2 He made the laws unalterable for a hundred years and organized the constitution in the following way.

3.33 Solon's Law-tablets: The Axones

Plutarch *Solon* 25.1–2

Like Drakon's homicide law (doc. 3.3), Solon's laws were also recorded on axones and numbered according to axon; Stroud (1978) 23, 27; Rhodes 131; Plut. *Sol.* 19.4, 23.4, 24.1–2; according to [Arist.] *Ath. Pol.* 7.1 (doc. 3.15) Solon's laws were inscribed on 'kyrbeis'. Plutarch saw fragments of the axones in the prytaneion and says that axones and kyrbeis were identical, though some ancient authors drew a distinction between their subject matter. Eratosthenes in the third century BC (*FGH* 241 F37ab) and Polemon in the second (*FGH* 241 F37c) also equated axones and kyrbeis. Most scholars accept that these were different words for the same objects (Ruschenbusch (1966) 14–22; Rhodes 132; Andrewes (1974) 21–28). Stroud (1979) argues, however, that axones and kyrbeis were two different sets of objects, wooden and bronze respectively (rejected by Rhodes 132, but not by Robertson (1986) 147–48). The axones were rectangular wooden beams, with four faces, fixed so the reader could revolve them. Whether they revolved on a vertical or horizontal axis is uncertain; see Rhodes 132–33. See the reconstruction in Stroud (1979) 46 fig. 1; compare Rhodes (1984) 123 fig. 1. For Kratinos (Kassel & Austin F300; Kock F274), note Robertson (1986) 148–53, who argues that this fragment is evidence that the kyrbeis prescribed a barley cake as the meal for the officials who dined in the prytaneion.

25.1 He laid down that all his laws were to remain in force for a hundred years, and they inscribed them on wooden axones which revolved in the oblong frames which surrounded them, of which small remnants were still preserved in the prytaneion in my time, and which were called, as Aristotle says, kyrbeis. **25.2** And Kratinos the comic poet wrote somewhere:

> 'By Solon and by Drakon, by virtue of whose
> Kyrbeis they now roast their barley.'

But some people say that the kyrbeis are specifically those recording sacred ceremonies and sacrifices, and that the others are called axones.

3.34 Solon in Egypt

Plutarch *Solon* 26.1 (Solon 28)

> So first he went to Egypt and spent time there, as he himself says (F28):
> 'At the Nile's outpourings, near the Canopic shore.'

REACTIONS TO SOLON'S LEGISLATION

Solon's seisachtheia adversely affected wealthy land-owners (not necessarily only the eupatridai), who no longer received the one-sixth rent previously paid by the hektemoroi (cf. doc. 4.2). More serious was the discontent with the constitution, politeia, of Solon, which had widened the basis for political participation; presumably this made the eupatridai, with their monopoly on political power broken, 'discontented'. Some of Solon's poems seem to have been a reaction to this discontent (cf. doc. 3.12).

3.35 Discontentment with Solon's Reforms

[Aristotle] *Athenaion Politeia* 11.1–2

Plut. *Sol.* 16.1 also mentions the discontent of both 'sides', but also that soon afterwards the Athenians established a festival called the 'Seisachtheia' to celebrate the measure (*Sol.* 16.4–5).

11.1 When Solon had organized the constitution in the manner narrated, since people kept approaching him and making a nuisance of themselves over the laws, criticizing some and querying others, and he wanted neither to alter them nor to stay there and be the object of attack, he went on a journey to Egypt for trade and to see the country, saying that he would not be back for ten years, as he did not think it right that he should stay there to interpret his laws but rather that everyone should follow what was written down. **11.2** Moreover many of the notables happened to be at variance with him because of the cancellation of debts, and both sides had changed their minds because what had been established had turned out contrary to their expectations. For the people had thought that he would have everything redistributed, while the notables had thought that he would put them back in the same position or change things only slightly. But Solon was opposed to both, and though he could have become tyrant by joining whichever side he chose, he preferred to antagonize both sides by saving his native land and passing the best laws.

3.36 Political Troubles after Solon

[Aristotle] *Athenaion Politeia* 13.1–3

Solon's policies did not solve all of the problems of Attica immediately. In the fifth year after his archonship and reforms there was an 'anarchia' (590/89), that is, no archon was elected, and again in the fifth year after that (586/5). The archonship of Damasias exceeded the year of his office, and presumably he had support for this, but he was ousted by force by his opponents; for the difficulties with the chronology of the *Ath. Pol.*, see also doc. 4.4. Damasias held the office in 582/1, 581/0, and two months of 580/79. The board of ten archons which replaced him has been viewed as either holding office for the remaining ten months of that year, or for the next year; this board may not have had an eponymous archon. Day & Chambers (1962) 172–73 accept that there were ten archons, but that the division into three groups is a fourth century view; see Figueira (1984) 461–62, who (447–73) discusses the board of ten archons and accepts the tradition as genuine, considering it to have been an aberration and an attempt by the eupatridai to reassert their influence. Following this passage, the *Ath. Pol.* 13.4–5 (doc. 4.2) goes on to describe the situation between Megakles, Lykourgos and Peisistratos. No precise chronological information is given for the years between c. 580 and 561, apart from continuing discontent amongst the Athenians. There was apparently no further dissension over the archonship, so presumably the Athenians accepted an unsettled state of affairs; Peisistratos was to provide the impetus for the next major upheavals.

13.1 So these were the reasons why Solon went abroad. After he had left, the city continued to be in turmoil, though they continued for four years in peace; but in the fifth year after Solon's archonship they did not appoint an archon because of the dissension (stasis), and again in the fifth year after that there was no archon for the same reason. **13.2** Then, after the same lapse of time, Damasias was chosen as archon and remained in office for two years and two months, until he was expelled from his office by force. Then, as a result of the dissension, they decided to choose ten archons, five from the well-born (eupatridai), three from the farmers (agroikoi), and two from the craftsmen (demiourgoi), and these held office for the year after Damasias. From this it is clear that the archon had the greatest power; for dissension always appears to have occurred over this office. **13.3** On the whole, however, their relations with each other continued in an unhealthy state, some having the cancellation of debts as the origin and reason for their unhappiness (for they had become poor because of it), while others were discontented with the constitution because of the great change that had taken place, and yet others because of their personal rivalries with one another.

SOLON AND TYRANNY

Fragments 9 and 11 were said by Diodorus to have been written to warn the Athenians of the impending tyranny of Peisistratos (Diod. IX.20.2–3); cf. Rihll (1989) 277–86 who argues that they refer to Drakon. Solon may well have been alive when Peisistratos first seized power in 561/0 and the historical context of fragment 10, according to Diog. Laert. 1.49, was Solon's rushing armed into the ekklesia to warn the Athenians about Peisistratos; the boule said that he was mad; cf. *Ath. Pol.* 14.2; Plut. *Sol.* 30.1–5; doc. 4.4); *Mor.* 794f. It is often overlooked that Kylon had attempted to become tyrant some three decades earlier, and that in Solon's time there were tyrannies in Greece, notably at Corinth and Sicyon. Solon could certainly have used his power as archon to become tyrant, like Pittakos in Mytilene, had he wished (doc. 2.24, cf. 2.15 for Theagenes of Megara); see Andrewes (1956) 89–91.

3.37 'Time will Prove my Madness'

Solon 9–11

9. From cloud comes the force of snow and hail,
And thunder arises from brilliant lightning;
A city of great men is perishing utterly, and through ignorance
The people have fallen into servitude to a ruler (monarchos).
For the man who has gone too far it is not easy for him to make land
Afterwards, but he should already have had all good things in mind.

10. A short time will prove my madness to the citizens —
It will be proved when truth comes to the fore.

11. If you have suffered dreadfully though your own baseness,
Do not ascribe this destiny to the gods;
You have yourselves exalted these men by giving them protection.
And because of this you now have wretched servitude.
Each one of you walks with the steps of a fox,
Everyone of you has an empty mind;
For you look to the tongue and the words of a wily man,
But see nothing that takes place in actions.

3.38 Solon Refuses to Become Tyrant

Plutarch *Solon* 14.4–9 (Solon 32, 33)

Solon refused to act as a tyrant, as he tells in his poetry: F32; F33; F34.7–8 (*Ath. Pol.* 12.3), cf. F36.21–25, F37.7–10 (doc. 3.12); see also *Ath. Pol.* 6.3 (doc. 3.11), 11.2; Plut. *Sol.* 15.1, *Comp. Sol. & Publ.* 2.5. Some people apparently ridiculed him for refusing to become a tyrant: F33; others encouraged him to seize power: Plut. *Sol.* 14.4. The oracle from Delphi is presumably apocryphal; see Parke & Wormell (1956) I.111, II.7 Response 15 (cf. Responses 16, 326); Fontenrose (1978) 290 Response Q67 (see also QQ 68–69).

14.4 The leaders of both sides kept urging Solon, recommending tyranny and persuading him to seize control of the city more boldly now he had become powerful .... **14.6** And some say that Solon received this oracle at Delphi:

'Seat yourself in the middle of the ship, steering
As the helmsman; many of the Athenians are your allies.'

14.7 His associates in particular reproached him, if he fought shy of sole rule (monarchia) because of its name, as if the virtues of the man who took it did not immediately turn it into a kingship, as had happened earlier in the case of Tynnondas in Euboea and in their own time in the case of Pittakos, whom the Mytilenaeans had chosen as their tyrant. **14.8** None of this moved Solon from his resolution, but he said to his friends, it is reported, that tyranny is a fine place to be, but there is no way down from it, writing to Phokos in his poems (F32):

'If I have spared (he says)
My country, and of tyranny and cruel violence
Not laid hold, defiling and disgracing my good name,
I am not ashamed; for thus I think I shall be more superior
To all mankind.'

From this it is obvious that even before his legislation he had a great reputation. **14.9** And as to what was said by many who mocked him for shrinking from tyranny, he wrote as follows (F33):

'Solon was not a deep thinker or a wise man;
For when the god gave him good fortune, he did not accept it.
After encompassing his prey, out of amazement he did not pull in the great
Net, failing in spirit and deprived of wits.
I would have chosen to have power, to have taken limitless wealth
And been tyrant of Athens only for a single day,
And then to have been flayed for a wineskin and had my posterity wiped out.'

3.39 Solon: the Man and his Priorities

Solon 23

Solon's travels are attested by these lines, as well as his love for the aristocratic sport of hunting (see the treatise 'On Hunting', probably by Xenophon; cf. doc. 6.33). An almost identical couplet appears in the corpus which was ascribed to Theognis (lines 1253–54).

Fortunate, he who has dear children, and whole-hoofed horses
And hunting hounds and a friend in foreign parts.

4

Peisistratos and his Sons

The archonship and legislation of Solon in 594/3 did not mean the end of strife in Attica, though the conflict between the rich and the poor was certainly defused to a great extent. In subsequent decades, there were difficulties over the archonship in some years (doc. 3.36), and as this office was the privilege of the wealthy, both the eupatridai and non-eupatridai, dissension amongst the wealthy must have been at the root of the problem. At the same time, even after Solon's reforms, there remained a group of dissatisfied poor. Three important political figures emerge by the 560s: Megakles, Lykourgos and Peisistratos. According to Herodotos (doc. 4.1), there were three staseis (singular: stasis), which can be translated as factions or parties: those of the coast under the leadership of Megakles the Alkmeonid, 'hoi paraloi', and those of the plain under Lykourgos, 'hoi ek tou pediou', while Peisistratos formed a third stasis, 'hoi hyperakrioi', meaning 'those from beyond the hills', also known by the *Athenaion Politeia* (doc. 4.2) as 'hoi diakrioi', 'men of the diakria'. The coastal region, paralia, stretches from Phaleron to Sounion, the west coast of Attica; it is here that the Alkmeonidai would have had their adherents, with their main centre probably at Alopeke, south of Athens. The plain referred to is the central plain, the valley of the Kephissos river, which adjoins the city, and Lykourgos probably had his main centre at Boutadai. The diakrioi were the inhabitants of the diakria, the area from Parnes to Brauron, the hilly north-east part of Attica; this area is separated from the plain of Athens by intervening hills.

Herodotos concentrates on the regional distinctions between the three groups (doc. 4.1). The *Ath. Pol.* 13.4 (doc. 4.2) emphasizes the regional distinction, stating that the name of each group came 'from the areas in which they farmed', but also gives a distinct political affiliation to each group. Lykourgos is described as the leader of the plain, presumably conservative landowners, who desired oligarchy, while Megakles pursued a 'middle-of-the-road' policy. Megakles, in fact, was able to ally himself with both Lykourgos, in overthrowing Peisistratos' first and second tyrannies, and also with Peisistratos, whom he helped to establish in power a second time through a marriage alliance, and then deposed when the marriage was, supposedly, not consummated (docs. 4.6, 4.8). Peisistratos' stasis, or party, consisted of the 'diakrioi' and he was 'a friend to democracy'. His party included not only regional adherents, but as the *Ath. Pol.* notes the poor as well, and Peisistratos combined leadership of the 'diakrioi' with the support of those economically disadvantaged by Solon's reforms, and those afraid of losing citizen rights. Peisistratos succeeded where Megakles and Lykourgos failed because he was able to transcend regionalism. While both Lykourgos and Megakles may have had adherents outside of their main area of support, where Peisistratos had the advantage was in being able to project himself as the leader not only of a certain region, but also of the poor and the discontented, and probably therefore of Athenians in general, whose support for him can be seen in the motion to award him a bodyguard.

Peisistratos' first two attempts at tyranny involved charades: on his first attempt he wounded himself and his mules and drove his chariot into the agora (doc. 4.3), and in the second the 'goddess Athena' herself restored him to power (doc. 4.6). His third tyranny was established through bloodshed and the use of outside help, and he also disarmed the people (docs. 4.9–13). Hostages were taken and sent to Naxos, and the Alkmeonidai and others went into exile (docs. 4.14–15). Later Athenians looked back upon Peisistratos' reign as a 'Golden Age' (doc. 4.16), in which the tyrant ruled mildly, gave financial aid to poor farmers (though not from disinterested motives), and was popular with both the ordinary people and with the wealthy class (or at least with those of this class who were not in exile).

Peisistratos was succeeded by his sons, the Peisistratidai, of whom Hippias and Hipparchos were the most important. Thucydides gives a favourable opinion of their reign (doc. 4.21), and they were known for their building projects (docs. 4.28–29). The Peisistratidai continued to rule by making use of the existing laws and by ensuring that 'one of their own people' was one of the magistrates (doc. 4.21). One of these was Peisistratos, son of Hippias, who held the archonship sometime between 522/1–511/0, possibly in 522/1 (docs. 4.24–26). A fragment of the archon-list gives the name of Miltiades as archon in 524/3; more surprising is the presence of Kleisthenes the Alkmeonid as archon in 525/4. The Alkmeonidai maintained that they had been in exile for the duration of the tyranny, but apparently a reconciliation had taken place by the year 525/4, and this and Miltiades' archonship seem to mark attempts at reconciliation with the aristocratic families who had previously left Athens (doc. 4.14). Hippias and Hipparchos ruled jointly until, in 514/3, Hipparchos was assassinated by Harmodios and Aristogeiton (docs. 4.30–31), after which the tyranny became harsher and Hippias took revenge through killing and exiling opponents (docs. 4.32–33), and planned a place of retreat for himself (doc. 4.34, cf. 4.39). An attempt by exiles, including the Alkmeonidai, to end the tyranny failed at Leipsydrion (doc. 4.35) and Hippias was finally overthrown with Spartan help (docs. 4.36–38). He made his way to Persia (doc. 4.39), from where he was to return in 490 with the Persians in their attack at Marathon (doc. 7.7).

Peisistratos and his sons ruled over Athens as tyrants, and yet the Solonian constitution continued to operate with elections held and the rights and privileges of each of the four Solonian classes intact. Peisistratos' first attempt at tyranny took place in 561/0, and the deposition of his son Hippias in 511/0; the family had accordingly determined Athenian politics for half a century.

THE THREE PARTIES

While Herodotos 1.59.3 (doc. 4.1) writes of Peisistratos' supporters as hoi hyperakrioi, 'those from beyond the hills', the *Ath. Pol.* 13.4 (doc. 4.2) writes of diakrioi, 'hillsmen'; cf. Plut. *Sol.* 29.1. Herodotos' term is sometimes preferred. But hyperakrioi, 'the men from beyond the hills' is a designation which would have been used by those for whom the hills were some distance, and thus by the men of the city and the plain to refer to the third group; diakrioi is probably the term which was used by Peisistratos and his supporters. For the diakrioi, the inhabitants of the diakria, the area from Parnes to Brauron, see Hopper (1961) 189–94. The *Ath. Pol.* is thus more correct in referring to the diakrioi, in that diakria is the actual name of a specific area, though the translation 'hillsmen' used here and by others needs caution: poor hillsmen existing on a subsistence livelihood is not an appropriate picture, as the diakria was as prosperous as the rest of Attica (cf. Frost (1990) 4). Support for each of the three groups could also have come from outside of their area; Peisistratos certainly had support from malcontents, as well as a group who were concerned about the possibility of losing citizen rights (doc. 4.2). Aristotle (*Pol.* 1305a 22–24) has Peisistratos as a tyrant exploiting the hatred of the wealthy; this might over-state the case, but the sources agree that the poor were amongst his adherents. See French (1957) 241–42, (1959) 46–57; Sealey (1960) 155–80; Hopper (1961) 189–219; Lewis (1963) 22–26; Holladay (1977) 40–56; Rhodes 184–87.

4.1 Peisistratos and his Rivals

Herodotos I.59.3

See Kinzl (1989) 5–8 for the implausible suggestion that the three regional divisions are anachronistic and reflect fifth rather than sixth century divisions. Fornara & Samons (1991) 151–57 accept Herodotos' account, but argue that Herodotos has Peisistratos *claiming* that he came forward for the hillsmen (their argument rests on their interpretation of τῷ λόγῳ in Hdt. I.59.3), that Herodotos regarded this claim as 'pretense or a piece of propaganda' because the hillsmen do not appear in the subsequent events, and that the *Ath. Pol.* expands Herodotos' account, and gives the struggle a tripartite regional division it did not really have. But the supporters of Lykourgos or Megakles also do not appear in the accounts, and the *Ath. Pol.* is correct in emphasizing that the struggle was in a sense regional, in that the three men drew on support from their local areas. Megakles was the grandson of the Megakles who married Agariste, daughter of Kleisthenes of Sicyon (doc. 2.4); the Alkmeonidai, who were banished following the Kylonian affair, were now back in Attica (cf. docs. 2.17–19), but they were to go into exile again when Peisistratos seized power for the third time, after Hipparchos' assassination, and after Kleomenes' second invasion of Attica. See Ostwald (1991) 137–48 for Herodotos and Athens. Doc. 4.3 follows on from here.

I.59.3 When the Athenians were in a state of dissension between the people of the coastland under Megakles son of Alkmeon and those of the plain under Lykourgos son of Aristolaides, Peisistratos fixed his sights on the tyranny and formed a third party, collecting partisans and coming forward representing himself as champion of the people beyond the hills (the hyperakrioi).

4.2 Peisistratos as Popular Leader

[Aristotle] *Athenaion Politeia* 13.4–5

The term demotikotatos ('a great friend to democracy', 'concerned with the interests of the people') is used here of Peisistratos, and given that he had the poor and underprivileged amongst his followers this is a reasonable description from a fourth century point of view; cf. Rhodes 186; Holladay (1977) 40. After the overthrow of the tyranny there was a review of the citizen body, and those who could not prove their citizenship were disenfranchised. Solon had encouraged immigrants to Attica (see doc. 3.28), and Peisistratos might also have done so. The disenfranchisement presumably took place because these individuals were guaranteed their citizenship by the tyrants (see Ostwald (1969) 141–42). It was presumably to these that Kleisthenes gave back citizenship (doc. 5.15). Doc. 4.4 follows on from here.

13.4 There were three parties; the first was that of the men of the shore, led by Megakles son of Alkmeon, and they seemed in particular to want a middle-of-the-road constitution. The second was that of the men of the plain; they wanted oligarchy, and were led by Lykourgos. The third was that of the hillsmen (diakrioi) with Peisistratos as their leader, who was apparently a great friend to democracy. **13. 5** The latter had moreover been joined by those who had lost debts they were owed and were now poor, and by those who were not of pure Athenian descent, who were now afraid; proof of this is that, after the tyrants were deposed, they held a vote on claims to the registration of citizens, on the grounds that many who were not entitled to were sharing citizen rights. Each party took its name from the area in which it farmed.

PEISISTRATOS' FIRST TYRANNY

According to Herodotos (doc. 4.3), the character of Peisistratos' first tyranny was similar to that of his third: he governed moderately and well, and it is stressed that Peisistratos made use of the existing (Solonian) laws and usages (doc. 4.3, cf. 4.5, 4.16), which must mean that the ekklesia met, the heliaia functioned, and elections were held for magistracies (but see doc. 4.21) and when Isagoras after the overthrow of the tyranny attempted to set up an oligarchy (508/7), he was opposed by the majority of Athenians (see docs. 5.2–3, 5.6). The dates of the first, second and third tyrannies are much debated: see Sumner (1961) 37–49; Hind (1974) 1–18 (discussing the views of Miller, Sumner, Hammond, Sanders, Jacoby); Davies (1971) 444–45; Ruebel (1973) 125–36; Rhodes (1976) 219–33, (1981) 191–99; Andrewes (1982) 399. The text of the *Ath. Pol.* is emended differently by modern authors to effect a consistent chronology; note that the translations in this section of the dates given by the *Ath. Pol.* have not been emended. Hind (1974) 7–8 provides a comparative list of chronologies proposed (up to 1974), and his own at 10–11; Rhodes (1976) 226–27, (1981) 195–96 has a table comparing the dates of Herodotos, Thucydides, Aristotle *Politics* and the *Ath. Pol.*

Rhodes' (1981) 198 chronology is as follows: first coup 561/0?; first expulsion 561/0 or 560/59?; second coup 557/6 or 556/5?; second expulsion 556/5?; third coup 546/5?; Peisistratos' death 528/7; assassination of Hipparchos 514/3; expulsion of the Peisistratidai 511/0. Note the discussions of the tyranny in Ure (1921) 33–67; Forrest (1966) 175–89; Andrewes (1956) 100–15, (1982) 392–416; Berve (1967) I.47–77,

II.539–63; Mossé (1969) 49–78; Jeffery (1976) 94–99; Lewis (1988) 287–302; Ober (1989) 65–68; Stockton (1990) 21–22.

4.3 Peisistratos as National Hero

Herodotos I.59.3–6

The Athenian capture of Nisaia (the main port of Megara) was part of the long-running dispute between the two states, which centred on Salamis; for Solon's part in this, see doc. 3.8. That Peisistratos was a general in this campaign indicates that he must already have had influence in Attica (cf. French (1959) 46). For Peisistratos and Nisaia, see Legon (1981) 136–39. Peisistratos' first bodyguard were club-bearers, armed to protect him from the attack of his rivals; his sons had spear-bearers, doryphoroi, like other tyrants (doc. 4.30); for such bodyguards, see docs. 2.11–12, 15, 40, 45.

I.59.3 Peisistratos devised the following plan: **I.59.4** he wounded himself and his mules and drove his cart into the agora, as if he had escaped from his enemies, who had tried to murder him as he was driving into the country, and asked the people to grant him a bodyguard; he had previously won a good reputation in his command against the Megarians, by his capture of Nisaia and other great deeds. **I.59.5** The people of the Athenians, deceived, picked out and gave him some of the citizens, who became not Peisistratos' spear-bearers, but his club-bearers; for they followed him around with wooden cudgels. **I.59.6** These joined in the revolt with Peisistratos and seized the acropolis. And so Peisistratos was master of the Athenians, but he neither disturbed the existing magistracies nor changed the laws, and governed the city in accordance with the status quo, ruling fairly and well.

4.4 Solon's Advice to the People

[Aristotle] *Athenaion Politeia* 14.1–3

There is a discrepancy in the statement that Peisistratos' first attempt occurred in the archonship of Komeas (561/0) and 32 years after Solon's reforms (594/3); see also doc. 3.36. Hegesias' archonship dates to 556/6. Despite the fact that the *Ath. Pol.* here gives Peisistratos five years of rule in his first period as tyrant, Rhodes 197–98 considers this first tyranny to have lasted only one year or less. Peisistratos is described as 'demotikotatos' once again (as at doc. 4.2). Plut. *Sol.* 30 gives essentially the same details as this passage. Aristion is sometimes identified with the gravestone bearing this name c. 510 in Peisistratid territory (*IG* I^2 1024; Friedländer 164; *LSAG* 75, 78n.42; Richter (1961) no. 67, pls. 155–58, 180, 211–12; cf. Rhodes 200), but this is probably a case of wishful identification.

14.1 Peisistratos, who seemed to be a great friend to democracy and had won an excellent reputation in the war against the Megarians, wounded himself and convinced the people that this was the work of his political opponents and that they should give him a bodyguard, Aristion proposing the motion. Once he had these 'club-bearers' as they were called, he rose up with their help against the people and seized the acropolis in the thirty-second year after the enactment of Solon's laws, in the archonship of Komeas. **14.2** It is said that when Peisistratos requested the guard, Solon spoke against it, and said that he was wiser than some and braver than others — he was wiser than all those who did not realise that Peisistratos was making an attempt on the tyranny and he was braver than all those who realised but were keeping quiet. When his words did not convince them, he brought out his weapons and placed them in front of his door, saying that he had helped his fatherland as far as was in his power (for he was already a very old man), and that he called on the others to do the same. **14.3** Solon's appeal at that point had no effect; Peisistratos took over the government and administered public affairs constitutionally rather than like a tyrant. But before his power had taken root, the parties of Megakles and Lykourgos came to an agreement and sent him into exile in the sixth year after his first coming to power, in the archonship of Hegesias.

4.5 Peisistratos Preserves Solon's Politeia

Plutarch *Solon* 30.5–31.5

Plutarch here stresses that Peisistratos maintained Solon's laws. Clearly the oath that the Athenians had sworn to observe the laws for ten (or a hundred) years (docs. 3.31–32), despite the years of anarchia, had had its desired effect. According to Plutarch, Aristion (called Ariston at Plut. *Sol.* 30.3) had proposed that Peisistratos should be granted a bodyguard of 50 club-bearers. For Solon's views on tyranny, see docs. 3.37–38.

30.5 The people ratified the proposal and did not even deal grudgingly with Peisistratos over the number of club-bearers, but allowed him to keep and openly take about with him as many as he wanted, until he seized the acropolis .... **31.2** When Peisistratos came to power, he won over Solon by treating him with respect and kindness and sending for him, with the result that Solon became his adviser and praised many of his acts. **31.3** For he preserved most of Solon's laws, abiding by them himself and compelling his friends to do so; for example, after he became tyrant he was even summoned to trial at the Areiopagos on a charge of murder and turned up to defend himself in due form, but his accuser failed to turn up in court; he wrote other laws himself, one of which lays down that those maimed in war should be maintained at the public expense. **31.4** Herakleides (F149 Wehrli) says that Peisistratos was copying Solon who passed this law earlier in the case of Thersippos who had been maimed. **31.5** But according to Theophrastos' account it was not Solon who was responsible for the law against unemployment, but Peisistratos, by which he made the country more productive and the city more peaceful.

PEISISTRATOS' SECOND TYRANNY

Megakles and Lykourgos joined forces to bring about the end of Peisistratos' first tyranny. They soon fell out, however, no doubt due to their different political ambitions, and because Megakles was losing out in the power struggle he patched up his differences with Peisistratos. The incident is an interesting insight into the 'balance of power' within Athenian society. Lykourgos and Megakles had to join forces to throw out Peisistratos, as neither of them was strong enough to dominate the state, but Lykourgos seems to have been more powerful than Megakles.

4.6 'Athena' Restores Peisistratos

Herodotos I.60.1–5

Even Herodotos found it difficult to believe that the Athenians were tricked by the ruse which Megakles and Peisistratos employed to effect his return. Connor (1987) 40–47, and Frost (1990) 7, argue that the ruse was a ritual charade, not unusual for the festivals of the time; but that for Peisistratos it was 'not simply a cynical act of political manipulation' is difficult to accept. Kleidemos *FGH* 323 F15 records the unlikely story that Peisistratos later married Phye to his son Hipparchos.

I.60.1 Not long afterwards the parties of Megakles and Lykourgos came to an agreement and drove Peisistratos out. Thus when Peisistratos was tyrant at Athens for the first time he was expelled because the tyranny was not yet deeply rooted, but those who drove Peisistratos out then began a fresh quarrel with one another. **I.60.2** As this discord was making life difficult for him, Megakles made proposals to Peisistratos asking if he were willing to marry his daughter and regain the tyranny on that condition. **I.60.3** When Peisistratos approved the idea and agreed to the conditions, they worked out for his return the most simple-minded ruse by far, that I have encountered (since the Greek nation has been distinguished from earliest times by being both cleverer and more superior to silly foolishness than the barbarian), and yet these men devised the following trick against the Athenians, who are supposed to be the wisest of the Greeks. **I.60.4** There was a woman in the village Paiania, whose name was Phye, who only lacked three fingers of four cubits in height (she was five feet six inches tall) and was handsome in other respects as well. They dressed this woman up in full armour and mounted her on a war-chariot, and when they had got her to pose in the attitude that would appear most distinguished, they drove into the city, having sent ahead advance messengers, who on their arrival in the city kept making the following announcement, as they had been instructed: **I.60.5** 'O Athenians, gladly welcome Peisistratos, whom Athena herself has honoured above all men and whom she restores to her own acropolis.' The messengers went around broadcasting these reports, and immediately rumour reached the villages that Athena was restoring Peisistratos. Those in the city were convinced that the woman was really the goddess, and offered this female their prayers and took Peisistratos back.

4.7 Phye: a Thracian Garland Seller

[Aristotle] *Athenaion Politeia* 14.4–15.1

The *Ath. Pol.* here gives Herodotos (I.60.4) as his source for one version of Phye's background, the only occasion on which he does so. The story that Phye was a Thracian garland seller (ie not an Athenian citizen), from Kollytos, a quarter of the city (Jacoby *FGH* Suppl. 3b 1.72), is probably a slander. Giving the demotic (see doc. 5.7) for a foreigner would be unusual (Jacoby *ibid.*; Rhodes 205).

14.4. In the twelfth year after this Megakles, harassed by strife between the parties, again made proposals to Peisistratos and, on the condition that Peisistratos married his daughter, restored him in a primitive and extremely simple-minded way. He broadcast the tale that Athena was restoring Peisistratos, and after discovering a tall and handsome woman called Phye, who according to Herodotos was from the deme Paiania, though some say that she was a Thracian garland-seller from the deme Kollytos, he dressed her up to resemble the goddess and brought her into the city with Peisistratos; and so he drove into the city on a war-chariot with the woman standing beside him, while those in the city fell down in worship and received him with awe. **15.1** This was how Peisistratos' first return took place.

4.8 Peisistratos Loses the Tyranny a Second Time

Herodotos I.61.1–2

Cf. *Ath. Pol.* 15.1: 'Afterwards, he was expelled for the second time about six years after his return (for he did not hold power for long, but was afraid of both parties because he refused to have sexual intercourse with Megakles' daughter, and secretly left the country).' The fact that Herodotos specifically states that Peisistratos 'left the country completely' seems to imply that after he was ousted from his first tyranny he had retired to his estates. The whole story of the non-consummated marriage is suspiciously detailed and should probably not be taken literally. It is more likely that having achieved power Peisistratos saw no further need to conciliate Megakles.

I.61.1 After recovering the tyranny in the manner described above, Peisistratos in accordance with his agreement with Megakles married Megakles' daughter. But since he had sons who were already young men and the Alkmeonidai were said to be accursed, he did not want to have children by his new bride and therefore did not have intercourse with her in the normal way. **I.61.2** Initially his wife kept this a secret, but afterwards, whether in answer to a question or not, she let it out to her mother and she to her husband. He was indignant at being insulted in this way by Peisistratos, and was so angry that he made up his differences with his political opponents. When Peisistratos learned of the actions taken against him, he left the country completely, and on his arrival at Eretria took counsel with his sons.

PEISISTRATOS IN EXILE

After fleeing Attica and arriving in Eretria, Hippias persuaded Peisistratos to win back the tyranny. Herodotos mentions that he was assisted by money from the Thebans and Argive mercenaries, while the *Ath. Pol.* 15.2 (doc. 4.10) adds that the hippeis of Eretria also assisted him, but does not explain why. Lygdamis was clearly acting on his own personal initiative in assisting Peisistratos, for Peisistratos installed him as tyrant over the Naxians when he regained the tyranny at Athens (doc. 4.14).

4.9 Peisistratos Gains Outside Assistance

Herodotos I.61.3–4

Lavelle (1992) 9n.14, 10, cf. (1986) 150, notes that while Hdt. I.61.4 writes of Argive 'misthotoi', which Lavelle translates as 'hirelings' ('mercenaries' is given below), the

Ath. Pol. 17.4 (doc. 4.18) states that Peisistratos had an Argive wife, and it was on account of this friendship (philia) that Hegesistratos, Peisistratos' son, was able to bring 1,000 Argives to Pallene. Perhaps the marriage alliance was important, but some money may also have changed hands. Hegesistratos was later sent to govern Sigeion; doc. 1.15.

I.61.3 Convinced by Hippias' opinion that they should try to win back the tyranny, they started collecting contributions from all the cities which were at all under obligations to them. Many supplied large sums of money, the Thebans surpassing everyone else in their gift of money. **I.61.4** And then, to cut a long story short, time passed and everything was ready for their return. For Argive mercenaries had arrived from the Peloponnese and a man from Naxos called Lygdamis turned up of his own accord and exhibited great eagerness to help, bringing with him both money and men.

4.10 Peisistratos' Movements while in Exile

[Aristotle] *Athenaion Politeia* 15.2

The *Ath. Pol.* here states that Peisistratos began his period in exile by settling a colony in Thrace, while Herodotos refers to Peisistratos' stay in Thrace only obliquely (see doc. 4.12). Cole (1975) 42–43 suggests that Rhaikelos was a joint Eretrian-Peisistratos venture. Peisistratos returned to Attica via Eretria; see doc. 4.11; cf. Rhodes 208.

15.2 First of all Peisistratos helped settle a colony at a place called Rhaikelos near the Gulf of Thermai, and from there he went on to the region about Pangaion, from where, after raising money and hiring mercenaries, he returned to Eretria. In the eleventh year he for the first time attempted to recover power by force, with the support of many others, especially the Thebans and Lygdamis of Naxos, as well as the hippeis who controlled the government in Eretria.

PEISISTRATOS RETURNS TO POWER FOR THE THIRD TIME

Peisistratos' third attempt at tyranny was not gained on the basis of popular support, but through the use of violence, backed by foreign supporters. But popular support for Peisistratos seems to have followed his third coup (though see doc. 4.14). The difficulties which Peisistratos had in retaining the tyranny on the first and second occasions indicate that Athenian politics were operating on a more sophisticated level than at Corinth or Megara, where tyrants came to power by attacking the wealthy; at Athens there was clearly not as much dissatisfaction amongst the poor as there had been in Solon's time. Peisistratos falls into the category of the typical tyrant: he was of aristocratic background, but able to harness the support of the poor and discontented (in addition to his regional adherents). But the role of the poor should not be down-played in the first attempt, and, in the second, Megakles formed an alliance with Peisistratos precisely because Peisistratos was a powerful figure, which related to the support of the poor, while in the third attempt the 'people' appear to have been in support of the coup: 'others streamed in from the villages who preferred tyranny to freedom' (Hdt. I.62.1). Given the rivalry between political figures and the role of the populace, attempts to focus purely on factionalism or a class-struggle do not adequately explain the politics of the period (cf. Ober (1989) 65n.30).

4.11 The Battle at Pallene

Herodotos I.62.1–63.2

Peisistratos landed at Marathon, both because of its proximity to Eretria, the hippeis of which were supporting his return, and because Marathon was in Peisistratid territory; Peisistratos was clearly still popular in the region. The opposing forces met at the temple of Athena Pallenis, in the deme Pallene (Lewis (1963) 33–34, 39). Here Peisistratos' opponents sat down to lunch, followed by dice or a siesta, whereupon Peisistratos, emboldened by a prophecy from a sooth-sayer (chresmologos), attacked; for the prophecy, see Lavelle (1991) 317–24. His policy of clemency and non-retribution was reflected in his method of government once tyrant (doc. 4.16).

I.62.1 They set out from Eretria and arrived back in the eleventh year after their departure. The first place they took in Attica was Marathon. While they were encamped there, their supporters from the city arrived, while others streamed in from the villages who preferred tyranny to freedom. **I.62.2** These assembled; meanwhile the Athenians from the city, while Peisistratos was collecting money and even afterwards when he occupied Marathon, took no action, but when they learnt that he was marching from Marathon towards the city, they came out to meet him. **I.62.3** They marched in full battle array against the returning exiles, while Peisistratos and his men, who had set out from Marathon and were marching against the city, met them at the temple of Athena Pallenis, where both sides took up their positions against each other. **I.62.4** There, under divine guidance, Amphilytos, a sooth-sayer from Akarnania, came up to Peisistratos, and pronounced the following oracle in hexameters:

'The cast is thrown, the net is spread,
The tuna-fish will come darting through the moonlit night.'

I.63.1 When he pronounced this with divine inspiration, Peisistratos understood the prophecy and saying that he accepted the oracle led his army into battle. The Athenians from the city were occupied with lunch at that point, and following their meal some of them were occupied with dice and others having a siesta. Peisistratos' men fell on the Athenians and routed them. **I.63.2** As they were fleeing Peisistratos came up with a most ingenious ploy, so the Athenians would be unable to rally in the future and would remain dispersed. He mounted his sons on horseback and sent them on ahead. Whenever they caught up with the fugitives, they told them as instructed by Peisistratos to be of good courage and each return home.

4.12 Peisistratos' Sources of Revenue

Herodotos 1.64.1

The river Strymon is in Thrace. Hdt. I.64.1 (cf. *Ath. Pol.* 15.2, doc. 4.10) is usually taken to mean that Peisistratos had access to silver mines in Thrace, not only before his third attempt at power, but also afterwards, and that the tyranny was wealthy as a consequence; but see Lavelle (1992) 5–21: Peisistratos is not noted in the sources as being wealthy, and his third attempt at power involved help from numerous sources (ie Peisistratos was not so wealthy from the Thracian venture as to manage his return to power without assistance). Athenian coinage during Peisistratos' tyranny varies markedly in its purity, indicating several sources for the silver, and the Wappenmünzen (for which see doc. 3.24) were modest coins having only a local circulation. The increase in the weight of the new coins which appear c. 525 after Peisistratos' death, the so-called 'owls', and the purity of the silver from which they were minted indicate that a new source of silver had became accessible (presumably Laureion, in Attica). Peisistratos raised revenue from a modest tax (doc. 4.16, cf. 4.21) and thus did not rely on silver from Thracian mines while actually tyrant. According to the *Ath. Pol.* 15.2 Peisistratos first joined in a colonial venture, and then moved on to the Mt. Pangaion region (east of the Strymon). Lavelle suggests that there was a Peisistratid settlement on the Strymon, an emporion exploiting the region. Peisistratos' involvement in Thrace was the beginning of a long Athenian association with the area (cf. docs. 1.6, 8.27).

I.64.1 The Athenians did as they were told, and in this way Peisistratos for the third time became master of Athens and established the tyranny on a firm footing with a large number of mercenaries and revenues from Attica and the river Strymon.

4.13 Peisistratos Disarms the People

[Aristotle] *Athenaion Politeia* 15.3–5

The *Ath. Pol.* here has Peisistratos disarming the people (cf. doc. 4.30 for Hippias). The account of Peisistratos' ruse can doubtless be accepted given his previous success with the Athena charade (docs. 4.6–7). For tyrants preferring citizens not to become involved in public affairs, cf. doc. 2.11. The *Ath. Pol.* speaks of Pallenis, rather than Pallene.

15.3 Now that he had won the battle at Pallenis, and captured the city and removed the people's weapons, he held the tyranny securely; he also seized Naxos and established Lygdamis as ruler. **15.4** He removed the people's weapons in the following way: he held a review in full armour at the Theseion and began to speak to the people, addressing them for a short time; when they said that they couldn't hear him distinctly, he told them to go up to the entrance gate (propylon) of the acropolis so he could make himself better heard. And while he was taking up time making his speech, the men assigned to this duty picked up the weapons and shut them up in the buildings near the Theseion and came and indicated this to Peisistratos. **15.5** When he had finished the rest of his speech, he told them about what had happened to their weapons, saying that they shouldn't be surprised or distressed, but should go away and see to their own affairs, as he was going to take care of all public business.

4.14 The Alkmeonidai Go into Exile

Herodotos I.64.1–3

While the source tradition regarding Peisistratos is quite favourable (see doc. 4.16) the third period of tyranny began with an act of violence (Hdt. I.64.3). Amongst those who fled were the Alkmeonidai: Megakles' role in overthrowing the second tyranny made their position in Attica untenable; for their going into exile again under Hippias, see doc. 4.35, cf. 4.33. Moreover, Peisistratos took hostages, presumably from families which might prove to be rivals. These were sent to Peisistratos' ally Lygdamis of Naxos.

I.64.1 He also took as hostages the sons of the Athenians who had remained and not immediately fled, and sent them off to Naxos **I.64.2** (for Peisistratos had conquered this island in warfare and put Lygdamis in power there) .... **I.64.3** So Peisistratos was tyrant of Athens, while as to the Athenians some of them had fallen in the battle and others had left the country and gone into exile with the Alkmeonidai.[1]

[1] The manuscripts read 'Αλκμεωνίδεω (Alkmeonides), Megakles' brother, who was the head of the family in 546, having succeeded Megakles, but Wesseling's emendation 'Αλκμεωνιδέων, the Alkmeonidai, is usually accepted; see Davies (1971) 373.

4.15 A Dedication of Alkmeonides son of Alkmeon

IG I^2 472 (*IG* I^3 1469)

Friedländer 167; Moretti 5 (cf. 4); Hansen 302; see Hdt. VI.125.5. A dedication by Alkmeonides, son of Alkmeon and brother of Megakles, is inscribed on a marble Doric capital at the sanctuary of Apollo Ptoios in northern Boeotia, celebrating a victory in the chariot race at the Great Panathenaia. *LSAG* 73, with 78n.30, notes (with others) that the victory was won in 546 but that the Alkmeonidai fled Attica as a result of Peisistratos' return 'before he (Alkmeonides) could make his dedication on the Akropolis' and hence made it at this sanctuary instead. Davies (1971) 373 suggests, however, that 'the primary historical value of the dedication (is) ... as a witness of the Alkmeonid response to the Theban support for Peisistratos' return in 547/6'; the view of *LSAG* is preferable.

I am the fa[i]r stat[ue of Phoi]bos son of [L]e[t]o;
Alkmeonides, [son of A]lkmeon
Who conqu[ered] with his [swift h]orses [d]edicated [me],
Which Ho[monymos so]n of Knop[ion] drove,
When the fest[ival] of Pallas was held in Athens.

PEISISTRATOS AS TYRANT

4.16 The 'Golden Age' of Peisistratos

[Aristotle] *Athenaion Politeia* 16.1–10

This document is extremely important for Peisistratos' reign. **16.2–3**: the *Ath. Pol.* stresses the assistance which Peisistratos gave to the farmers. Loans of money to the poor were presumably to reduce peasants' dependence on wealthy landowners and transfer their allegiance to Peisistratos; these loans may have been interest-free (Millett (1989) 23). **16.4**: for the tax of ten per cent, see discussion at doc. 4.21. That an increase in the farmers' prosperity meant an increase in Peisistratos' revenues which was sizeable enough to be commented upon supports the contention that during this third phase of the tyranny Peisistratos did not have revenue from silver in Thrace. As the poor had been supporters of Peisistratos it was now important to ensure the prosperity of this group. **16.6**: the story of the tax free farm is probably apocryphal. **16.7**: the tyranny of the sons is mentioned as being much harsher, see also docs. 4.32–33. For the Age of Kronos as a Golden Age, see Hes. *WD* 109–20. **16.8**: the incident of the Areiopagos, responsible for trying accusations of homicide, is favourably interpreted by the *Ath. Pol.*

However, Finley (1981) 83 sees this as the 'only joke ... in the entire corpus of (Aristotle's) surviving works'. But Arist. *Pol.* 1315b 21–22, Plut. *Sol.* 31.3 (doc. 4.5) refer to the same incident and it should be taken at face value. **16.9**: Although Peisistratos' third tyranny saw many go into exile, those of the gnorimoi (the wealthy class) that remained were won over by him. **16.10**: the punishment for establishing a tyranny was atimia, loss of citizen rights (see Rhodes 220–22). The deme or village judges will have precluded the necessity of disputants coming to the city (cf. 16.3). More importantly, judicial authority was not in the hands of the local nobility, to whom probably the disputants would otherwise have turned. The *Ath. Pol.* 26.3 (cf. 53.1) writes that the system of deme judges was instituted again in 453/2, so apparently they were discontinued at some stage.

16.1 This is how Peisistratos' tyranny was established initially and those were the changes it experienced. **16.2** Peisistratos, as I have said previously, administered the city's affairs with moderation and constitutionally rather than like a tyrant; for in general he was philanthropic and kind, and compassionate to wrong-doers, and moreover used to lend money to the poor to help them in their work, so they could make a living from farming. **16.3** He did this for two reasons, so that they would not spend time in the city but be scattered throughout the countryside, and, as they were moderately prosperous and busy with their own affairs, they would have neither the inclination nor the time to care about public business. **16.4** At the same time it happened that his revenue increased because the country was well-cultivated; for he exacted a tenth of the produce in tax. **16.5** On this account also he set up judges in each village and he often used to go himself into the country, to see what was going on and to reconcile disputants so that they would not come to the city and meanwhile neglect their work. **16.6** It was during one such tour of Peisistratos' that they say occurred the incident involving the man on Hymettos, who cultivated what was afterwards known as the 'tax-free farm'. For seeing someone labouring to dig land that was nothing but rocks, he was so amazed that he told his slave to ask what the farm produced; the man replied, 'Nothing but aches and pains,' replied the man, 'and it's of these aches and pains that Peisistratos ought to take his ten per cent!' The fellow replied this without recognizing him, but Peisistratos was pleased with his outspokenness and industry and made him exempt from all taxes. **16.7** And in general he did not impose burdens on the populace during his rule, but always maintained peace and made sure things were tranquil; for this reason it was often said in his praise that Peisistratos' tyranny was like 'life under Kronos'; for when his sons succeeded their government became much harsher. **16.8** And the most important of all his qualities mentioned was his natural benevolence and concern for the people. For in all matters he wanted to administer everything in accordance with the laws, not giving himself any advantage, and once when he was summoned to trial before the Areiopagos on a charge of murder, he turned up to make his defence, which frightened his accuser, who stayed away. **16.9** For this reason he remained in power for a long time and whenever he was expelled from power easily recovered it. For the majority of both the notables and the populace supported him; he won the former's support by associating with them socially, and the latter's by his assistance with their private affairs, and he was fair to both. **16.10** In those times all the Athenians' laws concerning tyrants were lenient, especially the law regarding the establishment of a tyranny. For the law went like this: these are the ordinances and ancestral customs of the Athenians, that if any persons should aim at being tyrant or if anyone should aid in setting up a tyranny, both he and his family shall be deprived of civic rights.

PEISISTRATOS' RELIGIOUS POLICY

Peisistratos and his sons were apparently scrupulous in their attention to religious matters. The square telesterion at Eleusis is usually attributed to Peisistratos; see Mylonas (1961) 67–70; Shear (1978) 9–10; cf. Boardman (1975) 1–12; Andrewes (1982) 412. It was also during Peisistratos' reign that the first dramatic tragedies seem to have been produced in Athens at the festival of the City Dionysia, honouring Dionysos Eleuthereus. Peisistratos must have overseen this development, and accordingly promoted this festival and the development of tragedy (see *FGH* 239 Marmor Parium 43; Knox (1978) 48; Andrewes 412; for the organization of the festival, see *Ath. Pol.* 56.3–4). It is sometimes suggested that this was part, with the Panathenaia, of making the city the focal point of Attica; for an alternative view, that the City Dionysia was established c. 501 to celebrate the new freedom enjoyed by Athens after the fall of the Peisistratidai, see Connor (1990) 7–32. The Panathenaia was possibly established in 566, and celebrated in the month Hekatombaion, with an especially magnificent, 'Great' celebration every fourth year. There is only circumstantial evidence that Peisistratos instituted the Panathenaia, but he certainly expanded it after his seizure of power (Morgan (1990) 208–12), and his sons, as can be seen in the account of the assassination of Hipparchos, took an active part in supporting it. Peisistratos has also been credited with the institution of the cult of Artemis Brauronia on the acropolis and the festival at Brauron, his home town. For Peisistratos and religious cults, see Andrewes (1982) 410–15; Connor (1987) 40–47; Frost (1990) 1–9; Morgan (1990) 13–16, 208–12.

4.17 Peisistratos and Delos

Herodotos I.64.2

The institution of the Dionysia and promotion of the Panathenaia indicate the development of 'civic cults', promoted by the tyrants, lessening the influence of aristocratic cults. The family of the Boutadai (later the Eteoboutadai) continued to provide the priestess for the cult of Athena on the acropolis, but the Panathenaia will have lessened the significance of this (Connor (1987) 40–47 suggests that Peisistratos in the chariot ruse was promoting the cult of Athena Paiania, as against that of Athena Polias (the cult dominated by the Boutadai) as a means of rivalling this cult); see Boardman (1972) 57–72, (1975) 1–3, for the suggestion that it was part of a policy of identification between Peisistratos and Herakles (but cf. Cook (1987) 167–69 who argues against the identification of Herakles and Peisistratos in Athenian art). The purification of Delos may have provoked Polykrates' conquest; cf. Parke (1946) 105–08; docs. 2.27, 12.27.

I.64.2 In addition Peisistratos purified the island of Delos, in consequence of an oracle, in the following way: he dug up the dead from the whole area within sight of the temple and transferred them to another part of Delos.

PEISISTRATOS' FAMILY

Peisistratos was married three times. The name of the first wife, an Athenian, is unknown; the sons of this marriage were Hippias, Hipparchos and Thessalos. Timonassa was the second wife, and mother of Iophon and Hegesistratos. Thirdly, Peisistratos married Megakles' daughter (see Table II). The Peisistratidai were the sons of Peisistratos, of whom the two most important were the eldest Hippias and Hipparchos, who shared power, with Hippias as the senior 'partner'. Thucydides I.20.2, VI.55 (docs. 4.19–20) sets out to prove that Hippias was the eldest. The fact that he had children and his brothers did not is not indisputable proof that Hippias was the eldest (Lewis (1988) 287 with n.4), but the other points seem convincing. The popular Athenian belief that Hipparchos was the eldest can be found in [Plat.] *Hipparch.* 228b, though *Ath. Pol.* 18.1 has Hippias as the eldest, presumably influenced by Thucydides' account. Despite Thucydides' attention as to who was the eldest, he himself refers to Hippias and Hipparchos as ruling jointly (doc. 4.21; cf. 4.32). Thucydides ascribes the belief that Hipparchos was tyrant to the fact that it was he who was assassinated: it would be natural to assume that the tyrannicides had killed *the* tyrant, rather than his younger brother. Peisistratos was probably born 605–600, Hippias in the late 570s. Hippias appears to have been old enough to counsel his father after the overthrow of the second tyranny, and was still alive in 490, when he landed at Marathon with the Persians. His son, Peisistratos, held an archonship before 511/0, possibly in 522/1 (see doc. 4.24). On Peisistratos' family, see Davies (1971) 445–55.

4.18 Peisistratos' Wives

[Aristotle] *Athenaion Politeia* 17.1–4

Hegesistratos was sent to be tyrant of Sigeion (doc. 1.15); of Iophon nothing is known. Hegesistratos and Thessalos (Thettalos in the *Ath. Pol.*) were two separate sons, despite the *Ath. Pol.*, who considers them the same person, and the *Ath. Pol.*'s story (doc. 4.31) that it was Thessalos who propositioned Harmodios contradicts Thucydides (doc. 4.30). Hegesistratos is described as a nothos (bastard) (Hdt. V.94.1; doc. 1.15), but in an age when marriage with women from other states, particularly amongst the aristocracy, was not unusual, this bastardry is either a misrepresentation or might have resulted because he was not introduced to Peisistratos' phratry (cf. Thuc. VI.55.1, where Hippias and his full brothers are described as gnesioi, legitimate).

17.1 Accordingly Peisistratos grew old in power and died after an illness in the archonship of Philoneus (528/7), having lived thirty-three years from the time when he first set himself up as tyrant, of which he had spent nineteen years in power, for he was in exile for the rest. **17.2** For this reason those who say that Peisistratos was loved by Solon and was a general in the war against the Megarians over Salamis are clearly talking nonsense; for this is impossible in view of their ages, as one can see from reckoning up the life of each and the archonship in which he died. **17.3** After Peisistratos died, his sons held on to power, carrying on managing affairs in the same way. He had two sons by his legal wife, Hippias and Hipparchos, and two by the Argive lady, Iophon and Hegesistratos whose surname was Thettalos. **17.4** For Peisistratos had married Timonassa, daughter of an Argive man whose name was Gorgilos, who had previously been married to Archinos of Ambracia a man of the Kypselid family; a consequence of this was his friendship with the Argives, and a thousand Argives brought by Hegesistratos fought on his side at the battle at Pallenis. Some say that he married the Argive woman when he was first in exile, others while he was in power.

4.19 Misconceptions about the Peisistratidai

Thucydides I.20.1–2

Here, and in the following passage, Thucydides corrects what he states are incorrect notions about the Peisistratidai; see Jacoby (1949) 158–59; Davies (1971) 446–47; Rhodes 189–90, 227–28. The Leokoreion (also at Thuc. VI.57.3; *Ath. Pol.* 18.3 (docs. 4.30–31)) was a shrine to the three daughters of Leos, sacrificed at a time of famine or plague to save the city; Thompson (1978) 101–02; Camp (1986) 47, 79. This passage is the beginning of a section in which Thucydides criticizes popular opinions about history and the work of his predecessors, and discusses his own methodology (I.20–22).

I.20.1 These are the historical facts I have discovered, though it is difficult to believe every single piece of evidence about them. For men accept each others' accounts of things of old, even if they took place in their own country, equally uncritically. **I.20.2** For instance the majority of Athenians think that Hipparchos, who was killed by Harmodios and Aristogeiton, was tyrant, and do not know that Hippias was ruling as the eldest of Peisistratos' sons, and Hipparchos and Thessalos were his brothers, and Harmodios and Aristogeiton on that very day and on the spur of the moment, having suspected in some way that information had been laid before Hippias by their fellow conspirators, kept away from him as aware of the plot, but wishing to achieve something and run the risk before their arrest, killed Hipparchos when they came upon him as he was marshalling the Panathenaic procession near the place called the Leokoreion.

4.20 The Evidence for Hippias' Seniority

Thucydides VI.55.1–3

Unfortunately, no details are provided for the altar and stele on the acropolis; the altar was presumably a thanksgiving for liberation from the tyrants and the stele outlawed them. Hdt. V.65.2 (cf. V.96.2) and *Ath. Pol.* 19.6 indicate that the Peisistratidai went into permanent exile; the law against tyranny at *Ath. Pol.* 16.10 presumably came into play at this point (see doc. 4.16), so the Peisistratidai and their descendants were now atimoi, without citizen rights; they were also probably condemned to death in absentia (Ar. *Birds* 1074–75); see Lavelle (1984) 17–19, (1989) 209–10. While no Peisistratidai remained in Attica, Hipparchos, son of Charmos, is described as a relation of the tyrants (*Ath. Pol.* 22.4 (doc. 5.9); Lyk. *Leokr.* 117; Plut. *Nik.* 11.8; Suda s.v."Ιππαρχος). It has been assumed that Charmos was married to Hippias' daughter (Davies (1971) 451), so indirect descendants remained in Athens (Hipparchos was archon in 496/5 and the first victim of ostracism, 488/7; see doc. 5.9; Table II). For a possible homosexual attachment between Hippias and Charmos, see Kleidemos *FGH* 323 F15.

VI.55.1 That Hippias was the eldest and ruler I contend strongly as I know it by report more accurately than others do, and anyone might learn it from this point: for he appears to have been the only one of the legitimate (gnesioi) brothers who had children, as is shown both by the altar and the stele concerned with the injustice of the tyrants which stands on the Athenian acropolis, on which no child of Thessalos or Hipparchos is listed, but five of Hippias, who were born to him by Myrrhine daughter of Kallias, son of Hyperochides; for it was likely that the eldest would marry first. **VI.55.2** And on the same stele he is listed first after his father, which is again not unnatural as he was the eldest son and the tyrant. **VI.55.3** Nor does it seems reasonable to me that Hippias could have seized the tyranny easily and on the spur of the moment, if Hipparchos had been in power when he was killed, and Hippias attempted to establish himself that same day; but he was an object of fear to the citizens and of obedience to his mercenaries because of his previous habits and took control because his position was secure, not being at a loss like a younger brother would have been, who had not previously had any experience of government.

THE REIGN OF THE PEISISTRATIDAI

Thucydides in the passage below sets out to correct what he claims are mistaken views about the tyranny. It is clear that the rule of the Peisistratidai was acceptable to the majority, and Thucydides briefly dwells on the main themes of their civic program of beautifying the city, their military success (cf. doc. 2.43), and their worship of the gods. Docs. 4.22–23 show Hipparchos' interest in the fine arts and poetry.

4.21 Thucydides' Judgement on the Peisistratidai

Thucydides VI.54.1–6

VI.54.2 (cf. 55.1–4): Thucydides here corrects the view that Hipparchos was the elder brother; see docs. 4.19–20. **VI.54.3**: In the love affair Aristogeiton as the older will have been the erastes, the lover, and Harmodios the eromenos, the beloved (Dover (1978) 41, 191). **VI.54.4**: The 'inconspicuous manner' was the slighting of Harmodios' sister, described at Thuc. VI.56.1–2 and *Ath. Pol.* 18.2 (docs. 4.30–31). **VI.54.5**: *Ath. Pol.* 16.4 mentions a 10% tax (δεκάτη) levied by Peisistratos; this could be a general term for tax (Gomme *HCT* IV.329–30; Rhodes 215; cf. Andrewes (1982) 407), or it can be assumed that there is no contradiction between the two passages and that the Peisistratidai reduced the tax to 5% (Stahl (1987) 197; cf. Andrewes 407), perhaps as a result of the presumed discovery of silver at Laureion; certainly the introduction of the fine 'owl' series seems to indicate a greater wealth for the tyranny of the sons than that of Peisistratos (see doc. 4.12). **VI.54.6**: the meaning of 'one of their own' (σφῶν αὐτῶν) is unclear; certainly the eponymous archonship was held by prominent members of other families (doc. 4.24), so supporters are presumably meant.

VI.54.1 Aristogeiton and Harmodios' deed of daring was undertaken because of an incident concerning a love-affair, and through a detailed description of it I will show that neither the other Greeks nor the Athenians themselves give an accurate account of their tyrants or their history. **VI.54.2** After Peisistratos died, still tyrant despite his advanced age, it was not Hipparchos, as most people think, but Hippias as the eldest who was in power. Aristogeiton, one of the citizens and a man of middling rank, was the lover and possessor of the beautiful Harmodios, then in the prime of youth. **VI.54.3** Harmodios was solicited by Hipparchos, son of Peisistratos. He was not won over and denounced him to Aristogeiton. Suffering the pains of love and fearful of the power of Hipparchos in case he might procure Harmodios by force, Aristogeiton immediately started plotting the downfall of the tyranny as far as was possible from someone in his position. **VI.54.4** Meanwhile after Hipparchos had again tried but got nowhere with Harmodios, he preferred to avoid violence and prepared in some inconspicuous manner, and as if unconnected with his actual motives, to insult Harmodios. **VI.54.5** Hipparchos' manner of government was not burdensome to the majority, and he ruled without exciting hatred; and these tyrants practised virtue and sagacity to the greatest extent, for they exacted from the Athenians only a twentieth of their produce, beautified their city, prevailed in their wars and made sacrifices at the temples. **VI.54.6** And in other respects this city continued to use the pre-existing laws, except in so far as they always made sure that one of their own people was in office.

4.22 Hippias the Politician and Hipparchos the Aesthete

[Aristotle] *Athenaion Politeia* 18.1

For these poets, brought to Athens by Hipparchos, see Knox (1978) 49–50. The recension of Homer's epics was ascribed to Peisistratos in antiquity; this has been both accepted and rejected by scholars; see esp. Davison (1955) 1–21 (rejecting this view), though there are firmer grounds for accepting that Hipparchos organized the recitation of the Homeric epics at the Panathenaia ([Plat.] *Hipparch.* 228b; Davison 10–13). Many tyrants attracted poets to their courts and fostered the development of poetry and the arts.

18.1 Hippias and Hipparchos were then in control of affairs owing to their positions and ages, but Hippias being the elder and a natural politician and man of sense was in charge of government. Hipparchos on the other hand was fond of amusement and engaged in love affairs and loved the arts (he was the one who brought Anacreon and Simonides and their schools and other poets to Athens).

4.23 Poets at the Court of the Peisistratidai

[Plato] *Hipparchos* 228c

Hipparchos sent a pentekonter for Anacreon the Teian to bring him to Athens, and persuaded Simonides of Keos to be his continual associate by great payments and gifts.

4.24 The Archon-List of 527/6–522/1

Meiggs & Lewis 6C (*IG* I^3 1031)

Miltiades was archon in 524/3 BC (Dion. Halic. VII.3.1; see Cadoux (1948) 110 with n.216; White (1974) 83), and this serves to date the others in the list. While retaining the existing laws, the Peisistratidai, as Thuc. VI.54.6 (doc. 4.21) states, ensured that 'one of their own people' held the magistracies; either this includes their supporters, or Thucydides may be referring not just to the eponymous archonships but the nine annual archonships as a whole (White (1974) 82). Peisistratos, son of Hippias, held the eponymous archonship (Thuc. VI.54.6–7; doc. 4.25) and the name Peisistratos can be restored here as the eponymous archon of 522/1, but this restoration is not certain.

The Alkmeonidai had gone into exile with Peisistratos' third attempt at the tyranny (doc. 4.14), but the archon list, with Kleisthenes holding the office the year before Miltiades, ie in 525/4, indicates that the Alkmeonidai were not in exile at this time. While it is possible that the Peisistratidai may have pursued a policy of reconciliation towards the Alkmeonidai, White (1974) 83–86 (cf. Lewis (1988) 288) argues that the choice of Kleisthenes as archon will have been made by Peisistratos rather than Hippias. That Peisistratos (rather than his sons) recalled the Alkmeonidai is perhaps supported by the fact that it is known that he recalled Kimon (Hdt. VI.103.2). As White and others point out, the evidence of the inscription contradicts the literary record, that the Alkmeonidai were in exile from 546 (the Battle of Pallene) until 510. They may have fallen out of favour once again after 525/4, possibly as a result of the assassination of Hipparchos, when many Athenians were exiled (doc. 4.33).

527/6 [On]eto[rides]
526/5 [H]ippia[s]
525/4 [K]leisthen[es]
524/3 [M]iltiades
523/2 [Ka]lliades
522/1 [..5..]strat[os]

4.25 Literary Evidence for the Archonship of Peisistratos

Thucydides VI.54.6–7 (Simonides 26b)

Page 240–41. The 'Twelve Gods' are presumably, but not certainly, the Twelve Olympians; this altar, in the agora, was a place of refuge and supplication (see Hdt. VI.108.4; Thompson & Wycherley (1972) 133). It was also important as the place from which distances were measured: Hdt. II.7.1. A verse inscription informs the reader that the distance from the harbour (at the Peiraieus) to the altar was 45 stades (*IG* II^2 2640 (*IG* I^3 1092 bis; Hansen 442), cf. *Agora* XIX, p.14 (c. 400 BC). For this altar, see Crosby (1949) 82–103; Thompson & Wycherley (1972) 20–21, 129–36; Camp (1986) 40–42; Shapiro (1989) 133–41; for a reconstruction, see Thompson & Wycherley 133, fig. 34 and Camp (1986) 41, fig. 23 (ph. of the visible remains, 41, fig. 24). Note Wycherley (1957) 119–22, nos. 363–78, for testimonia for the altar, with discussion. For the altar in the precinct of Pythion Apollo, see Boersma (1970) 53; Travlos (1971) 100; Wycherley (1978) 166–68; Shapiro (1989) 52 with n.30, cf. 59–60.

VI.54.6 Those who held the Athenians' yearly archonship included Peisistratos son of Hippias the tyrant, who had the name of his grandfather, and who as archon dedicated the altar of the twelve gods in the agora and that of Apollo in the Pythion. **VI.54.7** Afterwards the Athenian people built an additional length to the altar in the agora and erased the altar's inscription; but the inscription of the altar in the Pythion even today still clearly says in faint letters:

'Peisistratos son of Hippias as a memorial of his archonship
Erected this in the precinct of Pythian Apollo'.

4.26 Archaeological Evidence for the Archonship of Peisistratos

Meiggs & Lewis 11 (*IG* I³ 948)

IG I² 761; Friedländer 100; Page 240–41; Hansen 305. The archonship of Peisistratos, son of Hippias, cannot be securely dated. The archon list (doc. 4.24) is fragmentary but (c), line 6, has the letters -strat[os], sometimes restored as Peisistratos, which would date his archonship to 522/1 (Lewis (1988) 294). The restoration is not absolutely certain and the broader date span 522–510 (527/6–523/2 are occupied) should be retained. For a dating, on the basis of the lettering, to the fifth century, see Raubitschek *DAA* 450, who admits the difficulty which such a date implies for the evidence of Thucydides; but see also ML p.20. That there were Peisistratidai of direct descent through the male line still in Athens in the fifth century must be viewed as improbable, given the expulsion of the Peisistratidai in 511/0 and Hippias' involvement with the Persians (see *SEG* 39.42 for a discussion of a graffito on a geometric vase, Pisis<t>ratos, which is not proof that Peisistratos the younger was still in Athens in the 480s). When preconceived notions of letter dating conflict with the literary evidence the latter is always to be preferred (cf. docs. 6.38, 12.36). For a line drawing, see Lewis (1988) 295 fig. 30, a–b. Thuc. VI.54.7 states that the Athenians 'erased' the inscription and that the letters were 'faint', but ever since its discovery it has been noted that the letters are clearly cut and easy to read; Lavelle (1989) 207–12, listing previous scholarship, suggests that the inscription was not erased but plastered over.

Peisist[ratos s]on [of Hippias] as a memorial of his archonship
Erected this in the precinct of Pyth[i]an Apollo.

4.27 The Philaidai and the Tyrants

Herodotos VI.103.1–4

Miltiades the Elder, of the clan (genos) of the Philaidai (Table III), had established an Athenian presence in the Chersonese, presumably with Peisistratos' agreement, as Athenians accompanied him there. He ruled the area as tyrant, as did his successors, his nephews Stesagoras and Miltiades the Younger, who later fled the Chersonese in advance of the Persian invasion. Herodotos records a story that Kimon, the father of Miltiades the Younger, was murdered by the Peisistratidai, after being allowed to return by Peisistratos (cf. Hdt. VI.39.1). They may have thought that the presence of the head of the Philaidai in Attica was a political liability and in this case when they allowed the younger Miltiades to leave Attica to succeed to the tyranny in the Chersonese, they presumably did so in order that he would be out of the way. On the other hand, this might be an indication that the Peisistratidai had not murdered Kimon, and the fact that Miltiades the Younger was archon in 524/3 shortly after his father's 'murder' casts some doubt on Herodotos' story, especially since he was then sent officially to the Chersonese as tyrant; note too that Kimon the Elder was known as 'koalemos', 'booby' (Plut. *Kim.* 4.4). The dates of the three Olympic victories of Kimon were 536, 532, and 528, with his recall dated to 532; see Wade-Gery (1958) 157; cf. Davies (1971) 300. For the tyrants and the Philaidai, see Stahl (1987) 106–120. The context of this document is Hippias directing the Persians to land at Marathon (see doc. 7.7).

VI.103.1 Miltiades' father Kimon son of Stesagoras had, it so happened, been banished from Athens by Peisistratos son of Hippokrates. **VI.103.2** While an exile Kimon won the prize at the Olympic Games for the four-horse chariot race, and in winning this victory he carried off the same prize as Miltiades, his half-brother from the same mother. Later at the next Olympic festival he won with the same mares but waived the victory in Peisistratos' favour. **VI.103.3** For handing over the victory Peisistratos allowed him to return home with safe conduct. He won at the next Olympic festival too, with the same mares, but was killed by Peisistratos' sons, after Peisistratos' death; they set men to ambush him and killed him at night outside the prytaneion. Kimon was buried outside Athens, on the other side of the road known as 'the one through the hollow'; right opposite him are buried those mares who won the three Olympic victories. **VI.103.4** The mares of Euagoras of Sparta did the same, but they were the only ones. The elder of Kimon's sons Stesagoras was then living in the Chersonese with his uncle Miltiades, and the younger, Miltiades, who was named after Miltiades the founder of the Chersonese, with Kimon himself in Athens.

THE TYRANTS AND PUBLIC WORKS

The Athenian tyrants, like other Greek tyrants, were involved in public building projects (cf. doc. 2.40); while the building projects at Athens would not have created widespread employment, they would have been important for the tyrants' 'public-image' (cf. Thuc. VI.54.5, doc. 4.21). Shear (1978) 8, 11; Boersma (1970) 22; Shapiro (1989) 6, all suggest that tyrants may have deliberately vied with each other in their public works. For the Peisistratid building projects, see Boersma (1970) 11–27, with catalogue; Shear (1978) 1–19; besides the enneakrounos, these included the enlargement of the Eleusinian telesterion, the rebuilding of the temple of Athena Polias, commencement of the Olympieion (the temple of Olympian Zeus), the wall Hipparchos constructed for the Academy precinct (proverbial for its expense: Suda s.v. τὸ Ἱππάρχου τειχίον), and the fortifications at Mounichia (see doc. 4.35). For the Olympieion (doc. 2.40), begun by the Peisistratidai and completed by the Roman emperor Hadrian, see Wycherley (1964) 161–75; Boersma (1970) 25, 199; Shear (1978) 10; cf. Shapiro (1989) 112–17; for the altar of the Twelve Gods, see doc. 4.25 (Thuc. VI.54.6). It is also possible that the remains of a building in the agora represent the 'palace' of the tyrants: Shear (1978) 6–7.

4.28 The Enneakrounos: the 'Nine-Spouts'

Thucydides II.15.3–5

Cf. Hdt. VI.137.3; Paus. I.14.1. Thucydides attributes the enneakrounos to 'the tyrants'; Paus. I.14.1 to Peisistratos. The enneakrounos of Pausanias has been identified with a structure, the south-east fountainhouse, in the agora (see esp. Thompson & Wycherley (1972) 197–99, with figs. 50–51); archaeological considerations date it to c. 520 (Boersma (1970) 23; Shear (1978) 11) or more generally c. 530–20 (Camp (1986) 42); other fountain-houses were also built in Athens in the same period. Camp (1986) 42–43 argues that, while this fountainhouse in the agora does belong to the tyranny, it is not the enneakrounos of Thucydides. Pausanias places the enneakrounos in the agora, ie west of the acropolis, while Thucydides places it south of the acropolis; Thucydides is to be preferred, despite attempts (such as Wycherley (1957) 142) to weaken the sense of Thucydides' direction (cf. Owens (1982) 223). Black figured vases during this period begin to depict Athenian women and slaves at fountains; see esp. Keuls (1985) 235–40, pls. 208–212; Wycherley (1957) 137–42, nos. 434–55, for testimonia for the enneakrounos; Dunkley (1935–36) 172; Lang (1968); Boersma (1970) 23–24, 221;

Travlos (1971) 204–09; Shear (1978) 10–11, 15 n.43; Shapiro (1989) 6–7, 126; Owens (1982) 222–24; doc. 2.16 for the fountain-house of Theagenes.

II.15.3 Before the time of Theseus the city comprised what is now the acropolis, together with the area below it, especially that facing south. **II.15.4** This is the proof: the temples of the other gods as well (as that of Athena) are on the acropolis and those outside of it are generally situated in that part of the city, including the temples of Olympian Zeus and the Pythion and Earth (Ge) and Dionysos at Limnai (the 'marshy' quarter) .... The other ancient temples are also situated here. **II.15.5** Also the fountain, which is now called Enneakrounos ('Nine-Spouts'), since the tyrants built it like this, but which of old when the springs were visible was called Kallirrhoe ('Beautiful Stream'), used to be used for all purposes since it was so near, and from ancient times, as even today, it was customary to use the water before weddings and in other religious ceremonies.

4.29 The 'Hermai' of Hipparchos

(i)–(ii) [Plato] *Hipparchos* 229a–b; (iii) *IG* I^2 837 (*IG* I^3 1023)

(iii): Friedländer 149; *LSAG* 75, 78n.35; Hansen 304. Hipparchos set up hermai (singular: hermes) throughout Attica, according to [Plat.] *Hipparch.* 228c–229b, to educate the country Athenians, with each hermes having some moral maxim inscribed on one side, and a direction on the other to the effect that the hermes stood midway on the road between Athens and the relevant Attic deme. The only one that survives (no. iii below), served as a marker on the road from the deme Kephale to Athens; for a line drawing, see Lewis (1988) 293, fig. 29. These hermai would have kept Hipparchos' name before the popular eye and perhaps played a part in the notion that he and not Hippias had been *the* tyrant. A hermes was a short rectangular pillar with a head of Hermes (god of travellers) above it, with an ithyphallos carved on the front; the mutilation of the hermai in 415/4 (doc. 9.22) had important political consequences. For Hipparchos' hermai, see Pritchett (1980) 160–62; Whitehead (1986) 14; Lewis (1988) 292–93; Shapiro (1989) 125–32, esp. 125–28; for fragments of hermai with inscriptions, see Hansen 307, 312, 313.

i. 'A reminder of Hipparchos: walk thinking just thoughts.'

ii. 'A reminder of Hipparchos: do not deceive a friend.'

iii. 'Bright Hermes in between Kephale and the city.'

THE ASSASSINATION OF HIPPARCHOS

The motive of the tyrannicides was not political but stemmed from a love affair, when Harmodios' rejection of Hipparchos' advances led to the insulting treatment of Harmodios' sister. Although the assassination took place in 514/3, Herodotos has the tyranny continuing for another four years, which can be taken as 511/0 (Rhodes 233); Thuc. VI.59.4 (doc. 4.39) says the tyranny continued for three years and ended in the fourth; [Plat.] *Hipparch.* 229b has three more years of tyranny.

4.30 Thucydides on the Assassination of Hipparchos

Thucydides VI.56.1–58.2

Thucydides (cf. docs. 4.19–21) describes the original plan for the assassination and what went wrong. Harmodios and Aristogeiton had organized a plot for the day of the Great Panathenaia (the only day that citizens could carry arms, as Peisistratos had disarmed the citizens; doc. 4.13) and the plan seems to have been that they would kill Hippias first (and Hipparchos later), and that their fellow-conspirators would fall upon the body-guard. According to Thucydides, Hippias was at the Kerameikos, outside the city-walls, organizing the procession: it was the potters' quarter and a cemetery; see Wycherley (1978) 253–61. For Hipparchos' dream prior to his assassination, see Hdt. V.55–56; Shapiro (1990) 337–38 for the omens concerning the tyrants.

VI.56.1 So Hipparchos, as he intended, insulted Harmodios for having refused his offer; first they summoned his sister, an unmarried girl, to come and carry a basket in a procession, and then they sent her away saying that they had not invited her in the first place because she was not fit to take part. **VI.56.2** Harmodios took this badly, and Aristogeiton was even more incensed on his behalf. They had now arranged everything with those who were going to join with them in the deed, and were waiting for the Great Panathenaia, which was the only day on which those citizens who were to take part in the procession could gather in arms without arousing suspicion. They were to start, and the others immediately join in against the bodyguard. **VI.56.3** For safety's sake the conspirators were few in number; for they hoped that, if they started the venture off, those who had no prior knowledge of the plot would use their weapons and choose to liberate themselves. **VI.57.1** When the day of the festival arrived, Hippias was outside the city in what is called the Kerameikos with his bodyguard, arranging how each part of the procession should move forward, while Harmodios and Aristogeiton already holding their daggers proceeded to action. **VI.57.2** When they saw one of their fellow conspirators talking to Hippias in a friendly manner (Hippias being approachable by everyone) they were afraid, thinking that their secret had been disclosed and that they were already on the point of being arrested. **VI.57.3** They wanted first, if they could, to take revenge on the man who had wronged them and for whom they were risking everything. As they were they rushed inside the gates, came upon Hipparchos beside what is known as the Leokoreion, and immediately fell upon him rashly, one inspired by the anger of a lover and the other by insult, and struck and killed him. **VI.57.4** The mob gathered, and Aristogeiton at that point got away from the bodyguard, but was afterwards captured and roughly treated; Harmodios was straightway killed on the spot. **VI.58.1** When the news was brought to Hippias at the Kerameikos, he immediately proceeded not to the site of the incident but to the armed participants in the procession before they, being at a distance, perceived what had happened. He composed his countenance to give nothing away about the tragedy, pointed to a piece of ground and told them to move over there without their weapons. **VI.58.2** They went over there thinking that he had something to say, and he told his mercenaries to seize the weapons, and at once picked out those whom he blamed and anyone who was found carrying a dagger; for it was usual to carry shields and spears in the procession.

4.31 The *Ath. Pol.* on Hipparchos' Assassination

[Aristotle] *Athenaion Politeia* 18.2–6

The account of the *Ath. Pol.* varies from that of Thucydides in several respects: Thucydides' account is doubtless to be preferred. See Fitzgerald (1957) 282–86 for a discussion of the differences between the two accounts.

18.2 Thettalos was much younger and rash and insulting in his life-style, and it was from this that all their troubles started. He fell in love with Harmodios, but as he failed to obtain his friendship he could not contain his anger, but showed his bitterness in a number of ways and finally prevented Harmodios' sister from being a basket-carrier at the Panathenaia, as she was going to be, and cast some insult at Harmodios about being effeminate. Because of this provocation Harmodios and Aristogeiton perpetrated their deed in which they had many accomplices. **18.3** During the Panathenaic festival, while they were lying in wait for Hippias on the acropolis (for Hippias happened to be the one welcoming the procession and Hipparchos the one starting it off), they saw one of their fellow conspirators go up to Hippias in a friendly manner and thought that he was revealing the secret. As they wanted to achieve something before being arrested, they went down and killed Hipparchos as he organized the procession near the Leokoreion, acting without waiting for the others and thus ruining the whole plot. **18.4** Harmodios was killed immediately by the body-guard, while Aristogeiton was afterwards captured and tortured for a long period. Under torture he accused many who were of distinguished birth and friends of the tyrants. At first it was impossible to find any trace of the plot, but the story which is told that Hippias made the participants in the procession stand away from their weapons and searched out those that had daggers is not true; for at that point they did not carry arms in the procession, and it was not until later that the democracy instituted this. **18.5** Aristogeiton accused the friends of the tyrant, according to the democrats, on purpose, so the tyrants might act impiously and weaken themselves by killing innocent men who were their friends; others say that he did not make this up, but was actually disclosing his fellow conspirators. **18.6** And finally, as he was not able to die, do what he might, he stated that he would betray many others and persuaded Hippias to give him his right hand as a sign of good faith. As Aristogeiton took it, he taunted Hippias for having given his right hand to the murderer of his brother and so annoyed Hippias that he could not control his anger but drew his dagger and killed him.

THE TYRANNY BECOMES HARSHER

Clearly after Hipparchos' death the tyranny became far more oppressive, but Hippias feared not popular unrest but the aristocracy. It is this period which laid the foundation for the Athenians' later concept of tyranny as unacceptable. The group of exiles who wished to overthrow the tyranny in order to return to Attica made their first attempt at Leipsydrion, failed, and then sought outside help. Herodotos focuses attention on the Alkmeonidai, while the *Ath. Pol.* notes that they were the leaders of the exiles. This leadership will have derived from their prominence in Athenian society and presumably their previous role as rivals to Peisistratos.

4.32 The Harsh Tyranny of Hippias

Thucydides VI.53.3, 59.1–2

The context is the investigation following the mutilation of the hermai in 415, when the Athenians were suspicious that it was part of an attempt to overthrow the democracy. There is no evidence as to who lost their lives: perhaps it was those who were considered to have been implicated in the assassination plot.

VI.53.3 For the people, as they knew by report that the tyranny of Peisistratos and his sons had become harsh at the end and, besides, that it was not put down by themselves and Harmodios but by the Spartans, were always afraid and suspicious of everything .... **VI.59.1** In such a way, a lover's distress caused the beginning of Harmodios and Aristogeiton's plot and fear at the time their reckless venture. **VI.59.2** Following this the tyranny became harsher for the Athenians, and Hippias was now frightened enough to kill many of the citizens, at the same time looking outside of Athens for some chance of refuge should a revolution take place.

4.33 Hippias is 'Hated by All'

[Aristotle] *Athenaion Politeia* 19.1

Compare *Ath. Pol.* 16.7 (doc. 4.16), where the tyranny is said to have become harsher after the death of Peisistratos. Nevertheless, it was not until after Marathon that the tyrants became especially hated and there was a party of Peisistratid supporters that remained in Athens after their expulsion (see doc. 5.9).

19.1 After this the tyranny became much harsher; for to avenge his brother Hippias killed and exiled many people and became mistrusted and hated by everyone.

4.34 Hippias Seeks a Connection with Persia

Thucydides VI.59.3 (Simonides 26a)

Friedländer 138; Page 239–40; cf. Thuc. VI.59.2 (doc. 4.32). Hippias married his daughter to Aiantides of Lampsakos; for the epitaph and the term 'atasthalie', see Harvey (1985) 69–70. This connection gave Hippias a place in Persia (see doc. 4.39); cf. Arist. *Rhet.* 1367b 20–21. Thucydides' comment 'though an Athenian' is out of context here and relates to the period after 451/0 when Perikles' citizenship law (doc. 10.18) made marriages between Athenians and non-Athenians unattractive.

VI.59.3 At any rate after this, though an Athenian, he gave his daughter Archedike to a Lampsakene, Aiantides, son of Hippokles tyrant of Lampsakos, realising that they had great influence with the Persian king Darius. Her grave is in Lampsakos and has this inscription:

'This dust covers Archedike daughter of Hippias,
A man who was greatest in Greece of those of his time.
Though her father, husband, brothers and sons were tyrants,
She was not given to unseemly arrogance (atasthalie).'

4.35 A Drinking-Song about Leipsydrion

[Aristotle] *Athenaion Politeia* 19.2–3

Cf. V.62.1–2. For this skolion (drinking-song), see Bowra (1961) 383–84. Mounichia is a hill, on the eastern side of the Peiraieus, and faces Phaleron Bay; see Wycherley (1978) 263–65, with map at 264; Garland (1987) 160. Mounichia had an important place in Athenian history: the 400 (Thuc. VIII.92.5) and Thrasyboulos in 403 (*Ath. Pol.* 38.1) both made use of it. The failure of the exiles at Leipsydrion led to the Alkmeonidai seeking outside intervention (docs. 4.36–38).

19.2 In about the fourth year after Hipparchos' death, affairs in the city were so bad that Hippias attempted to wall Mounichia, so he could move there; while he was doing this, he was expelled by Kleomenes, king of the Spartans, as oracles kept being given to the Lakonians to put an end to the tyranny for the following reason. **19.3** The exiles, of whom the Alkmeonidai had assumed the leadership, were by themselves unable to manage to bring about their return, but were always suffering defeats. Among their other unsuccessful attempts they walled Leipsydrion, a place in the country below[1] Mount Parnes, where they were joined by some of the men from the city, but the tyrants besieged them and forced them to capitulate. As a result, after this disaster, they used to always sing the following in their drinking-songs:

'Alas! Leipsydrion, betrayer of comrades,
What men you have destroyed, brave
In war and of noble family,
Who then showed what their ancestors were like.'

[1] For the emendation of Wright (1892) 54n.2, accepted by Chambers (1986) in his Teubner edition, cf. Rhodes 235. Hdt. V.62.2 correctly has Leipsydrion above Paionia (a slight mistake for Paiania, see Rhodes *loc. cit.*).

THE OVERTHROW OF THE TYRANNY BY THE SPARTANS

The Alkmeonidai, after failing at Leipsydrion, decided to seek outside assistance. They did this, according to the Athenians, by bribing the Pythian priestess; see doc. 5.1, where Kleisthenes was the person responsible. Other examples of alleged bribery of the Pythia are Hdt. VI.66 (doc. 6.47); Thuc. V.16.2; Plut. *Mor.* 860c–d on this incident is rather naive in his defence of the Pythia. The Peisistratidai were able to call in outside help, and the Thessalians helped to defeat the first Spartan invasion, but were defeated by Kleomenes. Though the Peisistratid domination of Athens ends here, the Spartans c. 505–501 proposed to restore Hippias (see docs. 5.5, 6.37). On the Delphic oracle's instruction to liberate Athens, see Parke & Wormell (1956) I.145–47; II 35–36, Response 79; Fontenrose (1978) 53, 309 Response Q124.

4.36 The Alkmeonidai Bribe the Pythia

Herodotos V.62.2–64.2

Phaleron at this time was Athens' main port; cf. doc. 7.8; Hdt. VIII.66.1. Anchimolos, like other Spartans (except the kings on occasion) who died abroad, was buried where he fell (cf. doc. 6.13). The gymnasium at Kynosarges was across the Ilissos, south-west of the Olympieion; see Travlos (1971) 340; Wycherley (1978) 219, 229. The pelargic (or pelasgic) wall was the Mycenaean wall of the acropolis: Travlos (1971) 52; Wycherley (1978) 7–8, 177, 269; Thuc. II.17, with Hornblower (1991) 269–70. At Hdt. V.90.1 the Spartans, learning that the Pythia had been bribed, come to regret expelling the tyrants.

V.62.2 Then in their efforts to devise every scheme possible against the Peisistratidai, the Alkmeonidai got a contract from the Amphictyons to build the temple at Delphi, which is there now but was not then in existence. **V.62.3.** As they had become wealthy and were of a family which had always been well-regarded, the temple they completed was actually better than the plan, both in other respects and in the facade's being constructed of Parian marble, though it had been agreed that the temple was to be made of ordinary conglomerate. **V.63.1** The Athenians[1] indeed maintain that while these men were staying at Delphi they bribed the Pythia, to tell any Spartiates who came to consult the oracle either on private or public business to liberate Athens. **V.63.2** As the Spartans always received the same response, they sent Anchimolos,[2] son of Aster, a distinguished citizen, with an army to drive the Peisistratidai out of Athens, although they shared strong ties of hospitality with them; they considered the divine injunction more important than human relationships. **V.63.3** They sent them by sea in transport ships. Anchimolos put in at Phaleron and disembarked his troops, while the Peisistratidai, who had already learnt of this, summoned help from Thessaly, as there was an alliance between their two states. The Thessalians consented to their request and sent off a thousand cavalry and their king Kineas of Konde; when these allies arrived, the Peisistratidai devised the following plan: **V.63.4** they cleared the plain of Phaleron of all trees and crops and made the area fit for riding, and then sent a cavalry charge against the Spartans. It fell on them and destroyed many of the Spartans including Anchimolos, driving the survivors back to their ships. That was the end of the first expedition from Sparta, and Anchimolos was buried at Alopeke in Attica, near the temple of Herakles at Kynosarges. **V.64.1** Later (511/0), however, the Spartans dispatched a greater force against Athens, appointing King Kleomenes the son of Anaxandridas as the army's leader, and sending it this time not by sea but by land; **V.64.2** as they entered Attica the Thessalian cavalry were the first to engage with them, but were quickly overwhelmed, losing over forty of their men; the survivors immediately departed for Thessaly. When Kleomenes arrived at the city accompanied by those Athenians who wanted freedom, he besieged the tyrants whom he had confined within the pelargic wall.

[1] There is no reason to emend 'Ἀθηναῖοι 'Athenians' to Λακεδαιμόνιοι 'Spartans'.

[2] The manuscripts of Herodotos read 'Ἀγχιμόλιον, while the *Ath. Pol.* has 'Ἀγχίμολον; Anchimolos is adopted here; see Rhodes 237–38.

4.37 The Peisistratidai Surrender

Herodotos V.65.1–5

V.65.3: Kodros and Melanthos were mythical kings of Athens. The most famous son of Neleus was Nestor of Pylos the aged Homeric hero. It has been suggested that Peisistratos would have pressed this ancestry into service, and that Athenians would have been reminded of this descent, and Peisistratos' 'royal' background, either at the festival of the Dionysia or the Apatouria (Frost (1990) 9).

V.65.1 The Spartans would never have managed to dislodge the Peisistratidai at all (for they had not planned on a siege, and the Peisistratidai were well supplied with food and water) and after a few days siege would have departed for Sparta; but at this point an incident fortuitously occurred which was unfortunate for the Peisistratidai, but of use to the Spartans, for the children of the Peisistratidai were captured as they were being conveyed out of the country. **V.65.2** As a result of this all their plans were thrown into confusion, and in return for the children they submitted on the conditions the Athenians wanted, that they should leave Attica in five days. **V.65.3** They afterwards departed to Sigeion on the river Skamander, after ruling the Athenians for thirty-six years. In origin they came from the men of Pylos and were descended from the sons of Neleus, from whom came Kodros and Melanthos, who in former times as in-comers became kings of the Athenians. **V.65.4** For this reason Hippokrates gave his son Peisistratos the same name in memory of this, calling him after Peisistratos, the son of Nestor. **V.65.5** This was the way the Athenians were rid of their tyrants.

4.38 Delphic Money Pays the Spartans

[Aristotle] *Athenaion Politeia* 19.4–6

The *Ath. Pol.* alleges that the Alkmeonidai made money from contracting to build the temple of Apollo at Delphi, and used this money 'to pay for the Spartans' help'. Herodotos' account implies the opposite, that *because* the Alkmeonidai were wealthy they were able to complete the temple to grander specifications than necessary, and that while they were at Delphi, 'so the Athenians say', they took the opportunity to bribe the Pythian priestess. There are unsatisfactory discussions of the differences between these two main accounts in Forrest (1969) 277–86; Rhodes 236–37. The *Ath. Pol.* states that Athenian friendship with Argos was also a factor in the Spartans attacking Athens (see docs. 4.9, 18): the Spartans and Argives were old enemies and Kleomenes mounted a successful campaign against the Argives (see doc. 6.49, cf. 2.2).

19.4 So, as they kept failing in all else, they contracted to build the temple at Delphi, and thus acquired plenty of money to pay for the Lakonians' help. The Pythia used always to command the Spartans, when they consulted the oracle, to liberate Athens, to the point where she persuaded the Spartiates, although they had ties of hospitality with the Peisistratidai; the friendship which existed between the Peisistratidai and the Argives played no less a part in the Spartans' decision. **19.5** So first of all they sent off Anchimolos with an army by sea. When he was defeated and killed, because the Thessalian Kineas came to the assistance with a thousand cavalry, they were so angry at what had happened that they sent Kleomenes the king with a larger army by land, who, when he had defeated the Thessalians' cavalry which were preventing him from marching into Attica, shut Hippias up within what is called the pelargic wall and began to besiege it with the help of the Athenians. **19.6** While the siege continued, the children of the Peisistratidai happened to be captured as they were trying to get to safety; when they had been caught, the Peisistratidai came to terms on condition that their children not be harmed and, after having five days to remove their possessions, they surrendered the acropolis to the Athenians in the archonship of Harpaktides (511/0). Their tyranny had lasted for about seventeen years after the death of their father, making, when added to the time their father had ruled, a total of forty-nine years altogether.

4.39 Hippias Goes to Persia

Thucydides VI.59.4

Hippias made use of his family connections, his brother Hegesistratos at Sigeion (doc. 1.15), and then Aiantides, his son-in-law, before making his way to Persia, which was to be the home of many Greek exiles (for example, Demaratos and Themistokles, docs. 6.48, 8.4). He accompanied Darius on his expedition to Marathon and from his flight in 511/0 to his return in 490 was roughly a twenty year period (Thucydides has 'nineteen years').

VI.59.4 When Hippias had been tyrant of the Athenians for three more years and his reign had been ended in the fourth year by the Spartans and Alkmeonid exiles, he left under safe conduct, going to Sigeion and then to Aiantides at Lampsakos, and from there to King Darius. From there he set out with the Persians on their expedition to Marathon nineteen years later as an old man.

THE CULT OF THE TYRANNICIDES

The role of Harmodios and Aristogeiton in killing Hipparchos found public expression in regular cults, honours for their descendants, and statues in the agora, and they came to be accepted as a symbol of freedom and democracy in the fifth century; for the cult, see Rhodes 230; Taylor (1991) 5–9. By comparison, the role of the Alkmeonidai in organizing the expulsion of the Peisistratidai with Spartan assistance found no equivalent public expression. It was, however, clearly a subject for discussion: cf. docs. 5.6, 7.9). Jacoby (1949) 159–60 suggests that the emphasis on the tyrannicides was promoted by opponents of the Alkmeonidai (followed by Fitzgerald (1957) 276–77; Podlecki (1966) 129–41); however, Ehrenberg (1950) 515–48 argues that the tyrannicides were in fact promoted by Kleisthenes and the Alkmeonidai as a means of asserting the validity of the new (democratic) form of government at Athens. Fornara (1970) 155–80 criticizes both points of view; Taylor (1991) 24–25 summarizes the debate. Harmodios and Aristogeiton in subsequent history overshadowed the Alkmeonidai to such an extent that it is difficult to believe that the Alkmeonidai promoted their cult. Moreover, the popular view was more attuned to the tyrannicides, figures of heroic endeavour, than to the Alkmeonidai who bribed the Delphic oracle and encouraged the Spartans to invade Athens. The tyrannicides were buried in the Kerameikos, the resting place of other important Athenians (Paus. I.29.15).

4.40 Harmodios and Aristogeiton are Honoured as Heroes

[Aristotle] *Athenaion Politeia* 58.1

The polemarch made offerings to those who had died for the state in war and was also responsible for the offerings to the tyrannicides as heroes; enagismata (sing: enagisma, also enagismos) were sacrifices to chthonic deities and heroes. For the offerings to the tyrannicides, see Rhodes 651–52; Taylor (1991) xv, 5–8, 102; for enagismata in general, Nock (1944) 159, 161–62; Garland (1985) 110–13. The statues of the tyrannicides stood in the agora. The original statues by Antenor were taken by Xerxes when he sacked Athens, but new ones were made by Kritios and Nesiotes. The Antenor group would have been made soon after the expulsion in 511/0 (Taylor (1991) 13–15, with bibliography) and were replaced in 477/6 (*FGH* 239 Marmor Parium 54; see Brunnsåker (1971) 43–44). For the statues, see Brunnsåker (1971); Thompson & Wycherley (1972) 155–60; Taylor (1991) 8–9. Antiochos later restored to the Athenians the statues which Xerxes had taken away (Paus. I.8.5). Dem. XX.70 states that Konon was the first Athenian since Harmodios and Aristogeiton to have his statue set up by the state; throughout the fifth century, then, Harmodios and Aristogeiton were the only men to have official statues at Athens (Taylor (1991) 13). A pair of Roman marble statues at Naples have been confidently identified as copies of the statues of Harmodios and Aristogeiton by Kritios and Nesiotes; there are also fragments of other copies of the original statues; see Brunnsåker (1971) plates 1–3, 13–15; ph. at the frontispiece of Taylor (1991).

58.1 The polemarch makes the sacrifices to Artemis Agrotera (the huntress) and to Enyalios and organizes the funeral games for those that have died in war and is responsible for making the offerings (enagismata) to Harmodios and Aristogeiton.

4.41 Maintenance for the Tyrannicides' Descendants

IG I^{3} 131, lines 1–15

This decree lists those who were entitled to dine in the prytaneion at the expense of the state and is dated c. 440–432. See Thompson (1971) 226–37; Rhodes 308; Taylor (1991) 1–5; cf. docs. 10.2, 10.46, 9.39. According to Plut. *Arist.* 27.6, Aristogeiton's granddaughter who was living in poverty on Lemnos was brought back to Athens, and given a husband of good family and an estate.

(1) [....] was secr[etary vac. (2) It was resolved by the boule and the peop]le: (the tribe) Erechtheis h[eld the prytany], [.... was secretary, ...]thippos presided, [....]ikles [proposed the motion: there shall be public maintenance] in the prytaneion, first for [.... (5) i]n accordance with ancestral custom; then the descendants of Harm[odios and Aristogei]ton whoever is nearest in descent, [if there are no legitimate sons, shall ha]ve public maint[e]nan[ce, a]n[d] a[nyone else who receives maintenan]ce from the Athenians in accordance with what has been [gr]ant[ed ....] whom Apollo has appoint[ed] while they e[x]pou[nd (the oracles) (10) ....] maintenance, and for the f[ut]ure wh[om]ever [he appoints], these [are also to have maintenance] in the same way. And a[ll those who have won a victory at the festivals at Olympia] or Delphi or the Isthmus or Nem[ea or shall win a victory in future th]ey [shall have] public maintenance in the prytane[ion and the other

privileges in add]ition to public maintenance in accordance with what has [been written on the stele (15) i]n the prytaneion.

4.42 Inscription for the Statue Base of the Tyrannicides

Simonides 1 (*IG* I^3 502)

Friedländer 150; Page 186–89; Hansen 430. The first two lines of the following epigram were attributed in antiquity to Simonides, though Hipparchos, whom the tyrannicides killed, was in fact Simonides' patron (docs. 4.22–23; Ael. *VH* 8.2). Bowra (1961) 321–22 rejects the authorship of Simonides; Podlecki (1966) 135–37 accepts it; cf. Taylor (1991) 33. In 1936, a fragment of a statue base of the tyrannicides in the agora was discovered with the remains of two lines of letters; the first line can be restored as corresponding to the Simonidean couplet given here, and the second contains the letters of a second couplet. Whether the statue base belongs to the original group by Antenor or the later group by Kritios and Nesiotes is debated, with opinion inclining to the latter (Friedländer 150; Brunnsåker (1971) 90–98, with bibliography). See also Wycherley (1957) 93–98; Brunnsåker (1971) 84–98; cf. Thompson & Wycherley (1972) 156–57; Day (1985) 30–32; Taylor (1991) 32–33.

A great light arose for the Athenians when Aristo-
    geiton and Harmodios slew Hipparchos;
[..........]
    The two of them made their native land [?equal in laws]

DRINKING SONGS IN PRAISE OF THE TYRANNICIDES

Athen. 694c–696a collects several drinking-songs (skolia), four of which (695a–b) concern the tyrannicides Harmodios and Aristogeiton. There were clearly other versions of these songs (Bowra (1961) 393), and the change of subject in doc. 4.46 indicates that an oral tradition has affected the transmission and that some couplets have been randomly tagged onto others. See Podlecki (1966) 139–40; Ostwald (1969) 121–30; Fornara (1970) 178–80; Taylor (1991) 22–35; Bowra (1961) 373–97 for skolia generally.

4.43 Athens Attains Isonomia

Athenaeus *Deipnosophistae* 695a–b

At drinking-parties, singers traditionally carried a branch of myrtle; it is not an indication that the tyrannicides hid their daggers in myrtle; isonomia, 'equality before the laws' or 'equal rights', will have represented the return to the situation prior to the tyranny, when the state was not dominated by one family. Whether Kleisthenes usurped this term, isonomia, to describe his constitution is debated: Fornara (1970) 170–80 argues not; Ober (1989) 74–75 (with 75n.50 for bibliography) thinks he did.

In a branch of myrtle I shall bear my sword
Like Harmodios and Aristogeiton,
When the two of them slew the tyrant
And made Athens a city of equal rights.

4.44 The Tyrannicides Dwell in the Islands of the Blest

Athenaeus *Deipnosophistae* 695b

The tyrannicides are equated with the heroic warriors of the Iliad; heroes after death dwelt in the Islands of the Blessed (Hes. *WD* 170–73; Pind. *Olymp.* 2.68–77; cf. Hdt. III.26.1).

Dearest Harmodios, surely you are not dead;
They say that you are in the Islands of the Blessed,
Where dwells swift-footed Achilles
And, they say, brave Diomedes son of Tydeus.

4.45 The Murder of the Tyrant

Athenaeus *Deipnosophistae* 695b

In a branch of myrtle I shall bear my sword
Like Harmodios and Aristogeiton
When at Athena's festival
The two of them slew the tyrant Hipparchos.

4.46 Renown throughout the World

Athenaeus *Deipnosophistae* 695b

Here two couplets are conjoined; the first refers to the tyrannicides in the second person, the second in the third person; this second couplet is almost identical to that of doc. 4.43.

You both will always have renown throughout the world,
Dearest Harmodios and Aristogeiton,
Because the two of them slew the tyrant
And made Athens a city of equal rights.

4.47 The Song of Harmodios

Aristophanes *Pelargoi* (Schol. Ar. *Wasps* 1238a)

Kassel and Austin F444; Kock F430. The 'Word of Admetos' may have been a skolion of Peisistratid origin: Admetos was a Thessalian king (cf. doc. 13.64), and the Peisistratidai had Thessalian connections (docs. 4.36, 38). Here one character is obviously singing a Peisistratid song but is forced to change to a skolion in favour of the tyrannicides. See Bowra (1961) 377–79. Aristophanes also paraphrases the skolia in *Lys.* 631–33; cf. *Ach.* 980, 1093, *Wasps* 1225.

One was singing the 'Word of Admetos' to a myrtle-branch,
But the other forced him to sing the 'Song of Harmodios'.

5

Kleisthenes the Reformer

While Solon may have inadvertently done much to lay the foundations of Athenian democracy, it was the reformer Kleisthenes who established the democracy as such. After the overthrow of the tyranny of the Peisistratidai, Kleisthenes the Alkmeonid and another eupatrid, Isagoras, vied for power. Isagoras' election to the archonship in 508/7 must have been a great setback to Kleisthenes' ambitions. The people had been overlooked in this rivalry between Isagoras and Kleisthenes, and so, when Kleisthenes began losing out in the political struggle for influence among the upper-class hetaireiai, clubs, he counteracted with a masterstroke, gaining the support of the people by taking them into his hetaireia (docs. 5.1–2, 5.6). Not only were Kleisthenes' overtures welcomed, but the people were willing to besiege the Spartans on the acropolis rather than submit to Isagoras' planned oligarchy.

Isagoras persuaded Kleomenes to 'help in driving out the curse' (docs. 5.2–3, 5.6). The events of the Kylonian coup were still hanging over the Alkmeonidai (docs. 2.17–19), and Kleomenes drove out 700 families as accursed. His attempt to dissolve the boule, however, was met with resistance and the council refused to be disbanded (docs. 5.3, 6). Kleomenes, Isagoras and his supporters seized the acropolis, where they were besieged by the people. Kleomenes had apparently come with only a limited force, obviously unprepared for a siege, and on the third day the Spartans were allowed to leave under a truce, but those with them were 'imprisoned under sentence of death' (doc. 5.3). Isagoras left with Kleomenes, but in 506 Kleomenes attempted to establish Isagoras as 'tyrant' at Athens. This attempt failed through the opposition of the Corinthians and of Demaratos, Kleomenes' fellow king (doc. 5.5; cf. 6.21). Later, c. 505–501, a Spartan proposal to restore Hippias was rejected by Sparta's allies (doc. 6.37; cf. 2.7). With the departure of Isagoras and the Spartans in 508/7, and the return of Kleisthenes, his reforms could proceed unhindered.

Kleisthenes' reforms resulted in the political system undergoing major changes: the four Ionian tribes were abolished, and replaced by ten new ones, involving a division of Attica into trittyes and demes. Each new tribe was to contribute fifty members each year to the new boule, and the boule was increased in size, from 400 to 500 members. The main building block of the new organization were the demes, the villages of Attica, and in the new system there were 140 demes. These were grouped into thirty units known as trittyes (sing: trittys). There were ten city, ten inland and ten coastal trittyes (from the asty, mesogeios, and paralia); the number of demes in each trittys varied, but three trittyes went to make up each tribe. Each deme elected a number of members to the boule and was, in fact, a miniature polis, with its own assembly and officials, which voted on deme issues. The purpose of this re-organization was to re-orientate Athenian politics and weaken regional ties. Each citizen was a member of a tribe, which was made up of one city, one inland, and one coastal trittys, and thus each tribe brought together Athenians from all over Attica into one group. Regional ties which were thought to be particularly strong received special attention (see doc. 5.16) and the tribes also obscured the origins of individual citizens: it was not possible to tell from the tribal affiliation whether someone was a new citizen or not. Kleisthenes encouraged the Athenians to call one another by the deme names, but was not quite successful in this, and while they adopted the deme appellation they still retained the patronymic (see doc. 5.7).

Kleisthenes also introduced the procedure of ostracism according to the *Ath. Pol.* The Athenians did not make use of this procedure for many years, and the first ostracism took place after the battle of Marathon, in 488/7; the *Ath. Pol.* (doc. 5.9) states in explanation that the Athenians only then gained the confidence to make use of the procedure, and that they had hitherto been lenient towards the 'friends of the tyrants', who were the first victims. There was a quorum of 6,000, and the procedure involved a debate in the sixth prytany of the year as to whether or not an ostracism would be held, with the ostracism actually held in the eighth prytany. This means that someone ostracised in a particular archonship was actually ostracised in the second half of the year, and sometimes, as with other dates known to fall in a particular half of an archon year, this is indicated by underlining the second year: ie Hipparchos was ostracised in 487: 488/7. While it is possible that ostracism was introduced as a means of preventing those hostile to the demos from becoming too powerful, it is unlikely that it was advanced directly against the supporters of the tyranny. The people had not been opposed to the tyranny, and had not effected its downfall, and an attempt to ostracise the tyrants' supporters would have created a struggle between them and Kleisthenes. Hipparchos, possibly Hippias' grandson, the first to be ostracised, had in fact been eponymous archon in 496/5, indicating that the friends of the tyrants were still influential in the 490s. It will only have been Hippias' involvement with the Persian invasion at Marathon that discredited the tyrants and their friends in the popular imagination.

The constitution established by Kleisthenes was definitely democratic in character, though the four Solonian census classes remained in use as the determinant for qualification to office. Further changes were to take place in the fifth century, notably the appointment of archons by a procedure using both direct election and lot on a tribal basis (doc. 5.9), extension of the archonship to the zeugitai, Ephialtes' changes to the powers of the Areiopagos, and the introduction of pay for jury service (see docs. 8.10, 22; 10.16). Yet it was the reforms of Kleisthenes that made Athens a democracy and subsequent reforms were only aimed at making the state even more democratic.

5.1 Kleisthenes Renames the Athenian Tribes

Herodotos V.65.5–67.1

The deposition of the tyrants had been largely carried out through the machinations of the Alkmeonidai (though cf. 4.35, 5.6, 7.9), but this was not enough to secure their political prominence: Isagoras son of Teisander was also politically powerful. It was the struggle between Isagoras and Kleisthenes which led directly to the transformation of Attica into a democratic state. Ostwald (1969) 147–48 notes that the people were conspicuously absent from the attempts to end the tyranny, and it was only in 508/7 that the people were again important, having been previously ignored by both Isagoras and Kleisthenes. **V.66.1**: Isagoras was archon in 508/7, and his election to the archonship indicated his prominence: Andrewes (1977) 241; Kleisthenes had been archon in 525/4 (doc. 4.24). The reforms of Kleisthenes, since he was not archon, would have been introduced by him as a member of the ekklesia, backed by 'the people', who now supported him (Ostwald (1986) 16 with 16–17n.49). Herodotos places the renaming of the tribes prior to the interference of Kleomenes (cf. doc. 5.2), but it is unlikely that there was time to implement any of the other reforms at this point.

V.66.2: The Ionian tribes were named after the four sons of Ion. Ajax would have been one of the 100 names submitted to the Delphic oracle (see doc. 5.7). He is termed 'a neighbour' because of his association with Salamis; see Kron (1976) 171–72, and *passim* for a detailed treatment of the ten eponymous heroes and their cults. For the fourth century monument for the eponymous heroes in the agora, see Camp (1986) 97–100, with figs. 72–73; Hansen (1991) 48–49, 105–06; Zaidman & Pantel (1992) 85–86, with fig. 3; Kearns (1989) 80–102. For the Ionian tribes, see Hansen (1991) 28, 46.

V.65.5 This is how the Athenians were delivered from the tyrants; whatever they did or experienced worthy of being narrated after they had been liberated, prior to Ionia's revolt from Darius and Aristagoras the Milesian's arrival in Athens to ask for their help, I shall now recount. **V.66.1** Athens, which had previously been great, now became greater still after her deliverance from the tyrants. Two men held sway in Athens, Kleisthenes one of the Alkmeonidai, who was the one who according to report bribed the Pythia, and Isagoras son of Teisander, a man of reputable family, but the origins of which I am unable to recount; however, his relatives sacrifice to Carian Zeus. **V.66.2** These men began a struggle for power, and Kleisthenes, who was being worsted, took the people into his hetaireia. And later on he changed the Athenians' four tribes into ten, getting rid of the names derived from the sons of Ion — Geleon, Aigikores, Argades, and Hoples — and finding them the names of other heroes, who were Athenians, except Ajax; and he added him as a guest-friend (xenos), because he was a neighbour of the city and an ally. **V.67.1** I think that Kleisthenes in this was imitating his maternal grandfather Kleisthenes, tyrant of Sicyon.

5.2 Kleisthenes and Isagoras Struggle for Control

Herodotos V.69.1–70.2

Despite Herodotos' account, Kleisthenes of Athens' motives in renaming the tribes were very different from those of Kleisthenes of Sicyon (doc. 2.3). Tribal reforms are known from other states; Andrewes (1977) 242 points out that Sparta at some stage abandoned the three tribes which Tyrtaeus names (F19.8), and that there was also a tribal reform at Argos, probably in the mid-fifth century. Kleisthenes became the dominant political figure at Athens, but Isagoras had learnt the value of Spartan intervention, and the curse (docs. 2.17–19) was brought up against the Alkmeonidai. **V.69.2**: Phylarchs were leaders of tribes. **V.70.1**: Herodotos obviously does not believe the 'rumour' about Kleomenes' affair with Isagoras' wife, but includes it anyway. Doc. 2.17 follows on here. Rapke (1989) 47–51 unconvincingly argues that Kleomenes intervened because he perceived that Kleisthenes was attempting to set up a tyranny.

V.69.1 This is what the Sicyonian Kleisthenes did, and the Athenian Kleisthenes, being the son of Kleisthenes of Sicyon's daughter and named after him, seems to me to have imitated his namesake Kleisthenes because he despised the Ionians and did not want the Athenians and Ionians to have the same tribes. **V.69.2** So, as soon as he had added the Athenian people, which had previously been entirely left out of account, to his own party (moira), he renamed the tribes and increased their number. He created ten tribal leaders (phylarchs) instead of four, and divided the demes into ten and assigned them to the tribes. After winning the support of the people he was far more powerful than his opponents. **V.70.1** Worsted in his turn, Isagoras countered with this plan: he called for the help of Kleomenes the Spartan, who had been his guest-friend since the siege of the Peisistratidai. It was even rumoured that Kleomenes had had an affair with Isagoras' wife. **V.70.2** Kleomenes first sent a herald to Athens and expelled Kleisthenes and many other Athenians with him, calling them the 'accursed'. He did this at the suggestion of Isagoras, for the Alkmeonidai and their supporters were held to be guilty of this murder (of Kylon and his associates), while Isagoras and his friends had not been involved.

5.3 Kleomenes Attempts to Interfere Again

Herodotos V.72.1–4

As well as the Alkmeonidai, the 700 'accursed' families may have included families which had marriage ties with the Alkmeonidai. Isagoras was obviously seeking to destroy the influence of the Alkmeonidai in the state altogether. **V.72.1**: there is debate about which council, 'boule', is meant, the Solonian council of 400, Kleisthenes' new council of 500, or the Areiopagos. Kleisthenes is unlikely to have had time to organize the new boule of 500, and therefore it was presumably either the council of 400 or the Areiopagos. Hignett (1952) 94–95 (cf. Ehrenberg (1973) 68–69) considers it the Areiopagos, but the Areiopagos, with its membership moulded by decades under the tyranny, was more likely to have been hostile to Kleisthenes than Isagoras, who is referred to as a friend of the tyrants (doc. 5.6; cf. Rapke (1989) 50); Ober (1989) 68 inclines towards the boule of 400, as does Starr (1990) 13. As in the *Ath. Pol.* 20.3 (doc. 5.6), the dissolution of the council is here linked with entrusting government to Isagoras and supporters; the boule was the organizing body for the ekklesia, and an attempt to create an oligarchy of 300 would have needed to override the ekklesia.

At V.74.1 (doc. 5.5) Herodotos states that Isagoras left the acropolis with Kleomenes; *Ath. Pol.* 20.3 (doc. 5.6) has Kleomenes, Isagoras, and *all* those with them leaving the acropolis. Wade-Gery (1958) 136–37 suggested (on the basis of Schol. Ar. *Lys.* 273) that it was only *after* Kleomenes' later invasion (506) that Isagoras and his supporters were condemned to death (presumably *in absentia*). Isagoras himself probably died in exile in Sparta. Rhodes 246 sees *Ath. Pol.* 20.3 as 'careless' in the use of 'all', while Ostwald

(1969) 144n.6 suggests that 'all' refers to the Spartans alone: both suggestions would save Herodotos' account and mean that only Isagoras went into exile, and that the 300 supporters were put to death.

V.72.1 On the arrival of Kleomenes' order that Kleisthenes and the 'accursed' should be expelled, Kleisthenes himself withdrew from the city; but nonetheless Kleomenes then came to Athens with a small band of men, on arrival driving out, as under a curse, seven hundred Athenian families as Isagoras had suggested. After doing this he then attempted to dissolve the boule and entrust government to three hundred of Isagoras' adherents. **V.72.2** When the council resisted and refused to co-operate, Kleomenes, Isagoras and his supporters seized the acropolis. The rest of the Athenians, all of one mind, besieged them for two days; but on the third all the Spartans amongst them left the country under a truce .... **V.72.4** The Athenians imprisoned the others under sentence of death, amongst them Timesitheos of Delphi, of whose prowess and courage I could recount great things.

5.4 A Proposed Alliance with Persia

Herodotos V.73.1–3

The story of the Athenian embassy to Persia represents an alliance between Athens and Persia initiated by the Alkmeonidai; earth and water were the usual symbols of submission to the Persians. Horsley (1986) 99–107 believes that Kleisthenes was one of the ambassadors, and that the wrath of the demos which he incurred on the embassy's return (basing his argument on Cic. *de Legibus* 2.41) accounted for his 'disappearance from public life'. But this, like Cromey (1979) 129–47, rests on a misunderstanding of the nature of our sources. Kleisthenes disappears from the historical narrative after his reforms, because Herodotos is scarcely interested in Kleisthenes, while the *Ath. Pol.* after detailing Kleisthenes' reforms moves on to 501/0 and then ostracism (the first use of which was in 487). Kleisthenes presumably died several years after carrying out his reforms: there is no need to assume a political disgrace or sudden death.

V.73.1 After their imprisonment these were executed, after which the Athenians recalled Kleisthenes and the seven hundred families expelled by Kleomenes and sent messengers to Sardis, as they wished to make an alliance with the Persians; for they knew that they had made enemies of the Spartans and Kleomenes. **V.73.2** When the messengers arrived at Sardis and spoke as they had been instructed, Artaphernes son of Hystaspes, viceroy (hyparchos) of Sardis, inquired who these men were and what part of the world they inhabited who sought the Persians as allies; when he learnt this he gave the messengers this pointed reply: if the Athenians gave King Darius earth and water, he would conclude an alliance with them, but if they did not, then he bade them depart. **V.73.3** The messengers, on their own responsibility, said they would do so, as they wanted to make the alliance. But when they returned home, they were severely blamed on this account.

5.5 The Return of Kleomenes

Herodotos V.74.1–76

This expedition is dated to 506/5 (507/6 is also a possibility). The Spartans not only took their allies with them (the defection of the Corinthians and Demaratos' support of them led to the aborting of the attack), but arranged for the Boeotians and Chalkidians to attack on two other fronts. The Spartan threat dissolved, and the Athenians then defeated the Boeotians, on the same day crossing over to Euboea and defeating the Chalkidians. The prisoners were kept in chains and then ransomed for two minas each (cf. doc. 11.3); Herodotos saw the fetters on the acropolis. The Athenians dedicated one-tenth of the ransom money to Athena and made a chariot and four horses in bronze, consecrating it to the goddess (Hdt. V.77; cf. Paus. I.28.2). The inscription accompanying the dedication recorded by Hdt. V.77.4 (and Diod. X.24.3; *Anth. Pal.* VI.343; Aristeid. XXVIII.64) is also known from two marble fragments, see *IG* I^2 394 (*IG* I^3 501); *DAA* 168, 173; Friedländer 145; *LSAG* 75, 78n.43; ML 15; Page 191–93; Hansen 179. The fact that the Athenians won these victories indicated that the democracy could be militarily successful. This passage is important for an understanding of the workings of the Peloponnesian League; see doc. 6.37. **V.75.2**: see doc. 6.21.

V.74.1 Kleomenes felt that he had been treated insultingly by the Athenians in both word and deed and started collecting an army from the whole Peloponnese, without saying why he was collecting it, as he wanted to take vengeance on the Athenian people and establish Isagoras as tyrant; Isagoras had escaped from the acropolis with him. **V.74.2** So, while Kleomenes marched to Eleusis with a large force, the Boeotians by a preconcerted plan seized Oinoe and Hysiai, the furthermost villages in Attica, and the Chalkidians from the other side attacked and pillaged the Attic countryside. Although they were being attacked from both sides, the Athenians decided to put off dealing with the Boeotians and Chalkidians till later, and made a stand against the Spartans who were at Eleusis. **V.75.1** But when the two armies were just on the point of conflict, the Corinthians were the first to deliberate, coming to the conclusion that they were not acting rightly, and changed their minds and left, followed by Demaratos son of Ariston, who was king of the Spartiates and had jointly led out the expedition from Sparta, and who had not previously had a disagreement with Kleomenes. (**V.75.2**: *the Spartans thereupon make a law that both kings may not accompany the army.*) **V.75.3** At this point, when the rest of the allies at Eleusis saw that the Spartans kings were not in agreement and that the Corinthians had abandoned their post, they also withdrew. **V.76** This was the fourth time that the Dorians had come to Attica, twice invading as an act of war and twice for the good of the Athenian populace: the first occasion was when they founded Megara (this expedition is correctly dated to the time when Kodros was king of the Athenians), the second and third were when they came from Sparta to expel the Peisistratidai, and the fourth was this present occasion when Kleomenes led the Peloponnesians and invaded as far as Eleusis; this then was the fourth time the Spartans entered Attica.

5.6 Kleisthenes, Isagoras and Kleomenes

[Aristotle] *Athenaion Politeia* 20.1–5

Herodotos' statement (doc. 5.1) that Kleisthenes took the people into his hetaireia is more specific than *Ath. Pol.* 20.1, that he 'brought over the people to his side'. **20.5**: The skolion for Kedon is also given at Athen. 695e; see Bowra (1961) 383; West II.2 no.6; Rhodes 248; Page 403. Nothing else is known of Kedon apart from this epigram. The 'as well' means 'pour to Kedon in addition to the heroes of Leipsydrion'. How Kedon attacked the tyrants is not made clear, nor whether he died in the attempt (perhaps he did, on analogy with the heroes of Leipsydrion).

20.1 After the tyranny had been overthrown, Isagoras son of Teisander, who had been a friend of the tyrants, and Kleisthenes, of the family of the Alkmeonidai, were political rivals. As Kleisthenes was worsted by the hetaireiai he brought over the people to his side by promising to hand the state over to the populace. **20.2** Isagoras, who was losing out in the power struggle, then called again for the help of Kleomenes, with whom he had ties of hospitality, and persuaded him to join in driving out the curse, since the Alkmeonidai were thought to belong to the 'accursed'. **20.3** Kleisthenes secretly left the country, and Kleomenes arrived with a few men and expelled seven hundred Athenian families as under a curse; after doing this he attempted to dissolve the boule, and make Isagoras with three hundred of his friends masters of the city. However when the council resisted and the populace gathered in force, the supporters of Kleomenes and Isagoras fled to the acropolis and the people settled down and besieged them for two days, but on the third allowed Kleomenes and all those with him to leave under a truce, and recalled Kleisthenes and the other exiles. **20.4** Once the people had gained control of affairs, Kleisthenes became their leader and champion of the people. The Alkmeonidai had been primarily responsible for the expulsion of the tyrants and had consistently opposed them for most of the time. **20.5** Even before the Alkmeonidai Kedon had made an attack on the tyrants, and for this reason he too was celebrated in drinking-songs:

'Pour in honour of Kedon as well, steward, don't forget him,
If it is right to drink a toast to courageous men.'

5.7 Kleisthenes' Reforms

[Aristotle] *Athenaion Politeia* 21.1–6

The *Ath. Pol.* here deals with several reforms, which are discussed in the order of their appearance. **21.2**: The names and official order of the ten new tribes, which replaced the old four Ionian tribes of Attica, were (modern scholars give each tribe a Roman numeral): Erechtheis (I), Aigeis (II), Pandionis (III), Leontis (IV), Akamantis (V), Oineis (VI), Kekropis (VII), Hippothontis (VIII), Aiantis (IX), Antiochis (X). Further tribes, with reshuffling of demes, were created from the late fourth century BC. To inquire into backgrounds was now no longer feasible through tribes and to be a member of a tribe did not mean that one's ancestors had always been citizens. **21.3**: The Solonian boule had 400 members chosen from each of the four tribes, but the creation of a new system made a change inevitable, and a boule of 500, with 50 members drawn from each tribe, was formed. Each tribal contingent to the boule held a particular prytany, one-tenth of the year; these 50 members were known as prytaneis during their term of office; for the bouleutic calendar, see Rhodes (1972) 224–29.

21.4: Cf. Kinzl (1987) 25–33. Newly enfranchised citizens, of non-Athenian background, will presumably have had fathers with foreign names, hence Kleisthenes wanted the demesmen to address each other not by the formula 'Aristeides, son of Lysimachos', but by the formula 'Aristeides, of the deme Alopeke'. Custom, however, was too strong, and the use of the patronymic was not abandoned, but the demotic added to it: 'Aristeides, son of Lysimachos, of Alopeke' (see doc. 5.14; Kagan (1963) 45–46; cf. Winters (1993) 162–65). The demes were clearly arranged systematically into trittyes, but trittyes could well have been assigned by lot to tribes as the *Ath. Pol.* states, but this is uncertain (Rhodes 253). **21.5**: For demarchs, see doc. 5.20. For demes named after their 'founders', see Lewis (1963) 26, giving the examples of Boutadai, a city deme of Oineis (VI), and Paionidai, an inland deme of Leontis (IV).

21.6: Kleisthenes made demes, trittyes and tribes the basis of the political organization of Attica; for a detailed discussion, see note at doc. 5.17. The gene, phratries and priesthoods were, however, left intact. Kleisthenes did not pursue a policy as recommended later by Aristotle about phratries and religious cults (doc. 5.16); what he did do was to ensure that old religious organizations did not become political units in the new system. The ten eponymous heroes, for whom the tribes were named, were chosen by the Pythia out of 100 pre-selected heroes. It is possible that the Athenians presented the 100 names in a container, from which the she drew ten; in one instance in the fourth century the Athenians presented the Pythia with a choice of two containers (*IG* II^2 204.44–47).

21.1 So for these reasons the people put their trust in Kleisthenes. Then as leader of the populace in the fourth year after the overthrow of the tyrants, in the archonship of Isagoras (508/7), **21.2** he first of all assigned everyone to ten tribes instead of four, his aim being to mix them up, so that more might have a share in the constitution; from which comes the saying 'Don't investigate by tribes' to those wishing to inquire into family backgrounds. **21.3** Then he made the council five hundred instead of four hundred, fifty from each tribe; previously there were a hundred (from each tribe). He did not organize them into twelve tribes because he wished to avoid dividing them according to the pre-existing trittyes; for the four tribes consisted of twelve trittyes, with the result that he would not have succeeded in mixing up the population. **21.4** He also divided the country by demes into thirty parts, ten of them from the city area (asty), ten from the coast (paralia), and ten from the inland region (mesogeios), and he named these trittyes and assigned three by lot to each tribe, so that each tribe would have territory in all three regions. And he made those living in each of the demes fellow-demesmen, so that they should not address each other by their fathers' names and thus show up the new citizens, but would use the names of their demes; this is the reason why the Athenians call one another by their demes. **21.5** He also instituted demarchs who had the same responsibilities as the former naukraroi; for he created the demes to replace the naukrariai. He named some of the demes after their localities, and others after their founders, for not all of them were still connected with their localities. **21.6** But he allowed everyone to retain their clans, phratries and priesthoods according to ancestral custom. He assigned to the tribes ten eponymous heroes, whom the Pythia chose out of the one hundred founders (archegetai) who had been pre-selected.

5.8 The Oath of the Boule and the Strategia

[Aristotle] *Athenaion Politeia* 22.1–2

22.1: Kleisthenes' reforms certainly made the Athenian politeia (constitution) 'more democratic' than it had been before. The statement here that the tyrants did away with 'some of Solon's laws' contradicts the statements of other sources, including the *Ath. Pol.* (16.8) itself (docs. 4.3, 16, 21). **22.2**: The oath of the boule was introduced in the archonship of Hermokreon (501/0); for the difficulties with the date, see Rhodes 262–63, who emends 'fifth' to 'eighth'. Eliot (1962) 145–47; cf. Rhodes (1972) 1, 191–93, and others have taken the oath as evidence that this was the first year in which the Kleisthenic boule came into operation. However, the *Ath. Pol.* is simply reporting that an oath was imposed upon the boule, and his narrative implies that the boule was already in existence and that the oath was imposed several years after the reforms. For the oath, see esp. Rhodes (1972) 193–99; compare the oath sworn by the archons, *Ath. Pol.* 55.5.

Another change was the introduction of a board of ten strategoi in 501/0. Each tribe now elected a strategos, and fought as a military unit. Note Herodotos' description of the battle of Marathon (docs. 7.7–8), where there are ten strategoi and the polemarch (Kallimachos); despite the prominence of Miltiades in Herodotos' account, it is clear that Kallimachos as polemarch was the leader of the army. The strategoi were not a new creation: Phrynon was strategos in 607/6 (see doc. 1.15; Develin (1989) 32–33). In the fifth century the office of strategos became increasingly important as the prestige of the archonship diminished (see *Ath. Pol.* 22.5, 26.2). The strategia was an annual office which could be held repeatedly, through which individuals could gain prominence and influence in the state (cf. Ober (1989) 86–87; Stockton (1990) 32). Perikles held the strategia continuously from 443 to 429 (though the number of times he held the office was unusual) and the great leaders of the fifth century (Miltiades, Themistokles, Aristeides, Kimon, and Perikles) were all engaged in the military sphere. Direct election of the strategoi was unusual for Athens, as most offices (except the most important) were chosen by lot. The strategia, however, required military skill, which meant that the best candidates had to be chosen and re-election be permitted so that the best candidates could continue to be elected. The election of one strategos from each tribe mentioned by the *Ath. Pol.* does not seem always to have held (see doc. 8.12). For the concept of collective responsibility amongst the board of generals, see doc. 10.13.

The basic treatment of the strategia remains Fornara (1971), esp. 1–10 for 501/0, and 40–71 for a chronological list of known strategoi; see also West (1924) 141–60; Ehrenberg (1945) 113–34, (1950) 545–46; Hignett (1952) 347–56; Jameson (1955) 63–87; Jones (1957) 124–28; Dover (1960) 61–77; Lewis (1961) 118–23; Staveley (1966) 275–88, (1972) 40–47, 87; Bicknell (1972) 101–12, (1974) 156–57; esp. Ostwald (1986) 22–23, 62–66, 79, 203–04, (1988) 332–34; Hansen (1987) 50–52, (1991) 34, 52, 233–34; Sealey (1987) 127–28; Sinclair (1988) 17–18, 148, 171–72; Develin (1989) 3–4; Ober (1989) 86–88; Starr (1990) 42–43, 47–48; Stockton (1990) 105–06, 129–30.

22.1 Following these reforms, the constitution was far more democratic than that of Solon; for Solon's laws had been forgotten under the tyranny through lack of use, and Kleisthenes had made other new ones with the aim of winning popular support, amongst which the law concerning ostracism was enacted. **22.2** First of all, in the fifth year after these had been established, in the archonship of Hermokreon (501/0), they imposed on the boule of five hundred the oath which they still swear even today. Then they began electing the generals by tribes, one from each tribe, though the polemarch was in command of the whole army.

OSTRACISM

The Athenians employed ostracism in the fifth century to send certain political figures into exile for ten years. These individuals retained control of their property in Attica, and at the end of the ten years could return. A quorum was required, and an ostracism could take place once a year. For the large number of ostraka (c. 9000) discovered in the Kerameikos, still largely unpublished, see Willemsen (1968) 28–29; Thomsen (1972) 92–108; Lang 30; on the Kerameikos evidence for the candidates of 487/6, see Lewis (1974) 1–4; Williams (1978) 103–13; Lang 7–8. In addition to docs. 5.9–14, see also Pollux 8.19–20; Diod. XI.55.1–3; [Andok.] IV.3; and most recently Lang, which now supersedes previous publications of ostraka found in the Agora and on the north slope of the acropolis; Vanderpool (1970); Thomsen (1972).

Other studies include (a selection only): Broneer (1938) 228–44; Raubitschek (1947) 257–62, (1953) 113–22; Ehrenberg (1950) 543–45; Hignett (1952) 159–66; Hands (1959) 69–79; Kagan (1961) 393–401; Vanderpool (1968) 117–20, (1974) 189–93; Connor & Keaney (1969) 313–19; Keaney (1970) 1–11; Stanton (1970) 180–83; Mattingly (1971) 280–87, (1991) 1–26; Staveley (1972) 88–93; Karavites (1974) 326–35; Lang (1982) 75–87; Phillips (1982) 21–43, (1990) 123–48; Ostwald (1986a) 117–20; Figueira (1987) 281–305; ML 21; Ober (1989) 73–75; Stockton (1990) 33–41; there are 265 bibliographical entries at Martin (1989) 124–45. A late Byzantine account of ostracism (published by Keaney & Raubitschek (1972) 87–91) has the boule originally able to ostracise with a vote of more than two hundred of its members (hence the Solonian boule of 400 is probably meant); some scholars are inclined to accept this account (Develin (1977) 10–21, (1985) 7–15, with bibliography 7n.1; Longo (1980) 257–81), but it ought probably to be relegated to the status of other unreliable late material; Rhodes 268 prefers to be sceptical; cf. Starr (1990) 68n.13.

5.9 The *Athenaion Politeia* on Ostracism

[Aristotle] *Athenaion Politeia* 22.3–8

The *Ath. Pol.* lists as those ostracised (the name of the individual, the father, and the deme): 487 Hipparchos Charmou Kollyteus; 486 Megakles Hippokratous Alopekethen; 485 an unnamed friend of the tyrants; 484 Xanthippos Ariphronos Cholargeus; 482 Aristeides Lysimachou Alopekethen.

22.3: There is a discrepancy between a Kleisthenic date for the introduction of ostracism and its first use, nearly two decades later. For the statement of Androtion (*FGH* 324 F6), as preserved by Harpokration s.v. Hipparchos, that the law about ostracism had only just been passed prior to Hipparchos' ostracism, see Thomsen (1972) 11–60. **22.4**: Although, according to the *Ath. Pol.*, the law of ostracism was specifically introduced by Kleisthenes to drive out Hipparchos, son of Charmos, it was not until 488/7 that the Athenians first made use of ostracism; it is unlikely, then, that the *Ath. Pol.*'s statement is correct. Hipparchos' father, Charmos, may have married a daughter of Hippias: see Davies (1971) 451; doc. 4.20; Table II; cf. Carawan (1987) 195–96; Lavelle (1988) 131–35. The *Ath. Pol.* includes Megakles, son of Hippokrates, as one of the friends of the tyrants. This seems strange as Megakles was one of the Alkmeonidai (Davies (1971) 373), but cf. doc. 7.9. Certainly Kleisthenes in handing power over to the people did not secure his family from political misfortunes. **22.5**: In 487/6 partial sortition for the election of the archons was introduced. 500 candidates (prokritoi) were elected by the demes; from these the archons were chosen by lot. Staveley (1972) 38 accepts the *Ath.*

Pol., and 239n.59 defends it against Hignett (1952) 174; cf. Rhodes 273 who thinks there will 'hardly have been many more than' 500 eligible for the archonship.

22.6: The *Ath. Pol.* makes Xanthippos (Perikles' father; see Table I) the first person ostracised who was not connected with the tyranny; *Ath. Pol.* 28.2 describes him as the 'champion of the people'. His ostracism can only be explained in terms of political enmity of a different nature than that of connection with the tyranny; cf. Bicknell's suggestion (1972) 73–74 that Xanthippos was ostracised because of his connection with the Alkmeonidai; Hignett (1952) 188–89 sees the ostracisms of the 480s as the work of Themistokles. For Xanthippos' ostraka, see Lang 133–35; doc. 5.14 i. The third victim of ostracism, who was a friend of the tyrants, is often thought to have been Kallias Kratiou Alopekethen, represented by 763 ostraka (two from the agora; see the full bibliography of Lang 65–66). Several of the Kerameikos ostraka accuse him of being a Mede (doc. 5.14 iv); Bicknell (1972) 64–71 argues that he was an Alkmeonid. **22.7**: For the mine narrative, see doc. 7.21. Aristeides was ostracised in 483/2, and recalled when the Persians invaded; see docs. 5.12, 8.2.

22.8: The recall of the ostracised is also found in the Themistokles Decree (doc. 7.31); for the date of 481/0 for this recall, and the text of the *Ath. Pol.* here, see Rhodes 281. The motive for their recall was the expedition of Xerxes, and clearly the Athenians felt that these men could usefully serve the state, as Aristeides and Xanthippos did upon their return, both being elected strategoi in 479 (Hdt. VIII.131.3, IX.28.6). Themistokles was instrumental in having Aristeides recalled, seeing that the Athenians wanted him back (Plut. *Them.* 11.1, cf. *Arist.* 8.1), despite having been said to have been responsible for the ostracism in the first place: Plut. *Them.* 5.7, 12.6, *Arist.* 7.1–2 (doc. 5.12), 25.10. Hipparchos, the first to be ostracised as a friend of the tyrants in 488/7, presumably did not return, being later charged with treason and sentenced to death in absentia (not all accept this scenario, see Rhodes 282; Figueira (1987) 291–92): Hippias' involvement with the Persians at Marathon presumably will have made the return of any member of his family seem unwise. Megakles apparently returned; his son later held the office of secretary to the treasurers of Athena (Davies (1971) 381).

Philochoros (doc. 5.11) states that the ostracised were not allowed to come closer than Geraistos (the cape of south-east Euboea) and Skyllaion (in the Argolid), while the *Ath. Pol.* has the ostracised after the recall being compelled to live within the limits of Geraistos and Skyllaion. There has been much discussion of this discrepancy (to the bibliography at Rhodes 282, add Figueira (1987) 281–305). Most scholars argue that the clause in the *Ath. Pol.* be emended by inserting a negative, or ἐκτὸς (outside) for ἐντὸς (within), so that it reads that the ostracised were *not* to come within the bounds of Geraistos and Skyllaion. The *Ath. Pol.* as it stands would mean that the ostracised were to remain close to Athens, doubtless with the aim of keeping them away from Persian territory. Aristeides seems to have spent his period of his ostracism at Aegina (Dem. XXVI.6; Figueira (1987) 291n.31); Themistokles stayed at Argos (Thuc. I.135.3; Plut. *Them.* 23.1); Hyperbolos was assassinated on Samos (Thuc. VIII.73.3); there are unreliable traditions about others (Rhodes 282; cf. Figueira (1987) 294–96). But the requirement, if aimed against the ostracised collaborating with the Persians, could later have been relaxed. The emendation of the *Ath. Pol.* is therefore to be rejected.

22.3 In the twelfth year after this, in the archonship of Phainippos (490/89), they won the battle of Marathon, and after waiting two years after the victory, when the people were already more confident, they then (488/7) first used the law concerning ostracism, which was enacted because of suspicion of men in positions of power, because Peisistratos from being a popular leader and general had set himself up as tyrant. **22.4** The first man to be ostracised was one of his relatives, Hipparchos, son of Charmos of Kollytos, on whose account in particular Kleisthenes had made the law, as he wanted to drive him out. For the Athenians, employing the tolerance characteristic of a democracy, allowed those friends of the tyrants, who had not taken part in their crimes during the disorders, to continue living in the city; of these Hipparchos was leader and champion. **22.5** In the year immediately following, in the archonship of Telesinos (487/6), for the first time after the tyranny, they appointed by lot the nine archons by tribes from the five hundred pre-selected by the demesmen; previous ones had all been elected; and Megakles, son of Hippokrates of Alopeke, was ostracised. **22.6** So for three years they continued to ostracise the friends of the tyrants, on whose account the law was enacted, but after that in the fourth year they started removing anyone else who appeared too powerful; the first of those unconnected with the tyranny to be ostracised was Xanthippos son of Ariphron. **22.7** In the third year after that, when the mines at Maroneia were found (483/2), ... Aristeides son of Lysimachos was ostracised. **22.8** But three years later, in the archonship of Hypsichides (481/0), they recalled all those who had been ostracised, because of Xerxes' expedition; and for the future they resolved that anyone who was ostracised must <not> live within the limits of Geraistos and Skyllaion, or else they would entirely lose all citizen rights.

5.10 The Date when Ostracism was Decided

[Aristotle] *Athenaion Politeia* 43.5

The *Ath. Pol.* is describing the situation in the second half of the fourth century, which is generally assumed to apply also to the fifth century. In the sixth prytany of the year a vote about whether to hold an ostracism was taken, and if there were support for this, the actual procedure took place in the eighth prytany (see doc. 5.11).

43.5 In the sixth prytany, in addition to the matters already mentioned, they take a vote concerning ostracism, whether an ostracism should be held or not, and hear complaints about informers, both Athenians and metics, up to three of each, and against anyone who has made a promise to the people but failed to keep it.

5.11 Philochoros on Ostracism

Philochoros *FGH* 328 F30 [Lexicon Rhet. Cantab.]

There is debate about the number of votes required for an individual to be ostracised; Philochoros (and Pollux 8.19–20) has 6,000 votes required against an individual, while Plut. *Arist.* 7.6 (doc. 5.12) has a quorum of 6,000 in total, which seems more plausible; the individual who received most of the 6,000 votes would be ostracised (Jacoby *FGH* 3b Suppl. 1.317; Vanderpool (1970) 4; Thomsen (1972) 66–67, esp. n.23; Rhodes 270; Lang 2; 6,000 was a quorum for other procedures (Jacoby 1.317). Plut. *Arist.* 7.5 has a fenced off area, Philochoros has planks, while Pollux 8.19–20 has ropes, but planks were probably used, as a means of ensuring that all voters went through the official entrances. The ten entrances, one for each tribe, were presumably to identify the voters as citizens and ensure that they voted only once. Philochoros states that the period of ostracism was changed from ten years to five; Diod. XI.55.2 states that it was five; Plutarch does not mention any change, and it is fairly certain that the ten year period was always the case (Jacoby 317). For the ostracism of Hyperbolos, see Woodhead (1949) 78–83; Gomme

HCT V.257–61; Vanderpool (1970) 3; Sinclair (1988) 115–16; Lang 64 with bibliography; doc. 5.14 xii; the year 417 is usually assigned to this, though a date between 417 and 415 is possible.

The method of ostracism: Philochoros explains ostracism in his third book, writing as follows: 'Ostracism was like this; the people took a preliminary vote before the eighth prytany, to decide whether to hold an ostracism. When it was resolved to do so, the agora was fenced with planks, and ten entrances were left, through which they entered by tribes and deposited their ostraka, inscription-side down; the nine archons and the boule presided. When they had been counted up, whoever had received the most and not less than six thousand, had to settle his obligations regarding lawsuits in which he was a prosecutor or defendant in ten days and leave the city for ten years (but afterwards it became five), during which he could receive the income from his property, but not come any closer than Geraistos, the promontory of Euboea. Hyperbolos was the only disreputable man to be ostracised because of his depraved character, not on suspicion of aiming at tyranny; after him the custom was stopped. It had begun when Kleisthenes was passing laws, when he did away with the tyrants and wanted to expel their friends as well.

5.12 Aristeides 'the Just' is Ostracised

Plutarch *Aristeides* 7.1–8

Each of the voters wrote on an ostrakon (plural: ostraka), a piece of pottery, the name of the candidate whom they wished to ostracise, usually by scratching with an instrument; only a handful are painted, but painted ostraka are less likely to have survived (for example doc. 5.14 xii). Numbers of ostraka have been discovered in the Agora, on the north slope of the acropolis and in the Kerameikos. While the story below is obviously an invention to illustrate Aristeides' character, it does provide support for the fact that the illiterate participated in ostracisms. Ostraka with names already scratched on them could be handed out to voters: a well on the north slope of the acropolis yielded a find of 190 ostraka against Themistokles. His name was written in only fourteen different hands, and apparently the ostraka had been mass produced, and were probably dumped in the well without having been used (see Broneer (1938) 228–41; Phillips (1990) 134–36; Lang 142–58). This mass production of ostraka may have been for the purposes of selling them, but more probably for free distribution to voters by Themistokles' enemies. The ostraka often, but by no means always, include the name, the patronymic (ie father's name), and the deme of the individual that the voter wished to be ostracised.

7.1 So Aristeides at first found that he was loved because of his surname, but later envied, especially when Themistokles started spreading around the rumour to the people that Aristeides had done away with the law-courts by his judging and deciding everything and that, without anyone noticing, he had made himself sole ruler, without a bodyguard; and the people, proud because of their victory and thinking nothing too great for them, already found it hard to bear any name which had a reputation above the ordinary, **7.2** and they came together into the city from all sides and ostracised Aristeides, giving their jealousy of his reputation the name of fear of a tyranny. For banishment by ostracism was not a punishment for wickedness, but it was called for the sake of appearances the means of lowering and curtailing pride and power which had become too difficult to bear. In fact it was a humane way of relieving jealousy, which thus directed its malignant wish to cause harm, not into doing anything fatal, but into getting the person to change his residence for ten years. **7.3** And when ignoble and base men started being subjected to the practice, they stopped it, Hyperbolos being the last one to be banished by ostracism. The story is that Hyperbolos was ostracised for the following reason: Alkibiades and Nikias, the most powerful men in the city, were at odds. **7.4** So when the people were about to carry out an ostracism and were clearly going to write one or the other, they came to terms with each other and combined their two parties into one, and caused the ostracism of Hyperbolos. The people, incensed at this, left it off completely as a practice which had been abused and degraded, and abolished it. **7.5** What happened, to give a general account, was as follows. Each man took an ostrakon and wrote on it the name of the citizen he wished to get rid of, and brought it to a place in the agora which had been fenced round in a circle with railings. **7.6** The archons first counted up the total number of the ostraka there; if there were less than six thousand voters, the ostracism was invalid; then they sorted each of the names separately, and proclaimed the man whose name was written by the most people banished for ten years, but able to receive the income from his property. **7.7** So when the ostraka were being inscribed, it is said that one of the illiterate, a complete rustic, handed his ostrakon to Aristeides as one of the crowd, and requested him to write 'Aristeides' on it. He was surprised and inquired what harm Aristeides had ever done him. 'None', was the answer, 'I don't even know the fellow, but I'm tired of hearing him called "the Just" everywhere.' **7.8** When Aristeides heard this he said nothing, but inscribed his name on the ostrakon and gave it back.

5.13 Ostrakinda: a Children's Game

Scholiast to Aristophanes *Knights* 855

Here Aristophanes is playing on words. That individuals had to have 6,000 votes against them is almost certainly incorrect. Cf. Diod. XI.86–87 for ostracism in Syracuse; Thomsen (1972) 11–12. For ostrakinda, a chase game with two teams, see Golden (1990) 53–55.

Ar. *Knights*: 855: And if you are indignant and look to play 'ostrakinda'.
Scholiast: Ostrakinda is the name of a children's game. He means to say should you wish him to be ostracised. The method of ostracism was like this: the people voted to hold an ostracism, and when it was resolved, the agora was fenced with boards and ten entrances left. They entered through these by tribes and deposited the ostrakon, after placing their inscription on it. The archons and boule presided. When six thousand had been counted up (there could be more than this but not less), that man had to leave the city in ten days; if there were not six thousand, he was not banished. Not only the Athenians used to hold ostracisms, but also the Argives and Milesians and Megarians. Nearly all the most accomplished men were ostracised, Aristeides, Kimon, Themistokles, Thucydides (son of Melesias), and Alkibiades.

5.14 Examples of Individual Ostraka

Ostraka

i. Lang 134, no. 1065. An elegiac couplet. There are difficulties of interpretation (see Lang for full bibliography). The voter presumably regarded Xanthippos, Perikles' father, as 'accursed' due to his connection with the Alkmeonidai through his wife (see doc. 9.3; Table I); alternatively, he believed that all the leaders were accursed.

> This ostrakon says that Xanthippos, son of Ariphron,
> Does most wrong of the accursed leaders.

ii. Lang 36, no. 34: a more educated writer has helped out by adding 'son of Lysimachos' at the bottom; see Vanderpool (1970) 9, 16, figs 41–42.

’Αριστείδες	Aristeides	(correctly spelt)
[[Λυσι̣]]	son of Lysi.....	(left incomplete and crossed out)
[[’Αλοπεκεει]]	of Alopeke	(crossed out)
Λυσιμάχο	son of Lysimachos	(correctly spelt)

iii. Lang 138, no. 1097. See Vanderpool (1970) 9, fig. 21; Vanderpool identifies him as the son of Alkmeonides (see Lang 50–61, nos. 146–273), but Hippokrates son of Anaxileos is another possibility, who is known only from the ostraka (see Lang 61–62, nos. 274–282; cf. 62–64, nos. 283–306). Both were candidates for ostrakophoriai in the 480s. If Hippokrates is the son of Alkmeonides, it is possible that this Alkmeonides was the head of the Alkmeonid family who made the dedication at the sanctuary of Apollo Ptoios in the mid-sixth century when in exile after Peisistratos' return (see doc. 4.15). This, however, would date Hippokrates to an earlier generation than any other candidate for ostracism in the 480s (Lang 50).

> Vengeance on Hippokrates!

iv. Several of the Kerameikos ostraka have 'Kallias the Mede': Vanderpool (1970) 21; Thomsen (1972) 93, 97; cf. Lang 65–66, nos. 313–14. This Kallias is thought to be the 'friend of the tyrants' ostracised in 486/5 (doc. 5.9).

> Kallias the Mede

v. Lang 33, no. 14. Only five ostraka with the name of Alkibiades the Younger, son of Kleinias, are attested in the agora (Lang 33); this sherd was found adjoined to another identical sherd (no. 13) which suggests that neither was ever used.

> Alkibiades
> son of Kleinias

vi. Lang 98, no. 651. From the foot of a black-glazed skyphos, and hence presumably the ostrakon of one of the more well-to-do citizens. Perikles was never ostracised, though he must on a number of occasions have been a candidate at ostrakophoriai. This ostrakon may date to the ostrakophoria that he is said to have brought about to get rid of his rival Thucydides son of Melesias in 444/3 (Plut. *Per.* 14.3; doc. 8.23).

Perikles
son of Xanthippos

vii. Lang 116, no. 841. 386 ostraka bearing Themistokles' name have been found in the agora and 1893 elsewhere. While he was actually ostracised in the late 470s, the large numbers of ostraka bearing his name found in the agora, and perhaps those from the Kerameikos, may possibly come from the ostrakophoriai of the 480s. This, the rim and neck of a pithos, was the largest ostrakon found in the agora, weighing 522.5 grams.

For Themistokles
son of Neokles
of Phrearrioi

viii. Lang 94, no. 630. From the wall of a coarse unglazed pot; the fact that Megakles' patronymic is inscribed as Hippokartous rather than Hippokratous may imply an uneducated writer. Megakles, according to the *Ath. Pol.* 22.5 (doc. 5.9), was the second friend of the tyrants to be ostracised and his ostrakophoria took place in 486. According to Lys. XIV.39 he was ostracised twice. 4647 of his ostraka were found in the great Kerameikos deposit, suggesting that sherds from this ostrakophoria were deposited there. As the comments on these sherds refer to his morals (his adultery, luxury, stable of horses and pursuit of wealth) rather than his political sympathies as a friend of the tyrants (Lang 93; Bicknell (1975) 174), this may suggest that they come from a later ostrakophoria, though the fact that accompanying sherds bear the name of Themistokles and Kimon do not necessarily imply that this was the case (Lang 94).

[Me]gak[les]
[son of Hip]pokar[tes]

ix. Lang 89, no. 592. From a roof tile with black glaze, incised on the glazed side. Six ostraka with Kimon's name have been found in the agora, and 558 elsewhere. Kimon was probably ostracised in 461 (doc. 8.10); however, since several of the ostraka from the great Kerameikos deposit bearing Kimon's name were found in conjunction with ostraka inscribed with the names of Megakles and Themistokles, he may have been a candidate for ostracism as early as 486 when Megakles was ostracised (Lang 89).

Kimon
son of Miltiades

x. Lang 32, no. 10. From the knob of a large black-glazed lid. The elder Alkibiades, who had the same name, patronymic and demotic as his grandson Alkibiades the younger (Alkibiades son of Kleinias of Skambonidai), was ostracised, possibly in 460, the year after Kimon, and perhaps for the same reason, 'post-Ithome anti-Spartan feeling' (Lang 32). According to Lys. XIV.39 like Megakles he was ostracised twice.

[Alkibi]ades son of K[leinias]
[of Skamb]o<n>i<d>ai

xi. Lang 133, no. 1051. From a tile with a dull black glaze on its upper surface, incised through the glaze. Thucydides, son of Melesias was ostracised in 443, after setting himself up as a champion of the aristocracy and political rival to Perikles (see doc. 8.23).

For [Thucy]dides
[son of Mele]sias

xii. Lang 64, no. 308. From the wall of a large plain pot. This is one of the few painted ostraka; the final letters are no longer visible because the paint has faded. The ostrakophoria in which Alkibiades and Nikias reputedly plotted the removal of Hyperbolos is usually dated to 418/7, but 416 or 415 are also possible (cf. doc. 5.11).

Hyperbolos
son of Antiphanes

5.15 Citizenship Extended to Foreigners and Slaves

Aristotle *Politics* 1275b 34–38

Kleisthenes gave Athenian citizenship to many metics 'both foreigners and slaves'. The *Ath. Pol.* 13.5 (doc. 4.2) notes that after the tyranny many not of pure Athenian descent, who had supported Peisistratos and his sons, were disenfranchised. Kleisthenes gained their support by granting them citizenship. The slaves referred to by Aristotle are presumably manumitted slaves or their descendants; manumitted slaves received the status of metics. The foreigners would have been metics who came to Attica of their own free will. Bicknell (1969) 34–37 suggests that Kleisthenes enfranchised Peisistratos' foreign mercenaries, but see Lavelle (1992) 78–97. Oliver (1960) 503–07 (cf. Grace (1974) 353–68) questioned the traditional interpretation and argued that Kleisthenes enrolled foreigners and slaves 'in a classification as metics'; but see Kagan (1963) 41–46; Whitehead (1977) 143–47.

But perhaps there is even more of a difficulty here, regarding those who have obtained a share in the citizenship because change has taken place, for example Kleisthenes' actions at Athens after the expulsion of the tyrants; for he enrolled into the tribes a large number of metics, both foreigners and slaves. The doubt in respect of them is not who became citizens, but whether they are so unjustly or justly.

5.16 Kleisthenes Strengthens the Democracy

Aristotle *Politics* 1319b 19–27

Aristotle considers as a characteristic of extreme democracy the policy of including as many new citizens as possible in the citizen body, whether illegitimate or half-citizen, and he saw as significant the breaking down of private religious rites. Kleisthenes in the case of the Marathonian tetrapolis, which had its own joint religious activities, did not put an end to these (as *Ath. Pol.* 21.6 notes, he did not interfere with religious activities) but he did ensure that the tetrapolis did not function as a political unit. The Marathonian tetrapolis, made up of the four towns of Marathon, Oinoe, Trikorynthos and Probalinthos, sent religious embassies to Delphi and Delos, as distinct from those sent by the Athenian state, from the earliest times to the first century BC. It was therefore always a unit with a distinct religious organization, and Marathon certainly had Peisistratid associations. Kleisthenes broke up this unit: the deme of Probalinthos, which provided five bouleutai, and was thus reasonably populous, was detached from the other three and placed in a different coastal trittys; Rhamnous was joined to the other three to form a coastal trittys.

The four centres of the tetrapolis were therefore now split into two different tribes (Marathon, Oinoe, Trikorynthos in the tribe Aiantis (IX), and Probalinthos in the tribe Pandionis (III)). While these four demes continued their cultic activities as a unit, the important Probalinthos deme now had different political affiliations from the other three demes with regard to all the activities carried out on a tribal basis: it elected bouleutai, fought, and elected strategoi for a different tribe. Special effort was taken to detach Probalinthos, for it is an example of a deme detached from its trittys: it belongs to the coastal trittys of Pandionis, but the coastal trittys of the tribe Aigeis intervenes. Brauron, a Peisistratid centre, is in this Aigeis trittys, so Probalinthos, with its Marathonian Peisistratid connection, was deliberately not attached to this trittys, but was put with the Pandionis coastal trittys; cf. Traill (1986) 129, suggesting that Probalinthos belonged to the city rather than the coastal trittys of Pandionis (but the implications are similar). The Tetrakomoi provides a similar example: the four demes involved, Peiraieus, Phaleron, Xypete and Thymaitadai, were split into three different trittyes and hence tribes: Peiraieus and Thymaitadai to the tribe Hippothontis (VIII); Phaleron to Aiantis (IX); Xypete to Kekropis (VII). See Lewis (1963) 30–34; cf. Eliot (1968) 11; Ostwald (1969) 154; Thompson (1971) 77; Kearns (1985) 203; Rhodes (1986) 135; Whitehead (1986) 185). For religious activities in the demes, see Mikalson (1977) 424–35; Whitehead 176–222; Parker (1987) 137–47; docs. 5.18, 20, 10.20; cf. Lewis (1963) 35–36.

And there are also further practices like these which are useful with regard to this kind of democracy, which Kleisthenes employed in Athens when he wished to strengthen the democracy, like those who established democratic rule at Cyrene. For other tribes and phratries should be created, more than before, and private religious rites should be channelled into a few public ones, and everything should be contrived so that everyone mixes in with each other and former intimacies are dissolved.

DEMES

Attica was divided into thirty trittyes under Kleisthenes' reforms. There were ten city trittyes, ten inland trittyes, and ten coastal trittyes. Each trittys was made up of one or more demes. A deme was generally one village or town, and its surrounding territory. Membership of a deme was hereditary. An Athenian who moved to another deme retained membership in his original deme, and all Athenians remained registered in the deme in which their ancestor in the time of Kleisthenes had been enrolled. Many of the 'city' demes were not actually within the city-walls, but in its general vicinity. There were at least five demes within the walls: Koile, Kollytos, Kydathenaion, Melite and Skambonidai, which were presumably organized on quarters of the city. For an example of the arrangement of demes and trittyes within one particular tribe, see Map IV. For demes and trittyes, see especially Eliot (1962) 3–5; Lewis (1963) 26–30; Osborne (1985) 64–92; Whitehead (1986) *passim* provides the most detailed account. Traill (1975) 35–55, (1986) 125–40 lists known demes and evidence for their location.

The length of time required for Kleisthenes to organize the demes and trittyes into units is uncertain. Scholars agree that he would have carried out his reforms as soon as possible; Eliot (1962) 146–47 has argued that the organization would have taken several years, advocating the year 501/0, as this was the year in which the boule first took the oath (*Ath. Pol.* 22.2; doc. 5.8). However, the oath could easily date to several years after the introduction of the new boule. Kleisthenes came to prominence by promising the people power: to maintain this support, at least some, and probably the majority of his reforms, had to be carried out reasonably quickly. Thompson (1971) 72–79 considers that the demes were not rigidly defined on a territorial basis, and that a registration of demesmen simply took place in their home village. This meant that Kleisthenes did not have to establish the physical boundaries of demes and what was to constitute a particular deme will have been easy to determine (Andrewes (1977) 244).

The placing of demes into trittyes, however, was obviously more complex. A trittys was either a city, inland, or coastal collection of demes, but the demes making up a trittys were not necessarily contiguous. City demes as well could be non-contiguous with the other demes in a city trittys, as seems to have been the case with the city demes of Kollytos, Kolonos and Ankyle of the tribe Aigeis (II) (Lewis (1963) 27–28; Map IV). The boundaries of demes within the city itself, however, probably needed to be more accurately defined than the other demes, as population areas even in c. 508/7 presumably overlapped and boundaries were probably provided by roads, rivers and the like (Young (1951) 141–43; Thompson (1971) 75; Langdon (1985) 11–13; cf. Andrewes 244). There were occasionally 'divided' demes, two separate demes of the same name, one 'Upper' and one 'Lower', ie Upper Lamptrai and Lower Lamptrai; see Traill (1975) 6, 123–28; Whitehead 21 with n.70; note also the example of Upper and Lower Ankyle of Aigeis (II), Map IV.

The number of demes is now set at 140 (Acharnai as a split deme means that one extra deme is to be added to the previous canon of 139: Traill (1986) 123, 133–34, cf. (1982) 169). For *IG* II^2 2362, the fragment of the 'great deme list', see esp. Traill (1986) 52–78. Traill (1986) has a list of the demes and their tribes at 125–40; cf. Traill (1975) 73–103, esp. 76, with a list of the demes and their tribes at 109–12; cf. Whitehead 20–21, 369–73). The number of demes per trittys varied; the inland trittys of the tribe Aiantis (IX), for example, had only one deme, Aphidna (Whitehead 22; Traill (1986) 138), providing a quota of 16 bouleutai. The number of demes per tribe also varied: from six demes in the tribe Aiantis (IX), to twenty-one demes in the tribe Aigeis (II) (see Map IV). Clearly, the system was complex, as the ten tribes had to be roughly equal in population to ensure equal representation on the boule. The most important duty of the demes was the registration of its members, the demotai (see Whitehead 97–109), especially after Perikles' citizenship law of 451/0; the list of demotai in each deme constituted a record of Athenian citizens. The procedure for enrolment as a citizen in the fourth century is described by *Ath. Pol.* 42.1–2 (doc. 10.20), and it seems reasonable that this procedure or a similar one was inaugurated by Kleisthenes (*pace* Patterson (1981) 27).

It has been argued that Kleisthenes devised a system of demes, trittyes and tribes to give his family, the Alkmeonidai, prominence: Lewis (1963) 22–40; Forrest (1966) 199–200; Rocchi (1972) 13–44; Rhodes 254; Stanton (1984) 7–41; Sealey (1987) 122, cf. (1960) 173, but the evidence adduced for this is not sufficiently convincing, see Sinclair (1988) 4; Starr (1990) 15; Stockton (1990) 26, 60. Ober (1989) 68–75 does not consider the theory. Basically, this theory suggests that the Alkmeonidai were able to dominate three tribes; their strongholds south of the city were assigned to three tribes and were combined (in the same three tribes) with coastal areas in which they had influence (Forrest suggested four). Another theory, that the purpose of the ten new phylai was military in nature, is briefly criticized by Stanton (1984) 3–7. Whitehead 23n.77 dismisses Bicknell's (1972) 31–45 idea that bouleutic quotas in the demes of Kleisthenes' opponents were arranged to under-represent them. The main purpose of the system of demes and trittyes was to undermine regional tendencies.

5.17 Trittys Markers

The evidence for the names of trittyes (18 of the 30 names are known and several other possible identifications have been made) comes largely from fifteen trittys markers (Traill (1986) 93–113). The trittys markers are found in Athens and the Peiraieus, and they do not actually mark boundaries between trittyes; rather, they are 'marshalling stations for the army and navy' (Traill (1986) 112–13, cf. (1982) 165n.11; Dem. XIV.23;

cf. *Agora* XIX, p.15). Citizens would collect at the appropriate marker when called up for military service.

It has been argued that the Athenians sat in the ekklesia by tribes, or even by trittyes and most recently Stanton & Bicknell (1987) 51–92, Bicknell (1989) 83–100 argue (largely on the basis of one of the trittys markers, *IG* I^2 884 = Traill (1986) 96, no. 1 (*IG* I^3 1120): 'Trittys Lakiadai') that the Athenians in the ekklesia were seated according to trittyes (see also Siewert (1982) 10–13). Hansen (1988) 51–58, esp. 57–58, (1989) 163–65, (1991) 137–38, cf. *Agora* XIX, p.16, rightly argues against this interpretation. Seating arrangements on the Pnyx were not by tribe or trittyes, but were random, except that from 346/5 one tribe sat together in the front, nearest the bema (platform). *IG* I^2 884 (*IG* I^3 1120), a stele of Pentelic marble, is unlikely to have moved far as it is still held in place with lead in a block of red conglomerate rock, as found on or near the Pnyx. This means that the Pnyx area will have been one marshalling point for the forces. However, the smaller trittys markers may have been moved from their original location and so their find spots do not necessarily represent an actual marshalling point. In addition to the trittys markers, there were also throughout the Attic countryside rock cut inscriptions simply stating OPOC (with lunate sigma), 'horos'; these are known as the rupestral deme horoi. They served to mark the borders of demes, and were generally inscribed on 'horizontal expanses of natural rock'; see Traill (1986) 116–22.

The Pnyx had three major architectural phases, Pnyx I–III; Pnyx II involved extensive modelling at the end of the fifth century (Hansen (1982) 241–49, (1987) 12–14; see diagrams at Hansen (1991) 323–24). For the sanctuary of Zeus Hypsistos which was in use from the first to third centuries AD on the Pnyx, and is evidenced by the niches to be seen near the bema, see Forsén (1993) 507–21. Not all trittys markers are as well preserved as the two examples that follow.

i. A Trittys Marker (Paianieis — Myrrhinousioi)

IG I^2 898 (*IG* I^3 1127)

Re-edited by Traill (1986) 102, no. 12 Mid-fifth century; found in the Peiraieus. Myrrhinousioi is the coastal trittys and Paianieis the inland trittys of Pandionis (III).

Here the tri-
ttys Pai-
anieis en-
ds, and the trit-
[tys] My-
rrhinousi-
oi beg-
ins.

ii. A Tribe and Trittys Marker

IG I^2 900 (*IG* I^3 1131)

Re-edited by Traill (1986) 103, no. 13. Mid-fifth century; found in the Peiraieus. Tetrapoleis was the coastal trittys of Aiantis (IX); Cholargeis was the city trittys of Akamantis (V).

Here the tribe
Aiantis ends,
and the trittys T-
etrapoleis, and the tribe Akamantis beg-
ins, and the trittys
Cholargeis.

5.18 Catalogue of the Prytaneis of Tribe Aigeis (II)

Agora XV.38 (*IG* II^2 1749) lines 1–77

A deme provided members to the boule according to the population of that deme. This means that there were quotas for the deme, which are called bouleutic quotas, known from the fourth century (and onwards) and which are assumed to have been set by Kleisthenes (Whitehead (1986) 21); each deme was responsible for sending a certain number of men as its share of the fifty for its tribe to the boule. The bouleutic and prytany lists provide evidence for how many members a particular deme sent to the boule. There are several fragmentary prytany lists, and some in an extant state of preservation, particularly *Agora* XV.38 (*IG* II^2 1749) and *Agora* XV.44 (*IG* II^2 1750), which give the names of the fifty members, according to their deme, sent by a particular tribe to the boule; when this group of fifty held office for one-tenth of the year, they 'held the prytany'.

In the prytany list of Aigeis (II) below, there are four names under the heading of the deme Gargettos, indicating that this deme elected four members to the boule in 341/0 BC. The bouleutic quotas for the demes have been calculated; see Whitehead 369–73. The most detailed information is provided by Traill (1975), 'Tables of Representation' (end papers), and Traill (1986) 125–40, listing as far as the evidence permits the numbers each deme sent to the boule. Two entries in the table for the tribe Erechtheis (I), for example, are two city demes, Upper Agryle and Lower Agryle (an example of a 'divided' deme), whose quotas were, respectively, two and three members (bouleutai) for the boule. Larger demes provided a greater number of bouleutai: the inland part of the deme Acharnai, as opposed to the city part (for this as a split deme, previously assumed to be one deme, see Traill (1986) 133–34), provided a quota of 15 or 16 bouleutai of the 50 bouleutai from its tribe (for Acharnai, note Whitehead 23, 397–400). The smallest demes might share a bouleutic seat with another deme, taking it in yearly turns to provide the member for the seat: Traill (1975) 14, 19, 58, cf. (1986) 126; Whitehead 23. This system meant that there was equal representation throughout Attica on the boule. For the quotas for each deme in this inscription, see Traill (1975) end papers, (1986) 126–28; Siewert (1982) 20–21; Whitehead 369–70.

The quotas of the demes in Aigeis (II) are given here (the names of the 3 trittyes of Aigeis (II) are doubtful and given here in italics, as in Traill (1986) 110): City trittys (*Kollyteis*): demes: Kollytos, Kolonos, Bate, Upper and Lower Ankyle, Erikeia, Hestiaia, Otryne, Ikarion, Plotheia; Inland trittys (*Gargettioi*): demes: Gargettos, Erchia, Philaidai, Ionidai, Kydantidai; Coastal trittys (*Halaieis*): demes: Halai Araphenides, Teithras, Phegaia, Araphen, Myrrhinoutta, Diomeia; note that there are two pairs of brothers serving as prytaneis. For these demes, see Map IV: note that the location of Otryne, one of the city demes, is unknown.

The prytaneis of Aigeis, who were crowned by the boule and the people in the archon[ship] of Nikomachos (341/0) because of their virtue and justice, dedicated (this).

Column 1:

Erchia
Tharrias son of Tharrias
Kydias son of Lysikrates
Chaireas son of Paramythos
[Ph]ylarchos son of Paramythos
Xenokl[e]s son of Kallias
Polykleid[e]s son of Kallistratos
Ga[rg]ettos
Diodoros son of Philokles
Meixias son of Hegesias
Smikrias son of Philokedes
Ar[e]sias son of Pausias
Philaidai
Dionysios son of Hephaistion
Euthykles son of Ameinias
Euthydikos son of Ameinias
[K]ydantidai
Pythion son of Aischronides
Demostratos son of [D]emost[r]atos
Ionidai
Melieus son of Il[i]oneus

Column 2:

Ikarion
Timokritos son of Timokrates
Aristophanes son of Eukleides
Archenautes son of Archenautes
Eraton son of Eration
[A]rignotos son of Babyrias
Hestiaia
Poseidippos son of Kallikrates
Bate
Lysistratos son of Polyeuktos
From Kolonos
Kalliphanes son of Kallikles
Theages
Kollytos
Chairephon son of Thrason
Alexis son of Sosiades
Pherekrates son of Philokrates
Plotheia
Chairias son of Chairias
Otryne
Philinos son of Theodoros
Erikeia
Epameinon son of Epainetos

Column 3:

Halai
Lysimachos son of Lysipolis
Eubios son of Autosthenes
Apollodoros son of Archias
Eunostides son of Theophantos
Kallimedes son of Archemachos
Teithras
Demosthenes son of Demopho[n]
Demophilos son of Demokles
Ka[l]listratos
Prokleides son of Proxenides
Phegaia
Akeratos son of Archedemos
Theomnestos
Theodoros son of Theognis
Araphen
Elpinos son of Sosigenes
Kallimachos son of Mnesitheios
From Myrrinoutta
Theophilos
From Ankyle
Eubios son of Eubiotos
Diomeia
Dorotheos son of Theodoros
From Ankyle
Melesippos son of Melesias

(71) [Th]arrias of Erchia proposed the motion: that the tribesmen should decree, that since Poseidippos of Hestiaia, the treasurer (tamias) of (75) [th]e tribe, had performed his duties for t[he] tribesmen well [a]n[d just]ly and conducted on behalf of the prytane[is] all the sacrifices which had to be made, [h]e should be comm[ended] fo[r] his v[irtu]e [and ju]stice regarding the prytaneis [and be cr]ow[ne]d with a [cr]o[w]n of ol[ive].

5.19 The Finances of the Deme Plotheia, Tribe Aigeis (II), c. 420

IG I³ 258 (*IG* I² 1172)

For this inscription, see Finley (1952) 45, 96–97; Whitehead (1986) esp. 165–69. The deme Plotheia, of the city trittys of Aigeis (II) had a bouleutic quota of one, as doc. 5.18 indicates, and thus was one of the smallest demes. This is a decree of the deme assembly of the Plotheians. Lines 2–10 list the 'kephalaia': it is reasonable to translate this as 'capital', and to take the next eight sums as amounts of capital which are earmarked for particular purposes, with the ninth representing income from leases. The capital itself is not to be spent, but rather the interest on each of the sums listed is to be utilized for the purpose decreed: the demarch and two treasurers have funds, and money is put aside for five festivals (the Herakleion, Aphrodisia, Anakia, Apollonia, Pandia) and an 'immunity' fund (see below). In lines 30-31 the Plotheians make provision for participating in sacrifices with the Athenians as a whole and with the Epakreans. Traill (1986) 105–06 suggests that Epakreis was the inland trittys of Hippothontis (VIII), though it has generally been considered the inland trittys of Aigeis (II), because of its association with Plotheia in this decree; see Eliot (1962) 148; cf. *IG* I^2 901 (re-edited by Traill (1986) 103–04, no. 14; for *IG* I^2 899, see Eliot 148n.14). In either case Plotheia and Epakreis were situated in the region north of Mount Pentelikon and the decree suggests a regional association between the Plotheians and Epakreans.

The view that these sums are the interest rather than the capital can be safely set aside: a small deme like Plotheia is not likely to have spent nearly four talents on festivals a year, and a larger deme, Rhamnous, had capital of no more than ten talents in the 440s (Whitehead 167). The deme was careful with its resources, and financial officials are to be elected by the demesmen, demotai, to look after the capital which belongs to the deme. A special fund, the 'immunity', for which 5,000 drachmas are listed in line 7, is to be used for the sacrifices, hiera, and the officials are to make payments on behalf of the demesmen whenever it would otherwise have been necessary for the demesmen (as they presumably did before the decree was passed) to have met the expenses out of their own pockets. For all public sacrifices in which the Plotheians participate, the financial officials are to provide sweet wine, and up to 'half a chous' of wine for other sacrifices.

[Cap]ital
For the [de]march 1,000 drachmas
For the two [tre]asurers for the hiera throughout the year 5,000 drachmas
[F]or the Herakleion 7,000 drachmas
[F]or the Aphrodisia 1,200 drachmas
[F]or the Anakia 1,200 drachmas
[F]or the immunity 5,000 drachmas
[F]or the Apollonia 1,100 drachmas
[F]or the Pandia 600 drachmas
[Of l]eases 134 drachmas and 2 and a half obols

[It was r]esolved by the Plotheians: Aristotimos [proposed the mot]ion; that the officials ca[pab]le of handling the money are to be elected by lot [for each o]ffice, and these are [to look a]fter the money for the Plotheians; concerning whatever i[s d]ecreed they are to as[si]gn loan or interest in accordance with the decree loanin[g an]d exacting, and as much as is lent each y[ea]r they are to lend to wh[omev]er gives most interest, and who [persu]ades the official[s] who lend the money either [by sec]urity or by giving sureties. And from [both] the interest [a]nd the leases, instead of purchases f[rom the ca]pital or what c[om]es in from in[c]ome, they are to sacrifice the hiera at the [c]ommon festivals for the Plothe[ians] and for the Athenians on behalf of the community of the Pl[otheia]ns and for the quad[renn]ial festivals. And for the other sacrifices, wherever it is neces[sary] for all the [P]lotheians to pay mone[y for the s]acrifices, either to the Plotheians, or the Epakrean[s, or the A]thenians, the offi[cials, w]ho control the money for th[e 'immu]nity', are to pay it from the common fund on behalf of the demesmen; [and f]or all the public sacrifices, in which the Plotheians f[ea]st, (35) they are to provide swee[t] wine [from the] common fund, and for the other sacrifices u[p to half a chous for e]ach of those Plothei[ans] present [.....]

5.20 Law of the Deme Skambonidai, Tribe Leontis (IV), c. 460

IG I^3 244 (*IG* I^2 188)

LSCG 10. This is one of the earliest extant deme laws. The demes had their own official, the demarch (*Ath. Pol.* 21.5) and also their own assemblies, which passed decrees organizing local affairs (ie: *IG* I^3 242–45, 248, 250–51, 253–54, 256, 258 (doc. 5.19); *IG* II^2 1173–1221; these and others are listed by Traill (1975) 74–75n.10; Whitehead (1986) 374–93). The demarch was the most important official of the deme, and was introduced as part of the Kleisthenic reforms. Whitehead 121–139, esp. 122, identifies three main duties of the demarch: to convene the deme assembly, organize its proceedings (such as oath-taking and voting) and carry out its decisions. In this decree, the religious duties of the demarch, and his privileges, are indicated. The deme assembly will normally have met in its deme (for an explanation of the unusual case in Dem. LVII of the deme Halimous meeting in the city, see Whitehead 87–90). The deme Skambonidai had a bouleutic quota of three; for this inscription, see Whitehead 81, 83, 205 (the participation of metics in this sacrifice), 116–17, 142 (the euthynos conducts the euthynai (examinations) of deme officials), 128 (the perquisites of the demarch), 143–44 (deme tamiai, treasurers). B gives the oath sworn by some or all of the deme officials. The deme Skambonidai participated in the Synoikia, celebrating the political synoecism of Attica by Theseus: doc. 10.32; Mikalson (1975) 29–31, (1977) 430; Parke (1977) 31–32; Whitehead 179; in *LSCG Suppl.* 10A (dated to 403–399), the festival was apparently celebrated by the four pre-Kleisthenic tribes; see also Whitehead 43n.19, 87n.6; cf. Osborne (1985) 75, 234n.27. The sacred calendars of the demes Teithras, Eleusis, Marathon, Thorikos, and Erchia are examined by Whitehead 185–208; cf. Mikalson (1977) 424–32; Parker (1987) 144–47.

A

[....] th[e] end [....] an[d] allot the meat until the s[un (5) (sets). And if] not [....] s[e(l)l i]n the a[g]ora (10) and [.... let out] f[o]r con[tract] these [.... ex]cept the [....] the skin belongs to the dema[rch ....] (15) offer whatever sacrifice it is necessary to perform(?) and allot at the Dipolieia and Panathenaia (20) in the agora of Skambonidai as much as [....] a half-chous [....]

B

[.] to be proclaimed and sworn: I will als[o] keep safe (5) the common funds of Skambonidai and I will render the necessary to the euthynos (10) and I swear these things by the three gods (15) that they are not to render (any of) th[e] common funds to (20) the euthyno[s be]fore ....

C

[....] the de[march a]nd the hi[eropoi]oi [are to offer] to Leo[s a p]erfect (5) victim; allot[ment ... o]bols to e[ach] of the men of Skambonid[ai and] the metic[s are to receive a] share; in the agor[a of Sk]ambonida[i (10) ....] offer a [perfect victim] and allot [.... (15)] at the Synoi[kia] i[n] the city a per[fect victim a]nd se[ll t]he meat raw at the Epize[phyri]a (20) in the temple of Pythia[n (Apollo); .... a]nd [s]ell the meat raw [....] in the same w[ay?].

6

Sparta

Athens and Sparta are generally seen as the two main city states of ancient Greece. Their social and political organization, however, differed markedly. Sparta's political system consisted of two kings (there were two branches of the royal family, the Agiad and the Eurypontid, with a king from each branch; the Agiad was the senior branch), a council of elders known as the gerousia, which consisted of twenty-eight members and the two kings, a board of five ephors, and the Spartiates, full Spartan citizens, the assembly of which was known as the ekklesia. Sparta lies in the south-east Peloponnese, on the Eurotas river, with the Taygetos mountain range to the west separating it from Messenia. There were four villages making up Sparta, or Lakedaimon: Pitana, Mesoa, Limnai and Kynosoura; Amyklai, to the south, was incorporated at an early stage into Spartan territory (cf. doc. 10.1). The immediate territory was known as Lakonia. The Spartiates, Spartan citizens, were known as homoioi 'equals', but within Lakonia were two other main groups, the perioikoi and the helots who greatly outnumbered the Spartiates.

Central to Spartan history was the figure of Lykourgos. He was the lawgiver who supposedly established both the 'Great Rhetra' and the military system which was the basis of Spartan power. Lykourgos was said to have modelled the Spartan constitution on that of Crete (doc. 6.2); similarities between the two, however, would have been due to the fact that both were Dorian societies. While the Spartans saw him as a historical figure, it is more than possible that he was in fact a legendary creation, for while Tyrtaeus refers to the constitution which Delphi recognised, indicating that the reforms of Lykourgos were in existence when Tyrtaeus was writing during the Second Messenian War, he fails to mention Lykourgos (docs. 6.4–9). Nevertheless, it is convenient to speak of the reforms of Lykourgos, and it is now usual to date the so-called Lykourgan reforms to shortly after the Second Messenian War.

As early as the late eighth century BC Sparta had begun a series of wars to extend its territory; the First Messenian War is usually dated to 740–720 BC. The Messenians later revolted in what is termed the Second Messenian War, which took place about the middle of the seventh century and many scholars place the development of Sparta's military system to the aftermath of this war. The system adopted by the Spartans meant that they were always in a state of military preparedness, which makes sense only if there were some immediate and pressing threat. In taking Messenia they had also acquired a subject population which required constant vigilance. The helots, in fact, become the 'millstone' around the Spartans' neck, especially when the Spartans were away on campaign, and the helots' tendency to revolt was a factor which had to be considered in all Spartan foreign policy. In addition to adopting a military way of life to keep the helots under control, the Spartans also buttressed their control over the Messenians by a system of alliances, in which their allies had to come to their assistance if the helots revolted; in this way many Peloponnesian states came within Sparta's sphere of influence by the end of the sixth century. So, beginning with wars in the eighth century, Sparta had by the end of the sixth century established leadership over most of the Peloponnese.

Plutarch (relying on Aristotle) considers the 'Great Rhetra' as the work of Lykourgos, which subsequently had a 'rider' attached to it by the kings Polydoros and Theopompos. It is possible, however, that the 'rider' was in fact an original part of the Great Rhetra. Plutarch, who records the 'Great Rhetra', provides some explanatory notes about it and the difficulties of interpretation suggest that this probably does reflect an authentic decree (doc. 6.3). The Spartan assembly, like the Athenian ekklesia, had the final say about the proposals brought before it, but according to the 'Great Rhetra' only the 'elders and kings' could bring these proposals: the gerousia, in preparing the agenda, had a 'probouleutic' role. But the so-called rider to the Great Rhetra (doc. 6.4) provided that the assembly should not in any way alter the proposals but were to discuss those before them and vote on them; altered proposals were invalid. This meant that what the assembly was able to vote on was restricted. The rider, like the rhetra itself, indicates that the 'people' (damos) had 'sovereign authority' in the state, as they voted and made decisions: this is compatible with a hoplite system, in which the hoplites fought and had political power, and consequently the rhetra must date to a period when the military was organized along hoplite lines. The Spartan system had the training of the hoplite soldier as its focus, and the adoption of hoplite tactics and armour took place in the Greek world from c. 750–650 (cf. doc. 6.8). This is another argument for the reforms of the Spartan state taking place in the mid-seventh century, and not several centuries earlier, when hoplite warfare did not yet exist.

The Spartans evolved a military system which set them apart from the rest of the Greeks, not so much because of its general aim but because of its single-minded pursuit of military principles and practices. From early childhood they trained in the arts of war; this system was the agoge (doc. 6.34), while the system of public messes (docs. 6.30–31), where they ate together, was instituted to ensure that there would be conformity and uniformity of lifestyle amongst the Spartiates. The agoge was intended to create professional soldiers and this system worked well for about two centuries, and Sparta was strong enough to defeat Athens in 404 and bring about the end of its empire. But by the end of the fifth century there were signs that the system was breaking down and this was particularly reflected in the influx of wealth and the decreasing number of Spartiates.

LYKOURGOS 'THE LAW-GIVER'

Plut. *Lyk.* 1 records the opinions of ancient writers: that Lykourgos was contemporary with the establishment of the Olympic festival in 776 or earlier, that there were in fact two reformers called Lykourgos at different times, or that he was contemporary with the first kings. Herodotos (doc. 6.2) has him as the guardian of Leobotas which gives an approximately ninth-century date; cf. Thuc. I.18.1 (doc. 2.41). The military system, ascribed to Lykourgos, makes best historical sense in the aftermath of the Second Messenian War, dating to about the mid-seventh century, after which the Spartans had a subject population, the helots, to keep under control; for this date, see Wade-Gery (1958) 59, 66–69; Toynbee (1969) 221–26, 413–16; de Ste. Croix (1972) 91n.4; cf. Andrewes (1956) 73; Hooker (1988) 344; Hornblower (1991) 51–54; *contra*, opting for earlier dates, Forrest (1963) 157–79, (1980) 55–58; Hammond (1950) 62–64; Chrimes (1949) 305–47; while Finley (1975) 161–62 prefers c. 600 and Parker (1991) 25–47 c. 635/625–610/600. See also, for the date and hoplite armour and techniques, Snodgrass (1964) esp. 197–99, (1965) 110–22; Cartledge (1977) 11–27; and, more general accounts, Snodgrass (1967) 48–88; Ducrey (1986) 47–78; cf. Toynbee (1969) 250–60.

6.1 Lykourgos: Man or Myth?

Plutarch *Lykourgos* 1.1

1.1 In general nothing can be said concerning Lykourgos the law-giver that is not disputed, since there are different versions of his birth, travels abroad, death and above all his work on the laws and constitution, and least of all is there agreement about the times in which the man lived.

6.2 Lykourgos Reforms the Spartan Constitution

Herodotos I.65.2–66.1

For the oracle, see Parke & Wormell (1956) I.85–87, II.14 Response 29; Fontenrose (1978) 270, Response Q7 (not genuine). According to Xenophon (*Const. Spart.* 8.5) Lykourgos took his laws to Delphi, where they were approved by Apollo; cf. Plut. *Lyk.* 5.4, and 29.4–8 for the tradition of Lykourgos' second visit to Delphi, followed by his suicide. **I.65.4**: According to Plut. *Lyk.* 3.6 and Arist. *Pol.* 1271b 25–26, Lykourgos' ward was Charillos (also of the ninth century on traditional genealogies); for the modelling of the Spartan constitution on that of Crete, cf. Arist. *Pol.* 1271b 24–27; Plut. *Lyk.* 4.1–3. **I.65.5**: Herodotos is incorrect in attributing the ephorate to Lykourgos: this was a later addition, and the Great Rhetra does not mention it: see Cartledge (1979) 134.

I.65.2 The change to good government (eunomia) happened like this: Lykourgos, an esteemed Spartiate, went to Delphi to consult the oracle, and as he entered the shrine the Pythia immediately spoke as follows: **I.65.3**

'You have come, Lykourgos, to my rich temple
Dear to Zeus and all who have homes on Olympus.
I am in doubt whether to proclaim you a god or mortal;
But I hope that you are a god, Lykourgos.'

I.65.4 Some say that the Pythia in addition to this also revealed to him the Spartiates' constitution as it exists at the present time, but the Spartans themselves say that Lykourgos who was regent for Leobotas, his nephew, king of Sparta, brought the institutions from Crete. **I.65.5** For as soon as he became regent, he changed all the laws and made sure that these should not be transgressed. After this Lykourgos established military organization, the divisions (enomotiai), companies of thirty (triakades) and messes (syssitia), as well as the ephors and elders. **I.66.1** By these changes they became a well-ordered state, and they dedicated a temple to Lykourgos when he died and revere him greatly. Living in a fertile country and with a numerous population of men, they immediately shot up and flourished.

6.3 The Great Rhetra

Plutarch *Lykourgos* 6.1–9

There were originally three tribes, phylai, at Sparta (as was normal for Dorian states): Hylleis, Pamphyloi, and Dymanes (cf. Tyrtaeus F19.8). The obai, villages, have been identified by some scholars as the four villages of the 'polis' Sparta itself, plus nearby Amyklai. **6.2**: 'From season to season to apellaze' means to celebrate the festival of Apollo, the Apellai, and, according to Plutarch, to summon the assembly; these meetings were presumably once a month, but in the classical period were probably called as often as required (Forrest (1980) 47; cf. Jones (1967) 20–25; Staveley (1972) 73–76). **6.4**: Plutarch gives the places where meetings of the assembly would take place; the term 'apella' is used by some scholars in referring to the Spartan assembly, but this term was never actually used in the sources; Thucydides and Xenophon both use the word ekklesia (Thuc. I. 87.1, VI.88.10, esp. V.77.1, a quotation, in Doric dialect; Xen. *Hell.* III.2.23, IV.6.3, V.2.11); see Wade-Gery (1958) 38, 44; esp. de Ste. Croix (1972) 346–48. Plutarch continues by quoting the lines of Tyrtaeus (doc. 6.4, ll. 1–6). For the Great Rhetra, see Hammond (1950) 42–64; Andrewes (1956) 73–74; Oliva (1971) 71–102; Boring (1979) 20–23; Forrest (1980) 40–50; Parker (1991) 41; detailed discussions: den Boer (1954) 153–96; Wade-Gery (1958) 37–85; Butler (1962) 385–96; Toynbee (1969) 269–274; Parker (1993) 48–54, 59–60.

6.1 Lykourgos was so eager for this form of government (the elders) that he brought an oracle from Delphi about it, which they call a 'rhetra'. **6.2** It runs as follows: 'After dedicating a temple to Zeus Skyllanios and Athena Skyllania, forming tribes (phylai) and creating obai, and setting up a gerousia of thirty including the archagetai (founder-leaders), then from season to season apellaze between Babyka and Knakion so as to introduce and rescind (measures); †to the people should belong the agora† and the power.' **6.3** In this, 'forming phylai' and 'creating obai' refer to the division and allocation of the populace into groups, of which the former he named phylai, the latter obai. The kings are meant by archagetai, and to 'apellaze' is to hold an assembly, because he referred the origin and cause of his constitution to Pythian Apollo. **6.4** They now call Babyka .... and Knakion Oinous; and Aristotle says that Knakion is a river and Babyka a bridge .... **6.6** When the populace was assembled, Lykourgos allowed no one except the elders and the kings to put forward a proposal, but the people had the supreme authority to decide upon one which these laid before them. **6.7** Later on, however, when the people distorted and did violence to the motions by taking bits away and adding to them, the kings Polydoros and Theopompos added this to the rhetra: **6.8** 'If the people should choose a crooked ordinance (rhetra), the older-born and leaders are to set it aside,' that is they should not ratify it, but withdraw it entirely and dismiss the assembly, since they were altering and remodelling the proposal contrary to what was best. **6.9** And they persuaded the city that the god had commanded this addition, as Tyrtaeus perhaps recalls in these lines.

6.4 Apollo Proclaims the 'Rhetra'

Tyrtaeus 4

Lykourgos is not mentioned by Tyrtaeus, and Toynbee (1969) 276–83 argues that the 'Great Rhetra' was enacted in the mid-seventh century and that sometime between Tyrtaeus and Herodotos, the Spartans credited these reforms to a figure they called Lykourgos. Diod. VII.12.6 give 2 extra lines (following line 2 of this document: 'For thus the Lord of the Silver Bow, Far-shooting Apollo, / The Golden Haired spoke from his rich shrine').

They listened to Apollo and brought home from Delphi
The oracles of the god and his words of sure fulfilment:
The god-honoured kings shall begin the counsel,
For in their care is the lovely city of Sparta,
And the first-born old men; then the common men
Answering them with straightforward ordinances
Shall both speak what is good and do all things right,
Nor give this city any crooked counsel;
And victory and might shall attend the people.
For concerning this Apollo proclaimed thus to the city.

THE SPARTAN ETHOS

6.5 Eunomia: 'Good Order'

Tyrtaeus 2, lines 12–15

According to Strab. VIII.4.10 (362), this is part of an elegy entitled *Eunomia*. Tyrtaeus here clearly identifies himself as a Spartan, though according to later tradition like many other poets he was 'imported' to Sparta (see doc. 6.51).

For the son of Kronos himself, the husband of beautifully-crowned Hera,
Zeus, has given this city to the Herakleidai (descendants of Herakles),
With whom, leaving windy Erineos,
We arrived at this broad island of Pelops (the Peloponnese).

6.6 Victory over Messenia

Tyrtaeus 5

In the second half of the eighth century BC Sparta began a series of wars to extend its territory. The last Messenian victory in the Olympic games took place in 736; this, and the first Spartan victory in 716 at the Olympic games, as well as the approximate dates of Theopompos' reign in the eight century, gives a rough date for the First Messenian War, perhaps c. 740–20, or slightly later (see Parker (1991) 25–43 for the dating c. 690–670). Following this, Messenia was divided up amongst the Spartans. See Huxley (1962) 33–35; de Ste. Croix (1972) 89–90 with n.2; Jeffery (1976) 114–15; Hooker (1980) 99–101. The first two lines here are quoted by Paus. IV.6.5; lines 4–8 are given by Strab. VI.3.3 (279) in his account of the partheniai (see doc. 1.18).

.... To our king, Theopompos, friend of the gods,
Because of whom we took spacious Messene,
Messene good to plough, good to plant;
They fought for it for fully nineteen years
Unceasingly and always stout of heart
The spearmen fathers of our fathers;
And in the twentieth, leaving their rich fields,
The Messenians fled from the great mountains of Ithome.

6.7 An Exhortation to Fight for your Country

Tyrtaeus 10

The Second Messenian War broke out in the mid-seventh century, when either the Messenians revolted, or still unconquered Messenians decided to wage war on Sparta, perhaps as a result of the Argive victory at Hysiai (see doc. 2.2). Tyrtaeus, a contemporary of this conflict, exhorts the Spartans to victory, making clear the consequences of defeat; for the image of the 'archaic refugee', see Roisman (1984–86) 23–24; see also Adkins (1960) 73, (1972) 35–37. The Spartan army was organized in age-groups and the ephors proclaimed the age limit fixed for the campaign in question (Xen. *Const. Spart.* 11.2, *Hell.* VI.4.17; Anderson (1970) 243). For Tyrtaeus, see Hooker (1980) 71–73; Fitzhardinge (1980) 124–29; Hammond (1982) 351–52; for the Second Messenian War, see de Ste. Croix (1972) 89–90 with n.2; Jeffery (1976) 117–18; Forrest (1980) 69–71; Hammond (1982) 351–52.

To die after falling in the vanguard is a good thing
For a brave man doing battle on behalf of his native land.
But to leave his city and rich fields
To go begging is of all things the most painful,
Wandering with a dear mother and aged father
And with small children and a wedded wife.
Hateful shall he be amongst those, to whom he comes
Giving way to poverty and hateful penury,
And he shames his family, and belies his noble form,
And every dishonour and misery follow.
Thus there is no concern for a wanderer
Nor respect nor posterity hereafter.
Let us fight with courage for our country, and for our children
Let us die and never spare our lives.
Young men, remain beside each other and fight,
And do not begin shameful flight or fear,
But make your spirit great and brave in your heart,
And do not be faint-hearted when you fight with men;
Your elders, whose knees are no longer nimble,

Do not flee and leave them, those who are old.
For this is shameful, that fallen in the vanguard
An older man should lie before the youngsters,
His head already white and his beard grizzled,
Breathing out his brave spirit in the dust,
Holding his bloody genitals in his own hands —
Things shameful for the eyes and a sight to inspire wrath,
His flesh naked; but all things are seemly for a young man,
While he has the splendid flower of lovely youth,
Wondrous for men to behold, and desirable to women
While he is alive, and handsome when he has fallen in the vanguard.
But let each man plant himself stoutly and stay with both feet
Firmly stood upon the ground, biting his lip with his teeth.

6.8 The Spartan Phalanx

Tyrtaeus 11, lines 21–38

Tyrtaeus stresses that cowardice brings disgrace, and that bravery is shown in hand-to-hand combat in the front line. Note the use of hoplite tactics and armour; the final sentence addressing light-armed troops seems an addition to encourage helot or perioikoi troops fighting alongside the Spartans. The actual nature of hoplite warfare is debated: the 'push and shove' theory, for which see, recently, Holladay (1982) 94–97, is challenged by Cawkwell (1989) 375–89 (with bibliography), who envisages hand-to-hand combat.

Let each man plant himself stoutly and stay with both feet
Firmly stood upon the ground, biting his lip with his teeth,
His thighs and calves below and breast and shoulders
Covered with the belly of his broad shield;
In his right hand let him shake his mighty spear,
And let him wave the dreadful crest above his head;
In the doing of mighty deeds let him learn to do battle,
And not stand beyond the missiles holding his shield,
But let each man go close hand-to-hand and with his long spear
Or his sword let him wound and take his foe.
Let him set foot beside foot, rest shield against shield,
Crest on crest, and helmet on helmet
And let him fight his man with breast approached to breast,
Holding either his sword hilt or his long spear.
And you, light-armed soldiers, crouching beneath the shield
One from one side, one from another, cast your great sling-stones
And hurl your smooth spears at them,
Standing beside the men in heavy armour.

6.9 The Rewards of Courage

Tyrtaeus 12, lines 23–44

He who falls in the vanguard and loses his dear life,
Has brought honour to his city and his people and his father,

Many times through his breast and bossed shield
And breastplate pierced through from the front.
Young and old together lament him,
And all the city mourns with deep regret;
His tomb and children are notable amongst men
And his children's children and all his family after;
His great glory and his name will never perish,
But even though underground he becomes immortal,
For it was while he nobly stood and fought
For country and children that raging Ares took him.
But if he escape the fate of death that brings long woe,
And victorious wins the glorious boast of his spear,
All honour him, young and old alike,
And he after much contentment goes to Hades;
As he ages he has distinction amongst the citizens, nor does any
Wish to harm either his reputation or his right.
All alike in the seats of council, both the young, his age group,
And his elders, give way to him.
Now let every man strive to reach the peak of this prowess
And in his heart let him never relax from war.

6.10 The Songs of Tyrtaeus Instruct Spartan Warriors

Philochoros *FGH* 328 F216 (Athenaeus *Deipnosophistae* 630f)

Tyrtaeus was not only a poet but also the general responsible for the defeat of the Messenians in the Second Messenian War; cf. Plut. *Lyk.* 21, esp. 21.1–2 for Spartan music and songs, which were simple and character-building.

The warlike nature of the (pyrrhic) dance shows it to be a Spartan invention. The Spartans are warlike, and their sons learn by heart the marching songs (embateria), which are also called martial songs (enoplia). In addition, the Lakonians themselves in their wars sing the songs of Tyrtaeus from memory and move in time to them. Philochoros says that when the Spartans defeated the Messenians through Tyrtaeus' generalship they made it a custom in their expeditions, whenever they were dining and singing paeans, that one at a time they should sing the songs of Tyrtaeus; and the polemarch was to judge and give a prize of meat to the victor.

6.11 The Penalties for Cowardice

Xenophon *Constitution of the Spartans* 9.3–6

In Sparta the coward was the object of social ostracism; see Redfield (1977–78) 156; doc. 1.21 (Archilochos). The Spartans who had surrendered at Sphakteria (doc. 9.10) were disenfranchised, though this was later reversed. Cowards could not hold office (Thuc. V.34.2). Xenophon implies that membership of a mess would cease; they had to wear a cloak with coloured patches and have their beard partially shaven, and were forbidden to marry: Plut. *Ages.* 30.2–4; David (1989a) 9. For penalties for bachelors, see Plut. *Lyk.* 15.1–3, *Lys.* 30.7; Cartledge (1981) 95. See for cowardice and bravery, Hdt. VII.229–232, IX.71.2–4; Lewis (1977) 30–31; MacDowell (1986) 44–46.

9.3 Lykourgos clearly arranged that the brave should have prosperity, and cowards misery. **9.4** For in other cities whenever anyone shows himself to be a coward, he is only called a coward, and the coward goes to the agora in the same way as the brave man, and sits beside him, and exercises at the gymnasium with him, if he wants to; but in Sparta everyone would be ashamed to have a coward associated with him as a mess-mate, or as an opponent in a wrestling-bout. **9.5** Often such a person is left out unassigned when sides are picked for opposing teams in a ball game, and in choruses he is banished to the disgraceful positions, and even in the streets he has to make way, and on the benches give his place even to younger men. He has to maintain the girls of his family at home and give them the reason for their unmarried condition, while he has to suffer a hearth without a wife and pay a fine for that as well .... **9.6** When such dishonour is imposed upon cowards I do not wonder at their preferring death to such an ignominious and shameful life.

6.12 Spartan Battle Dress

Xenophon *Constitution of the Spartans* 11.3, 13.8–9

For the red uniform worn in battle, see David (1989a) 6; Xen. *Ages.* 2.7: Agesilaos' army appeared all bronze and crimson. For Spartan attention to their hair, see the references at David 6n.29; doc. 7.25 (Thermopylai). Cartledge (1993) 172 notes that according to Arist. *Rhet.* 1367a 28–32 long hair among the Spartans was the sign of a free man, since it is not easy for a long-haired man to perform any manual task. For Spartan weaponry, comprising shield (marked by the letter 'Λ', 'L'), spear, sword and body armour, see Anderson (1970) 16–19, 31–32, 38–39, 78–79; Lazenby (1985) 30–32. See Anderson 225–51; Lazenby 3–62 for detailed discussions of the organization of the army.

11.3 Regarding their equipment for battle, Lykourgos devised that they should have a crimson cloak and a bronze shield, thinking that the former has least in common with women's dress, and is most warlike; the latter can be very quickly polished and tarnishes very slowly. He also allowed those who had reached adulthood to wear their hair long, considering that they would thus appear taller, more noble, and more terrifying .... **13.8** When the enemy are close enough to see, a she-goat is sacrificed, and the law is that all flautists present are to play their flutes and no Spartan is to be without a garland; an order is also given to polish weapons. **13.9** Young men are permitted to enter battle with their hair groomed[1] and with a cheerful and glorious appearance.

[1] Taking the reading κεκτενισμένῳ 'combed' rather than Marchant's OCT emendation κεχριμένῳ (sc. ἐλαίῳ) 'anointed with oil'; some words may have dropped out of the text.

6.13 'With Your Shield or On It'

Plutarch *Sayings of Spartan Women* 16, 20 (*Moralia* 241f–242a)

Saying 16 (one of the most quoted — and mis-quoted — sayings from Greek history) overlooks the fact that most Spartans who were killed in battle were buried where they fell (Plut. *Ages.* 40.4). Both of the following *Sayings* stress the role expected of Spartan mothers (cf. docs. 13.19–20; Walcot (1987) 14) and serve as good examples of Spartan unwillingness to waste words; Cartledge (1978) 25–37, (1981) 92.

16. Another woman, handing her son his shield and encouraging him, said, 'Son, either with this or on this.' .... **20.** Another woman, hearing that her son had died in battle, on the spot where he had been positioned, said, 'Bury him and let his brother fill his place.'

6.14 Athenian Views of 'Good Old' Spartan Traditions

Aristophanes *Lysistrata* 1296–1320

This is the conclusion to Aristophanes' play *Lysistrata,* which was performed to Athenians at war with Sparta, at the Lenaia in 411 and won the first prize. While a comedy, with many parenthetical jokes against women and Spartans, Lysistrata's message was still meant to be taken seriously, and the chorus here, after the Spartan envoys have been entertained in the prytaneion, sings of the Sparta who was Athens' ally in the 'good old days' and Sparta's glorious traditions and festivals; cf. doc. 7.51; see Westlake (1980) 53–54. For girls' choirs in Sparta, see doc. 13.14.

Now leaving lovely Taygetos,
Come, Lakonian Muse, come to glorify
The god of Amyklai (Apollo)
Whom we revere
And the Lady of the Brazen House (Athena),
And the brave Tyndaridai (Castor and Pollux),
Who sport beside the Eurotas.
Come, come quickly,
Come, jump lightly,
So we can celebrate Sparta,
Who loves the choruses of the gods
And the sound of feet,
Where the maidens, like fillies
Beside the Eurotas
Dance, with their feet often
Bounding,
And their tresses waving
Like those of the Bakchai when they brandish the thyrsos and play.
The daughter of Leda (Helen) is at their head,
A pure and comely leader.
But come, bind your hair with a fillet,
And dance hand and foot
Like a stag; at the same time
Make a noise to help the dance along,
And celebrate again in song the almighty, all-conquering goddess of the
Brazen House.

THE SPARTAN CONSTITUTION

The Spartan constitution comprised two kings, the gerousia, the ephorate, and an assembly of Spartiates, ruling over a numerous class of perioikoi and helots; in addition to these, there was a system of upbringing, the 'agoge', and the mess system, participation in both of which was a prerequisite for citizenship. As Finley (1975) 175–76 notes, these features can be found in other Greek states, but at Sparta they were combined to effect a unique system: a state ruled by an elite of Spartiates whose prime concern was military preparedness, and one where 'polis and territory were not synonymous': Messenia, though ruled by Sparta, was not Sparta.

6.15 The Reasons for Sparta's Success

Plato *Laws* 691d–692a

Plato sees the dual nature of the kingship as a check on absolute monarchy; the 'double race' are the Agiad and Eurypontid royal houses. The third 'saviour' mentioned here is Theopompos, supposedly responsible for the institution of the ephorate; cf. Plut. *Lyk.* 7.1–3. Plut. *Lyk.* 5.10–11 makes the gerousia Lykourgos' main achievement, rather than the Great Rhetra, and sees it as the stabilising element of the constitution.

691d It seems as if there was some god who took care of you, who foresaw what was going to happen and engendered a double race of kings for you out of your one, thus contracting its powers to reasonable limits. **691e** And again after this a person (Lykourgos) whose human nature was mingled with some divine power, noticed that your government was still fevered, and so blended the prudent power of age with your natural audacious vigour, **692a** by giving the twenty-eight elders equal voting power in important matters to that of the power of the kings. Your third saviour saw that your government was still wanton and restive, so he imposed on it the power of the ephors as a kind of bridle, which was almost a power held by lot; and because of this measure your kingship, in as much as it had become a mixture of elements and a moderating power, has survived and itself been the reason for the preservation of the rest of the constitution.

6.16 The Election of the Gerousia

Plutarch *Lykourgos* 26.1–5

The powers of the gerousia were wide and they judged cases involving capital punishment, loss of citizen rights or exile: cf. Xen. *Const. Spart.* 10.2.

26.1 Lykourgos, as has already been said, himself appointed the elders at first from those who had been involved in his plan; later on he arranged that, when an elder died, the man whose merits were judged to be best of all those over the age of sixty should be appointed in his place. **26.2** And of all contests amongst mankind this seemed to be the most important and the one most worth fighting for; in it a man was judged not as the swiftest of the swift, nor as the strongest of the strong, but as the best and most prudent of the good and wise and would have as a lifelong prize for his merits, so to speak, total authority in the state, with supreme powers over death and loss of citizen rights and the most important issues generally. **26.3** The selection took place in this way: when the assembly had gathered, chosen men were shut up in a building nearby, where they could neither see out nor be seen, but could only hear the shouts of those in the assembly. **26.4** For as in other matters they judged the competitors by shouting, not all together but each man being brought forward as decided by lot and walking through the assembly in silence. **26.5** The men who were shut up had tablets, and so in each case they noted the volume of the shouts not knowing whom it was for, except that he was the first or the second or the third or whatever of those brought forward. And whoever received the most shouting and the loudest they proclaimed to be elected.

6.17 The Spartan Assembly Decides by Acclamation

Thucydides I.87.1–2

The very real importance of the ephors in the Spartan political system is made clear from the meeting of the Spartan assembly in 432, when the assembly voted for war. Sthenelaidas as ephor was clearly influential in this decision, against Archidamos' advice. de Ste. Croix (1972) 348–49 sees voting by acclamation as reflecting a lack of democracy, while Lewis (1977) 42 points to the anonymous nature of the system. For this speech, see Allison (1984) 9–16; Bloedow (1987) 60–66, both with bibliography.

I.87.1 After this speech, Sthenelaidas himself, as ephor, put the question to the Spartan assembly. **I.87.2** They actually make their decisions by shouting and not by voting, and he said that he could not distinguish which acclamation was the louder, because he wanted them to show their opinion clearly and thus be all the more eager for going to war ....

6.18 The Powers of the Ephors

Xenophon *Constitution of the Spartans* 8.2–4

The five ephors were elected annually, and there was no restriction on who could stand; see Chrimes (1949) 402–12; Michell (1952) 118–23; Huxley (1962) 38–39, 116n.239; Jones (1967) 26–30; Forrest (1980) 76–77; de Ste. Croix (1972) 130–31, 148–49, 327–28, 351–52.

8.2 Even the most important people in Sparta are very deferential to the magistrates and take pride in being humble and in running and not walking to answer whenever they are summoned, thinking that if they lead the way in strict obedience others also will follow; and this is what has happened. **8.3** It is also likely that these same men helped to establish the power of the ephorate too, since they realised that obedience is the greatest good, whether in a city, an army or a household; for the greater the power held by the magistrates, the more they considered that this would also impress the citizens with the need for obedience. **8.4** So the ephors have the power to fine whomever they wish, and have the authority to exact immediate payment, as well as the authority to put an end to magistrates' terms of office and even to imprison and put them on trial for their lives.

6.19 Sparta: Democracy or Oligarchy?

Aristotle *Politics* 1294b 19–34 (IV, ix)

Aristotle here points out the democratic and oligarchic features of the Spartan constitution. His judgement in this passage is less unfavourable than docs. 6.27–30, where he specifically criticizes Sparta's constitution and social system. He views Spartan kingship as having lasted so long because of its restricted powers: *Pol.* 1313a 18–33; for his criticisms, see *Pol.* 1271a 18–26.

Many people try to describe it as a democracy because its system has many democratic elements, for example, to begin with, the education of children (for the sons of the rich are brought up in the same way as those of the poor, and are educated in a manner which is also possible for the sons of the poor), and the same is the case in the next age-group, and when they become men (for thus there is no distinctive mark of being rich or poor) the arrangements for eating in the common messes (syssitia) are the same for everybody, and the rich wear such clothing as any of the poor could afford. Additionally, of the two most important offices the people choose the members of one and share in the other (for they elect the elders and share in the ephorate). Those who call it an oligarchy do so because of its many oligarchic features, for example that everyone is elected and no one chosen by lot, and that a few people have supreme authority to give sentences of death or exile, and many other similar points.

SPARTAN KINGSHIP

Hdt. VI.52–55 gives the Spartan account of the twins of Aristodemos and other traditions concerning the origins of Spartan dual kingship. The kings' power was not absolute, but was checked by both the gerousia and the ephorate. The heirs to the two thrones appear to have been exempt from the agoge required of other Spartiates: Plut. *Ages.* 1.4; MacDowell (1986) 43. For Spartan kingship, see Huxley (1962) 17, 117–18n.253; Jones (1967) 13–16; Oliva (1971) 23–28; Thomas (1974) 257–70; Forrest (1980) 28–29, 113; Proietti (1987) 74–78.

6.20 The Prerogatives of Spartan Kings

Herodotos VI.56–59

Herodotos in this passage lists the privileges of the kings in war and peace. **VI.57.1**: For the kings' double portions at meals (one to give away, not to eat), see Xen. *Const. Spart.* 15.2–5; 15.3 not only did the king get parts of beasts, but 'enough good land belonging to the cities of the perioikoi to ensure moderate means without excessive wealth.' **VI.57.2**: The Pythioi were officials who consulted the Delphic oracle on public affairs when the Spartans decided, probably in their assembly, to do so (Hdt. VI.57.2, 4, cf. 52.5; Xen. *Const. Spart.* 15.5; cf. Parker (1989) 154–55, esp. 170n.62). **VI.57.4**: Kleomenes had brought back from Athens the collection of oracles that the Peisistratidai had kept on the acropolis (Hdt. V.90.2). **VI.57.5**: Hdt. seems to imply here that the kings had two votes each, but Thuc. I.20.3 specifically contradicts this. **VI.58.3–59**: Spartans who died in battle were buried where they fell, but the bodies of kings were brought back to Sparta for burial (see esp. Plut. *Ages.* 40.4; Pritchett (1985) 241–42). The ceremony involving a bier presumably only took place when the body of the king could not be recovered; Leonidas was buried at Thermopylai, but his bones were later transferred to Sparta (Paus. III.14.1, with Pritchett (1985) 242n.425). For heroisation of Spartan kings, see Parker (1988) 9–10. This passage is part of doc. 6.47.

VI.56 The Spartiates have given their kings these prerogatives: two priesthoods, of Zeus Lakedaimon and Zeus Ouranios, and the power to declare war against any country they might choose; none of the Spartiates is allowed to hinder this, and if one should, then he is put under a curse. When they take the field, the kings are the first to go and the last to return; on campaign they are guarded by a hundred picked men; and on their expeditions they can use as many animals as they wish, and they keep for themselves the skins and chines of all that are sacrificed. **VI.57.1** This is in war, and in peace time their other prerogatives are as follows: whenever a sacrifice takes place at public expense, the kings are the first to sit down to dinner and are the first served, each being given twice as much of everything as the other guests; theirs is the right of making the first libation and they get the skins of the sacrificed animals. **VI.57.2** On the first and seventh days of every month each of them is given by the state a perfect victim for sacrifice at the temple of Apollo and a bushel of barley and a Lakonian quart of wine, and at all public games they have the privilege of specially reserved seats. It is their duty to appoint whomever of the citizens they wish as proxenoi and each of them chooses two Pythioi; the Pythioi are officials sent to Delphi, and they eat with the kings at public expense. **VI.57.3** If the kings do not attend dinner they are each sent at their houses two choinikes of barley and a kotyle of wine, and when they are present they are given double rations of everything; they are awarded this same honour when they are invited to dinner at the houses of private citizens. **VI.57.4** They guard the oracular responses, and the Pythioi also have knowledge of these. The kings have the sole right to make decisions on specific matters: concerning an heiress whom she should marry, if her father has not betrothed her, and concerning public roads. **VI.57.5** And if anyone wants to adopt a child, he must do it in the kings' presence. And they sit beside the elders in council, of whom there are twenty-eight; and if they are not present, those of the elders who are most closely related to them have the prerogatives of the kings and cast two votes and a third for themselves .... **VI.58.3** If one of the kings dies in war, they prepare a likeness of him and carry it to burial on a finely strewn bier. And when they bury a king, no public business takes place for ten days and no election is held, but they spend all these days in mourning. **VI.59** They also have another custom corresponding to Persian usage; when the king has died and another king is installed, the new incumbent cancels the debts of any of the Spartiates who owes money to the king or treasury. Amongst the Persians also when a king comes to the throne he remits outstanding tribute owed by all his cities.

6.21 A New Law for Kings on Campaign

Herodotos V.75.2

Kleomenes and Demaratos went as far as Eleusis in their invasion of Attica in 506, when the Corinthians decided to withdraw, followed by Demaratos (doc. 5.5); cf. Hdt. VI.50.2 (doc. 6.47) for corroboration that in official actions before this point it was normal for both kings to be with the army; Jones (1967) 15; Hooker (1980) 151. For images of the Tyndaridai accompanying the army, see Plut. *Mor.* 478a.

V.75.2 Because of this difference of opinion a law was made in Sparta that both kings should not accompany an army on campaign, for until now both used to go with the army; now one of them was exempted from military service and had to remain behind as well as one of the two Tyndaridai (Castor and Pollux); for before this both of these too were invoked as allies to accompany the army.

6.22 King Agis is Reprimanded

Thucydides V.63.1–4

This incident dates to 418. The advisory board appointed to oversee Agis curtailed his rights to begin wars (cf. Hdt. VI.56, doc. 6.20), and the incident underlines the accountability of the kings, while the threatened fine of 100,000 drachmas points to the fact that the kings could acquire wealth; cf. Thomas (1974) 268; docs. 6.43, 48.

V.63.1 When the Spartans returned from Argos after making the four months' truce, they blamed Agis very heavily for not having conquered Argos for them, for such a good opportunity, they thought, had never occurred before; as it was not easy to assemble so many allies of such quality. **V.63.2** But when it was also reported that Orchomenos had been captured, they became even more incensed and immediately decided in their rage, contrary to their usual procedure, that they ought to raze his house to the ground and fine him 100,000 drachmas. **V.63.3** However, he begged them to do none of these things, saying that when he next went to war he would atone for his faults by some noble deed, or they could then do as they wished. **V.63.4** So they held off carrying out the fine and razing his house, and for the time being made a law, which had not previously existed; this was that they should choose ten Spartiates as his associates and advisers, without whom he should have no authority to lead an army out of the state.

6.23 'Craftsmen in Warfare'

Xenophon *Constitution of the Spartans* 13.1–5

The omens were taken before crossing Sparta's frontiers when leading the army to war; these were known as the diabateria. Unfavourable omens could prevent a Spartan army from marching out: see Thuc. V.54.2, 55.3, 116.1; for favourable diabateria: Xen. *Hell.* IV.7.2; Jameson (1991) 202, 222n.12, 223n.17; Burkert (1983) 40 with n.22; Connor (1988) 13. For the passage below, see Lazenby (1985) 37; Parker (1989) 157; according to Arist. *Pol.* 1285a 3–16 kingship in Sparta was a 'perpetual generalship', and the kings had the power to kill only in cases of cowardice.

13.1 I will also give an account of the power and honour which Lykourgos gave a king on campaign. First of all, the city maintains the king and his staff while on service; the polemarchs share the same mess with him, so that they can always be at his side and take common counsel, if there should be need. Three of the homoioi also share the king's mess and take care of all the provisions for the others, so that they can give all their time to military matters. **13.2** But I will go back to how the king sets out with an army. First, while at home, he sacrifices to Zeus the Leader (Agetor) and the gods connected with him; and, if the omens are favourable, the fire-bearer takes fire from the altar and leads the way to the frontiers of the country; there the king again sacrifices to Zeus and Athena. **13.3** Only when the sacrifices to both gods show favourable omens, does he cross the country's frontiers; and the fire from these sacrifices leads the way without ever being put out, and all kinds of beasts for sacrifice follow. Whenever he offers a sacrifice, he always begins this work before daylight, wishing to be the first to win the god's goodwill. **13.4** The sacrifice is attended by polemarchs, captains, commanders of fifty men (pentekonteres), commanders of foreign troops, commanders of the baggage train, and any of the generals from the cities who chooses; **13.5** two of the ephors are also present, who do not interfere with anything, unless the king calls on them; they watch what each man does and see that everyone behaves properly. When the sacrifices are finished, the king summons everyone and gives the orders as to what has to be done. So, seeing these things, you would think that all others are novices in soldiering and the Spartans in reality the only craftsmen in warfare.

6.24 Oaths of the Kings and Ephors

Xenophon *Constitution of the Spartans* 15.6–9

15.6 Everyone rises up from their seats for the king except the ephors from their chairs of office. **15.7** And every month they exchange oaths with each other, the ephors on behalf of the city, and the king on his own behalf. The king's oath is that he will rule according to the established laws of the city, and the city's that while he holds to his oath they will keep the kingship undisturbed. **15.8** So these are the honours given to the king at home while he is alive, and they do not in any way greatly exceed those of private persons; for Lykourgos did not wish to inspire tyrannical pride in the kings nor to implant envy of power in the citizens. **15.9** But in the honours given to the king when he is dead the laws of Lykourgos wish to show that they have especially honoured Spartan kings not as men but as heroes.

6.25 Pausanias' Colourful Career

Thucydides I.130.1–132.4 (Simonides 19a)

I.130.1: Pausanias provides the first evidence of a phenomenon noted by Xenophon (*Const. Spart.* 14.1–4): Spartans abroad went 'bad', as there were opportunities for personal enrichment and a more relaxed lifestyle; cf. Thuc. I.77.6 (Brasidas provided a notable exception: Thuc. IV.81.3). **I.131.1**: the skytale was a length of wood for sending cipher messages; see Plut. *Lys.* 19.7–12; *LSAG* 57–58; Kelly (1985) 141–69;

West (1988) 42–46; cf. Boring (1979) passim. **I.132.2–3**: for the tripod and serpent column at Delphi, see also docs. 6.26, 7.44. Dem. LIX.98 (cf. Plut. *Mor.* 873c) relates that the Plataeans prosecuted the Spartans in the Delphic Amphictyonic Council for 1,000 talents for the offence; see Bonner & Smith (1943) 2 with n.10; Trevett (1990) 409–11; *contra* Fornara (1967) 291–94; for the epigram, see Page 217. Pausanias was tricked into betraying his treachery, but before the ephors could arrest him he took refuge in the temple of Athena of the Brazen House, where they walled him up, removing him only when on the point of death (Thuc. I.132.5–134.4): cf. Parker (1983) 33 with n.5 for death in temples. For Pausanias, see esp. Fornara (1966) 257–71; Powell (1988) 103–05.

I.130.1 Pausanias had even before this been held in high esteem by the Greeks because of his generalship at the battle of Plataea, but when he received this letter (from Artabazos) he then became far more conceited and was no longer able to live in the conventional way, but used to go out of Byzantium dressed in Persian attire and a bodyguard of Persians and Egyptians would escort him as he travelled though Thrace; his banquets were held along Persian lines and he was unable to hide what he intended, but clearly showed in unimportant matters what he planned to do later on in affairs of more importance. **I.130.2** He made himself inaccessible and everyone alike found him so difficult to deal with that no one was able to approach him; it was not least for this reason that the allies turned to the Athenians. (**I.131.1–132.1:** *Pausanias was recalled again and imprisoned by the ephors but released through lack of evidence.*) **I.132.2** He had given rise by his transgression of the laws and imitation of the barbarians to many suspicions that he did not wish to conform to conventional standards, and they began an investigation into all his actions to see if he had deviated at all from established rules of behaviour, as in the case of the tripod at Delphi, which the Greeks had dedicated as the first-fruits of their Persian victory, on which he had thought fit on his own initiative to have this couplet inscribed:

'Since as leader of the Greeks he destroyed the Persian army,
Pausanias dedicated this memorial to Phoibos (Apollo).'

I.132.3 The Spartans had immediately had this couplet obliterated from the tripod and they inscribed on it by name all the cities that had united in defeating the barbarian and erected the offering; even at the time this had seemed to be a crime of Pausanias', and after his recent conduct it appeared to be very much in line with his current intention. **I.132.4** They also learnt that he was intriguing in some way with the helots, and this was so: for he was promising them liberation and citizenship, if they would join him in revolt and help him to achieve all his aims.

6.26 Pausanias 'Ruler of Spacious Greece'

Nymphis *FGH* 432 F9 (Athenaeus *Deipnosophistae* 536a–b) (Simonides 39)

Page 254–55. The serpent column was not the only dedication of the time on which Pausanias arrogantly recorded his exploits.

Nymphis of Herakleia, in the sixth book of his work on his native land, says, 'Pausanias, who conquered Mardonios at Plataea, departed from Spartan customs and gave himself up to arrogance. When he was staying at Byzantium, he dared to inscribe, as if he himself had dedicated it, the bronze bowl dedicated to the gods whose shrines stand at the mouth (of the entrance to the Black Sea), and which happens to still exist today, with this epigram, forgetting himself through his luxurious lifestyle and arrogance:

"This memorial of his prowess is dedicated to Lord Poseidon
By Pausanias, ruler of spacious Greece,
At the Black Sea, by birth a Spartan, son
Of Kleombrotos, of the ancient family of Herakles".'

ARISTOTLE'S CRITICISMS OF THE CONSTITUTION

Although the Spartan constitution was widely admired by writers such as Xenophon and Plutarch, Aristotle in the *Politics* identified numerous defects in the Spartan system, judging it by its failure to maintain Spartan supremacy in the fourth century; see MacDowell (1986) 16–17.

6.27 Spartiate Numbers Decline

Aristotle *Politics* 1270a 29–b 6 (II, ix)

Prior to this passage Aristotle discusses the inequality of property ownership in Sparta (doc. 13.18). This shortage of men, oliganthropia, is reflected in the known figures of Spartiates. Lykourgos was said to have redistributed the land amongst 9,000 Spartiates (see doc. 6.41); Hdt. VII.234.2 has 8,000 Spartiates in 480; and 5,000 of these fought in 479: Hdt. IX.10.1, 11.3, 28.2, 29.1 cf. 12.2. Xenophon has 700 Spartiates at Leuktra in 371 of whom 400 fell (Xen. *Hell.* VI.4.15, 17); there were 700 Spartiates in 243 (Plut. *Agis* 5.6). See esp. de Ste. Croix (1972) 331–32; Cartledge (1979) 307–18; Cawkwell (1983) 385–400, esp. 385–90; Figueira (1986) 165–213; Hodkinson (1986) 378–406, (1989) 100–05.

1270a 29 So although the land was able to support 1,500 cavalry, and 3,000 hoplites, the number was less than 1,000. And events have themselves shown that the system was faulty: for the city could not withstand a single blow (Leuktra), but was destroyed because of the shortage of men. They say that in the time of the earlier kings they gave others a share in the citizenship, and so there was then no such shortage of men, although they were at war for so much of the time. They also say that there were once some 10,000 Spartiates; but whether these statements are true or not, it is better for the city to keep its numbers up through the equalisation of property. However, the law concerning the procreation of children is contrary to this amendment. **1270b 1** For the lawgiver, wishing there to be as many Spartiates as possible, offers inducements to the citizens to have as many children as they can; for they have a law that anyone who has three sons is exempt from military service, and anyone with four is exempt from tax. Yet it is clear that if many are born, and the land is correspondingly divided, inevitably many become poor.

6.28 The Ephorate

Aristotle *Politics* 1270b 6–35 (II, ix)

For the election of ephors, see also Arist. *Pol.* 1272a 27–33; for bribery of Spartans, see Finley (1975) 167–68, 240n.11; Lewis (1977) 33nn.45–46 for references; Hodkinson (1993) 250–52.

1270b 6 Moreover, the arrangements concerning the ephorate are also at fault. For this office has supreme authority in the most important matters, but its members come from the whole people, so that frequently men who are extremely poor get onto this board, and their poverty used to make them open to bribery. This has often been demonstrated in the past, and recently in the affair of the Andrians, in which certain ephors had been so corrupted by money that as far as was within their power they destroyed the entire city. And because the office is extremely powerful and equal to that of a tyrant, even the kings are compelled to curry favour with them, which has further harmed the constitution; for an aristocracy has turned into a democracy .... **1270b 28** They also have supreme jurisdiction in cases of importance, although being there by chance, and accordingly it would be better for them to decide them not on their own judgement but according to the written rules, that is the laws. The ephors' lifestyle, too, is not in accordance with the aims of the state; for it is excessively relaxed, while for the rest it is far too excessive in its austerity, with the result that they are unable to endure it but secretly evade the law and enjoy bodily pleasures.

6.29 The Gerousia

Aristotle *Politics* 1270b 35–1271a 18 (II, ix)

Xen. *Const. Spart.* 10.1; Plut. *Lyk.* 5.10–11 see the gerousia as having a balancing effect on the constitution; Aristotle, however, has numerous criticisms. The lawgiver referred to is presumably Lykourgos. For the qualifications for office, see Toynbee (1969) 266–69; de Ste. Croix (1972) 353–54; for a general discussion, Michell (1952) 135–40; Jones (1967) 17–19; Staveley (1972) 74–78; Forrest (1980) 46–47.

1270b 35 Their arrangements concerning the powers of the elders are also not faultless. One might suppose that as long as they are respectable men and sufficiently trained in manly virtue they would benefit the state, but it should be doubted whether they should possess for life supreme jurisdiction in cases of importance (for the mind, like the body, is subject to old age); **1271a 1** and when they have been trained in such a manner that the lawgiver himself has no confidence in their being good men, it is dangerous. For those who have had a share in this office have manifestly been guilty of taking bribes and have been corrupt enough to give away a lot of public property. Accordingly it would be better if they were accountable; but now they are not .... **1271a 9** As for the election of the elders the way it is decided is childish, and it is wrong that someone who is going to be thought fit for office should himself canvass it; for whether he wants it or not the man worthy of office is the man to hold it. Here the lawgiver is clearly doing what he does elsewhere in the constitution; for he makes the citizens ambitious and uses this in the election of the elders; for no one would canvass office unless he were ambitious. And yet nearly all deliberate crimes are caused by men's ambition and greed.

6.30 Spartan Financial Problems

Aristotle *Politics* 1271a 26–37, b 10–17 (II, ix)

Lykourgos instituted the practice whereby each of the homoioi had to make an equal contribution to the mess (Xen. *Const. Spart.* 7.3; cf. Plut. *Lyk.* 12.1–11). The inability of poorer Spartiates to make these contributions resulted in a declining number of citizens, particularly from the late fifth century onwards (see *Pol.* 1272a 12–16, cf. 1330a 6–8). Aristotle points out that the Spartan word for 'messes' was phiditia, not syssitia (andreia and syskenia were also found): see Michell (1952) 282; Toynbee (1969) 319. The messes formed an important part of the socialisation process for young Spartiates (Xen. *Const. Spart.* 5.5–6); the agoge was a prerequisite for membership: Xen. *Const. Spart.* 3.2–3, 10.7, discussed by MacDowell (1986) 42–43. See Michell (1952) 281–97; Toynbee (1969) 322–23; Hodkinson (1983) 251–54; Figueira (1984) 87–98; for Spartan lack of funds and cash-flow problems, note Thuc. I.80.3–4, 86.3, 142.1, 143.1.

1271a 26 Nor have the regulations concerning the common meals (syssitia), which are called 'phiditia', been well framed by the person who first established them. For the gathering should have taken place at public expense, as in Crete; but amongst the Lakonians each man has to contribute, even though some of them are extremely poor and unable to afford this expense, with the consequence being the opposite of the lawgiver's intention. For he wanted to make the system of common meals democratic, but under the current regulations it is not democratic at all. For it is not easy for the very poor to share in them, but this is their ancestral definition of citizenship, that anyone who is unable to pay their contribution can not be a citizen .... **1271b 10** The Spartiates' public finances are also badly managed. There is never anything in the state's treasury even though they are compelled to carry on great wars, and they are bad at paying taxes; because most of the land belongs to the Spartiates they do not look very closely at each other's contributions. The outcome has been quite the opposite of the beneficial state of affairs intended by the lawgiver; for he has made his city moneyless and its individuals greedy.

COMMUNITY LIFE IN SPARTA

6.31 Lykourgos Institutes the Public Mess System

Xenophon *Constitution of the Spartans* 5.2–4

As Xenophon notes, the Spartans did not have drinking-bouts (cf. docs. 6.32, 11.28; Plat. *Laws* 637a; MacDowell (1986) 113–14). According to Pausanias their main food was barley-bread (doc. 7.48). Cf. Plut. *Lyk.* 10–12; 12.12–13 for the 'black broth', the typical food of the Spartan mess: 'It is said that one of the kings of Pontos bought a

Lakonian cook for the sake of the broth, but was displeased after tasting it, at which the cook said, "To enjoy this broth, one must first have bathed in the river Eurotas."'

5.2 Lykourgos then noticed that the Spartans just like the rest of the Greeks were living at home, and, realising that this was responsible for their taking most things too easily, brought the common messes (syskania) out into the open, considering that this would reduce disobedience of orders to a minimum. **5.3** He assigned them a ration of corn, so that they would neither be gorged nor hungry. But they get many additional foods supplied from hunting expeditions; and there are times when the rich also contribute wheaten bread instead; so the table is never bare until they separate and go to their quarters, but neither is it extravagantly supplied. **5.4** He also put an end to the compulsory drinking of wine, which undoes both body and mind, and allowed each man to drink when he was thirsty, thinking that this would be the least harmful and most pleasurable way of drinking.

6.32 Drinking Customs at Sparta

Kritias 6

Kritias, who wrote a *Constitution of Sparta* now lost, praised Spartan moderation in drinking, each man using his own cup and drinking at his own pace; see esp. Usher (1979) 39–42; David (1989b) 1–25, esp. 5 for laughter at Sparta. For Kritias' praise of Spartan shoes, cloaks and goblets (which had an incurving rim to catch impurities, as the soldier often had to drink impure water), see F34; Plut. *Lyk.* 9.7–8; cf. doc. 12.40.

This also is a custom and practice at Sparta,
To drink from the same cup of wine,
Not to hand it round when you propose a toast,
Nor (pass the cup) to your right hand around the company ....

For drinking healths in wine-cups beyond measure
Straightway delights yet causes pain for all time;
But the Spartan habit is evenly disposed,
To eat and drink proportionately to prudence
And capacity to work; there is no day appointed
For intoxicating the body with unmeasured drinking.

6.33 Communal Ownership in Sparta

Xenophon *Constitution of the Spartans* 6.1–3

Communal responsibility for the discipline of boys at Sparta was intended to provide for strictness and conformity and was an important provision in a society in which fathers were absent from the home; see also Xen. *Const. Spart.* 2.10; Redfield (1977–78) 155; for children's discipline at Athens, see Golden (1990) 64–65.

6.1 In other cities each man has the charge of his own children, servants and property; but Lykourgos wished to ensure that, without doing any harm, the citizens might get some benefit from each other, and so gave each man authority over other people's children just like his own .... **6.2** If a boy is beaten by another's father and reports this to his own father, it is disgraceful if he does not give his son a further beating. To such a degree they trust each other not to give their children any disgraceful order. **6.3** He also permitted them to use other people's servants as well, should there be need. And he made hounds common property; so those who need some ask to take them on the hunt, and if their owner is not at leisure himself he is pleased to send them along. Similarly they also make use of each other's horses.

6.34 Spartan Training: the Agoge

Xenophon *Constitution of the Spartans* 2.1–8

Cf. Plut. *Lyk.* 16–19. According to Plutarch, the weak and deformed were exposed at birth (doc. 13.23). At seven years, boys were assigned to groups, each known as a boua, 'herd of cattle' (the term used in Spartan inscriptions; cf. Plut. *Lyk.* 16.7, who uses the term agele); for Athenian education, see Golden (1990) 60–64. Spartan boys could be joined in the agoge by others referred to as mothakes or mothones: Xen. *Hell.* V.3.9; Phylarchos *FGH* 81 F43; Ael. *VH* XII.43; Forrest (1980) 136; MacDowell (1986) 46–51. Some of these may have been sons of foreigners, sent to train in the Spartan system (such as Xenophon's own sons: Plut. *Ages.* 20.2; Diog. Laert. 2.54; cf. Plut. *Phok.* 20.4).

2.1 Other Greeks who claim to be educating their sons in the best possible way, as soon as the boys understand what is said to them straightway set over them servants as their escorts (paidagogoi), and send them to masters to learn letters and music and the exercises of the wrestling-school. In addition they soften their sons' feet with sandals, and coddle their bodies with changes of clothes; and they allow them as much food as their stomachs can take. **2.2** But Lykourgos, instead of each man privately appointing slaves as paidagogoi, gave the responsibility of the boys' charge to one of those from whom the most important offices are appointed, who is called the supervisor of education (paidonomos). He gave him the authority to muster the boys and oversee them, correcting them severely if any of them were lazy. He also gave him some of the older youths as scourge-bearers, so that they could punish them, when need be, and the result is that great self-respect and obedience are present in Sparta hand-in-hand. **2.3** And instead of softening their feet with sandals he ordered them to strengthen them by going barefoot, thinking that if they practised this they would go much more easily uphill, and descend more safely downhill, and that someone barefoot, if he were practised, would jump and spring and run more quickly than one in sandals. **2.4** And instead of being coddled with clothing, he thought that they should become accustomed to one cloak a year, considering that in this way they would be better prepared to face cold and heat. **2.5** He ordered the prefect (eiren) to provide just so much food that they would neither be weighed down from repletion nor lack experience of going hungry, thinking that those trained in this way would be better able, if they should have to, to toil without food, and last a longer time on the same food, if it were commanded, and need less cooked food, and be more tolerant of every kind of food and stay more healthy. He also considered that a regimen which made their bodies slim would do more to increase their height than one which dilated them with food. **2.6** On the other hand, so that they were not too distressed by hunger, though he did not allow them to take what they desired without trouble, he permitted them to relieve their hunger by occasionally stealing. **2.7** It was not because he was at a loss what to give them that he permitted them to contrive to provide their own food — no one, I think, could fail to see that. It is clear that anyone who is going to steal must both stay awake at night and deceive and wait in ambush during the day, and have spies prepared if he is going to steal something. So all this shows that he trained the boys like this because he wanted them to be more devious at procuring supplies and more warlike. **2.8** Someone might say, 'Why, then, if he thought stealing a good thing, did he impose many strokes on one who was caught?' 'Because', I reply, 'whatever men teach, they punish whoever does not do it well. So, the Spartans punish those who are caught for stealing badly.'

6.35 The Incredible Incident of the Boy and the Fox

Plutarch *Lykourgos* 18.1

In this incident, a exemplum of Spartan toughness, the virtue of stealing without being detected is emphasized. The reasons for stealing a fox are not exactly clear. For a longer version of this story, see Plut. *Mor.* 234a (*Sayings of the Spartans* 35); see also Plut. *Lyk.* 17.5–6; Michell (1952) 177–80; MacDowell (1986) 59–61; Proietti (1987) 49.

18.1 The boys take great care over their stealing, as is shown in the story of one who had stolen a fox cub and had it hidden under his cloak, for he endured having his stomach lacerated by the beast's claws and teeth, and died rather than be detected.

SPARTAN FOREIGN AFFAIRS

After failing to conquer Tegea in the first half of the sixth century, Sparta created a system of alliances, forming the Peloponnesian League, the 'Lakedaimonians and their Allies'. According to Hdt. I.68.6 Sparta had subdued most of the Peloponnese by c. 550; the allies were autonomous, and could speak and vote in the league assembly, but only the Spartans could convene an assembly, and the allies were bound by a majority vote. For the Peloponnesian League, see esp. de Ste. Croix (1972) 101–24, 333–42; also Larsen (1932) 136–50, (1933) 257–76, (1934) 1–19; Ehrenberg (1960) 112–19, 254–55; Burn (1962) 171–72, 188; Ryder (1965) 3, 12; Jones (1967) 44–47; Kagan (1969) 9–30; Toynbee (1969) 182–84, 206; Cartledge (1979) 147–48; Forrest (1980) 88–89, 99–100; Salmon (1984) 240–52; Jeffery (1988) 350–56.

6.36 A Spartan Treaty with Aetolia

Meiggs & Lewis 67 (bis)

Also *SEG* 26.46, 28.408, 32.398. As ML p.312 note this is 'the first inscribed classical Spartan treaty'. It was set up on the Spartan acropolis. The relationship between the Erxadieis and the Aetolians is unclear, but it is probable that the treaty was directly with the Erxadieis, who were a group of Aetolians (on the northern side of the Corinthian Gulf). A fifth-century date is almost certain: Peek (1974). Cartledge (1976) 91–92 suggests a date in summer 426 or 425/4; ML p.312 not before 426; Kelly (1978) 133–41 dates it to 388. The obligations of the Erxadieis outweigh those of the Spartans; while the Erxadieis must take part in Spartan offensives, the Spartans are under no obligations to reciprocate. For the obligation to have the same friends and enemies, a standard clause in Spartan alliances, see de Ste. Croix (1972) 108–10. Whether the Erxadieis were members of the Spartan alliance or of the Peloponnesian League (for the distinction, see de Ste. Croix 102–05) is not clear; Cartledge (1976) 91 suggests that 'geographical, military and political grounds' excluded them from the Peloponnesian League; see Peek (1974) 3–15; Cartledge 87–92; Kelly (1978) 133–41. For the Spartan treaty in which the Tegeates are not to make the Messenians citizens, see Arist. F592 (Plut. *Mor.* 292b); Jacoby (1944) 15–16; *contra* Hammond (1982) 355.

[Treat]y with the Aetolians. On [the following terms] there is t[o be friendshi]p and peace towards the [Aeto]lians [for ever] and alli[ance. ....]nmonos was se[er .... They shall [foll]ow wherever the Sp[artan]s lead both b[y land a]nd by sea, having t[he same] friend and the sa[me enemy] as the [Sp]artans. They will not put an e[nd] (to the war) without the S[partans], and shall sen[d fighters] to the same (opponent) as the S[partans]. They shall not [receiv]e exi[les] who have particip[ated in cri]mes. If anyone [leads an expedition against the] land of [the] Erxadieis for the purpose of making war, [the Spart]ans shall ass[ist] them with all the streng[th in their power;] and if anyone lea[ds an expedition] against th[e] land of [the Spart]ans [for the purpose of making w]ar, the E[rxadieis] shall assist them [with all the strength in their power ....]

6.37 The Corinthians Prevent the Restoration of Hippias

Herodotos V.91.1–93.2

In 506 the Spartans had summoned their allies and invaded Attica to set up Isagoras as tyrant, going as far as Eleusis; when informed of the expedition's purpose, the Corinthians pulled out (doc. 5.5). As de Ste. Croix (1972) 116 points out, the allies joined the Spartan expedition when called upon without knowing the purpose of their mission, and they must have been 'obliged to come at Sparta's call'. Later, upon learning that their expulsion of Hippias had been prompted by bribery of the Pythia, the Spartans planned to restore him, c. 505–01. In this passage they summon their allies to Sparta and their plans are attacked by the Corinthian representative Sokles (cf. docs. 2.7, 9; doc. 1.15 carries on from this passage); for Sparta as a deposer of tyrants, see docs. 2.5, 2.41–42; Plut. *Lyk.* 30.2. Larsen (1932) 140; de Ste. Croix (1972) 116, cf. 169, 211; Cartledge (1979) 147 et al. accordingly posit a change between the expedition of 506 and that of c. 505–501, arguing that the Spartans after the failure of the 506 expedition decided that it needed the majority backing of its allies, and a vote to bind the minority to the majority view. This system is seen in operation in 432 (Thuc. 1.67, 79, 87.4–5, 119).

V.91.1 The Spartans summoned Hippias son of Peisistratos from Sigeion on the Hellespont [where the Peisistratidai had taken refuge]. **V.91.2** When Hippias had arrived in response to the invitation, the Spartiates summoned envoys from their other allies as well and addressed them .... (**V.91.2–92.1**: *the Spartans acknowledge that they made a mistake in giving power to the Athenian people and plan to restore Hippias.*) **V.92.1** The majority of the allies did not approve of this speech, but while the rest kept quiet, Sokles the Corinthian spoke as follows: **V.92a.1** 'The sky will soon be beneath the earth and the earth in mid-air over the sky, and men live in the sea and fish live like men used to, now that you, Spartans, are preparing to put down democracies and install tyrannies in cities, than which there is nothing more unjust or more blood-thirsty among mankind' .... **V.93.2** The rest of the allies had meanwhile kept quiet, but when they heard Sokles speaking freely, everyone of them spoke up and supported Sokles' view, and called on the Spartans not to bring calamity to any Greek city. This concluded the matter.

6.38 A Spartan Dedication, c. 650

Meiggs & Lewis 22

Hansen 367; Pausanias V.24.3. This elegiac couplet was inscribed on the base of a statue discovered at Olympia. Pausanias dates it to the Second Messenian War but this has been rejected as too early because of the style of the lettering; see Buck (1955) 266, no.68. *LSAG* 196, no.49; Wallace (1954) 32–35; Huxley (1962) 88, followed by ML, considers it as evidence for problems with the Messenians c. 490 (Plat. *Laws* 692d, 698d–e; Strab. VIII.4.10 (362); Paus. IV.23.5–10), not accepted by den Boer (1956) 168–74; Lewis (1992) 102; cf. Pearson (1962) 401; note Hansen (1990) 170. The Second Messenian War provides an acceptable historical context for the dedication, and the fluidity of opinion regarding the lettering precludes its use as a criterion for dismissing Pausanias' explicit testimony, while the archaic nature of the dedication (cf. *LSAG* 196) fits such a date.

[Acce]pt Lo[r]d, Son of Krono[s], Olympian Zeus, a fine statue
From th[e] Spartans with propitiou[s sp]irit.

6.39 A Dedication for the Victory at Tanagra, 458/7

Meiggs & Lewis 36

Hansen 351; Paus. V.10.4. This inscription from Olympia is very heavily restored. The Argives and Athenians fought against the Spartans at Tanagra, the Ionians as allies of the Athenians; cf. Thuc. I.107.5 (doc. 8.16). For the Argive dead, see also ML 35. A phiale is literally a saucer or bowl, here used of a shield (which is the same shape).

[The temple] has [a golde]n [shield (phiale)], which in [Tanagra]
[The Spartans and their all]iance dedic[ated]
[As a gift (taken) from the Argives and Athe]nians and [Ionians],
[The tithe fo]r [victory] in the w[ar].

THE SPARTAN ECONOMY AND VIEW OF MONEY

6.40 Tyrtaeus on Spartan Unrest

Tyrtaeus 1 (Aristotle *Politics* 1306b 36–1307a 2 (V, vi))

Aristotle here refers to a fragment of Tyrtaeus which supposedly concerns Spartan discord and economic distress at the time of the Messenian Wars.

Discords also arise when some are too poor and others are well off. And this particularly happens in war-time; for this occurred in Sparta at about the time of the

Messenian War; and this is clear from Tyrtaeus' poem called *Eunomia*; for some were in such distress because of the war that they demanded a redistribution of land.

6.41 Lykourgos' 'Redistribution of Land'

Plutarch *Lykourgos* 8.1–8

There are several reasons for rejecting the notion that 'Lykourgos' distributed the land into 9,000 lots. Lykourgos' redistribution of land is not found in early writers (such as Herodotos, Xenophon, or Aristotle) and may well have been invented in the third century when such redistribution was proposed to help solve Sparta's decline as a military power (esp. Plut. *Agis* 7). There was certainly inequality in the distribution of land in the fourth century; cf. docs. 6.27, 30; 13.18. For Spartan inheritance laws, see Hodkinson (1986) 378–406. **8.7**: liquid produce means wine and oil (as opposed to grain).

8.1 A second and very revolutionary reform of Lykourgos was his redistribution of the land. **8.2** For there was dreadful inequality and many people who were penniless and without property were pouring into the city, and wealth was completely concentrated in the hands of a few. **8.3** So to drive out arrogance, envy, wrong-doing and luxury and those even older and greater political diseases, wealth and poverty, he persuaded them to pool the whole country and divide it up afresh, and to live with each other all as equals with the same amount of property for their subsistence, giving the first place by merit, **8.4** since there would be no difference or inequality between people, except what censure for base deeds and praise for good ones would determine. **8.5** Following his words by action, he allotted the rest of Lakonia to the perioikoi in 30,000 lots, and that tributary to the city of Sparta into 9,000; this was the number of lots for Spartiates. **8.6** But some say that Lykourgos allotted 6,000, and Polydoros added 3,000 afterwards; and some that Polydoros allotted half the 9,000 and Lykourgos the other half. **8.7** Each man's lot was enough to produce a return of 70 medimnoi of barley for a man, and 12 for his wife, and proportionate amounts of liquid produce. **8.8** He thought this would suffice for them, and that they needed sufficient food for vigour and health, and nothing more.

6.42 Spartan Currency

Plutarch *Lykourgos* 9.1–5

There was no Spartan silver coinage before the late fourth century, but individual Spartans could possess silver and gold (cf. doc. 10.41). Kings could be fined by the ephors, and Spartans were susceptible to bribery, so there were obviously inequalities of wealth. Plutarch, however, gives here the traditional view of the Spartan economy.

9.1 He attempted to divide up their movable property as well, to remove completely any inequality and diversity, but when he saw how badly they accepted its outright removal, he took another way and devised constitutional measures against their greed. **9.2** He first made all gold and silver coinage invalid and ordered that they should only use iron currency; and he gave a slight value even to a great weight and bulk of this, so that a sum worth ten minas needed a large storeroom in a house and a yoke of oxen to carry it .... **9.4** He next banished as foreign useless and superfluous crafts. And even with no one banishing them, the majority of them would probably have been driven out by the common currency, since there was no way of selling their products. **9.5** For the iron money could not be exported elsewhere in Greece, nor had it any value there, but was laughed at; as a result it was impossible to buy any foreign or trumpery goods, no cargo of wares sailed into their harbours, and Lakonia was visited by no rhetoric teacher, vagabond seer, keeper of hetairai, or any craftsman of gold or silver ornaments, because there was no coinage.

6.43 Sparta Becomes Wealthy in 404

Poseidonios *FGH* 87 F48c (Athenaeus *Deipnosophistae* 233f–234a)

There was an influx of gold and silver into Sparta after the establishment of Spartan control in 404 over what had previously been the Athenian empire: Xen. *Const. Spart.* 14.1–4; cf. Finley (1975) 168; Lewis (1977) 33–34; Hodkinson (1993) 152–64. For a deposit of money probably made illegally by a Spartiate at Tegea, see doc. 10.41. Despite Gylippos' great services to the state in Sicily (see Thuc. VII *passim*), he was nevertheless disgraced; cf. Plut. *Lyk.* 30.1.

The Spartans, though they were prevented by their customs, as the same Poseidonios relates, from introducing into Sparta and acquiring gold and silver, none the less acquired it, and deposited it with the Arcadians, their neighbours; later on they had them as enemies instead of friends, so that because of this enmity their breach of faith could not be called to account (by their government). In fact they relate that any gold and silver in Sparta before this had been dedicated to Apollo at Delphi, and when Lysander brought it into the city as public property he became the cause of many evils. For report says that Gylippos, who had liberated the Syracusans, starved himself to death after being convicted by the ephors of having stolen from Lysander's money. It is not easy for a mortal to be contemptuous of what has been dedicated to a god and given to him, I suppose, as his adornment and possession.

KLEOMENES: THE 'MAD' SPARTAN KING

Kleomenes was a crucial figure in the history of late sixth and early fifth century history. Kleomenes' first known act was in 519 when he advised the Plataeans to ally themselves with Athens (Hdt. VI.108; Thuc. III.55.1–3, 68.5; Hammond (1992) 143–45; Hornblower (1991) 464 correctly rejects attempts to down-date the event to 509), and his reign is usually dated therefore to c. 521 or 520 to 491 or 490. Herodotos' account is clearly following two divergent traditions and his negative remarks indicate that he had a hostile Spartan source, perhaps the relatives of Kleomenes' half-brothers, or of Demaratos. For Kleomenes' reign, see How & Wells (1912) II.347–53; Walker (1926) 137–40, 163–67; Munro (1926) 259–62; Huxley (1962) 77–96; Jones (1967) 48–55; Forrest (1980) 85–94; Hooker (1980) 150–57; Jeffery (1988) 356–57, 360–67; Griffiths (1989) 51–78; Cawkwell (1993) 506–27.

6.44 The Unusual Circumstances of Kleomenes' Birth

Herodotos V.39.1–42.2

Kleomenes had three half-brothers: Dorieus (cf. doc. 1.17), Leonidas, and Kleombrotos (Table IV). The ephors apparently had an interest in ensuring that the kings produced offspring; cf. Plut. *Ages.* 2.6 where the ephors fined Archidamos for marrying a short wife, as kinglets (basileidia), not kings (basileis), would be born of such a union.

V.39.1 Anaxandridas son of Leon was no longer king of Sparta; he had died, and Kleomenes son of Anaxandridas held the kingship, not because of his merit but by right of birth. For Anaxandridas had been married to his sister's daughter, of whom he was very fond, but had no children. **V.39.2** This being so, the ephors summoned him and said, 'Even if you do not look after your own interests, we can not permit the family of Eurysthenes to become extinct. You now have a wife, but as she is not bearing children, get rid of her and marry another one; and by doing this you will please the Spartiates.' He in reply said that he would do neither of these things, and that they were giving him very improper advice in suggesting that he should send away his present wife, who had done him no wrong, and marry another one; nor would he obey them. **V.40.1** In response to this the ephors and the elders consulted and made the following proposal to Anaxandridas: 'Since, then, we see that you are attached to the wife you have, do the things we suggest and do not object, otherwise the Spartiates might think up something for you less acceptable. **V.40.2** We do not ask you to divorce the wife you have, and you can continue to give her all the privileges she now has, but take another wife as well as her to give you children.' Anaxandridas agreed to their suggestion and after this had two wives and lived in two different households, which was in no way typical of Sparta. (**V.41.1–3**: *Not long afterwards the second wife gave birth to Kleomenes; Anaxandridas' first wife then became pregnant, giving birth to Dorieus, followed later by Leonidas and Kleombrotos.*) **V.42.1** Kleomenes, it is said, was not of sound mind and on the verge of madness, whereas Dorieus was first among all his age group and very confident that he would hold the kingship because of his merit. **V.42.2** So, feeling like this, when Anaxandridas died and the Spartans according to custom made the eldest Kleomenes king, Dorieus took this badly and, as he would not consent to being ruled by Kleomenes, he asked the Spartiates for a body of men and took them off to found a colony.

6.45 Kleomenes Proves Incorruptible

Herodotos III.148.1–2

Polykrates delegated the tyranny of Samos to Maiandrios, but Maiandrios was expelled c. 515 by the Persians (Hdt. III.142–147) and Polykrates' brother Syloson put into power.

III.148.1 Maiandrios escaped from Samos and sailed to Sparta; he arrived there, bringing the things he had taken with him at his departure from Samos, and used to act as follows: he used to set out gold and silver drinking cups and, while his servants were polishing them, would get into conversation with Kleomenes son of Anaxandridas, who was currently king of Sparta, and bring him home; and whenever Kleomenes saw the cups he would be deeply amazed and impressed, and Maiandrios would tell him to take away with him as many of them as he wanted. **III.148.2** Though Maiandrios said this on two or three occasions, Kleomenes was the most upright of men and did not think it proper to accept what was offered, but realising that if Maiandrios were to offer them to some of the other citizens he would get assistance in his plan of vengeance, he went to the ephors and said that it would be better for Sparta if the Samian visitor were to leave the Peloponnese, before he managed to persuade either him or another Spartiate to become corrupt. They took heed of this and Maiandrios was banished by public proclamation.

6.46 Three Months from the Coast!

Herodotos V.49.1–51.3

Between Maiandrios' and Aristagoras' visits, Kleomenes was active in Athenian affairs, deposing Hippias in 511/0, and attempting to support Isagoras in 508/7, with a further abortive invasion in 506. In 499 Aristagoras visited both Sparta and Athens seeking aid from mainland Greece for the cities of Asia Minor (cf. docs. 7.2–5). For Kleomenes' refusal of aid, see Larsen (1932) 136–50; Lateiner (1982) 137–38.

V.49.1 Aristagoras, tyrant of Miletos, arrived at Sparta when Kleomenes was ruling, and, according to the Spartans, went to talk to him taking with him a bronze map, on which the extent of the whole world was engraved including all the sea and every river. (**V.49.2–8**: *Aristagoras asks Kleomenes to rescue the Ionians from slavery and tells him how easy Persia will be to conquer and how wealthy it is.*) **V.49.9** Aristagoras said this, and Kleomenes answered him with these words: 'Milesian, I will put off answering you for two days.' **V.50.1** This is as far as they went at that point; when the day appointed for the decision came and they met as arranged, Kleomenes asked Aristagoras how many days' journey it was from the Ionian coast to the Great King. **V.50.2** Aristagoras, who had in other respects been clever and misled him well, in this made a mistake: if he wanted the Spartiates to invade Asia he ought not to have told him the truth, but he said that the journey took three months. **V.50.3** Kleomenes cut short the rest of his speech which Aristagoras had started to make about the journey, and said: 'Milesian, you must depart from Sparta before sunset; your proposal is totally unacceptable to the Spartans, for you want to take them a three months' journey from the sea.' **V.51.1** After saying this Kleomenes went home, and Aristagoras took a olive-branch and went to Kleomenes' house, and on entering begged Kleomenes, like a suppliant, to send away the child and listen to him; for Kleomenes' daughter, whose name was Gorgo, was standing beside him; she happened to be his only child and eight or nine years of age. Kleomenes told him to say what he wished and not hold back because of the child. **V.51.2** Thereupon Aristagoras began by promising him ten talents, if he would do what he requested. When Kleomenes refused with an upward motion of his head, Aristagoras went on offering more and more money, until he had promised him fifty talents at which the little child spoke out, 'Father, the stranger will corrupt you, if you don't go away.' **V.51.3** Kleomenes was pleased with his daughter's advice and went into another room and Aristagoras left Sparta for good, not getting another chance to speak about the journey to the Great King.

6.47 Antagonism between Kleomenes and Demaratos

Herodotos VI.49.2–50.3, VI.61.1–66.3

When the Persian designs on mainland Greece became obvious Kleomenes played an active part in dealing with the medising of Aegina. Kleomenes and Demaratos had previously fallen out during the abortive 506 campaign to Attica (cf. doc. 6.21). On the deposing of kings, see Parke (1945) 106–12, 108–09; for trials of kings, de Ste. Croix (1972) 350–52; David (1984) 131–40.

VI.49.2 The Athenians at once reacted violently against them for doing this, believing that the Aeginetans had given (signs of submission) out of hostility to themselves, and that they would join the Persian expedition against them, so, they gladly made use of the excuse and sent to Sparta accusing the Aeginetans of having acted like this as traitors to Greece. **VI.50.1** In response to this accusation Kleomenes son of Anaxandridas, king of the Spartiates, crossed to Aegina, intending to arrest the Aeginetans who were most responsible. **VI.50.2** When he tried to arrest them, some of the Aeginetans opposed him, and amongst them particularly Krios (Ram) son of Polykritos, who said that he would not succeed in arresting a single Aeginetan; for he was doing this without the knowledge of the Spartiate people, persuaded with bribes by the Athenians; for otherwise the other king would have assisted him. **VI.50.3** He said this at the command of Demaratos. As Kleomenes was driven from Aegina, he asked Krios his name; he told him what it was. And Kleomenes replied: 'You'd better cover your horns in bronze, Mr. Ram, as you're going to meet big trouble!' .... **VI.61.1** At this point, Demaratos was discrediting Kleomenes, who was in Aegina and working towards the common good of Greece; Demaratos was not doing this out of concern for the Aeginetans but through envy and malice. When Kleomenes returned from Aegina, he started considering how he might put an end to Demaratos' kingship, and used the following affair as his means of attack: when Ariston was king of Sparta, even though he had married twice, he had no children .... (**VI.61.2–62.2**: *Ariston falls in love with a friend's wife and tricks him into giving her up.*) **VI.63.1** In this way Ariston married his third wife, after divorcing his second. In a fairly short time, not having fulfilled her ten months, his wife gave birth to Demaratos. **VI.63.2** One of his servants reported to him that his son had been born, when he was sitting on his chair of office with the ephors. He knew the date at which he had married his wife and, counting up the months on his fingers, said with an oath: 'He can't be mine!' The ephors heard this, but did not at that point make anything of it; as the boy grew up, Ariston regretted what he had said; for he thought that Demaratos really was his son .... **V1.64** As time went on Ariston died, and Demaratos held the kingship. As it seems, it was fated that these events were to be publicly known and deprive

Demaratos of the kingship, through his quarrel with Kleomenes, first when Demaratos led the army back from Eleusis and then when Kleomenes went over to deal with the Aeginetans who had medised. **V1.65.1** So, eager to pay him back, Kleomenes came to an agreement with Leotychidas, son of Menares and grandson of Agis, who was of the same house as Demaratos, on condition that, if he made him king instead of Demaratos, he would assist him against the Aeginetans. **V1.65.2** Leotychidas was a particular enemy of Demaratos because of the following affair: Leotychidas had been betrothed to Perkalos, daughter of Chilon son of Demarmenos, but Demaratos schemed to deprive Leotychidas of his marriage, and got in first by carrying Perkalos off and marrying her. **V1.65.3** For this reason Leotychidas hated Demaratos, and so now, at Kleomenes' desire, Leotychidas accused Demaratos on oath, saying that he ought not to be king of the Spartiates, as he was not Ariston's son .... **V1.66.2** When this was referred to the Pythia by Kleomenes' design, Kleomenes then won over Kobon son of Aristophantos, an extremely influential person at Delphi, and Kobon bribed Periallos the prophetess to say what Kleomenes wanted. **V1.66.3** So the Pythia, when the messengers put the question to her, responded that Demaratos was not Ariston's son. But later this became publicly known and Kobon was exiled from Delphi, and Periallos deprived of her office.

6.48 Leotychidas and his Son Go to the Dogs

Herodotos VI.70.3–72.2

Demaratos initially remained in Sparta serving as an elected magistrate. Later, he fled to Persia, where he was welcomed by Darius. Leotychidas was soon exiled on a charge of bribery and Archidamos became the Eurypontid king (469–27) and played an important part in the Peloponnesian War, the first phase of which was called after him.

VI.70.3 Such was the fate of Demaratos who in this way reached Asia, he who had been quite outstanding among the Spartans in both actions and statesmanship, and had given them the honour of an Olympic victory in the four-horse chariot race, the only one of all the Spartan kings to have done this. **VI.71.1** When Demaratos was deposed, Leotychidas son of Menares succeeded to the kingship; he had a son Zeuxidemos, whom some of the Spartiates called Puppy (Kyniskos). Zeuxidemos did not become king of Sparta; he died before Leotychidas, leaving a son Archidamos .... **VI.72.1** Nor did Leotychidas grow old in Sparta, but Demaratos was avenged in the following way: when he was general of a Spartan army against Thessaly, and was just about to bring everything under his control, Leotychidas accepted a very large bribe. **VI.72.2** He was caught red-handed in his camp, sitting on a glove full of coins, and was brought before a court and exiled from Sparta, and his house was razed to the ground; he took refuge in Tegea and died there.

6.49 Kleomenes and the Unkindest Cut of All

Herodotos VI.74.1–84.3

Kleomenes by deposing Demaratos laid himself open to a charge of corruption. It is sometimes argued that Kleomenes made cause with the helots (see esp. Wallace (1954) 32–35); the evidence is mainly from Plat. *Laws* 692d that the Spartans were late for Marathon because of war with Messenia, but such a helot uprising is otherwise unattested. A large number of helots (35,000) went with the Spartans to Thermopylai in 479 (Hdt. IX.28.2, 29.1), which seems to preclude a helot uprising in 490 (Lewis (1992) 102). Griffiths (1989) 51–78 argues that many elements in Herodotos' account of Kleomenes' madness are folk-loric in nature, and that there are many similarities between the histories of the Persian king Cambyses and Kleomenes (70–71). **VI.76.1–83.2**: The campaign against Argos probably took place in 494, or a little earlier. The Argive army was defeated at Sepeia, and the survivors fled into a wood: Kleomenes lured some out, and then burned the wood; Griffiths (1989) 57–58 unnecessarily doubts the story of the holocaust. The Argives lost 6,000 men and used this to excuse themselves from participation in the war against the Persians (VII.148–52). **VI.84.1–3**: After Darius' invasion of Scythia in c. 513, a Scythian embassy visited Kleomenes, proposing a joint attack on Persia.

VI.74.1 After this, Kleomenes' schemes against Demaratos were detected and he became afraid of the Spartiates and retired secretly to Thessaly. From there he went to Arcadia where he began stirring up trouble, uniting the Arcadians against Sparta and making them take oaths that they would follow him wherever he might lead them .... **VI.75.1** When the Spartans learnt what Kleomenes was doing, they were afraid of him and brought him back home to the same power as before. He was slightly crazy even before this, but as soon as he returned he was overcome by madness: in fact when he met any of the Spartiates he used to thrust his sceptre into their faces. **VI.75.2** Because of this lunatic behaviour his relatives put him in the stocks; as he was imprisoned there, when he saw that his jailer was on his own he asked him for a knife; at first the jailer did not wish to give it to him, but Kleomenes threatened what he would do once he was released, and fearing his threats the jailer (who was one of the helots) gave him a knife. **VI.75.3** As soon as Kleomenes had the weapon he began mutilating himself from the shins; for he sliced his flesh into strips, proceeding from his shins to his thighs, and from his thighs to his hips and flanks, until he reached his stomach and while he was mincing this up he died. Such a fate, according to many of the Greeks, was owed to his bribing the Pythia to say what she did about Demaratos, but the Athenians say it was because he invaded Eleusis and destroyed the precinct of the goddesses, and the Argives for calling the Argive fugitives from the battle out of the shrine of Argos and massacring them, as well as holding the grove itself in such disrespect that he burnt it down .... **VI.84.1** The Argives say that it was because of this that Kleomenes went mad and died miserably, but the Spartiates themselves say that Kleomenes was not sent mad by any divine agency, but, because of his association with the Scythians, he had become a drinker of neat wine and this sent him mad. **VI.84.2** For the Scythian nomads, when Darius invaded their country, were eager to be revenged on him and sent to Sparta to make an alliance .... **VI.84.3** They say that when the Scythians came with this purpose in mind, Kleomenes associated with them too closely and from more contact with them than was proper learnt from them to drink his wine neat; and the Spartiates think he went mad because of this .... but in my view it was retribution on Kleomenes for what he did to Demaratos.

6.50 The Chorus Prepare to Besiege Lysistrata

Aristophanes *Lysistrata* 256–85

This passage, where the chorus of the *Lysistrata* prepare to besiege the heroine and her female colleagues on the acropolis, refers to Kleomenes' attempt to install Isagoras and his supporters as an oligarchy a century before (see doc. 5.3). The length of time supposedly involved — a siege of six years — is an obvious exaggeration; cf. Tritle (1988) 457. The chorus here is one of elderly Athenian citizens; for the Marathonian tetrapolis, see doc. 5.16.

Truly, many unexpected things
Happen during a long lifetime, alas!,
Since who would ever have expected,
Strymodoros, to hear that
Women, whom we have maintained
At home as a manifest evil,
Would take possession of the sacred image
And seize my acropolis,
And with bolts and bars
Make fast the propylaia? ....
By Demeter, they shall not laugh at us while I'm alive;
Since not even Kleomenes, who was the first to seize it,
Departed scot-free, but
Though breathing Spartan fury
Delivered up his arms to me and left,
With his tiny threadbare cloak,
Hungry,[1] filthy, unplucked,
And unwashed for six years.
Thus I savagely besieged that man,
Sleeping seventeen shields deep at the gates.
And these enemies to Euripides and to all the gods
Shall I not, as I am here, restrain them from such impudence?
No longer then may my trophy still be in Tetrapolis!

[1] Reading πεινῶν (Coulon, Budé, 1967), not πινῶν 'drinking' as in Hall & Gedart (OCT).

LATER VIEWS OF THE SPARTANS

6.51 The Spartans Import 'Professionals'

Aelian *Varia Historia* 12.50

The traditional view that after the Lykourgan reforms Sparta became a cultural and material desert is not completely accurate. The Spartans still had their festivals and contests and they competed at the Olympic games (Buck (1955) no. 71; Finley (1975) 164; Holladay

(1977) 118–19). Aelian's judgement, like that of many modern historians, is too harsh as Tyrtaeus, at least, was a Spartan; see Holladay (1977) 111–26; for Alcman, doc. 13.14.

The Spartans were ignorant of music; for their concern was with athletics and weapons. If they ever needed the help of the Muses in sickness or madness or any other public crisis, they used to send for foreigners such as doctors or purifiers in accordance to a response from the Delphic oracle. For instance they sent for Terpander, Thaletas, Tyrtaeus, Nymphaios of Kydonia and Alcman (for he was a Lydian).

6.52 Spartan Taciturnity

Plutarch *Lykourgos* 19.6–20.8

19.6 Lykourgos himself seems to have been given to brevity of speech and pointed utterances, if his recorded sayings can be taken as an indication. **19.7** For example what he said about government to someone who wanted to make the city a democracy: 'Make your own household a democracy first.' .... **20.5** Demaratos, when a miserable fellow was troubling him with untimely questions and kept on asking him, 'Who is the best of the Spartiates?' answered, 'The one most unlike you.' .... **20.7** Theopompos, when a certain stranger was displaying his goodwill, and kept saying that amongst his own citizens he was called a friend of Sparta, said, 'It would be better, stranger, for you to be called a friend of your fellow citizens.' **20.8** And Pleistoanax son of Pausanias, when an Athenian orator called the Spartans uneducated, replied, 'Your point is quite correct; for we are the only Greeks that have learnt nothing bad from you Athenians.'

6.53 Spartan Training Produces Wild Beasts

Aristotle *Politics* 1338b 9–19 (VIII, iv)

For Aristotle's other adverse comments on Spartan training, see *Pol.* 1338b 24–38, 1271a 41–b 6, 1333b 11–21, 1334a 40–b3. Aristotle's view of Sparta is of course conditioned by the time at which he is writing and contrasts with that of Xenophon and Plutarch.

In our times those states which have the best reputations for taking care of their children aim at creating the condition of an athlete, ruining both their appearance and their bodily growth, while the Spartans, who have not fallen into this error, make them like wild beasts by their physical exertion, on the grounds that this is particularly beneficial to courage. And yet, as I have often said, this care should not be directed towards one virtue only nor to this one in particular; and even if it should be directed towards this virtue they do not achieve even this. For neither amongst other animals nor foreign races do we see courage accompanying the most savage, but rather the gentler and lion-like dispositions.

7

The Persian Wars

For the Greeks the Persian Wars were of great significance, for in 490 and 480–79 the city-states of mainland Greece were faced with the prospect of becoming vassals of the Great Kings of Persia, Darius and Xerxes respectively. The failure of the Persian invasions meant that the Greeks of the mainland remained free — and that they went on to liberate their fellow Greeks of the islands, and the cities of the Asia Minor coast. Prior to his Marathon campaign in 490 Darius had already undertaken an expedition against the European Scythians c. 513 (which takes up most of Book IV of Herodotos' *Histories*) and he remained interested in the general area of Europe. By about 500 BC, just prior to the Ionian revolt, the Persians had control over the Greek cities of the Hellespont, Thrace and Macedon (cf. doc. 7.1). While the Ionian Revolt, led by Aristagoras of Miletos (doc. 7.2), brought the Athenians, and Eretrians, to Darius' attention, it is important to note that the Persian empire had already been expanding in that direction and it was probably inevitable that sooner or later it would have attempted to bring the Greeks of the mainland and the still unconquered islands under its sway. Persian activity north of Greece in the last two decades of the sixth century strongly suggests that the campaign at Marathon was intended as the start of Persian annexation of the Greek mainland. After the Ionian revolt collapsed in 494 with the defeat of the Ionians at the Battle of Lade and the capture of Miletos, various islands were reconquered in 493 by the Persians, and in 492 Mardonios set up democracies in many of the Greek states of Asia Minor.

In 490, the Persians, having sacked Eretria, landed at Marathon in Attica, the place where Peisistratos and his sons, including Hippias, had landed many decades previously in 546. The region may still have retained Peisistratid loyalties. While the Athenians with the Plataeans were preparing to fight the Persians, the messenger Philippides was sent to seek aid from Sparta, but the Spartans were celebrating a religious festival and could not come (doc. 7.7). Miltiades, the former tyrant of the Chersonese but now elected a strategos (general) for 490, was the hero of the day (see doc. 7.8 for details of the battle). A shield signal to the Persians was said to have been made during the course of the battle of Marathon; responsibility for this was attributed to the Alkmeonidai, but Herodotos attempted to absolve them from blame over this incident (doc. 7.9). The Persians, defeated at Marathon, managed to board their ships and made for Phaleron, the main Athenian port at the time, but the Athenians reached there before them. The Spartans arrived too late for the engagement but did tour the battlefield and congratulate the Athenians on their achievement.

The next Persian king, Xerxes, Darius' son, also demanded the submission of the Greek states. Among the cities who 'medised', or went over to the Persians, were the Boeotians, except for the Thespians and Plataeans (doc. 7.18) while the Greeks who were determined to oppose Persia formed the 'Hellenic League'. The Athenians sent to Delphi for an oracle in their hour of need, but the first that they received was so pessimistic that they requested a second (docs. 7.19–20). Themistokles was able to persuade the Athenians to accept the interpretation that the wooden walls, mentioned by the Pythia, referred to the Athenian fleet; he had already been instrumental in building up the Athenian navy (doc. 7.21). The Greeks decided to make a stand at Thermopylai and the Greek fleet was stationed close by, off northern Euboea. At Thermopylai, the allies under the command of King Leonidas of Sparta held off the Persians until they were betrayed by a local, Ephialtes, who showed the Persians a path through the mountain. Leonidas then dismissed most of the Greek forces who were with him; all those with Leonidas fell, and Simonides composed their epitaphs. While Leonidas fought the Persians heroically at Thermopylai, a naval battle took place at Artemision, the northern cape of the island of Euboea. Here the result was inconclusive (doc. 7.30). During the night after the battle, the Greeks fled from the Persians, having heard of the disaster at Thermopylai, and made their way to Salamis. Serious divisions between the Greeks were revealed there, centring around the best strategy with which to oppose the Persians.

At this point the evacuation of Athens took place (docs. 7.31–32), and shortly afterwards the Persians sacked and occupied it. With the Persian forces so near, many of the Peloponnesians wanted to retreat to the Isthmus, along which a wall had been built, but Themistokles threatened that the Athenians would sail off in their ships, and establish a new Athens in Italy and the decision was made to fight at Salamis. To ensure that the battle took place, Themistokles sent a message to the Persians that the Greek fleet was about to sail away, and that they should act quickly to stop this. The Persian fleet trapped the Greek fleet at Salamis, and there was now no choice: the Greeks had to fight (doc. 7.34). The campaign of Salamis was by no means the end of the war but it was a turning point, and the Persians were now on the retreat. There were two more important battles, the campaigns at Plataea (docs. 7.42–43) and at Mykale (doc. 7.46), which took place on the same day. The death of Mardonios at Plataea contributed significantly to the Greek victory, but the Greeks came extremely close to defeat. At the battle of Mykale the Greeks defeated the Persians and gained control of the Hellespont and the Aegean islands. The allied fleet then sailed for the Hellespont; when the allies reached Abydos, they found Xerxes' bridges already destroyed, and Leotychidas and the Peloponnesian allies returned home, while the others stayed to besiege Sestos (see Hdt. IX.106, 114.1–2). Herodotos' narrative ends soon after this, and is taken up by Thucydides, in the section known as the 'Pentekontaetia' (Thuc. I.89–117).

7.1 Persia: Darius' Mighty Empire

Aeschylus *Persians* 852–907

The Persians was produced in 472 and was thus presented to participants in the battle of Salamis only eight years after the event. Aeschylus himself served at Marathon (doc. 7.10) and possibly as one of the heavy-armed troops at Salamis on Psyttaleia. In this scene Xerxes arrives in rags as a visible sign of his great defeat at Salamis (the mother-city of the Salamis in line 892). The chorus in lamenting the defeat recalls the glories of Darius' reign, emphasizing his sway over all his subject territories, Greek especially. See for a recent treatment, with bibliography, Hall (1993) 116–30. For the vast tribute received by Darius from the satrapies of the empire, including the Greek cities of Asia Minor, see Hdt. III.89–97; Armayor (1978) 7; cf. Lewis (1985) 101–17.

Chorus of Persian Elders:
Alas!, it was a glorious and good
Life of social order that we enjoyed, while our aged
All-powerful, guileless, unconquerable King,
God-like Darius ruled the land;

Firstly, we displayed glorious armies,
Which everywhere administered tower-like cities,
And returns from war brought home
Unwearied, unscathed men who had achieved much,

And how many cities he captured, without crossing Halys river's ford
Or rising from his hearth,
Such as the Acheloan cities of the Strymon sea which neighbour
The Thracians' dwellings;

And those outside the marshes on the mainland built round with walls
Obeyed him as lord,
As did outspread Helle around the broad strait, and the embayed Propontis
And the mouth of the Black Sea,

And the sea-washed islands opposite the sea's headland
Lying close to this land,
Such as Lesbos and olive-planted Samos, Chios and Paros,
Naxos, Mykonos, and Andros, Tenos' nearby neighbour,

And he ruled the sea-girt isles lying in mid ocean,
Lemnos and the abode of Ikaros,
Rhodes and Knidos and the Cypriot cities Paphos and Soloi
And Salamis, whose mother-city is now a cause of lamentation;

The wealthy and populous cities, too, in the Ionian lands
Of the Greeks he ruled by his own will,
And possessed the unwearied strength of armed warriors
And allies of different nations;
While now in no doubtful manner we suffer these divine changes of fortune in war,
Overcome woefully by disasters on the sea.

THE IONIAN REVOLT

Aristagoras, tyrant of Miletos, was approached for aid by aristocrats exiled from Naxos; he sought assistance from Artaphernes, the satrap of Lydia, at Sardis, and Darius agreed to the plan. However, the expedition failed (see Keaveney (1988) 76–81). Realising the implications of his failure, and encouraged by Histiaios, the previous tyrant of Miletos, Aristagoras decided to stir up a rebellion of the Greek cities under Persian rule and most of the tyrants in these cities were deposed. The adoption of isonomia at Miletos, and presumably in the other Greek cities, indicates that there was a political desire for such a form of government and that whereas Herodotos gives a great deal of emphasis to the motives of Aristagoras, and to a lesser extent Histiaios, the cities involved had grievances (see Ostwald (1969) 109–11). For Aristagoras' about-face (from being a tyrant organizing a Persian led expedition to the leader of the revolt), see Murray (1988) 475, who compares him to Miltiades. For Herodotos' treatment (books V–VI), note Lang (1968) 24–36; Waters (1970) 504–08; Evans (1976) 31–37; Brown (1981) 385–93; for Histiaios and Aristagoras, Evans (1963) 113–28; Manville (1977) 80–91; for Histiaios: Chapman (1972) 546–68; Murray (1988) 486–87. Because of the involvement of Athens and Eretria, the Ionian Revolt brought the Greeks of the mainland to the attention of Darius (see doc. 7.4), who had already been involved in extending his empire in the expedition against Scythia c. 513.

7.2 Aristagoras at Athens

Herodotos V.97.1–3

Hippias had briefly returned to Greece for the abortive Spartan plan to restore him as tyrant in c. 505–501; he then urged Artaphernes to arrange for the subjugation of Athens: Athenian representatives sent to Sardis were told to take Hippias back, but they refused (Hdt. V.96). For Aristagoras' visit to Sparta see doc. 6.46; Larsen (1932) 136–50.

V.97.1 At this point, while the Athenians were thinking in this way and had already been brought into discredit with the Persians, Aristagoras the Milesian who had been driven out of Sparta by Kleomenes arrived at Athens .... (**V.97.1–2:** *he convinces the people of the wealth to be found in Asia and of the ease with which they will beat the Persians.*) It seems to be easier to impose on many people than on one, if he was unable to mislead Kleomenes, one man, and yet managed it with thirty thousand Athenians. **V.97.3** The Athenians were persuaded and voted to send twenty ships to assist the Ionians, appointing as their commander Melanthios, a distinguished citizen in every respect. But these ships were the beginning of troubles for both the Greeks and the barbarians.

7.3 The Burning of Sardis

Herodotos V.100–103.1

The Panionion was the religious centre of some of the Ionian cities of Asia Minor, the 'koinon' or league of the Ionians (see doc. 10.34). Representatives, probouloi, of the cities which planned to revolt met at the Panionion, though some of these, such as Lesbos (a Dorian island), were not members of the Ionian League *per se.* Military decisions were taken by these representatives (as Hdt. V.109.3, VI.7 indicate) and strategoi had been chosen (Hdt. V.38.2); see, for the league's role in the revolt, Lateiner

(1982) 132–35; for the history of the league, see Caspari (1915) 173–88; Roebuck (1955) 26–40. Athens' position as mother city of the Ionians may have been a factor in its support of the revolt (Hdt. V.97.2; see Connor (1993) 194–206); desire for control of the Hellespont region (note the Athenian interest in and control of Sigeion (doc. 1.15), now within the Persian sphere of influence), probably also played a part. These 20 Athenian ships (plus 5 from Eretria) made their way in 498 to Ephesos, and the troops disembarked and marched to Sardis. The severe defeat of the Ionians at Ephesos led the Athenians to decide to abandon the Ionians, perhaps reinforced by the political situation at Athens, with Hipparchos, probably Hippias' grandson, eponymous archon at Athens in 496/5 (see doc. 5.9).

V.100 The Ionians arrived with this fleet at Ephesos and left their ships at Koressos in Ephesian territory, while they marched up-country with a large force, using Ephesian guides. They marched along the river Cayster, crossed the Tmolos range, and when they arrived captured Sardis without opposition, everything that is except the acropolis; Artaphernes himself saved the acropolis with a large force of men. **V.101.1** They were prevented from plundering the city after its capture by the following: most of the houses in Sardis were made of reeds, even those made of brick having roofs of reed. A soldier set light to one of these and immediately the fire went from house to house until it spread over the entire town .... **V.101.3** When the Ionians saw some of the enemy defending themselves and others approaching in large numbers, they withdrew afraid to the mountains called Tmolos, from there by night departing to their ships. **V.102.1** And Sardis was burned, and in it a temple of the local goddess Cybele, which the Persians later used as an excuse for burning the temples in Greece in return. (**V.102.1–3:** *the Ionians are severely beaten by the Persians at Ephesos.*) **V.103.1** After this the Athenians completely abandoned the Ionians and even though Aristagoras kept sending messengers calling for their aid, they refused to help him. But though the Ionians were deprived of the alliance of the Athenians, none the less, in view of what they had already done against Darius, they carried on preparing for war against the King.

7.4 'Sire, Remember the Athenians'

Herodotos V.105.1–2

Cf. Hdt. VI.94.1. Athenian involvement in the Ionian Revolt meant that Athens was brought to Darius' direct attention. By Zeus, Herodotos means Ahura Mazda, Zeus' Persian equivalent.

V.105.1 When it was reported to King Darius that Sardis had been taken and burned by the Athenians and Ionians, and that the leader of the joint attempt to bring this about was Aristagoras of Miletos, it is said that first, when he learnt this, he paid no attention to the Ionians, knowing well that they would not escape punishment for their revolt, but asked who the Athenians were, and after learning this, called for his bow, took it, fitted an arrow and shot it up to the sky, and as he did so said, **V.105.2** 'Zeus, grant that I may punish the Athenians!' After saying this, he ordered one of his servants to say to him three times every day before dinner, 'Sire, remember the Athenians'.

7.5 The 'Capture of Miletos'

Herodotos VI.18, 21.2

The Battle of Lade in 494 was decisive: many of the Greeks deserted, and the Persians were victorious, going on to sack nearby Miletos. Aiakes, who had been deposed as tyrant of Samos in 499, bribed the Samian captains at Lade, who deserted, causing the majority of the Ionian contingents to do the same (Hdt. VI.13–14); see Lateiner (1982) 151–57; Shipley (1987) 107; cf. Mitchell (1975) 87–88. After the revolt collapsed Mardonios established democracies in many of the Greek cities. Hdt. VI.43.3 states that all of the tyrannies were put down but this seems not to have been the case and tyrants ruled several cities after the revolt: Samos, Halikarnassos, Chios, Lampsakos, and perhaps Kos (Austin (1990) 306). But the establishment of democracies in some cities will have been part of a Persian policy to partly ameliorate the reality of Persian rule; cf. Hdt. VI.42.1. No fragment of Phrynichos' 'The Capture of Miletos' produced probably in 494 survives; it greatly affected the Athenians because of their racial and cultural connections with the Ionians. His 'Phoenician Women', however, which dealt with the events of 480, is known from several fragments: Hall (1993) 115–16; Rosenbloom (1993) 159–96.

VI.18 When the Persians had conquered the Ionians in the sea battle, they besieged Miletos by land and sea and dug under the walls and brought up all kinds of siege engines, taking the entire city five years after the revolt of Aristagoras; and they enslaved the city, so the fate foretold by the oracle for Miletos took place .... **VI.21.2** The Athenians made it clear that they were very distressed by the capture of Miletos in a number of ways and especially when Phrynichos wrote and produced his play 'The Capture of Miletos', at which the theatre was moved to tears, and they fined him a thousand drachmas for reminding them of a domestic disaster and forbade anybody ever again to use this as a subject for a play.

7.6 A Troubled Time for Greece is on the Way

Herodotos VI.98.1–2

Mardonios, a son-in-law of Darius, was sent westwards by the King in 494/3. Thasos submitted, as did Macedonia under Amyntas. But in 492 Mardonios' fleet was wrecked rounding Mount Athos (Hdt. VI.44–45). He returned to Persia, and while he recovered Datis took command. A new policy emerged: to abandon for the moment the advance south along the mainland and instead to sail direct to Euboea, destroy Eretria for the part it played in the revolt, and then attack Attica. On the way, Datis subdued Naxos, sacking the city, including the temples. He was lenient at Delos, and this can be compared with the favourable treatment that Apollo's other important sanctuary, Delphi, received in the second Persian invasion. Datis made an offering on the Delian altar of 300 talents' weight of frankincense; nevertheless after his departure Delos was shaken by an earthquake. From there, Datis went on to attack other islands, where children were taken as hostages, and the city of Karystos in southern Euboea was besieged until it agreed to co-operate (Hdt. VI.95–99); for Datis, see Lewis (1980) 194–95; Balcer (1989) 129–32.

VI.98.1 After Datis had set sail from there, it was the first and last occasion (up to my time anyway) that Delos was shaken, according to the Delians, by an earthquake. God perhaps sent this to men as a portent of the evils that were going to follow. **VI.98.2** For in the time of Darius, son of Hystaspes, and Xerxes, son of Darius, and Artaxerxes, son of Xerxes, three generations in succession, Greece suffered more evils than in the twenty generations preceding Darius, some of which were caused by the Persians, others by the leading states themselves fighting for supremacy.

MARATHON, 490

Datis first captured Eretria and destroyed its temples, in revenge for the destruction at Sardis. Then the Persian force proceeded to Marathon, where the Athenians and the Plataeans alone faced the Persians. There are numerous treatments of the battle at Marathon, disagreeing on various points: Gomme (1952) 77–83; Burn (1962) 236–56; Hignett (1963) 55–74; Bengtson (1968) 44–46; Hammond (1968) 13–57 (esp. 13n.1 for earlier bibliography), (1988) 506–17; Burn (1969) 118–20; Bicknell (1970) 427–39; Green (1970) 30–40; Schreiner (1970) 97–112; Avery (1972) 15–22; Shrimpton (1980) 20–37; Evans (1984) 1–27, (1993) 279–307.

7.7 The God Pan Helps the Athenians

Herodotos VI.101.1–107.1

VI.102: Hippias landed at Marathon, as in 546. The involvement of Hippias with the Persian invasion led to a change in the fortunes of those who at Athens had been friends of the tyrants (see doc. 5.9). **VI.103.1**: Fornara (1971) 72–73 (see also Bicknell (1970) 427–31) argues (*contra* Hammond (1968) 48–50) that Herodotos has misrepresented the position of Kallimachos, for whereas the polemarch was not important when Herodotos was writing, Kallimachos in 490 was the real leader of the army, and Herodotos is incorrect in writing that Kallimachos was chosen by lot (VI.109.2). *Ath. Pol.* 22.2 (doc. 5.8) has the polemarch as the leader of the army; cf. Paus. I.15.3; Herodotos is probably wrong in giving Miltiades the most important position. For Miltiades, see Bicknell (1970) 431; Develin (1989) 56; for the strategoi at Marathon, see Bicknell 432–39; Develin 56–57. **VI.105.1–106.1**: Numerous cults grew out of both Persian invasions (Hdt. VI.105.3, cf. VII.189; Plut. *Them.* 22.1–3 (Themistokles' cult of Artemis Aristoboule); cf. also Bowden (1993) 55–56; Hall (1993) 127–29). Here, Herodotos mentions the epiphany of Pan: see Pritchett (1979) 23; Garland (1992) 47–63; for Pan's shrine at Athens, see Travlos (1971) 417–21; cf. doc. 7.11. There were three other epiphanies at Marathon: a giant hoplite, Theseus, and the hero Echtelos, as well as epiphanies at Artemision and Salamis: Pritchett 11–46 collects the evidence for these and other Greek military epiphanies. The Athenians had vowed at Marathon to dedicate a goat to Artemis for every Persian killed: they did not have enough goats, so commuted the vow to a slaughter of 500 a year, and were still carrying this out in the fourth century (Hdt. VI.117.1 has 6,400 dead Persians; see Xen. *Anab.* III.2.12; Pritchett (1979) 232; Jameson (1991) 210–11). **VI.106.3**: The Spartans frequently cancelled or broke off campaigns for religious reasons: see Holladay & Goodman (1986) 152–60; cf. doc. 6.23.

VI.101.1 The Persians brought their ships in to land in Eretrian territory at Tamynai, Choireai and Aigilia, and having put in to these places they immediately disembarked their horses and made preparations to attack their enemy .... **VI.101.2** A fierce attack took place against the wall and many on both sides fell over a six day period; on the seventh, Euphorbos son of Alkimachos and Philagros son of Kyneas, both notable citizens, betrayed the city to the Persians. **VI.101.3** They entered the city and stripped and burned its temples, taking revenge for the temples burnt at

Sardis, and enslaved the inhabitants, in accordance with Darius' orders. **VI.102** After conquering Eretria and waiting a few days they sailed to Attica, pressing the Athenians hard and thinking that they would do the same to the Athenians as they had to the Eretrians. Marathon was the most suitable part of Attica for riding and the closest to Eretria, and here Hippias son of Peisistratos brought them in to land. **VI.103.1** When the Athenians learnt this, they too set off to Marathon. They were led by ten generals, of whom the tenth was Miltiades, whose father Kimon son of Stesagoras, it so happened, had been banished from Athens by Peisistratos son of Hippokrates .... **VI.105.1** First, when they were still in the city, the generals sent to Sparta a herald Philippides, an Athenian and experienced long-distance runner; as Philippides reported to the Athenians, Pan met him on Mount Parthenion above Tegea. **VI.105.2** Calling Philippides by his name, he told him to ask the Athenians why they paid him no attention, even though he was well-disposed to the Athenians and had already often been of service to them, and would be again in the future. **VI.105.3** And the Athenians believed this to be true and when their affairs settled down again properly they set up a shrine to Pan under the acropolis, and from the time of this message have propitiated him with yearly sacrifices and a torch-race. **VI.106.1** So Philippides was sent by the generals, on which occasion he said Pan appeared to him, and was in Sparta on the second day after leaving the Athenians' city. On arriving he said to the authorities, **VI.106.2** 'Spartans, the Athenians request you to help them and not to look on as the oldest city of the Greeks encounters slavery at the hands of barbarians; for even now Eretria has been enslaved and Greece is the weaker by a famous city.' **VI.106.3** He addressed them as he had been ordered, and they were willing to help the Athenians, but they were unable to do it immediately because they did not wish to break the law; for it was the ninth day of the month, and they said that on the ninth day they could not march out until the moon became full. **VI.107.1** So they waited for the full moon, and meanwhile Hippias son of Peisistratos brought the barbarians in to land at Marathon.

7.8 Marathon: the Battle

Herodotos VI.109.3–117.1

VI.107.2–109.2: for Hippias' omens, see Bonner (1906) 235–38; Shapiro (1990) 337–38. **VI.111.3–113.2**: The complex manoeuvre will have been the result of forward planning and not a chance manoeuvre. The absence of the Persian cavalry in Herodotos' account of the actual battle is the subject of debate (cf. Hdt. VI.102). This absence is usually interpreted as one, if not the main, reason for the Greek success (but see Shrimpton (1980) 20–37; Evans (1984) 3, 10–14). For the topography of Marathon, see van der Veer (1982) 290–321, with references to previous bibliography. **VI.115–116**: see Hodge (1975a) 155–73, (1975b) 169–71 for a discussion of views on the time it would have taken the Persians to sail from Marathon to Phaleron. **VI.117.1**: Pausanias (I.32.3) saw the grave of the Athenians at Marathon, and the stelai on it giving the names of the Athenians killed, listed by their tribes. Herodotos' figure of 192 is normally accepted. The figure of about 6,400 Persian dead is also credible (but cf. Avery (1973) 757). Another source for the battle are the paintings in the Stoa Poikile, the 'Painted Stoa' in the agora at Athens, described by Paus. I.15.3 (for the Stoa itself, see Thompson (1976) 102–03; Camp (1986) 66–72; Diog. Laert. 7.5). Those of the Battle of Marathon date to c. 460, the earliest piece of evidence for Marathon (see Wycherley (1957) 31–45 for testimonia; Hammond (1968) 26; Bicknell (1970) 429–30; Shrimpton (1980) 22; Francis & Vickers (1985) 99–113; Castriota (1992) 28–32; cf. Harrison (1972) 370–78). The south frieze of the temple of Athena Nike on the acropolis has been interpreted as depicting the Battle of Marathon (Harrison 353–70, cf. Pemberton (1972) 303–310, esp. 307–08); for the Parthenon frieze as a monument to the Marathon dead, see Garland (1985) 92; cf. Castriota (1992) 134–83.

(**VI.107.2–109.2**: *The night before landing Hippias had a dream that he was sleeping with his mother, which he took to portend success. However, he lost a tooth on arrival and re-interpreted the dream as foreshadowing failure. The Athenians were joined by the Plataeans with every available man. The Athenian generals were against risking a battle, until Miltiades addressed the following speech to the polemarch Kallimachos.*) **VI.109.3** 'Kallimachos, it is now up to you either to enslave Athens or to liberate her and leave behind such a memory for all the life of men as not even Harmodios and Aristogeiton left behind them. Now indeed the Athenians are facing the greatest danger of any in their history, for if they submit to the Persians they will be handed over to Hippias and there is no doubt what they will suffer, but if this city prevails, she has it in her to become the first among Greek cities' .... **VI.110** By these words Miltiades won over Kallimachos; and with the opinion of the polemarch added to his it was determined that they should attack. After this the generals whose opinion had been on the side of attacking, when their day for presiding came round, each offered it to Miltiades; he accepted it but would not join battle until it was his day for presiding. **VI.111.1** When it came round to his turn, then the Athenians were drawn up into position for attacking; the polemarch Kallimachos was in charge of the right wing; for the Athenians at that time had a law that the polemarch commanded the right wing. Next to him came the tribes, in their correct order, following closely on each other; and last of all the Plataeans were drawn up on the left wing. **VI.111.2** Ever since this battle, whenever the Athenians conduct sacrifices at their four-yearly festival, the Athenian herald prays that the Plataeans too like the Athenians will have good fortune. **VI.111.3** The Athenians' order of battle at Marathon had the following consequence: as the army was stretched out to equal the Persian army, its centre was only a few lines deep so the army was weakest at this point, while each wing was numerically strong. **VI.112.1** When they were drawn up and the sacrificial omens were favourable, the Athenians were then given the word to move and advanced at a run against the barbarians. The space between the armies was not less than eight stades. **VI.112.2** When the Persians saw them attacking at a run they prepared to meet them, imputing total destructive madness to the Athenians, when they saw that they were so few, and that they were hastening on at a run with not even a horse or any archers in support. **VI.112.3** That was the barbarians' view, but the Athenians in close order engaged with the barbarians, and fought in a manner worthy of note. For they were the first Greeks, that we know of, to meet the enemy at a run, and the first to endure seeing Persian dress and the men who wore it; until then even to hear the name 'Persian' gave the Greeks cause for fear. **VI.113.1** The fighting at Marathon went on for a long time. The barbarians prevailed in the centre of the army, where the Persians themselves and Sakai were stationed; here the barbarians were victorious, breaking through and pursuing them inland, but on each wing the Athenians and Plataeans were victorious. **VI.113.2** As they conquered, they allowed the routed enemy to flee, and drawing both wings together fought those that had broken through their centre, and the Athenians were victorious. They followed the fleeing Persians, cutting them down, until they arrived at the sea where they called for fire and took hold of the ships. **VI.114** It was in this struggle that the polemarch Kallimachos was killed, after fighting with bravery, and also Stesilaos son of Thrasylaos one of the generals; Kynegeiros son of Euphorion took hold of the stern of a ship and had his hand cut off and died, and many other famous Athenians also lost their lives. **VI.115** In this way the Athenians took possession of seven ships, but the barbarians backed water in the rest and got away, picked up the Eretrian prisoners from the island on which they had left them, and sailed round Sounion to Athens, aiming to arrive at the city before the Athenians. Amongst the Athenians the Alkmeonidai were blamed for a plot which suggested this plan to the Persians; they were said to have come to an agreement with the Persians and to have held up a shield to them as a signal once they were on board. **VI.116** .... The barbarians in their ships lay off Phaleron (which was at that time the Athenians' port) riding at anchor, and then sailed back to Asia. **VI.117.1** In this battle at Marathon, about 6,400 of the barbarians were killed, and 192 of the Athenians.

7.9 The Shield Signal

Herodotos VI.120–124.2

Cf. VI.115. Hudson (1936–37) 443–59 argues that the shield signal was actually given by the Athenians to Miltiades to signal an 'opportune moment for attack'. But if so, this was forgotten by the time Herodotos wrote, for he is at a loss to assign responsibility and attempts to prove the innocence of the Alkmeonidai by stressing their role in the tyranny's downfall; for Herodotos as an Alkmeonid mouth-piece, see Forrest (1984) 3–4; cf. Gillis (1969) 133–45; Knight (1970) 30. That there was a shield signal has been denied by Ehrenberg (1973) 140, but the tradition at Athens was obviously strong and there is nothing intrinsically implausible about its having taken place (Hudson (1936–37) 446 discussing Lysander's shield signal at Aigospotamoi, Xen. *Hell.* II.1.27–28; Plut. *Lys.* 10–11). An obvious candidate is the pro-tyrant group at Athens, still strong in the 490s as attested by the election of Hipparchos, probably the grandson of Hippias, as archon in 496/5. For the time at which the signal could have been given, see Hodge & Losada (1970) 31–36. For the bribery of the Pythia, see docs. 4.36, 38, 5.1; despite Hdt. VI.123.1 the Alkmeonidai were not in exile for the whole of the tyranny (see doc. 4.24).

VI.120 Two thousand Spartans arrived at Athens after the full moon, and were in such haste to get there that they were in Attica on the third day after leaving Sparta. They had come too late for the encounter, but desired to see the Persians; they went to Marathon and looked at them. They then praised the Athenians' good work and went back home. **VI.121.1** I can not accept the story, which I find quite astonishing, of the Alkmeonidai signalling to the Persians with a shield, wanting the Athenians to be subject to the barbarians and Hippias; these men appeared to be greater tyrant-haters than even Kallias son of Phainippos and father of Hipponikos.

VI.121.2 Kallias was the only one of all the Athenians who dared, when Peisistratos was expelled from Athens, to buy any of his property when it was publicly advertised for sale, and who devised all sorts of other forms of hostility towards him .... **VI.123.1** And the Alkmeonidai were no less tyrant-haters than he was. So the slander surprises me and I can not believe it, that they should give a shield signal, they who were in exile for the whole period of the tyrants and through whose plan the Peisistratidai gave up the tyranny. **VI.123.2** So they were thus the liberators of Athens far more than Harmodios and Aristogeiton, in my view. For the latter aggravated the remaining members of the Peisistratidai by killing Hipparchos, and did not actually put an end to the tyrants at all, while the Alkmeonidai clearly did achieve liberation, if they did in truth bribe the Pythia to tell the Spartans to liberate Athens, as I stated earlier. **VI.124.1** Perhaps, however, they betrayed their country because they had some complaint against the Athenian people. But not so, because they had a better reputation among the Athenians and were more honoured than any others. **VI.124.2** So logic proves that they would not signal with a shield for any reason of that sort. A shield was held up, and it can not be said otherwise; for it was; but as to who held it up I am unable to say more than this.

7.10 Aeschylus' Epitaph

Aeschylus 2 (Athenaeus *Deipnosophistae* 627c)

Despite being one of the greatest of Greek tragedians from 484 until his death in 456, Aeschylus' epitaph focuses only on his service at Marathon; Vidal-Nacquet (1986) 311. His brother Kynegeiros also served at Marathon and was killed there (Hdt. VI.114). Aeschylus visited Hieron more than once and died in Sicily; see Herington (1967) 74–85.

Aeschylus, son of Euphorion, an Athenian, is covered by
This tomb; he died in wheat-bearing Gela.
The famous grove of Marathon can tell his valour
As can the long-haired Persian who knew it.

7.11 Miltiades Dedicates An Offering to Pan

Simonides 5

Page 194–95. A dedication for Pan's help; see Hdt.VI.105; cf. 7.34; for Pan in Athens, see Borgeaud (1988) 133–62; Garland (1992) 47–63. Miltiades was to die of gangrene after being fined 50 talents for not taking Paros: Hdt. VI.136; Plut. *Kim.* 4.4; doc. 12.34.

I, goat-footed Pan, the Arcadian, the enemy of the Persians
And ally of the Athenians, was set up by Miltiades.

7.12 The Athenians' Epitaph at Marathon

Simonides 21

Page 225–31. Probably inscribed with a list of the fallen on a stele at the grave-mound at Marathon; cf. doc. 11.13.

Fighting as Greece's champions the Athenians at Marathon
Laid low the might of the gold-apparelled Persians.

7.13 The Memorial of Kallimachos

Meiggs & Lewis 18 (*IG* I^3 784)

Hansen 256; Paus. I.15.3. This inscription is on the remains of an Ionic column dedicated on the Athenian acropolis after the victory at Marathon, possibly in 489. Kallimachos died at Marathon, but it seems that he vowed the offering before the battle and it was made on his behalf subsequently. The dedicated 'messenger' could be Iris or Nike (Victory). For a discussion of the monument, see Raubitschek (1940) 53–56 (with reconstruction of the column and inscription, 54 fig. 1).

[Kallimachos of] Aphidna [de]dicated [me] to Athena,
The me[ssenger of the im]mortals who have [homes] on O[lympus],
[.... Pole]marc[h] of the Athenians the battle
At Ma[rathon ....]
To the sons of the Athenians [....]

7.14 An Athenian Thank-offering for Marathon

Meiggs & Lewis 19

This was inscribed on a limestone base at the south wall of the Athenian treasury at Delphi, c. 490. The present letters were later reinscribed over the original ones in the third century. Paus. X.11.5 has the treasury being built from the spoils taken from the Persians at Marathon, but is assuming that the date of the dedication was that of the treasury, which could, however, have been earlier (ML p.35).

The Athenians (dedicated this) to Apoll[o] as fir[st-fr]uits [from the Pers]ians
Of the b[attle] of Marath[o]n.

7.15 An Athenian Epigram on ?Marathon

Meiggs & Lewis 26 (II) (*IG* I^3 503)

Hansen 2; Simonides 20b; Page 219–25; *IG* I^2 763. This is an inscription on one of two fragments of an Athenian monument base. The date is subject to much controversy, but the first part of the inscription (doc. 7.36) could refer to Salamis and the second, though inscribed later than the first, is apparently an epitaph for the dead at Marathon, possibly added after the original Marathon monument was destroyed by the Persians in 480. Cf. Raubitschek (1940) 57 fig.3; West (1970) 271–82; Lang (1974) 80. Vidal-Nacquet (1986) 310–11 notes that Marathon became an ideological model, and throughout the fifth century was glorified at the expense of Salamis and Themistokles' achievements.

They truly had an adam[ant ....] when the spear
Was set in front of the gates [....]
To burn the sea-girt [....]
City, turning bac[k] by force the Persian [....].

7.16 Marathon: 'the Victory'

Thucydides II.34.1–5

This passage is part of the funeral oration, delivered by Perikles in 431/0; see Garland (1985) 89–90, 92; Pritchett (1985) 107–118, 124 (94–259 for a detailed treatment of war dead in general). **II.34.1**: For the public burial of the war-dead, see the bibliography at Hornblower (1991) 292–93; cf. Travlos (1971) 302; Clairmont (1983) 29–45; Garland (1985) 90, 131. **II.34.5**: There are other examples of the Athenian war dead being buried where they fell, but Ostwald (1969) 175, accepted by Hornblower, argues from the syntax that Thucydides was aware of these and is giving what he considered to be the most important example. The Athenian dead were cremated and covered with a mound (soros) which can still be seen on the Plain of Marathon. The Plataeans were buried in a smaller mound, with the slaves (of the Athenians; whether Plataean slaves participated is uncertain) who had been freed before the battle: doc. 11.13; cf. Paus. VII.15.7, X.20.2; see Sargent (1927) 209–11; Hammond (1968) 14–18; Burn (1962) 253–54; cf. Notopoulos (1941) 352–54. Paus. I.32.4–5 mentions a monument to Miltiades and a commemorative trophy of white marble; see Vanderpool (1966) 93–106; cf. West (1969) 7–15. Cf. Paus. I.32.5 for the Persian dead who were dumped in a trench.

II.34.1 In the same winter the Athenians, following their ancestral custom, held a public funeral for those who had been the first to die in the war in the following way: **II.34.2** two days beforehand they put up a tent in which they place the bones of the dead, and each person makes what offering he wishes to his own departed; **II.34.3** then there is the funeral procession in which wagons carry coffins of cypress wood, one for each tribe, which holds the bones of that tribe's members. One empty bier, decorated, is carried for the missing, whose bodies could not be recovered. **II.34.4** Any one who wishes, both citizens and foreigners, can join in the procession, and women related to the dead are present lamenting at the tomb. **II.34.5** They place them in the public grave, which is in the city's most beautiful suburb, and they always bury there those who died in war, except those at Marathon: as they judged *their* valour to be outstanding, they made their tomb on the spot.

7.17 Old Marathon Men Discounted

Aristophanes *Acharnians* 692–701

Cf. Ar. *Knights* 781–85, 1333–34 for similar references to Marathon and Salamis, which have obviously become events hallowed by tradition at Athens: the *Acharnians* was produced in 425. Here the chorus protest about the way elderly men are treated by young upstarts in the law-courts.

Chorus of elderly men from the deme Acharnai:

How can it be proper to use the water-clock to destroy a grey-haired old man,
Who has played his part well, often wiping off the warm sweat of manly toil,
And who was a brave man at Marathon for his city?
Then, when we were at Marathon, we were the ones prosecuting the attack,
But now we are the ones wicked men prosecute, and get convicted too.

XERXES' CAMPAIGNS

Darius was apparently more determined than ever to deal with the Greeks, especially the Athenians (Hdt. VII.1). When he died in 486, his son Xerxes inherited the Persian empire and his father's grudge against the Greeks, though see Hdt. VII.5–7. For Xerxes' preparations, see Burn (1962) 317–20; Bengtson (1968) 47–51; Green (1970) 49–53. The Egyptian, Jewish, and Babylonian rebellions did not deter Xerxes (Balcer (1989) 132–36). On the domestic front at Athens in this period, Miltiades had died in disgrace, and several 'friends of the tyrants' had been ostracised (docs. 5.9, 12.34).

7.18 Xerxes Demands Submission

Herodotos VII.32, 131–133.1

Xerxes' heralds secured the medism of several Greek states, many of which were neighbours of Persian dominated areas of northern Greece. To 'medise' was to go over to the Persian side, to give signs of submission (earth and water), and/or to collaborate with the Persians: Graf (1984) discusses the terminology. **VII.132.2**: for the oath and tithe, see Pritchett (1979) 232–33. **VII.133.1**: The Greeks regarded heralds as inviolable; for the divine consequences to the Spartans, see Hdt. VII.133–137; Wéry (1966) 469–70, 479; Mosley (1973) 84, 87; Parker (1989) 154.

VII.32 When Xerxes arrived at Sardis, he first sent heralds to Greece demanding earth and water and ordering that they prepare meals for the King; he sent the demand everywhere except Athens and Sparta. He sent a second time for earth and water because he thought that all those who had not earlier given them to Darius when he sent would now be frightened into co-operating; so he sent his heralds as he wanted to find this out .... **VII.131** Of the heralds who had been sent out to Greece to make the demand, some arrived back empty-handed, others bearing earth and water. **VII.132.1** Of those who gave them, there were the following: Thessalians, Dolopians, Ainianes, Perraibians, Lokrians, Magnetes, Malians, Achaeans of Phthiotis, Thebans, and the rest of the Boeotians except for the Thespians and Plataeans. **VII.132.2** Against these the Greeks who were undertaking to fight the barbarians swore an oath. This oath said that they would make all those Greeks, who gave themselves up to the Persians without being compelled to do so, give a tithe of their property to the god at Delphi, if matters went well for them. This was the Greeks' oath; **VII.133.1** Xerxes did not send heralds to Athens and Sparta to make this demand because when Darius had sent earlier for the same purpose the former had thrown those making the demand into a pit, and the latter into a well, telling them to take earth and water from there to the King.

GREECE PREPARES FOR THE ATTACK

In 480, the Persian army crossed the Hellespont; Xerxes had two bridges of boats constructed, which were subsequently destroyed in a storm — he had the Hellespont lashed and branded as a punishment for this, and the engineers beheaded (Hdt. VII.33–36). To prevent a re-occurrence of the disaster which befell Mardonios' fleet (Hdt. VI.44), Xerxes had a canal cut through the Mt. Athos peninsula (see Isserlin (1991) 83–91). There is no need to believe Herodotos' figures; Aeschylus gives the number of Persian ships as 1,207 (*Pers.* 341–43; cf. doc. 8.14). The Athenians received no comfort from Delphi; the oracle in counselling the Athenians to flee did not so much medise as give an answer appropriate to the situation. Given the odds, the Pythia's first reply was understandable.

7.19 The Delphic Oracle Counsels Flight

Herodotos VII.140.1–3

The Athenians consulted Delphi in either 481 or 480; the latter date is probably to be preferred, being closer in time to the approach of the Persians (cf. Evans (1982) 26–28). The Pythia was said to have spontaneously advised flight. The nature of the Athenian inquiry may have been known to her beforehand, because the Athenians, like other inquirers, had to consult the Pythia through the agency of the Delphian proxenos of their city who accompanied consultants into the temple (Eur. *Andr.* 1103, cf. *Ion* 335, *Hel.* 146). Presumably all major states had such a proxenos at Delphi (*SIG*³ 548; 585). For the oracles, see Parke & Wormell (1956) II.41–42, *Responses* 94–95; Fontenrose (1978) 316–17, *Responses* Q146–147. Some historians doubt their historicity, but the unusual nature of the double response is good evidence for their authenticity (but cf. Georges (1986) 14–59). The story that the Persians were driven off from Delphi by supernatural forces (Hdt. VIII.36–39) was local colouring added later. Delphi was not afterwards blamed for its stance (*contra* Dodds (1959) 74–75; Lloyd-Jones (1976) 69) and the Greeks in general did not view it as having medised. It was consulted after the battle of Plataea (Plut. *Arist.* 20.4; Parke & Wormell (1956) II.46, *Response* 104; Fontenrose (1978) 320, *Response* Q156) and thanksgivings such as the serpent column were made there (doc. 7.44); cf. Evans (1988) 29.

VII.140.1 The Athenians sent envoys to Delphi as they wanted to consult the oracle; and once they had performed the customary rites at the temple, as they entered the sanctuary and sat down, the Pythia, whose name was Aristonike, proclaimed as follows: **VII.140.2**

'Wretched men, why do you sit down? Fly to the ends of the earth and leave
Your homes and the high peak of your circular city.
For neither the head nor the body remains firm,
Nor the lowest feet nor the hands nor is anything left
In the middle, but all are in an evil plight; for it is being devastated
By fire and wrathful Ares, driving his Syrian chariot.

VII.140.3 Many other towers too he will destroy, not merely yours;
He will give many shrines of the immortals to raging fire,
Which now stand drenched in sweat,
Shaking with fear, and down from the topmost roofs
Pours black blood, foreshadowing evil necessity.
But leave the shrine and spread a brave spirit over your ills.'

7.20 The Delphic Oracle and 'The Wooden Wall'

Herodotos VII.141.1–143.2

In an unprecedented move the Athenians, unhappy with the oracle which they had received, approached the Pythia for a second. In some respects their promise to remain there until they died was a threat: for the pollution of dying in temples, cf. doc. 6.25 (Pausanias). There were two interpretations at Athens of the second oracle: one was that the acropolis was meant, which was originally hedged round with a thorn-bush palisade (cf. Hdt. VIII.51.2, where a number of Athenians remained on the acropolis), but others took the 'wooden wall' as meaning the fleet. Robertson (1987) 17–20 has suggested that the 'wooden wall' was a reference to the wall across the Isthmus, originally planned to be of wood, but built as a more permanent structure; see Evans (1988) 25–30 for a critique. The reference to Salamis is difficult to understand if the wall of the Isthmus was meant.

VII.141.1 When they heard this the Athenian envoys were in a dreadful plight. They were about to give themselves up for lost under the evil which was prophesied, when Timon son of Androboulos, one of the most respected men in Delphi, advised them to carry olive-branches and go a second time to consult the oracle as suppliants. **VII.141.2** The Athenians followed his advice and said, 'Lord, respect these olive-branches which we are carrying and give us a better prophecy concerning our country; otherwise we shall not leave the shrine, but remain here until we die.' When they said this the prophetess prophesied for a second time as follows:

VII.141.3 'Pallas is not able to propitiate Olympian Zeus,
Though entreating him with many words and her shrewd wisdom.
But again I will speak this word to you, having made it firm as adamant:
Though all else shall be taken which the boundary of Kekrops
Has within it and the hollow of sacred Kithairon,
Far-sounding Zeus grants to the Trito-born (Athena) that the wooden wall
Only shall be unsacked, and help you and your children.

VII.141.4 Do not await the cavalry and infantry which come,
A great host from the mainland, at your ease, but withdraw
And turn your back; at some point you will meet it face to face.
O divine Salamis, you will destroy women's children
Either when corn is scattered or when it comes together.'

VII.142.1 This seemed to be, and was, milder than the earlier oracle, so they had it written down and returned to Athens. (**VII.142.1–3:** *There was debate in Athens as to whether the wooden wall referred to the acropolis or to ships: believers in the latter were concerned by the implication that they would be defeated.*) **VII.143.1** But there was a certain Athenian who had recently came to the fore, whose name was Themistokles, called the son of Neokles. He said that the diviners' opinions were not entirely correct, pointing out that if the word was really meant for the Athenians it would not have been expressed so mildly, but as 'O *cruel* Salamis' instead of 'O *divine* Salamis', if the inhabitants were going to die for its sake. **VII.143.2** But it was to their enemies that the god really referred in the oracle, not the Athenians. Accordingly he advised them to prepared to fight at sea, as the 'wooden wall' did mean this.

7.21 Themistokles Builds the Fleet, 483/2

[Aristotle] *Athenaion Politeia* 22.7

This is part of doc. 5.9. Themistokles was the architect of the build-up of the Athenian navy prior to the second Persian invasion and responsible for Athens becoming a maritime power; he had persuaded the Athenians to use the money from the mines to build 100 ships for use against Aegina (Plut. *Them.* 4.3: 100 ships, Hdt. VII.144: 200). Other sources have the ship-building as a public proposal; see Hignett (1963) 96–97; Burn (1962) 291–93; Bengtson (1968) 49; Green (1970) 53–56; Lenardon (1978) 51–56.

22.7 In the third year after this (the ostracism of Xanthippos son of Ariphron), in the archonship of Nikodemos (483/2), when the mines at Maroneia were found and the city had a surplus of a hundred talents from the workings, some people advised that the money should be divided up between the people, but Themistokles prevented this, refusing to say what he would use the money for, but telling them to lend the hundred wealthiest Athenians a talent each; if they were happy with the way the money had been spent, the cost would be the city's, and if not they could take back the money from the people to whom it had been lent. Getting it on these conditions, he had a hundred triremes built, each of the hundred men building one of them, and with these they fought the naval battle at Salamis against the barbarians.

7.22 The 'Hellenic League': the Greek Alliance

Herodotos VII.145.1–2

The unity which (some of) the Greeks were able to achieve in the face of the Persian invasion of 480 is usually cited as the main reason why they were victorious (eg Brunt (1953/54) 135; but cf. docs. 7.6, 7.50). Athens ceded military leadership, even of the fleet, to the Spartans (Hdt. VIII.2.2–3.1, cf. Plut. *Them.* 7.3–4): the fleet was under the command of Eurybiades; the land forces were under Leonidas. The 'Hellenic League' seems to have met first in 481, for the spies sent out to Persia as a result of this meeting found Xerxes still in Sardis. The League also sent ambassadors to various Greek states; for the oath sworn by the Greeks, note Hdt. VII.132.2 (doc. 7.18). According to Paus. III.12.6, there had been a previous meeting of various Greek delegates at the 'Hellenion' at Sparta; this is accepted by most scholars and the decision to form the league was presumably taken there (cf. Hignett (1963) 98n.1, sceptical of this evidence). Argos had a Delphic oracle excusing it from participation (because they were short on manpower after Kleomenes' massacre; doc. 6.49), and their demand for an equal share in the command of the forces was rejected (Hdt. VII.148–152). Gelon, tyrant of Syracuse, also refused to send aid; see doc. 2.33 (Brunt 158–62). The Cretans also received a Delphic oracle not to become involved: Hdt. VII.169. This Hellenic League remained in existence for some decades, and the Athenians renounced it only after the Spartans dismissed them from Mt. Ithome: Thuc. I.102.4 (doc. 8.9). The Hellenic League and the Peloponnesian Leagues were two different entities (Brunt 141–50), but it is possible that the Delian League was modelled on the Hellenic League; see Larsen (1944) 151, 154, (1955) 48, 57; Brunt 135–63; Hignett (1963) 97–102; Green (1970) 69–72; cf. Tronson (1991) 93–110 who argues that the Hellenic League was an 'ideological fiction' made up after the event.

VII.145.1 The Greeks who were loyal to the Greek cause now assembled and gave each other promises and guarantees, deciding in their discussion that the most important thing of all was to reconcile enmities and put a stop to existing wars between each other; of such wars which were taking place, the most serious was that between the Athenians and Aeginetans. **VII.145.2** Later on, when they learnt that Xerxes and his force were at Sardis, they decided to send spies to Asia to learn of the King's actions, and envoys to Argos to make an alliance against the Persians, and to send others to Sicily to Gelon son of Deinomenes, and others to Corcyra and to Crete, bidding them to come to the rescue of Greece. They hoped that Greece would be united and that they would all, in concert, take the same action, in as much as these dangers threatened all the Greeks alike. Gelon's power was said to be immense, greater by far than that of any other Greek.

7.23 The Magnificent Persian Force Goes Forth

Aeschylus *Persians* 73–91, 101–14

The Persian elders are anxious as to what is happening in Greece, having received no news; parents and wives are missing the Persian soldiers, and the whole country regrets the absence of the stalwart warrior, Xerxes, 'the flower of Persia'.

Chorus of Persian Elders:

The impetuous ruler of populous Asia
Against the whole earth is driving his wondrous army
In two parts, confident in those in charge on land and those strong by sea,
His stern commanders, himself a godlike light of a gold-begotten race.

Flashing from his eyes the dark glare of a deadly dragon
With many men and many sailors and urging on his Syrian chariot
He leads on a warrior host of archers against men famed for the spear.

No one's of such tried valour that he can withstand a mighty flood of men
And ward off with strong defences the unconquerable wave of the sea;
Persia's host is hard to fight and her soldiers are stout-hearted ....

By the gods' will Destiny has prevailed
From times of old, and imposed upon the Persians
The conduct of wars which destroy towers
And the turmoil of horsemen and the desolation of cities;

And they have learnt, when the broad-pathed sea
Grows white with a furious storm
To look upon the ocean plain
Trusting in their finely-turned cables and man-conveying devices.

7.24 Persia's Target

Aeschylus *Persians* 230–55

Atossa the Queen Mother has had an unfavourable dream portending Xerxes' defeat, and she therefore asks the chorus for information about Athens. This is obviously a dramatic device: as Darius' wife (also Cyrus' daughter, and previously wife of Cambyses, her brother) she should have known all about Athens and Darius' earlier invasion. At the end of the conversation a messenger arrives with the news of the battle of Salamis. This is clearly written from the point of view of the Athenian audience.

Atossa: I would like to learn this:
My friends, where on the earth do they say that Athens lies?
Chorus: Far off, at the setting-point of our Lord the Sun, as he declines.
Atossa: Does my son really desire to destroy this city?

Chorus: Yes, for all Greece would then be subject to the King.
Atossa: Do they then have such a multitudinous army?
Chorus: Yes, such an army that has driven off the Persians with great disaster.
Atossa: Is the bow-stretching arrow suited to their hands?
Chorus: Not at all; lances for close fight and shield-bearing armour.
Atossa: What else in addition? Sufficient wealth at home?
Chorus: They have a spring of silver, the earth's treasure.
Atossa: And who is their chief and lord over their army?
Chorus: Of no man are they called the slaves or subjects.
Atossa: How then can they await the approaching enemy?
Chorus: Well enough to have destroyed Darius' large and splendid host.
Atossa: Your words give dire food for thought for the parents of those going there.
Chorus: But I think you will soon know the whole account in truth;
For the running of this man seems to be Persian,
And he bears clear news of something, whether good or ill.
Messenger: O cities of all the land of Asia,
O Persian land, great haven of wealth,
How at one blow your great prosperity has been destroyed,
The flower of the Persians fallen and departed.
Alas!, it is bad to be the first to report bad news,
But I must unfold the whole catastrophe,
Persians — the whole barbarian host has perished!

THERMOPYLAI AND ARTEMISION

The Thessalians sent representatives to the Hellenic League at the Isthmus, where it was decided to send a force by sea to the pass at Tempe in May 480. The Athenians were commanded by Themistokles. The force of 10,000 returned soon after and Thessaly passed into Persian hands, largely due to Persian sympathisers (Hdt. VII.172–174; see Robertson (1976) 100–20). The Greeks met at the Isthmus and discussed war strategy, deciding to hold the pass at Thermopylai ('Hot Gates') and to send the fleet to Artemision (Hdt. VII.175–177). The Hellenic League, however, did not make all military decisions, as many of these had to be made in the field: the decisions to flee from Artemision, and fight at Salamis, were made by the military commanders on the spot. The defeat at Thermopylai meant that central Greece was now lost to the Persians. Both battles, Thermopylai and Artemision, took place in September 480.

7.25 Thermopylai

Herodotos VII.204–222

Leonidas went north, but the festival of the Karneia prevented the rest of the Spartan force from marching; see Sacks (1976) 232–48 for 19 Sept. 480 as the final day of Thermopylai; Hammond (1988) 591 has a chronological chart. Neither the Thespians nor the Plataeans medised and it is sometimes overlooked that not only did the Spartan force die, but also the Thespians (VII.222), as well as helots (VIII.25.1). See Buck (1987) 54–60, rejecting Herodotos' account of the Thebans deserting at Thermopylai and arguing that they medised only after the disaster at Thermopylai (note Hdt. VII.225.2, 233). For arguments about Leonidas' motives, see esp. Grant (1961) 14–27; Simpson (1972) 1–11. The Spartan stand did allow for the retreat of the other Greeks from the pass, losses were inflicted on the Persians, and Leonidas presumably felt that flight was ignominious: cf. doc. 7.48. Note the Persian spy's astonishment when he saw the Spartans exercising and combing their hair before the battle (Hdt. VII.208.3; cf. doc. 6.12).

VII.204 The other states each had their own generals, but the most generally respected was the Spartan Leonidas son of Anaxandridas, who was commander of the whole army .... **VII.205.2** He then went to Thermopylai with the 300 men he had chosen, who were in their prime and had living sons. He arrived also having picked up from the Thebans a force whose size I have mentioned, of whom Leontiades son of Eurymachos was in command. **VII.205.3** Out of all the Greeks the reason why Leonidas took pains to take only these was because it was strongly alleged that they were medising; so he summoned them to the war wishing to find out whether they would send help or would openly disown the Greek alliance. They did send troops, but their sympathies were elsewhere. **VII.206.1** The Spartiates had sent Leonidas and his 300 men on ahead, in order that the other allies might see them and join the expedition, and not medise, as they might do if they learnt that the Spartans were delaying; and afterwards, when the Karneia, which was what was preventing them, was over, they were going to leave guards in Sparta and come to the rescue as quickly as possible with their whole force. **VII.206.2** The rest of the allies also planned to do the same themselves; for the Olympic festival fell at the same time as these events; so because they did not expect the battle at Thermopylai to be decided so quickly they sent only advance parties. (**VII.207–220.4:** *Xerxes' initial attacks were unsuccessful, but finally the Persians learn of a track leading over the hills. Leonidas deliberately dismisses all the allied troops.*) **VII.221** Not the least evidence of this in my view is the case of the seer who accompanied this army, Megistias the Akarnanian, said to be descended from Melampous, who had foretold what was going to happen to them from the sacrificial victims, whom Leonidas clearly sent away so he should not die with them. Despite being dismissed he did not leave, but sent away his son, his only child, who was serving with him. **VII.222** The allies then were dismissed and left in obedience to Leonidas, and only the Thespians and Thebans remained except for the Spartans. Of these the Thebans remained unwillingly and against their wishes (for Leonidas kept them as hostages), but the Thespians stayed of their own accord, refusing to go and desert Leonidas and his companions, and instead remained and died with them.

7.26 The Epitaph of Megistias the Seer

Simonides 6

Page 195–96; Hdt. VII.228.3–4. Megistias of Akarnania had predicted his own death (Hdt. VII.219, 221); the Spercheios is just north of Thermopylai. Of all the epigrams ascribed to Simonides, this has one of the strongest claims to authenticity (as has 22: doc. 7.28). For Simonides' work relating to 480, see esp. Podlecki (1968) 257–75.

This is the tomb of famous Megistias, whom once the Persians
Killed when they crossed the river Spercheios;
A seer, who then clearly knew that the Fates of Death were approaching
But could not endure to forsake Sparta's leaders.

7.27 Leonidas

Simonides 7

Page 196–97; this is perhaps Hellenistic in date. The Spartan epitaph at Thermopylai was Simonides 22b.

The earth hides glorious men, Leonidas, who with you
Died here, king of spacious Sparta,
After they had awaited in war
The might of the Persians' many bows and swift-footed horses.

7.28 Epitaphs for the Greeks and the Spartans

Simonides 22 a & b

Page 231–34; see Hdt. VII.228: the dead were buried where they had fallen. 22a was an inscription for the whole force left with Leonidas; 22b was for the Spartans. These have very strong claims to being authentic works of Simonides.

a. Here against three million once fought
Four thousand from the Peloponnese.

b. Stranger, tell the Spartans that here
We lie, obeying their orders.

7.29 Epitaph for the Lokrians

Simonides 23

Page 235–36; Strab. IX.4.2 (425). Hdt. VII.203.1 mentions that the Opuntian Lokrians were amongst those with Leonidas at Thermopylai, but they were not at the final stand; the Lokrians commemorated here must have died in previous engagements (Page 235). The Lokrians subsequently went over to the Persians (Hdt. VIII.66.2).

These men who died for Greece against the Persians are mourned
By Opous, mother-city of the righteous-judging Lokrians.

7.30 Artemision

Herodotos VIII.16.1–18

Artemision is the cape at the northern point of Euboea; a naval battle was fought there at the same time as at Thermopylai. For Themistokles' bribery of Eurybiades and Adeimantos to stay and fight at Artemision, see Hdt. VIII.4–5. The battle at Artemision was inconclusive, though there had been some Greek successes in naval engagements on previous days. As at the battle of Salamis, Xerxes' large fleet hindered its own efforts by its lack of ability to manoeuvre.

VIII.16.1 As the forces of Xerxes sailed in their battle order to the attack, the Greeks at Artemision stayed quiet. The barbarians formed a crescent shape with their ships and encircled them to try to surround them. Thereupon the Greeks put to sea against them and engaged them. The two sides were about equal in this naval battle. **VIII.16.2** For Xerxes' fleet because of it size and numbers kept harming itself, with the ships in confusion continually falling foul of one another; nevertheless it kept fighting and did not yield; for they considered it dreadful to be turned to flight by fewer ships. **VIII.16.3** Many of the Greeks' ships were destroyed, and many men, but far more of the barbarians' ships and men .... **VIII.18** Thus they disengaged, with both sides glad to hasten to their anchorage.

SALAMIS

Even after Themistokles convinced Eurybiades the Spartan commander that the allied fleet had to fight the Persians, there were those who disagreed, and the decision was almost reversed. Themistokles' message to the Persian king encouraged Xerxes into the trap and ensured that the battle took place. Themistokles was the architect of the defeat of the Persians: by choosing the scene of the battle, where the smaller and fewer Greek ships had the advantage, he made victory over the Persians possible; for Artemisia, cf. doc. 13.25.

7.31 The Themistokles Decree, 480

Meiggs & Lewis 23

This decree was inscribed in the third century BC (less probably the late fourth century), and there is much debate about whether it is or at least reflects a fifth century original. It was discovered at Troizen in the Peloponnese, south of Athens and Salamis. Most of the Athenians sent their children (and wives) and slaves to Troizen, though some went to Aegina and Salamis (Hdt. VIII.41.1; Paus. II.31.7). Hdt. VII.144.3 implies some form of this decree: the Athenians decided to fight at sea against the Persians; cf. Dem. XIX.303; Plut. *Them.* 10.4. There is an extensive bibliography on this inscription; see the original publication of Jameson (1960) 198–223 with (1962) 310–15. Note also Chambers (1961–62) 306–16, (1967) 157–67; Dow (1962) 353–68; Pritchett (1962) 43–47; Jameson (1963) 384–404; Hignett (1963) 458–68; Burstein (1971) 93–110; Jordan (1979) 77–80; Mattingly (1981) 79–87; Hammond (1982) 75–93, (1986) 143–48; Robertson (1982) 1–44 (this list is not exhaustive; on balance the majority of scholarship is against the authenticity of the decree).

The inscription (lines 44–47) refers to the recall of the ostracised in 481/0 (Rhodes 281); cf. *Ath. Pol.* 22.8 (see doc. 5.9); Plut. *Them.* 11.1, *Arist.* 8. One of the recalled was Aristeides, ostracised in 483/2 (see docs. 5.9, 12, 14 ii), who played an important role in capturing Psyttaleia at the eastern end of the Salamis channel (cf. Aeschyl. *Pers.* 447–64 (doc. 7.34); Hdt. VIII.95; Plut. *Arist.* 9.1–4; Fornara (1966) 51–53; Green (1970) 196–97); Aristeides' role at Salamis (Hdt. VIII.79–81, Plut. *Arist.* 8, cf. *Them.* 12.6–8) was later exaggerated to counter the achievement of Themistokles; he was strategos at Plataea (doc. 7.43), and went on to play an important role in setting up the Delian League. The foreigners (ll. 14, 30) must be metics.

(1) [Gods]. It was resol[ved] by the boule and the people: Themis[tokl]es son of Neokles of Phrearrhioi proposed the motion: [to en]tr[u]st th[e] ci[ty] to Athena [who prot]ects Athens (5) a[nd to all the oth]er gods to guard an[d] ke[ep off the ba]rbar[i]an in defence of the country; and that [a]l[l] Athenian[s and the foreig]ners living in Athens should place [their chil]dre[n and wiv]es i[n] Troizen [.... ? in the protection of Theseus] the founder of the land; and that they should pla[ce] (10) t[he old people and the] moveable possessions on Salamis[; and that the treasurers and the p]riestesses should remain on the acropoli[s guarding the belongings of th]e gods; and that all the other Athe[nians and the for]eigners who have reached adulthood should embark o[n the prepar]ed two hundred ships and (15) resi[st] t[he barbarian on behalf o]f freedom, both their own [and that of the other Greeks], along with the Spartans and Corin[thians and Aeginetans] and the others who wis[h] to sh[are in the dange]r; and that the gene[r]al[s] should appoint [two hundred] trierar[chs, one for] each ship, (20) [beginning t]omorrow, from those who o[w]n both la[nd a]nd [hom]e in Ath[e]ns and who have legit[imate] childr[en and are not more th]an fifty years of age, an[d] should [a]ss[ign t]he ships t[o t]hem by lot; vv they should also choose [t]en ma[r]ines [for eac]h ship from those between twenty [and (25) thi]rty years of age and four archers; they should [a]lso ap[point by lot] the officers for the ships when they al[so] appoint [the trierar]chs by lot; the generals should als[o] list [the others ship] by ship on notice-[boards, the A]thenians according to the deme (lexiarchic) regist[ers (30) and the] foreigners from those registered wi[t]h the [pole]m[arch;] they should list them, assigning them [t]o two hundred divisions of [u]p to a hundred men each and inscribe for each [divis]ion the name of the trireme and the trierarch and the offi[ce]rs so that they may know on which trireme (35) e[a]ch [d]ivision should e[m]bark; and when al[l] the divisions have been assigned and allocated to the triremes, the boule and t[h]e general[s] are to man a[l]l the two hundred ships after [sa]crificing to propitiate Zeus the Almighty (Pankrates) and Athena and Victory (Nike) and Poseidon (40) the Preser[v]er (Asphaleios); and when the ships are manned, with one hundred of th[e]m they are to assist Artemis[i]on in Euboea, and with the other hundred around Salamis and the rest of Attica they are to lie in wait and guard the country. So that all Athenians may be united (45) in resisting the barbarian, those who have changed their residence for [ten] years are to go to Salamis and stay t[here until the peo]ple should decide about them; and those [deprived of civic rights ....]

7.32 The Athenians Abandon their City

Plutarch *Themistokles* 10.8–10

The fact that the incident with the dog is supposed to have happened to Xanthippos, Perikles' father, rather detracts from than adds to its credibility; however, such a feat is not intrinsically impossible, and Plutarch here well portrays the anguish with which the Athenians abandoned their city. For the warning of the serpent on the acropolis (its failure to eat the honey-cake persuaded the Athenians that Athena was in favour of their abandoning the city), see Hdt. VIII.41.2–3.

10.8 As the whole city sailed off, the sight filled some with pity, others with amazement at their courage, as they sent off their families in one direction, and themselves crossed over to the island without flinching at the lamentations, tears and embraces of their parents. **10.9** Those of the citizens left behind because of their old age were most pitiable, while the affectionate disposition of the tame, companionable animals was also touching, as, howling and longing to be with their owners, they ran alongside them as they embarked. **10.10** Among these was a dog belonging to Xanthippos, Perikles' father, who, the story goes, could not endure being parted from him, and who jumped into the sea and swam alongside the trireme and was cast ashore at Salamis, where he fainted and immediately died; they say that its tomb is the place named the Dog's mound, which even today is pointed out.

7.33 Themistokles Carries the Day

Plutarch *Themistokles* 11.2–5

This discussion between the allies took place at Salamis; cf. Hdt. VIII.57–63, for presumably a more accurate and detailed account, where it was Adeimantos the Corinthian commander (not Eurybiades) who made the initial remark and then accused Themistokles of being a man without a polis, to which Themistokles replied that the Athenians would sail to Siris in Italy. For Adeimantos, see doc. 7.37.

11.2 Eurybiades had command of the ships because of Sparta's reputation, but he was faint-hearted in the face of danger, wanting to set sail for the Isthmus, where the Peloponnesians' infantry was gathered, but Themistokles spoke against him. **11.3** It was at this point that he made the remark which has often been quoted; for when Eurybiades said to him, 'Themistokles, at the games they thrash those who start before the signal,' Themistokles replied, 'Yes, but they don't crown those who are left behind.' And when Eurybiades raised his staff as if to hit him, Themistokles said, 'Strike me if you like, but listen.' .... **11.5** When someone then said that it wasn't proper for a man without a city to instruct those who had one to abandon it and desert their country, Themistokles turned to him and said, 'We have abandoned our homes and walls, you rascal, because we did not want to be enslaved by lifeless things; but we have the greatest city in Greece, our two hundred triremes, which are now ready to help you, if you want to be saved by them, but if you go away and betray us again, the Greeks will soon hear that the Athenians have acquired a city as free and land no worse than that we cast off.' When Themistokles said this, Eurybiades was afraid that the Athenians might leave and abandon them.

7.34 The Battle of Salamis

Aeschylus *Persians* 348–471

Atossa the Persian queen, mother of Xerxes, here asks the messenger about the action. Hdt. VIII.90.4 (cf. 86) mentions that Xerxes watched the battle from the base of a hill across from Salamis; compare lines 466–67 below. Frost (1973) 118–19 points out that Xerxes sat on a diphros (Plut. *Them.* 13.1), and Dem. XXIV.129 mentions an argyropous diphros (silver-footed stool) amongst the barbarian loot dedicated on the acropolis. The diphros, according to Dinon *FGH* 690 F26, was the stool which a Persian king would use when he descended from his chariot. Xerxes did not sit on a throne watching the battle, but drove around in a chariot, and when the action became critical, got down from his chariot, and sat on his chariot stool. Note that the treasures of the Parthenon included several diphroi: doc. 10.6. For Themistokles' stratagem which persuaded the Persians to stay and fight, see Detienne & Vernant (1978) 313–34; cf. Hdt. VIII.75. Wardman (1959) 49–55, 59–60 stresses the pro-Athenian nature of the *Persians* and how it reflects the Athenian view that Salamis was the most important campaign of the 480–79 war, while Goldhill (1988) 189–93 argues that the *Persians* celebrates Athenian democratic ideology; see also Hillard (1991) 132–51. For Themistokles' reported human sacrifice of three Persian princes sons of Xerxes' sister before the battle, see Plut. *Them.* 13.2–5; Hughes (1991) 111–15.

Atossa: Is the city of Athens then still not sacked?
Messenger: Its defences are secure, while it has its men.
Atossa: And, tell me, what began the naval engagement;
Who started the battle, whether the Greeks,
Or my son, exulting in his multitude of ships?
Messenger: The whole evil was begun, my lady,
By some avenging spirit or evil genius that appeared from somewhere;
For a Greek man from the Athenian host
Came and said this to your son Xerxes:
That when the blackness of dark night should descend
The Greeks would not remain, but on the decks
Of their ships they would leap, one one way, one another,
And each would save his life in secret flight.
Straightway as he heard this, not knowing of the guile
Of this Greek or the jealousy of the gods,
Xerxes proclaimed this speech to all his captains:
That when the sun ceased illuminating the earth with his beams,
And darkness covered the precinct of the sky,
They should marshal the close array of ships in three lines
With other ships in a circle around the island of Ajax
To guard the entrances and surging straits;
If the Greeks should avoid an evil fate
And find some means of flight secretly with their ships,
It was decreed that each captain should lose his head.
Xerxes spoke this from a very cheerful heart,
For he did not know the future destined by the gods.
And they not in disorder but with obedient minds
Prepared their dinner, and meanwhile the seamen
Were fastening their oars around the well-fitting pins.
Now as the sun's light dwindled
And night came on, every man who was lord of the oar,
Every man who was master of arms, went to his ship;
Rank of each long ship encouraged rank,
And they sailed as each had been commanded;

All night long the ships' commanders
Kept all the mariners cruising at the oar.
And night was passing, and the Greek host did not at all
In any way attempt a secret exit;
But when, however, white-horsed day
Brilliant to behold, shone over the whole land,
First of all, resoundingly a noise from the Greeks
Echoed in praise like song, and at the same time clearly
The echo of the mountain rock returned the cry,
And fear seized all the barbarians, who
Had been deceived in their opinion; for not in flight
Were the Greeks then chanting the solemn battle-hymn,
But rushing into battle with cheerful courage.
And the trumpet with its battle-cry inflamed them all;
Immediately with the stroke of the dashing oar
They struck the deep sea-water at command.
Swiftly all were clearly plain in view;
First the right wing, well-disciplined,
Led on in good order, and next the whole fleet
Advanced, and one could hear in unison
A mighty shout: 'Forward, O sons of Greece, forward,
Liberate your native land, and liberate your
Children and your wives, the seats of your ancestral gods,
Your forebears' tombs; now the struggle is for your all.'
And from us a roar of Persian voices
Rose in answer, and no longer did time permit delay.
Immediately ship struck into ship its bronze-tipped
Prow; a Greek ship began the attack,
Smashing the whole of a Phoenician ship's
High stern, and each side directed one ship against another.
Initially, the stream of the Persian fleet managed to stand its
Ground; but when in the narrow strait the multitude of ships
Were gathered, and no help could be given to one another,
They struck each other with their bronze-tipped
Rams, and all their rowing gear was broke to pieces.
Meanwhile the Greek ships, with deliberation,
Circled and battered them on every side, ships' hulls
Were overturned, and no longer could one see the sea
Now filled with shipwrecks and men's slaughter;
And shores and reefs were full of corpses.
Each of our ships started rowing off in disorder,
As many as survived from the barbarian fleet ....
441 Those Persians in the prime of life,
Bravest in spirit and notable in birth,
And always amongst the first to show loyalty to the King,

Have died disgracefully by a most inglorious fate.
Atossa: This dreadful calamity has made me wretched, friends.
But by what death do you say that these men perished?
Messenger: There is an island in front of Salamis,
Small, poor anchorage for ships, which the dance-loving
Pan frequents along its sea-washed shore;
Here Xerxes sent these men, so that, when from the ships
The ship-wrecked enemy might seek safety on the isle,
They could slay the easily-mastered host of Greeks,
And save their own friends from the narrow straits of the sea,
Badly forecasting the future; for when god
Gave the Greeks the glory of the battle of the ships,
They straightway fenced their bodies round with well-wrought brazen
Armour, bounded from their ships, and
Encircled the whole island, so our men were at a loss
Where they might turn. Many times they were struck
By hand-thrown rocks, and from the bow's bowstring
Arrows fell upon them and destroyed them;
At last the Greeks rushed on them all at once
And struck them, cutting to pieces the wretches' limbs,
Until they utterly destroyed the life of all.
Now Xerxes, seeing the depths of his misfortunes, groaned lamentation;
For he had a seat in view of the whole host,
A high hill near the shore of the open sea;
Rending his garments, uttering a loud wail,
He gave orders immediately to his infantry,
And dismissed them in disorder and in flight. Such now,
Besides the previous one, is the disaster you must mourn.

7.35 The Athenians Review their Past Services to Greece

Thucydides I.73.2–74.3

The context is the debate at Sparta in 432 when the Spartans voted that the Athenians had broken the Thirty Years' Peace made in 446/5. **I.73.4**: The Athenians' statement that 'we were the only ones to face up to the barbarian' neglects the help given by the Plataeans (esp. Hdt. VI.108.6); see Loraux (1986) 157–58; Walters (1981b) 204–11. **I.73.4–74.1**: Cf. Herodotos (doc. 7.49) for a similar assessment of the Athenians' role in the second Persian invasion, probably derived from Athenian sources. **I.74.1**: There were actually 200 Athenian ships in a Greek fleet of 366 or 378; see Hdt. VIII.48, cf. VIII.1, 14.1, 61.2, 82.2; Gomme *HCT* I.234–35; Walters (1981a) 199–203; Loraux (1986) 403n.118; Hornblower (1991) 119. The honours for Themistokles after Salamis from the Spartans consisted of a crown of olive for wisdom, the best chariot in the city, and an escort to the border of Sparta by a special guard of honour of 300 hippeis: Hdt. VIII.124.2–3; Plut. *Them.* 17.3; see Jordan (1988) 547–71; cf. Pritchett (1974) 283–90.

I.73.2 We must speak of the Persian Wars, events which you yourselves know well, even though you may be tired of always hearing them referred to .... **I.73.4** Our view is that at Marathon we were the only ones to face up to the barbarian and when he came later, and we were not able to keep him off by land, we got into our ships with all our people and joined in the naval battle at Salamis, which prevented him from sailing against the Peloponnese and ravaging it city by city, for they would have been unable to come to each other's aid in the face of such a number of ships. **I.73.5** The best proof of this is the barbarian's own actions: once he had lost at sea, he withdrew as quickly as possible with the greater part of his host because his force was no longer adequate. **I.74.1** This then was the outcome, and it clearly demonstrated that Greece's destiny depended on her ships, and we contributed to this in the three most useful ways: in providing the greatest number of ships, the most intelligent general and our resolute courage; for of the four hundred ships a little less than two thirds were ours, Themistokles was in command, who was primarily responsible for the sea battle taking place in the narrow straits, which was very clearly what saved the situation, and because of this you yourselves gave him more honour than any other foreigner who visited you, **I.74.2** and we displayed by far the most audacious courage, we who, since no one helped us by land and the other states right up to our borders were already enslaved, decided to abandon our city and destroy our homes, not in order to forsake the common good of the rest of the allies nor by dispersing to become useless to them, but getting into our ships and encountering danger and not being angry with you that you had not come to our help earlier. **I.74.3** So our view is that we have helped you no less than you have helped us. For you came to fight from inhabited cities and ones you wanted to preserve for the future, and because you were afraid on your own behalf much more than on ours (at any rate when we were still safe you didn't appear); while we set out from a city that no longer existed and encountered danger on behalf of one for which there was little hope, and joined in saving you as well as ourselves.

7.36 An Athenian Epigram on Salamis

Meiggs & Lewis 26 (I) (*IG* I³ 503); Simonides 20a

Hansen 2; *IG* I² 763. For this inscription, see doc. 7.15. If the inscription is accepted as referring to Salamis, the mention of footsoldiers refers to the fighting on Psyttaleia. The Athenians set up a trophy on Psyttaleia, and one on Salamis to commemorate that victory (see Wallace (1969) 293–303, esp. 299–303; West (1969) 16–17).

[The glory] of these men's valou[r will] always [be undying]
[.... the gods allot;]
For both as footsoldiers [and in quick-sailing ships] they prevented
All Gree[ce f]rom [seeing the day] of slaver[y].

7.37 Adeimantos: Corinthian Commander at Salamis

Simonides 10

Page 200–02. Adeimantos commanded the Corinthians at Artemision and Salamis. Plut. *Mor.* 870f (*On the Malignity of Herodotos* 39), who records this epigram, notes that Herodotos pours abuse on Adeimantos for fleeing from Artemision (Hdt. VIII.5.1, 59, 61, esp. 94, esp 94.1).

This is the tomb of the famous Adeimantos, through whom
All Greece put on the garland of freedom.

7.38 Epitaph of the Corinthians who Died at Salamis

Simonides 11

Page 202–04; Hansen 131; ML 24; *IG* I^2 927 (*IG* I^3 1143). Plutarch *Mor.* 870e (*On the Malignity of Herodotos* 39) gives this epitaph and writes that the Athenians allowed the Corinthians to bury their dead on Salamis near the city. Hdt. VIII.94 records that the Corinthians at Salamis fled as soon as battle was joined and only returned once the Greeks were victorious. A marble block on Salamis has the remains of letters of the first two lines of this epitaph. See also the dedication of Diodoros, a Corinthian captain, in the temple of Leto: Simonides 13 (Page 206–07).

Stranger, we once lived in the well-watered city of Corinth,
But now Salamis, island of Ajax, holds us;
Here we took Phoenician ships and Persians
And Medes and saved holy Greece.

7.39 A Prayer by Corinthian Women

Simonides 14

Page 207–11; Plut. *Mor.* 871b (*On the Malignity of Herodotos* 39). Simonides wrote the epigram for the bronze statues which the women dedicated to Aphrodite (Kypris) in thanks for the safety of Corinth; cf. Theopompos *FGH* 115 F285a–b.

These women on behalf of the Greeks and their fellow citizens who fight hand-to-hand
Stand praying with heaven-sent power to Kypris;
For the goddess Aphrodite did not choose to the bow-carrying
Persians to hand over the acropolis of the Greeks (Corinth).

7.40 The Naxians Fight with Honour

Simonides 19a

Page 219. Plut. *Mor.* 869a–c (*On the Malignity of Herodotos* 36), uses another epigram of Simonides to attempt (unsuccessfully) to discredit Herodotos, this time Hdt. VIII.46.3, who states that the Naxians were initially sent to fight for the Persians, but Demokritos persuaded them to join the Greeks. Cf. Hellanikos *FGH* 323[a] F28 and Ephoros *FGH* 70

F187 who say, respectively, that the Naxians came to help the Greeks with six and five ships; Diod. V.52.3 writes that the Naxians were the first to withdraw from Xerxes' fleet, and participated at Salamis with distinction.

Demokritos was the third to begin the battle, when off Salamis
The Greeks met the Persians at sea;
He took five of the enemy's ships, and saved a sixth,
A Dorian, from capture at barbarian hands.

7.41 A Western Greek at Salamis

IG I² 655 (*IG* I³ 822)

DAA 76; Moretti 11; Page 407–08; Hansen 265. This inscription is from an inscribed statue base of Phayllos, found on the acropolis at Athens. Hdt. VIII.47 says that of the Western Greeks only the Crotoniates came to help, and he specifically mentions Phayllos as a past victor in the Pythian festival at Delphi. See Paus. X.9.2 on his victories, two in the pentathlon and one in the stadion, and the statue of him erected at Delphi.

Phayl[los was admired by a]ll,
For he was thrice [vi]ctor [in the games
At] Delphi, an[d captured ships
W]hich Asia se[nt forth].

PLATAEA

After the defeat of the Persian navy at Salamis in 480, Xerxes himself left Greece, leaving behind an army under the command of Mardonios to continue operations. Mardonios sent Alexander, king of Macedon, to Athens to suggest an alliance; the Spartans sent an embassy to Athens, which was assured that the Athenians had no intention of going over to the Persians (Hdt. VIII.136, 140–144; doc. 12.43). Mardonios then recaptured Athens ten months after Xerxes had first entered it. Before leaving, he burnt the city. When Mardonios again made overtures to the Athenians, Lykidas, a member of the boule who proposed accepting the terms, was stoned to death by the Athenians (as was his family; see Rosivach (1987) 237–41, 245; doc. 13.26 for this incident). The Spartans, after some delay, sent a force, once they had been convinced that if the Athenians went over to the Persians the Isthmus wall would be of no avail. With news of the Peloponnesian forces at the Isthmus (where the Peloponnesians received favourable omens), Mardonios retired to Boeotia. Here, Greeks who had medised joined him. See Hdt. IX.1–27; for the allied numbers at Plataea, see Hdt. IX.28–30.

7.42 Oath of the Athenians before Plataea

Tod II.204, lines 21–51

The antiquity of this is contested, but while Herodotos does not mention the oath before Plataea he speaks of a similar oath sworn before Thermopylai (VII.132.2 (doc. 7.18); cf. Diod. XI.3.3, Polyb. IX.39.5), and its formula is quoted in almost identical terms by Lyk. *Leok.* 81 and Diod. XI.29.2–3; cf. Theopompos *FGH* 115 F153. To 'tithe' a city was to sell it and its inhabitants and give a tenth of the proceeds to the gods; but cf. Brunt

(1953–54) 136–37. See Raubitschek (1960) 178–83, who argues for the authenticity of the oath; Loraux (1986) 156, 402n.106 (rejecting it). All the military terms used here are actually Spartan.

(21) The oath which the Athenians swore when they were about to fight against the barbarians: 'I shall fight as long as I live, and shall not consider being alive more important than being free, and I (25) shall not desert the commanding officer (taxilochos) nor the leader of the division (enomotarch), whether he is alive or dead, nor shall I depart unless the leaders (hegemones) go first, and I will do whatever the generals command, and those of the allied fighters who die (30) I shall bury on the spot and I shall not leave anyone unburied; and after conqu[e]ring the barbarians in battle I shall tithe the city of the Thebans, and I shall not harm Athens or Sparta or Plataea (35) or any of the other cities who joined in the battle, nor shall I suffer their being coerced by famine nor shall I keep off from them flowing waters whether they are friends or enemies. And if I abide by the things written in the oath, (40) may my city be free from sickness, and if I do not, may it be sick; and may my city not be sacked, and if I do not, may it be sacked; and may my <land> bear <fruit>, and if I do not, may it be unfruitful; and may women bear children like their parents, and if I do not, monsters; and (45) may cattle bear young like cattle, and if I do not, monsters.' After swearing this, they covered the sacrificed victims with their shields and called down a curse at the signal of the trumpet, that if they should transgress anything of what was sworn and should not abi<d>e (50) by the things written in the oath, pollution should be on those that swore it.

7.43 The Battle of Plataea

Herodotos IX.46.1–63.2

The battle of Plataea was said to have taken place on the same day as the battle at Mykale (Hdt. IX.100.2; doc. 7.46). IX.48–63 deserves to be read in full; note the importance which was attached to receiving favourable omens. The seer with the Spartans was Teisamenos, while Mardonios was also employing a Greek seer, Hegesistratos (the Spartans later found Hegesistratos divining at Zakynthos and killed him (IX.37.4); note Jameson (1991) 207, 220; cf. Bradford (1992) 27–33); both sides had omens favourable for defence and unfavourable for attack. Mardonios on the eleventh day of these omens called a conference urging action, arguing that as they had not harmed Delphi, they would be successful (see Parke & Wormell (1956) I.174, II. 43, *Response* 98; Fontenrose (1978) 318, *Response* Q150). The Persian cavalry, which presented the greatest threat to the Greeks, harried them and fouled the spring from which they drew water. The Greeks therefore decided to move position to the 'Island', formed by two channels of the river Asopos; this led to their forces splitting up, but most of the Greeks fled instead to Plataea, stopping outside the walls near the temple of Hera (see Nyland (1992) 81–87). When Pausanias ordered the Spartans to move, one of the commanders, Amompharetos, refused to obey, causing a delay. They finally reached the temple of Demeter, and here the Persians pressed their attack. Pausanias failed to go on the attack in the absence of favourable omens, but prayed to Hera, who then caused the omens to be auspicious.

IX.46.1 The Athenian generals came to the right wing and told Pausanias what they had heard from Alexander (commander of the Macedonians). He was fearful of the Persians at their account and spoke as follows: **IX.46.2** 'Since the engagement will be at dawn, you Athenians should stand opposite the Persians and we against the Boeotians and the other Greeks drawn up against us' .... **IX.47.1** As this pleased both, when dawn broke they changed their positions. But the Boeotians noticed what they were doing and reported to Mardonios. And when he heard, he himself tried to change position, placing the Persians so they faced the Spartans. When Pausanias learnt that this had happened, realising that his manoeuvre had not escaped notice, he led the Spartans back to the right wing; and Mardonios did likewise on the left. **IX.48.1** When they were back in their original positions, Mardonios sent a herald to the Spartans (**IX.48.1–61.3:** *Mardonios rebuked the Spartans for trying to give the place of danger to the Athenians. After heavy Persian harassment, the allied troops moved position to Plataea. As the sacrifices remained unfavourable Pausanias called on Hera for help.*) **IX.62.1** While he was still asking her help, the Tegeates rose first and moved against the barbarians, and immediately after Pausanias' prayer the omens were favourable for the Spartans as they sacrificed. When this occurred they too moved against the enemy and the Persians left off their bows and met them face to face. **IX.62.2** At first the battle took place at the Persians' shields (from behind which they were shooting). When these had fallen, a fierce battle took place near the temple of Demeter over a long period, where they came to close quarters; for the barbarians took hold of their spears and broke them. **IX.62.3** In courage and strength the Persians were not inferior, but they were without armour and untrained and not equal in skill to their opponents. Singly or in groups of ten, both more and less, they dashed out and threw themselves in a body at the Spartans and were killed. **IX.63.1** Mardonios happened to be there, fighting from a white horse and with his 1,000 best hand-picked Persians around him, and here particularly the Persians pressed hard on their opponents. While Mardonios was alive they resisted and defended themselves and killed many of the Spartans; **IX.63.2** but when Mardonios was killed and the troops drawn up around him, which were the strongest, fell, then the others took to flight and yielded to the Spartans. What most greatly disadvantaged them was their clothing, being without armour; for they were fighting without armour against hoplites.

7.44 The Serpent Column

Meiggs & Lewis 27

The serpent column at Delphi, with the names inscribed on the coils, was dedicated by the allies after Plataea in 479, but refers to the whole of the war and not just to this battle. Three intertwined serpents, worked in bronze, stood about six metres high, with a golden tripod atop. See *LSAG* pl.13, no.15 for a line drawing of part; each line of the translation below represents one coil. This serpent column was one of three dedications which the Greeks made from the spoils after the repulse of the Persians in 479: there was also a bronze statue of Zeus dedicated at Olympia and one of Poseidon at the Isthmus (Hdt. IX.81.1). The names of 31 states are listed (cf. Paus. V.23.1–3); the Tenians were inscribed later (see Hdt. VIII.82.1) and there are also some absentees — Croton, Pale, Seriphos, Mantineia, and the Lokrians (see ML pp.59–60). The Phokians melted down the gold tripod in the Third Sacred War (Paus. X.13.9). Constantine the Great took the column to Constantinople for his new hippodrome; there it remains today, without its heads. Pausanias inscribed his arrogant epigram on the tripod (Thuc. I.132.2; doc. 6.25), which was later erased.

These the | war | fought:
Spartans | Athenians | Corinthians
Tegeates | Sicyonians | Aeginetans
Megarians | Epidaurians | Orchomenians
Phleiasians | Troizenians | Hermionians
Tirynthians | Plataeans | Thespians
Mycenaeans | Keians | Melians | Tenians
Naxians | Eretrians | Chalkidians
Styrians | Eleians | Potidaeans
Leukadians | Anaktorians | Kythnians | Siphnians
Ambraciots | Lepreates.

7.45 Epitaphs from ?Plataea

Simonides 8 & 9

Page 197–200. Although attributed to Thermopylai in antiquity these probably belong to Plataea; the first is the epitaph of the Athenians, the second of the Spartans (cf. Paus. IX.2.5).

8. If dying nobly is the greatest part of valour,
To us above all others Fortune has granted this;
For after striving to crown Greece with freedom
We lie here enjoying praise that will never age.

9. These men gave their beloved country inextinguishable fame
And encompassed themselves with the dark cloud of death.
They died but are not dead, since their valour glorifies them from above
And brings them up from the house of Hades.

7.46 The Battle of Mykale

Herodotos IX.101.3–102.3

IX.101.3 Both Greeks and barbarians hastened to meet in battle, as the islands and the Hellespont were the prizes for victory. **IX.102.1** For the Athenians and those drawn up next to them up to about half way, their line of advance was along the beach and level plain, while for the Spartans and those next to them in the line it was across a gully and mountains; so while the Spartans were still on their way round, those on the other wing were already engaged. **IX.102.2** As long as the Persians' shields remained upright, they were able to repel the attack and did not have the worst of the battle; but when the host of the Athenians and their neighbours, so that the victory might be theirs and not the Spartans', encouraged each other and battled even more eagerly, from that point the affair had already changed markedly. **IX.102.3** For they forced their way through the shields and made a massed attack upon the Persians, who repelled them for some time but finally fled to the wall. The Athenians, Corinthians, Sicyonians and Troizenians (for they were drawn up in this order) followed and rushed in alongside them. Once the wall was taken, the barbarians were no longer concerned with resistance, but all except the Persians turned and fled.

7.47 Inscription on the Megarian Dead

Simonides 16

Tod *GHI* I.20. The introduction, dating to the fourth or fifth century AD, to this epigram, states that it was re-inscribed by the high-priest Helladios because it 'had been destroyed by time', and was the work of Simonides. Lines 3–4 refer to Artemision; lines 7–8 refer to Plataea (cf. Hdt. IX.69). Paus. I.43.3 writes of a mass-grave at Megara for the Megarians who died in the Persian Wars, while Wade-Gery (1933) 95–97, noting that those killed in the cavalry charge at Plataea were buried there (Hdt. IX.85.2), suggests that Pausanias saw not a tomb but a cenotaph at Megara; Nisaia was Megara's main port.

While striving to strengthen the day of freedom
For Greece and the Megarians, we received the fate of death,
Some under Euboea and Pelion, where stands
The precinct of the holy archer Artemis,
Some at the mountain of Mykale, some before Salamis,
< >
Others on the Boeotian plain, who dared
To come to blows with enemies fighting on horseback.
The citizens granted us together this privilege around the navel
Of the Nisaians in their people-thronged agora.

7.48 Spartan Commanders on the Persians

Plutarch *Sayings of the Spartans* (*Moralia* 225a–d, 230e–f)

Leonidas, son of Anaxandridas:

4. When the ephors said, 'Haven't you decided to do anything other than block the passes against the barbarians?' he said, 'In theory no, but in actual fact to die for the Greeks.' **6.** (cf. Hdt. VII.226.2) When someone said, 'It isn't possible even to see the sun because of the barbarians' arrows,' he said, 'How nice, then, if we are to fight them in the shade.' **10.** When Xerxes wrote to him, 'If you do not fight against the gods, but side with me, you can be monarch of Greece,' he wrote back, 'If you knew what was good in life, you would refrain from desiring what belongs to other people; as for me it is better to die for Greece than be monarch of the people of my race.' **11.** When Xerxes wrote again, 'Hand over your weapons,' he wrote back, 'Come and take them.'

Pausanias, son of Kleombrotos (cf. Hdt. IX.82):

6. After his victory over the Persians at Plataea, he ordered that the dinner prepared beforehand for the Persians should be served to his staff; as this was amazingly extravagant, he said, 'By the gods, these Persians are gluttonous fellows, in that they had so much and still came after our barley-bread.'

7.49 Herodotos' Assessment

Herodotos VII.139.1–6

VII.139.1 Here I feel compelled to express an opinion, which will be resented by most people, but nevertheless as it seems to me true I will not suppress it. **VII.139.2** If the Athenians had dreaded the approaching danger so much that they had abandoned their country, or if they had not abandoned it but stayed and submitted to Xerxes, no one would have attempted to resist the King by sea. And if no one had opposed Xerxes by sea, events on the mainland would have taken place like this: **VII.139.3** even if a number of walls had been built across the Isthmus by the Peloponnesians, the Spartans would have been betrayed by their allies, not willingly but by necessity, as one by one their cities were taken by the barbarian fleet, and the Spartans would have been isolated, and being isolated would have performed great deeds and died nobly. **VII.139.4** Either this would have happened, or before this, seeing the other Greeks medising they would have come to terms with Xerxes. In either case, Greece would have become subject to the Persians. I simply cannot understand the use of the walls built across the Isthmus when the King had control of the sea. **VII.139.5** And so anyone who said that the Athenians were the saviours of Greece would be perfectly correct: whichever side they had turned to would have prevailed; they chose that Greece should remain free, and they roused all the rest of Greece, which had not medised, and played the main part, after the gods, in driving off the King. **VII.139.6** Not even the dreadful and frightening oracles which came from Delphi persuaded them to abandon Greece, but they stayed firm and dared to await the invader of their country.

7.50 Greece's Finest Hour?

Plato *Laws* 692d–693a

In the discussion about the governments of the Peloponnesian states Argos, Messene and Sparta, the Athenian suggests that if the three states historically had combined into a single authority, the Persians would never have attacked Greece. Balcer (1989) 137–41 stresses the role which Xerxes' 'blunders' had in bringing about the Persian defeat.

692d After all, Kleinias, they defended themselves against the Persians disgracefully. By disgraceful, I don't mean to say that those who conquered them at that time both by land and by sea did not win splendid battles. But what I mean when I say disgraceful is that first of all only one of those three states fought to defend Greece, and the other two were so corrupted that one (Messene) even tried to prevent Sparta's attempts to come to Greece's aid, fighting her with all her might, **692e** while the other, Argos ... was called on to fight off the barbarians and yet neither answered nor helped out. Anyone who gave a lengthy account of the events of that war would have to criticize Greece for very unbecoming behaviour: in fact, to speak accurately, one might say that it didn't make any defence at all, but if it hadn't been for the joint determination of the Athenians and Spartans to ward off the approaching slavery, **693a** now nearly all the races of the Greeks would be mixed up with each other, as well as barbarians with Greeks and Greeks with barbarians, just like those nations whom the Persians rule over, who have been split up, then awkwardly mingled together, and who now live in scattered groups.

7.51 A Spartan Remembers the Old Days

Aristophanes *Lysistrata* 1242–70

In the final scene of the *Lysistrata*, performed in 411, after the celebratory banquet signalling the return of peace, a Spartan sings of the past triumphs of the alliance. The dipodia is a Spartan dance. Cf. doc. 6.14 for a further passage from the *Lysistrata*, praising the Spartans.

Spartan: My dear chap, take your pipes,
So I can dance the dipodia and sing
A fine song for the Athenians and us together.
Prytanis (to the piper):
Take then your pipes, by the gods,
As I take pleasure in seeing you dance.
Spartan: Send to this youth, O Memory,
Your Muse, who
Knows us and the Athenians,
When they at Artemision
Threw themselves like gods
Against the ships and beat the Persians;
While us Leonidas
Led like boars as we sharpened,
I think, our tusks; and much
Foam flowed around our jaws,
As well as down our legs.
For the Persian soldiers were as numerous
As the sands.
Huntress, beast-slayer,
Come hither, virgin goddess,
To our treaty,
To keep us united for a long time. And now
Again may fruitful friendship exist
Through our compacts,
And may we put an end to wily foxes.
O come hither, come,
O virgin huntress.

8

The Delian League and the Pentekontaetia

In 478 the Spartan Pausanias was dispatched as commander of the Hellenes, but at Byzantium his arrogance made him unpopular with the Ionians, and Athens began to assume the leadership of the recently liberated Greeks (doc. 8.3). The rationale behind the Delian League was the continuation of the war against the Persians, though the Athenians obviously realised at the time the benefits to be gained from such an alliance. However, that the league was intended primarily to pursue a war of liberation is implicit in the league's subsequent military activities, in which the last remnants of Persian power in Greek territory were defeated.

The states that joined Athens, the islands and Greek cities of Asia Minor that had been liberated from the Persians, did so of their own free will (except for Phaselis; doc. 8.25) and were autonomous, while League decisions were made in general meetings. As the allies grew tired of fighting many commuted their contributions to money, rather than supplying men and ships (doc. 8.3). The league undertook numerous military activities against the Persians and its own members, and the number of wars in which the Athenians engaged in this period is indicated by the casualty list for the Erechtheid tribe, commemorating, in 460 or 459, those who died in Cyprus, in Egypt, in Phoenicia, at Halieis, on Aegina, and at Megara 'in the same year' (doc. 8.12). The most important campaigns against Persians were those of the Eurymedon (docs. 8.5–6), Cyprus (doc. 8.13) and Egypt (8.11). The first steps in turning the Delian League into the Athenian Empire were taken when allies who revolted were forced back into the league. Naxos, for example, lost its autonomy, and had no choice as to whether to be a member: it had to pay tribute, participate in league military activities, and follow Athens' lead (doc. 8.3), and the Athenian action against Thasos (doc. 8.7) strongly suggests that Athens was motivated to engage in economic imperialism and to take over the mines for its own benefit.

In either 460 or 459, another important development took place, when Megara allied herself with Athens (doc. 8.15); this is considered the incident which heralded the start of the First Peloponnesian War. Athens welcomed the alliance as control of Megara was important for forestalling a Spartan invasion of Attica. There was direct conflict between Athens and Sparta at the battle of Tanagra in 458/7 (doc. 8.16), in which the Spartans were victorious, but this was only a temporary setback for the Athenians who shortly afterwards established themselves as masters of Boeotia. This was followed, c. 457, by the Athenian victory over Aegina, which was forced to tear down its walls, give up its fleet, and pay tribute. Aegina was amongst those who later encouraged Sparta to declare war on Athens. But Athenian control of Boeotia was short-lived, ending in 446 and Megara returned to the Peloponnesian fold in the same year. In 446/5 a Thirty Years Peace was agreed upon (doc. 8.18) and Athens returned to the Peloponnesians those places which it had seized during the conflict.

The pentekontaetia (the term is used by the scholiast on Thucydides I.89.1), the fifty years between the Persian invasions and the Peloponnesian War, is marked by a number of outstanding statesmen in Athens. After the repulse of the Persians, Themistokles set about rebuilding the walls of Athens (doc. 8.1), and Aristeides and Kimon took over direction of military campaigns. Themistokles was ostracised sometime in the 470s, indicating that political initiative had passed to others, in particular to Kimon. Kimon, though a conservative politician and a philo-Spartan was nevertheless an ardent supporter of the growth of Athenian power. He commanded the fleet in the 470s and 460s and was responsible for successful campaigns against the Persians. His downfall occurred when he persuaded the Athenians to assist the Spartans against the helots and perioikoi who had revolted, probably in 465. Ephialtes took advantage of his absence to carry out reforms to the Areiopagos which reduced its powers, which were then distributed to the boule, assembly, and law-courts (doc. 8.10). When the Spartans 'became afraid of the Athenians' boldness and revolutionary spirit' and sent them away (docs. 8.7, 9), Kimon's opponents seized upon the opportunity to have him ostracised. Ephialtes' reforms meant that political decisions were made solely by the people, either in the assembly or in the law-courts. But the statesman who particularly dominated Athenian politics in the 440s and 430s was Perikles, and despite opposition, notably from Thucydides, son of Melesias (doc. 8.23), he was instrumental in completing Athens' transformation into an imperialist power and radical democracy.

The period 500–431 was dominated by several key figures of whom Miltiades, Themistokles, Aristeides, Kimon, Ephialtes and Perikles were the most prominent, and each played an important role in the history of the period and the growth of Athenian power. Miltiades was architect of the victory at Marathon; Themistokles saved the day at Salamis; Aristeides was instrumental in organizing the Delian League which the Athenians transformed into an empire; Kimon extended Athenian control through the Aegean; and Ephialtes strengthened the democracy by giving more of the powers of the state to popular bodies. But each of these six individuals suffered the ebbs and flows of the political game: Miltiades died of gangrene after being fined fifty talents, Aristeides, Themistokles and Kimon, were ostracised, and Ephialtes, was assassinated. Perikles was to die of the plague in 429, but he and his associates had also faced prosecution, fines and on one occasion Perikles was possibly even demoted from the strategia: political life in Athens, even for a champion of the people, was certainly no sinecure.

8.1 The Athenians Rebuild their Walls

Thucydides I.89.3–93.7

Athens had been sacked first by Xerxes and later by Mardonios. The rebuilding of the walls was opposed by the Spartans, while Sparta's allies, according to Thucydides, were already wary of the growing power of Athens. Themistokles' stratagem of delaying tactics (cf. Plut. *Them.* 19.1–3; Diod. XI.39–40), allowed the Athenians time to rebuild their walls; the Athenian assumption that the Spartans might attack is understandable given the Spartan invasions of Attica in the sixth century. **I.89.3**: Thucydides implies that the city had walls before 479 (cf. Hdt. IX.13.2); see Vanderpool (1974) 156–60, arguing that the city wall was built by 566, and perhaps earlier. **I.93.1–2**: For the city walls, see Boersma (1970) 45–46, 154 (misinterpreting Themistokles' role); McNeal (1970) 312; Wycherley (1978) 10–13; cf. doc. 13.36, a grave stele built into the wall. **I.93.3**: The fortification of the Peiraieus had begun in Themistokles' archonship, 493/2; for the archon-year, see Dion. Hal. VI.34.1; Gomme *HCT* I.261–62; cf. Cadoux (1948) 116–17 with n.252; Develin (1989) 55; there is no need to doubt that Themistokles was archon in this year (Lenardon (1956) 401–19). For the Peiraieus walls, see Plut. *Them.* 19.3; Boersma (1970) 37–38; Wycherley (1978) 262; Garland (1987) 14–21, 163–65; Frost (1968) 115). Thuc. II.13.7 states that the wall around the Peiraieus and Mounichia was 60 stades in length. **I.93.4**: Note that Themistokles was the first to encourage the Athenians to exploit the possibilities which their navy offered for empire; cf. Plut. *Them.* 19.4–5, 20.1.

I.89.3 The Athenian people, when the barbarians had left their country, immediately started bringing back their children and wives and their remaining property from the places to which they had removed them for safety, and prepared to rebuild their city and walls; for only small sections of their surrounding wall were still standing and most of their houses were in ruins, with only a few surviving, in which the important Persians had had their quarters. **I.90.1** But when the Spartans heard what was being planned, they sent an embassy, partly because they would not have been pleased to see either the Athenians or anywhere else with a wall, but more because the allies were stirring them up, because they were afraid both of the size of the Athenians' fleet, which had previously not existed, and of the courage which they had displayed in fighting the Persians. **I.90.2** The Spartans, without showing the Athenians their wishes and their underlying suspicion, proposed that the Athenians should not fortify their city, but rather join them in pulling down any walls outside the Peloponnese which were still standing, so that the barbarians, if they should again invade, would not have a stronghold which they could use as a base, as they had recently been able to do from Thebes; and, they said, the Peloponnese would be sufficient for everyone both as a refuge and as a base of operations. **I.90.3** After the Spartans made these proposals, by Themistokles' advice the Athenians immediately sent them away with the reply that they would dispatch envoys to them to discuss these matters, and Themistokles told them to send him to Sparta as quickly as possible; the other envoys, however, who had been chosen to go with him should not be dispatched immediately, but should delay until such time as the Athenians had raised the wall to a height sufficient for them to fight from. Meanwhile the entire population of the city should build the wall, sparing neither private nor public buildings which might be of some use in the work, but demolishing everything ....

I.93.1 In this way the Athenians fortified their city in a short time. **I.93.2** Even today it is clear that the building took place in a hurry; for the foundations are laid in all sorts of stone and these were not shaped so as to fit together but each was laid just as it was brought forward, and many stelai from tombs and pieces of sculpture were built into the wall. For the boundaries of the city were greatly extended on all sides, and because of this they used everything they could find in their haste. **I.93.3** Themistokles also persuaded them to build the rest of the walls of the Peiraieus (which had been begun earlier during the year in which he was archon), thinking that it was a good site, having three natural harbours, and, now they had become a seafaring people, it would greatly benefit their acquisition of power **I.93.4** (for he was the first who dared to say that they should cleave to the sea), and he directly helped to establish their empire .... **I.93.7** He thought that the Peiraieus was a more valuable place than the upper city, and often advised the Athenians that if they were ever hard pressed on land they should go down to the Peiraieus and resist everyone in their ships.

THE ORIGINS OF THE DELIAN LEAGUE

The League began as a voluntary organization, when the allies approached Athens to replace the unpopular leadership of the Spartans under Pausanias. Thuc. I.96.1 states that the *pretence* for the alliance was 'that they were retaliating for what they had lost by ravaging the King's country'; ravage (see Jackson (1969) 12–16; cf. Meiggs (1972) 462–64) is a closer translation than plunder (Sealey's preference, (1966) 233–55). Thucydides' use of the term *pretence* may indicate his view that the Athenians used this to cover their real objective, power (Rawlings (1977) 1–8), though elsewhere (Thuc. III.10.2–3, VI.76.3–4) the liberation of the Greeks from Persian rule is also stressed; cf. Hdt. VIII.3.2, 108.4, 109.5, 132; IX.90.2, 106; *Ath. Pol.* 23.5; cf. Plut. *Arist.* 25.1. While Thucydides places an emphasis on the Athenian subjugation of the allies, using the pentekontaetia to describe how Athens became powerful enough to challenge Sparta (I.89.1), nevertheless he still gives a treatment of campaigns against the Persians, which is detailed in the case of the Egyptian campaign. Against Sealey's 'minimalist' view of the original purpose of the alliance, to engage in plundering, see Rhodes (1985) 5, 7, cf. Brunt (1953/54) 150; Robertson (1980) 74. The Athenians with their allies vigorously prosecuted the war against the Persians (see docs. 8.3, 5–6, 11–13), and during this time, as later, also dealt vigorously with revolts from the League. It would of course have been surprising if the Athenians in 478/7 had not realised the benefits which leadership of the allies, a large fleet and the promise of booty would bring them (French (1979) 140–41).

The Delian League was established in 478/7 (for the date, see Loomis (1990) 488–89nn.11–12). The allies were at first autonomous and made their decisions in general meetings, but Athens no doubt from the very beginning was the most influential member. Presumably, when the treasury was moved to Athens (on the motion of the Samians: Plut. *Arist.* 25.3) and Delos was no longer the headquarters of the league, the league meetings were no longer held, or at least important political decisions were now made at Athens. Whether the league was unicameral (Athens and the allied representatives meeting as one) or bicameral (the allies meeting and coming to decisions separately from the Athenians, as in the Second Athenian Confederacy) is debated; see Thuc. III.10.5, 11.4; Diod. XI.47.1; Hammond (1967) 50–52, 57–61; de Ste. Croix (1972) 303–07; cf. Meiggs (1972) 460–62; Culham (1978) 27–31; Ostwald (1982) 33. The allies who helped Athens besiege Sestos were probably the initial members of the league (see Hdt. IX.106, 114.1–

2; Thuc. I.89.2. Hdt. IX.106.4 mentions only the islanders, but see Gomme *HCT* I.256–57, followed by Hornblower (1991) 134–35); others will have joined as they were freed from the Persians. If the figure of 460 talents for the tribute in 478 can be trusted, it must be assumed that there was a fairly large membership from the beginning (cf. *ATL* III.194–224; Gomme *HCT* 1.290–95; Meiggs (1972) 50–58). There are numerous discussions of the Delian League: a basic starting point remains Hammond (1967) 41–61; see also Sealey (1966) 235–55; Kagan (1969) 38–48; Meiggs (1972) 42–49; de Ste. Croix (1972) 298–307; Rawlings (1977) 1–8; French (1979) 134–41, (1988) 12–25; Robertson (1980) 64–96; Rhodes (1985).

8.2 Aristeides' Role in Setting up the League

[Aristotle] *Athenaion Politeia* 23.3–5

Aristeides had been ostracised in 482, but was recalled before the Persian invasion (docs. 5.12, 14 ii). Thucydides believed that the allies were willing to let the Athenians take over the leadership from the Spartans because of their hatred of Pausanias (doc. 8.3; cf. Thuc I.95–96.1, 75.2). Herodotos, however, has the Athenians making Pausanias' behaviour the excuse for depriving the Spartans of their command (Hdt. VIII.3.2), while the *Ath. Pol.* has Aristeides encouraging the allies to break away from the Spartans; Kimon was also important in winning the allies over to the Athenian side (Plut. *Kim.* 6.2–3, 6–7). Pausanias was recalled, but his replacement was not accepted by the allies and returned to Sparta (Thuc. I.95.6–7; see also Plut. *Arist.* 23–25). For the lumps of iron being thrown into the sea as part of a treaty, see Plut. *Arist.* 25.1; Jacobsen (1975) 256–58; cf. doc. 1.11; this symbolised a permanent alliance (to last until the iron floated); Balcer (1974) 23 suggests that because of this Athens could argue that Naxos had broken the oath by its secession (cf. for members of the Peloponnesian League, Thuc. I.71.5–6).

23.3 At that time the leaders of the people were Aristeides son of Lysimachos and Themistokles son of Neokles. Themistokles' reputation was based on his military skill, Aristeides' on his statesmanship, as well as on being the most upright man of his time; for this reason the Athenians used the one as their general and the other as their adviser. **23.4** So these two organized the building of the walls together, although they were political rivals, but it was Aristeides who urged the Athenians to separate the Ionians from their alliance with the Spartans, after watching for the moment when the Spartans were in discredit because of Pausanias. **23.5** Accordingly it was also Aristeides who assessed the first tribute contribution from the cities in the third year after the naval battle at Salamis, in the archonship of Timosthenes (478/7), and he swore the oaths to the Ionians that they would have the same enemies and the same friends (as the Athenians), upon which they also threw the lumps of iron into the sea.

8.3 The Beginnings of Athens' Empire

Thucydides I.96.1–99.3

The details which Thucydides provides in this extract and the rest of the section on the Pentekontaetia are the basis for the history of the Delian League. **I.96.1–2**: The assessment of contributions to the war-effort was carried out by Aristeides: Thuc. V.18.5; *Ath. Pol.* 23.5; Plut. *Arist.* 24, 26.3. According to Thucydides the tribute was initially fixed at 460 talents; it rose to 600 talents under Perikles (Thuc. II.13.3; Plut. *Arist.* 24.3–

4), although the tribute-quota lists point to only approximately 430 talents being collected in 431. The re-assessment of the tribute in 425/4 raised it to 1460+ talents (*IG* I[3] 71; doc. 9.15). Probably all the assessment figures for tribute were 'ideal' and the fixed amount never collected in full. Hdt. VI.42.2 (cf. Isoc. IV.120) seems to imply that when the Ionian cities became members of the Delian League their assessment was made the same as they had paid the Persians (*ATL* III.275; de Ste. Croix (1972) 310, 313; Evans (1976) 344–48). **I.97.2**: Despite Thucydides' complaint about the lack of chronological accuracy in Hellanikos' *History of Attica* (*FGH* 323a T8) he has given a history which provides few clues with respect to absolute chronology (Rhodes (1985) 12; cf. McNeal (1970) 311). For the chronology of the pentekontaetia, see Gomme *HCT* I.389–413; Hammond (1955) 396–405; Unz (1986) 68–85; Badian (1988) 289–310. For Hellanikos, see Lenardon (1981) 59–70. For the term 'arche', as empire, see Winton (1981) 147–52.

I.98.1: For Eion (captured 476, *contra* Smart (1967) 136–38) and Skyros, see also Plut. *Kim.* 7–8.5; Diod. XI.60.1–2; for Kimon, see also doc. 8.5; Thuc. I.112.3–4 (cf. doc. 8.11); *Ath. Pol.* 26.1, 27.1, 28.2; Plut. *Kim.* esp. 6–8, 11–14, 15–18. **I.98.4**: The revolt of Naxos was the first occasion when the independence of an ally was not observed. The meaning of 'against the terms of the existing agreement' is debated, and there may have been a clause guaranteeing the allies' freedom; a more appropriate interpretation is perhaps that such action was 'unprecedented' and that the autonomy of the allies was taken for granted (Thuc. I.97.1, III.10.5, V.18.5; Meiggs (1972) 45–46; Ostwald (1982) 38–39, cf. 23–24; cf. *ATL* III.156–57). **I.99.1**: In the Pentekontaetia section Naxos, Thasos, Boeotia, Euboea, Megara, Samos and Byzantium are explicitly mentioned as having rebelled. Meiggs (1963) 2, cf. (1972) 112, notes that Erythrai, Miletos, Myous, and Latmos are absent from the tribute-quota lists of 454/3–453/2, and these states may have revolted due to the Hellenic disaster in Egypt; but for Miletos, see doc. 9.9 (*IG* I[3] 21); the regulations for Erythrai (doc. 8.26) can be viewed in this context. Chios, Lesbos and Samos, powerful states with their own navies, were accorded different treatment from the other allies according to *Ath. Pol.* 24.2, while Thucydides has Chios and Lesbos left with their navies (Thuc. I.19), and all the allies 'enslaved' except them (III.10.5).

I.96.1 After the Athenians took over the leadership in this way, with the allies willing that Athens should do so because of their hatred of Pausanias, they assessed which cities had to provide money and which provide ships for the war against the barbarian; for the pretence was that they were retaliating for what they had lost by ravaging the King's country. **I.96.2** And then for the first time the Athenians instituted the class of officials known as the Treasurers of Greece (hellenotamiai), who received the tribute (phoros); for that was what contributions in money were called. The tribute fixed at first was 460 talents. Their treasury was at Delos, and the meetings used to take place in the temple. **I.97.1** The Athenians were the leaders of the allies, who were at first autonomous and made their decisions in general meetings, and achieved many great things both in war and in the handling of affairs in the period between the current war and the Persian War, against the barbarians, their own allies who revolted and the Peloponnesians whom they came up against on various occasions. **I.97.2** I have written this and made this digression because this subject has been omitted by those writing before me, who have either narrated the events of Greek history before the Persian Wars or the Persian Wars themselves; the only one who has touched on this in his *History of Attica* is Hellanikos, and he mentioned it briefly and without chronological accuracy. At the same time it will show the way in which the Athenians' empire was established.

I.98.1 First of all the Athenians, with Kimon son of Miltiades in command, took by siege Eion on the Strymon, which was held by Persians, and enslaved the inhabitants. **I.98.2** Then they enslaved the inhabitants of Skyros, the island in the Aegean, which was inhabited by the Dolopians, and settled it themselves. **I.98.3** Next there was a war between them and the Karystians, without any of the other Euboeans being involved; eventually the Karystians surrendered on terms. **I.98.4** After this they made war on the Naxians who had revolted and brought them to terms after a siege. This was the first allied city that was enslaved against the terms of the existing agreement, and then it happened to each of the others as well. **I.99.1** There were various reasons for the revolts, the most important of which were falling into arrears with the tribute or contribution of ships and sometimes refusal to serve; for the Athenians were strict in exacting payment and, in applying compulsion, made themselves unpleasant to those who were not accustomed or willing to endure hardships. **I.99.2** In other ways, too, the Athenians were no longer as popular as rulers as they had been, and as they did not take a share in expeditions as equals it was easier for them to bring back to their side those who revolted. **I.99.3** For all this the allies themselves were responsible; for most of them, because they shrank from campaigns so they might not be away from home, agreed to pay a corresponding sum of money instead of ships. Thus the Athenians' fleet grew powerful from the money the allies contributed, and the allies had made themselves inadequately prepared and inexperienced in war when they revolted.

8.4 Thucydides' View of Themistokles

Thucydides I.135.2–138.6

Themistokles fell victim to ostracism in the late 470s, after having been a candidate in the 480s as well (see doc. 5.14 vii). **I.135.2**: After he was ostracised, Themistokles was tried *in absentia* on a charge of intriguing with the Persians; he was linked with the treason of Pausanias: Plut. *Them.* 22.1–23.6, *Arist.* 25.10; cf. Lenardon (1959) 23–48; Carawan (1987) 196–200; Bauman (1990) 22–28. **I.135.3**: Themistokles took up residence in Argos, which was well-disposed towards him as he had successfully opposed the Spartan suggestion that those who had not fought against the Persians not be allowed to be members of the Amphictyonic League (Plut. *Them.* 20.3–4; Forrest (1960) 226; Podlecki (1975) 29; Frost (1968) 120). While in Argos Themistokles may have helped stir up democratic feeling, as Mantineia, Elis and perhaps Tegea adopted democracies at this time (Forrest 221–41, esp. 226; Adshead (1986) 91–95, but see O'Neil (1981) 335–46). For his flight to Persia, cf. Plut. *Them.* 24.1–27.2. The siege of Naxos has been dated anywhere between 471 to 465; see Milton (1979) 257–75, esp. 257–67; cf. Rhodes (1970) 394; Frost (1980) 207. A late date for Naxos' revolt, c. 465 (Artaxerxes' accession), suits Thucydides' narrative. Plut. *Them.* 27.1 refers to authors who believed Themistokles met Xerxes, not Artaxerxes, but this is an invention by writers who preferred a meeting with the man Themistokles actually defeated, rather than his successor (Frost (1980) 214, listing the ancient sources). **I.137.3–4**: For Themistokles' meeting with the King, see Plut. *Them.* 28. A miscellany of late authors are collected in Bauer & Frost (1967), and there are also the 21 'Letters of Themistokles' (see Bauer & Frost 111–18); though inauthentic, being written in the second century AD, they have a framework of historical truth, based on Charon of Lampsakos (*FGH* 262 F11); Lenardon (1961) 28–40. **I.138.4**: Plut. *Them.* 31.5–6 states that Themistokles committed suicide by drinking bull's blood, or a quick poison; cf. Ar. *Knights* 81–84. Nicander *Alexipharmica* 312–34 gives various 'antidotes' for bull's blood, which is not in itself fatal; see Lenardon (1978) 197–99. **I.138.5**: Plut. *Them.* 32.6 records that Magnesia (on the Maeander) still honoured the descendants of Themistokles in his time; see Lenardon (1978) 148–52, 197–98, 201–03; Hornblower (1991) 224–25. **I.138.6**: Themistokles was buried in the Peiraieus, and seems to have been the object of a cult there (Paus. I.1.2, 37.1; Plut. *Them.* 32.5–6; Lenardon (1978) 203–06; Wycherley (1978) 265; Rusten (1983) 293n.15; Garland (1987) 147–48; Kearns (1989) 41). This extract follows on from doc. 6.25, Pausanias' treasonable conduct. Thucydides' eulogy of Themistokles is unusual in his *History*.

I.135.2 As a result of Pausanias' medising, the Spartans sent envoys to the Athenians to accuse Themistokles also, because of what they had discovered from the evidence against Pausanias, and urged that Themistokles be punished in the same way. **I.135.3** The Athenians agreed and sent men with the Spartans, who were prepared to help in catching him, with orders to bring him from wherever they should come across him (as it happened he had already been ostracised and was living in Argos, as well as travelling to the rest of the Peloponnese). But Themistokles became aware of this beforehand and fled from the Peloponnese to Corcyra, as he was the Corcyraeans' benefactor. (**I.136.1–137.2**: *He has to take refuge with his enemy Admetos, King of the Molossians, and then takes passage in a merchant ship and is conveyed, past the siege of Naxos, to Ephesos.*) **I.137.3** Themistokles rewarded the captain by a gift of money (after it had reached him from his friends at Athens and also from what he had deposited at Argos) and travelled inland with one of the Persians from the coast, sending ahead a letter to King Artaxerxes, Xerxes' son, who had recently come to the throne. **I.137.4** The letter said, 'I, Themistokles, have come to you, I who did most harm of all the Greeks to your house, during the time that I was compelled to defend myself against your father's invasion, but still more good, when his retreat took place and I was safe but he was in danger. My benefaction should be repaid (here he wrote of the advance warning of the withdrawal from Salamis and how the bridges had not been destroyed, which he pretended, falsely, was his doing), and now I am here, pursued by the Greeks because of my friendship for you, and able to do you much good. But I want to wait a year before I show you, in person, why I have come.' **I.138.1** The King, it is said, was amazed by his resolve and told him to do this. And Themistokles, while he was waiting, learnt as much as he could of the Persian language and the customs of the country; **I.138.2** at the end of the year he arrived at court and became more important there than any other Greek has ever been both because of the reputation he already had and the hope which he held out of subjugating Greece to Artaxerxes, but mainly because he gave proof of his intelligence in his behaviour. **I.138.3** Indeed, Themistokles displayed very clearly the force of his natural powers and in this, more than anyone else, he deserves admiration; through his native intelligence, and without studying something beforehand or considering it later, he was outstanding in judgements that had to be settled immediately with the least possible discussion, and by far the best forecaster of what was going to happen in the future; he had the ability to explain things he was engaged in, and even in things he had no experience of he did not fail to make satisfactory judgements; in particular he could see beforehand the better or worse in what was as yet unseen. To sum him up, because of the strength of his natural genius and his capacity for instant action, this man was outstanding in extemporising whatever was needed. **I.138.4** He died through an illness; some people say that he intentionally took poison, when he considered it impossible to accomplish what he had promised the King. **I.138.5** There is a monument to him in Asian Magnesia in the agora; this was the country he ruled, as the King gave him Magnesia for his bread, which brought in fifty talents a year, Lampsakos for his wine (which was thought to be the best district for wine of any of that time), and Myous for his meat. **I.138.6** They say that his relatives brought his bones home, at his request, and buried them without the Athenians' knowledge in Attica; for it was not possible to bury him as he was in exile for treason. So the careers of Pausanias the Spartan and Themistokles the Athenian, the most illustrious of any of the Greeks of their time, in this way came to an end.

THE AFTERMATH OF THE PERSIAN WARS

8.5 The Battle of the Eurymedon

Thucydides I.100.1

See also Plut. *Kim.* 12–13.3; Diod. XI.61. The years 469, 466, or c. 465–60 are all suggested as dates for the battle of the Eurymedon. The victory was celebrated by establishing a hero-cult of the river Eurymedon in the Peiraieus (Garland (1987) 22, 126, 235), a bronze palm with a gilded Athena on it was dedicated at Delphi (Paus. X.15.4), and the southern wall of the acropolis was constructed from the spoils (Plut. *Kim.* 13.5). The campaign brought new members into the league; Athens next had to turn its attention to Thasos and the campaign against Persia ended for the time.

I.100.1 After this there occurred the battles on land and sea at the Eurymedon river in Pamphylia, in which the Athenians and their allies fought against the Persians, and the Athenians were victorious in both on the same day under the command of Kimon son of Miltiades, and they captured and destroyed some two hundred triremes, the whole Phoenician fleet.

8.6 Victory at the Eurymedon

Simonides 46

Page 268–72; *Anth. Pal.* 7.258. This epigram was associated with Simonides and the Eurymedon in antiquity (Wade–Gery (1933) 82–86 accepts this); it is very similar to ML 48.45–48 (*IG* I[3] 1162; Hansen 6). The dead of the Eurymedon were buried in the Kerameikos: Paus. I.29.14; Pritchett (1985) 177–78.

These men beside the Eurymedon lost their splendid youth
Doing battle against the vanguard of the Persian archers
As spearmen, both on foot and in their swift ships,
And, dying, left behind the finest memorial of their prowess.

8.7 The Revolt of Thasos

Thucydides I.100.2–101.3

The revolt of Thasos, probably in 465, was another instance in which Athens used league resources to force a seceding member back into the league (cf. doc. 8.3). Finley (1965) 28–32; Meiggs (1972) 571; Ostwald (1982) 39 accept that it was a dispute about the control of resources; de Ste. Croix (1972) 43 postulates that Athenian intervention may have been invited by the emporia of the mainland which resented Thasian control (cf. docs. 9.28; 10.40); for Thasos' mines, see Hdt. VI.46.2–47.2. **I.100.3**: For Athenian attempts to colonize in this area, see doc. 1.6, 8.27, cf. 4.12. The colony dates to 465 with the massacre at Drabeskos occurring soon after. **I.101.2**: see doc. 8.9. **I.101.3**: Kimon was in command at Thasos (Plut. *Kim.* 14.2; cf. Diod. XI.70.1); on his return was charged at his euthyna with having been bribed by Alexander of Macedonia not to invade his country: *Ath. Pol.* 27.1; Plut. *Kim.* 14.2–15.1, *Per.* 10.5. For Perikles' prosecution of Kimon, see Plut. *Kim.* 14.5; *Per.* 10.6; Carawan (1987) 187, 202–05; Bauman (1990) 28–31. The trial may have been before the Areiopagos, and possibly Kimon's acquittal encouraged Ephialtes to curtail its powers in 462/1 (see Rhodes (1981) 335–36; Carawan (1987) 203; Bauman (1990) 29, 179n.59; but cf. Hansen (1975) 15–16).

I.100.2 Some time after this (the battle of the Eurymedon) it happened that the Thasians revolted from the Athenians because of a dispute concerning the trading-stations on the coast of Thrace opposite and the mine which they worked. With their ships the Athenians sailed against Thasos, won a naval battle and landed, **I.100.3** while at about the same time they sent ten thousand settlers of their own and their allies to the river Strymon to colonize what was then called Nine Ways (Ennea Hodoi), but now Amphipolis; they gained control of Nine Ways, which was held by the Edonians, but when they advanced into the interior of Thrace their force was destroyed at Drabeskos in Edonian territory by all the Thracians acting in concert, who saw the colonizing of the site of Nine Ways as an act of hostility. **I.101.1** Meanwhile the Thasians, who had been defeated in battle and were now under siege, called on the Spartans and urged them to come to their aid by invading Attica. **I.101.2** This the Spartans promised to do unbeknownst to the Athenians, and were about to do so when they were prevented by the earthquake which took place, in which both the helots, and the Thouriatans and Aithaians among the perioikoi, revolted and withdrew to Ithome. The majority of the helots were the descendants of the Messenians of old times who had then been enslaved; because of this they were all known as Messenians. **I.101.3** So the Spartans had a war on their hands with those at Ithome, while the Thasians, who were in the third year of the siege, came to terms with the Athenians, demolishing their wall and handing over their ships, and agreed to pay whatever they had to immediately as well as tribute for the future, and to give up both the mainland and the mine.

8.8 The Spartans Consider Invading Attica

Diodorus Siculus XI.50.1–3

According to Diodorus in 475/4 the Spartans regretted allowing the Athenians to take over command of the sea; the gerousia considered making war on the Athenians and the ekklesia was enthusiastic about the proposal. Some historians have doubted this story, for it finds no echo in Thucydides. But it is plausible that a few years after 478 the Spartans, seeing the growth of Athenian power, may have regretted giving up the command of the war against the Persians to the Athenians. Both Kagan (1969) 51–52, 378–79 and de Ste. Croix (1972) 170–71 accept the account, though the latter thinks 478 or 477 a more appropriate date.

XI.50.1 In this year the Spartans began to be angry about the fact that they had unaccountably lost the command of the sea; accordingly they were displeased with the Greeks who had rebelled from them, and kept threatening them with fitting punishment. **XI.50.2** When the gerousia was convened they debated about whether to make war against the Athenians over the command of the sea. **XI.50.3** Similarly, when the common assembly (ekklesia) met, the younger men and most of the others were ambitious to regain the leadership, considering that if they could do this they would have more wealth, and Sparta in general would become greater and more powerful, and the estates (oikoi) of its private individuals be greatly increased in prosperity.

8.9 The Helot Revolt

Thucydides I.102.1–103.3

The expedition to help Sparta cope with the revolt of the helots and perioikoi was opposed by Ephialtes (Plut. *Kim.* 16.9); Kimon was successful in having it sent. Plut. *Kim.* 16.9–17.3, cf. Diod. XI.63–64, has Kimon going to Sparta on two different occasions, which seems incompatible with Thucydides' evidence (but cf. for two campaigns: Hammond (1955) 377–79; Badian (1988) 304–10). There appears to have been one campaign, in which Kimon went with 4,000 hoplites (for this number, see Ar. *Lys.* 1138–44; cf. Plut. *Kim.* 16.8); in the next year Kimon was ostracised (see Lang 88–89, nos. 592–597; doc. 5.14 ix). **I.102.3**: Perhaps news of Ephialtes' reforms, enacted while Kimon was away, reached the ears of the Spartans, but recent Athenian activities against Naxos and Thasos were evidence for the Athenians' 'boldness and revolutionary spirit'; the Athenians were Ionians not Dorians. The Spartans' decision allowed Kimon's opponents to ally themselves with Argos, Sparta's enemy. Aeschylus refers, clearly with approval, to the new alliance in the *Eumenides* 289–91, 669–73, 762–74, produced in 458 BC: de Ste. Croix (1972) 183–84; Sommerstein (1989) 30. Bauslaugh (1990) 661–68 argues that two bronze spear butts (*LSAG* 177, 182n.4, pl.33 n.4; 203–04, 206n.3, pl.39 n.3) dedicated by the Methanioi, were dedications of spears taken from the Spartans and Athenians besieging Mt. Ithome; Methanioi appears to be the 'Messenian' spelling for Messenians. **I.103.3**: Naupaktos was to be important as an Athenian naval base; the Athenians took it from the Lokrians who had recently seized it (see Badian (1990) 364–69); the Spartans expelled the Messenians from there after the war: Diod. XIV.34.2–3; see Salmon (1984) 261–62; Lewis (1992) 118. 'Tenth' is often emended to 'fifth', but see McNeal (1970) 306–25. If the helots revolted in 465/4 or 464/3 and surrendered in 456/5 or 455/54, Thucydides' narrative is not chronological, for he then narrates Megara's joining Athens in 460–459; the easiest solution is to assume that Thucydides, in narrating the end of the revolt, got ahead of the chronological sequence of events (cf. Gomme *HCT* I.401–02).

I.102.1 As their war against those at Ithome was dragging on, the Spartans called on their allies, including the Athenians, for help; **I.102.2** and the Athenians came with a large force, under Kimon's leadership. The Spartans particularly called on the Athenians' help because they were thought to be good at siege operations, which from the length of the siege to date it was clear that the Spartans were not, or they would have taken the place by storm. **I.102.3** And it was because of this expedition that open dispute between the Spartans and Athenians first arose. For when the Spartans were still unable to take the place by storm, they became afraid of the Athenians' boldness and revolutionary spirit (as well as considering them at the same time not to be of the same race as themselves), in case, if they stayed on, they might be won over by those at Ithome and attempt some sort of revolution. So alone of all their allies they sent the Athenians away, not revealing their suspicions, but saying that they no longer had any need of them. **I.102.4** The Athenians, however, realised that they were not being sent away on any such acceptable grounds, but that some suspicion of them had arisen, and were offended, not considering it right that they should be treated like this by the Spartans. So, as soon as they returned home, they dissolved the alliance which had been formed against the Persians and became allies instead of the Argives who were the Spartans' enemies; at the same time both the Athenians and Argives made a sworn alliance on the same terms with the Thessalians. **I.103.1** However, the rebels at Ithome were unable to hold out any longer and in the tenth year they came to terms with the Spartans, on condition that they left the Peloponnese under a truce and never set foot in it again; if any of them were caught there, he was to be the slave of the man who captured him. **I.103.2** The Spartans had also had an oracle from Delphi prior to this that they should let the 'suppliant of Zeus' leave Ithome. **I.103.3** So the rebels left with their children and wives and the Athenians took them because of the hostility which they now felt towards the Spartans and settled them at Naupaktos, which they had captured from the Ozolian Lokrians, who had recently taken it.

CONSTITUTIONAL CHANGE IN ATHENS

In addition to the constitutional changes made by Ephialtes in 462/1 to the powers of the Areiopagos, other significant reforms include: *Ath. Pol.* 22.2 (501/0): the oath imposed on the boule and the election of strategoi, one from each tribe; 22.5 (487/6): use of partial sortition to elect archons (500 candidates directly elected and then ten chosen by lot); 26.2 (458/7): the zeugitai made eligible for the archonship; 26.3 (453/2): 30 circuit judges reintroduced; 26.3 (451/0): Perikles' citizenship law; 27.4: pay for jury service; see docs. 5.8, 8.22, 10.16, 18.

Before Ephialtes, the Areiopagos had guardianship of the laws, oversaw the magistrates (conducting dokimasiai and euthynai), and had supervision of the citizens (cf. docs. 3.1–2, 17). Ephialtes led a campaign against the Areiopagos and its members prior to the introduction of his reforms; see Sinclair (1988) 19 for the Areiopagos as an anomaly in a democracy. The method of election for archons introduced in 487/6 meant that membership of the Areiopagos was less prestigious than previously and under Ephialtes it was deprived of all but a few areas of jurisdiction: trials for deliberate homicide, arson and poisoning, and the protection of the sacred olive trees and other religious cases (see for example, Lys. VII.22; Dem. XXIII.22, 24, 66, LIX.78; Dein. I.6; *Ath. Pol.* 57.3, 60.2; Pollux 8.117). Its powers were distributed amongst the ekklesia, dikasteria and boule. It would have retained the right of prosodos (introducing motions) to the boule and ekklesia, but this right may have been little exercised. It is often assumed that Aeschylus in the *Eumenides* (produced in 458) which deals in large part with a trial for homicide of Orestes before the Areiopagos for the murder of his mother Clytemnestra shows support for Ephialtes' reforms. The role of the Areiopagos as a court of homicide is stressed: this could reflect Aeschylus' point of view that the council should have only this function. But Aeschylus also emphasizes that the Areiopagos fulfils an important role as a guardian of the state. Another message of the play is that the Athenians must avoid civil conflict; see Podlecki (1966) 127–29; Sommerstein (1989) 31–32; cf. Davison (1966) 93–107. For Ephialtes, see also *Ath. Pol.* 28.2, 35.2; Arist. *Pol.* 1274a 7–8; Plut. *Kim.* 13.4, 15.2–3, *Per.* 9.4, 10.7; Diod. XI.77.6. There is no satisfactory discussion of Ephialtes' reforms; see Hignett (1952) 193–213; Sealey (1964) 11–22, (1981) 125–34, (1987) 129–31, 143; Rhodes (1972) 201–07, (1981) 309–22; Wallace (1974) 259–69, (1985) 97–112; Stockton (1982) 227–28, (1990) 41–50; Carawan (1985) 120–22; Ostwald (1986) 47–77; Jones (1987) 53–76; Cawkwell (1988) 1–12; Sinclair (1988) 18–19; Develin (1989) 73; Ober (1989) 77–78; Roller (1989) 257–66; Hall (1990) 319–28; Starr (1990) 24–27; Hansen (1991) 36–37; Marr (1993) 11–19.

8.10 The Reforms of Ephialtes

[Aristotle] *Athenaion Politeia* 25.1–4

Ephialtes was the champion of the demos, and a strategos in the 460s, possibly in 465/4; see Plut. *Kim.* 13.4. **25.2**: During the absence of Kimon and 4,000 hoplites at Mt. Ithome (docs. 8.7, 9) Ephialtes put through legislation to curb the powers of the Areiopagos (Plut. *Kim.* 15.2, cf. *Per.* 7.8); their absence may have tipped the balance in the ekklesia in favour of the poor, the thetes, but the majority of the hoplites would have remained in Athens; Kimon on his return tried to reverse these changes (Plut. *Kim.* 15.3; unnecessarily doubted by Sealey (1981) 131), but he and his policy had been discredited and he was ostracised at the next opportunity, probably in 461 (Lang 88; doc. 5.14 ix). **25.3**: The presence of Themistokles here is anachronistic: he was in Persia at this time. One Archestratos, of whom nothing else is known, was associated with Ephialtes in these reforms; the Thirty in 404 erased their laws (*Ath. Pol.* 35.2; doc. 9.31). Perikles was also apparently involved with the reforms (*Ath. Pol.* 27.1; Plut. *Kim.* 15.2, *Per.* 9.5) but Ephialtes was clearly the main mover of the changes. **25.4**: For the assassination of Ephialtes, see Plut. *Per.* 10.7–8, who records the rumour that Perikles arranged the murder out of jealousy.

25.1 For about seventeen years after the Persian Wars the constitution remained unchanged under the supervision of the Areiopagos, although the Areiopagos was gradually declining. (And, as the populace increased in strength, Ephialtes son of Sophonides, who had a reputation for being incorruptible and upright with regard to the constitution, became champion of the people and attacked the (Areiopagos) council. **25.2** He first removed many of the Areiopagites, by bringing them to trial on the grounds of administrative misconduct; then in the archonship of Konon he took away all the council's additionally-acquired powers, through which it was the guardian of the constitution, and gave some of them to the Five Hundred (the boule) and some to the people and the law-courts.) **25.3** He did this with the assistance of Themistokles, who was a member of the Areiopagos and was about to be tried for collaboration with Persia .... **25.4** and not long afterwards Ephialtes too died, murdered by Aristodikos of Tanagra.

ATHENIAN MILITARY CAMPAIGNS

8.11 Disaster in Egypt, 460–54

Thucydides I.104.1–2, 109.1–110.4

Ktesias *FGH* 688 F14.36; Diod. XI.71.3–6, 74.1–4. **I.104.1–2**: Egypt became a Persian satrapy in 525; its revolt in 485 delayed the second Persian invasion of Greece. Thucydides places Inaros' revolt after Megara's alliance with Athens; the Athenians became involved in Egypt c. 460. **I.109.1**: Amongst the allies were the Samians; see ML 34, a dedication from Samos ('around lovely [Mem]phis [a battle] was brought abo[ut / by imp]etuous Ares between the ships of the Persians and the Gree[ks, and the Samians / took] fifteen [sh]ips of the Phoenicians') with addenda, where Inaros awards a prize to a Samian commander. **I.109.2**: Spartan susceptibility to bribery is well evidenced (doc. 8.18, cf. 8.8). While this first attempt to bribe the Spartans was unsuccessful, Persian funds were later to play a crucial role in the Spartan defeat of Athens. For Megabazos, see *ATL* III.168n.32, 253–54; de Ste. Croix (1972) 189–90; Lewis (1977) 50, 62, (1989) 230. **I.109.4**: Note the Persian capacity to undertake large-scale engineering works.

I.110.1–4: Thucydides is quite clear on the extent of the Hellenic disaster in Egypt: 200 ships initially followed by a relief force of 50 were mostly destroyed with few survivors (250 ships with crews of 180–200 men would mean casualties of up to 50,000, a disaster comparable to the Sicilian expedition). Ktesias, however, records that only 40 ships, not 200, went to Egypt from Cyprus and that they surrendered and their crews returned home. The two accounts cannot be reconciled despite attempts to do so: Gomme has most ships returning home after Memphis, leaving 40 behind, hence Ktesias' figure (*HCT* I.322), though Thucydides clearly gives the reader the impression that 250 ships and crews were lost. The disaster had little apparent affect on Athenian resources and Thucydides might need to be convicted of exaggeration: Westlake (1950) 209–16; Holladay (1989) 176–82; while Meiggs (1972) 101–08, 473–76 (cf. 439–41), prefers Thucydides' account; cf. Libourel (1971) 605–15. Cf. I.112.3–4 where later 60 ships leave the main force at Cyprus, to aid Amyrtaios, king of the marshes, and return safely.

I.104.1 Inaros son of Psammetichos, a Libyan, king of the Libyans who live near Egypt, set out from Mareia, the city beyond Pharos, and organized the revolt of most of Egypt from King Artaxerxes, and became its ruler, bringing in the Athenians as his allies. **I.104.2** They happened to be engaged in a campaign against Cyprus with two hundred ships of their own and their allies, and they left Cyprus and came to Egypt. After sailing from the sea up the Nile they gained control of the river and of two-thirds of Memphis, and started attacking the third part which is called the White Tower, inside which were those Persians and Medes who had escaped, as well as those Egyptians who had not joined in the revolt .... **I.109.1** Meanwhile the Athenians and allies were still in Egypt, and suffered all the different experiences of war. **I.109.2** At first, as the Athenians were in control of Egypt, the King sent to Sparta Megabazos, a Persian, with money to bribe the Peloponnesians to invade Attica so that the Athenians would have to return from Egypt. **I.109.3** But as this was unsuccessful, and the money was spent without results, Megabazos and the remainder of the money were recalled to Asia, and the King sent another Persian, Megabyzos son of Zopyros, with a large army (to Egypt); **I.109.4** he arrived and defeated the Egyptians and their allies in a battle on land, drove the Greeks from Memphis and finally shut them up on the island of Prosopitis, where he besieged them for a year and six months, when he drained the water from the channel and diverted it elsewhere, thus leaving the ships on dry land and turning most of the island into mainland, and crossed and captured the island on foot. **I.110.1** In this way the Greeks' venture failed after six years of fighting; a few out of the many involved got through Libya to Cyrene and were saved, but the majority were lost. **I.110.2** Egypt was again controlled by the King except for Amyrtaios, who was king of the marshes; it was impossible to capture him because of the size of the marshes, and the men of the marshes are the most warlike of the Egyptians. **I.110.3** Inaros the Libyan king, who had been responsible for these affairs in Egypt, was captured by treachery and crucified. **I.110.4** Meanwhile fifty triremes from Athens and the rest of the alliance had sailed out to relieve the force there and put in at the Menesian mouth (of the Nile), having no idea what had happened; and they were attacked by the infantry on land and the Phoenician fleet by sea and the majority of the ships were lost, though a few managed to get away. So ended the great expedition of the Athenians and their allies to Egypt.

8.12 A Casualty List of the Erechtheid Tribe, 460 or 459

Meiggs & Lewis 33 (*IG* I[3] 1147)

Cf. Thuc. I.104; Aristodemos *FGH* 104 F11.3. This inscription lists the war dead from the tribe Erechtheis (I) in 460 or 459. The army was organized along tribal lines (cf. doc. 5.17). The names of the war dead of all ten tribes were usually inscribed on one stele or adjacent stelai (ML p.75), but perhaps the great number of casualties explains this separate stele. The widespread nature of Athenian campaigns is seen here; Thucydides mentions all these except for Phoenicia. The list includes two generals from Erechtheis, Ph[ryni]chos (l. 6) and Hippodamas (l. 63). The election of one strategos from each tribe (cf. doc. 5.8), does not seem always to have held: while there is a possible example of two strategoi from the same tribe ('double representation') in 479/8, in 441/0 there is the first definite example of two strategoi, from Akamantis (V), Perikles and Glaukon: see Fornara (1971) 49; Develin (1989) 89. There are further examples in subsequent decades (see the list at Fornara 71; Lewis (1961) 118–23 (esp. 121); cf. Develin 3–4 with bibliography). In 432/1, there is an example of triple representation with three strategoi from Kekropis (VII). This document could date multiple representation to at least 460 or 459, but one strategos may have replaced the other: see Fornara 46; Develin 3, 74. The election of one strategos from each tribe was probably altered by at least 441/0, by a 'procedural reform' (Staveley (1972) 43; but cf. Bicknell (1974) 156–57); presumably the ten candidates who received the most votes were elected. Each of the strategoi was equal in power and responsibility (cf. doc. 10.13; see Hignett (1952) 348–54). The Athenians may have seen themselves as fighting a single 'war' (line 2), defending themselves against the Peloponnesians while they 'championed' Greece against barbarians (ML p.76).

(1) Of (the tribe) Erechtheis
These died in the war, in Cyprus, in Eg[y]-
pt, in Phoenicia, at Halieis, on Aegina, at Megara
in the same year.
(5) Of the [g]en[er]als:
Ph[....]chos .... (*there follows a list of 176 names in three columns*)
(62) general:
Hippodamas

8.13 The Campaign against Cyprus

Simonides 45

Page 266–68; Diod. XI.62.3 attributes this epigram to the battle of the Eurymedon. Simonides probably died shortly after 468 so obviously this is not his work.

From the time when the sea separated Europe from Asia
And impetuous Ares held sway over the cities of mortals,
No such deed of earthly men ever took place
On land and sea at the same time;
For on Cyprus these men destroyed many Persians
And took a hundred Phoenician ships at sea
Full of men; and Asia groaned loudly because of them,
Struck with both hands with the strength of war.

8.14 The 'Peace of Kallias'

All the evidence for such a peace is from the fourth century and later (Fornara (1977) pp.95–100 translates the relevant passages). Hdt. VII.151 alludes to an embassy of Kallias and other Athenians to Artaxerxes at Susa, and this is usually taken as the embassy concluding the Peace of Kallias in 449: cf. Badian (1987) 2, but Bloedow (1992a) 41–68 (cf. Fornara & Samons (1991) 171–75) shows that Badian's thesis that there were two Peaces of Kallias is untenable. If there were a Peace of Kallias, Thucydides' silence is interesting, but not impossible; Thuc. VIII.56.4–5, in fact, which points to restrictions on where the Persian fleet could sail, is a possible allusion to the Peace of Kallias. An absence of reported hostilities between Persia and Athens after Kimon's campaign with 200 ships against Cyprus in 451, during which he died, supports the statements that there was a peace, made by Kallias son of Hipponikos, between the two states at this time. The pre-occupation in subsequent decades to affairs in Greece and commitment to domestic building programs tends to suggest a formal peace. In favour of the Peace of Kallias is the possible treaty of 424/3 with Artaxerxes' successor Darius who came to the throne in that year: as treaties were made specifically with the King, they had to be remade on the accession of a new King (ML 70 (*IG* II^{2} 8); Meiggs (1972) 135; the dating is not accepted by all), so that this treaty could be seen as a renewal of an earlier one. Certainly, the current consensus is firmly in favour of the existence of the Peace (Badian (1987) 1n.5).

The Peace is usually dated to 449/8 (Diod. XII.4.4; cf. Lewis (1992) 122–23), and is held to have caused a crisis in the empire in the forties, reflected in the tribute-quota lists. There was one year in which tribute was not paid, perhaps because the reason for it, war against the barbarian, no longer existed (though see de Ste. Croix (1972) 311), and 449/8 is usually viewed as the missing year (as in *ATL* I.133, 175, II.13, III.278; *IG* I^{3} 263, p.243). The year 447/6, the second possibility, could indicate that there was widespread disaffection amongst the allies following the defeat of the Athenians at Koroneia in Boeotia. The suggestion has also been made that the quota of the tribute for 449/8 was not recorded because the entire tribute was allocated to a specific project, but it seems implausible that the Athenians would have deprived Athena of the quota (ML 50 p.135; Meiggs (1972) 154). It can perhaps be assumed that in 449/8 the allies refused to pay tribute because peace had been made. Collection of tribute recommenced after the 'missing year', and the tribute-quota list for the following year 448/7 indicates many partial payments, indicating difficulty in collecting the tribute. See esp. *ATL* III.277–81; Fornara (1977) pp.98–99; Lewis (1992) 123–25 (with 124 fig.3). For the Peace of

Kallias, see: Wade-Gery (1958a) 201–232; *ATL* III.275–300; de Ste. Croix (1972) 310–14; Meiggs (1972) 129–51, 487–95; Thompson (1981) 164–77; Walsh (1981) 31–49; Bosworth (1990) 1–13; Bloedow (1992a) 41–68; Lewis (1992) 121–27.

i. Isocrates IV *Panegyricus* 117–18

117 Our treatment of the barbarians for having dared to cross into Europe and for their excessive arrogance **118** ensured that they not only ceased making expeditions against us but even suffered their country to be ravaged; and we so abased their pride that they who had once taken to the seas with 1,200 ships launched no ship this side of Phaselis, but stayed quiet and waited better times, rather than trust in the forces they then possessed.

ii. Plutarch *Kimon* 13.4–5 (Kallisthenes *FGH* 124 F16; Krateros *FGH* 342 F13)

The Kyaneai are at the entrance to the Black Sea, the Chelidoniai are islands between Lycia and Pamphylia.

13.4 This achievement (the encounter at the Eurymedon followed by one at Syedra) so humbled the will of the King that he made that peace, which is much talked about, undertaking to keep a day's journey by horse away from the sea, and not to sail with a bronze-beaked warship past the Kyaneai (the Blue Rocks) or the Chelidoniai. Yet Kallisthenes denies that the barbarians made this peace, but says that he simply acted like this out of fear resulting from that defeat, and stayed so far away from Greece that Perikles with fifty ships and Ephialtes with thirty sailed beyond the Chelidoniai without a fleet from the barbarians coming to meet them. **13.5** But in the *Decrees*, which Krateros put together, copies of the agreements are described as having been made. It is also said that the Athenians dedicated an altar of peace as a result, and voted especial honours to Kallias the ambassador.

THE FIRST PELOPONNESIAN WAR

The dismissal of the Athenians from Ithome resulted in their allying themselves with Sparta's enemy, Argos. The Megarians approached Athens for an alliance in 460 or 459, as they were being attacked by Corinth; this alienated Corinth from Athens, and led to the outbreak of the First Peloponnesian War (which is a modern term). This war consisted of a series of conflicts, the main Spartan-Athenian confrontation being at Tanagra; Sparta did not take the war into Attica until 446. Holladay's view that Sparta in the First Peloponnesian War was not the aggressor seems to be the correct one, and after Tanagra, the Spartans did not press their advantage: it was Corinth that was the aggressive Peloponnesian (Holladay (1977) 54–63; Lewis (1981) 71–78, (1992) 111–20; but cf. de Ste. Croix (1972) 50–51, 180–83 and Salmon (1984) 260–69, 420–21 (answered by Holladay (1985) 161–62); note also Kagan (1991) 120–24). When Corinth complained in 432 of the Spartans' slowness to go to war this was probably an allusion to the First Peloponnesian War, in which Corinth and other allies of Sparta did most of the fighting (Thuc. I.68.2, 69.4–5, 71.4, 84.1, 118.2). In 451 the Athenians and Spartans agreed to a Five Years Peace.

8.15 The Megarians Join the Athenians

Thucydides I.103.4

Thuc. I.105 and following deals with clashes between the Athenians and Corinthians; see de Ste. Croix (1972) 181–82. Megara was important to Athens for it could block the invasion route from the Peloponnese; Pegai was at the eastern end of the Corinthian Gulf, and had strategic value (see de Ste. Croix (1972) 190–95); an Athenian expedition left here under the command of Perikles in 455/4 or 454/3 (Thuc. I.111.2–3, cf. II.102.2; Diod. XI.85; Plut. *Per.* 19.2–3) and attacked Sicyon and (unsuccessfully) Oiniadai in Akarnania (at the western end of the Corinthian Gulf, and therefore of strategic value; it was forced to join Athens in 424: Thuc. IV.77.2). Athenian control of Pegai (lost under the peace treaty of 446/5) meant that, as in Perikles' Corinthian Gulf expedition, the Athenians could avoid the long sail around the Peloponnese.

I.103.4 The Megarians also left the Spartans' side and allied themselves with the Athenians, because the Corinthians were attacking them in a war concerning boundary land. Thus the Athenians held both Megara and Pegai, and they built the Megarians the Long Walls from the city to Nisaia and manned them themselves. And it was primarily from this that the Corinthians' violent hatred for the Athenians first came into being.

8.16 The Battles of Tanagra and Oinophyta, 458/7

Thucydides I.107.1–108.5

I.107.1: There were two parallel 'Long Walls' from Athens to the city, as well as the Phaleric 'Long Wall' from Athens to the eastern side of the Phaleron harbour. The northern Long Wall and the Phaleric Wall were built first, being commenced before the battle of Tanagra and completed after Oinophyta. The Middle Wall (the southern Long Wall) was commenced in 446/5 after the Thirty Years' Peace. For these walls, see Boersma (1970) 156; Wycherley (1978) 262–63; Garland (1987) 22–26; plans at 157, 16, and 23 respectively. **I.107.4–6**: When Athens surrendered in 404, these walls were destroyed (see doc. 9.30); Badian (1988) 318n.43 is unnecessarily sceptical of the plot against the democracy. **I.108.1**: For Tanagra in 458, see also Diod. XI.80. See ML 35 for a stele at Athens listing the Argives killed at Tanagra (cf. Paus. I.29.8); see ML 36 (doc. 6.39) and Paus. V.10.4 for the golden shield dedicated at Olympia by the Spartans and their allies in thanks for this victory. The battle of Tanagra may also have led to the recall of Kimon (ostracised in 461): Plut. *Per.* 10.1–5, *Kim.* 17.8–18.1; Theopompos *FGH* 115 F88. Meiggs (1972) 111, 422–23 argues for a recall c. 452 after the Egyptian defeat; as does Unz (1986) 76–82; see also Connor (1968) 24–30; Kagan (1969) 91–92; de Ste. Croix (1972) 189n.79; Sealey (1976) 272–73; Badian (1987) 12–13. **I.108.2–3**: The Athenians' capture of Boeotia led to a ten year domination there (referred to as the 'land empire'). While it is generally assumed that the Boeotians had a different status from that of the members of the Delian League, Lewis (1981) 77n.43, (1992) 116n.72 suggests that the Boeotian cities Orchomenos and Akraiphia be read in the Athenian tribute-quota lists at *IG* I^3 260.IX 9 (453/2) and 259.III 20 (454/3) indicating that Athens treated Boeotia like the other areas it dominated. Certainly, the Boeotians as allies provided military contingents (Thuc. I.111.1). See, for Athenian control of Boeotia, Arist. *Pol.* 1302b 25; [Xen.] *Const. Ath.* 3.11; Buck (1970) 217–27; Boeotia was later lost in 447 (Thuc. I.113). **I.108.4**: So ended the long conflict between Athens and Aegina; Aegina henceforth paid an annual tribute of 30 talents. **I.108.5**: Tolmides' expedition was in

456/5. Corinthian Chalkis is meant, on the northern side of the Corinthian Gulf. The dockyards were at Gytheion.

I.107.1 At about this time the Athenians began to build their Long Walls down to the sea, one to Phaleron and the other to the Peiraieus .... (**I.107.2–3:** *Phokis had captured one of the towns belonging to Doris, the mother-city of the Spartans, and Sparta came to its assistance. The Spartans then had to consider how to return home.*) **I.107.4** The Spartans decided to remain in Boeotia and see what the safest line of march would be. Apart from anything else, they were urged in secret to do this by some Athenians who had hopes of overthrowing the democracy and preventing the building of the Long Walls. **I.107.5** But the Athenians marched out against them with their whole force, together with 1,000 Argives and contingents from their other allies: altogether they came to 14,000 men. **I.107.6** They made this attack because they thought that the Spartans had difficulties in getting back and because they had some suspicions about the plot to overthrow the democracy. **I.107.7** Some Thessalian cavalry also came to aid the Athenians in accordance with the alliance, though in actual fact they deserted to the Spartans. **I.108.1** A battle took place at Tanagra in Boeotia and the Spartans and their allies were victorious, though there were heavy losses on both sides. **I.108.2** The Spartans then went into the Megarid, cutting down trees as they went, and returned home through Geraneia and the Isthmus; the Athenians on the sixty-second day after the battle marched into Boeotia with Myronides in command, **I.108.3** and defeated the Boeotians in a battle at Oinophyta, gaining control of the country of Boeotia and Phokis. They demolished the walls of Tanagra and took as hostages a hundred of the richest of the Opuntian Lokrians, and then completed their own Long Walls. **I.108.4** After this the Aeginetans surrendered to the Athenians, which involved destroying their walls and handing over their ships and agreeing to pay tribute for the future. **I.108.5** And the Athenians sailed around the Peloponnese, with Tolmides son of Tolmaios in command, and burnt the Spartans' dockyards and took Chalkis, a Corinthian city, and landed and defeated the Sicyonians in battle.

8.17 The Second Sacred War

Thucydides I.112.5

This was the second 'Sacred War', which took place in 449. Hornblower (1992) 169–97 incorrectly takes Thucydides' relative silence on this matter (in that he gives no information about the Amphictyons) as an indication of his silence on important religious themes. Where Thucydides chooses, he provides information on numerous religious aspects of the war; see Oost (1975) 186–96; Powell (1979a) 15–31, (1979b) 45–50; Marinatos (1981) 138–40; Jordan (1986) 119–47. Delphi was to give its blessing to Sparta's declaration of war against Athens: Thuc. I.118.3, cf. 121.3.

I.112.5 After this the Spartans took part in what was called the Sacred War, and gained control of the temple at Delphi and handed it over to the Delphians; and once they had withdrawn, the Athenians then took the field, gained control of it and handed it back to the Phokians.

8.18 The Revolts of Euboea and Megara

Thucydides I.114.1–115.1

In 446, the revolts of Euboea and Megara, and Pleistoanax' invasion of Attica were important factors leading to the Thirty Years Peace. **I.114.1**: It is not stated why Euboea revolted in 446, unless the generic statements at Thuc. I. 98.4–99.2 (doc. 8.3) account for it; it has been suggested that the establishment of a cleruchy on Euboea c. 450 helped provoke the revolt (Gomme *HCT* I.340, Brunt (1966) 81; cf. Meiggs (1972) 123). **I.114.2**: Perikles may have bribed Pleistoanax to withdraw; see Thuc. II.21.1, V.16; Ephoros *FGH* 70 F193; Diod. XIII.106.10; Plut. *Per.* 22.2–4; Schol. Ar. *Clouds* 859; de Ste. Croix (1972) 197–99; Cartledge (1979) 230. Pleistoanax was exiled, but later an oracle from Delphi caused the Spartans to restore him as king (but his enemies accused him of bribing the Pythia; cf. doc. 9.19); for his place of exile, see Philippides (1985) 33–41. **I.114.3**: For the Hestiaians' capture of an Athenian ship and killing of the crew, see Plut. *Per.* 23.4. The Athenians settled at Hestiaia will have been cleruchs (Graham (1983) 170–72); *IG* I^3 41 is an Athenian decree regulating the affairs of the Athenian settlers at Hestiaia; cf. *IG* I^3 39 for Eretria; doc. 9.18 for Chalkis. **I.115.1**: In 446/5 the Athenians and Peloponnesians signed a Thirty Years Peace (see de Ste. Croix (1972) 293–94) which lasted for fourteen years (Thuc. II.2.1). In 425 Athens demanded that Nisaia, Pegai, Troizen and Achaea, surrendered by the terms of the truce, be returned (Thuc. IV.21.3).

I.114.1 Not long after this Euboea revolted from the Athenians; Perikles had already crossed over with an Athenian army, when it was reported to him that Megara had revolted and the Peloponnesians were about to invade Attica, and that the Athenian garrison troops had been destroyed by the Megarians, except for those who had managed to escape to Nisaia; the Megarians had brought in as allies the Corinthians, Sicyonians and Epidaurians. So Perikles swiftly brought the army back from Euboea. **I.114.2** And after this the Peloponnesians, with Pleistoanax, son of Pausanias in command, did invade Attica laying it waste as far as Eleusis and Thria, but they came no further than that and departed for home. **I.114.3** The Athenians again crossed to Euboea under Perikles' leadership and subdued the whole island, drawing up treaties with all the cities except the Hestiaians, whom they drove out and whose land they occupied. **I.115.1** Not long after returning from Euboea the Athenians made a thirty years' peace with the Spartans and their allies, and gave back Nisaia, Pegai, Troizen and Achaea, all of which they had taken from the Peloponnesians.

8.19 A Memorial for Pythion of Megara, 446

Meiggs & Lewis 51 (*IG* I^3 1353)

Hansen 83; cf. Diod. XII.5.2. After Megara revolted Athens sent a force into the Megarid under the command of Andokides; this army was guided back to Athens by Pythion, through a round-about route, presumably because of Pleistoanax's march to Eleusis. Athens continued to control Pegai despite Megara's revolt, but it was given up to Sparta when the Thirty Years Peace was made (doc. 8.18). The lines of verse, which do not correspond with the lines of the inscription, are followed here.

T[his] memorial [is] set [o]ver the body of the bravest of men.
Pythion of Megar[a] killed seven men,
And bro[k]e seven spears in their bodies,
Choosing valour and bringing his father honour among the people.
This man, who [s]aved three Athenian tribes
By leading them from Pegai through Boeotia to Athens,
Brought honour to Andokides with two thousand prisoners.
Having harmed no one among earthly men
He descended to Hades most blessed in the sight of everyone.
These are the tribes: Pandionis, Kekropis, Antiochis.

PERIKLES 'THE OLYMPIAN'

Perikles took over leadership of the democratic party some time after the assassination of Ephialtes. The institution of jury pay and his citizenship law of 451/0 (docs. 8.22, 10.18) were Perikles' two known political reforms. Another measure of Perikles' to advantage the people was his establishment of cleruchies in allied territory (doc. 8.21); Stadter (1989) 142 notes that his measures were 'statesman-like rather than demagogic'. Despite the ostracism of his political opponent Thucydides, son of Melesias (doc. 8.23), Perikles still faced opposition. When Pheidias, a friend of Perikles, was prosecuted in c. 438/7 for embezzling gold and ivory intended for the chryselephantine Athena (see doc. 10.3), Perikles was implicated. Pheidias was acquitted of embezzlement but prosecuted for impiety (asebeia) and put into prison, where he died, for including the likeness of Perikles and himself in the amazonomachia (battle of the amazons) on Athena's shield in the Parthenon; for this amazonomachia, see Castriota (1992) 143; for Pheidias, see Plut. *Per.* 31.2–5; Philochoros *FGH* 328 F121; Aristodemos *FGH* 104 F1.16; Diod. XII.39.1–2; Bauman (1990) 37; Kagan (1991) 185–86. That Aspasia was prosecuted, at about the same time as Pheidias, for impiety and acting as a procuress of free women for Perikles is doubted by some scholars; see doc. 13.29; Plut. *Per.* 32.1; Ostwald (1986) 195; Bauman (1990) 38; Kagan (1991) 184.

Diopeithes was responsible for the passing of a decree against those who did not believe in the gods. Anaxagoras of Klazomenai, a natural philosopher and another of Perikles' friends, was the target of the decree, which was an indirect attack on Perikles. Plutarch has Perikles arranging for Anaxagoras to leave the city; other sources state that he was prosecuted and fined: see doc. 9.32; Plut. *Per.* 4.6–5.1, 6.1–3, 16.7–9, 32.2–5 (cf. 32.6: Perikles stirred up the war with Sparta because of his impending prosecution over the misuse of public funds); Davison (1953) 39–45; O'Brien (1968) 93–113; Mansfeld (1979) 39–69, (1980) 17–95; Ostwald (1986) 195–98; Bauman (1990) 38–40; Kagan (1991) 22–24, 184, 186. For Diopeithes' law against impiety, see Ostwald (1986) 274–90, 528–33. These trials on religious grounds involving Perikles' associates were very probably aimed at Perikles; certainly in 430 he was fined (Thuc. II.65.3, cf. 59.3). Diod. XII.45.3–4 and Plut. *Per.* 35.4 have him deposed from the strategia; see Fornara (1971) 54; Develin (1989) 119. So Perikles did not have unbridled influence, as these prosecutions of himself and his associates prove that he was not considered to be above criticism. For Perikles' nickname 'the Olympian' (there was dispute as to whether it was on account of his oratory, buildings, or prowess as a statesman and general), see Plut. *Per.* 8.2–4; for his disproportionate head at birth, because of which nearly all his portraits showed him wearing a helmet, and which was a constant target for jokes from the comic poets who called him 'squill-head', see Plut. *Per.* 3.3–7; Ober (1989) 86–91 for Perikles.

8.20 The Revolt of Samos

Thucydides I.115.2–117.3

This document follows on from doc. 8.18. See also Diod. XII.27–28; Plut. *Per.* 24.1–2, 25.1–28.8; Meiggs (1972) 190–93. For the chronology of the revolt, 440–439, see Fornara (1979) 7–18, cf. Meritt (1984) 128–33. Plutarch's statement that Perikles' actions against Samos were inspired by Aspasia (doc. 13.29) can be safely rejected: he was primarily prompted by imperial considerations. **I.115.2**: The Athenians supported the Samian democrats who wanted a change in government, not simply on ideological grounds but because the 'private individuals' were presumably of sufficient prominence to be potentially powerful friends in the new political set-up. **I.115.3**: Miltiades the Younger had captured Lemnos, which became an Athenian cleruchy; see Jones (1957) 172–73; Brunt (1966) 80–81; Graham (1983) 174–88. **I.115.4**: While there may have been a Peace of Kallias with a cessation of formal hostilities (see doc. 8.14), Persian interference continued. Pissouthnes, son of Hystaspes, was satrap of Sardis, see Lewis (1977) 55, 59–61; his bastard son Amorges later rebelled. For Perikles' 'Congress Decree', which involved a Panhellenic Congress at Athens to discuss the rebuilding of the temples destroyed by the Persians, the sacrifices vowed when the Persians invaded, and keeping the peace, see Plut. *Per.* 17, esp. 17.1; Kagan (1969) 110–12; Meiggs (1972) 512–15; Stadter (1989) 201–09. It is possible that with the Peace of Kallias (though the date of Perikles' decree is uncertain), Perikles sought a new rationale for the Delian League; but the Spartans rejected the Congress, possibly because it implied Athenian leadership of the Hellenes. **I.117.3**: See *IG* I^3 363 (ML 55; Fornara (1977) 113) for the Athenian expenses of the Samian War paid for with money from the fund of the Treasurers of Athena. The Samian campaign provides the first example of borrowing temple funds for the prosecution of a war (Parker (1983) 173; cf. doc. 10.5). The cost was around 1200 or 1400 talents (Fornara (1979) 9–12; Shipley (1987) 118). It is debated how long it took the Samians to pay off the indemnity: before 431, and 414/3 have been suggested (see ML p.151). For possible references to payments, see *IG* I^3 68.21–22, 426 BC (ML 68.20–21; Fornara 133, doc. 9.14) and *Lactor*^{3} n.125. For the Athenian treaty with Samos, *IG* I^3 48 dated to 439/8 BC (ML 56; Fornara (1977) 115), see Plut. *Per.* 28.1; Diod. XII.28.3–4; Bridges (1980) 185–88. The Potidaea campaign was to cost the Athenians 2,000 talents.

I.115.2 In the sixth year (of the peace) war broke out between the Samians and Milesians over Priene, and, after getting the worst of the war, the Milesians came to Athens to protest loudly against the Samians. Some private individuals from Samos itself, who wished to install a democratic form of government, also supported them. **I.115.3** So the Athenians sailed to Samos with forty ships and set up a democracy, and took fifty children and an equal number of men from Samos hostage, and left them for safe keeping on Lemnos. They then left a garrison behind (on Samos) and returned home. **I.115.4** Some of the Samians, however, had not stayed behind but fled to the mainland, and they made an alliance with the most influential men (leading oligarchs) in the city and with Pissouthnes, son of Hystaspes, who was then governor of Sardis, gathered about 700 mercenaries, and crossed to Samos during the night. **I.115.5** First they rose up against the leaders of the democracy and seized most of them, and then they rescued the hostages from Lemnos and declared a rebellion, and handed over to Pissouthnes the Athenian garrison and officials who were there, and made immediate preparations for an expedition against Miletos. The

Byzantines also joined with them in the revolt .... (**I.116.1–117.1**: *The Athenians sent sixty ships, which were reinforced by others, under Perikles and nine other generals. Samos was blockaded, but while Perikles was preventing the arrival of the Phoenician fleet, the Samians defeated the Athenian fleet.*) **I.117.2** But, when Perikles returned, the Samians were again blockaded by the Athenians' ships. Later forty ships came to assist them from Athens under the command of Thucydides, Hagnon and Phormio, twenty more under Tlepolemos and Antikles, and thirty from Chios and Lesbos. **I.117.3** The Samians put up a brief fight at sea, but were unable to hold their own, and in the ninth month of the siege had to come to terms. They pulled down their walls, gave hostages, handed over their ships, and agreed to pay back the money, which had been expended, by instalments. The Byzantines also agreed to return to subject status, like before.

8.21 Perikles Sends out Cleruchies

Plutarch *Perikles* 11.4–6

The Athenians established several settlements abroad, both cleruchies and colonies, in the fifth century. Cleruchies were usually sent to the territory of allies which had revolted and involved the allocation of land to Athenian citizens who retained their citizenship, and would be loyal garrisons in allied states. They were an important part of Athenian control and were obviously unpopular with Athens' fifth century allies (see doc. 8.29). Colonies were sent out to captured territory, but the distinction between a colony and a cleruchy is not always clear in the sources. Numerous settlements were sent out in the fifth century, to Naxos, Andros, the Chersonese, Hestiaia (doc. 8.18), Chalkis, Mytilene, Thrace, Potidaea, Sinope, Amisos, Skyros, Eion, Aegina, Melos, Brea, Thourioi, Amphipolis, and perhaps Karystos: Thuc. I.98.2, I.114.3, II.27.1, III.50.2, V.116.4, VII.57.2; Andok. III.9; Aisch. II.175; Isoc. IV.108; Diod. XI.60.2, 88.3, XII.46.7; Plut. *Kim.* 7.3–4, 8.2–5, 14.1, *Per.* 11.5–6, 19.1, 20.2, 23.4, 34.2, *Mor.* 349c–d; Paus. I.27.5; Ael. *VH* VI.1; the islands of Lemnos and Imbros also had Athenian settlers (Andok. III.12; cf. Xen. *Hell.* IV.8.15).

When Strepsiades in Ar. *Clouds* 203 is told by one of Socrates' pupils that geometry is used to measure land, he automatically assumes that it will be used to divide up cleruchies. The establishment of cleruchies seems to have led to the reduction of the tribute assessed from the region involved: for example, the Chersonese in 453 paid 18 talents but less than 3 talents in 446, and Andros paid 12 talents in 450 but in the following year only 6 (Meiggs (1972) 121, 123, 159–60, 530; Lewis (1992) 126); Skyros, settled by Athenians, never paid tribute (*ATL* III.286). Meiggs 530 dates the Chersonese cleruchy to 447, and Naxos and Andros to 450. The cleruchy amongst the Bisaltai is often identified with Brea (see doc. 8.27). The foundation of Thourioi in southern Italy took place in 444/3 BC (a refoundation on the site of Sybaris). It was a Panhellenic colony, having Athenian settlers and an Athenian founder (the chresmologos, seer, Lampon), but with a greater number of other Greek colonists, including Herodotos. See also Ar. *Clouds* 331–32 with Schol.; Diod. XII.10.3–11.4; Strab. VI.1.13 (263); Plut. *Nik.* 5.3; Phot. s.v. *Thouriomanteis*; Ehrenberg (1948) 149–70; Jones (1957) 169; Wade-Gery (1958) 255–58; Kagan (1969) 154–69, 382–84, (1991) 127–30; de Ste. Croix (1972) 381; Meiggs (1972) 280, 304, 368; Rutter (1973) 155–76; Andrewes (1978) 5–8; Graham (1983) 35–37. For cleruchies, see Gomme *HCT* I.376–80; *ATL* III.284–97; Jones (1957) 167–77; Meiggs (1972) esp. 260–62, 530; Brunt (1966) 71–92; Ehrenberg (1952) 143–49; Graham (1983) 166–92, 209–10; Stadter (1989) 138–39; Figueira (1991), esp. 217–25.

11.4 For this reason Perikles chose at this point to relax the reins on the people more than ever before and aimed his policy towards their gratification, by constantly providing public festivals, feasts and processions in the city, thus keeping the city occupied with cultural pleasures, and by sending out sixty triremes each year, in which many of the citizens sailed with pay for eight months, and at the same time learnt and practised seamanship. **11.5** Besides this he sent 1,000 cleruchs (lot-holders) to the Chersonese, 500 to Naxos, half this number to Andros, 1,000 to Thrace to live alongside the Bisaltai, and others to Italy, when Sybaris was being resettled, which they named Thourioi. **11.6** In this way he lightened the city of a idle mob, who were trouble-makers because they had leisure, and relieved the poverty of the people, and by sending out settlers to live alongside the allies installed both fear and a garrison to prevent their rebellion.

8.22 Perikles Institutes Jury Pay

[Aristotle] *Athenaion Politeia* 27.3–4

Ephialtes' transference of judicial functions from the Areiopagos to the jury-courts (see doc. 8.10) gave the courts more political power and importance. The amount of jury pay was initially two obols per day (see docs. 10.16–17).

27.3 Furthermore Perikles was the first person to introduce pay for serving in the law-courts, as a measure to win popular favour and counteract the generosity of Kimon. For Kimon, who was as wealthy as a tyrant, not only performed his public liturgies munificently but maintained many of his fellow-demesmen; for any of the men from Lakiadai who wished could go to him each day and obtain enough for his needs, and all his land was unfenced, so anyone who wished could enjoy its produce. **27.4** Perikles lacked the resources for this kind of expenditure and he was advised by Damonides of Oe (who seems to have been the instigator of many of Perikles' measures, and it was for that reason that he was later ostracised) that since he was less well provided with private property he should give the people their own, and therefore Perikles brought in payment for the jurors; it was because of this, some people allege, that the courts deteriorated, as it was always the ordinary people rather than the better-off who wanted to be chosen.

8.23 Perikles and Thucydides, Son of Melesias

Plutarch *Perikles* 11.1–2, 14.1–3

Thucydides, son of Melesias, was Perikles' main opponent, and after his ostracism in 443 (the usually accepted date), Perikles was the outstanding figure in Athenian politics. Perikles' citizenship law of 451/0 indicates his importance by that date, and the 440s were dominated by him. Thucydides does not seem to have held any military commands; he was the champion (prostates) of the aristocrats. His main point of attack against Perikles seems to have been the misuse of allied funds for the adornment of Athens, but these accusations were doubtless greatly exaggerated as political invective (see Andrewes (1978) 1–5; Ostwald (1986) 185–88; Ober (1989) 88–89; Kallet-Marx (1989b) 252–66; Bauman (1990) 35–36, Kagan (1991) 106–08; Burke (1992) 217; but cf. the unlikely suggestions of Krentz (1984) 499–504. The main source on the opposition to Perikles on the part of Thucydides is Plut. *Per.* 11–12, 14 (cf. Plut. *Per.* 6.2–3, 8.5, 16.3; *Ath. Pol.* 28.2, 5; Plat. *Meno* 94d). Cf. docs. 10.7 (Plut. *Per.* 12.1–2), 11.38 (Plut. *Per.* 12.5–6) for Perikles' building program. For Thucydides' ostracism, see Lang 98 nos. 651–52, 132 nos. 1050–51 (doc. 5.14 xi). For Perikles' offer to pay privately for public works, see doc. 10.8.

11.1 The aristocrats had even before this recognised that Perikles had already become the most important of the citizens, but they were nevertheless anxious that there should be someone in the city to stand up to him and blunt his power, so it should not become a downright monarchy. They put forward Thucydides of Alopeke, a moderate man and relative of Kimon's, to oppose him. Thucydides was less of a soldier than Kimon, but was more effective as a speaker and politician, and by keeping his eyes open in the city and coming to grips with Perikles on the speakers' platform he soon introduced a state of balance into the political arena (politeia). **11.2** He did not allow the so-called 'landed gentry' to be scattered and mixed up with the people as they were before, resulting in their influence being overshadowed by the populace, but by separating them out and assembling them into a single entity he made them collectively into an important power-group, a counterweight in the scale, so to speak .... **14.1** Thucydides and his supporters kept denouncing Perikles for squandering money and wasting the revenues, and so Perikles asked the people in the assembly if they thought too much had been spent; when they all replied far too much, he said, 'Then let the cost be put down to my account, not yours, and I will have the inscriptions of the buildings dedicated to the gods made in my name.' **14.2** When Perikles said this, either they were amazed at his munificence, or else they wanted to vie with him for the repute from the public works, and they made an uproar telling him to spend from state funds and spare nothing in his expenditure. **14.3** And finally he took the risk of setting up a competition against Thucydides with an ostracism, and had him banished and put down the party formed against him.

THE TRIBUTE

The first tribute-quota list dates to 454/3; it is generally assumed that the treasury was moved in 454/3 to Athens because of the disaster which the Greeks suffered in Egypt (Rhodes (1985) 15). The Athenian tribute-quota lists provide evidence for the annual payment of tribute, phoros, by the allies and record the dedication by the Athenians of one-sixtieth of the phoros of each allied state to the goddess Athena (this was the aparchai, 'first-fruits'). For example, in the first entry of doc. 8.24, the 200 drachmas of the Pedasians represents one-sixtieth of the phoros they actually paid: their phoros was thus 12,000 drachmas (2 talents). The actual records of the full phoros payments have disappeared; the fact that the one-sixtieth was a dedication to Athena explains why these were inscribed on stone. The lists of the first 15 years from 454/3 were recorded on a single massive stele (3.663m x 1.109m x 0.385m); there are also fragments of a second, smaller, stele for the lists of 438/7–432/1. After 454, the tribute was reassessed every four years ([Xen.] *Const. Ath.* 3.5), and known changes in the tribute generally occur in years in which the Great Panathenaia was celebrated (450, 446, 434; but see doc. 9.15); payments were made by the allies at the Dionysia (see doc. 9.16; Ar. *Ach.* 502–06). From

443/2, cities were grouped according to region: Ionia, the Hellespont, Thrace, Caria, the Islanders; the Ionians and Carians are placed together from 438/7. Note that cities paying are listed by their ethnics rather than by the name of their cities. The basic starting point for any research on tribute or the empire is the monumental four volume study of Meritt, Wade-Gery, McGregor *The Athenian Tribute Lists* (1939–53): *ATL*. For assessments from the Peloponnesian War, see docs. 9.14–17. For an overview of the tribute, see Meiggs (1972) 234–54; Rhodes (1985) 15; this discussion owes much to the summary of ML 39.

8.24 The First Tribute-Quota List, 454/3

IG I^3 259 (Meiggs & Lewis 39)

ATL II.1. It appears that 454/3 was the only year in which the aparchai were totalled (*ATL* I, p.vii). The rather full preamble of the first list is also not repeated in subsequent years. A new fragment gives the archon as Aris[ton], which had previously been a restoration only. The preamble to the list and part of column III follow. See esp. *ATL* III.265–74.

(1) [These quotas, separately and a]ll to[gether fro]m the hell[enot]amiai for w[hom .... was secretar]y, were the fi[r]s[t to be a]udited [by the] thir[ty (logistai) for the goddess from the allied tribute, when] Aris[ton] was archon for the A[then]ians, a mina f[rom (each) talent]:

Pedasians 200 dr.
Astyreni[ans 8 dr. 2 ob.]
Byzantine[s 1500 dr.]
[K]amirians [900 dr.]
Thermaians
[on] Ikaro[s 50 dr.]
[D]aunio
-teichit[ians 16 dr.] 4 ob.
Samothra[cians] 600 dr,
Astypal[aians] 200 dr.
Mendai[ans 80]0 dr.
Selym[b]r[ians] 900 dr.
Aigant[ians 3]3 dr. 2 ob.
Neopo[litans from]
Mile[tos on White]
Pen[insul]a 300 dr.
Ko[lophon]ians 300 dr. ....
(*6 further names follow*)
Neopolitans 50 dr.
Maiandrians 66 dr. 4 ob.

ATHENS AND HER ALLIES

These decrees reveal how Athens regulated its affairs with the allies. The democratic constitution imposed on Erythrai (doc. 8.26) indicates Athens' trust in the demos. It appears that revolts against Athens and the imposition of democratic governments are linked (as at Erythrai and Samos), suggesting that oligarchs throughout the empire were less well-disposed to Athens than the demos and its leaders. The dating of many important inscriptions of the fifth century is subject to debate; some of those dated to the period of the pentekontaetia almost certainly do not belong there: see docs. 9.7, 9, 12, 16, 18, 20.

8.25 Relations with Phaselis, c. 469–50

IG I^3 10 (Meiggs & Lewis 31)

The orthodox dating for this decree is 469–450, while Mattingly dates it to after 428/7 (see Mattingly (1964) 37–39, (1966a) 216–17n.29, but the case is not overwhelmingly persuasive). Phaselis was a Greek city that had not wanted to leave the Persian fold for the

Greek, and was besieged by Kimon. The Chians intervened on Phaselis' behalf, and Kimon came to terms in return for ten talents and the Phaselites' help against the Persians; this provides an appropriate historical context for the decree (Plut. *Kim.* 12.3–4; cf. Thuc. II.69.1). The most important feature to note is the favourable judicial arrangements made for the Phaselites. Trial before the polemarch, rather than before an ordinary Athenian court, must have been a privilege; possibly trial in this court would take place sooner than in the ordinary courts, and so be less inconvenient to a Phaselite trader. Other cases were to be tried according to the previous treaty with the Phaselites. Why they were awarded this privilege (apparently an addendum to the original treaty) is unknown. See Wade-Gery (1958b) 180–200; Meiggs (1972) 231–32; Cohen (1973) 182–83; for 'cause of action' rather than 'contract', see de Ste. Croix (1961) 100–08.

(1) [It was reso]lved by the boule and the pe[ople; (2) (the tribe) A]kamantis [held] the prytany, [.]nasippos was secretary, Ne[....]des presided, Leo[n pr]oposed the motion: (5) this d[ec]r[ee is to be re]corded [for th]e Phaselites; whatever [c]a[us]e of action arises at Ath[ens involving] one of the [Ph]aselit[e]s, [the c]ase shall be tried at Ath[e]n[s] befo[re (10) the po]lemarch, just as for the Ch[ians, and] in no other place whatsoever. Oth[er cas]es will b[e] tried on treaty terms in accorda[nce with the existing] treaty with the Pha[selites]; the [....] (15) shall be abolished. And if a[ny other of th]e magistrates accepts a c[ase against] any Phaselite [...., i]f he convic[ts him, the convicti]on shall be void. [And] i[f (20) anyone viol]a[t]es what has been dec[reed, he shall o]w[e] ten thousand d[rachmas sac]red to Athena. Th[is decr]ee is to be record[ed by the secre]tary of the boule (25) [on a sto]ne [stele] and set [up on the acropolis] at the [ex]pense of th[e Phaselites] vacat

8.26 Regulations for Erythrai, c. 453/2

IG I^{3} 14 (Meiggs & Lewis 40)

The stele itself is now lost and there are many uncertain readings. The decree sets down the obligation of Erythrai to bring grain, or victims for sacrifice (depending on the restoration) to the Great Panathenaia, and represents 'an early stage in the conversion of an Athenian into an Empire festival' (ML p.91). The offering of a cow and panoply at the Panathenaia was to become a standard obligation for the allies (docs. 8.27, 9.15). That no arrangements are mentioned here for an alliance is usually taken to mean that Erythrai had been a member of the Athenian alliance and had then revolted (possibly a pro-Persian group was responsible); in 454/3 and 453/2 Boutheia (about 10 kms. north of Erythrai), part of the Erythraian peraia (district) is listed by itself with a quota of 300 drachmas, ie a tribute of three talents (*IG* I^{3} 260.X 5, cf. 259.V 19) whereas later it pays only 1,000 drachmas as part of the Erythraian syntely; Erythrai and the nearby towns in its peraia are listed as one tribute paying entity (for syntelies, see *ATL* I.446–49). It is usually assumed that Erythrai was in revolt, but that those loyal to Athens fled from Erythrai to Boutheia, and paid their dues from there to Athens (*ATL* I.486–87, II.57, III.252; Meiggs (1972) 112). Lines 35–46 are extremely fragmentary, but line 42 mentions a garrison and ten archers and line 46 a [phoura]rch (garrison commander) and garrison.

(1) [It was resolved by the boule and the people; .... held the prytany, (2) ....] presided, L[....]; (3) [the Erythrai]ans are to bring w[h]ea[t to] the Gre<at> Panathenaia <w>or[th not les]s than three minas and it is to be di[st]rib[ut]ed to [t]h[os]e Erythraians present (5) [....] by the hie[r]opo[i]oi [....] and if (they) bri[(ng)

....] wor[th] (less) than thre[e] min[as] in accordance with the [.... the] priest is to b<u>y wh[eat]; [and] the [peo]ple [.... d]rach[m(as) ... of m]eat [....] for anyone who wishes; of the Erythraians [b]y [l]ot [....] there [i]s to be a boule of one [h]undred and t[w]enty men; and the [....] in the <b>oule and [....] to be able to be a member [of the boule .... no]r anyone who [i]s less than th[i]rty [yea]rs of age; and prosecution will take place [against] anyone [w]h[o] is found gui[l]t[y]. No one is to be a member of the boule with[i]n four years [.... a]nd [t]he [supervis]ors (episkopoi) and [the] ga[rr]ison commander (phrourarch) shall choose by lo[t] and set [u]p [t]he n[ew] boule, and in future the boule and the [phrour]arch (will do it), not le[s]s than [t]hirty d[a]ys be[for]e [the bou]le goes out of office; [and] (the councillors) shall swear by [Z]eus an[d] Apo[l]lo and Deme[ter] callin[g down utter des]truction if they for[swear themselves .... a]nd utter destr[uctio]n on their chil[dr]en [....] over [sa]crificial victims [....] and t[h]e boule is to [b]u[rn in sacrifice] not l[e]ss (than) [....] and [i]f not, it shall be liable to a fine of a [th]o[us]a[n]d d[rachmas .... t]he people are to burn in sacrifice not less. [And the] boule is to sw[e]a[r as fo]llows: 'I shall deliberate as bes[t and] as j[u]s[tl]y as I [c]a[n] for the Erythraian populace and that of the Athenians and their [all]i[e]s [a]nd I shall not [rev]olt against the p[op]ulace of the Athenians nor [the] allies of the Athenians, neither I myself n[o]r shall I be per[s]uad[ed] by a[ny]one else [no]r [....] neither I myself nor shall I be [p]ers[uaded] by anyone [else .... (nor) shall I rec]eive back eve[n] one of the e[xil]es either [....] shall I be persu[a]de[d by anyon]e [of those] who f[le]d [to] the Persians without the approval of th[e] bou[le of the Athe]nians and the [p]eople, [n]or shall I banish any of those who remain [w]ith[out the approval] of the b[oule] of the Athenians and [the] people. And if a[n]y [Erythrai]an kills another of the Erythr[ai]ans, he shall be p[ut] to death if he is [jud]ged guilty [....] if he is [sen]tenced (to exile) he shall be exiled from al[l] th[e] Athenian allian[(ce)... and h]is property shall [bec]ome state-prop[erty] of the Erythraians. And if [an]yone [....] to t<h>e tyrants [....] of the Erythrai[a]ns and [....] he shall be put to death [....] childre[n] from hi[m .... the] children from [h]i[m....]

8.27 The Foundation of the Colony at Brea

IG I^3 46 (Meiggs & Lewis 49)

See also Kratinos F426 (Kassel & Austin *PCG*; Kock F395); Theopompos *FGH* 115 F145. The decree, which appears to belong to between c. 445 and the late 430s provides important information about fifth century Athenian colonization; an amendment (B) provides that Brea's colonists were to be thetes and zeugitai. For the bringing of a phallos to the City Dionysia (the carrying of the phallos, phallophoria, was part of the festival procession), see Krentz (1993) 12–16. The site is not known; Brea is sometimes identified with the colony 'amongst the Bisaltai', near Amphipolis: Plut. *Per.* 11.5; see Stadter (1989) 141; cf. Woodhead (1952) 57–62. The date is also uncertain; it has the tailed form of the letter rho, not found in precisely dated inscriptions after 438/7 (Meiggs (1966) 91, 93). Mattingly (1963) 258–61, (1966b) 172–92 argued for a lower dating (426/5) but now views Brea as in existence by the late 430s: (1970) 135, (1984b) 352–53. Woodhead's 438 date (cf. Kagan (1969) 182) remains a possibility; *IG* I^3 prefers c.

445. For Brea, see also *ATL* III.287–88; Ehrenberg (1952) 143–44; Mattingly (1966b) 172–92; Asheri (1969) 337–40; Kagan (1969) 182–86, 389–90; Graham (1983) esp. 60–64.

A

(5) [....] in respect of which he den[ounces or indicts (someone), let him pr]osecute. If he prosecutes [.... (let pledges by taken from him by)] the denouncer or the prosecutor. [....] are to be provided for them by the ap[oikistai (leaders) to obtain good] omens on behalf of the colony, [however many (10) the]y resolve. They shall elec[t ten men] as geonomoi, one from (each) tribe; these are to distribu[te the land.] And [Dem]okleides shall have [full p]owers to establish the c[olony], in the b[est way] he can. They shall leave [the prec]incts which have been set apart a[s they are, (15) and] not consecrate [ot]hers. And [they shall bri]ng a cow and a p[anoply] to the Grea[t] Panathenaia [and] a phallos [to the Dionysi]a. If anyone wages w[ar against the] colonists' [territ]ory, th[e cities] shall come to their aid [as quickly as] possible in accordance with the agreements whi[ch when (20) ....] was secretary were drawn [up for the citi]es in Thrace. An[d] they shall write [these things on a stel]e and set it up on the acropolis; the colonists are to pr[ovide t]he stele at th[eir own expense.] And [i]f anyone proposes a decree contrary to th[e stele or (25) a spea]ker counsels or [attempts] to invit[e (someone else) to res]cind or put an end to anything of what has been v[oted], he is to be [deprived of citizen rights] as are [his] children [and his pr]operty is to belong to the state and [a tith]e [be gi]ven to the [goddess], unless the coloni[sts] themselves [.... (30) req]uest. All [th]e soldiers who are enroll[ed to go as settlers], when they have com[e to Athens], are to be at Brea as se[ttlers within thi]rty days. [They shall le]ad out the colony within thir[ty days.] And [A]ischines shall accompany them and pr[ovide (35) the mon]ey vacat

B

(36) [Ph]antokles proposed the motion: concerning the col[o]ny at Brea, (let it be) as Demokl[e]ides proposed; and Phantokle[s] (40) shall be introduced by (the tribe) E[r]echtheis, the tribe holding the prytan[y], to the boule in it[s] first session; and thetes and ze[u]gitai are to go to [B]rea (45) as the colo[n]ists.

8.28 An Athenian Alliance with Rhegium, 433/2

IG I^3 53 (Meiggs & Lewis 63)

The preamble dates this treaty to 433/2 (the archonship of Apseudes). But the preamble is re-inscribed over an earlier version of the preamble, and the text following it is older, so in 433/2 the treaty must have been renewed; this is also the case for the treaty with Leontinoi: see *IG* I^3 54 (ML 64). Possibly Athenian involvement in Corcyra alerted the Greek world to impending war between Athens and Sparta, and Rhegium and Leontinoi (and other Ionian cities in Sicily) may have feared 'that Syracuse would take advantage of Athens' preoccupation to try to swallow them' (ML p.173). One of these envoys died in Athens and was publicly buried: 'Silenos son of Phokos, who was raised / By fortunate Rhegium as its justest citizen' (ML 63 p.175; *IG* II^2 5220 (*IG* I^3 1178); Hansen 12).

(1) [Gods. The envoys from Rhegium w]ho [made] the alliance [and took the oat]h were Kleandros son of Xen[...., ... (son of) ....]tinos, Silenos son of Phokos, [....

in Ap]seudes' archonship (5) a[nd in the boule of which Kritia]des was secre[tary] for the first time. vv [It was resolved by the bo]ule and the people, (the tribe) A[kamantis held the prytany, Ch]arias was secretar[y, Timoxenos preside]d, Kalli (10 spaces) [as proposed the motion: there shall b]e [an alliance] between the Athenians and (10) [Rhegians. And the] Athen[ians] shall swear [the oat]h [so that everything may be tru]stworthy and without deceit and str[aightforward on the part of the Athenians for]ever towards the Rhegians, [swearing] a[s follows: 'As all]ies we shall be trust[worthy and just and ste]adfast and sincere (15) [forever to the Rhegians and] we shall give assistance i[f they require anything ....']

8.29 The Second Athenian Confederacy, 377

Tod II.123 (*IG* II² 43), lines 1–41

When the Athenians established the Second Athenian Confederacy in 377, they aimed at avoiding features of the Delian League which had been unpopular: Marshall (1905) 16–20; Ryder (1965) 55–56; Meiggs (1972) 262; Cawkwell (1981) 41–47; Cargill (1981) 14–47. They kept their promise about cleruchies: two only are known from the fourth century, and they were sent to non-allies, Samos and Potidaea (at Potidaea's request, *IG* II² 114 (Tod 146)); but there were garrisons in some allied states; see Cawkwell 46, 51–52.

(1) In the archonship of Nausinikos. Kallibios son of Kephisophon of Paiania was secretary. In the [sev]enth prytany, held by Hippothonti[s]; (5) it was resolved by the bou[le an]d the people, Charinos of Athmon[on pr]esided; Aristoteles prop[osed the motion]: to the good [for]tune of the Athenians and of [t]he [all]ies of the Athenians in order that the Spa[rt]ans may allow the Greeks, (10) fr[e]e [and] autonomous, to live in peace holding [all] the[ir own land] in security [a]nd so that [the common peace] may be in f[o]rce and con[tinue for ever, which the Greeks] and the King [swo]re in accordance with the tre[aty], (15) the people are [to decr]ee: if anyone [of the Gr]eeks or of the barbarians [li]ving on [the mainland] or of the islanders, as ma[ny as] are [not subject to the Ki]ng, wis[hes to be] an all[y] of the Athenians [a]nd their allies, it shall be permitted to h[i]m, (20) being [fre]e and autonomous, li[ving un]der whatever constitution he wishes, neither receiving [a garris]on nor having a governor im[po]sed on him nor paying tribute, on t[he] same terms as the Chians and Thebans (25) an[d] the other allies. To those that have m[ad]e an alliance with the Athenians and their al[l]ies the (Athenian) people shall give up the properties of the Ath[e]nians which happen to be either private or [p]ublic in the co[untry of those ma]king (30) the alliance a[nd] shall give t[hem a p]ledge [concerning these. And if it h]appe[n]s with regard [to any] of the cities [making] the alliance with the Athen[ians] that there are [s]telai unfavourab[le] to them at Athens, [t]he boule which is at that time in office (35) sha[ll ha]ve authority to destroy them. And after the archo[n]ship of Nausikinos it shall not be permitted, either privately or publi[c]ly, for any Athenian to possess in t[h]e countries of the allies either a house or a plot of land, either by purchase (40) or through a mortgage or through any other means.

9

The Peloponnesian War and its Aftermath

Thucydides viewed the Peloponnesian War as the greatest disturbance that had ever affected the Greeks (doc. 9.1). A detailed reading of Thucydides' work is necessary for an in-depth understanding of his views of the war and of Athenian imperialism. This chapter assumes that Thucydides' history is an essential background to the study of this period and concentrates primarily on a few of the main historical events, and particularly on the epigraphic evidence which complements Thucydides' narrative. One of the main themes which emerges is the enhanced Athenian imperialism which accompanied the Peloponnesian War, particularly with regard to tribute payment, which became of prime importance for the Athens' prosecution of the war.

The Thirty Years' Peace of 446/5 did not last, and in 431 the Peloponnesian War broke out. Thucydides distinguishes between underlying and immediate causes of the war (doc. 9.2), and states that he is going to explain the grievances of each side against the other and the instances when their interests clashed. These specific instances were disputes over Epidamnos, Corcyra and Potidaea. But Thucydides also states that these specific instances obscure the real reason for the war, and at I.23.6 (doc. 9.2) he observes that the 'truest reason' for the war was the growth of Athenian power and the fear that this caused at Sparta. Some scholars are inclined to reject this argument, because in the ten years leading up to the outbreak of war in 431 Athens had not extended her power base: but the Spartans were aware that the Athenians were more powerful than they had been in 479 (cf. doc. 8.8) and Thucydides in writing of Spartan fear is not speaking of the short period immediately prior to the outbreak, for Athens had, in half a century, become a city with a far flung empire which had challenged Spartan supremacy.

The Peloponnesian war was dominated by great statesmen and generals, and in Thucydides' narrative figures such as Perikles, Kleon, Brasidas, Nikias, and Alkibiades are seen dominating the stage. But at Athens the war was conducted by the ekklesia, and it was there that debates were conducted and decisions made. Many decrees were passed in the course of the Peloponnesian War, and of particular importance are those concerning tribute payment (docs. 9.14–16). But the dating of many important Athenian inscriptions is subject to intense debate. Traditionally, there are two main epigraphic criteria for dating inscriptions for which there is no internal indication in their content as to dating: the form of the letters sigma (the most important 'letter form' criterion) and rho. The sigma with three bars was eventually superseded by a four-barred form; on orthodox dating the last three-barred sigma in a firmly dated inscription appears in 447/6, while tailed rho last appears in an absolutely dated inscription in 438/7. Mattingly has argued that these criteria are too rigid, and that several decrees dated to before c. 445 on the basis of having three-barred sigmas can be given later dates, many in the 420s. Many valuable fifth century Athenian inscriptions do not have a precise date, which means that their dating is subject to debate. But now that the Egesta decree (doc. 9.20) seems to provide a clear example of three-barred sigmas being used as late as 418/7, this reinforces the arguments of Mattingly for down-dating some inscriptions from their traditional dates in the 450s and 440s to the period of the Peloponnesian War, which is far more appropriate in terms of their content and tone. This debate is not purely an academic one. Its importance is that down-dating these decrees affects the picture of the development of Athenian imperialism. The best example is the coinage decree (doc. 9.12), which laid down that Athenian coinage and measures were to be used throughout the empire, prohibiting other silver coinage. There may have been distinct advantages to enforcing uniformity throughout the empire, but this nevertheless reflects an infringement of the freedom of the cities which had hitherto minted their own currency. The date of the decree is debated, but a date in the 420s is to be preferred to an earlier date c. 450–46. This down-dating significantly affects the picture of the development of Athenian imperialism; decrees seen traditionally as signs of Athens' increasing imperialism in the 450s and 440s can now be dated to the 420s with important implications for the conduct of the Peloponnesian War.

Thucydides' opinion that the allies wanted to revolt from Athens, particularly after the Sicilian expedition (doc. 9.24), needs to be set against the evidence showing that allies did remain loyal, such as Neapolis in Thrace and Samos (docs. 9.28–29). The Athenians, in fact, even despite the disaster in Sicily, managed to carry on the war and victory might still have been possible except for the finances which the Persians provided for the Spartans. The conduct of the war, of course, had not gone smoothly, and both Athenians and Spartans suffered reversals. At Athens, these led to discontent with the democratic constitution and two oligarchic revolutions: in 411 (docs. 9.25, 27) and 404 (doc. 9.31). The regime of the Thirty Tyrants in 404/3 was particularly brutal; even so, when democracy was restored, the Athenians declared an amnesty covering all except those chiefly responsible. But despite this amnesty, the people did not entirely forget these events, and in 399 Socrates was prosecuted on a charge of refusing to recognise the gods recognised by the state and introducing other, new divinities; he was also said to be guilty of corrupting the youth (doc. 9.38). While these charges may have been sincere, and a sign of unhappiness with the new 'scepticism' of the time (docs. 9.32–35), the Athenians inevitably recalled Socrates' long-standing association with Kritias, Charmides and Alkibiades (doc. 9.36), and Socrates was condemned to death (docs. 9.38–39), though he was, in Plato's view (doc. 9.41), 'of all the people we knew of that time, not only the best, but in general the most discerning and upright'.

THE OUTBREAK OF THE PELOPONNESIAN WAR

9.1 Thucydides and his History

Thucydides I.1.1–3

Thucydides' exile, incurred for his failure to come to the relief of Amphipolis on time in 424/3, gave him the opportunity of seeing the war from both sides (Thuc. V.26.5, cf. IV.104.4–105.1, 106.3–107.1).

I.1.1 Thucydides the Athenian wrote the history of the war between the Peloponnesians and Athenians, how they fought each other, beginning at the very outbreak, in the expectation that it was going to be a great war and more worth writing about than those of the past, judging from the fact that both states were in their prime and at the peak of preparation and seeing that the rest of the Greek world was aligned with one of the two, even those that were not immediately committed having it in mind to commit themselves. **I.1.2** This disturbance was the greatest which ever affected the Greeks, as well as affecting a great part of the barbarian world, and thus, so to speak, most of mankind. **I.1.3** For it has been impossible because of the passage of time to discover precisely what place before this war or still earlier, yet the evidence, from looking into it as far back as I can, leads me to conclude that these were not great periods in warfare or anything else.

9.2 The 'Truest Cause' of the War

Thucydides I.23.4–6

Cf. I.33.3, 88, 118.2. The 'truest cause' (alethestate prophasis) was Spartan fear, and the specific causes of complaint (aitiai) were Corcyra, Epidamnos and Potidaea, for which see Thuc. I.24–65, docs. 1.7–8. There are numerous discussions of the causes of the Peloponnesian War: Rhodes (1987) 154–65 is a good starting point; see also Andrewes (1959) 223–39; de Romilly (1963) 17–24; Kagan (1969) esp. 345–74; de Ste. Croix (1972) esp. 51–63; Edmunds (1975) 172–73; Sealey (1975) 89–109; Richardson (1990) 155–61.

I.23.4 The Athenians and Peloponnesians began the war when they broke the Thirty Years' Peace, which had been made after the capture of Euboea. **I.23.5** Regarding the reasons for their having broken it, I have already recorded first their causes of complaint and disputes, so that no one ever has to ask why such a great war came upon the Greeks. **I.23.6** For its truest cause, although the one least mentioned, I consider to have been that the Athenians by growing powerful, and making the Spartans afraid, compelled them to go to war. The causes of complaint which were openly expressed by both sides, because of which they broke the truce and went to war, were as follows.

9.3 Sparta's Ultimatum

Thucydides I.139.1–3

The Corinthians, because of Athens' siege of Potidaea, encouraged the Peloponnesian allies to send representatives to Sparta, where the Corinthians attacked the Athenians (Thuc. I.66–71), and Athenian delegates made a reply (I.72–78). The Spartans voted that the Athenians had broken the Thirty Years Peace of 446/5 (I.87–88) and then, having sought Apollo's approval for the war, called a meeting of their allies, at which the Corinthians made a second speech (I.118–24) and the Peloponnesian League voted for war (I.125, cf. VII.18.2–3). For the Corinthian speeches at Sparta, see esp. Crane (1992) 227–56, discussing the characteristics of the Spartans and Athenians as given in these speeches; cf. Thuc. VIII.96. While Thucydides did not include the Megarian decree as one of the 'aitiai', it was clearly important; cf. I.67.4, 139.1–2, 140.3, 144.2; Plut. *Per.* 29.4, 30; Ar. *Ach.* 515–40, *Peace* 605–14; for the authenticity of Plutarch's decrees, see de Ste. Croix (1972) 230–31, and 225–89 in general. MacDonald (1983) 385–410 argues that the Megarian decrees were not intended as economic measures, but to deprive Megara of political access to Megarian colonies, such as Byzantium, within the empire.

I.139.1 These were the demands which the Spartans made on the occasion of their first embassy and, like the demands which the Athenians made in return, they concerned the expulsion of the 'accursed'; later the Spartans came to the Athenians and demanded that they abandon the siege of Potidaea and allow Aegina to be autonomous, while above all and most explicitly they proclaimed that if the Athenians revoked the Megarian decree, in which the Megarians were forbidden to make use of the harbours of the Athenian empire and the Athenian agora, there would be no war. **I.139.2** But the Athenians did not give in on the other points and did not revoke the decree, accusing the Megarians of cultivating the sacred land and boundary land and of harbouring runaway slaves. **I.139.3** Finally the last embassy came from Sparta, consisting of Ramphios, Melesippos and Agesander, who said none of the things that the Spartans had usually raised earlier, but simply this: 'The Spartans want the peace to continue, and it will, if you would allow the Greeks to be autonomous.'

THE ARCHIDAMIAN WAR, 431–21

The first phase of the Peloponnesian war is named after King Archidamos, who invaded Attica in the early years of the first phase of the war, which began with Thebes' attack on Plataea in 431 (see doc. 12.35). Perikles advised the Athenians not to give in to the Spartan demands, but adopted a passive rather than an aggressive strategy in the defence of Attica; it is important to note that many Athenians were clearly against the war (Thuc. I.139.4) and Perikles must bear some of the responsibility for its outbreak (Thuc. I.127.2–3). For a good discussion of philia, friendship, and the ties between xenoi (guest-friends) in the Peloponnesian war, see Herman (1990) 87–99. The first invasion took place in summer, when the grain was ripe, and the Spartans hoped that they would defeat Athens in a few years (Thuc. V.14.3).

9.4 Perikles' Strategy

Thucydides II.14, 65.6–7.

Perikles successfully argued that the Athenians should not give in to Spartan demands, but also that they should not meet the Spartans in battle outside the walls (Thuc. I.139–44, II.13, 21–23, 59–65). The Athenians moved into the city (esp. II.13, 14, 17), even into temples and shrines except where absolutely forbidden, and the crowded conditions helped the spread of the plague. For Perikles' suspension of meetings of the ekklesia in 431, to prevent the people meeting and making 'wrong decisions' in the heat of their anger at the Spartan invasion, see Thuc. II.22.1; Kagan (1991) 234–35; Bloedow (1987) 9–27; Christensen & Hansen (1983) 17–31, (1989) 210–11; Hansen (1987) 22.

II.14.1 The Athenians took Perikles' advice and brought their children, women and other household possessions in from the country, even removing the woodwork from the very houses; they sent their sheep and cattle across to Euboea and the neighbouring islands. But they found this removal hard, as the majority of them had always been used to living in the country .... **II.65.6** Perikles lived on for two years and six months (after the start of the war); and when he died, his foresight regarding the war became even more apparent. **II.65.7** For he had said that they would come out of it on top if they bided their time, and looked after the fleet, and did not try to extend the empire while the war was on, and did nothing to endanger the city.

9.5 The Plague Strikes Athens

Thucydides II.47.2–3, 52.1–53.4

Perikles' plans for the conduct of the war could not take into account unforeseen events such as the plague, exacerbated by the overcrowding in Athens (II.52.1–2, cf. 17.1; Edmunds (1975) 70–75), and this was the first set-back in the Periklean strategy. In Thucydides' discussion of the plague there is a 'scientific' description of the symptoms, but as Lateiner (1977) 97 notes, 'over half the description of the plague concerns .... the social and religious effects' (cf. doc. 8.17). For the plague, from which Perikles himself died, see Page (1953) 97–119; Poole & Holladay (1979) 282–300, (1984) 483–85; Allison (1983) 14–23; Wylie & Stubbs (1983) 6–11; Mikalson (1984) 217–25; Scarrow (1988) 4–8; Marshall (1990) 163–70; Morens & Littman (1992) 271–304.

II.47.2 At the beginning of the following summer, the Peloponnesians and their allies, with two thirds of their forces as at first, invaded Attica (the Spartan king Archidamos son of Zeuxidamos was in command), and they took up their positions and started devastating the country. **II.47.3** And after they had been in Attica for only a few days the plague made its first appearance among the Athenians. It was said that it had previously broken out in a number of other places such as Lemnos, but nowhere else was it recorded to have been so virulent or caused such numbers of deaths .... **II.52.1** The existing suffering had been made far worse by the removal of people from the country to the city, and the incomers were affected the worst. **II.52.2** There were no houses for them, and, living as they did in the summer season in stifling huts, they died without hindrance, corpses of the dying lay on corpses, and the half-dead staggered around the streets and around all the fountains in their desire for water. **II.52.3** The temples in which they were living were full of corpses, who had died inside them; for as the disaster weighed so heavily upon them, men, not knowing whether they would continue to live, turned to neglect of sacred and holy things alike. **II.52.4** All the funeral customs, which had been followed up to now, were thrown into disorder and they buried the dead as best each could. Many turned to disgraceful means of disposing of the dead through lack of relatives because of the number of those who had already died; for they got to other people's pyres, before those who had piled them up, and placed their own corpse on them and set them alight, or when someone else was being burnt they threw on top the body they were carrying and made off. **II.53.1** In other respects as well for the city the plague was in great measure the beginning of lawlessness. For seeing the swift change of fortune of those who were rich and died suddenly, and of those who had earlier possessed nothing and then all at once inherited what the others had had, people began to venture more readily on acts of self-indulgence, which they had previously kept secret .... **II.53.4** Neither fear of the gods nor law of men was any restraint, and they considered it the same whether one worshipped the gods or not, since they saw everyone dying equally, and no one expected to live long enough for a trial to take place or to be punished for their offences, but they rather thought that the punishment had already been decreed and was hanging over them, and that it was reasonable to enjoy life a little before it arrived.

9.6 The Financial Decrees of Kallias, ?434/3

IG I³ 52 (Meiggs & Lewis 58)

ATL II.D1–2. The dating of these decrees is a matter of debate: they either belong to the Peloponnesian War, or are a preliminary to it; in either case it is appropriate to deal with them here. The orthodox dating is 434/3. The usual interpretation is that the treasures of temples in rural demes and the lower city have been moved onto the acropolis (cf. doc. 10.6) and this is seen as a security measure in the event of invasion, and it is argued that the decree can be set alongside Thuc. I.44.2: the prevailing opinion that war with the Peloponnesians was inevitable and therefore the alliance with Corcyra was attractive so that its navy would not pass to Corinth (cf. ML pp.158–59; Meiggs (1972) 519–23).

Mattingly argues for a lower date, 422/1: the creation of treasurers of the gods provided for in decree A 13–18, 27–29 are first indisputably found in 421/0 (*IG* I³ 472.5–11), and the vote of adeia, immunity, necessary for expenditures of more than 10,000 drachmas from Athena's fund are not found in connection with the payments for the Corcyraean squadrons in 433/2, but first in payments made by the Treasurers between 418/7 to 415/4 (no payments from 422/1–419/8 survive); see Mattingly (1964) 35–55, (1968) 450–85, (1975) 15–22, (1984b) 355–56; Fornara & Samons (1991) 176–78. There are, of course, other arguments for both higher and lower dates. See Kallet-Marx (1989a) 94–113 for a recent discussion of the decrees. As A has very few restorations these are not marked.

A

(1) It was resolved by the boule and the people; (the tribe) Kekropis held the prytany, Mnesitheos was secretary, Eupeithes presided, Kallias proposed the motion: repayment is to be made to the gods of the money which is owed, since Athena's

3,000 talents, which have been voted, have been brought up to the acropolis in our coinage. And it is to be repaid (5) from the money which has been voted for repayment to the gods, both that which is now in the hands of the hellenotamiai and the rest of this money, and also the money from the ten per cent tax when it has been farmed out. The thirty auditors (logistai) who are now in office are to calculate precisely what is owed to the gods, and the boule is to have full powers over the meeting of the auditors. The prytaneis together with the boule are to pay back the money (10) and cancel the debt when they pay it back, after searching the registers and account-books and anywhere else it might be recorded. The priests and the temple overseers (hieropoioi) and anyone else who knows of the records are to produce them. And the treasurers of this money are to be chosen by lot at the same time as the other magistrates, as are those of the sacred money (15) of Athena. These on the acropolis in the Opisthodomos are to administer the money of the gods as efficiently and piously as possible, and are to share in the opening and closing and sealing of the doors of the Opisthodomos with the treasurers of Athena. As they receive the treasures from the current treasurers, superintendents (epistatai) and hieropoioi in the temples, who now to have charge of them, (20) they are to count them up and weigh them in front of the boule on the acropolis and the treasurers who have been chosen by lot are to take them over from the current officials and record on one stele all the treasures, both that according to each of the gods, how much belongs to each, and the entire sum, with the silver and the gold both separate. And in future the treasurers who are in office are to record this (25) on a stele and draw up an account of the balance of the money and the revenue of the gods, and whatever is spent during the year, for the auditors, and submit to an examination at the end of their term. And they are to draw up accounts from Great Panathenaia to Great Panathenaia, just like the treasurers of Athena. And the stelai, on which they have recorded the sacred treasures, (30) are to be set up by the treasurers on the acropolis. When the money has been repaid to the gods, they are to use the surplus money for the dockyard and the walls [....]

B

(1) [It was resolved by the boule and the people: (the tribe) Kekropis held the prytany, Mnesitheos was secretary, E]up[e]ithes [presided, K]allias proposed the motio[n: ....] of stone and the go[lden Vict]ories (Nikai) and the Pro[pylaia;....] completely [....] are to use [....] (5) according to what has been decr[eed], and the acropolis [....] and they are to res[tor]e it by s[pending] ten talents each [yea]r until it has been [...] and has been resto[red as well as possible]; an[d t]he treasurers and [the superintend]ents are to [jointly s]upervi[s]e [the wo]r[k]. The archi[tect is to ma]ke [the pla]n [j]ust as for the Pro[pylaia; and he (10) is to see] to [it] with th[e superint]endents that the acr[opolis] is [....] as wel[l and as economically as possible] and that restora[tion is done to whatever is required. A]nd [the] rest of the mon[ey of] Athena's wh[ich is now on the acropolis a]nd whatever may be [br]ought up in [t]he fu[ture] they are not to us[e or to borrow f]rom it fo[r] a[ny] other reason [than] this more than ten tho[u]sa[nd drachmas, (15) except for restor]ation if any is necessa[ry]; and they are to us[e the money for] no [oth]er reason [unless] the people decr[ees] immunity as wh[en it decrees concerning the prop]erty tax. And if anyone [proposes

a motion or] puts it to the vo[t]e that without [immun]ity hav[ing been decreed]they should use t[he mon]ey of Athe[na's, he shall be liable to the s]ame (penalty) as someone who proposes a motion or puts [it to the vote] concerning the [prop]erty tax. For [al]l [the gods] (20) the helleno[tamiai] are to deposit d[uring th]e year [what is owed] to ea[ch with t]he treasurers [of Ath]ena. [When from] t[h]e two hundred ta[lent]s which [the people] de[creed] for repayment what is owed has be[en paid ba]ck to [th]e other gods, [the] treasures [of Ath]ena shall [be stored in the area] on the right-hand side of the Opis[thodomos, (25) and those of the other g]ods on the l[ef]t vacat [However many of th]e [sacre]d treasures are unweighed or un[counted, the] current [treasurers] together with the f[ou]r boards which dr[aw up the accounts from Pa]nathenaia to Pan[athena]ia are to we[igh] how much go[ld there is and silver] and silver gilt, [a]nd [count the] res[t ....]

9.7 Kolophon Swears Loyalty to the Athenians, 427 (or ?447/6)

IG I^3 37 (Meiggs & Lewis 47)

ATL II.D15. This decree makes use of three-barred sigmas and has therefore generally been dated to before c. 445, and a revolt of Kolophon at this time assumed as an explanation for this decree. However, Thuc. III.34 describes the foundation in 427 of a colony under Athenian direction at Notion, Kolophon's port: a pro-Persian group had seized upper Kolophon, and the citizens loyal to Athens fled to Notion, and there split into two groups, one of which received assistance from the pro-Persian group, while the other group fled. The Athenian general Paches took Notion and handed it over to this latter group. The Athenians sent out settlers to join them, with oikistai, and gathered together all the Kolophonians found in other cities for the purpose of the new settlement. The decree mentions Kolophonians; references to Kolophon are only in the restored part of the text, except at line 9 (but cf. reading at ML 47.9; see Mattingly (1992) 132–33), so the decree accords with Thucydides' narrative. See also Mattingly (1961b) 175, (1966a) 210–12, (1984b) 344, for a dating on epigraphic grounds to 427; cf. ML 47 pp.123–25, arguing against the later date. Lines 1–37 are poorly preserved and therefore omitted.

It is appropriate at this point to deal with the main letter forms used for dating criteria. The sigma with three bars was eventually superseded by a four-barred form; the three-barred sigma last appears in a firmly dated inscription in 447/6 (*IG* I^3 265), so c. 445 is usually taken as the date at which these sigmas went out of use; on this criterion, undated inscriptions with three-barred sigmas are dated to before c. 445. Four-barred sigmas first appear in *IG* I^3 264; 448/7. The tailed rho last appears in a firmly dated inscription in 438/7 (*IG* I^3 445); see Meiggs (1966) 91–98, esp. 97; cf. Henry (1978) 75 with 106n.3. Mattingly has long questioned these formal dating criteria by letter form on both historical and epigraphic grounds. While, on orthodox dating, all absolutely dated decrees with a three-barred sigma date to before c. 445, this does not mean that all inscriptions with three-barred sigmas must automatically fall within this period, especially given that the sample is small, and the criterion ought not to have been given the status of indubitable proof. Many of Mattingly's arguments have been criticized. The use of laser technology, however, now seems to prove that three-barred sigmas and tailed rhos appear as late as 418/7, strengthening his previous arguments (see doc. 9.20). This chapter accepts many of Mattingly's dates; note also Fornara & Samons (1991) 182–87.

(38) [The secret]ary of the b[oule] is to record [this] decre[e and the oath on a stone stele on the acropolis at the expense (40) of t]he Kolopho[nians; and at Kolophon

the] oikistai [(sent) to Kolophon] are to reco[rd these things and the oath on a stone stele] and set [it up in a place which] the law of the [Koloph]onians [assigns. The Kolophonians are to swear: 'I shall act and sp]eak and advise [as fittingly and best I can con]cerning the people of t[he Athenians and concerning the colon]y; and I will not re[bel against the people of the Athenians either in w]ord or in de[ed, either I myself nor shall I be persuaded by anyone else; a]nd I will cherish th[e people of the Athenians and I shall not dese]rt (to the enemy); and [I will not put down] demo[cracy at Kolophon, either] I [m]yself nor [shall I be persuaded by] an[yone else, either by revolt]ing (and going over) [to another] city o[r by stirring up dissension here. And in accordance with the oa]th [I shall confirm t]he[se things] as true [without deceit and without violating the terms, by Z]eus and by Apo[llo and by Demeter, and if] I should tran<s>gre[ss these things may both I myself and] my [fa]mily [be utterly destroyed for all time, but if I keep the oath may] m[a]ny [good things] be mine' ....

9.8 The Mytilene Debate, 427

Thucydides III.36.2–4, 37.2

After Perikles, other leaders took over, who according to Thucydides were less capable (II.65.10; cf. *Ath. Pol.* 28.1). Kleon, however, was successful as a politician, and his portrait suffers a great deal from Thucydides' dislike. Perikles and Kleon pursued similar policies (Woodhead (1960) 299–300; cf. Marshall (1984) 23–27), but Kleon's style of leadership, his background, and his possible involvement in having Thucydides exiled over Amphipolis may explain this bias. For Aristophanes' portrait of Kleon, see Dorey (1956) 132–39.

In 428, Lesbos (except Methymna) under the leadership of Mytilene revolted from Athens (Thuc. III.2–19, 26–28, 35). Kleon states in the Mytilene debate that the empire is a tyranny and in this echoes Perikles (compare Thuc. II.63.2 with III.37.2, cf. 40.4; II.61.2 with III.38.1). This raises the question of whether the Athenian empire was popular amongst its subjects. de Ste. Croix (1954/55) 1–41, in what is still the classic treatment, believes that the demos in allied states was pro-Athenian and the empire benefited the majority of its subjects, noting the case of Mytilene where the demos supported the Athenians (though some argue this was only when the situation was becoming desperate). See, however, Bradeen (1960) 257–69 who argues that allies were willing to forego the advantages of being allies in order to have autonomy; also Pleket (1963) 70–77; Quinn (1964) 258–59; Starr (1988) 114–23. Each incidence of revolt needs to be looked at independently, but the cases of Neapolis (doc. 9.28) and Samos (doc. 9.29) are good examples of loyal allies. There is no doubt that the Athenians committed atrocities, as at Melos (doc. 11.2); the Spartans, however, were no better (de Ste. Croix 14–15; see references at doc. 11.2) and Thucydides' view that when the war broke out the allies wanted to revolt, and that the whole Hellenic world was against Athens after the Sicilian expedition, is inaccurate.

After the surrender of Mytilene, the Athenians, on the motion of Kleon, decided to deal harshly with the Mytilenaeans. On the next day, many regretted the decision, and the debate was re-opened. On the previous day Kleon had proposed (and carried) the decree for the executions, and Diodotos had opposed it. They both spoke again. Diodotos is otherwise unknown (see Ostwald (1979) 5–13). Thucydides does not give the first debate, only the second; see Andrewes (1962) 64–85; de Romilly (1963) 156–71; Winnington-Ingram (1965) 70–82; Immerwahr (1973) 28–29; Macleod (1978) 64–78; Connor (1984) 79–95; Hussey (1985) 129–31. For discussions of Kleon, see esp. Cornford (1907) 110–

28; Gomme (1962) 112–21; Westlake (1968) 60–85. Woodhead (1960) 289–317 has the most detailed arguments for reappraising Kleon. For the history of the relationship between Lesbos and Athens, see Quinn (1981) 24–38.

III.36.2 They then discussed what to do with the other prisoners and in their anger decided to put them to death, not only the ones in their hands but all the other adult male Mytilenaeans and sell the children and women into slavery. Their anger against Mytilene was caused by their revolt, even though they were not subject-allies like the others, and the Athenians' violent reaction was particularly reinforced by the fact that the Spartans' ships had dared to venture to Ionia to support them; for they thought that this showed that the revolt had been long pre-meditated. **III.36.3** So they sent a trireme to Paches to tell him what had been decided, ordering him to kill the Mytilenaeans immediately. **III.36.4** On the following day, however, there was a sudden change of heart and they began to reflect upon the cruelty and severity of the decision, destroying a whole city rather than just those responsible .... **III.37.2** (Kleon) 'What you fail to perceive is that your empire is a tyranny imposed on people who plot against you and are governed unwillingly.'

9.9 Agreement with Miletos, 426/5 (or 450/49)

IG I^3 21

ATL II.D11. This is a poorly preserved text, but despite the many restorations much of importance about the empire can be gleaned from it, especially details concerning judicial arrangements between Miletos and Athens. This inscription has been dated to the mid-fifth century on the basis of having the three-barred sigma. The archon's name in line 86, cf. 61, is, however, Euthynos, and a Euthynos was archon in 426/5. The text of Diod. XII.3.1 has, however, been emended to change the archon of 450/49 from Euthydemos to Euthynos, allowing this decree to be dated to that year, which fits in with the view of those who believe that three-barred sigmas do not appear after c. 445; but this emendation is not warranted. The evidence that there was a revolt at Miletos in the late 450s (Meiggs (1972) 112, 115–16, 564–65) is now not so secure, as a new fragment of *IG* I^3 259 perhaps shows Miletos paying tribute in 454/3, along with Leros and Teichioussa; see Mattingly (1981a) 113–17, (1984b) 340–42; (1987) 68–69, (1992) 131–32. Given the lack of precise evidence for a revolt in the 450s, the uncertain emendation, and the probability that three-barred sigmas appear as late as 418/7 (see discussion at doc. 9.20), this decree belongs in 426/5 until better arguments are produced against this dating.

(1) [Agr]ee[ment] with the [Mi]lesi[ans. (2) It was resolved] by the boule an[d the people; ....is held the pr]yta[ny, ... was secretary, ...]or presided, [Euthynos was archon; the co]mmissioners (syngrapheis) drew up [as follows: the c]ustomary sacrifices are [to be paid] to th[e gods, a]nd [the people are to elect im]mediately five m[en from everyone] (5) o[ver fifty years of] ag[e, and refusal shall not be allowed them o]r sub<s>ti[tution, and these are to be off]icials and .... (*lines 10–24 appear to deal with the supply of troops by Miletos.*) (26) [.... of the al]lies what would not be (good) for the Athe[nians .... he] shall be [deprived of citizen rig]hts and h[is] property [belong to the state and a tithe be given to the goddess]; and [the] trials for Milesians are to be [....] (30) drachmas from the tith[e ... the] court-fees are to be deposited with [the officials .... a]nd [the] trials are to be at Athens in [....

Antheste]rion and Elaphebolion; [and the ....] having distributed and allotte[d ....] (35) two of the archons a[nd .... and the payment is to be giv]en to the jurors from th[e court-fees ....] they are to provide the law-c[ourt .... in the months that] have been laid do[w]n or they shall be liable [to examination .... t]o the archons of the Ath[enians ....] (40) to Athens to the epimelet[ai ....] just as before and [....] the fi[ve] are to see that [.... la]w-court sits [....] shall be for those who proceed [.... (45) t]he officials of the Athen[ians ....] to be pa[i]d; and the (cases) over one hundr[ed drachmas .... o]n a stele [an]d for the decree[s ....] not to destr[oy] or to deal fraudule[ntly. .... And if anyone tran]sgresses them in any way, there shall [b]e an indictment against him be[fore the ....]; (50) they shall bring [hi]m forward either to one [....; and the] court is [to assess] what penalty or f[ine] is pr[op]er .... (*lines 52–70 and 72–82 are not translated here.*) (71) [.... a]nd the fi[ve] are to admin[ister the oath ....] (83) [.... t]he boul[e .... the g]arrison; of the decr[e(es) .....] may be accom[plis]hed, the boule is to have full po[wers .... (85) let them s]end of[f the] two guardships and the [....] in the archonship of [Euth]ynos [[....]]

9.10 Pylos, 425

Thucydides IV.38.5–39.3

For the whole episode, see Thuc. IV.3–41, with the commentary of Wilson (1979); Plut. *Nik.* 7.1–6. The general Demosthenes was responsible for the fortification at Pylos in the Peloponnese; the Spartans responded to this by putting troops onto the nearby island of Sphakteria. Events turned against the Athenians; Kleon accused the strategoi of incompetence, at which Nikias challenged him to take the command himself; Kleon, according to Thucydides, attempted to back out when he realised Nikias was in earnest, but gave in and promised to bring the Spartans on Sphakteria to Athens within twenty days or kill them there. And he succeeded in bringing them back, strongly suggesting that Thucydides misread what happened at the meeting of the ekklesia and that Kleon had positive information from Demosthenes. The Athenians established a garrison at Pylos, helots deserted to Pylos, and Lakonia was raided. The Athenians refused to negotiate with the Spartans for the return of the captured Spartiates; the Athenians decided to kill the prisoners if the Spartans invaded Attica (Thuc. IV.41.1). There were no further Spartan invasions of Attica from 425 until Dekeleia was fortified in 413 (doc. 9.23). For Kleon's reward for this success, see doc. 10.2. For the Pylos campaign, see de Romilly (1963) 172–93; Marshall (1984) 19–36; Strassler (1988) 198–203, (1990) 110–25; Flower (1992) 40–57. For Demosthenes, see Westlake (1968) 97–121, 261–76 and for Nikias 86–96, 169–211.

IV.38.5 The numbers of those who were killed and taken alive on the island were as follows: altogether 420 hoplites had crossed to Sphakteria; of these 292 were captured alive and the rest were killed. About 120 of those taken alive were Spartiates. Few of the Athenians had been killed, as no pitched battle had taken place. **IV.39.1** The total period of the siege on the island, from the sea-battle up till the battle on the island, was 72 days. **IV.39.2** For about 20 of these days, in which the (Spartan) envoys had been absent over the peace-treaty, the Spartans were allowed provisions, but for the rest of the time they lived on what was smuggled in .... **IV.39.3** The Athenians and Spartans now both withdrew their forces from

Pylos and returned home, and Kleon's promise, although a mad one, had been fulfilled; for he had brought the men back, as he had undertaken to do, in 20 days.

9.11 Athenian Spoils from Sphakteria

Agora B, 262

The Athenians inscribed and dedicated the shields which they had taken from the Spartans at Sphakteria; Pausanias saw them in the Stoa Poikile (I.15.4) and one of these has been discovered in the agora. For a photograph and line drawing, see Camp (1986) 71–72, figs. 45, 46.

'The Athenians from the Spartans at Pylos (dedicated this).'

9.12 Athenian Decree on Coins, Weights and Measures, c. 425

Meiggs & Lewis 45 (*IG* I³ 1453)

ATL II.D14. This decree forbids the minting of silver coinage in the allied cities and imposes the use of 'Athenian coins, measures and weights' (para. 12). The Athenian officials in the cities or otherwise the local officials are to be responsible and copies are to be set up in the agora of each city (10). The dating of the decree is a matter of controversy. The discovery of a small fragment from Kos, which has Attic lettering and three-barred sigmas led some scholars to redate the decree from its previous position 430–15 to before c. 445, the three-barred sigma being held not to occur after c. 445; not all scholars accepted the new dating for the decree. In fact a new fragment, the seventh copy, published in 1988 is also in Attic script but from the Troad, specifically Hamaxitos, which is known not to have joined the empire until 427 (Mattingly (1993) 99–102).

If the criterion that three-barred sigmas predate c. 445 can safely be abandoned, there is no obstacle to assigning a later date to the decree. Mattingly (1992) 137, (1993) 101 points out that the numismatic evidence now indicates that continuous minting of coins took place in the north Aegean mints of Abdera, Akanthos, Mende, Maroneia and Ainos through the 440s, 430s and into the 420s. The coinage decree can be set alongside the Reassessment Decree of 425, which is also imperialistic in tone, and is more appropriate to the attitude adopted by Kleon and his successors. Certainly the parodying of the decree in Aristophanes suggests a date relatively close to the production of *Birds* (doc. 9.13). *IG* I³ 90, probably dated to the 420s (its mason cut several other decrees of the 420s), is a 'supplement' to the coinage decree, and may well have been passed within a few years of it (Mattingly (1987) 70–71). For the decree, see also Mattingly (1961b) 148–88, (1984a) 498–99, (1987) 65–71. Evidence of vase container types is also important: these seem to indicate that the new measures were not in use in the 440s and 430s, though this evidence needs further examination; see Mattingly (1971) 295–96, (1981b) 78–86. The text is composite, based on the existing copies; the numbers refer to clauses. The translation does not adopt the lengthy restorations of *ATL* II.D14.

(1) [.... gov]ernor[s in the c]ities or (local) off[icials .... (2) The] hellenotam[iai .... are to m]ake a record; i[f not ....] of any of the [c]ities, [anyone who wishes shall immediately] br[ing the offenders before t]he heliaia of th[e thesmothetai]; and [t]he thesmothe[t]ai within fi[ve days shall ins]titute [trial proceedings for the infor]mers against each (offender). (3) If anyone, either one of the [citiz]ens or a foreigner, [other than t]he gover[nors in t]he cities does not act in accor[dance with what has been

decr]eed, he shall be [depriv]ed of citizen rig[hts and his pro]perty [b]e confiscated and a [tithe] (given) to the goddess. (4) [And if there] ar[e n]o Athenian governors, the official[s of each city] shall s[ee that all that is in the d]ecree [is carried out; and] if they do not act in accordance with wh[at has been decreed, there shall be a prosecution at Athens against] these [off]icials, the penalty being [loss of citizen rights. (5) In th]e mint [after receiving] the sil[ver they shall mint no l]ess than half and [....] the cities; [the superintendents (of the mint) shall always] exa[ct a fee of three] drachmas per mi[na; they shall co]nvert [the other half within .... months] or [be] liab[le .... (6) Whatever is le]ft over of the silve[r that has been exacted they shall mint and hand] over either to the gene[rals or to the .... (7) Wh]en it has been handed over, [....] and to Hephaist[os .... (8) And if anyo]ne propo[ses or] puts it to the vote regardi[ng these things that it be permissible] to use or le[nd foreign curren]cy, [he shall be denounced immediately before] the Eleven; an[d] the [Eleven] shall p[unish him with de]ath; and [if] he disputes this, let them br[ing him before the jury-cou]rt. (9) Th[e people] shall elect heralds [.... what has been decre]ed, one to the isl[ands, one to Ionia, one to the Hellespo]nt, and on[e] t[o the regi]on of Thrace; [the generals are to prescribe the route for each] of th[ese and s]end them [off; and if they do not, each one shall be liable] at his examination (to a fine of) [t]en thou[sand drachmas. (10) The o]fficial[s i]n the cities [are to set] up t[his] decree [after recording it on] a stone [ste]le in the agora of [each ci]ty and the superint[endents (are to do this) in front of] the mint; [the Athenians] shall s[ee] to this, [i]f they themselves are not willing. (11) The herald who makes the journey shall request of the[m] all that the Athenians [c]omma[nd]. (12) The secretary of the [boule] shall make an addition to the oath of the boule [for the future as fo]llows: 'If anyone mints silver coina[ge] in the ci[ties a]nd does not use [Athen]ian co[ins], weights and mea[sures, but foreign coin]s, measures and weights, [I will punish an]d f[ine him in accordance with the form]er decree which Klearch[os proposed.' (13) Anyone is to be allowed to hand ov]er the foreign money [which he possesses and convert it in the same way wh]enever he wishes; and the ci[ty is to give him in exchange our own currency]; eac[h man shall bring h]is (money) [to Athens and deposit it at the mi]nt. (14) Th[e] superintend[ents (of the mint) are to re]cord [everything handed over by each person] and set [up a stone stele in front of the min]t for whoever wi[shes] to look at it; [and they are also to record the total of the] foreign [currency, both the silver and the gold] separ[ately, and the total of ou]r silv[er ....].

9.13 New Laws in Cloud-Cuckoo-Land

Aristophanes *Birds* 1035–42

Performed at the Great Dionysia 414 this is clearly a reference to the coinage decree, which must have been relatively recent.

Decree-seller: If an inhabitant of Cloud-Cuckoo-Land commits an offence against an Athenian –

Pisthetairos: What is this dreadful thing now, this book?

Decree-seller: I am a decree-seller and I have come here
Bringing new laws to sell you.
Pisthetairos: What?!
Decree-seller: That you shall use the measures of Cloud-Cuckoo-Land
And its weights and decrees just like the Olophyxians.
Pisthetairos: As for you, you're going to use those of the Olotyxians ('always weeping'), right now!

THE TRIBUTE IN THE PELOPONNESIAN WAR

The tribute was vital to the Athenian conduct of the war (cf. doc. 8.24), and various measures were taken to ensure its efficient collection. Kleonymos moved a decree for the election in allied cities of tribute collectors along with various measures designed to ensure effective collection (doc. 9.14). This was followed by a reassessment of the tribute in 425 (doc. 9.15). Kleinias' decree (doc. 9.16) almost certainly dates to after Kleonymos' (doc. 9.14) and further tightens up tribute payments.

9.14 Appointment of Tribute Collectors in 426

IG I^3 68 (Meiggs & Lewis 68)

ATL II.D8. Kleonymos, the proposer of the decree, is persistently vilified by Aristophanes (*Wasps* 19–20, 592–93, *Ach.* 88–89); Kleonymos' role in tightening up tribute collection as evidenced by this decree shows that he was an important figure, and presumably sympathetic to Kleon's attitudes towards the collection of tribute (for which see doc. 9.17). The inscription is surmounted by a relief depicting jars and sacks in which the tribute was brought to Athens. Each of the allied states were to elect tribute collectors in their cities, who were made responsible for the collection of tribute. Note the various other provisions to ensure that the tribute is paid; these provisions are further strengthened in Kleinias' decree (doc. 9.16). The importance of collecting the tribute for the war is made explicit (lines 28–29). There was to be a similar decree for Samos, Thera and other cities (lines 21–25) for payments which were not for tribute; presumably these were war indemnities (see ML p.187).

(1) [....] (2) Tribu[te]; it was resolve[d] by the boule and t[he people]; (the tribe) Kekropis held the pryta[n]y, Polemarchos [was secre]tary, Onasos preside[d, (5) K]leonym[os proposed the motion: al]l the cities that brin[g] tribute to the [Ath]en[ians are to elect] in each city [tribute collectors, so that] from all part[s] the [whole tribute may be collected for the Athe]n[ians] or [the collectors will be] held [liable ....] lacuna (11) [.... for the hellenotamiai], which[ever prytan]y [is in of]fic[e shall] of ne[cessity hold an assembly concerning the cities twenty days after] the Dionys[ia; and they shall public]ly ma[ke known those ci]ties wh[ich (15) pa]y t[he tribute, and those whi]ch do not pa[y, and th]ose whi[ch (pay) in part]; and [they shall se]nd fi[ve men t]o the de[faulters in order that] they may exa[ct the tr]ibute; [and the hel]lenota[m]iai are to re[cord] on a notice-board the [cities that have fail]ed to pay the tri[b]ute (20) and [the names] of those that brin[g it a]nd place it [on] each occasion in fron[t of the (statues of) the heroes. Th]ere is also to be [a similar d]e[c]re[e] for the Samians and Theran[s] concerni[ng t]he money which it is nec[essary for them to pay exc]ept for the election of [t]he men, and the same for

a[ny oth]er ci[t]y which has agreed to bring mo[n]ey (25) to Ath[ens]. The [pryta]ny of Kekropi[s] is to set up this decree on a s[te]le on the acropolis. P[....]kritos proposed the amendment: that th[e re]st be as Kleonym[os proposed]; and [s]o that the Athen[ians] may as we[ll and as eas]ily as possible carry on [t]he wa[r, an assem]bly [is to be held to]morrow and [(this) resolution] brought [before] the people; (30) it was resolved by the [boule and the people: (the tribe) Kekr]opis held the prytany, Po[lemarchos was secretary, H]ygiainon presided, [Kleonymos proposed the amendment: that the res]t be as in the previou[s decree ....] lacuna (35) [.... (39) ep]imeletai shall be elected for th[e other cases concerning] the Athenian monies in accor[dance with the d]ecree [which has been enacted] and o[ne] of the generals [shall be assigned to sit] alongside them whenever [a case is to be judge]d concerning one of the [cities]; and if anyone schemes [to prevent] the tribute decree [from bein]g [effective or] the tribute [from being broug]ht (45) to Athens, [anyone who wishes] from that ci[ty] may in[dict h]im [for treason be]fore the epimeletai; [and] th[e epimeletai shall br]ing him before the j[ury-court] within a month [of the] arrival of [the s]ummoners (kleteres). There shall be t[wice as] many [summoners] (50) as there are men against whom anyone w[ishes] to bring an indictment; [and if it co]nvicts anyone the [ju]ry-court is to dec[ide his proper p]unishment or [f]ine; and the he[ralds, however ma]ny there [mi]ght [be], whom the prytaneis wi[th the boule have electe]d, are to send to the cities i[n the pr]ytany of [Kekropis], (55) so that [the men who] are to collect the tribute may be elec[ted], a[nd (their names) be recordedin th]e council chamb[e]r; [the poletai are to let] out the contract for the stel[e] vacat Collec[tors of tr]ibute (60) [fr]om the ci[ties]; vacat

9.15 Reassessment of Athenian Tribute, 425/4

IG I^3 71 (Meiggs & Lewis 69)

ATL II.A9. This decree was proposed by Thoudippos. The amount of tribute being collected had become inadequate (lines 16–17), and a new assessment was made, probably under Kleon's influence; note the various measures outlined in the decree to this effect, in particular that reassessment must take place at every Great Panathenaia, and allied states are to bring a cow and panoply to the Great Panathenaia (see Barron (1964) 47; cf. doc. 12.6). It is an optimistic assessment: tribute payments are greatly increased, and the total seems to have come to 1460–1500 talents. But while Thoudippos' assessment shows between 380–400+ cities being assessed, the aparchai (tribute-quota lists) for the 430s never have more than 175 paying states. Many will have been small cities, such as Carian ones known not to have paid tribute since the 440s: 'all cities which had ever paid were listed' (ML p.194). The aim is a comprehensive reassessment, and the increase for cities that paid regularly will have had the desired effect of raising more tribute. Eisagogeis (sing.: eisagogeus) were magistrates who brought cases into court.

(1) G[ods.] (2) Ass[essme]nt of [tr]ib[ute.] (3) It was resolved by th[e boule and the people; (the tribe) Leontis] held the pr[ytany, ...]on was sec[retary, ... pres]ided, Thoudi[ppos proposed the motion: that heralds be sent] out of the [contractors (?) whom the boule] el[ects, to th]e (5) cities, two [to Ionia and Caria], two t[o Thrace, two] to the is[lands, and two to the Hellesp]ont; [and] the[se are to announce in the] government [of] e[ach city that ambassadors] are to ar[rive (in Athens) in the month

Mai]makterio[n. They are to choose by lot thirty ei]sagogei[s]; and [the]se [are to elect a secret]ary and assis[tant secretary from amongst themse]lves; and the b[oule is to immediately ele]ct [ten me]n [as assessors (of the tribute)]; these [within five da]ys from when [they have been elected and sworn their oaths shall record (the names of) the cities or] for e[ach] day eac[h shall pay a thousand drachmas. T]he commissioners for oa[ths (horkotai) are to administer the oath to the assessors on the same day that] they are [elected or each will be liable to th]e same pena[lty. The] eis[a]g[ogeis are to be res]pon[sible for the law-suits concerned with the tribute, as] the [people should de]cree; [and the eisagogeus who is chosen by] lot an[d t]he polemar[ch are to prepare the cases for trial in t]he heliaia [just like the ot]her [cases judged by] th[e he]liasts; and i[f the assessors do not assess the] citie[s] in accorda[nce with the l]aw-[suits, each of th]em [will be fined] t[en] thousand drach[mas] at their examination [in accordance with the law]; and the [nomo]theta[i] are to es[t]ablish a new [jury-court] of a th[ousand jurors. A]s [the tribute] has be[co]me too little, the [new assessments] are to be dra[wn up all prop]ortionate[ly with the] help of the [bou]le, [as was done in the la]st magistracy, [during the] month [P]oside[io]n; [and] they are to co[nduct business every day fr]om the new mo[on in] the sa[me way in order that] the tri[b]ute [may be ass]ess[ed] in the [month] Po[sideion; and a full boule] is to conduct busi[ness] co[ntinuously in order that the a]ss[ess]ments m[ay] be made, un[less the peop]le [decrees otherwise]; and they are not [to asse]ss t[h]e [new] tribu[te] for a[n]y c[ity at les]s th[an it pa]i[d before] unless so[me difficulty is sh]ow[n, such as] i[t]s region being un[able to pay more. This re]solution [and this de]cr[ee and the tr]ibu[te] which is assess[ed for each city] the se[cretary of the boule shall re]co[rd on two] stone [st]el[a]i and [set up, one in the cou]ncil [cham]ber [and] on[e on the acropolis; and] th[e] poletai [are to let out the contract] and the k[o]llakret[ai are to provide] t[he money. In future a declaration is to be made to the c]it[i]es concerning the tr[ibute before t]he Gr[e]at [Panathenaia; and the prytany which] ha[p]pens to be in of[fice] shall in[troduce the assessments during the P]anath[e]naia; [and if the prytaneis do not at that time introd]uce them t[o] the people a[nd do not decree a law-co]urt concerning the [tribute and do not conduct the business at that time du]ring t[heir] period in office, [each of the p]r[ytaneis] shall ow[e a hundred drachmas sac]red t[o A]then[a a]nd a h[undred] to th[e] public treasury [and at their examination each of the pr]yta[neis shall pay a fine of a thou]sand [dra]chmas. [An]d if anyone else bri[ngs a motion that] t[he] assess[ments of th]e [cities shall n]ot be made [during] the G[reat P]a[nathena]ia in the pryta[ny which fi]rst [holds of]fice, he is to [be] de[prived] of citizen rights [and] his pr[operty] be co[nfiscate]d [with a tith]e given to the goddess. [The] p[r]yt[an]y [of (the tribe) Oine]is is of necessity to b[ri]ng these proposals before [the] people, whe[n the] expedi[tion has arrived], on the second day [direct]ly aft[er the sacri]fices. And i[f it is not c]omp[l]eted on th[is day, it is to be dealt] with fi[r]st on the [ne]x[t day continu]ously [un]til it has been [c]omp[l]eted during th[e aforesai]d[1] prytany; an[d] if they do [n]ot br[in]g it before [the peop]le or do [not] co[mp]l[e]te it during their term [of office], e[ac]h of the [prytan]eis [at their examination] are to be fined ten thousand dr[achm]as [for] preventing the contrib[ution of tr]ibut[e for th]e expe[dit]ions. The [her]alds who are su[mm]oned[2] a[re to be br]ough[t b]y the public summo[ners (kleteres) in order that t]he boul[e can ju]dg[e wh]ether they appe[ar] not [to be perform]ing their duties corr[ectly. Th]e [rou]tes for the heral[ds who are to set out are to be prescribed according to t]he oa[th by th]e asse[ssors, (indicating) to wh]ere [they sh]ould pr[oc]e[e]d, so that th[ey] shall not [proceed in undisciplined fashion; and the heralds] are to be [co]m[pe]ll[ed] to proclaim the ass[ess]ments to the c[ities wh]erever [the magistrates] think be[st; and the people is to de]cr[e]e [whatever] is to be sa[id to the] c[ities con]cerning the [a]ssessments an[d the decr]e[e] and any[thing else which] t[he prytaneis introduce conc]erning what is ne[cessary. The generals are to see that t]he cities p[a]y [the tribute as so]on a[s the boule has jointly made t]he assessme[nt of the] trib[u]te, in order that there may be [sufficient money for the people for the] w[ar; and the generals] are to be obliged to give [consideration every year] co[ncerning the tr]ibute, [invest]ig[ating by land an]d sea fi[rst of all how mu]ch it is necessary [to expend] either o[n the exp]edi[tions or on anything else; and they are] al[ways to introduce cas]es [concerning] t[h]is [at the] fir[st session of t]he boule [without consulting the heliaia and t]he other jury-courts, unless [the] peop[le decrees that they introduce them once the jurors have] fi[rst made] a deci[sion. Th]e k[olakretai] are to p[ay] to the heralds who are to set out th[eir remuneration .... proposed the amend]ment: that the rest be as the boule resolved; [but] the [assessments] as many as [are made on individ]ual c[ities are to be declared to t]he jury-court, when [it is dealing] with assess[ments, by the pr]ytanei[s] who happen to be in o[ffic]e and th[e sec]ret[ary of the boule, s]o that [the juror]s can [a]p[prove] t[hem] v It was resolv[ed] by the boule and the people: (the tribe) A[igeis he]ld the prytan[y, Phil]ip[pos was secretary, ...]oros pres[ided], Thoudippos proposed the motion: all [the ci]ties [whose] tribute [was asse]ss[ed during t]he [boule of which Pleisti]as [was secr]etary for the first time, in the archonship of Stratok[les, are to bring] a co[w and panop]l[y to] the Gr[eat Panath]enaia; an[d] they are to take part [in] the procession [in the same way as colo]n[ists vvv] The boul[e] of which [Pl]eistias [was secr]e[tary] for the f[irst time and the heliaia ass]essed [as follows] the tri[bute for th]e cities [i]n the [a]rchonship of Stratokl[es] in the [period of] office of [th]e [eis]agog[ei]s of whom Ka[.... was se]c[retary ....].

(There follows a list in four columns of the cities, according to district.)

[1] An alternative is to read with ML 'in the prytany of Leontis'.
[2] An alternative is to read with Bannier, *IG* I^3 *app. crit.* and ML 'those summoned to trial'.

9.16 Kleinias' Decree on Tribute Payment, 420s (or ?447)

IG I^3 34 (Meiggs & Lewis 46)

ATL II.D7. Kleinias' decree was aimed at ensuring that the tribute was paid and in the correct amount. The date of this decree is also disputed. Alkibiades' father, who died in battle in 447/6, was called Kleinias (an uncommon name) and this serves as a possible but by no means certain identification with the Kleinias who proposed this decree. The tone of the decree, with its emphasis on tightening up tribute collection, is often placed in the context of 447, when there were problems with the payments of tribute (many states are absent from the list in 447, or pay less tribute; cf. doc. 8.14). Epigraphic grounds are provided by the letter forms: for example, curved upsilons as in this decree are rare (but not unparalleled) after the 430s.

Certainly, however, these epigraphic criteria are not conclusive (Fornara & Samons (1991) 179). Other considerations point to a date in the 420s. Thoudippos' decree (doc. 9.15) made the bringing of cow and panoply to the Great Panathenaia compulsory; Kleinias' decree reinforces this by providing penalties for failing to do so (lines 34, 41–43), so it can be argued that Kleinias' decree logically follows on from Thoudippos': Mattingly (1961b) 153, (1970) 131–33; Fornara & Samons (1991) 181. Fornara & Samons (1991) 179–81 (cf. Mattingly (1992) 137 with n.49) also argue that the Kleinias decree was passed after Kleonymos' tribute decree (*IG* I^3 68, doc. 9.14; 426 BC) as the method of collecting tribute in Kleinias' decree is more sophisticated then that of Kleonymos'; *contra* ML p.186, see also pp.120–21; Meiggs (1972) 166–67.

(1) Gods. (2) It was resolved by the boul[e and the] people: (the tribe) Oineis held the pry[tany, Sp]oudias was secretar[y, ...]on (5) presided, Klein[ias proposed the motion: th]e boule and the off[icials in] the cities, and the [commissio]ners (episkopoi) are to see th[at] the tribute [is co]llected each [y]ear (10) and bro[ught] to Athens; they are to a[rran]ge seals for the cities, so t[hat] it is impossible for those b[ringi]ng the tribute to do wrong; an[d] after [the] city has written on (15) a tablet whateve[r tr]ibute it is sending, it is to seal it with its se[a]l and send it off to Athens; those who bring it are to gi[ve] up the tablet in the boule to be read wh[e]n they pay the tribute. The prytaneis, after the Dio[ny]sia, are to call an assembly for the (20) hellenotami[ai to r]eport to the Athenians which of the cities have pai[d their tribute i]n full and which defaulted, separately, however many [there may be]; and the [Ath]enians are to choose fo[ur] men and [send them to] the cities to give a receipt for t[he tribute which has been paid an]d to demand (25) what was not [paid from the default]ers, two of them to sail t[o the cities of the islands and to Ionia on] a swift trireme, [and two to the cities of the Hellespont an]d to Thrace; [the prytaneis] are to b[ring this matter before the] boule and th[e people immediately after the Dionysia and co]nsider (30) i[t continuously until it is complet]ed. If any Ath[enian or ally commits an offence with regard to th]e tribute, which [the cities] must [send to Athens after writing it on a tabl]et for those bringi[ng it, he is to be p]rosecuted before [the prytaneis by a]nyone who wishe[s, Atheni]an (35) or a[lly. The pryta]neis are to br[ing] before the council [any indictment w]hich has been brough[t or] each will be [lia]ble at their examination [to a fine of ten thousand drachm]as for bribe[ry]; th[e boule is not] to have the power [to decide sentence on anyo]ne it convicts, [but is to immediate]ly [br]ing him before t[he heliaia]; and when someone is found [guilt]y, (40) [the pry]taneis should m[ake] proposals as to what punishment or f[ine] they think ri[ght for him. And i]f anyone commits an offence regarding the bri[ngin]g of the cow or [the panopl]y, there [shall b]e a similar indictmen[t] against him a[nd punishment i]n the same way. The [hellen]o[tamiai are to record] and [display o]n a wh[itened] notice-board (45) [both the assessme]nt of the tribute and [the cities as many as pay in full an]d rec[ord .... *c. 10 lines are missing*] (57) [.... the] boule ente[ring office is also to deliberate concerning the men who bring the tribute; the boule is to re]port to the peop[le for each city in turn a]ll those of the men who b[ring money to Athens who have been re]corded [on the

notice-board in the boule] as ow[ing (money). (61) A]nd [if] any of the cities di[sputes the pay]ment [of the tribute], saying that it h[as paid ....] the government of the [city; ....] the cities and (65) [....] not be permitted [to prosec]ute [....] the pr[osecutor] shall be liable [for the fine of the defend]ant, [if he is acquitted]; the prosecution is to take pl[ace before the polemarch in the month Gamel]ion; if anyone d[isputes ....] summons, the boule af[ter deliberating ....], (70) the [eisagogeis] are to bring [before the heliaia in turn those who owe] tribute [to the Athe]nians [in accordance with the notice-b]oard for information; [.... of the current] and last ye[ar's] tribute [....; the boule af]ter framing a preliminary decree is to in[troduce ....] (75) on the next d[ay to the people; .... of t]he election to con[duct business ....] vacat

9.17 Kleon and Athenian Tribute

Aristophanes *Knights*, 303–27, 1030–34, 1067–72

Kleon held a military command at Pylos, as a strategos, but this is best viewed as an extra-ordinary command (see Develin (1989) 130); he was also strategos in 424/3, 423/2 and 422/1 (Fornara (1971) 59, 61–62; Develin (1989) 133, 136, 138). But Kleon's influence was primarily due to his ability in the ekklesia; this is often contrasted with Perikles who was continually elected to the strategia. However, Perikles and Kleon were both influential in the ekklesia because they were persuasive orators, and they pursued similar policies: both were for war against Sparta, and both were imperialistic; cf. Cairns (1982) 204. Pope (1988) 283–84 suggests that Thucydides' dislike of Kleon was because Thucydides saw Perikles as the leader of the polis as a whole, whereas Kleon led 'the mob'. Kleon was of prosperous background and belonged to the liturgic class: Connor (1971) 151–58; Davies (1971) 318; Finley (1974) 17; Ostwald (1986) 202–03, 214–15.

For Kleon and the ekklesia, see esp. Ostwald (1986) 208, 228; and 201 where he notes that not the term 'demagogos', but rather 'prostates (champion) of the demos' was usual for leaders such as Kleon, Hyperbolos, and Kleophon (demagogos was yet to acquire sinister overtones). These 'champions' were also active in the law-courts (Ostwald 208–13) and jurors' pay was raised from two to three obols in 425 or 424, possibly by Kleon; see doc. 10.16; Meiggs (1972) 331; Ostwald (1986) 223. The *Knights* was performed at the Lenaia in 424, winning first prize. It was an attack on Kleon, who was now at the peak of his reputation because of the victory at Sphakteria. The son of Hippodamos, line 327, is Archeptolemos, who tried to end the war. For the ships sent to collect silver, see Thuc. II.69.1, III.19.1. Philostratos, line 1069, is a standing joke in Aristophanes; cf. *Lys.* 957 where he is also called 'dog-fox'; see Meiggs (1972) 322. In the second passage the sausage-seller is quoting oracles which supposedly concern the state; presumably Kleon used to call himself the watch-dog of the people.

i. The chorus of knights (hippeis) addresses Kleon:

You loathsome blackguard, †you loudmouth†, of whose audacity
305 The whole world is full, and the entire assembly, and taxes
And law-suits and law-courts! You mud-raker,
310 You have stirred up our entire city,
And quite deafened our Athens with your shouting,
313 As from the rocks above you keep a lookout for tribute as if it were tuna fish ....
Haven't you from the very beginning shown your shamelessness,

325 Which is the orator's only protection?
Trusting in this you milk all the foreigners from whom you can get money,
Being first and foremost; and the son of Hippodamos weeps as he looks on.

ii. The Sausage-seller:
1030 'Watch well, Erechtheides, the dog Cerberus, the kidnapper,
Who wags his tail and keeps his eye on you, while you dine,
And gobbles up your meat, when your attention wanders;
And like a dog always creeps round to the kitchen unnoticed
At night-time to lick clean the plates — and the islands' ....
1067 'Aigeides, watch the dog-fox, lest he trick you,
Who bites silently, the crafty thief, the wise and wily one.'
Do you know what this means?
Demos: Philostratos the dog-fox!
Saus.-seller: It doesn't mean that — but Kleon here who on each occasion
Asks for swift ships to levy money;
Apollo Loxias tells you not to give him them!

9.18 Athenian Regulations for Chalkis, 424/3 (or 446/5)

IG I^3 40 (Meiggs & Lewis 52)

ATL II.D17, III p.297. This is extremely important evidence for Athens' treatment of an ally which had revolted. The stele has both tailed and untailed rhos, the former not occurring in any precisely dated inscriptions after 438/7 (Meiggs (1966) 92, 94), which suggests a higher rather than lower date for those inclined to regard this as a fixed epigraphic criterion. Euboea revolted in 446 (Thuc. I.114), and this revolt is usually seen as the historical context for these regulations; see esp. ML 52 pp.140–44. Mattingly, however, argues that a date in the 420s is more appropriate as the decree shares phraseology with decrees of the 420s; he also points to Athenian military activity against Euboea in 424/3 (*FGH* 328 F130); Mattingly (1961a) 124–32, (1966a) 201–02, (1992) 135–36.

(1) It was resolved by th[e b]oule and the people: (the tribe) Antiochis held the p[ryt]any, Drak[on]tides presided, Diognetos proposed the motion: that the boule and the jurors of the Athenians are to swear the oath as follows: 'I shall not expel the Chalkidians (5) from Chalkis, nor shall I lay waste the city, nor shall I deprive any individual of his citizen rights, nor shall I punish anyone with exile, nor shall I arrest anyone, nor shall I kill anyone, nor take anyone's property without trial without the consent of the people of the Athenians, (10) nor shall I put anything to the vote without due notice either against the state or even against a single individual, and if an embassy arrives I shall introduce it to the boule and the people within ten days, when I hold the prytany, as far as is possible. I shall gua[r]antee these things (15) to the Chalkidians while they obey the pe[o]ple of the Athenians.' An embass[y] is to arrive from Chalkis and administer the oath to the Athenians along with the commissioners for oaths and record the names of those who took it. The ge[n]erals are to see that everyone [t]akes the oath. (20) vacat The Chalkidians

are to swear as follows: 'I shall not re[v]olt from the [p]eople of the Athenians by any me[a]ns or device either in word or deed, nor shall I obey anyone who does revolt, and (25) if anyone revolts I shall denounce him to the Athenians, and I shall pay the tribute to the Athenians, which I persuade them (to accept), and I shall be as good and upright an ally as I can, and I shall help and defend the people of the Athenians, (30) if anyone does wrong to the people of the Athenians, and I shall obey the people of the Athenians.' All the Chalkidians who are adults are to swear; and whoever does not swear is to be deprived of citizen rights and his property belong to the state and (35) a tithe of his property be consecrated to Zeus Olympios. An embassy of Athenians arriving at Chalkis is to administer the oath along with the commissioners for oaths at Chalkis and record the names of those Chalkidians who took it. vacat (40) Antikles proposed the motion: with good fortune for the city of the Athenians the Athenians and Chalkidians are to take the oath, just as the people of the Athenians decreed for the Eretrians; and the generals are to see that it takes place as soon as possible. (45) The people are to immediately choose five men to administer the oath when they arrive at Chalkis. Regarding the hostages, they are to reply to the Chalkidians that the Athenians have for now resolved to leave things as decreed; but when (50) it seems good, after deliberation they will make the excha[n]ge as seems good and suitable for the Athenians and Chalkidians. And the foreigners in Chalkis, who living there do not pay taxes to Athens, or who have been granted exemption from tax by (55) the people of the Athenians, are otherwise to pay tax to Chalkis, just like the other Chalkidians. The secret[a]ry of the boule is to inscribe this decree and oath at Athens on a stone stele and set it up (60) on the acropolis at the expense of the Chalkidians, and at Chalkis the boule of the Chalkidians is to inscribe it and set it up in the temple of Zeus Olympios; this has been decreed for the Chalkidians. vv The sacrifices prescribed by the oracles (65) on behalf of Euboea are to be made by Hierokles and three others, whom the boule is to choose from its own members, as soon as possible; the generals are to join in seeing that this takes place as quickly as possible and [s]upply the money for this vacat (70) Archestrato[s] proposed the amendment: that everything else should be as Antikles proposed, but that the Chalkidians are to have control of punishments against their own people at Chalkis just like the Athenians at Athens, except for cases where the penalty is exile, death or loss of civic rights; and concerning these there is to be right of appeal (75) to Athens to the heliaia of the thesmothetai in accordance with the decree of the people; and concerning the defence of Euboea the generals are to see to this as best they can, so that everything be as excellent as possible for the Athenians. (80) The oath.

9.19 The End of the Archidamian War

Thucydides V.16.1

Brasidas was successful in Thrace in detaching several cities from the Athenian alliance, notably Amphipolis in 424/3 (Hunter (1973) 23–41). Kleon as strategos in 422/1 led his troops against Amphipolis, and thus forced Brasidas to battle, in which the two leaders lost their lives. Thucydides' bias against Kleon is nowhere more clear than in the narrative of his death; Ostwald (1986) 217: 'Thucydides goes so far as to describe Cleon's death, quite wantonly and unnecessarily, as a coward's'; see also Woodhead (1960) 303–17; Westlake (1962) 276–87; Anderson (1965) 1–4.

Nikias and Pleistoanax both wanted peace, for personal motives according to Thucydides, for Pleistoanax was under attack for the military difficulties Sparta had experienced (cf. doc. 8.18). The Athenians, who had confidently rejected peace offers after their victory at Pylos, had been defeated at Delion and at Amphipolis, and were concerned about the loyalty of their allies; Sparta was being raided from Pylos and Kythera (which Nikias had captured) and the helots were deserting. The Peace of Nikias, 421, was rejected by Sparta's allies; Amphipolis was not returned to Athens. But hostilities were largely suspended except for the Battle of Mantineia (418), and Athens had several years in which to recover from the Archidamian War. For the terms of the Peace of Nikias and the 50 year alliance into which the Athenians and Spartans subsequently entered, see Thuc. V.14–24.

V.16.1 Now the Athenians had been defeated again, at Amphipolis, and both Kleon and Brasidas were dead. They were the two men, one on each side, who had been most opposed to the peace, Brasidas because of the success and honour he had gained from the war, and Kleon because he thought that in peace time his villainy would be more obvious and his attacks on others less credible. Now, then, was naturally the time when the men who aimed at the leadership in each city, Pleistoanax son of Pausanias king of Sparta and Nikias son of Nikeratos, who had had more success in his military commands than anyone else, made even greater efforts to secure peace.

9.20 Alliance of Athens and Egesta, 418/7 (or 458/7 or 454/3)

IG I[3] 11 (Meiggs & Lewis 37)

The dating of this decree is more than usually controversial, and now may have been solved by the use of laser technology, despite Henry's scepticism about the technique. The dating is important for Athens' interest in the west. Thucydides does not mention this alliance, though on the 418/7 dating it must have been recent when the Egestaeans came to Athens from Sicily to seek Athenian help in 416/5. If the alliance dates to the 450s it indicates Athenian activity in Sicily at that time; but 418/7 would fit into the historical context of the Sicilian expedition, which Egesta played an important role in starting.

In line three, the last two letters '-on' of an archon's name can be read. As Mattingly (1986) 167 notes the 'rounded, tailed rho and three-bar sigma' have consigned the inscription to c. 450. The archon's name can be restored as Habron, the archon of 458/7, or Ariston, archon in 454/3. But some scholars claim to see the phi of Antiphon's name, the archon of 418/7 (as others claim to see the beta of Habron); see esp. Mattingly (1986) 167–70, with bibliography (cf. Mattingly (1976) 42–44). Euphemos can be restored in line 15, but this is not completely certain; however, a Euphemos was negotiating a treaty with Camarina in 415/4, and his restored presence here, an alliance between Athens and another Sicilian city, is attractive.

The application of new technology, however, changes the picture dramatically. Chambers et al. have measured the spaces between letters, taken 'image enhancement' pictures, and have applied laser beams to the stone: the latter revealed a 'phi of nearly perfect shape' under the surface of the stone, caused by the impact of the mason's chisel as he carved the letters of the decree (Chambers (1992) 27); the full case is set out by Chambers, Gallucci, Spanos (1990) 38–63, and Chambers (1992) 25–31 (with photographs); Chambers (1993) 171–74 provides a simplified version, and replies to the scepticism of Henry (1992) 137–46, cf. (1993) 49–53. If there is enough unanimity on this reading and acceptance of the validity of the use of laser technology and its interpretation, the decree will need to be redated (with consequences for the dating criteria involving the three-barred sigma). Tréheux (1991) 469 and Mattingly (1992) 129–30 accept Chambers' findings.

(1) [The alliance and o]at[h] of the A[th]enians and Egestae[ans. (2) It was resolved by the boule and t]he [people; ....is] held the prytany, [.... was secretary ....]o[.... presided, ...]on was archon, Ar[chi]a[s proposed the motion: concerning the Egesta]eans [.... to t]a[k]e [th]e [o]a[th (5) ....] as ma[n]y [v]ictims [....] to s[wea]r [t]he o[at]h. [The gene]rals are to se[e th]at [all] sw[ear .... (10) (with) t]he oath-commissioners so th[at ....] Eg[estaean. ....]; the secretary of the boule is to in[sc]r[ibe] this [dec]ree and the [oa]t[h on a stone stele on the ac]ropolis; [and the poletai are to let out the contra]ct; and th[e] kolakretai are to pro[v]id[e the money]. The E[gestaean] embassy is to [be invited t]o hospitality [in the prytaneion at the] customary time. v (15) Euphe[mos proposed the amendment: that the rest be as the b]oule resolved; and in future when e[nvoys of the Egestaeans arrive, the h]erald is to intro[duce .... th]e e[nvoys ....] lacuna [These are the envoys] of the Egestae[ans who swore the oath: (20) ....]ikinos, Ap[....] vacat

9.21 The Sicilian Expedition

Thucydides VI.1.1, 15.2–4

The most ardent supporter of the Sicilian expedition was Alkibiades. His removal from command, because of his implication in the mutilation of the hermai and the profanation of the Eleusinian Mysteries (Thuc. VI.28–29, 53, 60–61), was one of several factors which led to the failure of the expedition. For Alkibiades, see de Romilly (1962) 195–213; Westlake (1968) 212–260; Ellis (1989); Forde (1989); Vickers (1989) 267–99; Bloedow (1992b) 139–57; that he was aiming at tyranny, cf. Thuc. VI.28.2; Seager (1967) 6–18. Nikias opposed the expedition, but his advice that the expedition needed to be greater than the Athenians thought led to them voting a large force (see esp. VI.24.1).

For the debate between Nikias and Alkibiades about sending an expedition to Sicily, see Hunter (1973) 123–44; Edmunds (1975) 120–30; Bloedow (1990) 1–19. For a treatment of the expedition, see Kagan (1981) 157–372. Buck (1988) 73–79 argues that the Sicilian expedition was not foolhardy imperialism but an attempt to win further manpower with which to defeat Sparta, and was a well-considered part of Athenian strategy. Thuc. II.65, that the expedition failed because the force was not given adequate support, seems to be contradicted by the reinforcements sent to Sicily. For the first Sicilian expedition in the 420s (427–24), see Thuc. III.86, IV.58–65; de Ste. Croix (1972) 221–22; Meiggs (1972) 320–21.

VI.1.1 In the same winter (416/5) the Athenians again started wanting to sail against Sicily, with a greater force than that which Laches and Eurymedon had had, and conquer it, if they could. The majority of them were ignorant of the size of the island and the large numbers of its inhabitants, both Greek and barbarian, and of the fact that they were taking on a war not much less in scope than that against the Peloponnesians .... **VI.15.2** The most enthusiastic advocate of the expedition was Alkibiades son of Kleinias, who wanted to oppose Nikias, since he was Nikias' constant opponent in political life and because Nikias had attacked him in his speech. Additionally, he desired to be in command and hoped that Sicily and

Carthage would be captured through his agency, which would, if he were successful, simultaneously bring him personally wealth and fame. **VI.15.3** For he was held in high esteem by his fellow-citizens, and was thus more enthusiastic about his horse-breeding and other expenses that his estate warranted, which was mainly responsible for the later destruction of the Athenians' city. **VI.15.4** For the majority were afraid of the extent of the lawlessness of his life-style and his attitude towards every single thing in which he was involved, and turned against him, thinking that he was aiming at tyranny.

9.22 The Mutilation of the Hermai, 415

Thucydides VI.27.1–28.2

VI.27.1: Alkibiades was implicated in the mutilation of the hermai and he with others was also accused of having taken part in a mock celebration of the Mysteries. Thucydides writes that the faces of the hermai were mutilated, and it is not necessary to assume that he implies that the phalloi were also smashed off (cf. Gomme *HCT* IV.288–89). For the mutilation, see Osborne (1985) 64–67; while Ar. *Lys.* 1094 might point to the mutilation of the ithyphallos, this is not conclusive (cf. Osborne (1985) 65). For a detailed commentary on the mutilation and profanation, see Gomme *HCT* IV.264–88, and MacDowell (1962) 6–10, 181–85. The property of those convicted of the mutilation and profanation was confiscated and sold; for the inscriptions recording the sale in 414/3, see *IG* I[3] 421–30; *Agora* XIX P1, p.70; doc. 11.12. **VI.28.2**: Cf. VI.15.4. For Alkibiades' ostentation and extravagance, see Plut. *Alk.* 9.1, where he bought an exceptionally fine dog for 70 minas and cut off its tail; when his friends rebuked him for this, he replied that he had done it to give gossip material to all of Athens, to prevent them saying anything worse about him.

VI.27.1 Meanwhile, all the stone hermai in the city of Athens (these are typically Athenian square pillars, many of which stand both at the doorways of private houses and in temples) in a single night had their faces mutilated. **VI.27.2** No one knew who had done it, but large public rewards were offered to informers to find out who the offenders were and furthermore a decree guaranteed immunity to anyone, whether citizen, foreigner or slave, who knew of any other act of impiety which had taken place and wanted to give information about it. **VI.27.3** They took the matter extremely seriously; for it seemed to be an omen for the expedition and at the same time part of a revolutionary conspiracy to overthrow the democracy. **VI.28.1** Information was accordingly presented by some metics and slaves, not about the hermai at all, but about the mutilation of some other statues which had been done by young men as a drunken jest and also about the sacrilegious celebration of the mysteries in private houses. **VI.28.2** One of the people they accused was Alkibiades. And those who particularly disliked him, as an obstacle in the way of their acquiring firm control of the people, took this up, thinking as well that if they could drive him out they would step into first place, and so they exaggerated the affair and cried up the (profanation of the) mysteries and the mutilation of the hermai as part of a plan to overthrow the democracy, pointing out as proof of the fact that Alkibiades had had a hand in it the rest of the lawless and undemocratic behaviour apparent in his life-style.

9.23 The Fortification of Dekeleia, 413

Thucydides VII.19.1–2, 27.3–4

Recalled from Sicily to face trial, Alkibiades went instead to Sparta (Thuc. VI.88.9–92) and argued that the Spartans should send aid to the Sicilians and fortify Dekeleia, about fourteen miles north of Athens (VI.91); this was undertaken in 413 (VII.19–20.1; cf. Plut. *Alk.* 23.2). The Corinthians in 432 had mentioned the possibility of establishing fortresses in Attica (I.122.1). Agis in 410, however, seeing many grain ships sailing into Peiraieus, said that there was no point wasting time denying the Athenians access to their land if grain was coming in by sea. In fact Lysander in 405, prior to the defeat of the Athenians at Aigospotamoi, sailed to the Hellespont to prevent grain-ships sailing out to Athens; the war was brought to an end by starving Athens into submission (Xen. *Hell.* II.1.17, cf. I.1.35–36; cf. doc. 10.38). See Bugh (1988) 82–83 for the use of Athenian cavalry against Dekeleia. Doc. 11.14, the desertion of Attic slaves, follows on from here.

VII.19.1 At the very beginning of the following spring, as early as possible, the Spartans and their allies invaded Attica; the Spartan king Agis, son of Archidamos, was in command. They first ravaged that part of the country which lay around the plain, and then they fortified Dekeleia, assigning the work city by city. **VII.19.2** Dekeleia is approximately 120 stades from the Athenians' city, and is about the same, or not much further, from Boeotia. The fort was built to do damage to the plain and the best parts of the country and was visible from the Athenians' city .... (*1,300 Thracian peltasts arrive in Athens for the Sicilian Expedition; as they are each paid a drachma a day, they are thought too expensive to use against Dekeleia*). **VII.27.3** From the time when Dekeleia had been initially fortified in this summer by the whole army, then to be occupied by garrisons from the different cities in succession attacking the country, it had done a great deal of harm to the Athenians, and amongst the worst had been the destruction to property and the loss of manpower. **VII.27.4** For previously the invasions had been short and for the rest of the time had not prevented the enjoyment of the land; but now they were stationed there continuously; sometimes an even greater force invaded, and sometimes out of necessity the existing garrison overran the country and plundered it, and with Agis, king of the Spartans actually present, who considered the war a very high priority, the Athenians were done a great deal of harm.

9.24 The Failure of the Sicilian Expedition, 413

Thucydides VIII.1.1–2.2

Thucydides in Books VI & VII gives a detailed account of the Sicilian expedition and its failure. Athens refused to give in, despite the enormous losses in Sicily, and seems to have recovered quickly from the disaster; Hornblower (1991a) 143–44 argues that Thucydides has exaggerated the extent of the losses suffered: Athens was not defeated for another eight years (Thuc. II.65.12), and when in 410 the Athenians defeated the Spartans at Cyzicus, Sparta wanted peace (Diod. XIII.52). In fact, it was only the intervention of the Persians and their financial support of Sparta that caused Athens' downfall. The older men (VIII.1.3) were probouloi, 'preliminary advisers'.

VIII.1.1 When the news reached Athens, for a long time they did not believe that the expedition could have been so utterly destroyed, even when this was clearly reported to them by those soldiers who had been there and escaped; and when they did recognise the facts, they were angry with the speakers who had been united in favour of the expedition, as if they had not voted for it themselves, as well as furious with the sooth-sayers and seers and all the others who had originally by means of divination led them to believe that they would take Sicily. **VIII.1.2** They had nothing but grief on every side and after what had happened they were not only frightened but, quite naturally, extremely shocked .... **VIII.1.3** Nevertheless, they resolved, as far as circumstances allowed, that they would not give in, but equip a fleet, getting the timber from wherever they could, and raise money, and make sure that their allies, especially Euboea, stayed loyal, and reduce the expenses of government in the city, and appoint a board of older men, who would be able to give them preliminary advice on the present situation, whenever there was occasion. **VIII.1.4** Because of their immediate fear, as is always the way with a democracy, they were ready to behave in an orderly manner. They carried out what they had resolved upon and so ended the summer. **VIII.2.1** But in the following winter because of the great disaster that the Athenians had experienced in Sicily, all the Greeks suddenly turned against them, those that were not allies of either side thinking that they should not stay out of the war any longer, even if they were not invited to join in, but should attack the Athenians of their own accord, for they believed that, if things had gone well in Sicily, each of them would have been attacked by the Athenians, and they also thought that the rest of the war would be brief and it would be good to participate in it. The Spartans' allies, for their part, were even more eager than before to be quickly relieved from the sufferings they had long endured. **VIII.2.2** And in particular the subjects of the Athenians were ready, even if not able, to revolt, because they were not judging dispassionately, and would not even countenance the possibility that the Athenians would be able to survive the coming summer.

9.25 The Rule of the 400

[Aristotle] *Athenaion Politeia* 29.5, 31.1, 32.3

See also Thuc. VIII.48–54, 63–77, esp. 65.3, 81–82, 86, 89–98; *Ath. Pol.* 29.1–34.1; Plut. *Alk.* 25–27. The Athenians were unwilling to abolish the democracy in 411, but gave way when confronted by the argument that this was the only way of obtaining financial aid from the Persians (Thuc. VIII.53–54, cf. 47–48, noting that the suggestion originally came from Alkibiades). The oligarchy failed: the majority of the fleet at Samos was opposed to oligarchy; one of the oligarchs, Theramenes, later one of the Thirty, expressed dissatisfaction with it, and there was rivalry amongst the 400, and Phrynichos, one of the main movers of the oligarchy, was assassinated (see doc. 9.27; Thuc. VIII.92.2). The hoplites were unhappy with the thought of surrender to Sparta. The revolt of Euboea (cf. doc. 9.26) was also important and the 5,000 took over, a constitution of which Thucydides approved (VIII.97.2). Full democracy was soon restored in 410.

See for the 400 & 5,000, Hignett (1952) 268–80; de Ste. Croix (1954–55) 26–28, 30, (1956) 1–23; Gomme *HCT* V.184–256; Lintott (1982) 135–55; Harris (1993) 243–80. The entry of Persia on the side of the Spartans was crucial to Spartan victory. Sparta made treaties with Persia in return for financial assistance: Thuc. VIII.18, 36–37, 57–58; an important feature of these was that territory and cities which belonged to the King or had in the past belonged to his ancestors were to be the King's. For a detailed account of Spartan-Persian relations, see Lewis (1977) 83–135.

29.5 After this they organized the constitution in the following way: it should not be permitted to spend Athens' revenues for any other purpose than the war, and all officials should serve without pay for the duration of the war, except the nine archons and the prytaneis who were in office, who would each receive three obols a day ... **31.1** The committee drew up this constitution for the future and the following for the present crisis: there would be a council of 400 in accordance with tradition, 40 from each tribe, appointed from a pre-selected number of the age of thirty or more elected by their fellow-tribesmen .... **32.3** Once this constitution was established the 5,000 were chosen but only nominally, while the 400 together with the ten generals with full powers entered the council chamber and started ruling the city.

9.26 Eretria Revolts from Athens, 411

Meiggs & Lewis 82 (*IG* XII.9, 187A)

In the summer of 411 thirty-six Athenian ships were defeated off Eretria by the Spartan admiral Agesandridas, and Eretria immediately revolted followed by the rest of Euboea except for Oreus (Thuc. VIII.95); this caused panic at Athens as Euboea was of more use to them than Attica itself (VIII.96.2); they had sent their sheep and cattle there when they moved into Athens (II.14). The Spartan fleet included some ships from Taras (Tarentum), of which Hegelochos may have been in command. The fact that the people are not mentioned in line 2 suggests that Eretria at this point was ruled by an oligarchy. Other allies were more loyal: see docs. 9.28–29.

(1) Gods. (2) It was resolved by the boule: Hegelochos of Taras is to be proxenos and benefactor, both he (5) a[n]d his sons, and both he and his sons shall be granted public maintenance, whenever they s[ta]y here, and immunity from public burdens (ateleia), and the privilege of front seats (proedria) at the games, since he joined in liberating the city (10) from the Athenians.

9.27 Honours Paid to Phrynichos' Assassins, 409

IG I[3] 102 (Meiggs & Lewis 85) lines 1–24

Osborne (1981) D2. Phrynichos was assassinated on his return from Sparta in the autumn of 411; this was followed by other events leading to the overthrow of the 400. See ML 85 pp.262–63 for a discussion of the evidence of Lysias. This decree grants Thrasyboulos, of Kalydon, Athenian citizenship for his role in the restoration of democracy (see Thuc. VIII.73.4, 75.2, 76.2, 81.1); it also gives honours to other conspirators involved in the assassination of Phrynichos.

(1) [In the] a[r]chon[sh]ip of [Glauki]ppos. (2) [Lobon of] Kedoi was secretary. (3) [It was resolved by the] boule and the people: (the tribe) Hippothonti[s held the

prytan]y, Lobon was secretary, Philistide[s (5) presided], Glaukippos was archon, Erasinides propos[ed the motion]: that Thrasyboulos, who is a brav[e] man [with regard to the peop]le of the Athenians and eager to d[o whatever] good [he c]an, [is to be commend]ed; and in return for the good he has do[ne both the city] and the peo[p]le of the Athenia[ns (10) he is to be crowned with a golden cr]own, [and the crown] be mad[e at a cost of a thousand dr]achmas; [and] the [hellenotamiai are to give the mone]y. And [the herald Dionysios is to proclaim at the] festival the reasons [why the people have crowne]d [him]. Diokles proposed the amendment: (15) [that the rest be as the boule resolved]; and that Thrasy[boulos] should be [an Athenian, and h]e [should be enrolled in] which[ever tribe a]nd phratry [he wishes]; and that the rest which has been d[ecreed by the people should b]e [valid] for Thrasyboulo[s; and he should be able to acquire f]rom the Athenians (20) [anything else] as [well which seems right on] account of his good [deeds towards the people of the Athenians.] And [the secretary] is to recor[d what has been decr]eed; an[d five men] are to be elected [immedia]tely from the boule, wh[o] are to de[termine what por]tion shall belong [to Thrasyboulos].

9.28 Athens Honours Neapolis in Thrace, 409–407

IG I^3 101 (Meiggs & Lewis 89)

The first decree dates to 409; the date of the second decree is uncertain, but Thasos revolted after the Sicilian expedition and was regained by Athens in 407 (see further ML p.274). The decrees praise Neapolis (modern Kavalla) for not revolting from Athens despite being besieged by Thasos and the Peloponnesians, noting its continued loyalty, and promises protection by Athenian generals and officials. The double square brackets in lines 7 and 8 indicate that these words were erased, and lines 58–59 specifically refer to this erasure. See de Ste. Croix (1954/55) 8; Pleket (1963) 76–77 (cf. docs. 1.20–22). Even late in the war, Athens could rely on the loyalty of at least some of its allies.

(1) [Go]d[s. (2) The N]ea[p]olita[ns] near Thas[os. I]t was resolved by the b[o]u[le] and the people; (the tribe) Leontis held the pryt[any], (5) Sibyrtiade[s was sec]retary, Chairimenes presi[ded, Gl]aukippos was archon, [....]theos proposed the motion: the Neap[olitans] near Thasos are to be [com]mended, [firstly [[because they are colonists of the Thasians]] and though bes]ieged [[by them]] and the Pelo[ponn]esians they did not ch[oose to rev]ol[t from the Atheni]ans, and also because they have b[een] good me[n towards both the (10) ar]m[y and the peo]ple of t[he Athenians an]d th[e allies] lacuna [....] (25) and lent 4 talents, 2,000 drachmas [.... as the generals of the Atheni]ans requested so that they might ha[ve it for the war; instalments shall be m]ade to them from the mon[ies which come] from the harbour [of Neap]olis. The [generals] on [Thasos each y]ear are to [record] what has been received from [them (30) until] it has been [complete]ly repaid; and they are to do this as [long as they are at war with] the Thasians. That which [the Neapolitans from Thrac]e are n[ow] giving, [they gave] both willingly and voluntar[ily to the hellenotam]iai — 5 talents, 4,800 drachmas — and they ar[e] eager [to do whatever go]od [they can], having themselves promised this in both w[ord and deed to the (35) cit]y of the Athenians. In return for [this] benefa[ction the]y shall [now] and in the futur[e have

favours] from the Athen[ians] because they are go[o]d men, and [th]ey are [to have access] to the boule and pe[o]ple f[irst after the sacrifices, because] they are benefactors of the Athenians. Th[e envoys are to hand over to the se]cretary of the boule [all the reco]rds (40) of what the Neapolitans ga[ve, what is now being given] separately and [the re]st [separately], and [the secretary] of the boule is to inscr[ibe] this decree on a stone stele and set it [up on the acropolis at the expense of th]e Neapolitans; and in Neapolis they are to [inscribe it and set] it up (45) on a [stone] stel[e] in the temple of the Parthenos. [The embassy is also to be invited] to hospitality at the pryta[neion tomorrow vvvv] To Oinobios of Dekeleia, general, 3 talents, 600 [and 34 drachmas, 4 obols].

(48) Axiochos proposed the motion: the Neapolitans from [Thrace] are to be commended [because they are good men] both to the army and the city of the Athenians, and becau[se they have made war against Thasos and besie]ged it (50) with the Athenians, and because when they fought [at sea with the Athenians they were victorious], and [they joined in the fighting by land the w]hole time, and because they are benefactors of the Athenia[ns] in other respects. [And in return for th]ese [good deeds] they shall have [favours from the A]thenians just as was voted by t[he peo]ple. [An]d so that they are n[ot wronged in any way eith]er by a private individual or by the government of a city, both the g[eneral]s who h[old offic]e at any given time are [all to se]e to whatever they might require, and also the off[i]c[i]als of the Athenians [who provide for their city] at any gi[ven time] (55) shall protec[t] the Neapolitans and be eager to do whatever they [bid them]. And now they shall acquire from th[e p]eople of the Athenians whatever seems go[od .... Concerning] the first-fruits for the Parthenos w[hich] were before given to the [god]dess the matter [shall be considered] in the assemb[ly for th]em. In the ear[lier] decree the secretary of the boule shall make a [co]rrection a[nd on it wri]te instead of 'the colon[y of the Thasi]ans' that 'they fought through to the end of the war w[ith the Athenians'. And ....] (60) and P[....] and [.....]ophantos are to be commended in as much as they now say a[nd do good on behalf of the people of the Athe]n[ians and because] they are eager to do whatever g[ood] they can [to the army and the city for the future just] as in the past. And they are to be invited to hos[pitality tomorrow v .... proposed the amendment: the rest to be as the] boule resolved; and [the first-fruits which the p]eople [of the Neapolitans] v[o]ws is to be set [apart] for the Parthenos [just as before] vacat

9.29 Athens Honours the Samians for their Loyalty in 405/4

IG I^3 127 (Meiggs & Lewis 94)

Osborne (1981) D4–5; Thuc. VIII.21. The grant of 405/4 was reaffirmed in 403/2, the date of this inscription. The Samian demos overthrew the oligarchy which came to power there in or before 412, and Athens conferred autonomy on the democracy. In this decree the Athenians honour their loyalty (cf. Quinn (1981) 23), for after the battle of Aigospotamoi, in which Lysander defeated the Athenians, the Greek states deserted Athens except for Samos, where the people slaughtered the aristocrats and seized the city, but later many of the people left under an agreement with Lysander who besieged the city in 404 (Xen. *Hell.* II.2.6, 3.6); see Meiggs (1972) 356–58; Shipley (1987) 131–33.

Lysander imposed a decarchy (a government of ten men) here as elsewhere, and he was honoured by the (remaining) Samians who gave him cult worship: a statue was dedicated at Olympia and the festival of Hera renamed the Lysandreia; cities built altars and made sacrifices to him (Duris *FGH* 76 F26; Shipley 133–34); no doubt this contributed to Lysander's fall from favour at Sparta (Hamilton (1979) 87–90).

Kephisophon of Paiania was secretary. All the Samians who were on the side of the people of the Athenians vacat It was resolved by the boule and the people; (the tribe) Kekropis held the prytany, Polymnis of Euonymon was secretary, Alexias was archon, Nikophon of Athmonon presided; proposal of Kleisophos and his fellow prytaneis: the Samian envoys, both those who came here formerly and those here now, and the boule and the generals and the other Samians shall be commended because they are good men and eager to do whatever good they can, and because in their actions they seem to have acted rightly for the Athenians and Samians; and in return for the benefits they have given the Athenians, because of their high esteem for them and the good things they are proposing for them. It has been resolved by the boule and the people that the Samians are to be Athenians, governing themselves however they wish; and so that these things may be as advantageous as possible for both, as these men themselves say, when peace comes, then concerning the other matters there shall be common deliberation. They shall use their own laws and be autonomous, and act in other respects in accordance with the oaths and the treaties which have been agreed by the Athenians and Samians. Concerning the disputes which might take place against each other they are to grant and submit to law-suits according to the existing agreements. [I]f any emergency arises on account of the war and earlier about the constit[ut]ion, just as the envoys say themselves, they are to deliberate and act according to present circumstances [a]s seems to be best. Concerning the peace, if it should come, it is to be on the same terms for those who now inhabit Samos [j]ust as for the Athenians. If it is necessary to wage war, they are to make prep[a]rations as best they can acting with the generals. [I]f the Athenians send an embassy anywhere, the Samians present are also to send with it [an]yone they wish, and shall offer whatever good advice they can. They shall be given the use of all the triremes which are now at Samos when they have had them refitted as [they th]ink fit; and the names of the trierarchs whose ships these are shall be recorded by [the en]voys for the secretary of the boule and the generals, and if there is any [.... (debt)] recorded in the public treasury from when they took over the triremes, the dockyard superintendents are to [wipe all of it] out totally, but they are to g[et in] the equipment [as quickly as possible] for the public treasury [an]d compel those who possess [any] of it to hand it over [intact. An amendment proposed by Kleisophos and] his fellow prytaneis: the rest to be as the boule proposed, [but a privilege is to be granted to those Samians who ha]ve come, as they themselves request, and [they] are to be assigned [immediately] in ten parts [to the demes and th]e tribes. [The generals] are to pro[vide] travelling expenses [for the envoys a]s quickly as possible and Eumachos and [all] the [other Samians who have com]e [with Eumachos] are to be commended since they are [good] men [with regard to the Athenians; and Eum]achos [shall be invited] t[o d]inner at the prytaneion [for tomorrow. T]he secret[ary of the bou]le with the [generals is to inscribe what has been decreed on a stone stele and set] it up on the acropoli[s, and the hellen]otamiai [are to provide (40) the money; and (the Samians) are to inscribe it at Sa]mos in the same way [at their] own ex[pen]se.

THE FALL OF ATHENS

Despite the protests of the Kerykes and Eumolpidai, the families in charge of the Eleusinian sanctuary and its rites, Alkibiades was recalled to Athens and elected strategos for 407/6 (cf. doc. 12.3). But the defeat of the Athenian fleet at Notion led to Alkibiades' deposition as strategos in 406 and his self-imposed exile in the Chersonese. The Athenians won the battle at Arginousai in 406 (cf. doc. 10.13) but in the following year, 405 Lysander refurbished the Spartan allied fleet and built more ships. He visited Cyrus (son of the Great King) who gave him funds, with which he paid the rowers' wages and Persian money flowed more freely than before into the Spartan war-effort (Xen. *Hell.* 5.1–5.9, II.1.13–15). For Lysander, see Proietti (1987) 79–88; Due (1987) 53–62.

9.30 The End of the Line for Athens

Xenophon *Hellenika* II.2.10–11, 2.16–23

Lysander sailed to the Hellespont (Xen. *Hell.* II.1.17) to prevent grain ships sailing down the Hellespont to Athens (cf. doc. 10.38). The Athenians sailed to Aigospotamoi opposite Lampsakos, and for four days sailed out to meet Lysander in battle, which he refused. Alkibiades, from his fort on the Chersonese, advised the Athenians to move a better site, for at the end of each day the crews had to scatter to find food, but Alkibiades' advice was ignored; it may well have saved the Athenians from defeat had it been taken. Lysander launched a surprise attack and captured most of the ships and their crews (Xen. *Hell.* II.1.21–32; Diod. XIII.105.1–106.5; Strauss (1983) 24–35). This, in 405, was the last battle of the Peloponnesian War and the Athenians now feared that they would suffer what they had inflicted on their own enemies: Xen. *Hell.* II.2.3–4 (doc. 11.3). Theramenes participated for a second time in an oligarchic revolution (see doc. 9.25).

II.2.10 The Athenians, under siege by land and sea, were at a loss what to do, since they had neither ships nor allies nor food; they thought that there was no escape from suffering what they had done to others, not out of revenge but wrongly and arrogantly to men from small cities, for no other reason than that they were allies of the Spartans. **II.2.11** Because of this they held out, restoring citizen rights to those deprived of them, and although many were dying of starvation in the city they did not start discussions about peace terms. (**II.2.11–15:** *The Athenians send envoys to the Spartans declaring their willingness to become their allies while retaining their walls, but this proposal is rejected by the ephors, and they are reduced to despair.*) **II.2.16** With affairs in Athens in this state, Theramenes said in the assembly that if they were willing to send him to Lysander, he would return with the information as to whether the Spartans were holding out over the walls because they wanted to enslave them or to obtain a guarantee of good faith. He was sent and spent three months or more with Lysander, waiting for the time when the Athenians would be ready to agree to anything that was said because of their lack of food. **II.2.17** And when he returned in the fourth month, he reported in the assembly that Lysander had kept him for that period, and then told him to go to Sparta as he did not have the authority to answer a question of that sort, only the ephors. After this Theramenes was chosen as one of ten ambassadors to Sparta with full powers. **II.2.18** Meanwhile Lysander sent Aristoteles, an Athenian exile, with others who were Spartans, to report to the ephors that he had told Theramenes that they had full authority to decide on matters of war and peace. **II.2.19** When Theramenes and the other ambassadors were at Sellasia and were asked with what proposals they had come, they replied that they had full powers to make peace, and so the ephors ordered them to be summoned. And when the envoys arrived, they called an assembly, in which the Corinthians and the Thebans in particular, and many others of the Greeks as well, spoke against making peace with the Athenians, and in favour of destroying the Athenians. **II.2.20** But the Spartans refused to enslave a Greek city which had done great service at the time of Greece's greatest danger, and offered peace on condition that they pull down the Long Walls and those of the Peiraieus, hand over all except twelve ships, take back their exiles, have the same enemies and friends as the Spartans and follow them by land and sea wherever they should lead. **II.2.21** So Theramenes and his fellow ambassadors brought these terms back to Athens. As they entered the city a great crowd gathered around them, afraid that they had returned unsuccessful; for it was not possible to delay any longer because of the number who were dying of starvation. **II.2.22** On the following day the ambassadors announced the terms on which the Spartans would make peace; Theramenes was their spokesman, and said that it was necessary to obey the Spartans and destroy the walls. Though a few people opposed him, a far greater number agreed with him, and it was resolved that they should accept the peace terms. **II.2.23** After this Lysander sailed into the Peiraieus and the exiles returned and with great enthusiasm they began to tear down the walls to the music of flute-girls, thinking that that day was for Greece the beginning of freedom.

THE RULE OF THE THIRTY TYRANTS

Intimidated by Lysander, the ekklesia voted that thirty men be elected to codify the ancestral laws under which they would govern (Xen. *Hell.* II.3.2; *Ath. Pol.* 34.3); Agis withdrew from Dekeleia. The Thirty obtained a garrison from Sparta and with its backing they arrested all their opponents (Xen. *Hell.* II.3.13–4; cf. *Ath. Pol.* 37.2). Theramenes opposed the ruthless nature of the rule of the Thirty, but was forced to drink hemlock by Kritias (Xen. *Hell.* II.3.15–56). Thrasyboulos, in exile in Thebes, first seized the fort of Phyle on the Athenian-Theban frontier, then Mounichia in the Peiraieus (doc. 9.27, cf. 11.26). The Thirty were deposed, and replaced by a board of Ten for the purpose of ending the civil war; these, however, sent to Sparta for help, and in turn were replaced by another board of Ten, who worked for peace. King Pausanias came with a force from Sparta, but after initial fighting with the democrats at Peiraieus, arranged peace and an amnesty in conjunction with the Ten (Xen. *Hell.* II.4; *Ath. Pol.* 38.3–4; Harding (1988) 186–93). Democracy was restored. The most detailed discussion of the Thirty Tyrants is Krentz (1982); see also Hignett (1952) 285–98, 378–89; Anderson (1974) 47–60; Whitehead (1982/83) 105–30; Ostwald (1986) 460–96; Strauss (1986) 89–120.

9.31 The Thirty Tyrants

[Aristotle] *Athenaion Politeia* 34.2–35.4, 39.6

See also Xen. *Hell.* II.3–4. **35.2**: For Solon's 'ambiguous' laws, see doc. 3.23, 35. For Ephialtes' laws concerning the Areiopagos, see doc. 8.10. The jurors, particularly with their jurisdiction over dokimasia and euthyna procedures, were associated with democracy. **35.4** For the Thirty's treatment of metics, see doc. 11.24; for the metics who took part in the restoration of the democracy, see doc. 11.26. **39.6** The reconciliation took place in 403/2. For the amnesty agreement, see esp. Loening (1987). In the interests of unity, the state paid back the money the Thirty had received from the Spartans (*Ath. Pol.* 40.3). The property of the Thirty Tyrants, the ten governors of the Peiraieus, and the Eleven, and the first group of Ten who replaced the Thirty, was confiscated and sold by the poletai in 402/1, see Lewis (1966) 177–91; Walbank (1982) 74–98; *Agora* XIX, P2 pp.70–74.

34.2 In the following year, the archonship of Alexias (405/4), the Athenians had the misfortune to lose the sea-battle at Aigospotamoi, as a result of which Lysander became master of the city and set up the Thirty in the following way. **32.3** Peace had been made on condition that the Athenians should live under their traditional constitution. The democrats tried to preserve the democracy, of the notables those who belonged to the hetaireiai and the exiles who had returned after the peace treaty were eager for oligarchy, while those who did not belong to any hetaireia and who otherwise appeared to be among the best of the citizens aimed at the traditional constitution; these included Archinos, Anytos, Kleitophon, Phormisios and many others, but their particular champion was Theramenes. But Lysander sided with the oligarchs and the people were intimidated and compelled to vote for the oligarchy. The decree was drafted by Drakontides of Aphidna. **35.1** In this way the Thirty were established in the archonship of Pythodoros (404/3). Once they had become masters of the city, they ignored all the resolutions concerning the constitution except for appointing 500 bouleutai and the other officials from a pre-selected 1,000, and chose as supporters for themselves ten governors of the Peiraieus and eleven guardians of the prison and 300 whip-bearers as their attendants, thus keeping the city under their control. **35.2** At first they were moderate towards the citizens and pretended that they were administering the traditional constitution, and took down from the Areiopagos the laws of Ephialtes and Archestratos concerning the Areiopagites, and annulled the laws of Solon which were ambiguous, and removed the power of the jurors, on the grounds that they were emending ambiguities in the constitution .... **35.3** So this is what they did at first, and they eliminated the informers (sykophantai) and those mischievous and wicked men who gain favour with the people contrary to their best interests, and the city was pleased with this, considering that they were doing this for the best. **35.4** But when they had firmer control of the city, they spared none of the citizens, but put to death those who were noted for their property, family and reputation, because this removed their own fear and they wanted to appropriate their property; and in a short space of time they had done away with no less than 1,500 .... (*Thrasyboulos and the exiles occupy Phyle and Mounichia and the Thirty are deposed.*) **39.6** There was to be a total amnesty concerning the past actions of everyone except the Thirty, the Ten, the Eleven and the governors of the Peiraieus, and not even them if they would submit to an examination (euthyna). The governors of the Peiraieus were to be examined among the men of the Peiraieus, and those who held office in the city amongst those who had taxable property there. Then those who wished could leave. Each side was to pay back separately the money it had borrowed for the war.

SOCRATES AND THE 'NEW EDUCATION'

By the mid-fifth century Athens had become the acknowledged leader of Greece in intellectual matters and attracted a number of philosophers and sophists (Guthrie (1967) 64; Ostwald (1986) 243), who were a professional group who made a living as itinerant teachers, especially of rhetoric, the technique of winning over opinion in the assembly and courts. The term sophists only acquired a pejorative sense during the fifth century; see Armstrong (1949) 21–24; Guthrie (1971b) 27–44; Rankin (1983) 29; Roberts (1984) 219–26. Since religion was both the cornerstone of morality and 'good order' and an integral part of the life and tradition of the city-state, the wide-spread questioning of traditional concepts of religion and conventional beliefs (cf. doc. 9.5) naturally provoked a dramatic reaction. Many of these 'sceptics' were from the periphery of the Greek world: perhaps interaction with different cultures played some part in their attitudes towards established ideas and concepts.

Socrates was born in Athens in 469, the son of Sophroniskos a stone-mason or sculptor, and Phainarete a mid-wife; according to the *Phaedo* (96a–99d; but cf. Plat. *Apol.* 19c, 18b; Xen. *Mem.* IV.7.1–8) he had an interest when young in natural philosophy, including Anaxagoras' concept of Mind, until he realised it was a set of physical theories: see Guthrie (1971a) 101–02; Blum (1978) 140–45; Roberts (1984) 232–34; Vlastos (1991) 160–62. Socrates saw active service as a hoplite in the Peloponnesian War at Potidaea in 432, Delion in 424 and Amphipolis in 422 (Plat. *Apol.* 28e); at Potidaea he saved Alkibiades' life (Plat. *Symp.* 220d–e; according to Diog. Laert. 2.23 he saved Xenophon's life at Delion). For Socrates' ugliness (pot-belly, flat-nose, pop-eyes), see Guthrie (1971a) 66–69. Socrates was unusual in that he did not teach (at least for fees) but questioned, and the essence of the Socratic method was to convince the interlocutor that he knew nothing. For an intensive discussion of the Socratic method, see Santas (1979) 59–179. Socrates believed that virtue was knowledge, and that no one does wrong willingly, for vice is only due to ignorance: Armstrong (1949) 30–32; Guthrie (1967) 76, (1971a) 130–42; Santas (1979) 183–94; Vlastos (1991) 222–24.

9.32 Anaxagoras of Klazomenai

Anaxagoras 12

Anaxagoras began his philosophical activity in Athens in 456/5 and remained there for 27 years; Perikles and Euripides were among his pupils. His scientific speculations led to his being prosecuted for impiety and he died at Lampsakos. His most famous theories were that the sun, moon and stars were red-hot stones and that the sun was larger than the Peloponnese (Hippol. *Refut.* I.8.6–7). For his relationship with Perikles, see Plut. *Per.* 4.6–5.2, 16.7–9, 32.2–5; de Romilly (1992) 11–12; for Diopeithes' law against impiety, asebeia, of c. 430 and the fear of atheism in the 420s, see Montuori (1981) 110–11, 169–73; Ostwald (1986) 274–90, 528–33; cf. Momigliano (1978) 188, 192. However, Anaxagoras' book was on general sale in Socrates' time for a drachma or less (Plat. *Apol.* 26d); see Armstrong (1949) 16–18; Warner (1958) 37–40; Kirk & Raven (1960) 362–94; Rankin (1983) 131–37; Roberts (1984) 229–31; Carter (1986) 141–52.

For Mind is the finest of all things and the purest, and has all knowledge about everything and has the greatest power; and Mind controls everything, all things that have life, both the greater and the lesser. Mind also controlled the whole rotation, so that it began to rotate in the beginning. And at first it began to rotate from some small point, but now it rotates over a greater area, and it will rotate over a greater area still. And the things which are mixed together and separated off and divided are all known by Mind. And whatever was going to be and whatever that was then but is not now, and whatever is now and whatever will be, Mind arranged all of them, including this rotation in which now the stars rotate and the sun and the moon, and the air and the aether which are being separated off.

9.33 Nature versus Law

Antiphon 44

For Antiphon, an Athenian sophist, and his teaching, see Guthrie (1971b) 107–13, 285–94; Rankin (1983) 64–68; Ostwald (1986) 260–61; de Romilly (1992) 115–16, 182–85, 208–09. Antiphon recommended a discipline capable of banishing misery and argued that nature (physis) should be followed rather than law (nomos); cf. Ar. *Clouds* 1075–78. Protagoras of Abdera, according to Plat. *Prot.* 317b, had been the first to call himself a sophist and take fees for teaching; his teaching was largely based on the art of persuasive speaking and he coined the phrase 'to make the weaker argument the stronger' (F6a–b); his dates are generally placed at c. 490 – c. 420. He was a sceptic with regard to the Olympian religion, and may have been exiled from Athens; like Anaxagoras, he was a friend of Perikles (Plut. *Per.* 36.5). His most famous saying was (F1), 'Man is the measure of all things, of those that are that they are, and of those that are not that they are not.' For Protagoras, see Guthrie (1971b) 262-69; Rankin (1983) 30-35; de Romilly (1992) 75-85.

So justice is not transgressing the legal usages of the city in which one is a citizen. Accordingly a man can best conduct himself in accordance with justice, if he upholds the great laws in the company of witnesses, and when alone without witnesses the dictates of nature; for the dictates of the laws are accidental (epitheta), but those of nature compulsory; and the dictates of the laws are agreed by consent not by natural evolution, while those of nature have evolved naturally and have not been agreed upon. So if a man who transgresses legal usages does so unnoticed by those who have agreed on them he avoids both disgrace and punishment; otherwise he does not; but if someone violates against possibility any of those laws implanted by nature, even if he does so unnoticed by all mankind, the evil is no less, and even if all see, it is no greater; for he is not harmed because of an opinion but because of truth.

9.34 A Sophist's View of Socrates

Xenophon *Memorabilia* I.6.1–3, 6.10

Socrates was well-known for wearing the same cloak, summer and winter, and for going barefoot, for which he was satirized in the comic poets (see Ar. *Clouds* 103, 363; cf. *Birds* 1282; Guthrie (1971a) 40–41); he himself stated (Plat. *Apol.* 23b) that the mission imposed on him by the oracle at Delphi had reduced him to extreme poverty. In Plat.

Symp. 174d–175c, when on the way to dine with Agathon, he stopped in a neighbour's porch and refused to move, turning up halfway through dinner, and Alkibiades relates how at Potidaea Socrates walked barefoot across the ice, and stood motionless for 24 hours in contemplation (*Symp.* 220b–d). For his teaching on self-control, see Xen. *Mem.* I.5.1–6, II.1.1–13, IV.5.1–11.

I.6.1 Antiphon approached Socrates with the intention of taking his companions away from him, and in their presence spoke as follows: **I.6.2** 'Socrates, I always thought that philosophers ought to become happier people; but you seem to me to have derived the opposite from philosophy. At all events, you live in such a way that not even a slave under a master would be able to endure; your food and drink are of the poorest kind, and you not only wear a poor cloak, but wear the same one summer and winter, and always go barefoot and without a tunic. **I.6.3** Besides you won't take money, which gladdens its receivers and makes those who possess it live more freely and pleasantly. The teachers of other occupations try to make their students imitate themselves, but if you are disposed to make your companions do that, you must think yourself a teacher of misery.' .... **I.6.10** 'You seem to think, Antiphon, that happiness comprises luxury and extravagance; but my view is that wanting nothing is divine, and to want as little as possible comes closest to the divine, and as that which is divine is supreme, that which approaches nearest to the divine is nearest to the supreme.'

9.35 The Socrates of the 'Clouds'

Aristophanes *Clouds* 218–48

Socrates was made fun of not only by Aristophanes in the *Clouds*, first performed in 423, but by at least four other writers of Old Comedy — Kallias, Ameipsias, Eupolis and Telekleides; see Dover (1971) 65–66, 69–70; Guthrie (1971a) 39–57, 101–04; cf. Ar. *Birds* 1282, 1553–55, *Frogs* 1491–99; Xen. *Oec.* XI.3, *Symp.* VI.6; Plat. *Apol.* 18b–d, 19c, *Phaed.* 70 b–c, *Symp.* 221b. The portrayal of Socrates here is a conflation of the views of various thinkers, including the 'air-theories' of Diogenes of Apollonia, who was said to regard the air as god (Rankin (1983) 138) as well as the rhetorical skills of the sophists. de Romilly (1992) 10 points out that the play is also unfair to the sophists, but it shows how concerned the city was with the crisis in values brought by the new philosophers: see Dover (1971) 54–58; de Romilly (1992) 75–84. For Aristophanes' portrait of Socrates, see Richardson (1970) 59–75; Dover (1971) 50–77; Nussbaum (1980) 71–76; cf. Nichols (1987) 7–28; Tarrant (1988) 116–22; Green (1989) 112–19. Montuori (1981) 108–09 suggests that Strepsiades' extravagant son Pheidippides in the *Clouds* may be a portrait of Alkibiades, whose mother Deinomache was the daughter of Megakles (cf. doc. 13.59); for Alkibiades in Ar. *Birds*, see Vickers (1989) 267–99.

Strepsiades: Tell me, who is this man hanging from the hook?
Student: It's him.
Strepsiades: Who's him?
Student: Socrates.
Strepsiades: Socrates! Could you give him a shout for me?
Student: You call him yourself! I haven't got the time.
Strepsiades: Socrates!
My dear little Socrates!

Socrates: Why do you call me, mortal creature?
Strepsiades: First, I entreat you, tell me what you're doing up there.
Socrates: I walk on air and contemplate the sun.
Strepsiades: If you want to be contemptuous of the gods, why do you do it
From a basket, and not from ground-level?
Socrates: I would never discover the truth of astronomical phenomena
If I did not suspend my mind and combine
My fine thought with the air itself.
If I were on the ground and looked upward from below,
I would discover nothing; for the earth forcibly
Draws to itself the moisture from thought
In exactly the same way as happens with watercress.
Strepsiades: What?
Thought draws moisture into watercress?
Do come down to me, my dear Socrates,
And teach me what I've come for.
Socrates: What have you come for?
Strepsiades: I want to learn to be a speaker.
Because interest rates and hard-hearted creditors
Are laying me waste, and my goods are being seized for debt.
Socrates: How did you manage to get into debt without noticing it?
Strepsiades: A horsy disease — terrible at devouring people! — has destroyed me.
But teach me the one of your two arguments,
Which never pays its debts. Whatever fee
You charge, I swear to you by the gods I'll pay it!
Socrates: What gods are you swearing by? The first thing to learn
Is that gods are not current coin with us.

9.36 Alkibiades Practises the Socratic Method on Perikles

Xenophon *Memorabilia* I.2.39–46

Socrates' aim was to elicit definitions from his interlocutors, particularly of terms relating to ethical ideas such as justice, arete (virtue) and courage. Socrates states in Plato's *Apology* that one of the reasons for his unpopularity was the fact that a number of upper-class young men attached themselves to him because they enjoyed hearing people cross-questioned, and took him as their model; as a result, people were angry with Socrates for filling young persons' heads with wrong ideas (*Apol.* 23c); cf. Xen. *Mem.* I.2.9; see Roberts (1984) 243–47; Ostwald (1986) 229–73; Rankin (1987) 68–87. Green (1989) 117 compares the way Pheidippides can run intellectual rings round his father Strepsiades in the *Clouds*, with the way Alkibiades here confutes his uncle Perikles.

I.2.39 While Kritias and Alkibiades were Socrates' associates they were out of sympathy with him for the whole of that time, and right from the very beginning what they were aiming at was leadership of the city. For even while they were Socrates' companions they tried to converse not with others, but mainly with leading politicians. **I.2.40** It is actually reported that Alkibiades, before he was twenty years of age, held the following conversation about the laws with Perikles, his guardian, and the city's champion. **I.2.41** 'Tell me, Perikles,' he asked, 'could you teach me what a law is?' 'Why, certainly,' replied Perikles. 'Then please teach me,' said Alkibiades. 'For whenever I hear men being commended for observing the laws, I think that no one can justly obtain this praise without knowing what a law is.' **I.2.42** 'Well, Alkibiades,' said Perikles, 'there is nothing very difficult about what you want, in your wish to understand what a law is; laws are all those things which the assembled people have approved and enacted, through which they declare what ought and ought not to be done.' 'Is this the case whether they think it right to do good or evil?' 'Good, of course, young man, but not evil.' **I.2.43** 'But if, as happens under an oligarchy, not the majority but a minority meet and enact what ought to be done, what's this?' 'All that, after deliberation, the sovereign power in the city ordains ought to be done, is called a law.' 'And if a tyrant controls the city and enacts what the citizens ought to do, is this also a law?' 'Yes, whatever a tyrant as ruler ordains is also called a law.' **I.2.44** 'But what is force, or the negation of law, Perikles? Isn't it when the stronger without persuasion forcibly compels the weaker to do whatever he chooses?' 'Yes, that is my view', replied Perikles. 'Then whatever a tyrant enacts and compels the citizens to do without persuasion is the negation of law?' 'I believe so,' replied Perikles, 'and I withdraw my statement that whatever a tyrant enacts without persuasion is a law.' **I.2.45** 'And whatever the minority enacts, without persuading the majority but by using its power, should we call that force, or not?' 'Everything, I think,' replied Perikles, 'that a person compels someone else to do without persuasion, whether by enactment or not, is force rather than law.' 'So whatever the whole people enacts without persuasion, by using its power over the possessors of property, would be force rather than law?' **I.2.46** 'Alkibiades', said Perikles,' when we were your age we used to be very clever at these sorts of things too; for the sorts of things we studied and exercised our skill on then, are exactly the same as those that you seem to like practising now.' 'Perikles,' answered Alkibiades, 'I only wish I'd known you when you were at your cleverest in such debates!'

9.37 Socrates and the Delphic Oracle

Plato *Apology* 20e–21a

For the oracle given to Chairephon (a prominent disciple of Socrates in the *Clouds*) by the Pythia, see also Xen. *Apol.* 14. For this consultation, see Guthrie (1971a) 85–86; Daniel & Polansky (1979) 83–85; Brickhouse & Smith (1989) 87–100; Vlastos (1991) 288–89 with n.152; cf. Montuori (1981) esp. 57–86, 133–39. Blum (1978) 181–85; Kraut (1984) 270–74 discuss the paradox involved in Socrates' claim to wisdom being based on his knowledge of how little he knows; cf. Guthrie (1971a) 122–29. In *Apol.* 23a–b, the oracle's meaning is that Socrates' highly limited form of wisdom is the most that human beings can accomplish, and real wisdom is the prerogative of god. Socrates explains his habit of questioning others as his attempt to prove the oracle wrong.

20e Gentlemen, please do not interrupt me if I seem to be making an arrogant claim, for what I'm going to say is not my opinion; I'm going to bring forward an unimpeachable source. For as witness to my wisdom, such as it is, I am going to call the god at Delphi. Of course you know Chairephon. He was a friend of mine from boyhood **21a** and a friend to democracy and took part in your recent expulsion and restoration. You know what Chairephon was like, how impetuous he was over anything he had started. Well on one occasion he actually went to Delphi and dared to ask the oracle — as I said earlier gentlemen, please don't interrupt — whether there was anyone wiser than myself. And the Pythia replied that there was no one wiser. And as he is dead, his brother will give evidence about this.

9.38 Socrates and his 'Daimonion'

Plato *Apology* 31c–32d

Socrates was accused of being guilty of refusing to recognise the gods recognised by the state and introducing other, new divinities (apparently his daimonion); he was also said to be guilty of corrupting the youth. For these charges, see Finley (1977) 64–73; Brickhouse & Smith (1989) 109–28, (1992) 14–34, who argue that these charges were intended to be taken seriously, despite Socrates' past association with Kritias, Charmides (and Alkibiades) which the amnesty prevented the prosecution from addressing directly; for Socrates' political affiliations, see Guthrie (1971b) 298–304; Kraut (1984) 194–244; Rankin (1987) 68–87; Brickhouse & Smith (1989) 171–73. For the daimonion, the divine voice which guided Socrates, see Guthrie (1971a) 82–85; Brickhouse & Smith (1989) 237–57; Vlastos (1991) 280–87; Xen. *Mem.* I.1.2–4, IV.8.1, *Apol.* 5, 12–13. See Woozley (1971) 299–318; Santas (1979) 33–38; Kraut (1984) 17–24 (reviewed by Irwin (1985–86) 400–15) for a discussion of Socrates' principles.

In Plat. *Gorg.* 473e Socrates relates how, when he was chosen by lot as epistates (in charge of presiding for the day over the boule), he caused a laugh by being ignorant of the procedure for putting a motion to the vote; cf. Xen. *Mem.* I.1.18, according to whom Socrates was epistates (in charge of procedure) at the Arginousai debate (doc. 10.13). For Socrates and his circle as 'apragmones' (unconcerned with public life), see Carter (1986) 183–86; cf. Ar. *Frogs* 1498, *Clouds* 316, 334.

31c Perhaps it may seem to be strange that I should go around giving advice like this and taking an interest in private affairs, but not dare publicly to address your assembly and give counsel to the city. The reason for this is what you have heard me mention on many previous occasions, that I am subject to a divine and supernatural experience (daimonion), **31d** which Meletos made fun of in his indictment. It started in my childhood, a sort of voice, which when it comes always stops me from doing something that I was going to do, and never encourages me. This is what opposes my taking part in politics .... **32a** Gentlemen, I have never held any office in the city, except for being a member of the boule; **32b** and it happened that my tribe Antiochis was holding the prytany when you decided to judge *en masse* the ten generals who had not picked up the survivors in the sea battle, illegally, as you all realised later. On that occasion I was the only one of the prytaneis who opposed your acting against the laws, and voted in opposition; and while the orators were ready to inform against me and arrest me, with you ordering and clamouring for them to do so, **32c** I thought I ought to run the risk on the side of law and justice rather than support you in your unjust decision through fear of prison or death. This happened while the city was still a democracy; and when the oligarchy came to power, the Thirty in their turn summoned me and four others to the tholos and ordered us to escort from Salamis Leon of Salamis for his execution, and they issued many similar orders to a number of other people, wishing to implicate as many people as possible in their crimes. On that occasion I, however, **32d** showed again not by words but by deeds that death was no concern at all to me, if that is not too strong an expression, but that I was entirely concerned not to do anything unjust or impious. That government, though it was so powerful, did not terrify me into doing anything unjust, but, when we left the tholos, the other four went to Salamis and arrested Leon, and I went off home. And I would probably have been executed for this, if the government hadn't shortly afterwards been overthrown.

9.39 Not a Potion, but a Pension

Plato *Apology* 36b–e

At Plat. *Apol.* 36a Socrates says that had only 30 jurors voted the other way he would have been acquitted: so it seems that 280 voted for conviction, 221 for acquittal. After the prosecution had proposed the death-penalty, it was up to Socrates to propose a counter-penalty that the jury would accept; according to Xen. *Apol.* 23, Socrates refused to name a counter penalty; cf. Xen. *Mem.* IV.8.6–8; Higgins (1977) 41; Gray (1989) 136–40; Vlastos (1991) 291–93. According to Diog. Laert. 2.42, 80 more votes were cast for the death penalty than for conviction (making the vote 360 to 141); see Brickhouse & Smith (1989) 230–32, who at 214–25 argue that Socrates' eventual suggestion of a fine of a mina (after an initial suggestion of 100 drachmas), guaranteed by his friends who included Plato and Krito (38b), was reasonable, and that his statement that he deserved maintenance in the prytaneion was recognisably ironic and intended to remind the jurors of Xenophanes B2 (doc. 10.46).

36b So Meletos wants the death-penalty. All right; what penalty shall I propose to you as an alternative, gentlemen? Clearly it must be deserved; so, what penalty do I deserve to suffer or what fine, in view of the fact that I have not led a quiet life, but have ignored what most people care for — making money, a comfortable family life, rank as a general or public speaker, other official positions, and political clubs and factions which are features of our city, considering myself **36c** to be too honest in reality to survive if I went in for such things, and so instead of going into something which was going to be of no benefit to either myself or you, I went to each of you in private to do you, as I think, the great possible service. I tried to persuade each of you not to care for his own interests before his own-well being, how he might become as virtuous and wise as possible, and not to care for the interests of the city before the city itself, and in all other concerns in the same way — **36d** so what do I deserve for behaving in this way? Some reward, gentlemen, if I have to propose what in truth I deserve; and also a reward which would be suitable for myself. Well, what suits a poor man who has benefited the city and who needs leisure for giving you exhortation? There is nothing more appropriate for such a person, gentlemen, than maintenance in the prytaneion, which is far more appropriate in fact for me than for any of you who has won at the Olympics with a horse or pair or team; such a person makes you seem to be successful, but I really do, and he does not need the maintenance, whereas I do. **36e** So if I have to propose a penalty in accordance with justice, I propose this, maintenance in the prytaneion.

9.40 Socrates Dismisses Xanthippe

Plato *Phaedo* 59d–60a

According to Walcot (1987) 14, Socrates was a failure when measured by the standards of his own contemporary society, as his statement at *Apol.* 36b indicates. His poverty and hardihood were certainly well-known, as was his refusal to enter public life, and this attitude doubtless irritated his wife Xanthippe, who was herself known for her irritability (see doc. 13.30). If Plato's description of Socrates' rather offhand dismissal of her here was typical of Socrates' domestic behaviour perhaps this partially explains her notoriously bad temper. At *Phaed.* 116b Socrates' children, two small boy and an older son, and the women of the household come to say farewell to him.

59d We assembled earlier than usual on that occasion; for on the previous day, when we left the prison in the evening, **59e** we learnt that the boat from Delos had arrived. So we encouraged each other to meet at the usual place as early as possible. When we arrived, and the porter who was accustomed to answer the door came out to us, he told us to wait and not to go in until he told us. 'The Eleven are releasing Socrates from his chains', he said, 'and informing him that he is to die today.' After waiting a short while he came and told us to go on in. So we entered and found Socrates just released, **60a** and Xanthippe, you know her, holding his little boy and sitting beside him. When Xanthippe saw us, she wailed and made the sort of remark you'd expect from a woman: 'Socrates, this is the last time you and your friends will be able to talk together!' Socrates looked at Krito and said, 'Krito, let someone take her home.' And so some of Krito's servants led her away lamenting and beating her breast.

9.41 A Cock for Asklepios

Plato *Phaedo* 117a–118

Socrates refused to allow his friends to arrange for his escape from prison (Plat. *Krito* esp. 44b–46a). On the day fixed for the execution, he asked that the hemlock be brought in, even though Krito reminded him that he need not drink it till late at night: *Phaed.* 116d–117a; see Vlastos (1991) 233–35 for Socrates' cheerfulness at facing death. For a discussion of Socrates' dying words, see Most (1993) 96–111, who argues that he is not thanking Asklepios for healing him of the sickness of life by the cure of death; rather, Asklepios was thanked for aiding recovery from illness (see docs. 12.7–9). Plato is recorded at 59b as being absent through illness, and it is possible that here Socrates foresees Plato's recovery, and requests a thank-offering to Asklepios for healing Plato.

117a Krito, after hearing this, made a sign to his servant who was standing nearby. The slave went out and after a considerable time came back with the man who was to administer the poison, carrying it already pounded up in a cup. When Socrates saw the man he asked, 'Well, my good fellow, you're the expert in these matters, what do I have to do?' 'Only drink it and walk around,' he replied, 'until your legs feel heavy, and then lie down; **117b** it will then act on its own.' As he said this he handed the cup to Socrates. Socrates took it quite cheerfully, Echekrates, without a tremor or change of colour or countenance, but looked up at the man with his usual bull-like gaze and said, 'What do you say about pouring a libation from this drink? Is it allowed or not?' 'We only make up, Socrates,' he replied, ' just as much as we think is a sufficient dose.' **117c** 'I see,' he said. 'But I suppose that I am allowed, and indeed ought, to pray to the gods that my migration from this world to the next might be prosperous. So this is my prayer and may it be granted.' As he said this he held his breath and drank it down calmly and with no sign of distaste. Most of us had up to this time been able to hold back our tears, but when we saw that he was drinking and then had actually drunk it, we were able to no longer, but my tears despite myself flooded forth, and I covered my face and mourned my loss — not for him, but for my own fate in losing such a friend. **117d** Even before me Krito had gone out because he wasn't able to restrain his tears. And Apollodoros, who even previously hadn't stopped crying, now roared aloud weeping and grieving so violently that he caused everyone present to break down except Socrates himself. 'Really my friends,' he said, 'what an extraordinary way to behave! That was my main reason for sending the women away, so they wouldn't offend like this, **117e** for I have heard that one ought to die in auspicious silence. Calm yourselves and be brave.' His words made us ashamed of ourselves and we restrained our tears. Socrates walked around and then said that his legs were feeling heavy and laid down on his back — that was what the man told him to do. This man, who was the one who had given him the poison, kept his hand on Socrates and after a little while examined his feet and legs, and then gave his foot a hard pinch and asked if he could feel anything, and Socrates said no. **118** He then did the same to the calf of both his legs, and moving upwards like this showed us that Socrates was becoming cold and numb. He then felt him again and said that when it reached his heart Socrates would be dead. The coldness was already nearly as far as his abdomen, when Socrates, who had covered his face, uncovered it and said (these were his last words), 'Krito, we ought to offer a cock to Asklepios; pay the debt, and don't forget it.' 'It shall be done,' said Krito. 'Is there anything else?' Socrates made no reply to the question, but after a little while he stirred and when the man uncovered him his eyes were fixed. When Krito saw this, he closed his mouth and eyes. This was the end, Echekrates, of our friend, who was, we might say, of all the people we knew of that time, not only the best, but in general the most discerning and upright.

10

The Polis: the Greek City-State

The central focus of civilization for the Greeks, after the oikos or family unit, was the city state or polis (plural: poleis). Much of the history of the Greeks is the history of the interaction between the cities of Greece. Aristotle's well-known statement that 'Man is a political animal' in fact should be translated as 'man is a creature who lives in a polis' (Arist. *Pol.* 1253a 2–3). To the Greeks the fact that they lived in a city-state was proof that they were a civilized people. City-states were generally independent, and though various cities at different times attempted to dominate the other cities in Greece, these attempts were generally short lived. The cities, rather than uniting with each other, were prone to fight amongst themselves, and nearby neighbours were often the most implacable enemies. While there was a concept of national identity when faced with an outside enemy, as when during the Persian Wars the Hellenic League was formed to combat Xerxes (doc. 7.18), most Greeks saw themselves not primarily as Greek, but as a member of their city-state.

Apart from links with a mother-city which had sent out a colony, individual communities preferred to be self-sufficient, though many states were members of leagues, larger organizations formed to protect smaller cities or contribute to the power of the largest city-state in the region, such as the Peloponnesian League and Boeotian federation (doc. 10.33, cf. 6.36–37). Athens was to gain power over a number of cities through the Delian League. There could also be cultural and religious unions between different cities (doc. 10.34). But in general not only were city-states politically independent of each other, but each had its own army, and could also have its own calendar and system of currency. While the Greek states shared several cultural features, such as the same language, religious beliefs, and system of writing, there were still differences between states: there were dialectical variations, each state had its own tutelary deities with different cults names and festivals, and there could be differences of alphabet (cf. doc. 1.9).

From the available sources, it is possible to obtain a clear impression of some of the economic priorities of Greek city-states. Obviously by the fifth century the import of grain was of great importance to certain states like Teos (doc. 10.39), and there was legislation to stop corruption and consumer exploitation, as in the wine trade at Thasos, which not only regulated when wine could be sold, but specifically prevented adulteration and retail dealing, in terms which imply that these were a common occurrence (doc. 10.40). The most specific evidence for the economy of a city-state of course derives from Athens: doc. 10.43 concerns the Athenian control of trade during the days of her empire, and docs. 10.44–45 her taxation and customs duties. But all cities would have had their own system of taxation, both direct and indirect (see doc. 10.25), and in the sixth as well as the fifth century most states would have had quite complex taxation and commercial systems in place.

Most of our evidence about the workings of city-states comes from Athens. This was an unusually large city, with several important urban areas, such as Eleusis, and various villages (demes) scattered throughout the territory of Attica. Every citizen had the right to vote and also to speak in the assembly, which in fifth-century Athens was the decision-making body (docs. 10.12–13; cf. 2.21 for Mytilene). Nevertheless there were constitutional constraints on it, and from Kleisthenes' time the agenda for the meeting was drawn up beforehand by the boule, the council of 500, which served rather like a standing committee. Of the 500 councillors, 50 were chosen from each of the ten tribes and one of the tribes was in office ('held the prytany', each prytany being one-tenth of the year) at any one time, the 50 councillors from that particular tribe being responsible for the day-to-day business that came up in the boule and procedure in the assembly, such as putting questions to the vote. But the procedure did not always run normally, as after the battle of Arginousai in 406 (doc. 10.13). In the seventh and sixth centuries the most important officials of Athens had been the archons: there were nine of these — the basileus (or king) archon, the eponymous archon, after whom the year was named, and the polemarch, plus six thesmothetai. In the time of Kleisthenes, the archons were joined by a tenth, the secretary of the thesmothetai, and now corresponded to the new ten tribes, and one archon was elected from each. In fact, in the fifth century the most important officials were the ten generals (strategoi), who were appointed annually, one from each tribe, but were eligible for re-election and thus became the real political leaders of Athens as well as the commanders of the forces.

Perikles' 'funeral oration' is a valuable document for the Athenians' concept of the responsibilities of a citizen in a democracy as well as making clear the fact that Athens in particular prided itself on its independence and political system (see doc. 10.9). Nevertheless, there was no 'model' for a city-state, and it would be unwise to take Athens as the norm: Sparta was in many respects the very antithesis of Athens, in political structure and constitution, society, economy and culture. All Greek city-states were different and possessed their own constitutions and political and social usages (cf. docs. 10.23–31), but all were of course equally important to their inhabitants, whose lives revolved entirely around this integral component of Greek civilization and culture.

ATHENS: 'THE VIOLET-CROWNED CITY'

Pindar F64 : 'Rich, violet-crowned and famed in song,
Bulwark of Greece, glorious Athens.'

Finley (1963) 46 estimates Athens' total population in 431 as between 250,000 and 275,000: approximately a third of these would have lived in Athens itself; cf. Gomme (1933) 29, 37–48, who suggests a citizen population for Athens and the Peiraieus in 430 of 60,000 (172,000 for Attica as a whole; Attica is approximately 1,000 sq. miles in area); Sinclair (1988) 223–24; Starr (1990) 33. Ober (1989) 32 notes that Thucydides, even in 411 after drastic losses (VIII.66.3), emphasizes the number of inhabitants and the fact that not all the citizens were known to each other (in Aristotle's ideal polis, *Pol.* 1326b 16–17, all the citizens would be able to know each other); Ober suggests a number of at least 20,000–40,000 citizens throughout most of the fifth and fourth centuries. Ruschenbusch (1985) 253–63 estimates the total number of Greek poleis to have been around 700, though not all of these would necessarily have existed in the fifth century. For a general discussion of the Greek city state, see esp. Kitto (1957) 64–79; Ehrenberg (1960) 28–102; Finley (1963) 45–88; cf. Rhodes (1986a) 108–71. The Athenians were exceptionally proud of their city; Aristophanes laughs at them for having been flattered by envoys describing Athens as 'violet-crowned' (*Ach.* 636–40; cf. *Knights* 1329).

10.1 A Comparison of Athens and Sparta

Thucydides I.10.2

See Hornblower (1991) 34 for this description of Sparta inhabited by villages, and not 'synoecised' into one community like Athens; for the synoecism of Athens, see doc. 10.32, and, for her great buildings, docs. 10.7, 11.38.

I.10.2 If the Spartans' city were to become deserted, and only the temples and foundations of buildings were left, I think that the people of that time far in the future would find it difficult to believe that the Spartans' power had been as great as their fame implied (and yet they inhabit two-fifths of the Peloponnese, and are in command of all of it as well as of many allies outside it; nevertheless, it has not been synoecised into a city, nor does it possess costly temples and buildings, but consists of a number of villages in the early Greek manner, and would seem an inferior place), whereas if the same thing were to happen to Athens, from its visible remains one would assume that the city had been twice as powerful as it actually is.

10.2 The Basis of Power in Athens

Aristophanes *Knights* 162–67

Demosthenes the slave is here trying to persuade the sausage-seller to take over the government; performed in 424, this is a bitter satire against Kleon, who was granted dining-rights in the prytaneion after his victory at Pylos, and who was said to have come late to a meeting of the assembly and asked that it be adjourned because he had guests to entertain (Plut. *Nik.* 7.7; Ostwald (1986) 204; Starr (1990) 43); the sausage-seller is here promised Kleon's heritage — he can control the sources of Athens' prosperity and political power, override the boule, and cut the generals down to size in the courts at their euthynai (examinations); cf. for rewards for public life, Sinclair (1988) 179–86. For Aristophanes' summons before the boule for his portrayal of Kleon, probably in the (lost) *Babylonians*, see esp. Bauman (1990) 53–60; Halliwell (1991) 64–66; cf. [Xen.] *Const. Ath.* 2.18; see also docs. 10.16–17. For the very abusive tone of the verb λαικάζειν in line 167 (even by the standards of Attic comedy), see Jocelyn (1980) 35.

Demosthenes: Look over here,
Can you see the rows of all these people?
Sausage-seller: Yes I can.
Demosthenes: Of all of these you will be chief,
And of the agora and the harbours and the Pnyx;
You'll tread on the boule and humble the generals,
Throw people into prison, and suck penises in the prytaneion.

10.3 Pheidias' Statue of Athena, 440/39

IG I^3 458a

This statue, the cult-image of the Parthenon, was begun in 447/6 and dedicated in 438; cf. Thuc. II.13.5 (doc. 10.5); Philochoros *FGH* 328 F121; Plut. *Per.* 13.14. The total cost may have been between 700 and 1000 talents; cf. Gomme *HCT* II.22. For the charges against Pheidias of impiety and embezzling gold and ivory intended for the statue, see Plut. *Per.* 31.2–5; Ostwald (1986) 192–94; Bauman (1990) 37–38; Kagan (1991) 184–85; and see note at doc. 8.20.

Kichesippos of the deme Myrrhinous was sec[r]etary for the commissioners of the sta[t]ue. Receipt from the treasurers for whom Demostratos of Xypete was secretary 100 talents. The treasurers (were) Ktesion, St[r]osias, Antiphat[e]s, Menandros, Th[ym]ochares, Smokor[d]os, Pheideleid[es]. vacat
Gold was bought, weight 6 talents, 1,618 drachmas, 1 obol; the cost of this was 87 talents, 4,652 drachmas, 5 obols.
Ivory was bought: 2 talents, 743 drachmas.

10.4 Building Accounts of the Parthenon, 434/3

IG I^3 449

This is the best preserved of the Parthenon building accounts, of which the fifteen years 447/6 to 433/2 are recorded on the four sides of a marble stele. The accounts start with the balance from the previous year and the year's income of the board of annual commissioners, the main grant coming from Athena's treasurers (here less than normal at 4 talents as the project was nearing completion). Note that the non-Athenian Lampsakene and Cyzicene staters remain in the treasury unchanged. The Antikles who proposes the motion may be the same Antikles as in doc. 9.18; for the Parthenon's construction, see Burford (1963) 23–35; Kagan (1991) 157–67.

For the commissioners for whom Antikles was secretar[y] in the (year of) the fourteenth boule in which Metagenes was first secretary, when Krates was the Athenians' archon. Receipts for this year are as follows:

1,470 dr.:	Balance from the last year
(381) 7[4]:	[Lamps]akene gold staters
27 $^{1}/_{6}$:	C[yzic]ene [gold] staters
(385) 25,000 dr.:	From [the treasur]ers of the goddess' [t]reasu[ry] for whom Krates of Lamptr[ai] was se[c]retary
1,372 dr.:	From gold so[ld off], weight 9[8] drachmas; payment for this
1,305 dr. 4 ob.:	From ivory [so]ld off, weigh[t 3] talents, 60 drachmas; payment for t[his]
(395)	EXPENDITU[R]ES:

[....]200:	For purchase[s]
---2 dr. 1 ob.:	

	For wages:
1,926 dr. 2 ob.:	For the worke[rs at Pentelikos and those who load the stone on the wagons]
(401) 16,392 dr.:	[Wa]ges for [the sculpto]rs of the ped[iment-sculptures]
------------------	
[1],800 dr.:	For mo[nth]ly wages
[..]11 dr., 2 ob.:	
------------------	
(405)	BALANCE FOR T[HIS YEAR]

-----	
[74]:	[Lampsakene gold staters]
[27 $^{1}/_{6}$]:	[Cyzicene gold staters]

10.5 Athens' Resources at the Outbreak of War

Thucydides II.13.3–5

Perikles is here pointing out the city's resources to the people of Athens at the outbreak of the Peloponnesian War; cf. doc. 10.6. Parker (1983) 173nn.168–69 discusses the financing of wars by public borrowing from temple funds, as in Athens' Samian campaign of 440 (*IG* I^3 363); he considers that Perikles implies the payment of interest, which seems initially to have been paid at more or less the going rate, but later dropped to a nominal rate, and most of the capital was never repaid.

II.13.3 Perikles told the Athenians to take courage from the fact that the city had nearly 600 talents a year coming in as tribute from the allies, quite apart from the rest of the revenue, and that they still had on the acropolis 6,000 talents in coined silver (at its greatest the reserve had amounted to 9,700 talents, from which they had paid for the Propylaia of the acropolis and the other buildings and for Potidaea). **II.13.4** There was also uncoined gold and silver in the shape of private and public dedications and all the sacred accoutrements used in the processions and festivals, and Persian spoils and other things of the same kind, amounting to not less than 500 talents. **II.13.5** And to this he added the many possessions of the other shrines, which they could make use of, and if nothing else were available to them, the gold decorating the statue of the goddess herself. He pointed out that there was 40 talents weight of pure gold on the statue, all removable. But he said that if they used it to ensure their own safety, they had to replace no less an amount afterwards.

10.6 Inventory of the Treasures of the Parthenon, 422/1

IG I^3 351

For these treasures, many of which would have been spoils of war, compare Croesus' dedications at Delphi: Hdt. I.50 (cf. doc. 12.21), cf. IX.80, where the helots at Plataea steal Persian plunder, including short Persian swords (ll. 9, 17); cf. doc. 9.6.

Gods [....] The following was handed over by the four boards, who gave th[eir account from the Great Panathenaia t]o the Great P[anathenaia, to the tr]easurers, for whom Presbias son of Semi[os of Phe]gaia was secretary. [The treasurers, for whom Pres]bias son of Se[mios of Phegaia] was secretary, handed over to the treasurers for whom Nikeas son of Eu[thykles of Halimous was s]ecret[ary, to Euphemos] of Kollytos and his colleagues in the Parthenon: crown of g[old, weight of th]is 60 drachmas; bow[ls (phialai) of gold, five, we]ight of these 782 drachmas; uncoined gold, weight of this 1 drachma, [4 obols; drinking-cup (karchesion)] of g[o]ld, its ba[se silver g]ilt, sacred to Herakles of Elaious, weight of th[is 138 drachmas]; two nails, silver [underneath, gi]lt, weight of these 1[8]4 drachmas; mask, silver underneath, gi[lt, wei]ght of this 116 drachmas; ph[ialai of si]lver, 138 drachmas; horn of silver; weight of these 2 talents, 3,30[7 drachmas. By number] as follows: short Persian swords set [in gold, 6]; standing crop set in gold, ears of corn, 1[2; br]ead-baskets wooden underneath, gilt, [2; cense]r, wooden underneath, g[ilt], 1; girl on a stele, gilt, [1]; bed, wooden under[neath], gil[t, 1; gorg]on mask, skull overlaid [with gold; hor]se, griffin, front part of griffin, griffin, head of lion, nec[kl]ace of fl[owers, ser]pent, these overlaid with gold; [helmet, overlaid] with gold; shields, overlaid with gold, wooden underneath, 15; b[eds, Chian] work, [7; beds], Milesian work, 10; sa[bres], 9; swords, 5; breastplates, 1[6]; shields with devices, 6; shields c[overed with bronze, 3]1; chairs, 6; footstool[s, 4; camp]-stools (diphroi), 9; lyre, gilt, 1; lyres of ivory, 4; lyres 4; [table inlaid] with ivory; helmets [of bronze, 3; f]eet of beds, overlaid with silv[er, 13; small leath]er shield; phialai of silver, 4; small [cup, silver] underneath, 2; horse [of silver; weigh]t of these 900 drachmas. Shields, overlaid with gold, wooden underneath, [2]; short Persian sword, overlaid [with gold, unw]eighed; phial[ai of silver, 8, we]ight of these 807 drachmas; drinking-cups (poteria) from Chalkis of silver, 4, weight [of these] 124 drachmas; flute-[case from Methy]mne of ivory, gilt; shield from Lesbos, with device; hel[met from L]esbos, of Illyr[ian bronze; phia]lai of silver, 2; drinking-cups (karchesia) of silver, 2; weight of these 580 drachmas. Lesbian [cups (kotyloi)] of silver, 3, wei[ght of these 3]70 drachmas; crown of gold, weight of this, 18 drachmas, 3 obols; crown of gol[d, weig]ht of this 2[9 drachmas]; crown of gold [of Athena N]ike, weight of this 29 drachmas; crown of go[ld, wei]ght of this 3[3 drachmas]; crown of gold [of Athena N]ike, weight of this 33 drachmas;

tetradrachm [of gold, w]eight of this 7 drachmas, [$2\ {}^{1}/_{2}$ obols; onyx on] a gold ring, unweighed.

10.7 Perikles' Building Program

Plutarch *Perikles* 12.1–2

Perikles' opponents in the assembly criticized his building program as misuse of funds contributed by the allies; cf. docs. 8.23, 11.38. On whether tribute funded the Parthenon, see Kallet-Marx (1989) 252–66, who argues that the accusations are greatly exaggerated (the Parthenon itself probably only cost some 460–500 talents: Stanier (1953) 68–76; Kallet-Marx 261–62), and that there is no reason to suppose that tribute chiefly paid for the Parthenon. On the Parthenon frieze, see Castriota (1992) 184–229.

12.1 But what brought most pleasure and adornment to Athens, and the greatest amazement to the rest of mankind, and is the only evidence that the tales of Greece's power and ancient prosperity are not lies, was Perikles' construction of monuments. But this of all his measures was the one most maligned and slandered by his enemies in the assembly .... **12.2** 'Greece must be outraged,' they cried, 'and consider this an act of blatant tyranny, when she sees that with the contributions she has been compelled to make towards the war we are gilding and beautifying our city, like some vain woman decking herself in precious jewels and statues and temples worth thousands of talents.'

10.8 Care of Athens' Water Supply, c. 435

IG I^3 49

ATL II.D19. This inscription concerns Perikles and his sons Paralos and Xanthippos (and other unspecified sons; doc. 13.29) and the improvement of Athens' water supply, which was to receive first priority after the first-fruits to Athena; see Mattingly (1961) 164–66; Meritt & Wade-Gery (1963) 105–06; Thompson (1971) 329–32. Perikles and his sons had apparently offered to pay some of the costs themselves, but the people decided to use the money from the tribute instead. See Plut. *Them.* 31.1 for the bronze statue of a girl carrying water, which Themistokles dedicated out of the fines imposed on those convicted of tapping or diverting the public water; for superintendents of the springs, see Arist. *Pol.* 1321b 26; [Arist.] *Ath. Pol.* 43.1; *IG* II^2 215 & 338; cf. Plat. *Laws* 758e.

[...... Hipp]oniko[s proposed the motion: ....] eac[h .... are to receive pay of a d]rachma for [each day, and they are to look after the spring an]d the conduit [for the water .... Nikomachos proposed the amendment: that the] rest be as resolved [by the boule, ...] so that they flo[w .... so that for m]inimum cos[t .... the prytaneis who by lo]t are the first to hold offic[e, ... in the first of the] regular assemblies immed[iately after the sacred matters. .... is go]od for the people of the Athe[nians .... no]t occur and it shall turn out for the Athe[nians .... p]roposed the amendment: that the rest be as Nikoma[chos proposed; and that Perikles and Par]alos and Xanthippos and the (other) so[ns be commended; and expenditure (on this) shall be made from the money] that is pa[id] into the tribute of the Athenians, [once the goddess has rec]eived [from them] her accustomed portion vacat

THE WORKINGS OF ATHENIAN DEMOCRACY

The two most important democratic institutions were the assembly and the law-courts; in the fifth century all citizens over eighteen years of age were members of the assembly, but in the fourth century citizens had to be twenty years of age: Jones (1957) 108–116; Ehrenberg (1960) 54–59; Finley (1963) 67–73, (1981) 81–88, (1983) 70–84; Andrewes (1971) 184–205; Sinclair (1988) 114–27; Powell (1988) 280–92; Ober (1989) 7–8; Starr (1990) esp. 39–48; Stockton (1990) 67–84; Hansen (1991) 88–89. Pay for attending meetings of the assembly was possibly introduced shortly after 403 (Stockton (1990) 72; cf. [Arist.] *Ath. Pol.* 62.2). The assembly met regularly, 40 times a year, at least in the fourth century (*Ath. Pol.* 43.3), and approximately 6,000 citizens, the quota needed for an ostracism, appear to have regularly attended: Hansen (1976) 115–34, (1987) 20–24, (1991) 130–36; Stockton (1990) 71; however, less than 5,000 citizens, according to Thuc. VIII.72.1, were accustomed to attend during the Peloponnesian War. For the assembly in other Greek states, see Ehrenberg (1960) 52–55. A majority of Athenian citizens served at least once in their lives on the boule so it was a representative council; members could only serve twice and had to be at least 30 years of age (see Hansen (1980) 167–69); the qualifications of officials could be challenged beforehand through the dokimasia (Adeleye (1983) 295–306), and they had to submit to examination (euthyna) at the end of their term; pay for bouleutai was introduced possibly in the 450s and certainly by 412/11; in the fourth century it was 5 obols a day, with an extra obol for the prytaneis who dined in the tholos: Hansen (1991) 253; *Ath. Pol.* 62.2. See Finley (1983) 74; Jones (1957) 105–08; Ehrenberg (1960) 59–65; Rhodes (1972) 1–16; Hansen (1983) 1–23 (fourth century); Osborne (1985) 42–46, (1990) 266–67; Sinclair (1988) 84–88, 106–14; Powell (1988) 292–96; Stockton (1990) 84–95. Bouleutai, like other magistrates, wore a myrtle crown as a badge of office, and had seats of honour in the theatre (Rhodes (1972) 13; Stockton (1990) 86; see doc. 13.61). For citizens who preferred non-involvement in politics, see Carter (1986) esp. 99–130.

10.9 The Duties of a Citizen: Perikles' 'Funeral Oration'

Thucydides II.37.1–40.2

Perikles is here stressing the ideals of radical democracy, and praising the Athenian way of life, especially as opposed to the Spartan; he is perhaps more concerned with proclaiming an ideal worth fighting and dying for, rather than recording reality; see Loraux (1986), esp. 172–220; Carter (1986) 26–28; Ostwald (1986) 183; Sinclair (1988) 191–96; Ober (1989) 295; Raaflaub (1990) 56–57; Starr (1990) 36–37; Stockton (1990) 183–87; Harris (1992) 157–67; cf. doc. 13.27.

II.37.1 We possess a constitution which does not imitate the laws of our neighbours: in fact we are an example to others rather than imitating anyone else. And the constitution's name is democracy, because the majority manage its affairs, not just a few; as regards the laws, everybody is equal when private disputes are being settled, and as regards the criteria used to pick out anyone for office, what counts is not his belonging to a particular class, but his personal merit, while as regards poverty, as long as he can do something of value for the city, no one is prevented by obscurity from taking part in public life. **II.37.2** We conduct our political life with freedom, especially freedom from suspicion in respect of each other in our daily business, not being angry with our neighbour if he does as he pleases, not even giving him the sort of looks which, although they do no harm, still hurt people's feelings .... **II.38.2** And because of the city's size, all kinds of things are imported from all over the earth, so that it seems just as natural to us to enjoy the goods of other men as those of our own production .... **II.40.1** We love good things without extravagance and we love wisdom without cowardice; we use wealth as an opportunity for deeds rather than as something to boast about, and there is nothing disgraceful for anyone in admitting poverty — what is disgraceful is not taking steps to escape it. **II.40.2** In the same people there is a concern at the same time for their own affairs and for those of the city, and even those primarily concerned with their own business are not lacking in knowledge of the city's affairs; indeed, we are unique in considering the man who takes no part in the affairs of the city not as one who minds his own business, but as one who is totally useless.

10.10 The Amenities of the City of Athens, c. 425

[Xenophon] *Constitution of the Athenians* 2.9–10

In 1.13 the author complains that it is the wealthy who pay for liturgies, and sees a popular motive behind it, so that the poorer citizens become wealthy and the rich poorer. Finley (1981) 91 calls this treatise, 'a skilfully contrived political pamphlet, with an unconcealed oligarchic bias'; see Ostwald (1986) 188–91; doc. 11.20.

2.9 The people, realising that it is impossible for each of the poor to offer sacrifices, hold banquets, set up shrines and govern a great and beautiful city, have discovered a way of having sacrifices, shrines, festivals and sanctuaries. So the city sacrifices numerous victims at public expense, but it is the people who banquet and who are allocated the victims. **2.10** And while some of the wealthy have their own private gymnasia, baths and dressing-rooms, the people have built for their own use many wrestling-schools (palaistrai), dressing-rooms and bath-houses; and the mob enjoys far more of these than the aristocrats and the wealthy.

10.11 Liturgies

Lysias XXI *On a Charge of Taking Bribes* 1–5

The defendant, apparently on a charge of corruption, was eighteen in 411/0 and gives us an account of his public services down to 404/3; he states that in eight years he spent over 10 talents on liturgies. For liturgies in Athens, and the way in which the richer individuals financed certain state activities, often in this way buying influence and gratitude (cf. Lys. XXV.12–13), see Jones (1957) 100–01; Finley (1985) 150–53; Rhodes (1986b) 136–42; Stockton (1990) 107–08; cf. for Lysias himself, doc. 11.24. The eisphora was a levy imposed on the wealthy from time to time to meet special military costs. Davies (1967) 33–40 concludes that in the fourth century there were more than 97 annual liturgical appointments, and over 118 in a Great Panathenaic year, and this did not include some 300 trierarchs; cf. Gabrielsen (1987) 7; Osborne (1991) 130–31. For the liturgical class and the threshold for liability for liturgy service (3 talents), see Davies (1981) 15–37; cf. Rhodes (1982) 1–19; Carter (1986) 110–11.

1 I was judged of age in the archonship of Theopompos, and was appointed choregos for tragedy, spending 30 minas, and, two months later at the Thargelia, 2,000 drachmas where I won with a male chorus, as well as 800 drachmas in the archonship of Glaukippos on pyrrhic dancers at the Great Panathenaia. **2** In the same archonship I also won with a male chorus at the Dionysia, spending 5,000 drachmas including the dedication of the tripod, and, in the archonship of Diokles, 300 on a cyclic chorus at the Lesser Panathenaia. In the meantime I was trierarch for seven years and spent six talents. **3** And though I have incurred such expenses and been daily in danger on your behalf on service abroad, nevertheless I made contributions, one of 30 minas and one of 4,000 drachmas, to special taxes (eisphorai). And when I returned in the archonship of Alexias, I immediately produced games at the festival of Prometheus, and won a victory, after spending 12 minas. **4** And afterwards I was made choregos for a children's chorus and spent more than 15 minas. In the archonship of Eukleides, I was choregos for comedy for Kephisodoros and won, spending, including the dedication of the costumes, 16 minas. I was also choregos at the Lesser Panathenaia with beardless pyrrhic dancers and spent 7 minas. **5** I have won a victory with a trireme in the competition at Sounion, spending 15 minas; and this is apart from sacred embassies and processions of maidens in honour of Athena Polias (arrephoriai) and other such duties, in which my expenditure has been more than thirty minas. If I had wanted to perform my liturgies according to the actual regulations, I would have spent less than a quarter of what I have enumerated.

10.12 Assembly Procedure

Aristophanes *Acharnians* 17–27

Though the *Acharnians* was performed in 425 during the Archidamian War when many country-dwellers were cramped together in the city, they still apparently had to resort to the vermilion-painted rope to pull people into the assembly; this perhaps shows the lack of attention of the people to public duty (Carter (1986) 78), though Powell (1988) 284; Sinclair (1988) 116 suggest that instead it implies problems with starting on time; Powell 284 cites the statement of a scholiast that anyone who was smeared with paint by the rope had to pay a fine. The meetings began early in the morning with religious preliminaries, and were generally over by midday: Stockton (1990) 72; Hansen (1991) 136–37; cf. Ar. *Ekkl.* 122–31, for the wearing of wreaths by speakers at the assembly and the initial lustral purification. For the archers keeping order, see Rhodes (1972) 146, (1986a) 106; doc. 11.7; in Plat. *Prot.* 319b, Socrates remarks that if anyone tried to advise the assembly, and the citizens thought that the speaker was not an expert in that area, they would jeer and boo until he sat down or was forcibly removed on the order of the prytaneis. In the fifth century the Athenians were seated, either on the ground, or perhaps on cushions: Hansen (1991) 137 (cf. doc. 5.17); voting was by show of hands (cf. doc. 11.22), except in exceptional cases: Hansen (1990) 225; Osborne (1990) 266–67.

Dikaiopolis (a die-hard countryman):
Never, from the time when I began to wash
Have I been so tormented by soap under my eyebrows
As now, when a regular assembly is due to be held
At dawn, and the Pnyx here is deserted —
People are chatting in the agora and here and there

Avoiding the vermilion rope.
Even the prytaneis haven't come, but they'll arrive
Late, and then jostle as you'd expect
To try and get on the front bench,
All pouring in together; but that there'll be peace,
They don't care at all — O city, city!

10.13 The Trial of the Generals after Arginousai

Xenophon *Hellenika* I.7.9–15

In 406 the Athenians sent every available man (including slaves: doc. 11.15) to aid the Athenian fleet blockaded at Mytilene by the Spartans. They were victorious at Arginousai, but a storm prevented the generals from rescuing those cast into the sea. Six of the eight generals involved returned to Athens, and they were brought before the assembly. When darkness fell (so votes by hands could not be counted), the boule was instructed to draw up a probouleuma (preliminary decree) for the following day's assembly; an enemy of the generals, Kallixenos, secured passage in the boule of a resolution that the assembly should simply vote to acquit or condemn, by ballot, all six defendants together without further discussion; despite Socrates' refusal as one of the prytaneis to cooperate (cf. doc. 9.38), the generals were convicted and executed, one of them being Perikles' son by Aspasia. Note the probouleutic function of the boule, and the fact that popular feeling in the assembly could override normal procedures. The Athenians soon regretted what they had done: Xen. *Hell.* I.7.35; doc. 9.38. See Andrewes (1974) 112–22; Ostwald (1986) 62–66, 431–45; Sealey (1987) 49–50, 86; Sinclair (1988) 169–73; Starr (1990) 47–48; Bauman (1990) 69–73; see also Lang (1990) 24–29, who discusses the political affiliations of all six generals.

I.7.9 Then they held an assembly, to which the boule presented its proposal, Kallixenos bringing the motion as follows: since the Athenians have heard both those who brought charges against the generals and the generals' defence in the previous assembly, they are all to vote by tribes; and two urns will be provided for each tribe; and for each tribe a herald shall proclaim that whoever thinks the generals to be guilty of not picking up those who had won the naval battle shall place his vote in the first urn, and whoever thinks them to be not guilty, in the second. **I.7.10** And if it is decided that they are guilty, they shall be punished with death and handed over to the Eleven and their property confiscated, and a tithe to belong to the goddess .... **I.7.12** Euryptolemos and Peisianaktos and some others brought a charge against Kallixenos of having made an unconstitutional proposal. And some of the people commended this, but the majority shouted that it would be dreadful if the people were not allowed to do what they wanted. **I.7.13** In addition, when Lykiskos proposed the motion that these men should be judged by the same vote as the generals unless they withdrew their charge, the mob again created an uproar, and they were forced to withdraw their charges. **I.7.14** Some of the prytaneis declared that they would not put the question to the vote contrary to law, but Kallixenos again mounted the speakers' platform and made the same accusations against them. And they (the crowd) shouted that all who refused should be taken to court. **I.7.15** The prytaneis, terrified, all agreed to put the question to the vote except for Socrates son of Sophroniskos; he declared that he would not do anything against the law.

10.14 Public Salaries in Fifth Century Athens

[Aristotle] *Athenaion Politeia* 24.3

The *Ath. Pol.* is here recording Aristeides' policy towards the populace, resulting in their 'taking control of the empire'. Finley (1985) 172–73 calls the arithmetic here preposterous; nevertheless the passage outlines the essential quality of the Athenian system, payment to citizens for performing their citizen duties. Immediately prior to the revolution of 411, participation in public affairs was supposedly limited to not more than 5,000 (Thuc. VIII.65.3; Sealey (1987) 6, 133). Sinclair (1988) 201–02 discusses the amount of money expended on state pay in the later fifth century; see also Burke (1992) 217–18; Hansen (1980) 151–73 for the number of magistracies in Athens, who argues that the *Ath. Pol.* is correct in numbering them at 700. The 'prytaneion' refers to those who dined at public expense; instead of 'ships carrying the tributes' perhaps 'ships carrying the guards' should be read; the phrase 'from the tribute collections, the internal taxes and the allies' also reads strangely as the allies and tribute are surely synonymous; for the problems involved in the readings of this passage, see Rhodes 300–09.

24.3 They also gave the masses a comfortable standard of living, as Aristeides had proposed. For it came about that more than 20,000 people were maintained from the tribute contributions, the taxes and the allies. For there were 6,000 jurors, 1,600 citizen archers, plus 1,200 cavalry, 500 members of the boule, 500 guards of the dockyards, plus 50 guards on the acropolis, about 700 officials at home, and about 700 abroad. In addition, when they afterwards went to war, there were 2,500 hoplites, 20 guard-ships, and other ships carrying the tributes with 2,000 men chosen by lot, as well as the prytaneion, and orphans, and jailers; for all of these received their maintenance from the state.

10.15 A Disabled Tradesman

Lysias XXIV *On the Refusal of a Grant to an Invalid* 6

This was probably written after the restoration of the democracy in 403. Every year the boule examined the claims of disabled persons, and, if they could show cause, would allow them a pension of an obol a day. In this case a small tradesman who ran a shop has been accused of not being disabled. Late in the 4th century eligibility for public support was restricted to those with property less than 300 drachmas (3 minas): [Arist.] *Ath. Pol.* 49.4, who states that the person should be so disabled as to be unable to work; Jameson (1977–78) 122n.6. Clearly this tradesman is very poor, and not to have slave help appears unusual even at this economic level; but see Wood (1983) 45–47 for a discussion of the speech's discrepancies, which perhaps mean that it may not be a genuine speech by Lysias. Rhodes (1972) 175–76 discusses the boule's role in scrutinising such cases.

My father left me nothing, and I ceased maintaining my mother on her death only two years ago, and I do not yet have any children to look after me. I possess a trade from which I can obtain only slight support, which I work at with difficulty, and I am as yet unable to procure someone to relieve me of this. I have no other income besides this and if you deprive me of it, I am in danger of ending up in the most dreadful position.

10.16 The Delights of Jury Pay

Aristophanes *Wasps* 605–12

The *Wasps*, performed in 422, is in many respects a satire on the jury-courts. Anyone over 30 could serve as a juror, and the official number of jurors was 6,000 (600 from each tribe); see *Wasps* 662 (doc. 10.45), [Arist.] *Ath. Pol.* 24.3, 63.3. At this period, jurors were assigned by lot to one of the ten courts, and the juries were selected by lot from those who turned up on the day; Sinclair (1988) 225 suggests that the courts sat between 150–60 and 200 days a year (not on assembly or festival days). A full court for important public cases needed 501 jurors, private suits had 201 or 401. Perikles introduced jury pay of 2 obols a day (doc. 8.22), which was raised to 3 obols probably in 425 or 424 (Andrewes (1971) 204; Ostwald (1986) 222–23; Todd (1990) 155). A family of four, living frugally, might have subsisted on less than 2 and a half obols a day for their food in the late fifth century: Markle (1985) 277–81, 293–97; Sinclair (1988) 129; Todd 156–58; cf. Jones (1957) 135. Jury pay would have been a useful source of support for the elderly, would have allowed craftsmen some leisure to serve on juries (Markle 266), and would have been acceptable to farmers who would not lose income (Todd 168–69); but it would not have been sufficient as a sole source of income. For keeping small change in one's mouth (and swallowing it), see also *Birds* 502–03. Philokleon is speaking here.

But the most enjoyable thing of all of these, which I had forgotten,
Is when I get home with my pay, and everyone joins
In welcoming me back for my money, and first of all my daughter
Gives me a wash and rubs my feet with oil and bends down to kiss me
And calls me daddy, and fishes out the three obols with her tongue,
While my wife brings me a barley cake to win me over
And sits down beside me and presses me: 'Eat this,
Try this.'

10.17 A Satire on Jury-Court Procedure

Aristophanes *Wasps* 836–62, 894–97

Bdelykleon (Kleon-hater), whose father Philokleon (Kleon-lover) is a confirmed and obsessive juror, tries to keep him from the courts by setting up a mock trial at home. For Kleon as a dog, see doc. 9.17; his deme was Kydathenaion (cf. line 895). Labes is meant to represent the general Laches; this is a parody of Laches' trial before a heliastic court for embezzlement during his generalship in Sicily in 426/5 (Ostwald (1986) 212). The courts in the later fifth century possessed some political jurisdiction in the examination of the incoming and outgoing magistrates (dokimasiai and euthynai), who may have comprised some 700 (doc. 10.14): see Ostwald (1986) 66–77; Stockton (1990) 96–103; Hansen (1990) 233–39; Starr (1990) 25–27, 46; cf. Rhodes (1972) 166–71. Aristophanes is here satirising Kleon's control of the jury-courts and his use of them against opponents (cf. Bauman (1990) 49–60): Philokleon is itching to inflict a harsh penalty by drawing a long furrow in his voting-tablet (cf. *Wasps* 106–08); if the defendant was found guilty the jurors then voted between the penalties proposed by the prosecutor and the defendant (cf. doc. 9.39). The jurors were a feature of Athenian life: in *Clouds* 208, Strepsiades refuses to believe that Athens is on the map he is shown because he cannot see the jurors.

Bdelykleon: Whatever is the matter?
Sosias (a slave): Why, that dog Labes just
Rushed into the kitchen, snatched up

A fresh Sicilian cheese and ate the lot!
Bdelykleon: So this is the first case to be brought before
840 My father: you can be there as prosecutor.
Sosias: Not I indeed; actually the other dog has said
That he will prosecute, if someone brings the indictment.
Bdelykleon: Very well, bring them both here.
Sosias: I'll certainly do that.
Bdelykleon: What's that?
Philokleon: The pig-pen from the Hearth.
Bdelykleon: Do you want to commit sacrilege?
Philokleon: No, it's so that
846 I can begin 'from the hearth' (from the start) and squash someone.
But come on, hurry up; I have my eye on condemning a defendant.
Bdelykleon: Hold on while I get the notice-boards and charge-sheets.
Philokleon: Damn it, you're wasting time and driving me mad with these delays.
850 I'm longing to plough furrows in the space on my voting-tablet!
Bdelykleon: There you are.
Philokleon: Call the case.
Bdelykleon: Very well. Who's
The first?
Philokleon: Blast! I'm cross
That I forgot to bring out the urns.
Bdelykleon: Hey, where are you dashing off to?
Philokleon: To get the urns
Bdelykleon: There's no need.
855 I brought these small jugs.
Philokleon: Splendid. Now we have everything
We need, except a water-clock.
Bdelykleon: Well, what's this? (he produces a chamber-pot) Not a water-clock?
Philokleon: You've provided everything, and all expeditiously (like an Athenian).
Bdelykleon: Let someone bring fire as quickly as possible
861 And myrtle-wreaths and incense from indoors,
So we can first pray to the gods.

The indictment:
Bdelykleon: Now hear the indictment. Prosecution
895 By The Dog of Kydathenaion against Labes of Aixone
That he wronged one Sicilian cheese by eating it
All by himself. Penalty a figwood dog-collar.

CITIZENSHIP

The Greek word for citizenship was politeia, which also meant constitution and the body of citizen members: citizenship was the basis on which the constitution rested. There were clear political and legal distinctions between citizens on the one hand and metics and slaves on the other; one of the more severe punishments for a citizen was atimia, or loss of citizen rights: Ehrenberg (1960) 39–42; MacDowell (1978) 67–75; see Finley (1963) 48–50, for the minority that constituted the community proper in a city state. A citizen in Athens had the right to attend the assembly, and be a magistrate or juror when over thirty, own property and attend all festivals, and had a privileged position at law: Hansen (1991) 97–99. Before Kleisthenes' reforms every citizen belonged to a phratry, which was the criterion for citizenship; nevertheless in the fifth century, it is still reasonable to assume that all or most citizens belonged to a phratry as well as a deme, as grants of citizenship included the right to choose one's own phratry (Flower (1985) 234; doc. 9.27; cf. Davies (1977–78) 109–10). Many Athenians would also have belonged to clubs, hetaireiai, some of which were political, some purely social; see Thuc. VIII.54.4; Rhodes (1986b) 138–39; Sinclair (1988) 141–45; Osborne (1990) 268–77. Starr (1990) 60 sees the hetaireiai as primarily social ('to celebrate those symposia depicted on Athenian vases with drinking cups and attendant scantily clad girls') except in the upheaval of 411, when they openly displayed their upper-class political sympathies.

10.18 Perikles Changes the Law on Citizenship

[Aristotle] *Athenaion Politeia* 26.4

More rigorous regulations regarding citizenship were brought in by Perikles, perhaps because of the growing size of the citizen body, or so that Athenians could find citizen husbands for their daughters. There were possibly a large number of mixed marriages and dubious cases of citizenship at this point; see Humphreys (1974) 88–95, who believes that the law's main aim was to stop the contracting of marriage-alliances with leading families in other states (*contra* Walters (1983) 329–32, who suggests it was to preclude the legitimacy of sons of Athenian fathers and slave women); see Patterson (1981) *passim* for an in-depth discussion; Walters (1983) 314–36. MacDowell argues (1976) 88–91, that providing both parents were Athenians nothoi (bastards) could perhaps be citizens after 451/0, though they were excluded from the father's phratry, and from his property if there were legitimate children; cf. Walters (1983) 317. But see Davies (1977–78) 105–21; Sealey (1984) 111–33; Just (1989) 55–62; and Patterson (1990) 40–73, who believes that nothoi were non-citizens from the time of Solon.

26.4 In the archonship of Antidotos (451/0), because of the number of citizens, it was decided on a motion of Perikles that a person should not have citizen rights unless both of his parents had been citizens.

10.19 The Plataeans Become Athenian Citizens

[Demosthenes] LIX *Against Neaira* 104

The Plataeans allied themselves with Athens in 519, and fought with them against the Persians at Marathon. [Demosthenes] quotes a decree conferring citizenship on the Plataeans, after Plataea was destroyed by Sparta in 427 (Thuc. III.68.3); rather than settle in Athens, most of them set up a new city at Skione; see MacDowell (1978) 71.

Hippokrates proposed the motion: that the Plataeans are to be Athenians from today, with full rights like the rest of the Athenians, and share in all the things which the Athenians share, both sacred and profane, but they shall not be eligible for any priesthood or rite which belongs to a particular family or the nine archonships, but their descendants shall be. And the Plataeans shall be distributed among the demes and tribes. Once they have been so distributed, it will no longer be possible for any Plataean to become an Athenian, unless he is awarded it by the Athenian people.

10.20 Registration as a Deme Member

[Aristotle] *Athenaion Politeia* 42.1–2

Youths were registered as deme members after their 18th birthday, when the deme members voted as to whether they were the correct age, and whether they were eligible for membership; if anyone was judged to be ineligible as not-free, he was allowed to appeal to the court. In the fourth century, the ephebes at the age of eighteen had two years of military service before being entered on the register of citizens (the pinax ekklesiastikos) of their deme: Garland (1990) 183–87; Hansen (1991) 88–89. For deme meetings and officials, see Osborne (1990) 268–71, cf. 277–85; for the supportive links between members of a deme, see doc. 8.22 (for Kimon); Rhodes (1986b) 135–36; for religious activities in the demes, see Mikalson (1977) 424–35; Sourvinou-Inwood (1990) 311–16; Zaidman & Pantel (1992) 81–85; Osborne (1985) 178–81; Whitehead (1986) 176–222; cf. the Plotheia decree *IG* I^3 258 (doc. 5.19, cf. 5.20).

42.1 The present arrangement of the constitution is as follows: those whose parents have both been citizens have the right to be citizens, and they are enrolled amongst the demesmen at the age of eighteen. When they are enrolled, the demesmen decide by vote under oath concerning them, first if they appear to be the legal age, and if they do not appear to be, they again return to the status of boys, and secondly if the candidate is free and has been born in accordance with the laws. When they decide that someone is not free, he appeals to the law-court, and the demesmen choose five men from amongst themselves as his accusers, and if it appears that he had no right to be enrolled, the city sells him (into slavery); but if he wins his case, the demesmen are compelled to enrol him. **42.2** After this the boule examines those who have been enrolled, and if anyone appears to be younger than eighteen years, it fines the demesmen who enrolled him. When the young men (ephebes) have been examined, their fathers assemble by tribes, take an oath, and elect three of their tribesmen over the age of forty, whom they consider to be the best and most suitable to supervise the young men, and from these the people elects by vote one from each tribe as guardian and from the other Athenians a superintendent for all of them.

10.21 Phratry Membership

Philochoros *FGH* 328 F35a (Photios s.v. ὀργεῶνες)

Phratries were primarily concerned with the entitlement of potential members to membership and the ritual ceremonies which accompanied the acceptance of new members. The orgeones are members of the phratry, but their exact nature is unclear; homogalaktes means 'men of the same milk' (cf. Arist. *Pol.* 1252b 16–18), gennetai 'members of clans (gene)'; see Andrewes (1961) 1–15; Lacey (1968) 25–27; Frost (1976) 69; Osborne (1990) 272, 274; Sourvinou-Inwood (1990) 316–17. Zaidman & Pantel (1992) 88–89 suggest that associations of orgeones, which were upper-class in origin, offered sacrifices at their own expense on the altars of gods and heroes in Attica. This law possibly dates to 451/0. For phratries in Attica in 621/0, see doc. 3.3.

Philochoros has also written concerning the orgeones: 'the phratry members are to be compelled to accept both the orgeones and the homogalaktes, whom we call gennetai.'

10.22 Of Zeus of the Phratry, 396/5

IG II² 1237 lines 1–2, 9–38, 114–26

The phratriarch was the president of the phratry, probably of the Dekeleians in this case, the Demotionidai being a privileged clan (genos) within that phratry. The Apatouria was an Ionian festival (Hdt. I.147.2) lasting for three days during Pyanopsion at which children were presented to the phratry members as new members. On the first day (Dorpia) the fellow-phratry members feasted together; the second day was given over to sacrificing, especially in honour of Zeus Phratrios and Athena Phratria; and on the third day (koureotis) young boys were admitted to the phratry, their change of status being celebrated by sacrifices (the meion and koureion), both of which probably took place on this day. The koureion sacrifice accompanied a dedication of a lock of the boy's hair to Artemis to celebrate his passage out of childhood, hence the name: Davies (1977–78) 109; Tyrrell (1984) 68–69; Garland (1990) 179–80; Zaidman & Pantel (1992) 66. According to Andok. I.127 the father had to swear on the altar that he was introducing a legitimate (gnesios) son to the phratry; Davies (1977–78) 109n.27 suggests that this may reflect a public law of the state imposed on phratries, possibly Perikles' citizenship law: see Just (1989) 56–60 for the criteria for membership of a phratry. Line 120 makes it clear that the mother's name and her father's name and deme have to be recorded; for the association of women with phratries, see Gould (1980) 40–42, who argues persuasively against the birth of female-members being declared to the phratry of their father; cf. Golden (1985) 9–13. Andrewes (1961) 1–15 suggests that there were a large number of phratries, probably as many as there were aristocratic gene; however, the statement of the *Ath. Pol.* F2, that originally in Athens there were 4 tribes, 12 phratries and 360 gene, is not generally taken to be historically correct. Flower (1985) 232–35 takes *IG* II² 2344, a list of twenty phratry members, to be the dedication of a full phratry (rather than of a 'thiasos' within a phratry), and concludes that by the end of the fifth century there may well have been a very large number of phratries in Athens (but see Hedrick (1989) 126–35). For this inscription, and for phratry records, see Thompson (1968) 51–68; Sealey (1987) 13–16; Osborne (1990) 271–72; cf. Sourvinou-Inwood (1990) 316–20; Zaidman & Pantel (1992) 86–88. For phratries in other states, see docs. 1.24, 1.31, 10.28.

(1) Of Zeus of the Phratry. The priest Theodoros son of Euphantides vv inscribed and set up the stele. The priest is to be given the following perquisites from sacrifices: (5) from every meion a thigh, a side-cut, an ear, and three obols of silver; v from every koureion a thigh, a side-cut, an ear, a cake made from a choinix measure of flour, a half-kotyle of wine and a drachma of silver. vacat (9) The following was resolved by the members of the phratry, when Phormio was archon of the Athenians and Pantakles of Oion was phratriarch. Hierokles proposed the motion: all those who have not been adjudicated on in accordance with the law of the Demotionidai (15) the members of the phratry shall immediately adjudicate on, swearing by Zeus of the Phratry and taking their ballot from the altar; whoever appears to have been introduced without being entitled to be a phratry member, the priest (20) and the phratriarch are to delete his name from the tablet of the Demotionidai and the copy, and the man who introduced the person who has been rejected shall be liable to pay a fine of a hundred drachmas sacred to Zeus of the Phratry, and this money (25) the priest and the phratriarch are to exact or be liable to pay the fine themselves. In future the adjudication (on new members) is to take place in the year after the sacrifice of the koureion, on the koureotis day of the Apatouria.

The (phratry members) are to take their ballot from the altar. (30) If anyone wishes to appeal to the Demotionidai regarding the grounds on which he has been rejected, he is allowed to do so; the house of the Dekeleians shall elect as judges five men over thirty years of age, (35) and the phratriarch and the priest shall take their oaths to undertake their duties most justly and not to allow anyone who is not entitled to phratry membership to belong to the phratry .... (114) Menexenos proposed the amendment: that the rest be resolved by the phratry members regarding the introduction of the children in accordance with the previous decrees, but, so that the members of the phratry may know which men are going to introduce (new members), there is to be recorded with the phratriarch in the first year (of the child's life) or in that of the koureion his name and his father's name and deme, and his (120) mother's name and her father's name and deme, and the phratriarch is to make a record of the names submitted and set [this up in a place which the Dek]eleians frequent, [and the priest] is to record it on a [white-washed] notice-boa[rd] and set it up in the sanctuary (125) of Leto. And [this] d[ecree is to be recorded on the] stele ....

CITY STATES AND THEIR LAWS

10.23 A Law from Dreros in Crete, 650–600

Meiggs & Lewis 2

This may be the earliest surviving Greek law on stone, and is the earliest which has survived complete. It forbids the repeated tenure of the office of kosmos, probably the chief magistracy, within ten years. The demioi may be financial supervisors and the twenty perhaps the council. The use of the word city may, or may not, imply the participation of the assembly; cf. Starr (1990) 6.

(1) May god be kind (?). The city has decided as follows: when a man has been kosmos, for ten years (2) that same man shall not be kosmos; if he should become kosmos, wha[te]ver judgements he gives he shall himself owe double, and (3) he shall lose rights to office as long as he lives, and whatever he does as kosmos shall be nothing. (4) The swearers shall be the kosmos, and the demioi and the twenty of the c[it]y.

10.24 The Popular Boule at Chios, 575–550

Meiggs & Lewis 8C

The role of the people has already by this point become considerable, and the popular boule can apparently judge appeals; cf. doc. 3.19 for this inscription's possible relevance to the council of 400 of Solon at Athens; Starr (1990) 9. The Hebdomaia was a festival to Apollo celebrated on the seventh of every month.

(1) Let him appeal to the boule of the people; on the third day after the Hebdomaia, (5) the boule of the people with power to inflict penalties[1] is to assemble, with fifty men chosen from each tribe; it shall transact the other business (10) which concerns

the people and in particular all the lawsui[ts whi]ch ari[se] subject to appeal in the month (15) [....]

[1] Taking ἐπιθώιος actively with ML rather than passively 'under penalty of a fine for non-attendance', as with *LSJ*^{9} 635.

10.25 Immunity from Indirect Taxation at Cyzicus

SIG^{3} 4, lines 5–12

This sixth century inscription grants exemption (ateleia) from certain indirect taxes to the descendants of two citizens who died for their country. It was reinscribed in the first century BC, and was therefore presumably still current; see Nixon & Price (1990) 145, who translate the 'nautos' as a tax on the movement of goods by boat; Starr (1977) 174–75 on indirect taxes.

(5) In the prytany of Maiandrios. The city has given the son of Medikes and the sons of Aisepos and their descendants exemption from taxes and maintenance in the prytaneion, with the exception of the nautos, the tax for the use of the public scales, the tax on the sale of horses, the tax of twenty-five per cent, and the tax on the sale of slaves; (10) they shall be exempt from all the others; the people swore about these over the sacrificial victims. The city gave this stele to Manes son of Medikes.

10.26 A Lokrian Community Settles New Territory

Meiggs & Lewis 13 A & C

This law dated to c. 525–500, on a bronze plaque from western Lokris, deals with the regulations concerning the settlement of new territory, including rules to protect the new settlers; it appears in particular to define pasturage-rights, but the term epinomia may instead refer to inheritance, as translated here; text C has also been inserted as an omitted line (see ML p.23). The lots are only allowed to be sold in cases of real need, which implies the desire to keep the property (kleros) in the family, and the colony, not the mother-city, is to have the right of decision as to whether they need reinforcements under the necessity of war. The fact that they already have temples, elders and a citizen assembly suggests that these are not new settlers from another area, but members of an existing settlement who are assimilating a new stretch of agricultural land; see Buck (1955) no. 59; *LSAG* 104–06, with pl.14; Larson (1968) 54; Austin & Vidal-Nacquet (1977) 231–33; Graham (1983) 56–57, 65.

(1) This law concerning the land shall be in force for the division of the plain of Hyla and Liskara, both the separate lots and the public ones. The right of inheritance (epinomia) shall belong to the parents and the son; if there is no son, to the daughter; if there is no daughter, (5) to the brother; if there is no brother, by degree of relationship let a man inherit according to the law. If there is no (such man), the one who inherits (?) shall have the right to give the property to whomever he wishes. Whatever a man plants, he shall be immune from its seizure. Unless under compulsion of war a majority of the one hundred and one men chosen from the best citizens decides that at least two hundred fighting-men are to be brought in as additional settlers, whoever (10) proposes a division (of land) or puts it to the vote

in the council of elders or in the city or in the select council or who causes civil dissension concerning the division of land, he and his family for all time shall be accursed and his property confiscated and his house be razed to the ground just as for the law on murder. This law shall be sacred to Pythian Apollo and the gods who dwell with him; on the man who transgresses it may there be destruction for himself and his family and his property, but may (the god) be propitious to the man who observes it. The la[nd] shall belong [half] to the previous settlers, half to the additional settlers. Let them distribute the valley portions; exchange shall be valid, but the exchange shall take place before the magistrate.

10.27 A Treaty between Oiantheia and Chaleion

Buck (1955) no. 58

This treaty between two small states of western Lokris is recorded on a bronze tablet of the mid-fifth century. The first document guarantees reciprocal rights to the citizens of each when on the other's territory, specifically the prevention of seizure of persons or property in enforcement of existing claims on the other party; the second consists of regulations regarding the legal rights of foreigners. The proxenos ('guest-friend') presumably bears witness that the foreigner has been resident there for a month or more; Austin & Vidal-Nacquet (1977) 246–47, however, translate 'witness'. For symbola, agreements between pairs of states, originally agreements on legal aid to be granted to the citizens of one state in the other state, which then became primarily commercial treaties, see Tod I.34; *LSAG* 106, with pl.15; Ehrenberg (1960) 104–05; Larsen (1968) 54–57; MacDowell (1978) 220–21; Finley (1985) 161–62.

A

No one is to carry off an Oiantheian foreigner from Chaleion territory, nor a Chaleian from Oiantheian territory, nor his property, even if anyone is making a seizure; but the person who has made the seizure may be seized with impunity. The property of foreigners may be seized at sea with impunity, except from the harbour of either city. If anyone makes a seizure unlawfully, (the penalty is) four drachmas; and if he holds what has been seized for more than ten days he shall be liable to pay half as much again as the value of what he seized. If a Chaleian resides in Oiantheia or an Oiantheian in Chaleion for more than a month he shall be subject to the legal procedure there. If the proxenos acts falsely as proxenos, he shall be fined double.

B

If those who judge suits concerning foreigners are divided in opinion, the foreigner who brings the suit shall choose jurors from the best citizens, exclusive of his proxenos and private host, in suits involving a mina or more, fifteen men, in those involving less, nine men. If a citizen brings a suit against another citizen in accordance with the treaty, the magistrates shall chose the jurors from the best citizens after having sworn the five-fold oath. The jurors shall take the same oath and the majority is to prevail.

10.28 An Eleian Law c. 500

Buck (1955) no. 61

This law appears to free from liability the family and phratry of an accused person, and to prevent his maltreatment.

(1) The law (rhetra) of the Eleians. The phratry, family and property (of an accused man) shall be immune. If anyone makes a charge (against them), he shall be prosecuted as in (the case of) an Eleian. If he who has the highest office and the magistrates (basileis) do not exact the fines, each of those who fails to exact them shall pay a fine of ten minas sacred to Olympian Zeus. (5) The hellanodikas shall enforce this, and the board of public workers (demiourgoi) shall enforce the other fines (which have not been exacted); if the hellanodikas does not enforce it, he shall pay double in his accounting. If anyone maltreats a man who is accused of a charge involving a fine, he shall be lia[bl]e to the fine of ten minas, if he does so intentionally. And the secretary of the phratry shall incur the sa[m]e (fine), [if] he [wr]ong[s an]yone. The t[a]blet sacred at Olympia.

10.29 A Sixth Century Eleian Law

Buck (1955) no. 64

This is the conclusion of an inscription, the first tablet of which has been lost. Compare the procedure in Sparta (docs. 6.3–4), where the assembly was not allowed to propose changes to motions. The restoration of the last sentence is uncertain.

If he commits fornication (?) in the sacred precinct, he shall pay the penalty by sacrificing an ox and complete purification, and the official (?) (thearos) the s(a)me. If anyone gives judgement contrary to what is written, the judgement shall be invalid, and the rhetra of the people shall be final in judging; anything of what is written may be amended if it seems better with regard to the g(o)d, by withdrawing or adding with (the approval of) the whole boule of (f)ive hundred and the people in full assembly. (Chan)ges may be made three (t)imes (?), (5) adding or withdrawing.

10.30 An Alliance between Elis and Heraia c. 500

Meiggs & Lewis 17

Heraia is in western Arcadia; this was passed prior to Elis' synoecism. For a similar alliance, cf. doc. 6.36, a Spartan treaty with Aetolia.

(1) The covenant (rhetra) of the Eleians and the Heraians. There shall be an alliance for one hundred years, starting with this year. If there shall be any need either of word or deed, they shall combine with each other both in oth<er> matters and in (5) war. If they do not combine, the offenders are to pay a talent of silver sacred to Olympian Zeus. If anyone offends against these writings, whether private individual, official, or the state, he is to be liable to the penalty (10) written here.

10.31 An Treaty Between Knossos and Tylissos c. 450

Meiggs & Lewis 42B, lines 2–17

This is part of an inscription defining relations between Argos and the two Cretan states Knossos and Tylissos; Tylissos, possibly a dependency of Argos, is being protected against Knossos; the Argives do not have the power of veto when the two cities are in agreement, but are able to break a tied vote; for a discussion, see Merrill (1991) 16–25. This fragment, found at Argos, deals with the sharing of plunder and the export of goods.

[The Tylissians ma]y plunder the la[nd of th]e A[ch]a[rnaians] exce[pt] for th[e parts bel]onging to the city [of the Knossians]. What[ever] we both win together [from the enem]y, (the Tylissians) shall in a div[ision] have a third part of everything [taken by l]and, and th[e] half of everything t[hat is taken by] sea. The Knossians shall have the t[it]he of whatever we seize in co[mm]on; the fin[e]st of the spoils shall be s[e]nt to Delphi by both jointly, and the rest shall be dedicated [to Ares at Knos]sos by both jointly. Ex[port shall be all]owed from Knossos to Tylissos and from Tylis[sos to Knosso]s; but i[f] (a Tylissian) exports beyond, let him pay as much [as the Kn]ossians, and goods from Tylissos may be exported whever[ever he desires.] [T]o Poseidon the Knossia[n priest shall sa]crifice at Iutos. To Hera in the Heraion [bot]h shall sacrifice [j]ointly a [c]ow, and they shall sacrifice before the Hyakinth[ia ....]

LEAGUES, UNIONS AND FEDERATIONS

Synoecism (synoikismos) is the amalgamation of communities to form a single city-state. According to Cavanagh (1991) 106 in classical sources the term synoecism can mean simply the collaboration of different groups in the founding of a city (Thuc. III.93.1 (doc. 1.19), cf. I.24.2, VI.5.1) but, as here, can also mean the foundation of a larger state by merging a number of independent communities (cf. Thuc. III.2.3); for synoecism in Sicily, see Hdt. VII.156.2–3. For the synoecism of Eleian cities into one community as late as 471/0, see Diod. XI.54.1; cf. doc. 10.1. For fifth and fourth century federations and leagues, see Ehrenberg (1960) 122–31; Rhodes (1986a) 172–220.

10.32 The Synoecism of Athens

Thucydides II.15.1–2

Thucydides is here describing how, according to Athenian tradition, Theseus reorganized Attica, making Athens the single political centre; see Humphreys (1978) 130–31; Sealey (1987) 109; Starr (1990) 7; Hornblower (1991) 262–64. For the Synoikia, a festival in honour of Athena celebrating Athens' political union, see Parke (1977) 31–32, who believes this to have been an archaic rite; doc. 5.20, for the festival as celebrated in the deme Skambonidai in the mid-fifth century; and *LSCG Suppl.* 10A for the fact that the festival, even in the last years of the fifth century, appears to have been celebrated by the phylobasileis (heads of tribes) of the four pre-Kleisthenic tribes.

II.15.1 In the time of Kekrops and the first kings down to Theseus, the people of Attica had always lived in cities, each of which had their own administrative building (prytaneion) and officials, and unless there were some danger they did not join in consultation with the king, but each of them would govern itself and make its own decisions; and some of these on occasion actually made war on Athens, like Eumolpos and the Eleusinians against Erechtheus. **II.15.2** But when Theseus became king, being an intelligent as well as a powerful man, he organized the country primarily by dissolving the council chambers (bouleuteria) and governments of the other cities and bringing them together into the present city, making one council chamber and one seat of administration, and compelling everyone to belong to this one city, though they could look after their own affairs just as before. With everyone uniting in it, it was a great city that was handed down by Theseus to posterity; and he inaugurated the Synoikia (celebration of union), a festival in honour of the goddess, which the Athenians still keep at public expense even today.

10.33 The Boeotian Federation

Thucydides V.38.1–3

Thebes took the lead of the Boeotian cities in about the seventh century; under Theban supremacy there was a federal army under the command of boeotarchs (commanders of Boeotia); Thebes was only one of 9, later 10, league members, but there were 11 representational districts, of which each supplied to the federal army approximately 1,000 hoplites and 100 cavalry, and one boeotarch and 60 councillors to the federal government. The autonomy of the individual cities was limited by the compulsion to adopt a certain moderately oligarchic constitution; the government of the individual cities, and it seems of the league as well, was in the hands of a council, divided into four sections, which took it in turns to transact business: Larsen (1955) 31–40, 45–46; Ehrenberg (1960) 123–24; Hdt. VI.108 (for the events of 519). This passage relates to 421/0.

V.38.1 Meanwhile the boeotarchs, Corinthians, Megarians and envoys from Thrace resolved to exchange oaths with each other that they would come to each other's help on any occasion when requested, and that they would not make war or peace without common consent, and that the Boeotians and Megarians (who were acting in concert) should conclude a treaty with the Argives. **V.38.2** But before the oaths were taken the boeotarchs communicated these proposals to the four councils of the Boeotians, which have the supreme authority, and advised them that oaths should be exchanged with all the cities who were willing to form a defensive alliance. **V.38.3** But the members of the councils refused to agree to this proposal, fearing that they might be acting in opposition to the Spartans, by entering an agreement with the Corinthians who had revolted from them.

10.34 The Panionion

Herodotos I.141.4–142.4, I.148.1

Twelve of the Ionian cities and islands of Asia Minor formed a 'league' (koinon) which met at the Panionion, from which other Ionians were excluded. At the Panionion, a temple dedicated to Poseidon, on the north side of Cape Mykale, they celebrated a festival called the Panionia; see Larsen (1955) 27–31; Ehrenberg (1960) 121–22 and 122–31 for other leagues, such as those of the Thessalians and of the Molossians; Emlyn-Jones (1980) 10–35. The league continued meeting after their defeat by the Persians: Hdt. I.170.1. For the Panionion and its festival, the Panionia, see Caspari (1915) 173–88; Magie (1950) I.65–66, II.866–69; Roebuck (1955) 26–40. Because of wars in the Mykale region, the Panionia was moved to Ephesos (Diod. XV.49.1); Hornblower (1982) 241–45 suggests that this took place prior to 424 and that by the 'Ephesia', Thuc. III.104.3 (doc. 12.27) is referring to this relocated festival. See Hdt. I.144 for a similar league, the Dorian pentapolis ('five cities') of Asia Minor and Rhodes, who shared a temple, the Triopion, where they held the Games of Triopian Apollo.

I.141.4 When the news was reported back to the cities, the Ionians all fortified their cities and gathered at the Panionion, all except the Milesians; for Cyrus had given them alone the same terms as Croesus had done; the rest of the Ionians resolved to send messengers to Sparta to ask them for help .... **I.142.3** Miletos is the most southerly of the cities, and after it Myous and Priene; these are settled in Caria and speak the same dialect. The following are in Lydia: Ephesos, Kolophon, Lebedos, Teos, Klazomenai and Phokaia. **I.142.4** These cities share a dialect completely different to those previously mentioned. There are also three remaining Ionian cities, of which two are on the islands of Samos and Chios, and one, Erythrai, is founded on the mainland. The Chians and Erythraians speak the same dialect, while the Samians have one peculiarly their own .... **I.148.1** The Panionion is a sacred place on Mykale, facing north, jointly dedicated by the Ionians to Poseidon of Helikon; Mykale is a cape of the mainland running out towards Samos in a westerly direction, and here the Ionians from the cities used to gather and celebrate the festival, which they called the Panionia.

TRADE AND COMMERCE

For Greek trade and its relationship to colonization, see esp. Isager & Hansen (1975) 19–49, for the fourth century; Starr (1977) 55–78, and note (1987) 119, where he estimates that at the height of its empire Athens directly ruled 179 states, which may have included 2 million Greeks; Hahn (1983) 30–36. Nixon & Price (1990) 165–66 stress the extent to which inter-state trade was routine. For symbola, commercial treaties, see Ehrenberg (1960) 104–05; MacDowell (1978) 220–21; Finley (1985) 161–62. Agriculture was the economic basis of Athenian, as of all Greek, society; Osborne (1985) 142 estimates that perhaps 45% of Athenians were landowners, though his evidence is primarily fourth century. Garnsey (1988) 132–33 (who believes that the productive capacity of Attica has been underestimated, 89) notes that the outbreak of the Peloponnesian War was a crucial turning-point in terms of grain production; thereafter the Athenians became more actively dependent on imports; Foxhall (1993) 134–45 notes the effects of warfare on farmers.

10.35 The Wealth and Power of Corinth

Thucydides I.13.2–5

Corinth had always been a commercial emporion because of its position on the Isthmus, even when most communication was overland and before it had a navy; hence its wealth. When traffic by sea became more common, the Corinthians acquired a navy, put down piracy, and opened a market on both sides of the Isthmus; cf. doc. 2.6. For the diolkos, the stone runway for moving ships and goods across the Isthmus, see note at doc. 2.39; Starr (1977) 70; Salmon (1984) 136–39, and for the Corinthian economy in general, 132–58; for a general overview of Corinthian history, see Freeman (1950) 83–101; doc. 1.7 for colonies. Finley (1963) 46 estimates Corinth's population at c. 90,000; Salmon 168 at 70,000, including slaves. For Corinth as 'wealthy', see *Iliad* II.570.

I.13.2 The Corinthians are said to have been just about the first to involve themselves with naval matters along modern lines, and it was at Corinth, it is said, that the first triremes in Greece were constructed .... **I.13.5** As the Corinthians had founded their city on the Isthmus they had always possessed a trading-station (emporion), as the Greeks of ancient times travelled more by land than by sea, with those from within the Peloponnese and those outside of it having to pass through Corinthian territory to make contact with each other. And the Corinthians grew rich and thus powerful, as is shown by the early poets, who called the place 'wealthy'. And when the Greeks began to take more to the sea, the Corinthians acquired ships and put down piracy, and since they were able to provide a double emporion (for traders by land and sea) they made their city powerful with the money that flowed in.

10.36 Siphnos' Revenues Distributed

Herodotos III.57.1–2

The islanders of Siphnos used to divide the proceeds of their mines amongst themselves every year; cf. doc. 7.21 (Themistokles' use of silver to build ships instead of sharing it out amongst the Athenians; cf. Hdt. VII.144.1). Nixon & Price (1990) 155 note Siphnos' treasury at Delphi as evidence for its prosperity. The context of this document is the joint expedition by Samian exiles and the Spartans against Polykrates (doc. 2.28); the Samians asked the Siphnians to lend them 10 talents. When this request was refused they attacked the island and forced the Siphnians to pay them 100 talents (Hdt. III.58.3–4). For the Thasians' revenue from their mines, see Hdt. VI.46.2–47.2.

III.57.1 The Samians who had made the expedition against Polykrates, since the Spartans were going to desert them, sailed off to Siphnos; **III.57.2** they were in need of money, and at that time Siphnos' affairs were at the height of their prosperity, and they were by far the richest of the islanders, in as much as their gold and silver mines on the island were so productive that with a tenth of their output they furnished a treasury at Delphi equal to the richest ones there; and every year they used to share out the yield of the mines amongst themselves.

10.37 The Berezan Lead Letter, c. 500

Chadwick (1973) 35–36

The text used is that of Chadwick (1973) in preference to that of Merkelbach (1975); cf. Bravo (1974) 111–87 with pl. This inscription, on a lead tablet, was found on the island of Berezan near Olbia, a Milesian colony on the Black Sea. It is a letter from Achillodoros, who was travelling on a business trip on behalf of Anaxagoras. His cargo has been confiscated by Matasys, who has attempted to reduce Achillodoros to slavery, presumably in order to settle an outstanding claim against Anaxagoras. Matasys claims that Anaxagoras has deprived him of what ought to be his, that Achillodoros is

Anaxagoras' slave, and that he is therefore liable to seizure by Matasys as compensation. Achillodoros here writes to his son Protagoras to let him know what is happening and to tell him to inform Anaxagoras. He tells his son to get the rest of the family to safety in the city, where they can appeal to the magistrates against an attempt to enslave them; Euneuros may be another of Achillodoros' sons. See Chadwick (1973) 35–37 for the Milesian dialect; Miller (1975) 158–60 conjectures that Achillodoros and Matasys are in Olbia, and Anaxagoras and Protagoras in Miletos, the city of line 12.

Protagoras, your father sends you this message: he is being wronged by Matasys, for he (Matasys) is reducing him to slavery and has deprived him of his cargo vessel. Go to Anaxagoras and say to him: he (Matasys) says that he (Achillodoros) is the slave of Anaxagoras, and says, 'Ana[xa]goras has my property, male slaves, female slaves, and houses.' But he (Achillodoros) complains loudly and says that there is nothing between him and Matas[ys], and says that he is free and that there is nothing between him and Mata[sys]. But what there is between [Ma]tasy[s] and Anaxagoras they themselves know between them. Tell this to Anaxagoras and his (Achillodoros') wife. He (Achillodoros) sends you another message: take your mother and your bro[t]hers, [wh]o a[r]e among the Arbinatai, to the city, and Euneuros will come himself to him (?Achillodoros) and then go [s]traight down. Reverse: The lead of Achillodoros; addressed to his son and to Anaxagoras.

10.38 The Grain Trade

Herodotos VII.147.2–3

This passage is the earliest explicit reference to the grain trade. Hahn (1983) 33–34 notes the importance for grain production both of the Black Sea region (cf. doc. 1.12), and of the west (Hdt. VII.158.4; cf. doc. 2.33, where Gelon promised to ship sufficient grain to Greece for the duration of Xerxes' invasion). Early in the Peloponnesian War (426/5) Athens gave permission for Methone to import a specified amount of grain from Byzantium (*IG* I^3 61, 34–41) and evidently the Hellespontophylakes (the 'guards of the Hellespont') would not usually allow the passage of grainships without a licence from Athens; Jameson (1983) 12; cf. *IG* I^3 63, 10–19 for Aphytis. Clearly in normal times the allies could manage without importing grain: in the Peloponnesian War Athens' aims in Sicily were spoken of in terms of denying grain to the Peloponnese, not of securing it for herself (Thuc. III.86.4); cf. Xen. *Hell.* II.1.17, for Lysander's stopping the grain ships sailing through the Hellespont to Athens, before the battle of Aigospotamoi. For Athens' preoccupation with the grain supply in the fourth century, see Burke (1990) 5–7.

VII.147.2 When Xerxes was at Abydos he saw boats from the Black Sea sailing through the Hellespont with cargoes of grain, carrying it to Aegina and the Peloponnese. His counsellors, on learning that they were enemy ships, were prepared to capture them, and kept their eye on the King awaiting his order. **VII.147.3** Xerxes asked them where the boats were sailing; they answered, 'They are carrying grain, sire, to your enemies.' His reply was, 'Are not we sailing there ourselves, equipped, among other things, with grain? So what harm are they doing in transporting our grain for us?'

10.39 Public Imprecations at Teos c. 470

Meiggs & Lewis 30 A & B, lines 8–28

The following curses are to be pronounced three times each year by certain magistrates against those who endanger the community, including those who prevent the import of grain, showing its great importance to the community that imported it, and against pirates; Hahn (1983) 33; Jameson (1983) 12; Strubbe (1991) 37–38. For the Teians' colonization of Abdera, see doc. 1.11; some of the Teians returned later (Strab. XIV.1.30 (644)) and Teos appears in the Athenian tribute lists. The aisymnetes is apparently a magistrate. For Thucydides on piracy as a way of life in his own time amongst the Ozolian Lokrians, Aetolians, and Akarnanians, see I.5.1–6.2; cf. Hom. *Od.* III.71–74.

A

(1) Whoever makes drugs that are poisonous (to use) against the Teians as a community or against an individual, that man shall die, both himself (5) and his family. Whoever prevents grain being imported to the Teian land by any cunning or contrivance either by sea or by the mainland, (10) or re-exports it after it has been imported, shall die, both himself and his family.

B

.... (8) Whoever in future is aisymnetes in Teos or in the territory of Teos [....] (11) knowingly betra[ys] th[e] cit[y and territory] of Teos or th[e] men [on the i]sland or (15) on the s[ea] here[after or the] Aro[i]an fo[rt; or who in] future commits trea[son or rob]bery or receives brigands (20) or commits piracy or receives pirates knowingly, who carry off (plunder) from the territory of Teos or from the [s]ea; or who plots [some e]vil against the Teian (25) community knowingly either w[ith] Greeks or with barbarians shall die, both himself and his family.

10.40 The Wine Trade on Thasos c. 425–400

Pleket *Epigraphica* I, no. 2

The wine trade was obviously of extreme importance to Thasos. The second part of the inscription forbids the import of foreign wine into the area of the mainland which the Thasians controlled, the Thasian peraia, and the Thasian landowners are presumably ensuring the sale of their own produce, free from foreign competition; see de Ste. Croix (1972) 43 n.80; Nixon & Price (1990) 152. In lines 12–13, the selling of wine retail (literally by the kotyle, or jug) is also forbidden; cf. Pleket no. I, p.8 for a law on wine and vinegar dating to c. 480, where transgressors of the law pay a sixth of a mina to Athena and Apollo and another to the person who denounces them to the authorities. Lines 10 and 15 also show that adulteration of wine was a problem in need of legislation.

I

(1) Neither sweet wine nor wine from the crop on the vi[nes shall be bo]ught before the first of Plynterion; whoever trans[gresses] and buys it, shall be bound to pay stater for stater, one [half] to the city and the other half to the prosecutor. The law-suit shall be as [for] cases of violence. (5) But if someone buys wine in wine-jars (pithoi) the purchase shall be valid, if (the seller) has stamped a seal on wine jars.

II

[.... the] penalties and deposits shall be the same. If no one [puts down a d]eposit (does not prosecute), the commissioners of the mainland are to bring the case. Whenever they win, all the penalty is to belong to the city; but if the commissioners do not bring the case, though they have learnt of the matter, they shall be liable to pay a double penalty; whoever wishes shall bring the case in the same way, and he shall have half the penalty, and the magistrates (demiourgoi) shall grant the case against the commissioners in the same way. No Thasian ship shall import foreign wine within Athos and Pacheia; if it does, (the owner) shall be liable to the same penalties as for adulterating the wine with water, and the helmsman shall be liable to the same penalty; and the law-suits and the deposits shall be the same. Nor shall anyone sell wine by the kotyle either from amphorai or from a cask or from a false (non-regulation) wine-jar (pithos); and whoever sells it, the law-suits and the deposits and the penalties shall be the same as for adulterating (wine) with water.

10.41 A Spartiate Deposits Money at Tegea c. 450

Bogaert *Epigraphica* III, no. 29 A & B

LSAG 212–13 (27) with pl. 41; Buck (1955) 267, no.70. This bronze plaque, originally from the temple of Athena Alea at Tegea, contains two contracts, one cancelled by deliberate erasure, presumably when replaced by the second. It is likely, as the dialect is not true Arkadian, that Xouthias was one of the Spartiates evading Spartan currency regulations by depositing money at Tegea; see doc. 6.43.

A

For Xouthias son of Philachaios 200 minas (are deposited); if he comes himself, let him take it; but if he dies, it shall belong to his children, when they are five years after the age of puberty. If none of his offspring s[u]rvive, it shall belong to those who are judged his heirs. The Tegeate[s] are to decide according to the law.

B

For Xouthias son of Philachaios are deposited 400 minas of silver. If he is alive, let him take it himself; but if he is not alive, let his legitimate sons take it, when they are five years after the age of puberty; and if they are not alive, let his legitimate daughters take it; and if they are not alive, let his illegitimate sons take it; and if his illegitimate sons are not alive, let his nearest relations take it; and if they dispute about it, the Tegeates are to decide according to the law.

10.42 The Mystery of the Missing Amphorai

Herodotos III.6.1–2

III.6.1 From all of Greece, and from Phoenicia as well, earthenware jars full of wine are imported into Egypt throughout the year, yet one could say that not a wine jar is to be seen anywhere. **III.6.2** Obviously, one should ask, where are these disposed of? I will explain this. Each mayor (demarch) has to collect all the wine jars from his city and send them to Memphis, and the people of Memphis have to fill them with water and take them to the waterless regions of Syria.

10.43 Athenian Control of Trade under the Empire

[Xenophon] *Constitution of the Athenians* 2.11–12

For Athens' need to import timber and corn (referring specifically to 374), see Xen. *Hell.* VI.1.11. Athens had a long-standing need for timber, particularly during the days of her empire; see Borza (1987) 32–45; cf. Burke (1990) 5–12; Meiggs (1982) 192–217.

2.11 They alone of Greeks and barbarians are able to possess wealth. For if a city is rich in timber for ship-building, where will it dispose of it unless it has the consent of the rulers of the sea? If a city is rich in iron, copper or flax, where will it dispose of these unless it has the consent of the rulers of the sea? But it is from these very things that my ships are made, timber from one place, from another copper, from another flax, from another wax. **2.12** In addition, they will not permit exports elsewhere to wherever any of our rivals are, on pain of not being allowed use of the sea. And I, though I do nothing, have all these things from the land because of the sea, while no other city has two of them; the same city does not have timber and flax, but where there is most flax the land is smooth and timberless; the same city does not even have copper and iron, nor do any two or three of the rest come from a single city, but one from this and one from that.

10.44 Customs Duties at the Peiraieus

Andokides I *On the Mysteries* 133–34

Like most other taxes, the 2% customs duty levied by Athens was not collected by a government agency but farmed out to the highest bidder. At this percentage the volume of traffic was approximately 1800 talents in 399, and presumably was much greater under Athens' 'empire'. See Finley (1985) 164 on the harbour tax, levied at the same rate on all imports and exports; there was no concept of protecting home production or encouraging essential imports. No tribute was collected in the years 414/3 to 411/0, and the Athenians instead imposed 5% harbour dues throughout the empire; they seem to have already had a 2% harbour tax in place (Thuc. VII.28.4; *ATL* I.153, III. 91; Nixon & Price (1990) 149).

133 Agyrrhios here, that honest man, two years ago was chief contractor for the tax of two per cent. He bid thirty talents for it and those people he meets under the poplar tree all had shares in it with him; you know the kind of people they are. I think they met there with two purposes, to be paid for not outbidding him and to get a share in a tax-collecting business sold at a low price. **134** When they'd made a profit of six talents and realised what they were on to and how valuable it was, they all combined, gave the other bidders a share and put in a bid for the tax again for thirty talents. Since no one else put in a rival bid, I came forward before the boule and kept raising their offer, until I got the contract for thirty-six talents. After getting rid of those men and providing you with guarantors, I collected the money and paid it over to the city, without making any loss by it, as my partners and I made some small profit; and I'd ensured that those men didn't share out between them six talents of your money.

10.45 Revenues at Athens

Aristophanes *Wasps* 655–64

Here Bdelykleon lists Athens' revenues, to prove to his father that the jury-courts only receive a small proportion of the state's income; he is calculating on every juror serving 300 days a year, surely an over-estimate; for the *Wasps*, see also docs. 10.16–17.

Bdelykleon: Listen now, daddy darling, and relax your forehead a little.
First of all make a rough calculation, not with counters but on your fingers,
Of the tribute which comes to us from all the cities together,
Then apart from this the taxes, besides, and the many one-per-cents,
Court deposits, mines, market-taxes, harbour dues, rents for public land, confiscations;
From these we get a total of nearly 2,000 talents.
Now take away from this a year's pay for the jurors,
6,000 of them — 'for no more than these yet dwell in our land' —
And we get some 150 talents.
Philokleon: So the pay we've been getting is not even a tenth of the revenue!

10.46 The Heroes of the City State

Xenophanes 2, lines 1–14

Successful victors in the games could be awarded a state pension or a monetary reward by their city: cf. Plut. *Sol.* 23.3 (a victor at the Isthmian games awarded 100 drachmas); Diog. Laert. *Sol.* 1.55 (a victor at Olympia 500 drachmas). Socrates also asked for maintenance in the prytaneion (doc. 9.39; cf. 4.41); Xenophanes and Socrates seem to have had similar views of their own merits.

But if anyone were to win a victory through swiftness of foot
Or through competing in the pentathlon, in the precinct of Zeus
Beside the streams of Pisa at Olympia, or in wrestling
Or through possessing the painful art of boxing,
Or in that dreadful kind of contest which they call the pankration,
To the citizens he would be more glorious to behold
And would win a conspicuous seat of honour at the games
And would get maintenance out of public stores
From the city, as well as a gift for him to put by as treasure;
So too if he won with his horses, he would obtain all these things —
Though not deserving of them like I am. For better than the strength
Of men or of horses is my wisdom.
But opinion about this is random, nor is it right
To prefer strength to noble wisdom.

11

Labour: Slaves, Serfs and Citizens

Slavery and servile labour played a very important part in the economy and society of Greek city-states throughout Greek history, and slaves are in fact documented as early as the Mycenaean age in the Linear B tablets. Without slaves, metics and serfs, the face of Greek society would have changed markedly, and they were an essential component of Greek life throughout the archaic and classical periods. It is difficult to estimate the actual numbers of slaves in any city at any given time, but Thucydides (doc. 11.14) tells us that when the Spartans fortified Dekeleia in Attica in 413 more than 20,000 Attic slaves deserted, a large part of them skilled manual workers; these would not of course have included slaves employed in the city itself.

To the Greeks there was a very important distinction between slave and free and there was little or no moral dilemma for the Greeks about owning slaves. Slaves had either been captured in war (docs. 11.2–3); or they had been born and bred in the house or on the estate (cf. docs. 11.6, 9) and thus were an integral part of the family, over whom the master of the house had almost total rights. In addition, some slaves would have been unwanted new-born children who had been exposed by their parents; a further means of enslavement was through piracy and kidnapping (docs. 11.1, 4–5). Moreover, while Solon had put an end to agricultural debt-slavery in Athens, it obviously still existed elsewhere as can be seen in the Gortyn law code (doc. 11.16).

Kidnapping and the slave trade were profitable occupations: Herodotos (doc. 11.1, cf. 2.10) describes how the Chian Panionios made his living by castrating and selling good-looking boys. Yet while death was the penalty for abducting people as slaves (see doc. 11.4), the slave trade and slave traders were simply a fact of life (docs. 11.2, 4–5). A slave could be an expensive commodity: Nikias the wealthy estate owner and general is said to have paid a talent for an overseer for his silver mine (doc. 11.10), the equivalent of 12,000 times a day's pay for a juror (doc. 10.16). For those with large numbers of slaves, hiring them out was obviously a profitable way to make money: slaves were hired out to work the mines, and Nikias cleared an obol per man per day for 1,000 men (doc. 11.11). In times of war slaves were a useful source of manpower, and those slaves who fought in wartime might be given their freedom, and sometimes even citizenship. The first slaves are recorded as fighting for Athens at the time of the first Persian invasion, and those slaves who served as rowers at Arginousai in 406 were given their freedom (doc. 11.15).

The legal position of slaves could of course vary between different states. The Gortyn law code (doc. 11.16) gives us information about the status of slaves and serfs in Crete, as well as clearly showing the status of children born to slaves or serfs (col. IV). Slaves in general were subject to the whims or wishes of their master, whose rights were almost absolute, though it appears that masters were not however allowed to kill their slaves. Socrates (doc. 11.18) lists the punishments of idle or recalcitrant slaves with no hint of disapproval, and in Athens slaves could only give evidence in a court of law under torture (doc. 11.17). Athens and a number of other Greek cities also included a class of metics (immigrants, or resident foreigners). By the fifth century metics at Athens had become a large and important class; while not citizens, they had specific and very well-protected rights, and in return contributed a great deal to the state's revenues as well as serving in the fleet (docs. 11.21–26). Lysias, the orator, and his brother Polemarchos were metics who owned a shield factory (doc. 11.24); another well-known metic was Aspasia, who was said to run her own business training young girls as hetairai (doc. 13.29). Under certain specific conditions, metics could be granted citizenship: those metics who helped restore the democracy in 403 appear to have been made citizens and their occupations are listed in doc. 11.26.

Crete was not the only Greek state to possess a class of serfs. The best known of such states was Sparta, which depended on its helots for agricultural production, but we also find a similar class, the penestai, in Thessaly (doc. 11.32). The Spartans were also surrounded by the perioikoi, literally 'neighbours', who were politically subject to Sparta but had their own cities and some internal independence. Tyrtaeus the Spartan poet of the Second Messenian War gives us details of the regime imposed on the helots by the Spartans after their final conquest of Messenia (see docs. 11.27). There were, therefore, various types of slavery and forced labour in the Greek world. That slaves were an essential part of Greek life can be seen by the important part they play in Greek drama, and most dramatic productions include one or more slaves as members of the *dramatis personae* who are integral to the plot (docs. 11.40–44). These plays present slaves to an Athenian audience in a variety of environments and situations and show how deep-rooted an institution slavery was in Greek culture and society.

Naturally, of course, free Greeks themselves also worked in various ways. In certain classes of society agriculture, rather than trade, was considered the business of a 'gentleman' (docs. 11.36–37), and even in the heyday of fifth century Athens traders in the sense of retail manufacturers could be looked down on, and were to a large degree metics who had been encouraged to settle in Athens. Nevertheless, Solon and Hesiod mention a number of occupations in the archaic period (docs. 11.33–34), and while a 'citizen economy' like that of Athens was made up of a myriad of small farming households, obviously a large proportion of Athenian citizens were also traders, artisans, and workmen, and it would be unwise to ignore this very important class of labour.

ENSLAVEMENT AND THE SLAVE TRADE

Solon's legislation put an end to debt-slavery in Attica, and from this point Athenians did not own slaves who were Athenians. The main sources of supply for slaves were warfare and piracy, as well as the sale by traders of non-Greeks; for slaves and slave traders, see Finley (1981) 167–75; Garlan (1988) 45–55. For the extent to which classical Greek thought saw the world in terms of polarised antitheses, Greeks and barbarians, men and women, free and slave, see Cartledge (1993) 168–73, and 175–78 for the degree to which slavery was central to the Greeks' mentality, way of life, and civilization. For Greek, and especially Athenian, slavery, see Jones (1957) 12–15; Andrewes (1971) 146–56; Webster (1973) 40–48; Finley (1973) 62–74, 78–80; Vogt (1975) 1–14; Starr (1977) 90–91; Finley (1981) 97–106; de Ste. Croix (1981) 133–47; Roberts (1984) 31–40; Wiedemann (1987) 11–18; Powell (1988) 318–21; and Garlan (1988) 19–23 (on terminology and personal names). Finley (1959) 164; Jameson (1977–78) 122 note that the most developed form of chattel slavery appears in those societies, like Athens, where citizens were allowed the greatest individual and intellectual freedom.

11.1 A Slave Trader Meets his Just Deserts

Herodotos VIII.105.1–106.4

Herodotos' account of Hermotimos' revenge for his castration highlights the way Greeks felt about the castration of slaves, but does not mean that they saw anything improper or cruel in slavery as an institution or in slave trading as a profession. For slaves as one of the main items traded between local peoples and Greek colonies, see Finley (1962) 51–59; Graham (1984) 6–8, who notes that Seuthes, prince of the Odrysian Thracians, paid for his hire of Xenophon's men in 400 by selling his captives in the slave markets of the Greek cities of the coast (Xen. *Anab.* VII.3.48, 4.2, cf. 5.2). Cf. Hdt. V.6.1, where some of the Thracians have the custom of selling their children into slavery.

VIII.105.1 Hermotimos had been captured by enemies and sold, and Panionios, a man from Chios, bought him, who made his living by the most vile profession; for he used to acquire boys who possessed a degree of beauty, castrate them and take them and sell them at Sardis and Ephesos for a lot of money. **VIII.105.2** For amongst the barbarians eunuchs are more highly regarded for their complete trustworthiness than the uncastrated. Amongst the many whom Panionios had castrated in the course of his profession was Hermotimos. But Hermotimos had not been entirely unfortunate, because he was sent from Sardis to the King with other gifts and as time passed was more highly valued by Xerxes than all his other eunuchs. **VIII.106.1** Now when the King was at Sardis, launching his Persian expedition against Athens, Hermotimos went down on some business to a part of Mysia, which the Chians own, called Atarneus, and there he found Panionios. **VIII.106.2** Recognising him, he spoke to him for a long time in a friendly manner, first narrating to him all the benefits which he'd had from what Panionios had done, and then promising to do the same for him in return if he brought his family (to Sardis) and settled there; Panionios gladly accepted the offer and brought his children and wife. **VIII.106.3** And when Hermotimos had him with his whole family in his power, he spoke as follows: 'You have made your living by the vilest profession practised by all mankind. What evil had I or any of my family ever done to you or yours that you should make me a nothing instead of a man? You thought that your actions then would escape the notice of the gods; but they are just and have brought you, whose actions were so vile, into my hands, so that you can not complain of the vengeance I am going to take.' **VIII.106.4** After reproaching him like this, he had Panionios' sons brought before him, and Panionios was compelled to castrate all four of them, which he did; and when he had done that, his sons were compelled to castrate him. In this way Hermotimos got his revenge on Panionios.

11.2 Athens Captures Melos

Thucydides V.116.2–4

Cf. Thuc. V.85–113 for the 'Melian Dialogue'. The Melians were initially non-aligned with either Athens or Sparta and when faced with hostility from Athens went over to Sparta; for a Melian contribution to the Spartan war-fund, see ML 67, dated possibly to 427. The Athenians blockaded the island and took it in 416/5. Some Melian survivors were later restored by Lysander (Xen. *Hell.* II.2.9). Cf. Thucydides on the Athenian capture of Skione (V.32.1), Plataea by the Spartans and Thebans (Thuc. III.68.1–3), Hysiai by the Spartans (V.83.2), and the debate over Mytilene in 427: Thuc. III.36–49 (doc. 9.8); Dover (1973) 39–42. See Xen. *Hell.* I.6.13–15 for the behaviour of the Spartan Kallikratidas in 406, who sold the Athenian garrison of Methymne into slavery but refused to sell the Methymnaeans. For the fate of women as slaves in wartime, see Schaps (1982) 202–06; Cole (1984) 111–13; cf. doc. 11.42.

V.116.2 At about the same time the Melians captured another part of the Athenians' blockading wall, where there were not many guards. **V.116.3** As this had happened, another force came out later from Athens, with Philokrates son of Demeas in command, and as they were heavily besieged, and some treachery took place, the Melians surrendered of their own accord unconditionally to the Athenians. **V.116.4** And the Athenians killed all the Melian men they took in the prime of life, and enslaved the children and women; and they settled the spot, later on sending out five hundred colonists.

11.3 The Athenians Fear Similar Treatment

Xenophon *Hellenika* II.2.3–4

Athens' expansion during the fifth century ensured her at intervals a good revenue from slaves; at the beginning of the Delian League the Athenians enslaved the inhabitants of Eion and then Skyros (Thuc. I.98.1–2; doc. 8.3), and though Hykkara was only a small Sicilian town the Athenians received 120 talents for their captives (Thuc. VI.62.3–4). See Thuc. VII.87.3–4 for the 7,000 prisoners from the Sicilian expedition, many of whom were sold by the Syracusans into slavery. The standard ransom asked for prisoners of war in the sixth and fifth centuries seems to have been 2 minas: Hdt. VI.79.1 (Spartans); cf. V.77.3 (Athenians); Thuc. V.49.1 (Eleians). In 405, after Aigospotamoi, the Athenians feared that they themselves would be enslaved; clearly no one in the Greek world could be entirely certain of escaping slavery (see doc. 9.30).

II.2.3 The Paralos arrived at Athens at night and the disaster was reported, and lamentation passed from the Peiraieus along the Long Walls to the city, one man telling the news to another. As a consequence, no one slept during that night, because they were grieving not only for those who were lost, but far more than that for themselves, as they thought that they would now suffer the same as they had done to the Melians, who were colonists of the Spartans, after subduing them by siege, and to the Histiaians and Skionaians and Toronaians and Aeginetans and many others of the Greeks. **II.2.4** On the next day they held an assembly, at which they resolved to block up all the harbours except one, repair the walls, station guards and make the city ready for a siege in all other respects as well.

11.4 Death for Slave Abduction

Lysias XIII *Against Agoratos* 67

Agoratos, by birth a slave and an informer for the Thirty, is being tried c. 399 under the restored democracy for the murder of one of the Thirty's victims. Here Lysias, in attacking his character and family, is describing one of Agoratos' brothers as a kidnapper of slaves.

Now there were four brothers, jurors. One of them, the eldest, was caught in Sicily making secret signals to the enemy and was crucified on a plank by Lamachos. The next abducted a slave from here to Corinth, and was caught again abducting a young female slave from there, and was thrown into prison and put to death.

11.5 Thessalian Kidnappers as Social Necessities

Aristophanes *Wealth* 509–26

In this, the last play of Aristophanes, produced in 388, Chremylos plans to have Ploutos, the blind god of wealth, cured by Asklepios so that in future, being able to see, he will share his gifts out equally to everyone. Poverty, however, tries to argue him out of this plan on the grounds that no slave-traders will bother to traffic in slaves when everyone is equally wealthy. For this passage, see Vogt (1975) 31; Wood (1983) 42, who argues that it does not prove that in the real Attic world peasants normally employed a slave or slaves, though it does, of course, imply that slavery was taken for granted.

Poverty: If what you desire happened, it certainly wouldn't benefit you.
For if Ploutos could see again to divide himself up evenly,
No person would study a craft or skill any more;
And with both of these vanished who would want
To be a smith or build ships or sew or make wheels,
Or make shoes or bricks or do the laundry or tan hides,
Or break up the earth with his plough and harvest the fruits of
Demeter,
If you could live in idleness and neglect all these things?
Chremylos: You're talking nonsense. All the things you've just mentioned
Will be done by our servants.
Poverty: So where will you get servants from?
Chremylos: We'll buy them with money of course.
Poverty: But who's going to sell them,
When he's got money?

Chremylos: Someone who wants to make a profit,
A merchant from Thessaly from amongst all those kidnappers.
Poverty: But there won't even be a single kidnapper
According to your plan. What wealthy man would want
To risk his life doing something like that?
So you'll have to do the ploughing yourself and dig and all the rest
And you'll have a much more painful life than now.

SLAVES: THEIR OCCUPATIONS AND TRAINING

For estimates of the number of slaves in classical Attica, see Gomme (1933) 37–48, who suggested for 430 that the population of Athens and the Peiraieus would have been 60,000 citizens (rather over a third of the citizen population of Attica), 25,000 metics, 25,000 slaves belonging to citizens, 10,000 belonging to metics, and 35,000 industrial slaves; Wood (1983) 39–41; see also Finley (1959) 151, who suggests an average of 3 to 4 slaves to each free household, and (1981) 102, for an estimate of 60–80,000 slaves overall in Attica (cf. de Ste Croix (1957) 56 for the 420s); Andrewes (1971) 148 suggests approximately 80–100,000 slaves at the time of Athens' greatest prosperity; Jameson (1977–78) 122–23 believes that the majority of Athenians households would have had one or more slaves; Balme (1984) 145 that many families even of hoplite status probably had no slaves; Garlan (1988) 61 suggests that 'average' peasants owned at least three slaves, but this is on the evidence of Aristophanes; Isager & Hansen (1975) 31–34 postulate a total slave population for Attica of at least 150,000 in the fourth century and an annual replacement requirement of at least 6,000 slaves. For the importance of slaves as agricultural workers, see Finley (1959) 148–49; Jameson (1977–78) 124; Wood (1983) 1–47, who argues, 21–31, that there were other options available to Athenian landowners; Ober (1989) 25–27; cf. doc. 11.14. For slaves in 'industry', see Finley (1959) 150. The disabled tradesman (doc. 10.15), who cannot afford a slave, is often taken as evidence that slave help was possible even for the poorest classes (Jameson (1977–78) 122–23 with n.6; Finley (1981) 97–98); but cf. Wood (1983) 45–47.

11.6 Slaves as Shepherds

Sophocles *Oedipus Tyrannus* 1121–41

This episode leads to the revelation that Oedipus has killed his own father, Laios, and married his mother, Iocasta: Oedipus is questioning Laios' former shepherd (a trusted servant, born in the household), and asking whether he knows the Corinthian shepherd to whom the former shepherd had originally given Oedipus, rather than exposing him on the slopes as instructed. Cf. Thuc. III.73 for slaves as agricultural workers on Corcyra in 427.

Oedipus: You there, old man, look at me now and answer
1122 What I ask you. Did you once belong to Laios?
Servant: Yes, not a purchased slave, but reared in his house.
Oedipus: What task or occupation was your care?
Servant: For most of my life I tended the flocks.
Oedipus: And which regions did you most frequent?
Servant: Sometimes Kithairon, and sometimes the neighbouring country.
Oedipus: Then you must have known this man, at least from report?

Servant: Doing what? What man do you refer to?
Oedipus: This one here; have you encountered him before?
Servant: Not enough for me to speak straightway from memory.
Corinthian: And no wonder, master. But I will definitely
Remind him, though he knows me not. For I know well that
He remembers when in the region of Kithairon —
He had two flocks, and I had one —
I associated with this man for three whole years
From spring till Arcturus rose for six months at a time;
When winter came to the sheepfold
I would drive mine back, and he his to Laios' farmstead.
Did this happen as I say or did it not?
Servant: You speak the truth, although of long ago.

11.7 Public Slaves: the Archers

Schol. to Aristophanes *Acharnians* 54

The archers, who kept order in Athens in the assembly and boule (Rhodes (1972) 146, (1986a) 106; cf. Ar. *Knights* 665) are caricatured in Ar. *Thesm.* 930–1231; cf. *Lys.* 433–55, *Ach.* 54. For the archers, originally 300 in number, see Finley (1980) 85–86; Hansen (1991) 124; Lavelle (1992) 78–97. Lewis (1990) 254–58 discusses other public slaves in Athens such as the public executioner and torturers, road workmen, and mint workers.

The archers were public slaves, a thousand in number, who originally lived in tents in the middle of the agora, but later moved to the Areiopagos. They were called Scythians or Peisinians.

11.8 A Slave Woman is More Useful than a Wife

Hesiod *Works and Days*, 405–06

Hesiod is giving advice to the small farmer, who is expected to own one or more servants; cf. 502–03, 765–67; and 602–03, where he advises acquiring a servant-girl with no children (for a servant nursing a child is a nuisance). The woman's chief task would have been that of preparing food, especially grinding wheat and barley (Jameson (1977–78) 138). On Hesiod's slaves, see Nussbaum (1960) 213–20; Garlan (1988) 37. Line 406 may be a later addition; it was apparently not known to Aristotle (*Pol.* 1252b 11–12).

First of all you should acquire a house and a woman and an ox for the plough,
— A female slave, not a wife, who can follow the oxen as well.

11.9 Successful Household Management

Xenophon *Oeconomicus* 9.5, 9.11–12

Isomachos here relates to Socrates how he showed his new wife her home (cf. doc. 13.57 where the wife promises to care for all sick slaves). Particularly important for the smooth running of the household was the choice of housekeeper; for living quarters in a Greek house, see Walker (1983) 81–91; Jameson (1990) 191–92.

9.5 I showed her the women's quarters as well, divided from the men's quarters by a bolted door, so that nothing which ought not to be could be taken out from within and the servants did not produce children without our approval. For good servants who have produced children are for the most part more loyal, but the bad ones who have found a mate become more ingenious at doing mischief .... **9.11** When we appointed our housekeeper, we considered which woman seemed to us to be the most temperate with regard to her stomach, wine, sleep and consorting with men, and additionally the one who appeared to us to have the best memory and the forethought not to annoy us by her carelessness, and to think how she might earn a reward by gratifying us. **9.12** We taught her to be well-disposed towards us by sharing our joys with her when we were pleased, and if something made us miserable by calling on her sympathies. And we trained her to be eager that our household should prosper by making her acquainted with it and sharing our success with her.

SLAVE PRICES

The price of a slave could vary markedly, depending on her or his skills and age. Factories staffed by slaves were very profitable (doc. 11.24); it was also usual to leave a slave to work on his own at his trade and be responsible for his keep, while he paid a regular sum to his master; the term for this was 'living apart' (Andrewes (1971) 148–49; Jameson (1977–78) 123). Slaves could also be hired out to another employer (docs. 11.11, 26).

11.10 Nikias Pays a Talent for a Slave

Xenophon *Memorabilia* II.5.2

For slaves in mining and quarrying, see Finley (1959) 149: as many as 30,000 slaves may have been at work in the Athenian silver mines and processing mills; Sinclair (1988) 197. Mines were state property, but leased out by agreement to individuals.

'Antisthenes,' said Socrates, 'do friends have certain values, like servants? For one servant may be worth perhaps two minas, another less than half a mina, another five minas, and another even ten; Nikias son of Nikeratos is said to have paid a talent for a overseer for his silver-mine.'

11.11 Mineworkers Hired out by Nikias

Xenophon *Revenues* 4.14–15

4.14 Those of us who have been interested in the matter have long ago doubtless heard that Nikias son of Nikeratos once acquired 1,000 men in the silver-mines and that he hired them out to Sosias the Thracian, on condition that Sosias paid him a clear obol a man a day, and always kept the numbers constant. **4.15** And Hipponikos too had 600 slaves let out on the same terms, who brought him a clear mina a day, while Philemonides had 300 who brought him half a mina.

11.12 The Auction of Confiscated Slaves

IG I^3 421, col. I, 33–49 (Meiggs & Lewis 79A)

The property of the men accused of having mutilated the hermai in 415, the hermokopidai ('hermai-cutters'), was confiscated and auctioned (*IG* I^3 421–30; *Agora* XIX P1, p.70). The list of prices received at auction for 16 domestic slaves belonging to Kephisodoros, a metic, is given here (cf. Andok. I *On the Mysteries* 15). The average price per slave is 157 drachmas, though this may have been below full market value; the majority of the slaves were barbarians. The first column represents the sales-tax paid by the buyer, the second the price, and the third the sex and ethnic origin of the slave. Cf. doc. 10.37, for an attempt to enslave a free man as compensation for property seized.

Property of Kephisodoros, a metic [living] in the Peira[ieus]

2 dr.	165 dr.	A Thracian woman
1 dr. 3 obols	135 dr.	A Thracian woman
[2] dr.	170 dr.	A Thracian
2 dr. 3 obols	240 dr.	A Syrian
[1] dr. 3 obols	105 dr.	A Carian
2 dr.	161 dr.	An Illyrian
2 dr. 3 obols	220 dr.	A Thracian woman
1 dr. 3 obols	115 dr.	A Thracian
1 dr. 3 obols	144 dr.	A Scythian
1 dr. 3 obols	121 dr.	An Illyrian
2 dr.	153 dr.	A man from Colchis
2 dr.	174 dr.	A Carian child
1 dr.	72 dr.	A little Carian child
[3] dr. 1 obol	301 dr.	A Syrian
[2] dr.	151 dr.	A Melitt[enian (man or woman)]
1 dr.	85[..] dr. 1 ob.	A Lydian woman

SLAVES IN WAR

On the use of Athenian slaves in warfare, see Sargent (1927) 201–12; Hanson (1992) 222–23. It was customary to have slaves with the army, to carry the baggage and perform menial tasks, like preparing the food; cf. Thuc. IV.101.2 (Delion), VII.13.2, VII.75.5 (Sicily). At Potidaea in 428, there were 3,000 slaves, one for each Athenian hoplite in the garrison, for each of whom their master received one drachma a day for maintenance (Thuc. III.17.4). Rowing was a citizen's duty (Thuc. I.14.3); for metics in the navy, cf. doc. 11.23. Slaves that fought either in the army or with the fleet were manumitted.

11.13 Slaves at Marathon, 490

Pausanias I.32.3

Cf. Paus. VII.15.7. Sargent (1927) 209 records that there were only three occasions (Marathon, Arginousai and Chaironeia) when the Athenians called for slaves to be soldiers or sailors and offered them emancipation; this does not take into account *IG* II^2

1951 (see doc. 11.15). Herodotos' account (doc. 7.8) does not mention that slaves took part in the battle at Marathon, but Sargent 209–10 notes that his account is very much slanted towards glorification of the occasion, and the activities of individuals. See Paus. I.29.7 for public burial of the slaves died alongside their masters who fought against Aegina before the Persian invasion, and the stele proclaiming that 'they behaved bravely in respect of their masters'.

There is a village, Marathon, equidistant from the city of the Athenians and Karystos in Euboea; it was here that the barbarians landed in Attica and were defeated in the battle and lost some of their ships as they were putting off. There is a grave for the Athenians on the plain and on it are stelai with the names of the dead, each according to their tribes, and another grave for the Plataeans of Boeotia and for the slaves — for that was the first occasion on which slaves fought as well.

11.14 Slaves Desert in the Peloponnesian War

Thucydides VII.27.5

Dekeleia had been fortified in 413 and used as a permanent hostile post against Attica (doc. 9.23), which caused Athens great hardship from devastation of the countryside and loss of manpower, including the desertion of a large number of slaves. Thucydides obviously believed that this was a great blow to Athens; the numbers of skilled workmen (cheirotechnai) who deserted perhaps give some clue as to the total number of slaves in Attica, though this may be no more than an estimate by Thucydides: see Wood (1983) 19; Hornblower (1987) 36. Hanson (1992) 210–28 believes that Thucydides is basing his estimate on the number of landowning Athenians citizens, and assuming that every Attic farmer at the time owned a slave. Many of these deserting slaves, who might have been miners but were more probably agricultural workers, did not achieve their freedom but were acquired by the Boeotians: *Hell. Oxyrhynchia* 17.4; Hanson (1992) 217–20; cf. Jameson (1977–78) 136. Chian slaves also deserted to the Athenians in 411: according to Thucydides (VIII.40.2) there were more slaves in Chios than in any other city except Sparta. For the effects of warfare on farmers, see Hanson (1983) esp. 37–63; Foxhall (1993) 134–45. This passage follows on from doc. 9.23.

VII.27.5 For they were deprived of the whole of their country, and more than 20,000 slaves deserted, of whom the majority were skilled manual workers, and they lost all their flocks and draught animals.

11.15 Slaves Fight at Arginousai and are Made Free

Xenophon *Hellenika* I.6.24

For Aristophanes' approval of the decision to grant citizenship to the slaves who fought at Arginousai, see *Frogs* 687–99 (and cf. 33–34, 190–91: it was obviously a current issue); Arnott (1991) 18–23. Slaves who fought for Athens may also have been freed after Aigospotamoi, or on some other occasion between 410 and 390: see *IG* II^2 1951, in which slaves, many of them owned by the officers, appear to make up 20–40% of the oarsmen; Davies (1977–78) 120; Garlan (1988) 166. The use of slaves as rowers at Arginousai was unprecedented in Athens (Sargent (1927) 276–77; MacDowell (1978) 72), though there were slaves on the seven Chian ships blockading the enemy fleet in 411 (Thuc. VIII.15.2), and 800 on Corcyra's ships in 432 (Thuc. I.55.1).

When the Athenians heard of what had happened and about the blockade, they voted to go to the rescue with a hundred and ten ships, embarking all those who were of age, both slaves and free men; and they manned the hundred and ten ships in thirty days and set sail. Many of the hippeis even went aboard.

THE LEGAL POSITION OF SLAVES

See especially MacDowell (1978) 79–82; Christensen (1984) 25, and cf. 23–32 for the Theseion as a slave refuge, where slaves could demand resale because of abuse by their masters; Cartledge (1993) 173–75; see Sinn (1993) 88–109 in general for sanctuaries as places of refuge. See Garlan (1988) 40–45 for the slave as a possession with no legal standing, but with certain legal safeguards; Fisher (1992) 58–60, 65–67 for the possibility of an act of hubris against slaves (cf. Dem. XXI.46–47; Athen. 267a). In law, the slave was primarily seen as a possession of his or her master; see doc. 13.47 for the Cretan penalties for rape of a slave or serf, which vary with the social class of the victim and offender; Cole (1984) 102–03, cf. 108–11, suggests that sexual assault of a slave in Athens would have required a fine of 50 drachmas, half that for violating a free person, paid of course to the owner; for the probable prohibition against killing slaves, see MacDowell (1978) 80; Antiphon V *On the Murder of Herodes* 46–48.

11.16 Serfs and Slaves in the Gortyn Law Code

Willetts *The Law Code of Gortyn*

Crete possessed a tradition of patriarchal slavery, long after commercial slavery had become the dominant form of servitude in other parts of Greece; Willetts (1967) 13, (1977) 169–74; cf. Finley (1981) 135–39; Garlan (1988) 99–101. The serfs had rights, such as that of tenure of the house in which they lived and were seen as part of the estate. They possessed money, could marry and divorce, and their wives had their own property. A serf could even marry a free woman. But chattel-slaves and the slave market are also mentioned below; and clearly in Crete slavery for debt was still possible; cf. de Ste. Croix (1981) 162–65. In Crete, a stater was worth two drachmas.

Suits concerning ownership of actual or alleged slaves

(col. I) Gods. Whoever is going to contend whether someone is a free man or a slave is not to seize him before trial. But if he seizes him, (the judge) is to condemn him to pay ten staters for a free man and five for a slave, whoever he belongs to, and he is to give judgement that he should release him within three days. But if he does not release him, he is to pay a stater for a free man and a drachma for a slave (10) for each day until he does release him; and the judge on oath is to decide as to the time. But if he denies that he seized him, the judge is to decide on oath, unless a witness testifies. And if one side contends that he is a free man and the other that he is a slave, those who testify that he is a free man are to win. And if they contend about a slave, each saying that he is his, (20) if a witness testify, the judge is to judge according to the witness, but is to decide on oath if they testify for both sides or for neither. After the one who has him is defeated, he is to release the free man within five days and give back the slave in hand. But if he does not release nor give back, (the judge) is to judge that the (winning side) should receive in the case of a free man

(30) fifty staters and a stater per day until he releases him, and in the case of a slave ten staters and a drachma per day until he gives him back in hand .... (56) But one who seizes a man condemned (for debt) or a man who has (col. II) mortgaged himself is to be immune from punishment.

Property rights of serfs

(col. III.40) If a female serf be separated from a serf while he is alive or if he should die, she is to have her own property; but if she takes away anything else, that is grounds for a trial .... (52) And if a female serf should bear a child while separated, it is to be taken to the master of the man who married her, in the presence of two witnesses. (col. IV) And if he does not accept it, the child shall belong to the master of the female serf; but if she marries the same man again within a year, the child is to belong to the master of the male serf; and the oaths of the one who brought it and the witnesses shall have precedence .... (18) If a female serf who is unmarried conceives and bears a child, the child shall belong to the master of her father; but if her father is not alive, it shall belong to the masters of her brothers.

Ransomed prisoners

(col. VI.46) If anyone of necessity gets a man, who is away from home, set free from another city at his request, he shall belong to the one who ransomed him (50) until he pays what is owed. But if they do not agree about the amount, the judge is to decide on oath with reference to the pleas.

Mixed marriages

(col. VI.56) If a slave goes (col. VII) to a free woman and marries her, their children shall be free. But if the free woman goes to the slave their children shall be slaves. And if there are free and slave children of the same mother, if the mother dies and there is property, the free children are to have it; but if she had no free children, the heirs are to have it.

Purchase of slaves in the slave-market

(col. VII.10) If someone buys a slave from the market-place and does not terminate the agreement within sixty days, the one who has acquired the slave will be liable if he (the slave) has done any wrong before or after (the purchase).

11.17 Slaves Give Evidence under Torture

Antiphon V *On the Murder of Herodes* 29–32

This speech was probably delivered c. 415. Cf. Lysias IV *On a Wound by Premeditation* 10–17, where the defendant proposes to have a slave-girl tortured, whom he alleges to be the common property of himself and the accuser, and who was the cause of the quarrel in which the accuser had gained a black eye. Slaves could only give evidence in a law-court under torture; cf. doc. 13.49; MacDowell (1978) 245–47; Finley (1980) 94–95; Garlan (1988) 42–44; Todd (1990) 27–28, 33–35. A party to a suit could refuse the challenge to have one of his slaves tortured; otherwise, the methods of torture employed were drawn up in an arrangement between the parties involved, which made provision for compensation to be paid to the slave's master if the slave were permanently disabled as a result; cf. a parody of such tortures in Ar. *Frogs* 618–22, which included racking, hoisting, scourging, cudgelling, and pouring vinegar up the nose and heaping bricks on the victim.

29 When they found the blood, they said that it was there that Herodes had been killed; but when this was not possible, as it turned out to belong to the animals for sacrifice, they desisted from that line of argument and seized and tortured the men. **30** The first whom they tortured there straightaway said nothing foolish about me; the other whom they tortured a number of days later, and who had been in their company during the preceding period, was the one who was persuaded by them to tell lies about me. I will produce witnesses to this. (Witnesses) **31** You have heard evidence as to how much later the man was tortured; now pay attention to the torture itself, what it was like. For the slave, to whom they had doubtless promised his freedom and who had to look to these men for putting an end to his sufferings, hoped to gain his freedom and wanted to be delivered immediately from the torture. I think you know already that with regard to those who do the greatest part of the torturing **32** it is in their favour that the tortured say whatever is going to gratify them; for in them lies their possible advantage, especially if those about whom they are lying do not happen to be present. But if I had ordered him to be stretched on the rack for not telling the truth, that in itself would doubtless have deterred him from telling lies about me.

11.18 The Punishments Appropriate for Slaves

Xenophon *Memorabilia* II.1.15–17

As part of an exhortation on the virtues of self-control, Socrates is here explaining to Aristippos, a rather intemperate and independent companion of his, that his beliefs and taste for high-living would not prevent his being enslaved by wrong-doers.

II.1.15 Socrates: 'Who would want to have in his household a man who didn't want to work and who enjoyed a luxurious lifestyle? **II.1.16** Let us consider how masters treat such servants. Do they not control their lecherousness by starving them? Prevent them stealing by locking up anywhere they might steal from? Stop them running away by putting them in fetters? Drive out their laziness with beatings? What do you do when you find one of your servants is like this?' **II.1.17** (Aristippos) 'I punish them with every kind of misery until I can compel them to behave like a slave should.'

11.19 Solon Legislates against Slave Activities

Aischines I *Against Timarchos* 138–39

Cf. Plut. *Sol.* 1.6; Golden (1984) 317–18 suggests that, as places of exercise were favourite meeting-places for citizens and their admirers, Solon is therefore presumably guaranteeing the special status of the homosexual relationship between free Athenians; see also Murray (1990) 145. For gymnasia and athletic nudity, see Glass (1988) 155–73, esp. 160–63 for Solon's legislation regarding pederasty.

138 Our fathers, when they were legislating on our everyday pursuits and what nature compels us to do, forbade slaves to do the things they thought ought to be done by free men. 'A slave,' says the law, 'is not to take exercise or anoint himself in the wrestling schools (palaistrai)' .... **139** Again the same lawgiver said, 'A slave shall not be the lover of a free boy nor follow him around or else receive fifty lashes from the public scourge.'

11.20 Slaves, Metics and Citizens are Indistinguishable

[Xenophon] *Constitution of the Athenians* 1.10

This was written c. 425 by an author of very 'right-wing' views. For the 'graphe hybreos' (indictment for hubris) and the crime of treating a citizen as if he were a slave, see Fisher (1990) 123–38, (1992) 36–68, 86–97; Murray (1990) 139–45; Cartledge (1993) 174.

Slaves and metics are allowed the greatest licence at Athens, and you are not allowed to strike any of them there, nor will a slave stand aside for you. Why this is the local custom, I will tell you: if it were the law that a slave or metic or freedman could be struck by a free man, you would often hit an Athenian thinking that he were a slave; for the people there are no better dressed than slaves and metics, nor is their appearance any better.

METICS

For the status of metics in Athens, see Davies (1977–78) 115–16; by the end of the fifth century, their obligations and rights included the payment of the 'metoikion' tax after residence of a month (one drachma per month for a man, and half a drachma for a woman not in her husband or son's oikos); access to certain festivals, such as those of the deme in which they resided, as in *IG* I^3 244 (doc. 5.20), and those of the city as a whole (at the festival of the Lenaia metics could serve both in the chorus and as choregoi: Davies (1967) 34); registration with the polemarch who represented their judicial interests; and liability to pay liturgies and the war-tax (eisphora) and for military service. They could not vote or own land or houses (their official designation was 'resident in' a deme; see doc. 11.26); they also needed a citizen patron, or prostates, or would be liable to prosecution (see doc. 13.55). Slaves who were manumitted acquired the status of metics; for metics and their legal position, see MacDowell (1978) 76–79.

For metics generally, see Andrewes (1971) 143–44; Finley (1973) 78–79, 162–64; Whitehead (1977) esp. 17–20, 69–98; Starr (1977) 87–89; Roberts (1984) 28–31; Vidal-Nacquet (1986) 237–40; Powell (1988) 317–18; Sinclair (1988) 28–30. For Thrasyboulos, see doc. 9.27, Whitehead (1977) 157–59. Gomme (1933) 47 suggests a population of 25,000 metics in Athens c. 431, owning 10,000 slaves; see Whitehead 97–98 who does not give a specific estimate; Roberts 38–40 estimates some 20,000 metics in 431; Salmon (1984) 159–63, believes that the number of metics in Corinth, despite its trade and manufacture, was significantly less than that in Athens. Perikles in 431 led an army of 10,000 citizen and 3,000 metic hoplites into the Megarid (Thuc. II.31.1–2); cf. Thuc. I. 143.1, II.13.6–9, III.16.1; Whitehead (1977) 42. Duncan-Jones (1980) 102–04 postulates some 12,000 metic hoplites in 431, though they may not normally have been used in the striking force; for metics in the navy, see doc. 11.23.

11.21 The Definition of a Metic

Aristophanes of Byzantium F38 (Nauck)

Aristophanes of Byzantium (c. 257–180) gives us the 'earliest of the retrospective definitions of the term' (Whitehead (1977) 7). Note that the specified period before becoming a metic was only a month: cf. doc. 10.27, a treaty in which after a month's residence 'foreigners' from the other Lokrian city became subject to the local legal procedures; Whitehead 7–10.

A metic is anyone who comes from a foreign city and lives in the city, paying tax towards certain fixed needs of the city; for a number of days he is called a parepidemos (visitor) and is free from tax, but if he outstays the time laid down he becomes a metic and liable to taxation.

11.22 The Danaids as 'Metics' in Athens c. 460

Aeschylus *Suppliant Women* 600–14

Danaos had 50 daughters, and his brother Aigyptos 50 sons, who tried to force the Danaids to marry them; the Danaids, the chorus here, fled to Argos with their father and Aeschylus imagines their being granted metic status in Argos. There is no evidence that metic status was formally regularised by this point (Davies (1977–78) 116; Whitehead (1977) 35), but *IG* I^3 244 (doc. 5.20) dated to c. 460, clearly refers to metics and it is likely that Aeschylus is referring to metics as a definite class; according to Plutarch, Solon had actively encouraged foreign craftsmen to settle in Athens (docs. 3.27–28). For the frequent references to metics in tragedy (including the *Antigone*, line 852), see Whitehead 35–38, and, in comedy (including three plays now lost entitled *Metics*, by Krates, Pherekrates and Plato the comic poet), 39–40; cf. Ar. *Ach.* 507–08, where the metics are called the 'bran' to the Athenians' 'grain'.

Danaos: Children, take heart; the decrees of this country's
People have resolved everything well.
Chorus: Greetings, old man, who bring me welcome news.
Tell us in what way it was finally decided,
How the people's sovereign hand prevailed.
Danaos: It was resolved by the Argives, with no wavering,
So as to make my old heart young again;
The whole people, with right hands raised,
Made the air quiver as they brought these words to pass:
We are to be metics of this land, free and
Protected, with complete inviolability,
And no one, inhabitant or stranger, can
Remove us; and if violence be used,
Any of the landowners who does not help us
Will lose his rights and be exiled by popular decree.

11.23 Nikias Addresses the Metics in Sicily

Thucydides VII.63.3–4

On the eve of the final defeat in Sicily in 413, Nikias addressed the troops. In this passage he turns to 'those who have been considered Athenians', who are serving as sailors (the implication is that they form the predominant part of the fleet; Duncan-Jones (1980) 102); these are almost certainly the metics in the fleet, though he could be referring to the subject-allies. Whitehead (1977) 43 considers that he is referring to metics and flattering them by not mentioning their status. For a (probably) metic helmsman (kybernetes), a prestigious position, between 414 and 406, see Jordan (1975) 142; 150–51 for metic flute-players with the fleet in the fifth century; and for metics as sailors, see 103, 210–12; doc. 7.31. For the importance placed on metics in 411, see Ar. *Lys.* 580 (doc. 13.60).

VII.63.3 And as for the sailors I advise you — indeed I entreat you — not to be overly depressed by our disasters, as we now have better armament for our fighting men on deck and more ships; you must bear in mind that enjoyment you have had, which is worth preserving: for until now you have been considered as Athenians, even though you are not, through your knowledge of our speech and your imitation of our way of life, and have been admired throughout all Greece, and have had no less a share than you deserve in the advantages of our empire, while in the respect shown you by our subjects and in your freedom from ill treatment you have had even more than your share. **VII.63.4** So that you, the only people with whom we freely share our empire, do not betray it now, despise the Corinthians whom you have often defeated, and the Sicilians, none of whom thought of resisting us when our fleet was in its prime, and beat them off, and show that even in sickness and disaster your skill is better than anyone else's strength, which is a matter of luck.

11.24 The Thirty Attack Wealthy Metics

Lysias XII *Against Eratosthenes* 4–20

Lysias was himself a metic, and owner of a shield factory with his brother Polemarchos; cf. doc. 11.12 for the personal property of the metic Kephisodoros. See also doc. 13.58, where Socrates lists a number of successful slave-run businesses and Dem. XXVII.9 for the two factories left by Demosthenes' father. For the financial benefits which metics brought to Athens, see Xen. *Revenues* 2.1.

4 My father Kephalos was persuaded by Perikles to come to this country, and lived here for thirty years, and neither we nor he have ever appeared in any case as prosecutor or defendant .... **6** Theognis and Peison stated in the Thirty concerning the metics, that there were some who had a grudge against their government and so they had the best possible pretext for appearing to punish, while in fact making money; for the state was completely impoverished and the government needed money .... **8** They divided up the houses and began their activities. They found me entertaining guests, whom they drove out and then handed me over to Peison, while the others went to the workshop and began recording the slaves. I asked Peison if he would take money to save me. He agreed, provided it was a lot. **9** So I said that I was prepared to give him a talent of silver and he agreed to do this. I knew that he thought nothing of gods or men, but decided under the circumstances that it was still essential to have his oath on this. **10** When he had sworn that he would take the talent and save me, calling down utter destruction on himself and his children if he broke his oath, I went into my room and opened the chest. Peison noticed this and came in, and when he saw what was inside he called two of his servants, and told them to take what was in the chest. **11** He had now not what was sworn, jurors, but three talents of silver and four hundred cyzicenes, a hundred darics and four silver cups .... (**16–17:** *Polemarchos, Lysias' brother, is arrested and made to drink hemlock.*) **19** They had seven hundred shields of ours, they had all that silver and gold, copper, jewellery, furniture and women's cloaks, more than they had ever thought to acquire, and a hundred and twenty slaves, of whom they took the best, and gave the rest to the state, and showed the degree of insatiability and disgusting greed they had reached in this revelation of their characters: for the golden earrings of Polemarchos' wife, which she happened to be wearing, Melobios took from her ears as soon as he came into the house. **20** And we did not find any mercy at their hands even in regard to the smallest part of our property. But they injured us because of our money as much as others might have done through anger at great crimes, and we did not deserve this from the city, but had defrayed the cost of all our choruses (as choregoi), and contributed to many special taxes (eisphorai), and shown ourselves to be well-conducted, and performed all the duties laid on us, and had not made a single enemy, and ransomed many Athenians from the enemy.

11.25 A Mixed Work-Force on the Erechtheum, 408/7

IG I^3 476, lines 199–218

Citizens, metics and slaves are listed as having been paid for taking part in the fluting of a column of the Erechtheum. Citizens are given their deme of origin, metics are described as living in a deme, and slaves as belonging to a particular person. Of the workmen, the status of 86 can be identified: 24 are citizens, 42 metics, and 20 slaves; see Randall (1953) 199–210; Finley (1973) 79–80, (1980) 100–01; Roberts (1984) 33–34; Garlan (1988) 65 (where 24 metics is obviously an unintentional error). The citizens in this inscription filled the positions of overseeing architect and under-secretary, and with the exception of one woodcarver and one labourer who laid roof tiles, all the others were masons, carpenters and sculptors; the metics, while still outnumbering the citizens in these occupations, pursued all the minor specialised trades; all the slaves were skilled, being either masons or carpenters. The rate of pay was a drachma per day for skilled labour, and citizens and metics have their slaves working alongside them; Markle (1985) 295–96 calculates that because of the low cost of feeding and clothing slaves the profits from their work could be enormous. See Randall 205, tables 3 & 4, for the relation of civic status and trade to demes and 208, table 7, for rates of pay.

(199) The ne[xt] (column): Simias l[iving in] Alopeke [1]3 dr.; Kerdon 12 dr. 5 ob.; Sin[dron belonging to Sim]ias 12 dr. 5 ob.; Sokles belonging to Ax[iopeith]es 12 dr. 5 ob.; Sannion belonging to Si[mi]as 1[2 dr. 5] ob.; Epieikes belonging to [S]imias 1[2 dr. 5] ob.; (205) So[s]andros belonging to Simias 12 dr. 5 ob. [Th]e next: [O]nesi[mos] belonging to Nikostr[a]tos 16 dr. [4] ob.; Eudo[xo]s li[vin]g in Alopeke 16 dr. [4 ob.; Kl]eon 16 dr. 4 ob.; Sim[on l]iving in [Ag]ryle (210) 16 dr.

[4] ob.; [Ant]idotos belonging to [Glau]kos 16 dr. 4 ob.; E[udi]kos 16 dr. [4] ob. [The ne]xt: Theug[enes] of Peiraieu[s 15] dr.; Kephisoge[nes of P]eiraieu[s 15 dr.; T]e[u]kros (215) [livi]ng in [Kyda]thenaion 15 dr.; Kephi[sodo]ros liv[ing] i[n Skamb]onidai 15 dr.; Niko[stratos] 15 dr.; Theug[iton] of Peirai[eus] 15 dr.

11.26 Metics are Honoured with Citizenship, 401/0

Osborne (1981) D6 (*IG* II^2 10)

Thrasyboulos (cf. doc. 9.27), a democrat who defeated the Thirty in 403 by entering the Peiraieus and seizing Mounichia, was joined by metics, to whom he seems to have promised citizenship, though not all the honorands here are necessarily metics. Whitehead (1984) 8–10 argues persuasively, against Krentz (1980) 298–306; Osborne (1981, 1982), that this inscription enfranchises some 1,000 metics, and that citizenship and not isoteleia (favoured metic status), as restored here in line 9 of face A, was awarded to all those involved. For the wives of enfranchised metics remaining metics, and not becoming citizens, see Carey (1991) 84–89. Cols. II–III of face B are given here.

A

(1) [Lysiades was se]cretary, [Xenainet]os was archon. [It was resolved by the boule and the people: (the tribe) Hippothontis held the prytan]y, Lysiades was secretary, Demophilos pre[sided, Thrasyboulos proposed the motion: so that the foreign]ers who took part in the return from Phyle or who [assisted] those who ret[urned in the return to the Peiraieus should be awarded suitable honours,] (5) it is to be decreed by the Athenians that they and their descend[ants] are to have [citizenship, and they are to be allocated immediately to the tribes in ten parts.] The magistrates are to ap[ply] the same laws to them [as to the other Athenians. And all those who came afterwards,] and joined in the battle at Mounichia, and [preserved] the [Peiraieus, and all those who stood by the demos in the Peiraieus w]hen the reconciliation took place, and did what was ord[ered, who are domiciled in Athens, are to have isoteleia in accordance with the p]ledge [given][1] just [as for the A]thenians. And they [....]

B

Chairedemos, a farm(er)
Leptines, a (coo)k (mageiros)
D[e]metrios, a carp(enter)
Euphorion, a mulet(eer)
K[e]phis[o]doros, a buil(der)
[He]gesias, a garden(er)
Epameinon, a donkey (driver)
.[..]opos, an olive(....)
[Gl]au[k]ias, a farm(er)
[.....]n, a nut(....)
[Diony]sios, a farm(er)

Be[n]diphane[s, a d]ig[....]
Em[p]o[r]ion, a [fa]r[m(er)]
Paid[i]kos, a b[a]k[e(r)]
Sosi[a]s, a ful[l(er)]
Psammis, a fa[r]m(er)
Ergesis
[...]m[.....]o
Euk[o]lion, a hired [lab]our(er)
Kallias, a statue (maker)
Of (the tribe) Aigeis
Atheno[g]i[t]on [....]

[1] Here following the suggestion of Whitehead (1984) 8–10.

HELOTS, PERIOIKOI AND SERFS

Unlike most other slaves in Greek states, helots were not foreigners, but a subject people working their own lands in a state of servitude. They had property rights of a kind, after paying a ratio of produce to the Spartans, and well outnumbered the Spartiates; Finley (1959) 158–4. For helots as a self-perpetuating class of slaves with their own families and possessions, see Finley (1973) 63–64; Cartledge (1979) 160–77; de Ste. Croix (1981) 147–50; Powell (1988) 248–52; Talbert (1989) 22–40. While slaves in Athens were manumitted on serving in the armed forces, Sparta depended on helots in her army, with 35,000 at Plataea (see Hdt. IX.28.2, 29.1, cf. doc. 7.25); this made them a dangerous political force with a potential for revolt: Vidal-Nacquet (1986) 164–65; Garlan (1988) 153–55. For the perioikoi, see Ridley (1974) 281–92, who argues against their being basically an industrial and commercial class; Cartledge (1979) 178–85; cf. Vidal-Nacquet (1986) 175–83, 212–13; Garlan (1988) 95–97. They also served as hoplites, as at Plataea (see Hdt. IX.11.3, 28.2).

11.27 Messenian Tribute and Servitude

Tyrtaeus 6, 7 (Pausanias IV.14.4–5)

For the amount each allotment (kleros) was supposed to produce, see Plut. *Lyk.* 8.7 (doc. 6.41), 24.2; Figueira (1984) 98–109. For mourning for Spartan kings, cf. Hdt. VI.58.

IV.14.4 The Messenians themselves were treated by the Spartans in the following way: first they made them take an oath that they would never rebel against them or attempt any form of revolution. Secondly, while the Spartans imposed no fixed tribute on them, they used to bring half of all their agricultural produce to Sparta. It was also laid down that at the funerals of kings and other magistrates both men and women should come from Messenia in black clothes; and a penalty was imposed on transgressors. **IV.14.5** As to the punishments with which they maltreated the Messenians, this is written in the poems of Tyrtaeus (F6):

Just like donkeys oppressed with great burdens,
2 Bringing to their masters of grievous necessity
Half of all the produce their land bears.

That they were compelled to join in their mourning (for their masters) he has shown in these lines (F7):

Lamenting their masters, both their wives and themselves,
2 Whenever the baneful fate of death should overtake one.

11.28 The Spartans' Callous Treatment of Helots

Plutarch *Lykourgos* 28.8–12

Cf. docs. 6.31–32 for Spartan attitudes to alcohol; the quotation at 28.11 is from Kritias F37 (Diels II). According to Myron of Priene *FGH* 106 F2 the Spartans imposed all forms of insults on the helots, including the wearing of dog-skin caps, and fined the owners of helots who grew fat. For the helot revolt, see docs. 8.7, 9.

28.8 In other ways too the Spartiates treated the helots harshly and brutally; for example they would compel them to drink a large quantity of unmixed wine and then would bring them into the messes to show the young men what drunkenness was like, **28.9** and used to order them to sing songs and perform dances which were ignoble and ridiculous, but to refrain from those appropriate for free men .... **28.11** This distinction can be clearly seen in the saying that at Sparta a free man is really free and a slave really a slave. **28.12** I believe that such harsh treatment on the part of the Spartiates came later, particularly after the great earthquake, when the helots are said to have to have risen up with the Messenians, done terrible damage to the country, and posed a serious threat to the city.

11.29 Drastic Measures for Dealing with Helots

Thucydides IV.80.2–5

Brasidas in 424 proposed taking a small force against Athens' possessions in Thrace, one of his reasons being to keep the helots occupied. The Spartans voted in 421 that these helots be freed, and settled them at Lepreon with the neodamodeis, literally 'new citizens' (Thuc. V.34.1, presumably helots who had been liberated after military service); see Thuc. V.67.1, VII.19.3, 58.3, VIII.5.1; Lazenby (1985) 14; Figueira (1986) 197; see Andrewes (1978b) 99; Jordan (1990) 37–69. Talbert (1989) esp. 31–33 considers that the helots' potential for revolt has been over-exaggerated and that the Spartiates were for the most part confident of their helots' loyalty. Helots served in Sicily; see Thuc VII.19.3, 58.3.

IV.80.2 At the same time they were glad of an excuse to send out some of the helots, as they were afraid, in the present state of affairs with Pylos in enemy hands, that they might start some sort of revolution. **IV.80.3** Also on one occasion, because they were afraid of the difficulties they could cause and their numbers (for the Spartans' measures respecting the helots have concentrated almost entirely on security), they proclaimed that the helots should pick out all those who claimed to have done best service to Sparta in their wars, implying that they would be freed, but they were actually conducting a test, as they considered that those with spirit who came forward first to claim their freedom would also be those most likely to turn against Sparta. **IV.80.4** So they picked out about 2,000, who crowned themselves with garlands and made the round of the sanctuaries as if they were now free, but not long afterwards they caused them to disappear and no one knows in what way any of them died. **IV.80.5** And so on this occasion the Spartans were glad to send out 700 hoplites with Brasidas, while the rest of the army he took with him from the Peloponnese he had hired as mercenaries.

11.30 The Krypteia: the Spartan 'Secret Service'

Plutarch *Lykourgos* 28.1–7 (Aristotle F538)

Cf. Thuc. IV.80.4; Plat. *Laws* 633b; see Vidal-Nacquet (1986) 112–14. David (1989) 13 considers this to be a primitive rite of passage which was 'preserved and institutionalised in the pseudo-primitive Spartan society'. Powell (1989) 181 suggests from Plut. *Lyk.* 28.4 that there may have been a curfew in force, hence the killing of helots on the roads at night: certainly the actions of the krypteia would have enforced a *de facto* curfew.

28.1 In all this there is no trace of the injustice or arrogance, of which some accuse Lykourgos' laws, considering that while they are well equipped to produce valour, they fail to produce justice. **28.2** Their so-called 'krypteia', if this really was one of Lykourgos' institutions, as Aristotle says, may have given Plato as well this idea of Lykourgos and his constitution. The krypteia was like this: **28.3** the supervisors of the young men from time to time would send out into the countryside in different directions those who appeared to be the most intelligent, equipped only with daggers and basic provisions. **28.4** During the day they would disperse into obscure places to hide and rest, but at night they would make their way to the roads and kill any helot they caught. **28.5** Often too they would go through the fields and do away with the sturdiest and most powerful helots .... **28.7** And Aristotle also says specifically that the ephors, when first they took up office, would declare war on the helots, so that killing them would not involve ritual pollution.

11.31 The Helots' View of the Spartiates

Xenophon *Hellenika* III.3.6

The leaders of the conspiracy against the Spartan king Agesilaos (397) believed that they were aware of the secret feelings of all non-Spartans; here an informer reveals the secrets of the plot to the ephors. The hypomeiones ('inferiors') *may* have been Spartiates who had undergone the agoge but could not make mess-contributions (Xen. *Hell.* III.3.6; Lazenby (1985) 16–17). Kritias F37 (Diels II) states that the Spartiates at home removed the handles off helots' shields; being unable to do this in war-time, because of the need for speedy use, they always carried their spears in case the helots attempted mutiny.

The leaders said that they were privy to the feelings of all the helots, neodamodeis, hypomeiones and perioikoi: for whenever amongst these mention was made of the Spartiates, no one could hide the fact that he would be glad to eat them — even raw.

11.32 Thessalian Serfs

Theopompos *FGH* 115 F122 (Athenaeus *Deipnosophistae* 265b–c)

For the penestai, Thessalian serfs, cf. Xen. *Hell.* VI.1.11; for those of Crete, doc. 11.16; Starr (1977) 163 considers Thessaly and Crete as fringe areas of the Greek world, where nobles were unchecked by other forces; cf. de Ste. Croix (1981) 150–54. Theopompos believes the Chians to have been the first Greeks to institute chattel-slavery. The Byzantines also made serfs of Bithynians in Asia Minor: Phylarchos *FGH* 81 F8; see Garlan (1988) 102–06; cf. Beringer (1982) 20; Rihll (1993) 100–05.

After the Thessalians and Spartans, the Chians were the first of the Greeks to use slaves, but they did not acquire them in the same way as these. For, as we shall see, the Spartans and Thessalians constituted their slave population out of the Greeks who had previously lived in the territories which they now hold, the Spartans taking over the Achaean territory, the Thessalians that of the Perrhaiboi and the Magnesians, and they call the people they enslaved helots and penestai respectively. But the Chians acquired barbarians as slaves and paid money for them.

CITIZEN LABOUR

There were of course, in Athens at least, and probably in most Greek cities except Sparta, large numbers of free men engaged in labour, either manufacturing, or retail trade, or working their own land. The ideal life-style for the Athenian citizen was to own a farm and support a family on the produce from that land, while having sufficient freedom from work to engage in social and political life (Jameson (1977–78) 124; Starr (1977) 92–95; de Ste. Croix (1981) 506; Roberts (1984) 37; cf. Wood (1983) 15). For Aristotle's denigratory attitude towards 'banausic' (artisan) occupations, see Balme (1984) 140–52; Cartledge (1993) 172–73; for the banausic arts in general, see Wood (1983) 4–6, (1988) 137–45. Naturally, not all industry, retail trade and manufacture was in the hands of metics; for citizen workers in these areas, see Finley (1959) 145; Ridley (1974) 283–84; Whitehead (1977) 117–19; Garlan (1980) 6–22; Welskopf (1980) 23–25; doc. 11.26.

11.33 Maxims for Prosperity

Hesiod *Works and Days* 20–26

While Hesiod assumes that the farmer will have slave labour, he also sees it as necessary for the farmer to work hard; Finley (1959) 145–46; cf. doc. 11.8. He states explicitly that hard work is not degrading, though it is part of man's condition in the 'Iron Age' of the world and a disagreeable necessity; cf. lines 42–46, 174–79, 298–319, 381–82, 397–400; Nussbaum (1960) 217; Balme (1984) 141–42. He also sees hard work as the preserve of the craftsman and artisan, and provides evidence for the existence of crafts and trade. For Hesiod's view of trade as 'a supplementary form of income for well-off farmers', see Hahn (1983) 30; for the risks and profits involved in trade, see esp. lines 236–37, 618–45. Cf. Theognis 173–78 for poverty as the worst thing that can befall a man.

Moreover Strife rouses even the helpless to work;
For a man craves work when he looks at the next man
Who is rich, who hastens to plough and plant
And set his house in good order; and neighbour is jealous of neighbour
As the latter hastens after riches; this strife is good for mankind.
And potter is angry with potter, and craftsman with craftsman,
Beggar envies beggar and minstrel envies minstrel.

11.34 The Professions

Solon 13, lines 43–66

Solon here lists the ways that men can justly acquire wealth; see Crane (1992) 244–47; cf. docs. 3.25, 27; de Ste. Croix (1981) 185 notes that the hired farm labourer is depicted no more unfavourably than other men who have to work; for doctors, cf. doc. 2.30.

All exert themselves in different ways: one wanders the fishy sea
Desiring in his ships to bring home gain
Tossed by dreadful winds,
Quite unsparing of his life;
Another ploughs the land abounding in trees every year
And works for hire, his care the curved ploughs;
One who has learnt the works of Athena and Hephaistos skilled in many crafts
Brings in his livelihood with his hands,

Another through being taught the gifts of the Olympian Muses,
And who knows full measure of lovely wisdom;
Another person Lord Apollo the Far-shooter has made a seer;
He knows the evil that comes to a man from afar,
For on him the gods attend; but what is destined
No bird (omen) or sacrifices will in any way ward off.
Others have the work of Paian (the gods' healer), who knows many drugs,
Doctors: but they have no efficacy;
For often from a small ache comes great pain,
And no one can relieve it by giving soothing drugs;
Although he can touch a man disordered by dreadful diseases
And with his hands suddenly make him well.
Fate brings both evil and good to mortal men,
And the gifts of the immortal gods can not be avoided.
There is danger in all forms of work, nor does one know
Where a matter once begun will end.

11.35 The Spartan Way of Life

Xenophon *Constitution of the Spartans* 7.1–2

Herodotos (II.166.2–167.2) lists societies which view trade as unsuitable for a citizen: not only the Kalasirians (Egyptian warriors) but 'the Thracians and Scythians and Persians and Lydians and nearly all the barbarians consider those who learn a craft and their descendants as inferior to other citizens, while they consider those who are exempted from manual work to be noble, and especially those who concentrate on war' (II.167.2); among the Greeks the Spartans in his view despise craftsmen most, while the Corinthians look down them least of all. For citizen participation in crafts in Corinth, see Salmon (1984) 162–64. Xenophon is giving the idealised view of Sparta: for Spartan art and crafts, see Cartledge (1976) 115–19; and cf. Hdt. VI.60 for the hereditary nature of the occupations of herald, flautist and slaughterer (mageiros) in Sparta (presumably all military occupations).

7.1 In other states, I suppose, everyone makes as much money as they can; for one person farms, another owns ships, another is a merchant, and others support themselves by different crafts. **7.2** But at Sparta Lykourgos forbade free men to touch anything to do with making money, and instructed them only to think about those activities which provide cities with freedom.

11.36 Socrates on Artisans

Xenophon *Oeconomicus* 4.2–3

Despite the views of Socrates here, it is likely that a large number of Athenians supported themselves by labour of various sorts, and that contempt for 'banausic' crafts was limited in Athens to the aristocratic class. When he questioned Charmides as to why he was too shy to speak in the assembly, Socrates listed, as the people who made up the assembly, fullers, cobblers, builders, smiths, farmers, merchants and 'dealers in the agora who think of nothing but buying cheap and selling dear': Xen. *Mem.* III.7.6; cf. Plat. *Prot.* 319d; Balme (1984) 140–52; Markle (1985) 275. Note Perikles' statement in the 'Funeral

Speech' (Thuc. II.40.1; doc. 10.9) that poverty is no disgrace: what is disgraceful is not taking steps to escape it. For Socrates' view of agriculture as the healthiest and most leisured occupation for a gentleman, see Xen. *Oec.* 6.8–9.

4.2 'Well said, Kritoboulos', replied Socrates, 'For the trades of artisans as they are called are decried and are understandably held in contempt in our cities, for they disfigure the bodies of those who work at them and supervise them, compelling them to remain seated and stay within doors, and sometimes to spend all day at the fire. When bodies become enervated, the souls become much more sickly. **4.3** And moreover these artisans' trades as they are called leave no free time for attending to one's friends and the city, with the result that such men appear to be inadequate both in their relationships with friends and as defenders of their countries. And in some cities, and especially those which have a warlike reputation it is not permissible for any of the citizens to work at the trades of artisans.'

11.37 Eutheros Falls on Hard Times

Xenophon *Memorabilia* II.8.1–6

Eutheros is apparently a man of property who has fallen on hard times (cf. doc. 13.58). Socrates suggests that he should hire himself out as an estate manager; clearly Athenians of this class were reluctant to take on salaried employment, but obviously it was a possibility, and bailiffs were not always slaves (Wood (1983) 21; *contra* de Ste. Croix (1981) 181–82). Clearly working for someone else does not befit a 'gentleman'; see Millett (1989) 28–29.

II.8.1 On seeing another old friend after a long time, Socrates said, 'Where have you come from Eutheros?' 'From abroad when the (Peloponnesian) war ended, Socrates,' he replied, 'And now I'm living here. Since we lost our foreign property, and my father left me nothing in Attica, I'm now compelled to stay here and engage in physical labour to obtain my provisions. I think that that's better than begging from anyone, especially as I have nothing against which I can borrow.' **II.8.2** 'And how long, said Socrates, 'do you think your body will be strong enough to earn your provisions by working for hire?' 'By Zeus,' he said, 'not long.' 'And when you get older it is clear that you will need to spend money, but no one will be willing to give you a wage for physical labour.' **II.8.3** 'That's very true.' 'Then wouldn't it be better for you to take up at once the sort of work that would also be viable for you when you're older, and approach someone who has more property who needs someone to assist him, and supervise his tasks and help bring in the crops and look after his estate, helping yourself by helping him?' **II.8.4** 'I would find it hard to endure slavery, Socrates.' 'But those who are in charge in the cities and look after public affairs are not thought more servile on that account, but are thought even more free.' **II.8.5** 'Yet, Socrates, I could never undertake to become accountable to anyone.' 'But Eutheros, it is not at all easy to find a job where one does not have some censure .... **II.8.6** So you should try to avoid fault-finders and look for those who are considerate and undertake those things you are able to perform, and keep away from any that you can't, and whatever you do give it your best and most zealous attention. In this way, I think, you are least likely to find censure, and you are most likely to find help in your difficulties, and live most easily and in greatest security and with a good competence for you old age.'

11.38 Perikles and Citizen Labour

Plutarch *Perikles* 12.5–6

Perikles' program would have provided employment for a number of skilled workers, at least some of them citizens: cf. docs. 8.23, 10.7; Frost (1976) 70–71; Ostwald (1986) 183–84, 187; Kallet-Marx (1989) 252–66; Burke (1992) 217. de Ste. Croix (1981) 189–90 argues that it was unlikely that the main purpose of such works was to provide employment, and that it would mainly have involved metics, foreigners and other slaves; but this is on the assumption that few citizens were artisans, which is arguable (cf. de Ste. Croix 114–15, 124–25; docs. 11.37, 39; but note Andrewes (1978a) 1–5).

12.5 The military campaigns provided incomes from public funds for those who had their youth and strength, but Perikles wished that the undisciplined artisan mob should also have a share in the payments. He did not want it to receive pay for being lazy and idle, so he brought before the people great construction projects and undertakings which would require the involvement of many crafts for works that would take a long time to complete, so that those who stayed at home, no less than those who were with the fleet or on garrison duty or on expeditions, should have a reason for benefiting from and sharing in the public funds. **12.6** The raw materials to be used were stone, bronze, ivory, gold, ebony and cypress-wood, while the trades which fashioned this material were to be those of carpenters, modellers, coppersmiths, stone-masons, gilders, workers in ivory, painters, embroiderers and engravers, as well as the carriers and suppliers of these materials — merchants, sailors and pilots by sea, and by land cartwrights, keepers of draught animals, muleteers, rope-makers, weavers, leatherworkers, road-makers and miners.

11.39 A Craftsman Dedicates a Tithe to Athena

IG I[2] 678 (*IG* I[3] 766)

Friedländer 134; Hansen 230. Fragments of a base of Parian marble from a dedication on the acropolis at Athens. The craftsman appears to have dedicated his own work as a tithe; this dedication may have been made by a metic rather than a citizen.

[It is good] for the skilled to ex[e]rcise their ski[ll a]ccordin[g to their craft];
[For he who] has a craft ha[s] a bet[t]er [life].
[.... dedicat]ed a tit[he] to Athena.

THE DRAMATIC SLAVE

11.40 The Garrulous Old Nurse of Orestes

Aeschylus *Libation Bearers* 747–65

Orestes returns to Mycenae planning to murder his mother Clytemnesta and her lover Aegisthus. To make his task easier, he arrives in disguise, and reports that he (Orestes) is dead. For wet-nurses (tithai) and nannies (trophoi) and their role in caring for children, see Vogt (1975) 105–09; Golden (1984) 309–10, (1990) 146–49; Garland (1990) 113–18; doc. 13.23.

Nurse: Well I've never yet endured such a blow!
I've born my other troubles with endurance,
But dear Orestes, my soul's care,
Whom I took from his mother and brought up,
The times he cried and got me out of bed!
The many tedious things I went through
For nothing; a baby knows no better and you've got
To nurse it like an animal; why not? It's how it thinks;
For a babe still in swaddling clothes can't say
If it's hungry or thirsty or wants to pee.
Children's insides are young and act instinctively.
I used to foretell these, but often
I'd be wrong, and I'd be washing the baby clothes,
For laundress and nurse were both the same person.
And I had these two duties
When I took Orestes from his father;
And now I'm wretched to hear that he's dead!
Well, I'll go to that man who's this house's
Ruin; he'll be pleased to hear of this.

11.41 Helen's Loyal Servant

Euripides *Helen* 722–33

On noble slaves in tragedy, see Vogt (1975) 15–23; cf. doc. 13.64. Garlan (1988) 15, 18 warns, of course, that slaves in tragedy should not be arbitrarily related to 'real life'.

Now I remember again your wedding
And recall the lamps which I carried as I ran
Beside the four horses yoked together; and you in your chariot
As a bride with him (Menelaos) left your happy home.
It's a base slave that does not revere his masters' affairs
And rejoice with them and share in their troubles.
I would be, a servant though I am,
Numbered amongst the noble
Slaves — not free in name,

But at least in mind; for this is better than for one man
To suffer two ills — to have a base mind
And to hear himself called slave by those around him.

11.42 The Fate of Women in Wartime

Euripides *Trojan Women* 235–52, 272–78

Hekabe, wife of Priam and queen of Troy, after the capture of Troy hears her own fate and that of her daughters and daughters-in-law from Talthybios, the Greek herald. Compare Hector's poignant foreshadowing of Troy's capture by the Greeks and Andromache's future fate as a slave: Hom. *Iliad* VI.447–63.

Talthybios: Hekabe, you know me from my frequent journeys to Troy,
236 Coming here as herald from the Greek host,
Known to you, lady, formerly,
I, Talthybios, come to announce news.
Hekabe: †Dear women, this† was our former fear.
Talthybios: You have now been allocated, if this was what you feared.
Hekabe: Alas! For what
242 City of Thessaly or Phthia
Or the land of Kadmos are we destined?
Talthybios: You have each been assigned to a different man, not all together.
Hekabe: Who is assigned to whom? Which Trojan woman does good luck await?
Talthybios: I know; but you must learn one at a time, not all together.
Hekabe: My child then,
Tell me, wretched Cassandra, who has obtained her?
Talthybios: King Agamemnon chose her specially.
Hekabe: For his Spartan wife
251 To be a slave? O misery!
Talthybios: Not so, but for his bed as a concubine ....

Hekabe: What of the wife of bronze-hearted Hector,
Poor Andromache, what is her fate?
Talthybios: The son of Achilles too chose her especially.
Hekabe: And whose servant am I, who leans on her stick
276 With her aged hand as if on a third foot ?
Talthybios: Odysseus, king of Ithaca, has obtained you as his slave.
Hekabe: Oh woe!

11.43 A Utopia without Slaves

Krates *The Wild Animals* (Athenaeus *Deipnosophistae* 267e–f)

Kassel & Austin F16; Kock F14. This is from a fifth century comedy of which fragments remain; here automation is promised as an alternative to slaves; see Vogt (1975) 29–30; Garlan (1988) 131–32.

A: Then won't anyone own a male or female slave?
Will each man, even old ones, have to look after themselves?
B: Not at all; I am going to give everything the ability to move around.
A: So what will that achieve? B: Each piece of equipment
Will come when called for. 'Set yourself beside me table.'
'That one — get yourself ready.' 'Get kneading, bread basket.'
'Pour, ladle.' 'Where's the cup? Go and wash yourself out.'
'Barley cake, rise.' 'The pot ought to disgorge the beets.'
'Fish, get moving.' 'But I'm not cooked yet on the other side.'
'Then why don't you turn over and give yourself some oil and a sprinkle of salt?'

11.44 Slaves as a Stock-joke in Comedy

Aristophanes *Frogs* 1–20

Obviously to bring on a slave or slaves with stock jokes to commence a comedy has become a stereotyped convention: cf. Ar. *Knights* 1–149, *Wasps* 1–135. Harsh treatment of slaves appears to be considered amusing: see Golden (1990) 161. On slaves in Aristophanes, see Ehrenberg (1943) 165–91, who notes that Xanthias, being a Greek, is not a typical Athenian slave (171); cf. Vogt (1975) 5–14; Garlan (1988) 16–18.

Xanthias: Shall I tell one of the usual jokes, Master,
Those at which the audience always laugh?
Dionysos: Yes, whatever you like — all except 'what a load I've got!',
Watch that one; I feel sick enough already.
Xanthias: What about some other joke?
Dionysos: Anything but 'what a bad way I'm in!'
Xanthias: Then what? Shall I say something really funny?
Dionysos: Yes
With confidence; but just don't say —
Xanthias: What?
Dionysos: Shift your load and say you want to 'ease yourself'.
Xanthias: Not even that I'm carrying such a tremendous load that
10 If someone doesn't remove it I'm going to fart?
Dionysos: Definitely not, please — keep it for when I'm about to vomit.
Xanthias: So why did I have to carry all this baggage,
If I can't make any of the jokes that
14 Phrynichos and Lykis and Ameipsias always do?
Dionysos: Well, you can't; when I'm a spectator
17 And see one of these stage-tricks,
I come away more than a year older.
Xanthias: This thrice wretched neck of mine —
It's 'in a bad way' and can't say anything funny.

<<>>

12

Religion in the Greek World

Homer and Hesiod recorded numerous stories about the gods, and their works reflect many of the beliefs about the gods held by the Greeks in the period under discussion (cf. doc. 12.10). In the *Iliad* the gods have many negative characteristics: they are jealous, capricious, cruel, selfish, devious, petty, vindictive, and obstinate, behaving, in fact, exactly as human beings do. The traditional view of the gods in Homer was not without its sceptics and a number of the pre-Socratic philosophers as part of their questioning of conventional beliefs criticized the traditional mythology of the Olympian religion and its ceremonial and rites of worship (see docs. 12.12–16; cf. 9.32–35). But these sceptics only serve to confirm the rule: most Greeks believed in the gods about which Homer and Hesiod wrote, and traditional Olympian religion remained the normal form of belief in the period under discussion.

Traditional Greek religion lacked written guidelines, and most Greek religious practices were traditionally handed down from generation to generation. Without a set of holy books, the Greeks sought to learn the will of the gods through the use of oracles, and by interpreting omens which they believed were sent by the gods. Through the use of oracles in particular the Greeks believed that they could consult the gods directly. There were several oracular centres throughout Greece, the most famous being at Delphi, where a priestess, the Pythia, sat on a tripod in the temple of Apollo, answering questions which were put to her by inquirers. The priestess was the medium of Apollo, god of prophecy: when she spoke it was believed that the god was speaking through her. Consultants would customarily inquire about a number of problems: why there was a plague in their city, whether they should send a colony to Sicily, or why they were childless or their crops had failed (docs. 12.21–22). Another way to seek knowledge of the future was by the use of divination, for which the customary procedures were to sacrifice an animal, examine the liver, and interpret from this the will of the gods (doc. 12.20), or to study the flights of birds (doc. 12.19).

The Greeks considered their right to go to Panhellenic sanctuaries and worship there as very important. Major sites, such as Olympia and Eleusis, proclaimed sacred truces for the pious pilgrims who wished to participate at their festivals and these truces came into effect for the period immediately before, during and after the major celebration at these sites. Prior to the celebration of the Eleusinian Mysteries, an annual event, messengers would be sent out throughout the Greek world to announce a sacred truce under the terms of which all who wished were to be allowed to travel to and return from Eleusis in safety (see doc. 12.4). Panhellenic festivals were very much a part of the Greek way of life and the right of worshippers to travel to and from these festivals was carefully protected (doc. 12.25). The major festivals attracted participants from all over the Greek world and even tyrants from Sicily and Greek kings from Cyrene regularly sent chariots to compete at the Olympic and Pythian games, while poets such as Pindar and Bacchylides celebrated their victories (docs. 2.37–38; 1.26). There were also, of course, festivals held by individual cities for the benefit of their citizens, as well as festivals which were restricted to a particular group of Greeks. The Ionians had a cult centre on the island of Delos, and Thucydides, reflecting his general interest in religion as it impinged on political events, has a long description of the festival there, and quotes extracts from the *Homeric Hymn to Apollo* which describe the festival on Delos in the archaic period, when the Ionians came together to give the god pleasure with boxing, dancing and singing (doc. 12.27, cf. 10.34).

Another important aspect of religious beliefs concerned the afterlife. In the *Odyssey*, Homer paints a very gloomy picture of the afterlife (doc. 12.30, cf. 13.3). The souls of the deceased wander around in the underworld, as spirits, leading a shadowy existence without pleasure. But this idea of a shadowy afterlife did not appeal to all of the Greeks, many of whom participated in ceremonies which gave them hopes for a better afterlife. These ceremonies are known as mystery celebrations, the most famous of which were the Eleusinian Mysteries, celebrated at Eleusis in Attica (docs. 12. 1–6). Another example of personal religion was the cult of the healing god Asklepios and it was to Asklepios that the Greeks turned in cases of personal sickness. The main healing centre of Asklepios in Greece was at Epidauros, in the eastern Peloponnese, where the sick slept in a special building, the abaton, set aside for this purpose, and hoped that during the night the god Asklepios would appear to them in a dream and heal them. It was very much a case of faith healing: carrying out the proper rituals, praying, and then during the night hoping for a vision of the god which would bring about a cure (docs. 12.7–9).

Religion permeated the life of the city-state: the life of the citizen revolved around innumerable festivals, of the city, phratry and deme (cf. docs. 10.20–22, 5.19–20). Public religion centred on the sacrifices offered at such festivals, which involved public feasting which strengthened ties of kinship and solidarity within the polis. Each city had its own temples and shrines, and tutelary deities, and Athens was full of hermai, small representations of Hermes in stone outside individual houses (cf. doc. 9.22). Yet despite the fact that the various Greek cites each had their own especial deities and festivals, Herodotos tells us that two of the most important characteristics of the Greeks were the fact that they had a common language, and the same religion (doc. 12.43). Religion was therefore a significant determinant of Greek identity and an important part of the common heritage which distinguished Greek from barbarian.

THE ELEUSINIAN MYSTERIES

Participants in the Eleusinian Mysteries were bound to secrecy, on pain of death, but the ceremonies seem to have been based to some extent on the adventures of Demeter as related in the *Homeric Hymn to Demeter*, probably written down in the seventh century (doc. 12.1). The hymn tells how Persephone, the daughter of Demeter, was carried away by the god Hades. Demeter roamed the world looking for her daughter until, exhausted, she came to Eleusis, where she was looked after by the local people. Eventually an agreement was worked out whereby Persephone returned to the earth for spring, returning to Hades and the underworld for winter, for which her absence was believed to be responsible. Demeter in gratitude for their help gave to the Eleusinians ceremonies which ensured a happy afterlife for the participants. The Athenians administered the Eleusinian Mysteries, both Greater and Lesser, as a state cult (cf. docs. 12.4–6). On the day after the initiates (mystai) had walked from Athens to Eleusis, there was a night time celebration at which the actual initiation took place, and in the darkened hall called the telesterion the secret of a blessed afterlife was revealed to them. Since Demeter was connected with agriculture, there may well have been an agricultural symbolism in the objects revealed to the initiates, such as an ear of wheat. Participation was open to all adults, men, women or slaves: the only criteria were the ability to speak Greek and innocence of murder. Children, however, were excluded from the Eleusinian Mysteries and all the mystai were adults except for the 'child of the hearth', whose role was to propitiate the goddess on behalf of all the initiates. Children were perhaps excluded because the mysteries involved a comprehension of the rites, and an understanding of the revelation which was at the core of the ceremony; Porph. *Abst.* IV.5; Sokolowski (1959) 3; Mylonas (1961) 236–37; Clinton (1974) 98–114; *Hesp.* 49 (1980) pp.263–68, side A, line 41, p.285); Burkert (1983) 254, 280, (1987) 52, 151n.115. For the mysteries, see esp. Mylonas (1961) 224–316; Burkert (1983) 248–97; Osborne (1985) 174–78; and Ostwald (1986) 161–69 on the laws relating to Eleusis. For the sanctuary, see esp. Clinton (1993) 110–24.

12.1 Demeter Grieves for the Loss of Persephone

Homeric Hymn to Demeter 198–211, 476–82

On arrival at Eleusis, Demeter sat and neither laughed nor tasted food or drink: *Hom. Hymn Dem.* 200, cf. 49–50, 129, 302–04; Callim. *Hymn Dem.* 12. It is probable, therefore, that the pilgrims to Eleusis fasted in imitation of the goddess. For the kykeon, which Demeter drank as it was 'holy' (lines 206–11), see Richardson (1974) 224, 344–48, with bibliography. According to Sophocles, the mysteries were locked 'by a golden key (of silence) on the tongue' (*Oed. Col.* 1050–53); see Guthrie (1950) 289; Mylonas (1961) 224–29; Richardson (1974) 304–08; Parke (1977) 56; Burkert (1983) 248–56.

A long while Demeter sat upon the stool silent and mourning,
Nor did she greet anyone by word or sign,
But unsmiling, without tasting food or drink,
She sat pining with longing for her deep-girded daughter,
Until with jests true-hearted Iambe
Joked many times and turned the holy lady
To smile and laugh and have a joyous heart;
And afterwards also she delighted her with her moods.
Metaneira filled and gave her a cup of honey-sweet wine,
But she refused it; for she said it was not right
To drink red wine, but told them to mix

Meal and water with delicate pennyroyal and give it her to drink.
Iambe made the kykeon and gave it to the goddess as she bade;
And the lady Demeter received it for the sake of the rite ....

To all Demeter revealed the conduct of her rites and mysteries —
To Triptolemos and Polyxeinos and Diokles as well —
Dread mysteries, which one may not in any way transgress or learn of
Or utter; for great reverence for the gods checks the voice.
Happy is he of mortal men who has seen these things;
But he who is not initiated in the rites, who has no part in them,
Has no share of such things, dead, down in mouldy darkness.

12.2 The Revels of the Initiates

Aristophanes *Frogs* 312–36

Here the god Dionysos and Xanthias see in the underworld the happy life enjoyed by the initiates. Diagoras of Melos in the fifth century trivialised the mysteries by telling people about them, and thus dissuaded people from being initiated. He was therefore sentenced to death: Ar. *Birds* 1072–73; Diod. XIII.6.7; the Arab source Al-Mubassir (trans. in Jacoby *FGH* 3b *Suppl.* 1.198; cf. Woodbury (1965) 188–90). There was a reward of one talent for the person who killed Diagoras and, the scholiasts add, two talents if he was brought in alive; see Jacoby *FGH* 3b *Suppl.* 1.199–201, *Suppl.* 2.165–67.

Dionysos: Didn't you hear it?
Xanthias: What?
Dionysos: A sound of flutes.
Xanthias: Yes I did, and a certain
Very mystical air of torches breathed on me.
Dionysos: Be quiet, let's crouch down and listen.
Chorus: Iakchos, O Iakchos!
Iakchos, O Iakchos!
Xanthias: That's it master — the initiates
Are sporting somewhere here, whom Herakles told us about.
At any rate they are chanting Iakchos, like Diagoras does.
Dionysos: I think so as well. It'll be best
To keep quiet, so we can know for sure.
Chorus: O Iakchos, highly honoured, who dwell here in your abode,
Iakchos, O Iakchos,
Come here to dance through this meadow
To your pious celebrants,
Shaking about your head
The full-fruited myrtle
Garland, striking with bold
Foot the unbridled
Sportive rite,
Which has full share of the Graces, the pure and holy
Dance among your pious mystai.

12.3 Alkibiades Returns to Athens, 407

Xenophon *Hellenika* I.4.20–21

Cf. Plut. *Alk.* 34.3–7. To celebrate the Greater Mysteries the Athenians traditionally made the journey from Athens to Eleusis by land, on the nineteenth of Boedromion, a distance of some 22 kilometres, but since the Spartan fortification at Dekeleia (doc. 9.23) they had gone by sea instead. Alkibiades, however, in 407 led out the army by land, protecting the mystai during their procession to Eleusis; see Benson (1928) 273–78; Kagan (1987) 290–91; Ellis (1989) 89–90. The sacred objects which had been removed from Eleusis on the fourteenth were now returned on the nineteenth, accompanied this time by those seeking initiation; see *LSCG Suppl.* 15; Mylonas (1961) 252–58; Parke (1977) 65–67; Burkert (1983) 277–80, (1985) 286–87; for the date: *IG* II^2 1078.18–22; Mylonas (1961) 256–57n.151; Mikalson (1975) 59. The majority of Athenians may well have been initiates: see Andok. I.11–12 (where the assembly is cleared of non-initiates); Sealey (1987) 84; for the vision of dust arising as if from the marching of 30,000 men from Eleusis (the citizen body comprised approximately 30,000), see Hdt. VIII.65, cf. V.97.2; Plut. *Them.* 15.1, *Phok.* 28.1–2; cf. Poseidonios *FGH* 87 F36.51; Paus. I.36.3.

I.4.20 When Alkibiades had spoken in his defence in the boule and assembly, saying that he had not committed sacrilege and had been wronged, after other such things had been said and no one spoke in opposition because the assembly would not have tolerated it, he was proclaimed commander-in-chief with supreme powers, on the ground that he would be able to restore the city's former power. First of all he led out all the soldiers and conducted by land the mysteries which the Athenians had been conducting by sea because of the war; **I.4.21** then he collected a force of 1,500 hoplites, and 150 cavalry and 100 ships.

12.4 Regulations for a Sacred Truce for the Mysteries, c. 460

IG I^3 6B

There were sacred truces for the Eleusinian Mysteries, both Lesser and Greater, as well as for the major Panhellenic events. The length of the truces for the mysteries was fifty-five days, covering the period before, during and after the celebration itself. The terms of the truce indicate that cities which did not observe the truce would not be allowed access to the mysteries. Sacred truces did not mean that warfare ceased throughout the Greek world, but ensured that those participating in the festivals involved were to be inviolable. The truces for the Eleusinian Mysteries, as for the Olympic festival, were announced by special ambassadors known as spondophoroi, 'truce-bearers'; for the truces, see Pritchett (1971) 121–24n.28; Rougemont (1973) 94–98. In 420 the Spartans were excluded from the Olympic games for attacking Eleian territory during the sacred truce, and remained excluded for over 20 years: Thuc. V.49.1–50.4; see Popp (1957) 127–32; Rougemont (1973) 94–98, 102; Sordi (1984) 20–23. The Lesser Mysteries were a purificatory preparation for the Greater Mysteries (Schol. Ar. *Wealth* 845; cf. Polyaen. V.17.1); whether they were a prerequisite is debated; they were compulsory according to a scholiast on Plat. *Gorg.* 497c; see Mylonas (1961) 243; Burkert (1983) 266n.7; while Parke (1977) 60 and Clinton (1974) 13n.13 doubt their compulsory nature; cf. Simms (1990) 183n.1. If there were large numbers of participants, then it appears that the Lesser Mysteries would be held twice (*IG* II^2 847.22–24; cf. Mylonas (1961) 239n.81), which would strengthen the argument that the Lesser Mysteries were a compulsory preliminary for initiation into the Greater.

[.... t]hat (5) done inadverte[ntly by a si]ngle, that done [inte]ntionally by a dou[ble (penalty)]. There shall [be a tr]uce (spondai) for the initi[ates], (10) both th[e ep]optai [and for t]heir foll[ow]ers and for the [pro]perty of the [for]eigners (15) and for all the [Athe]ni[a]ns; the beginni[ng] of the perio[d] of the truce shall be (20) Metageitnion fro[m] the full moon [t]hrough Boedr[o]mion and [P]yanopsion (26) until the tenth of the month. The truce shall be (in force) in a[l]l those (30) cities which use the shrine and for the Athenians there in those (35) same cities. For the Lesser Mysteries the [t]ruce shall b[e] from (40) Gamelion from the [fu]ll moon throug[h] Antheste[ri]on and Elaphebolion (46) until the tenth of the month.

12.5 Regulations for the Mysteries, c. 460

IG I^3 6C

In order to be initiated, the initiates had to pay various fees to cult personnel. The Eumolpidai and the Kerykes were the Eleusinian families which had charge of the Mysteries; see Clinton (1974); Burkert (1987) 37. It is usually held that each mystes had his or her own individual mystagogos, who was responsible for overseeing their initiation, but the evidence for this comes from a restoration in this inscription which has been taken to provide for individual myesis, initiation, with a penalty if group myesis occurred (lines 26–30 as restored by Meritt (1945) 70–71, 77, but subsequently questioned (1946) 251; see also Sokolowski (1959) 4; Richardson (1974) 20–21; Simms (1990) 186–87). For individual myesis, see Mylonas (1961) 237, 249; Parke (1977) 62 with 194n.54; Burkert (1985) 287 with 460n.20 incorrectly citing *LSCG Suppl.* 15. But it is possible to read the text as having no reference to individual initiation, and leaving aside the restored text, there is no other evidence for it as a requirement. The hieropoioi were sacred officials.

(5) [....] obol[....] the hier[opoioi shall receive a ha]lf-ob[ol each d]ay [from e]a[ch] initiate. The pries[te]ss of Demeter (10) shall [r]ec[e]ive at the Le[s]ser My[st]eries an obol from [ea]ch [in]itiate and [at the G]reater Mysteries an o[bol from] each [initi]ate; a[ll the obo]ls [shall belong] (15) to the two goddes[s]es [except 1],600 [dr]achmas. From the 1,[600] drachm[as the p]riestess [shall provide] for expenses [a]s (20) was done previously. The E[u]m[olpid]ai and the Ker[y]kes shall recei[ve from e]ach initia[te] fi[ve obols from me]n and [three from] wome[n]; it shall not be p[ermitted to initiate an underage in]itiate (25) except for the one [initiat]ed from the [hearth]. The Kerykes shall init[iate ....] each of the initiates [and the Eumolpid]ai the s[am]e; [....] more they shall be fine[d 1,000] (30) dra[ch]mas. T[hose] of the Kerykes and Eu[molpidai who are ad]ults shall perform the initiation; the sacred mone[y ....] the Athen[ians....], as long as they wi[sh, as] for (35) the [money] of Athen[a] on the acropolis; and [th]e hieropoioi are to administer the m[oney ....] on the acropolis (39) [....] (41) the orphaned child[ren and the in]itiates each [.... Th]ose initiates at Ele[usis ....] in the hall (aule) [within the san]ctuary, (45) and those in the city [....] in the Eleusinion. [T]he priest of the altar and t[he cleanser] of the two godde[ss]es and the priest o[f .... sh]all each receive [.... from (50) e]ach initiat[e ....]

12.6 The Offering of First-Fruits at Eleusis, c. 422

IG I^3 78

See Jameson (1983) 10 for the administration involved in collecting 1/600 of all barley and 1/1200 of all wheat grown in Attica and by Athens' allies, and possibly by other Greek cities as well; in 329/8 Eleusinian wheat was sold at prices fixed by the assembly, presumably below the market price. The hierophant was the most important of the Eleusinian officials, as he revealed the rites to the initiates. For the appointment of epistatai, superintendents, responsible for the revenue of the two goddesses, see *IG* I^3 32.

(1) [Timo]tel[e]s of Acharn[ai] was secretary. [It was resolv]ed by the boule and the people; (the tribe) Kekropis held the prytany, Timote[les was s]ecretary, Kykneas presided: the commissioners (syngrapheis) d[re]w up the following: that the Athenians are to offer to the two goddesses the first-fruits of the grain in accordance with ancestral custom and the (5) oracle from Delphi, from every hundred medimnoi of [b]arley not less than a sixth of a medimnos, from every hundred medimnoi of wheat not less than one twelfth of a medimnos; and if anyone produces more or less than t[hi]s he is to offer first-fruits in the same proportion. The demarchs are to collect (it) by deme and they are to hand it over to the hieropoioi (10) from Eleusis at Eleusis. (The Athenians) are to construct at Eleusis three storage pits, in accordance with ancestral custom, wherever seems to be suitable to the hieropoioi and the ar[ch]itect from the money belonging to the two goddesses. They are to deposit there th[e gr]ain which they receive from the demarchs. The allies are also to offer first-fruits in the same way. The cities are to choose (15) [co]llector[s] for the grain, according to the way in which it seems to them best for the grain to be collected; when it has been collected, they are to send it to Athens; and those who bring it are to hand it over to the hieropoioi from Eleusis at Eleusis. If they do not receive it within five days after it has been reported, although those from the city from which the g[ra]in [comes] have offered it, (20) the hieropoioi are to be liable to a fine of a thousand drachmas [eac]h; and they are to receive it from the demarchs in the same way. The boule is to chose [her]a[ld]s and send them to the cities an[no]uncing what is [now] being decreed by the people, for the present as quickly as possible, and for the [f]uture whenever the boule decides. The hierophant and the (25) torch-bearer (daidouchos) are to proclaim at the mysteries that the Greeks are to offer first-fruits in accordance with ancestral custom and the oracle from Delphi. They are to record o[n] a notice-board the weight of the grain received from the demarchs accord[ing t]o each [de]me and that received from the cities according to ea[ch] city and [s]et it up in the Eleusinion at Eleusis and in the cou[ncil ch]amber. (30) The boule is also to make a proclamation to all [t]he other Gr[e]ek cities, in whatever way seems to be feasible, tel[li]ng them how the Athenians and the allies are offering first-fruits, and not ordering t[he]m but encouraging them to offer first-fruits, if they wish, in [ac]cordance with ancestral custom and the oracle from Delphi. The hieropoioi (35) are also to receive (grain) that anyone brings from these cities in the same way .... (59) And concerning the first-fruits of olive oil Lampon

shall draw up a draft and show it to the boule in the ninth prytany; and the boule shall be compelled to bring it before the people.

ASKLEPIOS THE HEALER

Individuals who consulted the healing deity Asklepios slept overnight in the abaton, an 'incubation' centre, and hoped that the god would appear to them in a dream and cure them or prescribe a cure; for the abaton, see Burford (1969) 50–51, 62–63, 82; Tomlinson (1983) 67–71. In general, consultation of Asklepios involved preliminary sacrifice and the payment of a consultation fee. The three major Panhellenic shrines (Asklepieia) were at Epidauros, Kos in the Aegean, and Pergamon in Asia Minor. There were also local Asklepieia, and the shrine of Amphiaraos at Oropos dealt with visitors from both Boeotia and Attica, while the Asklepieion at Lebena attracted the sick from all over Crete. For the cult of Asklepios, see esp. Farnell (1921) 234–79; Guthrie (1950) 242–53; Kerényi (1960); Burkert (1985) 215, 267–68; Luck (1985) 141–42; Martin (1987) 50–52; for the healing centre at Oropos, the Amphiaraion, see Petropoulou (1981) 39–63; doc. 12.21.

12.7 Asklepios is Introduced to Athens in 420

IG II² 4960a, lines 2–13

Asklepios' popularity as a healing god spread throughout the fifth and fourth centuries. He was introduced to the Peiraieus in the late 420s and from there to Athens, along with his sacred snake, in 420 (Aleshire (1989) 7–11; Garland (1992) 116–35); Zea is a small harbour at the Peiraieus. For a detailed treatment of the Asklepieion at Athens, beneath the acropolis, see Aleshire (1989), (1991); at Corinth: Roebuck (1941). As well as his snake Asklepios also had sacred dogs, and the assistance of Hygieia, Health.

[.... (2) when (the god) ca]me up fr[om] Zea at the time of the Gre[at Mysteri]es he was taken to the El[eusinio]n (5) and [having summ]oned his sn[ake] from his home he [bro]ught it hither in Telemachos' [chariot ....] At the same time Hyg[ieia] arrived, (10) [and] in this way this whole [sanctu]ary was established during the archonship of [Astyphi]los of Ky[dantidai].

12.8 The Iamata: Testimonia to Asklepios' Cult

IG IV², 1, no. 121–22, 1, 4, 20, 42

A iama (plural: iamata) was a cure. The pilgrims who visited Epidauros left behind dedications as thanks for their cures; in the fourth century BC the priests at Epidauros gathered together the individual testimonia, and presumably also oral versions of cures, and had them inscribed on stelai, some of which still survive. Some of the cures appear to be fantastic, but the cult at Epidauros functioned for nearly a millennium, and drew its clientele from all over the Greek world. For a translation of iamata 1–43, see Edelstein & Edelstein (1945) I.221–29. For the Epidaurian iamata and Asklepieia in general, see Dodds (1971) 168–71. Dillon (1994), with bibliography, argues that no medical attention was available and that the cult relied on auto-suggestion and faith-healing.

1 Kleo had been pregnant for five years. After she had been pregnant for five years she came as a suppliant to the god and slept in the abaton; as soon as she left it and

was outside the sanctuary she bore a son, who as soon as he was born washed himself from the spring and walked about with his mother. In return for this she inscribed on her offering, 'The size of the tablet is not wonderful, but the god is, in that Kleo was pregnant with the burden for five years, until she slept in the temple and he made her healthy.' **4** Ambrosia of Athens blind in one eye. She came as a suppliant to the god. As she walked about in the sanctuary she laughed at some of the cures (iamata) as incredible and impossible, that the lame and blind should be made healthy just by seeing a dream. She slept and saw a vision: the god seemed to stand beside her and say that he would make her well, but that as payment he would require her to dedicate to the temple a silver pig as a memorial of her ignorance. When he had said this, he cut the diseased eyeball and poured in some drug. When day came, she left cured. **20** Lyson of Hermione a blind boy. While wide-awake he had his eyes healed by one of the dogs of the temple and went away cured. **42** Nikasiboula of Messene slept (in the abaton) for the sake of offspring and saw a dream; it seemed to her that the god approached her with a snake creeping behind him, and that she had intercourse with it; and afterwards two sons were born to her within a year.

12.9 The God Wealth is Healed by Asklepios

Aristophanes *Wealth* 659–671, 727–41

Aristophanes, in his play *Wealth*, gives a comic description of a night in an Asklepieion, where Ploutos, the god Wealth, is cured of blindness; here Karion, the slave of Chremylos, is reporting the success of Wealth's cure to Chremylos' wife. Ploutos first bathes in the sea (ll. 656–58); for ritual bathing, see Edelstein & Edelstein (1945) II.149; Parker (1983) 212–13. At the Amphiaraion there was the provision that women were to sleep on one side of the altar, and men on the other (*LSCG* 69.43–47); intercourse in temples was forbidden (Hdt. IX.116–20, cf. II.64; Paus. VIII.5.12; cf. Parker (1983) 74).

Karion: Then we went to the god's precinct.
And there on the altar our cakes and preparatory offerings
We dedicated, food for Hephaistos' flame,
And after putting Wealth to bed, in the proper way,
Each of us set our mattresses in order ....
When he'd put out the lamps
And ordered us to go to sleep, the god's
Servant told us, if anyone heard a noise,
To be silent, so we all lay there in an orderly manner.

Karion: Then the god sat down beside Wealth;
First of all he examined his head,
Then taking a clean linen cloth
He wiped his eyelids; and Panacea
Covered his head with a purple cloth
And his whole face; the god then made a clucking noise
And two serpents rushed from the inner shrine —
They were absolutely enormous!
Wife: Dear gods!

Karion: They crept gently under the purple cloth
And appeared to lick his eyelids all round;
Before you could drink down ten cups of wine
Wealth was standing up, mistress, and could see!
I clapped my hands for joy
And woke up my master, and the god immediately
Disappeared, with the snakes, into the inner shrine.

THE OLYMPIAN RELIGION AND ITS CRITICS

12.10 The Birth of Zeus

Hesiod *Theogony* 466–91

Ouranos was overthrown and castrated by his son Kronos, who was to be the father of the Olympian gods; Kronos attempted to avoid the prophecy that he too would be overthrown by his offspring by swallowing his sons; see esp. Caldwell (1989) 161–64, cf. 146–52.

Kronos kept no careless watch, but looked carefully
And swallowed down his children; and endless grief seized Rhea.
But when she was about to bear Zeus, father of gods and men,
Then she beseeched her dear parents,
Both Earth (Ge) and starry Heaven (Ouranos),
To devise with her some plan, so that she might unnoticed bear
Her dear child, and that Retribution might pay Kronos back for his own father
And the children great Kronos, crafty of counsel, had swallowed down ....
They sent her to Lyktos, to the rich land of Crete
Where she was about to bear the last of her children
Great Zeus; mighty Earth received him from her
In broad Crete to nourish and to rear.
There she came bearing him swiftly through the black night,
First to Lyktos; and taking him in her hands she hid him
In a deep cave, in the secret places of divine earth,
On densely wooded mount Aigaion.
But in his place she wrapped a great stone in swaddling clothes and put it
In the hands of the great lord son of Heaven, king of earlier gods;
And he took it in his hands and placed it in his belly,
Wretch, not knowing in his heart that
In place of the stone his son, unconquered and unworried,
Was left behind, who by force and hands was soon to overcome
And drive him from his rank, himself to reign amongst the immortals.

12.11 Pheidias' Statue of Zeus at Olympia

Pausanias V.11.1

The chryselephantine (gold and ivory) statue of the seated Zeus, over forty feet high, was housed in the temple at Olympia, built in the 460s; Pheidias made the statue about thirty years later; see Coldstream (1985) 78–81.

The god sits on a throne and is made of gold and ivory; on his head is a garland in imitation of olive shoots. In his right hand he carries a Victory (Nike) also of ivory and gold, and she has a ribbon and on her head a garland; in the god's left hand is a sceptre adorned with every kind of metal, and the bird sitting on the sceptre is the eagle. The god's sandals are of gold, as is his cloak; on the cloak both figures of animals and flowers of the lily are embroidered.

12.12 The Gods of Homer and Hesiod

Xenophanes of Kolophon 11

Xenophanes lived c. 570–c. 475, and challenged traditional notions about the gods (cf. doc. 1.1). He also had theories about cosmology, that the sun came into being daily from small pieces of fire collected together, and that there were innumerable suns and moons (Hippol. *Ref.* I.14.3). He seems to have been compelled to leave Ionia as a young man, and from then on lived primarily in Sicily. See Kirk & Raven (1960) 163–81; esp. 168–69; Guthrie (1971) 226–35; Freeman (1971) 20–24; Emlyn-Jones (1980) 133–4; Rankin (1983) 135–46; de Romilly (1992) 103–11.

Both Homer and Hesiod have attributed all things to the gods,
As many as are shameful and a reproach amongst mankind,
Thieving and adultery and deceiving each other.

12.13 'In Their Own Image'

Xenophanes of Kolophon 15

Xenophanes points out that humans portray the gods as anthropomorphic, but that there is no reason for supposing that they are. He perceives that different races attribute to the gods their own characteristics; cf. F16, 'The Ethiopians say their gods are snub-nosed and black, the Thracians that theirs have grey-blue eyes and red hair.'

But if oxen and horses and lions had hands
Or could draw with their hands and create works like men,
Horses would draw pictures of the gods like horses,
And oxen like oxen, and each would make their bodies
Just like the bodily form that they themselves had.

12.14 Purification in Blood

Herakleitos 5

For Herakleitos of Ephesos, see Kirk & Raven (1960) 182–215, esp. 211; Guthrie (1967) 43–47; Freeman (1971) 24–34; Emlyn-Jones (1980) 143–61; Robinson (1987). Parker (1983) 371–72 notes that Herakleitos emphasizes the nature of purification (presumably from homicide) by sacrifice involving the shedding of blood; the blood of the murder is washed away by the blood of the sacrifice.

They purify themselves by defiling themselves with other blood, just as if one were to step into mud to wash off mud. A man would be thought mad if anyone were to observe him acting in this way. And they pray to these statues, as if one were to talk gossip to houses, not knowing at all of what nature gods or heroes are.

12.15 Reincarnation

Empedokles of Akragas 117

Empedokles wrote in the mid-fifth century BC. His work *On Nature* gives a physical explanation of the universe (based on the belief that there were four eternally distinct substances, Fire, Air, Water and Earth); another work was on *Purifications*, which seems to reflect the Pythagorean belief in transmigration, though Empedokles, unlike the Pythagoreans, believed in the kinship of all creatures and that he himself had transmigrated into animals and plants as well as men; see Kirk & Raven (1960) 320–61; Freeman (1971) 51–69; Lambridis (1976) 119, 144.

For already I have been born as a boy and a girl
And a bush and a bird and a dumb fish leaping out of the sea.

12.16 The New Education

Aristophanes *Clouds* 365–73

Socrates is here attempting to educate the ignorant old Strepsiades who wants to learn the new rhetoric so he can win law-suits and not pay back his debts. In this play Aristophanes is attributing to Socrates a number of beliefs and practices which actually belonged to other sophists, such as Protagoras, and pre-Socratic philosophers, such as Anaxagoras and Diogenes of Apollonia. For Socrates' 'teaching' in the *Clouds*, see also doc. 9.35.

Socrates: The Clouds are the only goddesses, all the others are just nonsense.
Strepsiades: But Zeus! Come on now, doesn't the Olympian god exist?
Socrates: Who's Zeus? You're talking rubbish, there is no Zeus.
Strepsiades: What do you mean?
Who rains then? Tell me that first of all.
Socrates: Why, they do; and I can teach you this with clear proofs.
Come on, have you ever seen it raining without Clouds?
Yet he should be able to rain from a clear sky, when these are out of town.
Strepsiades: By Apollo! You've confirmed this by your argument;
Yet before I really thought that Zeus was urinating through a sieve!

HEROES

Many of the heroes worshipped in classical times represent a rediscovery of ancient tombs and, from the eighth century on, rediscovered graves of the Mycenaean period became the objects of cults. Since power resided with the vestiges of the hero's mortality, the cult of a hero centred on those bones: the hero was a localised semi-divine figure. For Sparta's recovery of the bones of Orestes from Tegea, see Hdt. I.67–68; Huxley (1979) 145–48; for Kimon's discovery of the bones of Theseus on Skyros, see Plut. *Kim.* 8.5–7; Podlecki (1971) 141–43. The heroes were chthonic deities, dwelling beneath the earth; other chthonic deities were Trophonios, who had an oracular centre at Lebadeia, and Asklepios. The main differences between the rituals employed for Olympian and chthonic deities are summarised by Guthrie (1950) 221–222: bloodless offerings were often made to the chthonic deities (such as honey, fruits of the earth); the Olympians had temples, chthonic deities caves or graves. See also Nock (1944) 141–74; Burkert (1985) 203–08.

12.17 Oedipus Bequeaths his Bones to Athens

Sophocles *Oedipus at Colonus* 1518–34

Oedipus here states that his grave will protect the Athenians, and be a bulwark against the Thebans; see Kearns (1989) 208–09.

Oedipus (to Theseus, King of Athens):
I will teach you, son of Aigeus, what
For this city will remain untouched by age.
I will myself straightway show you the place,
Without a guide's help, where I must die.
Never tell this to any man,
Either where it is hidden or whereabouts it lies;
And this will always serve for your defence
Better than many shields and the imported spear of neighbours.
But these mysteries, which may not be spoken of,
You will yourself learn, when you go there alone;
Since neither to any of your citizens might I reveal it
Nor to my own children, though I love them.
But you must always preserve it, and when to life's end
You come, only to your eldest son
Reveal it, while he should show it to his own successor.
And thus you will inhabit this city unmolested
By the men of Thebes.

12.18 Kleomedes: The Last Hero

Pausanias VI.9.6–8

For these Delphic responses, see Parke & Wormell (1956) I.353–54, II.38–39 Response 88; Fontenrose (1976) 130, 323 Response Q166 (not genuine); cf. Fontenrose (1968) 73–79. Parke & Wormell I.354–55 also discuss the case of the poltergeist Polites, companion of Odysseus, whose ghost attacked local inhabitants until appeased by an annual offering of a virgin.

6 At the Olympic festival before this (492 BC) they say that Kleomedes of Astypalaia while boxing with Ikkos of Epidauros killed him during the contest. When he was convicted of foul play by the umpires (hellanodikai) and deprived of his victory, he became mad through grief and returned to Astypalaia. There he attacked a school of some sixty children and overthrew the pillar which supported the roof. **7** The roof fell on the children, and he was stoned by the townsmen and took refuge in the sanctuary of Athena; he got into a chest standing in the sanctuary and pulled down the lid, and the Astypalaians laboured in vain in their efforts to open the chest. Finally they broke open the boards of the chest, but found no Kleomedes, either living or dead, so they sent men to Delphi to ask what had happened to Kleomedes. **8** They say that the Pythia gave them this response:

'Kleomedes of Astypalaia is the last of heroes:
Honour him with sacrifices as he is no longer a mortal.'

So from this time the Astypalaians have paid honours to Kleomedes as a hero.

DIVINATION: OMENS AND ORACLES

Inquirers could receive a spoken message from the gods through the medium of a priestess or priest at oracular centres such as Delphi, Olympia, Delos, Dodona and Didyma, as well as that of the god Ammon at Siwah in Egypt. In addition to divination through oracles and dreams, there were various other methods employed: oionomanteia (the observation of the flight of birds), hieroskopia (examination of the internal organs of a sacrificed beast); and 'signs by the way'; a sneeze on the right was also favourable. For oracles and divination in general, see Bouché-Leclercq (1879–82) which remains the classic account; Halliday (1913); Nock (1942) 472–79; Nilsson (1961) 121–39; Bloch (1963); Flacelière (1965); Pollard (1965); Parke (1967); Luck (1985) 229–51; Parker (1985) 298–326; divination at Athens: Mikalson (1983) 39–49, cf. (1991) 87–114; Garland (1984) 80–83; Powell (1988) 383–413; at Sparta: Hodkinson (1983) 273–76; Parker (1989) 154–60; Thebes: Symeonoglou (1985) 155–58. There are numerous works on Delphi, see Parke & Wormell (1956) I esp. 17–45; Flacelière (1965) 33–50; Pollard (1965) 17–39; Lloyd-Jones (1976) 60–73; Fontenrose (1978) esp. 196–232 (with Green (1989) 91–111); Burkert (1983) 116–30, (1985) 115–17; Price (1985) 128–54; Morgan (1990) 148–90; Zaidman & Pantel (1992) 121–28; for Olympia: Parke (1967) 164–93; Dodona: Parke (1967) 1–163, 259–79; Ammon: Woodward (1962) 5–13; Delos: den Adel (1983) 288–90; Didyma: Fontenrose (1988a); Lebadeia: Paus. IX.39; Clark (1968) 63–75.

12.19 Sixth Century Divination at Ephesos

LSAM 30 (*SIG*[3] 1167)

This is the only inscription which lists several possible bird movements and their interpretation. It seems to suggest an official site from which observations were taken; cf. Eur. *Bakch.* 346–50; Paus. IX.16.1; cf. Soph. *Ant.* 999. Birds were so common a form of omen that the word for omen is often simply 'bird', as in Hesiod *WD* 828; cf. doc. 11.34, line 56. For oionomanteia, see Halliday (1913) 246–71; Pollard (1977) 116–29; Pritchett (1979) 101–08; Dillon (1995) for this inscription and divination in general.

[....] if (the bird) [flyi]ng [from right to left] disappear[s (from view) (the omen is) fav]ourable; if it raises it[s l]eft wing, [flies a]way and disappears (the omen is) un[fav]ourable; if fl[y]ing from l[ef]t to right it disap[p]ears on a straight course (the omen is) unfavourable; but if after raising its [rig]ht wing, [it flies away and disappears (the omen is) favourable ....]

12.20 Prometheus Teaches Man Divination

Aeschylus *Prometheus Bound* 484–95

Prometheus, amongst his other gifts to mortals, taught the art of divination, especially oionomanteia and hieroskopia. 'Signs by the way' were phenomena one encountered as one went about daily life, which could be interpreted as ominous: see also Xen. *Mem.* I.1.3. In Xen. *Hell.* IV.7.7 a lobeless sacrifice led to the termination of a military campaign; for the portents of Aegisthus' fate revealed through sacrifice, see Eur. *Elect.* 826–29; and Soph. *Ant.* 998–1011 for the portents preceding Antigone's death.

I marked out many ways of divination,
And was the first to discern among dreams those which must
Take place in reality, and doubtful utterances
I made known to them and signs by the way;
The flight of birds with crooked talons I distinguished
Exactly, those which by their nature are auspicious
And the ill-omened, and the mode of life
Each has, and what enmities
Towards each other and loves and companionships,
And the smoothness of entrails and what colour
The gall bladder should have to please
The gods, and the speckled symmetry of the liver's lobe.

12.21 Croesus Consults Delphi

Herodotos I.53.1–54.2

Croesus, concerned at the rising power of Persia, sent envoys to consult a number of Greek oracles. He considered Delphi and the Amphiaraion at Oropos to be the only genuine oracles, and Herodotos states that in addition to an immense sacrifice he sent magnificent gifts to Delphi, including a lion of gold weighing 10 talents, 2 huge mixing-bowls, 4 silver casks, the figure of a woman in gold, said to represent his baker, and his own wife's girdles and necklaces. The Delphians in return granted him and the people of Lydia citizenship and other privileges (see Parke (1984) 209–32). For promanteia, by which the Delphians granted to either individuals or communities the right of consulting the oracle first, before other inquirers, see Sokolowski (1954) 169–71; the Athenian tetrapolis had promanteia at Delphi (cf. doc. 5.16). There were special days set aside for consultation; traditionally, consultations had taken place in the month of Bysios, but, presumably by classical times, these had been extended from once a year to once a month, except during winter: Plut. *Mor.* 292e, 398a. At any one time in the classical period there were two other 'Pythias' in addition to the one in office and their duties rotated. The Pythia could be married at the time of taking up office and set her husband aside for the course of her duties; see *SIG*^{3} 823a; Parke & Wormell (1956) I.44). The response here is a classic case of Delphic ambiguity.

I.53.1 Croesus instructed the men who were going to take these gifts to the shrines to ask the oracles if he should make war on Persia and if he should seek the help of another allied army. **I.53.2** When they arrived at their destinations, the Lydians dedicated the offerings, and consulted the oracles, asking, 'Croesus, King of Lydia and other nations, believing that these are the only oracles among mankind, has given you gifts worthy of your divination, and now inquires of you if he should make war against the Persians and if he should seek the help of another allied army.' **I.53.3** This is what they asked, and the response of both oracles was the same, prophesying to Croesus that if he made war against the Persians, he would destroy a great empire; and they advised him to find out which of the Greeks were the most powerful and to ally himself with them. **I.54.1** When Croesus learnt the oracles which had been delivered, he was delighted with the responses, and, as he confidently expected to destroy the kingdom of Cyrus, he sent yet another present to Delphi, after ascertaining the number of inhabitants, two gold staters for each man. **I.54.2** The Delphians in return gave Croesus and the Lydians in perpetuity the right of promanteia and exemption from dues (ateleia) and front seats at the festival, and allowed anyone who wished to become a citizen of Delphi.

12.22 The Cost of the Pelanos

LSCG Suppl. 39

Before consultation took place an offering of the pelanos, a cake, had to be made outside and a full sacrifice was also necessary within the temple prior to the consultation: cf. *Ion* 226–29. In this inscription, which probably dates to the last two decades of the fifth century, the pelanos seems to have been commuted into a tax or sum of money. The consultation fees which seem to have varied from state to state are here set down for the Phaselites. See Parke (1939) 59–65; Parke & Wormell (1956) I.43n.62.

(1) These things (were resolved) by the Delphians: the Phaselites are to give seven drachmas two obols in Delphian currency for the pelanos for a public (consultation), a private individual four obols. (5) Timodikos and Histiaios were the theoroi (from Phaselis), Herulos the magistrate.

12.23 The Eclipse during the Sicilian Expedition

Thucydides VII.50.3–4

The Athenians were preparing to move, when an eclipse of the moon took place and Nikias insisted that they stay for the further 27 days recommended by the seers; in this he followed the opinion of the majority of the troops. The eclipse occurred on 27 August 413; see also Plut. *Nik.* 4.1–2; Powell (1979) 25–28. Pausanias also waited for favourable omens at Plataea, though under attack: Hdt. IX.61.3–62.1 (doc. 7.43).

VII.50.3 When the Athenian generals saw that the Syracusans had been reinforced by another army and that their own position, far from improving, was daily becoming worse in every respect, and was becoming particularly difficult because of the sickness among the men, they regretted that they had not withdrawn earlier and as even Nikias was no longer so opposed to this, except that he did not approve of an open vote, they gave notice as secretly as possible for everyone to be prepared to sail out of the camp when the signal to do so was given. **VII.50.4** And they were about to sail out, and everything was ready, when there was an eclipse of the moon, which happened to be full. Most of the Athenians took this so seriously that they bade the generals wait, and Nikias (who was rather too inclined to divination and such matters) said that he would not even discuss how the move should be made until, as the seers prescribed, they had waited thrice nine days. It was for this reason that the Athenians delayed and stayed on.

FESTIVALS

By at least the eighth century an athletic contest was held at Olympia (the traditional date was 776), and similar games may already have existed at Delphi; by the early fifth century Delphi, Olympia, Isthmia and Nemea had become the heart of an institutionalised festival circuit on the Greek mainland (the 'periodos'); see Morgan (1990) 39–49, 212–23.

12.24 Provisions for an Andrian Choir Visiting Delphi

LSCG Suppl. 38

Andros sent this theoria, sacred embassy, to Delphi, probably in the fifth century, and made detailed arrangements for its procedure. The architheoroi who were in charge of the theoria and the other officials had their food supplied for them. As there was a choir it is likely that the theoria was being dispatched to participate in the Pythian festival (for which, see Fontenrose (1988b) 121–40). For the inscription, see Daux (1949) 59–72.

A

.... (6) The following are [n]ot to pay for their gra[in] or b[ea]ns(?): the three architheoroi, the seer, the commander, the herald, (10) the flautist, the helmsman, the b[o]atswain, the s[t]eward. The following shall receive a s[k]in: the heral[d], the flautist, the boatswain, each of the public priests. The (Delphians) are to provide (15) food on the first day; barley-cake, meat, wine as mu[c]h as they wish and the ot[h]er things as suitable. For the (next) two days apart from grain let ea[c]h put down (20) both boy and man an A[e]ginetan ob[o]l for each day; and the architheoroi are to consecrate half (of these obols); the costs (of the cult) are: (25) four obols for the p[el]anos, two for the metaxen[i]a, six for the priest at ea[c]h s[acr]ifice. Let the pri[vate] individual receive the third p[art] of the skins (30) which he sacrifices [e]xcept for the ones sacrificed for consultation or p[urifica]tion, and all those on the embassy (theoria) [....] vac

B

[....] (4) The boule is to elect from those sailing to Delph[i] five men and take their oaths; they are to not pay for food on account (10) of this office; and they are to have the power to fine the disorderly up to five drac[hma]s for each (15) day. Whomever they [f]ine let them record (their names) in the boule.

12.25 Access to Panhellenic Sanctuaries Guaranteed

Thucydides V.18.1–3

Cf. Thuc. IV.118.1. The first clause, given below, of the Peace of Nikias in 421 allowed everyone to consult Panhellenic oracles and attend festivals in safety.

V.18.1 The Athenians and Spartans and their allies made a treaty and swore to it, city by city, as follows: **V.18.2** 'Concerning the temples which are common to all, anyone who wishes may, in accordance with ancestral custom, offer sacrifices in them, travel to them, consult the oracle, and attend the festival, being guaranteed security both by land and sea. The sanctuary and the temple of Apollo at Delphi and the Delphians are to be independent and have their own taxes and courts, both the people and their territory, in accordance with ancestral custom. **V.18.3** This treaty is to be in force between the Athenians and their allies and the Spartans and their allies for fifty years, without deceit and without harm both by land and sea.'

12.26 Alkibiades Competes in Style at the Olympics

Plutarch *Alkibiades* 11.1–12.1

Cf. Thuc. VI.16.2; Alkibiades entered seven chariots in the same race; for a woman victor, see doc. 13.17. A win at the games was very prestigious for the city (cf. docs. 9.39, 10.46); there were also political advantages to attending festivals: when the Chians in 411 were preparing to revolt, the Athenians while attending the Isthmian festival gained a clear idea of the situation (Thuc. VIII.10.1).

11.1 The horses Alkibiades bred were renowned everywhere, as was the number of his chariots; for no one else, either a private individual or a king, had ever entered seven at the Olympics, and he was the only one to do so. **11.2** And to have won with them the first, second and fourth prizes, as Thucydides says, and the third according to Euripides, surpasses in brilliance and renown all ambition in this field .... **12.1** This success was made all the more brilliant by the distinction shown him by the different cities. For the Ephesians erected for him a magnificently adorned tent, and the city of Chios provided fodder for his horses and a large number of victims for sacrifice, and the Lesbians gave him wine and other provisions which enabled him to give many people lavish entertainment.

12.27 The Delian Games

Thucydides III.104.1–4

Cf. Diod. XII.58.6–7; the purification was carried out because of the plague (doc. 9.5). The Ionians had previously held a festival at Delos and the Athenians in 426 revived it. For Peisistratos' purification, see doc. 4.17; for Athens' connections with the sanctuary of Apollo on Delos, see Morgan (1990) 205–08; cf. den Adel (1983) 288–90. **III.104.3**: the Ephesia may have originally been the Panionia, the Ionian festival moved to Ephesos because of wars in the Mykale region (Diod. XV.49.1); see doc. 10.34; Hornblower (1982) 241–45. For Nikias' liturgy at Delos, see Plut. *Nik.* 3.5–8.

III.104.1 The same winter (426/5) the Athenians purified Delos in accordance with some oracle. Peisistratos the tyrant had previously purified it, though not all of it, just as much of the island as could be seen from the temple; but at this time all of it was purified in the following way. **III.104.2** They removed all the graves of those who had died on Delos and proclaimed that for the future no one was to die or to give birth there, but had to be taken over to Rheneia .... It was then after the purification that the Athenians first celebrated the Delian Games, which were held every fifth year. **III.104.3** There had also been in days of old a great gathering of the Ionians and neighbouring islanders on Delos; for they used to come to the festival with their wives and children, as the Ionians do now at the Ephesia, and they would hold a contest there in athletics and music and the cities would bring choruses. **III.104.4** Homer in particular shows that this was so in these verses, which come from his hymn to Apollo:

'But it was on Delos, Phoibos, that your heart especially took delight,
Where the long-robed Ionians gather together
With their children and wives on your sacred street;
There in boxing and dancing and singing
They think of you and rejoice, when they hold your contest.'

SANCTUARIES AND CULT REGULATIONS

Sanctuaries were often walled, to set them aside from the profane world of humans. There were often specific regulations for sanctuaries and they could not be used for sleeping, unless they were dedicated to a healing god. The dress of worshippers was often subject to specific requirements (Mills (1984) 255–65; Culham (1986) 235–45), accommodation was confined to certain areas (Dillon (1990) 64–88), sexual activity was restricted (Parker (1983) 85–86; Burkert (1985) 87), and the types of food which the worshippers could eat might also be prescribed (Parker (1983) 357–65); who was to have access to temples could also be restricted (Hewitt (1909) 83–91). Prior to the battle of Delion, the Boeotians complained that 'the Athenians had fortified and were living in Delion, and all the things men do on unhallowed ground were taking place there' (Thuc. IV.97.2–98.7; cf. III.96.1 where Demosthenes camped with his army in the precinct of Nemean Zeus). For a largely architectural treatment of the major sanctuaries, see Tomlinson (1976).

12.28 A Spring of the Nymphs at Delos

LSCG Suppl. 50

This inscription concerning the nymphs' sacred spring dates to the fifth century BC. The prohibition against dumping manure was typical of Greek sanctuaries, and must have reflected a real problem (see *LSCG* 57, 78, cf. 115; *LSCG Suppl.* 53). For the purificatory power of water, particularly for use prior to ritual observances, such as making libations and sacrifices, see Parker (1983) 226–27, 371; Burkert (1985) 79, 86; cf. Hesiod, who warns against urinating or defecating in streams: *WD* 757–59, cf. 727–32; West (1978) 335–38; Parker (1983) 291, 294. For the protection of trees at sacred sites, see in general: Sokolowski (1960) 376–80; Parker (1983) 164–65; Jordan & Perlin (1984) 153–59; cf. Hughes (1980) 45–49. The penalty for cutting vine-props from ground sacred to Zeus and Alkinous on Corcyra was one stater for each stake: see Thuc. III.70.4–6.

(1) Do not wash anything in the spr[in]g, or sw[im in t]he spring, or [th]ro[w] i[n]to the spri[ng manure or (5) anything els]e. Pe[nalty]: 2 [s]acr[e]d drachmas.

12.29 The Cult of Enyalios at Lindos on Rhodes

LSCG Suppl. 85, lines 1–30

Enyalios was a war deity, probably to be equated with Ares; cf. docs. 4.40, 1.21. Here all soldiers are to pay a tax to the cult and initially their general is made responsible for collecting the money to be paid from the soldiers. For the 'sixtieth' compare the one-sixtieth of the phoros (tribute) made over to Athena by the Athenians; see Pritchett (1979) 324–26. *IG* I^3 138 is another example of a cult levy on military pay.

[It was resolved by the boule and th]e people, Oi[.... p]resided, S[....] was secretary, Ag[ath]archos proposed the motion: those [who] make exp[edi]tions from Lindos [either] at p[u]b[li]c or at private expense should [pa]y a six[tiet]h [of th]eir pay to E[nya]lios; [th]e genera[l] is to e[x]act the m[on]ey and hand it [over] to t[h]e priest; and in f[utu]re from the booty t[he] individuals th[emselves] are to ha[n]d it [o]v[e]r to the priest; the [p]rie[st] is to [g]ive an account to the bou[le] each yea[r] and is to [h]and (it) over to the incoming pri[est]. The commissioners are to re[c]ord [what] the generals [ho]ld themselves and for the futu[re those who] make an expediti[on]. A [sacrific]e [to Eny]alios is to be made by the pry[taneis] who are in offi[ce] in the mo[nt]h of [Ar]ta[miti]on; they are [to sacrif]ice to Enyal[ios a bo]ar, a dog and a goat.

DEATH & FUNERAL CUSTOMS

The dead were cremated or inhumated; cremation was the most popular form of burial at Athens in the last quarter of the fifth century. The ashes and bones from the funeral pyre were placed in an urn, which was then buried. Funerary fashions changed: in archaic Athens larger than life statues of kouroi and kourai, sphinxes, or mounds marked grave sites; competition for space in the Kerameikos meant that this practice was later abandoned. Classical tombs were largely marked by stone reliefs or lekythoi (sing.: lekythos, a vessel for holding oil), many of marble rather than of clay like their prototypes. The most common lekythoi, buried with the dead, were the 'white-ground' lekythoi, covered with white slip, often decorated with scenes which were mythological or funerary in nature. Other grave goods were buried with the deceased and an obol might be placed in the mouth of the dead, but this practice was by no means universal: Morris (1992) 105–06. For the afterlife, see Mikalson (1983) 74–82; Burkert (1985) 194–99; see Richter (1961), esp. 1–4 for a catalogue of Athenian archaic gravestones. Inscribed stelai marking graves were the norm: there are 10,000 epitaphs on stone from classical Athens (Morris (1992) 156). For a good discussion of funerals and family tombs in Attica, see Humphreys (1980) 96–126; for epitaphs at Athens, see Meyer (1993) 99–121, esp. 106–12; for examples, see docs. 13.31–38.

12.30 Odysseus Visits the Underworld

Homer *Odyssey* XI.473–91

The view of the afterlife represented in this passage was widely held, and it was to escape this that individuals were initiated into the Eleusinian Mysteries. If the mysteries had a Mycenaean origin, it is probable that the two versions of the afterlife had always existed side by side. The Homeric afterlife was more suited to the heroic lifestyle of the warrior chieftains of the *Iliad*: as Hades had nothing to offer, it was important to live gloriously and achieve immortality through heroic exploits. It was the psyche, the phantom of the deceased (cf. doc. 13.3) that went to Hades; see Burkert (1985) 195–97. Here Odysseus meets Achilles, the bravest of all the Greek (Achaean) warriors. Odysseus has consulted the dead by a special ritual which does not appear to have classical counterparts, digging a pit, pouring libations of milk and honey, wine, and water, sprinkling barley-meal, and cutting the throat of the victims so their blood flowed into the pit (*Od.* XI.23–36). The blood draws the dead, and when they drink it they remember their past life and can speak.

'Son of Laertes, ordained by Zeus, Odysseus of many devices,
Dauntless one, what still greater deed can you devise in your heart?
How have you dared to come down to Hades, where the dead
Dwell without their wits, the shadows of outworn mortals?'
So he spoke, and I answered him in reply,
'Achilles, son of Peleus, bravest of the Achaeans,
I came in need of Teiresias, in case he might give me
Counsel how I might arrive at rocky Ithaka;
For I have not yet come near Achaea, nor set foot on
My island, but have always met with evils; but you, Achilles,
No man was ever more fortunate than you or ever will be.
For before, when you were alive, we honoured you like the gods,
We Argives, and now again you are a great ruler of the dead
Down here; you should not grieve at being dead, Achilles.'
This I spoke, and he immediately said in answer,
'Do not praise death to me, noble Odysseus.
I would rather be a serf (thes) labouring for someone else,
Even for a landless man, who had no livelihood,
Than be king over all the departed dead.'

12.31 Antigone Buries her Brother Polyneikes

Sophocles *Antigone* 426–31

After Oedipus, Antigone's father, died, bequeathing his body to Athens (doc. 12.17), her two brothers killed each other fighting for the kingship of Thebes. Kreon, Antigone's uncle, has decreed that Polyneikes, the invader and traitor, should remain unburied. Antigone, however, buries her brother's corpse and is caught by the guard. For Electra's prayers and libations at her father's tomb, see Aeschyl. *Libation Bearers* 87–151.

The guard (who has captured Antigone in the act):
Thus she, when she saw the body bare,
Cried out in lamentation, invoking
Dreadful curses on those who did the deed.
Straightway in her hands she carried thirsty dust,
And from a well-wrought brazen ewer
Honoured the corpse with threefold libations.

12.32 The Dead at Potidaea, 432

IG I^2 945 II (*IG* I^3 1179)

Hansen 10. Potidaea was one of the conflicts immediately prior to the outbreak of the Peloponnesian War; it revolted from Athens in 432 and was reduced two years later; this epitaph honours the Athenians who died in this campaign. Socrates took part in the preliminary fighting and saved the life of Alkibiades (Plat. *Apol.* 28e, *Symp.* 219e–220e). Mikalson (1991) 115 (cf. (1983) 77) compares the mention of aether (the upper air) here with mentions of aether in Euripides; aether also occurs in a personal epitaph, *IG* II^2 11466; see also Guthrie (1950) 262–64; Kirk & Raven (1960) 200–01.

Aether has received their souls [and earth] their bod[ies];
They d[ied] at the gates of Potidaea;
Some of their enemies have the grave as their portion, oth[ers fled]
And put the wall as their truest hope [of life].

12.33 Funerary Rites on Keos

LSCG 97A

SIG^3 1218. A funerary law from Iulis on Keos, dating to the second half of the fifth century. The legislation is sumptuary in nature, as Garland (1989) 11–13 notes (see 1–11, 13–15 for other examples; cf. doc. 13.48); see Parker (1983) 35–36 for the emphasis on the avoidance of pollution; cf. Morris (1992) 107–08. For funerary rites, the laying-out (prothesis), the funeral cortege (ekphora), and the burial, see Kurtz & Boardman (1971) 142–61 (200–01 for this law); Zaidman & Pantel (1992) 72–78; and cf. doc. 13.64.

These are the laws concerning the de[a]d; bu[r]y the dead person as [f]ollows: in three white clo[t]hs, a spread, a garment, [and a c]overlet — there may be l[e]s[s] — worth no[t] more than 300 dr[ach]mas. Carry it out on a wedge-foo[t]ed bed [a]nd do not cover (the b[i]e[r]) completely with th[e clot]hs. Bring not m[ore] than three choes of wine to the tomb and not mor[e] than on[e] chous of olive oil, [and] bring back [the v]essels. [Carry] the de[a]d man, [c]overed over, u[p to the t]omb in silence. [P]erform the preliminary sacrifice according to an[cestral custom.] Bring [t]he bed and its c[over]ings from th[e] t[o]m[b] indoors. On the following da[y] first [sp]rinkle the house with se[a water], then wash it with w[a]ter having a[noi]nted it with ear[th]; when it has been sprinkled throughout, the house is purified and sacrifices should be made on the h[earth]. The women who [g]o [t]o the fune[ral] are to leave [the t]omb before the men. [Do not c]arry out the rites performed on the thirt[ieth day] in honour of the deceased. Do not put a cup (kylix) under the [be]d, do not pour out the water, and do not bring the swee[pi]ngs to the tomb. Whenever someone [d]ies, whe[n he is ca]rried out, no women should go t[o] t[he ho]use other than those polluted (by the death). The mother and wife and si[sters a]nd daughters are po[lluted], and in addition to these not m[ore than f]ive women, children [of the d]aug[hters and of the c]ousins, no [o]ne else. Those po[lluted] wash[ed] from head to foot [.... a p]ouring [of wat]er are pu[rif]ied [....]

WOMEN AND THEIR RELIGIOUS ROLE

Although excluded from the political life of the polis, women played a vital role in its religious life (Pomeroy (1975) 75). Female deities usually had priestesses and numerous cults were under the jurisdiction of women; the most important priesthood in all of Greece was arguably that held by the Pythia. In Athens, the priestess of Athena Polias (Guardian of the City) played an important part in Athenian history on at least two occasions, unsuccessfully refusing admittance to the temple to Kleomenes, and supporting the evacuation of Athens by reporting that the sacred snake had failed to eat its honey-cake (Hdt. V.72.3–4, VIII.41.2–3; cf. doc. 7.31, line 11 where the priestesses remain on the acropolis in 480). Priests and priestesses were responsible for the administration of the sanctuaries, purificatory rituals and the overseeing of sacrifices, and, generally, for the guardianship of the sanctuary's treasures. For these duties, they were entitled to a share of the sacrifices. See Mikalson (1983) 86; Finley (1985) xv–xvi; Muir (1985) 193–94; Garland (1990b) 77–81; Zaidman & Pantel (1992) 49–52; for women and religion in Athens, see Pomeroy 75–78.

12.34 Miltiades and Sacrilege on Paros

Herodotos VI.134.1–135.3

Following his triumph at Marathon, the Athenians granted Miltiades the Younger a fleet of seventy ships with which he attacked Paros, but unsuccessfully. In this episode he met with an accident, and returned home. Herodotos' account does not make clear exactly what Timo's advice to Miltiades was, but there are overtones of sacrilege in this incident. Demeter's title here is Demeter Thesmophoros: for the Thesmophoria, see doc. 12.39.

VI.134.1 What I have so far narrated is what all the Greeks say happened, but from here on the account is that of the Parians themselves: as Miltiades was getting nowhere one of the prisoners, a Parian woman whose name was Timo, an under-priestess of the chthonic deities, approached him. When she saw Miltiades she counselled him, if he really wanted to take Paros, to do what she suggested. **VI.134.2** After she had given him her advice, Miltiades went to the hill in front of the city and jumped over the fence around the sanctuary of Demeter Thesmophoros (the law-giver) as he was unable to open the doors. After jumping over he went towards the shrine (megaron) to do something inside, whether to disturb in some way the things which ought not to be touched or something else; but when he got to the doors he was immediately overcome by terror and went back the way he had come, but in leaping down the wall he sprained his thigh. Some people say he struck his knee. **VI.135.1** Miltiades was in a bad way as he sailed back to Athens, and he was returning without money for the Athenians and without having succeeded in taking Paros, having just besieged it for twenty-six days and ravaged the island. **VI.135.2** When the Parians learnt that Timo, the under-priestess of the goddesses, had instigated Miltiades' actions, they wanted to punish her for this, and sent messengers to Delphi as soon as they were free of the siege; they sent to inquire if they could put the priestess of the goddesses to death for giving information to the enemy which might have led to her country's capture and for revealing to Miltiades mysteries that ought not be divulged to the male sex. **VI.135.3** But the Pythia did not allow this, and said that Timo was not guilty of these offences, but it had been necessary for Miltiades to come to a bad end, and Timo had only put in an appearance to bring about his misfortunes.

12.35 Chrysis, Priestess of Hera at Argos

Thucydides II.2.1, IV.133.2–3

Another priestess of importance was Chrysis who served Hera for 56 and a half years at Argos. Thucydides uses her (together with the ephorate at Sparta and the archonship at Athens) to date the Theban entry into Plataea and the outbreak of war in 431.

II.2.1 The thirty years' truce which was signed after the capture of Euboea remained in force for fourteen years; but in the fifteenth year (431), which was the forty-eighth year of the priestess-ship of Chrysis at Argos, when Ainesias was ephor at Sparta and Pythodoros still had two months to go as archon at Athens, six months after the battle of Potidaea, at the beginning of spring, rather more than 300 Thebans (commanded by the boeotarchs Pythangelos son of Phyleidas and Diemporos son of Onetorides) came armed at about the first watch of the night and entered Plataea in Boeotia, an ally of Athens .... **IV.133.2** Also in the same summer (423) the temple of Hera at Argos burnt down, after Chrysis the priestess had placed a lighted lamp near the garlands and then fallen asleep, which resulted in her not noticing that they caught fire and blazed up. **IV.133.3** Chrysis, afraid of the Argives, immediately fled by night to Phleious; and they appointed another priestess named Phaeinis according to the established procedure. Chrysis, at the time of her flight, had been in office for eight years of the war and half of the ninth.

MYRRHINE, PRIESTESS OF ATHENA NIKE

Three inscriptions testify to the life and importance of Myrrhine, a priestess of Athena Nike. The inscription appointing her as priestess was found on the acropolis; on the reverse side of the stele a further inscription dated to 424/3 (*IG* I³ 36; ML 71) authorised payment of her salary. For the dating of the inscription of her appointment to c. 448, see Mattingly (1961) 168–71; Meritt & Wade-Gery (1963) 110–11. However, it has recently been redated more realistically to c. 430: Mattingly (1982) 381–85. For a lekythos depicting a youthful figure, generally dated to c. 420–410, which might have been part of Myrrhine's funeral monument, see Clairmont (1979) 103–10. The priestess was appointed by lot from all Athenian women, so it was not an office confined to aristocratic families, like many of the traditional priestly offices; her epitaph, which proudly proclaims her status, shows that the incumbent served for life. Myrrhine has been tentatively identified with the Myrrhine of the Lysistrata, performed at the Lenaia in 411, but this identification is uncertain, and the name is not uncommon: cf. *IG* I² 1009 (*IG* I³ 1248), found in the deme Kephale, 'I am the [to]mb of Myrrhine, who died of the [pla]gue.' On the appointment of priests and priestesses in Athens and their duties, see Sourvinou-Inwood (1990) 320–22; for this priesthood, Jordan (1979) 32–33.

12.36 The Appointment of the Priestess of Athena Nike

IG I³ 35 (Meiggs & Lewis 44)

As well as appointing a priestess for Athena Nike and providing her with a annual salary of 50 drachmas (equal to 100 days jury-pay for a citizen) and perquisites from the sacrifices, the decree also provides for doors to be constructed for Nike's sanctuary (and the letting out of the contract), and preliminary arrangements for the building of a temple and stone altar. For Kallikrates, one of the period's most famous architects, see Plut. *Per.* 13.7; *IG* I³ 45.

(1) [(The tribe) Leontis held the prytany. It was resolved by the boule and th]e [peo]pl[e: .... presided, Gl]aukos proposed the motion: [for Athena Ni]ke a priestess, [who is to be chosen (5) by lo]t from a[ll] Athenian women, [shall be appoi]nted, and the sanctuary is to be furnished with doors in accordance with the specifications

which Kallikrates draws up. The poletai are to let out the contract in the prytany of Leontis. The priestess is to be paid (10) fifty drachmas and receive the legs and hides from public sacrifices. A temple shall be built, in accordance with the specifications Kallikrates draws up, and a stone altar vacat (15) Hestiaios proposed the amendment: three men are to be chosen from the boule. These are to draw up the specifications wit[h] Kallikra[te]s and in[dicate to the bou]le the way in which the con[tract will be let out ....]

12.37 Epitaph for Myrrhine, Priestess of Athena Nike

SEG 12.80

This epitaph found on Mount Hymettos is dated to c. 405; see Clairmont (1979) 103–10, with pl. XXX(1), who suggests that Myrrhine's father Kallimachos may have been archon in 446/5. If the lekythos discussed by Clairmont is that of the priestess, the fact that she is veiled may have indicated her married state. Myrrhine means myrtle-branch, or myrtle-wreath, an appropriate name for a priestess.

This far-seen tomb is that of the daughter of Kallimachos,
Who was the first to tend the temple of Nike;
Her name shared in her good fame, for by divine
Fortune she was called Myrrhine. Truly
She was the first who tended the statue of Athena Nike
Chosen by lot out of everyone, Myrrhine, by good fortune.

12.38 An Athenian Girl's Service to the State

Aristophanes *Lysistrata* 638–51

Here a chorus of well-born Athenian women list their religious activities, which include having been an arrhephoros, a bear at the Brauronia, and a kanephoros at the Panathenaia (see docs. 4.30–31). The arrhephoroi were young girls, seven to eleven years of age, who worked on the peplos, robe, for Athena which was carried in procession at the Panathenaia, and had other cult duties on the acropolis. They were also involved in the Arrhephoria, a nocturnal festival in the month Skirophorion, in which they 'carried the symbols of Athena Polias'; Paus. I.27.3; see Pomeroy (1975) 76; Burkert (1983) 150–54, (1985) 228–30, (1992) 250–51; Garland (1990a) 187–91; Zaidman & Pantel (1992) 67; cf. doc. 10.11 for the arrhephoria (maintenance of these girls) as a liturgy; see Davies (1967) 37. Certain Athenian girls served as arktoi, bears, at the sanctuary of Artemis at Brauron. The festival at Brauron and the cult of Artemis Brauronia on the acropolis may have been instituted by Peisistratos: Morgan (1990) 13–16; see Simon (1983) 86. The Brauronia festival was celebrated every four years ([Arist.] *Ath. Pol.* 54.7; Ar. *Peace* 872–76; Peppa-Delmousou (1988) 255–58); this involved a theoria from Athens to Brauron. See Burkert (1983) 63n.20, (1985) 151; Sourvinou-Inwood (1990) 1–14; Garland (1990a) 187–91; Golden (1990) 78; Pantel & Zaidman (1992) 67; Osborne (1985) 157–72.

Chorus of old women:
For we, all you citizens, have been trying to speak words
Useful to the city;
Naturally, since it reared me splendidly in luxury.
As soon as I was seven years of age

I carried the symbols of Athena Polias;
Then when I was ten years old
I ground the corn for Artemis;
And then I was a bear at the Brauronia,
Wearing the saffron-coloured robe;
And as a beautiful girl I was a basket-carrier with a necklace of dried figs.
Do I not then owe it to the city to give it some good advice?
Even if I am a woman, do not grudge me this,
If I introduce something better than the present state of affairs.
For I have a share in the contribution — I contribute men.

12.39 A Male View of Activities at the Thesmophoria

Aristophanes *Thesmophoriazousai* 76–85, 623–33

The Thesmophoria was celebrated in honour of Demeter and Kore (Persephone) and was observed throughout Greece in autumn. In Athens, it was held in Pyanopsion (October); the women left their homes for the three day festival and set up tents in the sacred area on the acropolis. It was a secret all-female citizen celebration for married women, and the rites seem to have been conducted to assist the fertility of the seed for the coming crop. The sacred animals of Demeter, pigs, were thrown into a pit in the summer, along with serpents and phalloi, both made of dough. On the first day of the Thesmophoria the women retrieved the remains, and mixed these with grain placed on the altars. On the second day they fasted (they also abstained from sex for three days prior to and for the duration of the festival: Tyrrell (1984) 69–70; Burkert (1979) 44, 164n.38). On the third day, the pig remains and seed were scattered on the fields for fertility. See Harrison (1922) 120–62, (1925) 266; Pomeroy (1975) 77–78; Parke (1977) 82–88, 158–60; Brumfield (1981) 70–103; Mikalson (1983) 21, 122n.38; Tyrrell (1984) 69–71; Burkert (1985) 242–46; Lefkowitz (1986) 56–57; Winkler (1990) 193–200; Zaidman & Pantel (1992) 42, 188. Mnesilochos takes part in disguise to defend Euripides, whose 'slander' of women is a stock joke in Aristophanes (cf. *Frogs* 1050–51; doc. 6.50), as is their love of alcohol. Kleisthenes was a notorious effeminate, here shown on the side of the women.

Euripides: This very day it will be decided
Whether Euripides is to live or die!
Mnesilochos: How can it? The courts aren't going to be judging
Today, nor is the boule sitting.
After all, it's the second and middle day of the Thesmophoria!
Euripides: It's this that I think is going to put an end to me.
The women have been plotting against me,
And today at the Thesmophoria they'll be holding
An assembly to plan my destruction!
Mnesilochos: What for?
Euripides: Because I write plays and say bad things about them.

Kleisthenes: Have you ever been up here before?
Mnesilochos: Of course!
Every year!
Kleisthenes: Who's your tent-mate?

Mnesilochos: Oh, what's-her-name.
Kleisthenes: That's no answer!
Woman (to Kleisthenes): Go away. I will question her properly
About last year's rites; you stand aside,
For, as a man, you may not hear. You there, tell me
629 Which of the rites was the first shown to us?
Mnesilochos: Well now, what did come first? We drank!
Woman: And what did we do after that?
Mnesilochos: We drank each other's health!
Woman: You heard that from someone! What came third?
Mnesilochos: Xenylla asked for a basin, as there wasn't a chamber-pot.

PERSONAL PIETY

12.40 Libations to the Gods at a Symposium

Xenophanes of Kolophon B1

Xenophanes here describes his idea of the perfect, pious, dinner party; cf. doc. 6.32.

For now the floor is clean and everyone's hands
And the wine-cups; one (boy) puts woven garlands on our heads,
Another offers fragrant unguent in a bowl (phiale);
The mixing-bowl stands full of cheer;
And another wine, which says it will never run dry,
Gentle and smelling of flowers, is ready in the wine-jars;
In the middle frankincense gives off its sacred odour,
And there is water, cold, sweet and pure;
Yellow loaves and a table of honour carrying cheese and rich honey are at hand;
And the altar in the middle is completely covered with flowers,
And singing and festivity fills the house.
First cheerful men should celebrate the god in hymns
With auspicious speech and pure words,
And they should make libation and pray for the power to do
What is righteous; and they should drink as much as will allow them
To arrive home without a servant, unless they are very old.
And one should praise the man who displays good qualities after drinking,
For having memory and energy in praising virtue,
Not conducting the battles of the Titans and Giants,
Nor the Centaurs, fictions of older days,
Nor of violent discords; there is nothing good in these:
What is good is always to have consideration towards the gods.

12.41 Inscriptions from the Vari Cave near Athens

IG I^2 784–85, 788–89 (*IG* I^3 977, 980, 982)

Archedamos of Thera was a nympholeptos, one 'seized by the nymphs'. In the fifth century he embellished a cave in Attica, near Vari, which can still be visited today. The interior has several wall reliefs as well as inscriptions, and Archedamos planted a garden for the nymphs, and built them a dancing-floor. The entrails from sacrifices had to be washed out of the cave and the dung cleaned out. For nympholepsy, see Connor (1988) 155–89, esp. 166–74.

IG I^2 784 (*IG* I^3 977): Archedamos of Thera planted (this) garden to the Nymphs.

IG I^2 785 (*IG* I^3 977): Arched[a]mos of Thera also bu[il]t a dancing-floor for the dancin[g] Nymph.

IG I^2 788 (*IG* I^3 980; Hansen 321): Archedamos of Thera, raptured by Nymphs (the nympholeptos), furnished the cave at the request of the Nymphs.

IG I^2 789 (*IG* I^3 982; *LSCG* 9): Was[h] the en[t]rails outside and clean out the dung.

12.42 A Family from Sybaris Rescued off Lindos

Friedländer 126

A wooden group of cow and calf from the temple of Athena at Lindos on Rhodes, probably of the sixth century. When Diagoras of Melos (see doc. 12.2), was on Samothrace and a friend pointed out the votive paintings, he retorted that those who perished at sea did not have the opportunity to dedicate pictures (Cic. *Nat. Deor.* 3.89; van Straten (1981) 78).

Amphinomos and his sons from spacious Sybaris
When their ship was saved dedicated this tithe.

THE GREEKS AND THEIR IDENTITY

12.43 Religion as Part of the Greek Heritage

Herodotos VIII.144.2

When the Spartans heard that Mardonios had sent Alexander to the Athenians with a proposal that they make terms with Persia, they sent envoys who were present when the Athenians gave their answer. This was the Athenians' reply to the Spartans.

VIII.144.2 There are many important reasons which prevent us from doing this, even if we so wished, the first and greatest being the burning and demolishing of the statues and temples of our gods, which we must avenge with all our power rather than making terms with the agent of their destruction. Furthermore there is the fact that we are all Greeks, sharing both the same blood and the same language, and we have the temples of our gods in common and our sacrifices and similar life-style, and it would not be right for the Athenians to betray all these.

13

Women and the Family

Within the framework of tribes (phylai) and clans (gene) Greek society was essentially based on the family, on the oikos (or household), which was composed of a combination of free people and slaves. The family was under the power of the head of the household, and it was a tightly bound unit with complex hierarchical relationships. The term oikos covered not only the members of the nuclear family, but the whole physical and economic unit, including property, slaves and land, and there was strict limitation of succession by inheritance, only to be broken under specific circumstances. The oikos was also a religious unit, which placed particular emphasis on maintaining the tombs of the family's ancestors. Apart from their membership of the family, all or most Athenian males were enrolled in the phratry, or brotherhood, of their father. Indeed before the reforms of Kleisthenes in 508/7 citizenship depended on membership of a phratry. After this, while phratry-membership was not legally necessary, failure to be able to prove it was considered suspicious and those whose claims to citizenship are disputed regularly demonstrate their membership of a phratry as well as of a deme (cf. doc. 5.7; cf. docs. 10.20–22).

As the oikos was simultaneously property unit and family, questions of property, inheritance and marriage were inextricable, and to a great extent the legislation concerning heiresses and marriage was primarily concerned with the preservation of the family property and the survival of the oikos (docs. 13.47–48). Typically a man would marry when the property was divided on the death or retirement of his father, and establish his own oikos, and thirty or thirty-five appears to have been a normal age for a man to marry (doc. 13.65, cf. 13.9): prior to this age a man might have indulged in a homosexual relationship with a young boy (cf. docs. 13.52, 13.24; cf. 4.21, 30–31). Athenian law provided that sons succeed their fathers unless disinherited and all sons had a share in the inheritance, which could result in the creation of small estates (doc. 13.9; cf. 13.18 for Sparta). But often when there were no sons, estates were left in the possession of epikleroi (singular: epikleros); these were heiresses, daughters who had no brother natural or adopted, and in their case both the estate and the daughter together could and should be jointly claimed by the nearest male relative in an order of strict precedence (doc. 13.47; cf. 13.48); doc. 13.50 demonstrates how complex families could become as a result.

The legislation of Perikles in 451/0 decreed that a man's parents both had to be citizens for him to be a citizen likewise (doc. 10.18), resulting in a need for

Athenians to be able to prove legitimacy. This meant that adultery on the part of a wife could threaten the legitimacy and standing of all of her children. Sexual misconduct had always of course been considered highly reprehensible (doc. 13.48, cf. 13.51), and adultery was an offence not just against the husband but against the oikos generally. Not merely the need for chastity but patterns of work made a basic spatial division between men and women the norm: it was expected that women should live inside the house and see to the care of the house, children and servants, as well as contributing to the household's economy through their weaving (docs. 13.57–58). Nevertheless, despite middle-class conventions, many lower-class women did work (docs. 13.54–55) and women on the whole were not confined at home except by their duties. Poets of the archaic period, such as Hesiod and Theognis, give a realistic picture of the influence and status of a wife and her position in the family and are worth careful consideration. They are often used as evidence for a misogynistic viewpoint (such as doc. 13.8), but even the work of Semonides (doc. 13.13) highlights the importance of a wife's contribution to the home's prosperity and comfort; they certainly do not imply that women in this period were generally kept in seclusion. Similarly documents on Spartan women, while they often present an idealised picture of Spartan society, do not suggest that Spartan women were anything but respected within their families and in enjoyment of freedom relatively unknown elsewhere in the Greek world (docs. 13.14–22).

Much of the discussion concerning attitudes towards women in classical Athens has centred around the works of the tragedians. If heroines such as Clytemnestra and Medea (see docs. 13.62–63) are considered to have been directly modelled on the women of fifth century Athens, then clearly such women can hardly have been secluded or down-trodden. But these awesome protagonists were in origin pre-classical mythological figures, presented in the context of traditional tales. What is important in these cases is not only the choice of the plots in themselves, but the ways in which the tragedians have presented the story and the conflicts in which they chose to portray women. Valuable evidence is also provided by the works of Aristophanes, who wrote in great detail about women and their activities for the amusement of audiences of contemporary Athenians. To take his humour literally would be to misinterpret his point of attack greatly: his jokes cannot be taken as entirely representing Athenian men's views of their wives, with their emphasis on women's propensity to drink and sexual misdemeanours (cf. docs. 12.39, 13.59). Rather it shows that the Athenians were prepared, in comic productions, not only to poke fun at their wives (or *other people's* wives), but also to present on stage characters such as Lysistrata, whose views on society and politics are meant to be taken seriously by both actors and audience alike (see doc. 13.60). As with sources for all social history, each piece of evidence regarding women and the family must be considered in its social and historical context. Nevertheless, while women were politically and legally disadvantaged *vis-à-vis* their menfolk, it would be rash to assume that for this reason they were considered by their society as inferior and negligible members of their families and households.

SAPPHO OF LESBOS

The poet Sappho was a contemporary of Alcaeus and the tyrant Pittakos; born on Lesbos c. 620, she is said, like Alcaeus and his brother, to have spent some time in exile. Some 41 of her poems survive, mostly incomplete, as well as a number of fragments attributed to her; her main theme is love, and her poetry in general is written for a circle of aristocratic girls and women, although some of her work is intended for a wider audience. In antiquity Sappho was known as the 'tenth Muse', though she is only mentioned in passing by Herodotos (II.135.1). For the aristocratic and elitist nature of the poetry of Sappho, Alcaeus and Anacreon, see Arthur (1973) 38–43. On Sappho's poetry and the traditions within which she is working, see Stigers (1981) 45–61; Winkler (1981) 63–89, (1990) 162–87; Snyder (1989) 13–34; for Sappho and her environment, see Pomeroy (1975) 53–55; Burnett (1983) 209–28 (who follows the traditional view of Sappho as 'school-mistress'); Snyder (1991) 1–19; Parker (1993) 309–51, esp. 341–46.

13.1 The Intensity of Passion

Sappho 31

The scene is a dinner party, the circumstances of which are unspecified. There are no grounds for the traditional view that this is a wedding scene and the man in this poem the bridegroom, and that Sappho is describing her feelings for her favourite pupil who is leaving her for a husband; see Page (1955) 30–33. For an analysis of this poem, see Robbins (1980) 255–61; Burnett (1983) 229–35; Winkler (1990) 178–80; Snyder (1989) 18–21, (1991) 10–14, who notes (18) that in this poem Sappho appears to focus on matters not generally addressed by male writers of her time, such as detailed descriptions of the inner emotions of love and desire .

1 That man seems to me to be equal to the gods, who sits opposite you and listens close to you to your sweet voice

5 And your lovely laughter, which flutters my heart in my breast. For when I look at you for a moment, then I no longer have the power to speak,

9 But my tongue †has broken†, at once a subtle fire has stolen under my skin, with my eyes I see nothing, my ears hum,

13 †A cold sweat pours over me†, a trembling seizes me all over, I am paler than grass, to myself I seem to be little short of death.

17 But all must be endured, since †even a poor man† ....

13.2 'Whatever One Loves'

Sappho 16

For a defence of this poem against the comments of Page (1955) 55–57, see duBois (1984) 95–105, who notes that, contrary to the Homeric poems, Helen is here seen as an autonomous subject, not a passive object traded between men; cf. Winkler (1990) 176–78; Burnett (1983) 277–90; Snyder (1989) 22–24, (1991) 8–10.

1 Some say a host of cavalry, others of infantry, and others of ships to be the most beautiful thing on the black earth, but I say it is whatever one loves.

5 It is very easy to make this understood by everyone, for she that far surpassed mankind in beauty, Helen, her husband, who was best of all,

9 Deserted and went sailing off to Troy, with no thought at all of her child or dear parents, but (Love) led her astray ....

13 .... (?she) has reminded me now of Anaktoria, who is no longer near;

17 I would rather see her lovely walk and the bright radiance of her face than the Lydians' chariots and fully-armed infantry.

13.3 To an Uneducated Woman

Sappho 55

1 When you have died, there you will lie, and there will be no recollection of you nor †longing† ever after; for you have no share in the roses

3 From Pieria (home of the Muses). But unseen in the house of Hades also, you will go to and fro among the shadowy corpses, flown from our midst.

13.4 Sappho's Daughter

Sappho 132

For Gyges of Lydia and his wealth, see doc. 2.1. Sappho 98 is also addressed to her daughter Kleis; see Snyder (1989) 33–34.

I have a beautiful daughter, who resembles golden flowers, my darling Kleis, for whom I would not exchange all Lydia† or lovely ....

13.5 The Girl from Lesbos

Anacreon 358

According to Athen. 599c the following lines were said to be addressed to Sappho by Anacreon. Cf. Alcaeus 384, 'Dark-haired lady, holy, sweetly smiling Sappho'.

Once again, with his purple ball
Golden-haired Love (Eros) has struck me
And now with the girl in embroidered sandals
He invites me to play;
But she, for she comes from Lesbos, a lovely place
To dwell in, finds fault
With my hair, for it is white,
And is agape for some other — girl.

13.6 Praxilla's 'Hymn to Adonis'

Praxilla 747

Telesilla was a renowned Argive poetess of the fifth century, who according to Plutarch *Fine Deeds of Women* 4 (*Moralia* 245c–f) mobilised the Argive women to fight off Kleomenes; cf. Hdt. VI.77.2. She seems mainly to have written hymns for women. Praxilla of Sicyon, according to Eusebius, like Telesilla was writing in the mid-fifth century and Athenaeus (694a) reports that she was famous for her drinking songs. However, her reputation as a poetess was not always of the best and Zenobios (IV.21) records the expression 'sillier than Praxilla's Adonis' as used of foolish people. Adonis in mythology was a mortal beloved by Aphrodite, killed boar hunting. Here he is listing what he most misses from the world above; see Snyder (1989) 54–59.

The most beautiful thing that I leave behind is the light of the sun,
The next the shining stars and the face of the moon
And also ripe cucumbers and apples and pears.

EARLY MORALISERS AND MISOGYNISTS

Despite the overall tone of the works of the poets of the archaic period (Hesiod was writing c. 700 BC, Semonides in the mid-seventh century, Theognis 640–600, Hipponax c. 540) it is important to note the specific causes of complaint with which some of these early writers charged women (both Semonides and Hipponax, like Archilochos, were renowned for their abusive talents). It is significant that wives are seen as having a very great impact on a man's comfort and livelihood, and the 'misogynistic' works do not treat women as a negligible factor in their lives: certainly there is little if any concept of women being kept in seclusion. For women's work and its perceived role in society in Hesiod and Semonides, see Sussman (1984) 79–93; while it might be argued that Hesiod denies woman a role in the economy (*Theogony* 590–601), the same is not true of Semonides; cf. Arthur (1973) 7–26, 46–47; Pomeroy (1975) 32–56.

13.7 Odysseus Entreats Princess Nausikaa

Homer *Odyssey* VI.178–85

Odysseus has here been shipwrecked on the coast of Phaeacia, and the first person he sees is the young princess Nausikaa, who has left the palace to wash clothes. For an in-depth portrait of a harmonious and loving marriage in Homer, see *Iliad* VI.371–502 (Hector, Andromache and their infant son Astyanax); for Odysseus and Penelope's reunion, see Hom. *Od.* XXIII.85–365; see Pomeroy (1975) 16–31 for women in Homeric epic.

Show me the town, and give me a rag to wrap round myself,
If only a wrapper you brought here for your clothes.
And in return may the gods grant you all that you desire in your heart:
A husband and a home and the accompanying unity of mind and feeling,
Which is so desirable; for there is nothing nobler or better than this,
When two people, who think alike, keep house
As man and wife; causing great pain to their enemies,
And joy to their well-wishers; as they themselves know best.

13.8 Pandora

Hesiod *Works and Days* 57–82

Pandora (the 'all-endowed') was given by Zeus to mankind in revenge for Prometheus' theft of fire; she removed the lid from a storage jar thus allowing all the evils to escape; cf. Hes. *Theogony* 570–89; see Walcot (1984) 40–41 for her characterization in this passage. Here Zeus is speaking.

'I will give them instead of fire an evil, in which all
May delight in their heart and lovingly embrace it, evil though it is.'
Thus spoke the father of gods and men and laughed out loud;
And he told renowned Hephaistos as quickly as possible
To mix earth with water, and place in it human voice
And strength, and liken it in face to the immortal goddesses
With the lovely and beauteous form of a maiden; and bade Athena
Teach her handiwork, to weave the intricate web;
And golden Aphrodite to shed grace on her head
And painful desire and cares that gnaw the limbs;
While to place in her a shameless mind and wily nature
He charged Hermes the messenger and slayer of Argos.
So he spoke, and they obeyed the lord Zeus, son of Kronos.
Immediately the renowned Lame God (Hephaistos) fashioned from earth
The likeness of a modest maiden through the counsels of the son of Kronos;
The goddess grey-eyed Athena girt and clothed her;
The divine Graces and august Persuasion
Put necklaces of gold around her skin; and the
Lovely-haired Hours crowned her with spring flowers;
And Pallas Athena equipped her with all kind of adornment.
In her breast the messenger, the Argos-slayer,
Contrived lies and crafty words and a wily nature
At the will of loud-thundering Zeus; and the herald of the gods
Put speech in her, and named this woman
Pandora, because each of those who dwell on Olympus
Gave her a gift, a bane to men who eat bread.

13.9 Maxims for Prosperity

Hesiod *Works and Days* 370–78, 695–705

Hesiod is often considered to have been unsympathetic towards women and their social role because of his portrait of Pandora: Arthur (1973) 23–25; Pomeroy (1975) 2; Lloyd-Jones (1975) 18–21; Sussman (1984) 88–89. But in the *Works and Days* he clearly distinguishes between wives whom men choose for themselves, and women who are simply out for what they can get. His description of a marriageable young girl (*WD* 519–22), 'a tender maiden who stays indoors with her dear mother, not yet experienced in the works of golden Aphrodite, who washes well her soft body and anoints herself with oil', shows that his view of women's sexuality was not entirely negative. Line 370 is generally taken as spurious: Starr (1977) 225 n.41.

See that the wage promised to a friend can be relied on;
Even with your brother smile and get a witness;
†For trust† and mistrust together have ruined men.
Do not let a woman who decorates her buttocks deceive you,
By wily coaxing, for she is after your granary;
Whoever trusts a woman, trusts thieves.
There should be an only son to preserve his father's house;
For thus wealth will increase in the home;
He who leaves another son should die old ....

In the prime of life bring a wife to your home,
When you are not much short of thirty,
Nor yet much above: this is the right age for marriage;
Your wife should be four years past puberty, and be married in the fifth.
You should marry a maiden, so you can teach her diligent habits,
And marry especially one who lives near you
Looking well about you, so your marriage is not a source of malignant joy to your neighbours.
For a man acquires nothing better than a wife —
A good one, but there is nothing more miserable than a bad one,
A parasite, who even if her husband is strong
Singes him without a torch and brings him to a raw old age.

13.10 Youth and Age do not Mix

Theognis 457–60

A young wife is not suitable for an elderly husband;
For she is a boat that does not obey the rudder,
Nor do anchors hold her; and she breaks her mooring cables
Often at night to find another harbour.

13.11 A Happy Man

Theognis 1225–26

Theognis is here writing to his friend Kyrnos, urging him too to marry. See Theognis 183–92 for unsuitable marriages between 'good' and 'base' people because of greed for possessions.

Nothing, Kyrnos, is sweeter than a good wife;
I am a witness to the truth of this, and you should become so for me.

13.12 A Woman's Two Best Days

Hipponax 68

Hipponax of Ephesos was a master of abusive writing; he was banished from Ephesos and went to live at Klazomenai; for his poetry, see Burnett (1983) 98–104.

There are two days on which a woman is most pleasing –
When someone marries her and when he carries out her dead body.

13.13 The Sow, the Bitch, the Mare and the Bee

Semonides of Amorgos 7, lines 1–6, 12–20, 57–70, 83–93, 106–18

Semonides in this poem portrays women in ten different guises modelled on animals: all are distinctly uncomplimentary, except for the 'bee'. Lefkowitz (1983) 32 points out that the life of the 'good woman' in this passage is dedicated to serving her husband; Walcot (1984) 46, in his attempt to argue that Greek attitudes towards women were conditioned by men's fear of women's sexuality, notes that the good wife is like the bee in her indifference to sex. But the emphasis of the poem seems to be primarily on creature comforts within the household: note the complaint that it is impossible to entertain a dinner-guest properly once you are married (cf. doc. 13.30). For Semonides, who may have led the Samian colony to Amorgos, see Lloyd-Jones (1975) 15–18, 22–25.

God made the female mind separately
In the beginning. One he made from a bristly sow,
And everything in her house mixed with mud
Lies in disorder and rolls around the floor;
While she unclean in unwashed garments
Sits on the dunghills and grows fat ....

Another he made from a bitch, a quick runner, daughter of her own mother,
Who wants to hear and know everything,
And peers and wanders everywhere
Barking, even if she sees no human being.
A man cannot stop her with threats,
Not even if in anger he knocks out her teeth
With a stone, nor if he speaks to her gently,
Even when she is sitting amongst guests,
She continuously keeps up her incurable yapping ....

Another is the child of a dainty long-maned mare,
Who diverts menial tasks and toil to others.
She will neither touch a mill or pick up a sieve,
Nor throw the dung out of the house,
Nor sit at the oven avoiding the soot.
She makes her husband acquainted with necessity;
Every day she washes the dirt off herself
Twice, sometimes thrice, and anoints herself with perfumes,
And always has her thick hair
Well-combed and garlanded with flowers.
Such a wife is a fine sight
For other men, but proves an evil to the one she belongs to,
Unless he is a tyrant or king
Who takes pride in such things ....

Another is from a bee; the man who gets her is fortunate;
For on her alone no blame settles,

And his livelihood flourishes and increases because of her,
And she grows old with a husband whom she loves and who loves her
Bearing him a fine and well-reputed family.
She is pre-eminent among all the women,
And a godlike grace plays around her.
Nor does she take pleasure in sitting amongst the women
Where they tell stories about love.
Such wives of those granted to men
By Zeus are the best and the wisest ....

Where there is a woman, a man cannot even in his house
Heartily entertain a guest who has arrived.
And she that seems to be most prudent,
Turns out to be the most outrageous;
And while her husband is agape for her, the neighbours
Rejoice seeing that he too is deceived.
Each man takes care to praise his own wife,
And find fault with his neighbour's;
We do not realise that the fate all of us is alike.
For this is the greatest evil that Zeus has made,
Binding us with an unbreakable fetter,
From the time when Hades received those
Who went fighting for a woman's sake ....

SPARTAN WOMEN AND FAMILIES

Contemporary sources for sixth and fifth century Spartan women tend to be few and far between. However, the documents below by Aristotle and Xenophon are not written so much later that they cannot be taken as in some measure relevant to the period. Other documents of interest for Spartan women include: 6.11, 6.13–14, 6.44, 6.46–47. See esp. Pomeroy (1975) 35–42; Redfield (1977/78) 146–61; Cartledge (1981b) 84–105; Kunstler (1987) 31–48. For the 'Lakonian key' (Ar. *Thesm.* 421–23), which was used in Sparta not to lock up women but possibly foreigners, see Whitehead (1990) 267–68.

13.14 A Spartan Girls' Choir

Alcman 1, lines 39–101

Alcman was a Spartan poet (though he was later said to have come from Sardis: cf. doc. 6.51). From internal evidence his works can be dated to the later seventh and perhaps early sixth century, as he mentions the Eurypontid king Leotychidas (c. 625–600) in 5, F2. He was especially noted for his hymns written for girls' choirs (partheneia). In this passage, the girls appear to be offering a robe to a goddess. The expressions of desire by women for women can be compared to those in the poetry of Sappho; see Pomeroy (1975) 55–56; cf. Scanlon (1988) 187–88; Mulroy (1992) 55; Parker (1993) 325–31. Most of the names mentioned are those of the girls in the choir: Hagesichora means choir-leader, the role that she fills as 'choragos', while Ainesimbrota may be the trainer of the girls, or, as Parker 330 suggests, the mother of the four girls mentioned in lines 74–77. The Pleiades may be the constellation, or possibly a rival chorus, and the peace that the choir achieves due to Hagesichora may be victory in the competition; an Ibenian horse is a much faster breed than the Kolaxaian. For a discussion of the interpretation of this poem, see Fowler (1987) 70–72, cf. 93. For girls' choirs in Sparta, see also doc. 6.14.

39 I sing of the light of Agido: I see her like the sun, which Agido calls to shine on us as our witness; but our illustrious choir-leader (Hagesichora) does not allow me either to praise her (Agido) or to criticize her; for Agido[1] appears to be pre-eminent as if one were to set a horse among grazing beasts, a strong, thunderous-hoofed prize-winner of winged dreams.

50 Do you not see? The race-horse (Agido) is Venetic; but the hair of my cousin Hagesichora blooms like unmixed gold; and her silver face — why do I tell you distinctly? This is Hagesichora; and the second in appearance after Agido runs like a Kolaxaian horse against an Ibenian; for as we carry a robe to the Dawn Goddess (Orthria) the Pleiades rise through the ambrosial night like the star Sirius and fight us.

64 For so much excess of purple is not enough to defend us, nor cunningly wrought serpent of solid gold, nor Lydian headband, adornment of dark-eyed girls, nor the hair of Nanno, nor even godlike Areta, or Thylakis and Kleesithera, nor will you go to Ainesimbrota's house and say, 'If only Astaphis were mine, and Philylla were to look at me, and Damareta and lovely Ianthemis'; but Hagesichora oppresses me (with passion).

78 For is not Hagesichora of the beautiful ankles present here, and near Agido .... does she not praise our festival? Gods, receive their .... (prayer); for fulfilment belongs to the gods. Choir-leader, if I might speak, I myself am a young girl (parthenos), like an owl, I screech in vain from the roof; and I especially desire to please Dawn, for she was the healer of our pains; but because of Hagesichora the girls set foot on lovely peace.

92 .... and in a ship too one must listen to the helmsman; and she (?Hagesichora) is not more melodious than the Sirens, for they are goddesses, but this choir of ten sings as well as eleven girls; it sounds like a swan on the streams of the Xanthos; and she with her lovely blond hair .... (4 lines are missing).

[1] Reading, with Fowler (1987), αὔτα not αὐτὰ.

13.15 To 'Dress like a Dorian'

Anacreon 399

Accounts of the dress worn by Spartan women, or the lack of it, are substantiated by a fragment of Anacreon quoted by the scholiast on Euripides' *Hekabe* (line 934). The Dorians were the racial group of whom the Spartans were the best-known representatives. For the scanty clothing of Spartan girls, either nakedness in religious processions, or a revealingly split mini-chiton (chitoniskos), see Cartledge (1981b) 91–92; Scanlon (1988) 189; the bronze statuette of the female runner on the front cover is from Dodona, c. 600.

For women to 'dress like a Dorian' means to show themselves naked, as in Anacreon:

'Take off your chiton and dress like a Dorian.'

13.16 The Upbringing of Spartan Girls

Xenophon *Constitution of the Spartans* 1.3–8

Xenophon appears to be giving a reasonably accurate picture, despite perhaps a certain degree of gullibility, of the traditions which in his view had made Sparta great. He gives a useful contrast of Spartan upbringing of girls with that found in the rest of Greece. However, his account of Spartan dual households (including elderly men inviting youngsters into their house to sire children), while generally accepted, is at variance with Herodotos' account of Anaxandridas' double marriage (doc. 6.44), and, despite his account of bachelors siring children out of wedlock, Spartiates were expected to marry or else suffer penalties (cf. doc. 6.11). For this passage, cf. Plut. *Lyk.* 15; Kritias F32; Cartledge (1981b) 90–97; Scanlon (1988) 185–216.

1.3 First, to begin at the beginning, I will start with the begetting of children. Elsewhere those girls who are going to have children and are considered to have been well brought up are nourished with the plainest diet which is practicable and the smallest amount of luxury food possible; wine is certainly not allowed them at all, or only if well diluted. Just as the majority of craftsmen are sedentary, the other Greeks expect their girls to sit quietly and work wool. But how can one expect girls brought up like this to give birth to healthy babies? **1.4** Lykourgos considered slave-girls quite adequate to produce clothing, and thought that for free women the most important job was to bear children. In the first place, therefore, he prescribed physical training for the female sex no less than for the male; and next, just as for men, he arranged competitions of racing and strength for women also, thinking that if both parents were strong their children would be more robust .... **1.6** In addition he put a stop to each man marrying when he wished, and laid down that men should marry when in their physical prime, thinking that this too would contribute to the production of fine children. **1.7** He saw, however, that if an old man had a young wife, such men particularly guarded their wives, and wanted to prevent this; so he arranged that the elderly husband should bring in any man whose physical and moral attributes he admired to produce children. **1.8** And if anyone did not want to live with a wife, but desired remarkable children, he made it legal for him to have children by any fertile woman of noble birth he might see, providing he first persuaded her husband.

13.17 Kyniska: Olympic Victor, 396

Pausanias III.8.1

Kyniska daughter of Archidamos won the chariot race at the Olympic Games in 396 and 392, and is evidence of the fact that Spartan women controlled a large proportion of Sparta's wealth as early as 396 (cf. doc. 13.18). Paus. III.15.1 states that there was a heroon (hero-shrine) to her at Sparta and a statue of her by Apelles at Olympia (VI.1.6, cf. V.12.5). She is praised at *Anth. Pal.* 13.16; see *IG* V 1.235, a Doric capital with Kyniska's name at Sparta; Moretti pp.40–44; Lee (1988) 104n.4; Xen. *Ages.* 9.6. Olympic chariot-races were later won by other Spartan women: Hodkinson (1986) 402.

Archidamos also had a daughter whose name was Kyniska, who was extremely ambitious of winning at the Olympic Games and was the first woman to breed chariot horses and the first to win an Olympic victory. After Kyniska Olympic victories were gained by other women, particularly from Sparta, but no one was more distinguished for their victories than she was.

13.18 Aristotle on Spartan Women

Aristotle *Politics* 1269b 39–1270a 31 (II, ix)

In this passage Aristotle discusses the lack of control exercized over Spartan women and the problem caused in Sparta by the failure to limit the size of inheritances and dowries. Aristotle was writing his *Politics* between c. 335 and 323, though the discussion about Spartiate numbers below relates to Sparta's defeat at Leuktra in 371. For a discussion of this passage, see Hodkinson (1986) 386–406; Redfield (1977–78) 158–61; Cartledge (1981b) 84–105; cf. doc. 6.41.

1269b 39 Now, this licence of the women, from the earliest times, was to be expected. **1270a** For the men were absent from home for long periods of time on military expeditions, fighting the war against the Argives and again against the Arkadians and Messenians; when they were at leisure they gave themselves over to the legislator already prepared by military life (in which there are many elements of virtue), while they say that Lykourgos attempted to bring the women under his laws, but they resisted and he gave up his attempt .... **1270a 23** And nearly two-fifths of the whole country is in the hands of women, both because there have been numerous heiresses, and because large dowries are customary. And yet it would have been better to have regulated them, and given none at all or small or even moderate ones. But at present it is possible for a man to give an heiress to whomever he chooses, and if he dies intestate, the person whom he leaves as his heir may give her to whomever he wishes. Accordingly, though the country was able to support 1,500 cavalry and 30,000 hoplites, the number fell below 1,000.

13.19 'Spartans: The Only Women who Bear Men'

Plutarch *Lykourgos* 14.1–8

For the accuracy of Plutarch's account, note doc. 6.1, where Plutarch is unable to provide accurate details of Lykourgos' life and times, but nevertheless writes a biography. His *Life of Lykourgos* is, however, well worth reading. In *Sayings of the Spartans* (Plut. *Mor.* 225a) Gorgo is said to have asked Leonidas when he left for Thermopylai what instructions he had for her: his reply, 'To marry good men and bear good children'.

14.1 Since Lykourgos regarded education as the most important and finest duty of the legislator, he began at the earliest stage by looking at matters relating to marriages and births .... **14.3** For he exercized the girls' bodies with races and wrestling and discus and javelin throwing, so that the embryos formed in them would have a strong start in strong bodies and develop better, and they would undergo their pregnancies with vigour and would cope well and easily with childbirth. **14.4** He got rid of daintiness and sheltered upbringing and effeminacy of all kinds, by accustoming the girls no less than the young men to walking naked in processions and dancing and singing at certain festivals, when young men were present and watching .... **14.7** The nudity of the girls had nothing disgraceful in it, for modesty was present and immorality absent, but rather it made them accustomed to simplicity and enthusiastic as to physical fitness, and gave the female sex a taste of noble spirit, in as much as they too had a share in valour and ambition. **14.8** And so they came to speak and think in the way Leonidas' wife Gorgo is said to have done. For when some woman, who must have been a foreigner, said to her, 'You Lakonian women are the only ones who can rule men', she replied, 'That is because we are the only ones who give birth to men.'

13.20 The Mother of Brasidas

Plutarch *Lykourgos* 25.8–9

For Brasidas, see docs. 1.6, 9.19. Spartans were noted for their taciturnity and brevity of speech and Spartan women for their concept of honour: cf. docs. 6.13, 6.52; 2.28; Cartledge (1978) 25–37, (1981b) 92.

25.8 Brasidas' mother, Argileonis, when some of the Amphipolitans came to Sparta and visited her, asked them if Brasidas had died nobly and in a manner worthy of Sparta. **25.9** When they extolled her son and said that Sparta had no one else like him, she said, 'Don't say that, strangers — Brasidas may have been noble and brave, but Sparta has many better men than he.'

13.21 Lampito: a Typical Spartan Woman?

Aristophanes *Lysistrata* 77–82

Lysistrata has called together the women of Athens to reveal her plans for making peace, and they are awaiting the arrival of women from other Greek cities.

Myrrhine: Here's Lampito approaching now.
Lysistrata: Dearest Lakonian! Welcome, Lampito!
How beautiful you appear, darling.
What lovely colour you have, what physical vigour!
Why, you could throttle a bull!
Lampito: I think I could, by the two goddesses.
For I keep in training and practise my buttock-jumps.

13.22 Spartan Buttock-Jumps

Pollux *Onomastikon* IV.102

'Bibasis' was a kind of Lakonian dance, in which prizes were awarded not only to children but also to girls; one had to leap and touch the buttocks with one's feet, and the jumps were counted, hence the (anonymous) inscription in honour of one of these girls,

'Who once did a thousand at bibasis, the most ever done'.

13.23 The Trials of a Spartan Baby

Plutarch *Lykourgos* 16.1–2

This passage seems at variance with the necessary qualifications for Spartiate status — completion of the agoge and ability to pay the mess contribution; see docs. 6.30, 6.41; cf. 13.18. Nevertheless it may well reflect Spartan attitudes, and Greek views generally, towards deformity in new-born children. Plutarch also tells us that in Sparta babies were washed in wine to test whether they were epileptic, swaddling clothes were not used, and children were not allowed to be fussy about their food or afraid of the dark, and Spartan wet-nurses were very much in demand (cf. doc. 11.40). On infant exposure in Greece, see Harris (1982) 114–16; Engels (1980) 112–20, (1984) 386–93; Patterson (1985) 103–23; Garland (1990) 84–96; cf. Golden (1981) 316–31.

16.1 The father of a newborn baby did not have the power to decide whether to rear it, but carried it to a certain place called a meeting-place (lesche), where the eldest of his fellow-tribesmen sat. They examined the infant, and if it was sturdy and robust, they told him to rear it, and allocated it one of the 9,000 lots of land. **16.2** But if it was weak and deformed, they sent it off to the so-called Place of Exposure (Apothetai), a place like a pit by Mount Taygetos, considering it better for both the child itself and the city that what was not properly formed with a view to health and strength right from the very beginning should not live.

13.24 An Idealization of Spartan Pederasty

Xenophon *Constitution of the Spartans* 2.12–14

For such relationships, cf. Plut. *Lyk.* 17–18; on Spartan pederasty and its possible origins, see Cartledge (1981a) 17–36, who makes clear that Xenophon's attitude is probably here reflecting the homoerotic proclivities of his patron Agesilaos II; cf. Garland (1990) 137–41. For normal Greek attitudes to homosexuality (and the relationship between the lover, erastes, and the younger partner, the beloved or eromenos), see Dover (1973) 65–67; Just (1989) 147–50; docs. 4.21, 13.39–40, 52.

2.12 I think I ought also to say something about love affairs with boys; for this also relates in some way to education. Some of the other Greeks, like the Boeotians for instance, live together, man and boy, as if they were married, or, like the Eleians, they win the youth by means of favours. On the other hand there are some who entirely prevent lovers from conversing with boys. **2.13** Lykourgos' views were in contrast to all of these; if someone of suitable character admired a boy's soul and tried to make him into a blameless friend and associate with him, he commended this and considered it the finest form of education; but if someone appeared to desire a boy's body, he thought this to be quite disgraceful and laid it down that at Sparta lovers should refrain from molesting boys no less than parents refrain from sleeping with their children or brothers their sisters. **2.14** I am, however, not surprised that people disbelieve this; for in many cities the laws do not oppose passionate attachments to boys.

THE 'HISTORICAL' WOMAN

It is unwise to take literally any perceptions of society even when depicted by a contemporary author. The well-known passage in the funeral oration delivered by Perikles, and its brief comment on the duties of women who have lost their husbands, has to be taken in the context both of the funeral speech as a whole, and the aims and message of Perikles (as perceived by Thucydides) in delivering it at this point. For women in Thucydides, and the generally marginal role that they play in his history, see Wiedermann (1983) 163–70; Harvey (1985) 67–90; for women in Herodotos, Lateiner (1985) 93–96. Useful works for an introduction to the position of women in ancient Greece include: Gomme (1925) 1–25; Seltman (1955) 119–24; Lacey (1968) 100–18, 151–76; Richter (1971) 1–8; Arthur (1973) 7–58; Just (1989) 105–52; see also docs. 2.4, 4.34, and 12.34–39 for women and their religious role.

13.25 Artemisia Strikes Again

Herodotos VIII.87.1–88.3

Artemisia was tyrant of Herodotos' own city, Halikarnassos, and thus a Greek and ruler of Greeks, the power having passed into her hands on the death of her husband. She sailed with Xerxes' fleet, even though she had a grown-up son, furnishing five ships of war. She was the only one of his commanders who advised Xerxes not to fight at sea (VII.99.1–3; VIII.68.1–69.2) and the Greeks set a special reward of 10,000 drachmas for her capture (VIII.93.1–2). For Herodotos' portrait of Artemisia, see Dewald (1981) 107–10; Lateiner (1985) 9–95; Munson (1988) 91–106.

VIII.87.1 The following actions of Artemisia increased her reputation with the King even more. **VIII.87.2** When the King's side had reached a stage of total disorder, Artemisia's vessel was at that point being pursued by an Athenian ship; as she was unable to escape it (for in front of her there were other friendly ships, and hers happened to be the nearest to the enemy), she decided to act as follows, and this turned out to be much to her advantage; while she was pursued by the Athenian ship, she drove straight at one of her own side's vessels, one from Kalynda, which was carrying the Kalyndian king Damasithymos. **VIII.87.3** Whether she had had some quarrel with him while they were still in the Hellespont I cannot say, nor if she did this deliberately, or the Kalyndian ship just happened to be in the way by chance. **VIII.87.4** Anyway she rammed and sank it, and was lucky enough to gain a two-fold advantage by so doing; for when the trierarch of the Athenian ship saw her ramming one of the barbarians' ships, he thought that Artemisia's ship was a Greek one or was deserting from the barbarians and fighting for the Greeks, and so turned to attack others. **VIII.88.1** This then was one benefit, that she escaped and was not killed, and the other was that she happened, in injuring her own side, to gain an even better reputation with Xerxes. **VIII.88.2** For it is said that the King was watching and saw her ramming the ship, and one of the bystanders remarked, 'Sire, do you see how well Artemisia is fighting and that she has struck an enemy ship?' He asked if it really was the work of Artemisia, and they said that they knew her ship's figurehead very well; they thought that the ship which had been sunk belonged to the enemy. **VIII.88.3** She was also lucky, as was said, that no one from the Kalyndian ship was saved to accuse her. Xerxes' remark on what was told him is said to have been, 'My men have become women, my women men.'

13.26 Athenian Widows Make their Point

Herodotos V.87.1–88.3

According to Herodotos, who is describing the supposed origins of the enmity between Athens and Aegina, when the Athenians attacked Aegina to recover the statues of Damia and Auxesia originally made of Attic olive wood, which the Aeginetans had taken from Epidauros, all the Athenians except one were killed. The sole survivor also came to a bad end; as a result the women's dress was changed from a pinned peplos to an unpinned chiton. Clearly in times of national excitement women were freely able to take to the streets; see Schaps (1982) 206–07, 209–10. Cf. Hdt. IX.4–5, where Lykidas suggests that Mardonios' proposals be put before the assembly; the Athenians stoned him to death and the Athenian women got together and stoned his wife and children; see Rosivach (1987) 237–45; on women in Greece in wartime, see Schaps (1982) esp. 193–96.

V.87.1 This is what is said by the Argives and Aeginetans, and the Athenians agree that only one of their men was saved and reached Attica; **V.87.2** but according to the Argives this one man survived after they had destroyed the Athenian army, and according to the Athenians it was an act of God, and even this one man did not survive but was killed in the following way. He arrived at Athens and reported the disaster. When the wives of the other men who had gone on the expedition to Aegina learnt this they were angry that he alone out of all of them should have been saved, so they surrounded the fellow and jabbed the brooches from their dresses into him, each of them asking him where her husband was. **V.87.3** In this way he was killed, and this deed by their women seemed to the Athenians to be even worse than the disaster. The only way in which they could punish the women was to change their style of dress to the Ionian; for before this Athenian women wore Dorian dress, very similar to that at Corinth, but they now changed it to a linen tunic so the women would not use brooches .... **V.88.2** The Argives and Aeginetans then passed this law that in both their countries brooch-pins should be made half as long again as they had been and that in the sanctuary of these deities (Damia and Auxesia) women should particularly dedicate brooches .... **V.88.3** And the Argive and Aeginetan women because of the conflict with Athens, from that time up to the present, have worn even longer pins than in the past.

13.27 Women in Perikles' 'Funeral Oration'

Thucydides II.45.2

For a consideration of this much-quoted passage it is essential to look at the funeral speech as a whole (II.34.1–46.2; cf. doc. 10.9) and to compare Perikles' advice to those who have lost their sons (or brothers or fathers), who have died with honour. In context, it could be argued that Perikles is advising women here, as the widows of men who have died nobly, to restrain their grief as much as possible, rather than generally proclaiming that women should always be neither seen nor heard; see Gomme (1925) 15–16; Lacey (1964) 47–49; Richter (1971) 3–4; Harvey (1985) 67–90; Andersen (1987) 33–49; cf. Schaps (1977) 323–30. For women's social role as mourners in this passage, see II.34.4; cf. docs. 12.30–33, 13.48 for funerary practices and legislation.

'I should perhaps say something about the virtue appropriate to women, to those of you who will now be widows, and I shall simply give one brief piece of advice. Your renown will be great if you do not behave in an inferior way to that natural to your sex, and your glory will be to be least mentioned amongst men concerning either your virtue or your faults.'

13.28 Women Fight in the Corcyraean Civil War, 427

Thucydides III.74.1

When the Corcyraeans were split by civil war women joined in the fighting; cf. Thuc. II.4.2, where women and slaves at Plataea threw stones and tiles from the roofs at the invading Thebans; Harvey (1985) 73–74.

The women also joined in the fighting with daring, throwing down roof-tiles from their houses and enduring the uproar in a manner unnatural to their sex.

13.29 Aspasia and Perikles

Plutarch *Perikles* 24.2–9

While Plutarch's picture of Aspasia may be somewhat romanticised, it is clear that though a metic she was one of the educated and well-known hetairai and hostesses of Athens. Perikles had been unhappily married to a near relative, whom presumably he had married as an epikleros; see Thompson (1967) 278–80. Aspasia bore Perikles a son, Perikles junior (for whom see doc. 10.13), who had no citizen rights, because of Perikles' law of 451/0, but was made a citizen at Perikles' request; see *Ath. Pol.* 26.4, Plut. *Per.* 37.2; for Perikles' reputation with other women, see Plut. *Per.* 13.15–16; 28.4–7; 36.6; 38.2. For Thucydides' failure to mention Aspasia, see Harvey (1985) 79; for her trial for impiety, see Plut. *Per.* 32.1, 5; doc. 8.20; for her acquaintance with Socrates, Xen. *Mem.* II.6.36. Cf. Plutarch's description of Elpinike, sister of Kimon, Plut. *Kim.* 4.6–8; for Elpinike's marriage to Kallias (without a dowry), see Cox (1988) 186.

24.2 It seems that Perikles took these measures against the Samians to please Aspasia, so this would be a suitable place to discuss this woman and the art or power she possessed by which she won over all the leading citizens and even provided the philosophers with a subject for long and important discussions. **24.3** It is agreed that by birth she was a Milesian, the daughter of Axiochos; and they say that she was trying to rival Thargelia, an Ionian woman of times of old, in setting her sights at the most influential men .... **24.5** They say that Perikles was attracted to Aspasia because of her wisdom and political awareness; and Socrates used to visit her sometimes with his acquaintances, while his close friends used to bring their wives to listen to her, even though she practised a calling that was neither decent nor respectable, since she brought up young girls as hetairai .... **24.7** Perikles' affection for Aspasia seems to have been quite romantic. **24.8** For his wife was a relation of his, who had been married first to Hipponikos, to whom she bore Kallias the wealthy, while to Perikles she bore Xanthippos and Paralos. When they found that they could no longer live together, Perikles handed her over to another man with her consent, and he took Aspasia as his companion and loved her to an unusual degree. **24.9** And they say that when he left home and returned from the agora he used to greet her every day with a kiss.

13.30 An Untrainable Wife: Socrates and Xanthippe

Xenophon *Symposium* 2.8–10

Xanthippe, whose name, with its 'hippos' (horse) termination, may suggest that she was from the aristocracy, is said once to have scolded Socrates and overturned the dinner-table when he brought home an uninvited guest, Euthydemos, from the palaistra. Euthydemos was about to leave in anger, when Socrates said, 'At your place, the day before yesterday, didn't a hen fly in and do precisely this? — yet we weren't annoyed at it.' (Plut. *Mor.* 461d; cf. Xen. *Mem.* II.2.1–14, Socrates' advice to his eldest son Lamprokles, when irritated with his mother.) Socrates may have been married twice, to Xanthippe and Myrto; for a discussion, see Fitton (1970) 57–66; Thompson (1972) 214–25; cf. Walcot (1987) 14–15; for Socrates' views of women's capabilities, see Wender (1973) 84–87. For her dismissal from the room prior to Socrates' death, see doc. 9.40.

2.8 Then another girl began to accompany the dancing-girl on the flute and a boy stood beside her and handed her the hoops until he had given her twelve. She took them and as she was dancing kept throwing them whirling in the air, observing the proper height to throw them so as to catch them rhythmically. **2.9** And Socrates said, 'What this girl is doing is only one proof among many others that woman's nature happens to be no worse than man's, although lacking in judgement and bodily strength. So if any of you has a wife, let him confidently teach her what he would like to have her know.' **2.10** At which Antisthenes said, 'So how is it, Socrates, that you think like that and do not train Xanthippe, but live with a wife who is the most difficult to live with of all women in existence, and, I think, of all women past and future as well?' 'Because,' he replied, 'I see that those who wish to become horsemen do not acquire the most docile horses but high-spirited ones. For they think that if they can manage these, they will easily handle all the others. And I want to deal with and associate with mankind and I have got her, knowing well that if I can stand her, I can easily live with all the rest of mankind.'

INSCRIPTIONAL EVIDENCE

See Nielsen et al (1989) 411–20 who, on the basis of sepulchral inscriptions c. 400 to c. 250, suggest that grave monuments were so reasonable in price that most Athenians could afford them, and that tombstones commemorated a cross-section of the population; Humphreys (1983) 88–118 discusses a number of monuments and their family groupings; for dedications by women, see Schaps (1979) 71–73. Lefkowitz (1983) 40 believes that grave inscriptions offer only limited information, but, while they often have little literary value, they do provide useful evidence about the ways in which mothers, sisters, wives and daughters were seen by their families; cf. note to doc. 12.30.

13.31 Xanthippe, Periander's Great-Great-Grand-daughter

Simonides 36

Page 251–52. For Periander and the Kypselid tyrants of Corinth, see docs. 2.6–14; for Archedike, daughter of Hippias, see doc. 4.34. In this epitaph it is the stele which is speaking to the passer-by. (This is not the same Xanthippe as in doc. 13.30.)

I shall mention her; for it is not right that here the glorious wife of Archenautes
Should lie in death unnamed
Xanthippe, great-great-grand-child of Periander, who once in high-towered
Corinth, where he was sovereign, commanded the people.

13.32 Thessalia

Friedländer 32

Hansen 119. A marble stele possibly of the sixth century from Thessaly. In the first two lines Thessalia speaks for herself; Acheron is a river in the underworld.

I died when an infant and did not yet re[a]ch the flower of my youth,
But came first to tearful Acheron.
Her father Kleodamos son of Hyperanor and her mother Korona
Set me here as a monument to their daughter Thes(s)alia.

13.33 Learete of Thasos

Friedländer 60

IG XII 8.398; Hansen 161. Dated to the early fifth century.

Truly beautiful is the monument which her [fa]ther erected over dea[d]
Learete; for we shall no [lon]ger se[e] her alive.

13.34 Phrasikleia

IG I^2 1014 (*IG* I^3 1216)

Friedländer 80; Hansen 24. An anonymous epitaph on a statue base for an otherwise unknown girl, from Attica, probably of the sixth century; for a discussion of the statue and inscription, see Svenbro (1993) 9–25.

The tomb of Phrasikleia: I shall be called maiden forever,
Because I won this name from the gods instead of marriage.
Aristion of Par[os m]a[d]e [me].

13.35 Timarete for her Dear Dead Son

Friedländer 140

IG XII 9 285; Hansen 108. A stele from Eretria, probably sixth century or slightly later.

Hail, passers-by; I lie here in death.
Come hither and read what man is buried here:
A foreigner (xenos) from Aegina, his name Mnesitheos.
My dear mother Timarete set up this monument for me,
An imperishable stele on the top of the mound,
[Which] will say th[ese] words to passers-by fo[re]ver,
'Timarete set this up for her dear dead son'.

13.36 A Mother's Command

Friedländer 69a (*IG* I^3 1226)

Hansen 61; from the Wall of Themistokles, a block of poros, probably mid-sixth century.

Splendid [.... of ....]rylides, whose tomb here
His [s]ons constructed at their [mo]t[h]er's command.

13.37 Potalis for her Husband

Friedländer 74

IG VII 3501; Hansen 111. A stone, with outlines of figures, of perhaps the late sixth or early fifth century from Tanagra in Boeotia. If the reconstruction in line one is correct, Mantitheos' wife Potalis was afterwards buried with him.

[Potalis] placed this [ste]le over her [dear] dead h[usb]an[d]
M[antitheo]s, who was skilled in hospitality and ho(r)semanship.
Potalis.

13.38 Gnatho's Sister

IG I^2 975 (*IG* I^3 1210)

Friedländer 161; Hansen 37. A marble disk with spiral inscription; Attic, perhaps c. 530.

This is the tomb of Gnatho. His sister buried him after nursing him in mental illness.

13.39 An Oath for Love of a Boy

IG I^2 920 (*IG* I^3 1399)

Friedländer 59; Hansen 47. A slab of marble from the Attic countryside, with crude archaic lettering, c. 500, recording the heroic love of Gnathios for a younger boy, for whom he swore an oath that he would go to war; the boy presumably erected this as a memorial to Gnathios; see Dover (1978) 124.

Here a man sw[o]r[e a sol]emn oath for lo[v]e of a boy
To mingl[e] in strife and tearful war.
I am sacred to Gnathios of Eroiadai, who lost his lif[e] i[n war].

13.40 Lysitheos Loves Mikion

IG I² 924 (*IG* I³ 1401)

This inscription from the acropolis at Athens may have been written by the beloved about his older lover, which would make it unusual; see Dover (1978) 123; cf. doc. 13.24.

Lysitheos says that he loves Mikion more than anyone in the city since he is brave.

13.41 A Parian Girl Marries

Archilochos 326

Anth. Pal. VI.133. This epigram (considered spurious by West (1971) I.106) is probably from Paros where there was a temple of Hera and was copied in antiquity from an actual dedication. The unveiling of the bride was one of the formal elements of the wedding-ceremony, and the veil could be consecrated to Hera, goddess of marriage.

Alkibia dedicated the sacred veil for her locks
To Hera, when she attained lawful wedlock.

13.42 A Royal Offering

Anacreon *Epigrammata* 7

The label on a garment dedicated in an unknown temple in Thessaly by Praxidike and Dyseris, wife of Echekratidas ruler of Larissa, at the beginning of the fifth century.

Praxidike made and Dyseris designed
This garment; the skill of both is united.

13.43 A Western Greek Dedicates a Mirror to Athena

Friedländer 166

IG XIV 664; Hansen 395. An early fifth century dedication of a female bronze statuette on an Ionic capital, part of a mirror stand, from Poseidonia (Paestum).

Phillo, daughter of Charmylidas, (dedicated) a tithe to Athena.

13.44 From Nikandra, Prominent amongst Women

Friedländer 46

IG XII.5 1425b; Hansen 403. This inscription was carved on the right thigh of an archaic female statue at Delos dedicated to Artemis and is dated to c. 650–625.

Nikandra dedicated me to the Far-Darter who delights in the arrow,
The daughter of Deinodikes of Naxos, prominent amongst ot(h)er women,
The sister of Deinomenes, and n[ow] wife of Phraxos.

13.45 A Prayer by Man and Wife

Friedländer 144

IG XII 5.1 215; Hansen 414. Possibly early fifth century, or before, from Paros.

Demokydes and Telestodike having made a vow in common
Erected this offering to virgin Artemis
On her sacred ground, the daughter of aegis-bearing Zeus;
To their family and livelihood give increase in safety.

13.46 Inscriptions on Possessions

Friedländer 177

(c) A lekythos from Cumae in Italy; cf. Strubbe (1991) 37, who describes it as a Protocorinthian aryballos, dating to the seventh century.

I am Tataia's flask: whoever steals me will become blind!

(e) *CIG* 545. Possibly a lover's gift from one male youth to another.

The cup (kylix) of Kesiphon; if anyone breaks it
He shall pay a drachma, because it is a gift from Xenyllos.

(h) *IG* VII 3467; Hansen 446. A black kantharos (drinking cup with large handles) from Thespiai, dated to the second half of the fifth century.

Mogeas gives this cup as a gift to hi[s] wife Eucharis
Daughter of Eutretiphantos, so she may drink her fill.

(m) An Attic black figure cup, allegedly found at Taras (Tarentum), with the inscription scratched on the foot.

I am Melosa's prize; she beat the girls in carding.

THE LEGAL STATUS OF WOMEN

For women in Greek inheritance law, see Schaps (1975) 53–57, (1979) 25–47: generally in Greece women inherited in preference to more distant male relatives, but were excluded by men of the same degree of relationship as themselves; the position of daughters (but not sisters) in the Gortyn law code is exceptional. See also doc. 10.26 for Lokris; Lacey (1968) 125–50; MacDowell (1978) 95–99, (1989) 10–21; Gould (1980) 43–46; Just (1989) 89–104; for Spartan heiresses, see Hdt. VI.57.4 (doc. 6.20, cf. 13.18). For marriage and the married woman in Athenian law, see Patterson (1991) 48–72; for the marriages of first cousins in Athens, see Thompson (1967) 273–82; for dowries, see Harris (1993) 73–95. For sexual offences and the penalties for sexual assault, see Cole (1984) 97–113 (Athens and Gortyn); Cohen (1991) 98–132; Fisher (1992) 104–09.

13.47 The Gortyn Law Code

Willetts *The Law Code of Gortyn*

This law code from Crete dates to c. 450, and seems to be the result of a revision of earlier laws by the legislative body of Gortyn; its provisions differ somewhat from Athenian practice. Daughters had a specific portion of the inheritance rather than a dowry, and in some cases heiresses could have a say in whom they married; see Willetts (1967) 18–29, (1977) 164–76. The apetairoi were not full citizens, but had a relatively free economic status. They may have included those unable to pay their mess contribution, or have been the sons of a citizen and a serf or slave: Willetts (1967) 12–13; cf. Lacey (1968) 208–16.

Rape, Seduction, Adultery

(col. II.2) If a person commits rape on a free man or free woman, he shall pay one hundred staters (200 dr.), and if on someone belonging to the house of an apetairos ten; and if a slave on a free man or woman, he shall pay double; and if a free man on a male or female serf, five drachmas; and if a male serf on a male or female serf, five staters. If a person seduces by force a female slave belonging to the house, he shall pay two staters; but if she has already been seduced, one obol if in day-time, two obols if at night; and the slave's oath shall have precedence. If a person attempts to have intercourse with a free woman who is under a relative's guardianship, he shall pay ten staters if a witness testifies. If someone be taken in adultery with a free woman in her father's house or brother's or husband's, he shall pay one hundred staters; but if in someone else's house fifty; and if with the wife of an apetairos ten; but if a slave with a free woman he shall pay double; and if a slave with a slave five. The captor should proclaim in the presence of three witnesses to the relatives of the person caught that he must be ransomed within five days; and to the owner of the slave in the presence of two witnesses; but if he is not ransomed, the captors may deal with him as they wish; but if anyone declares that he has been taken by deceit, the captor is to swear in a case involving fifty staters or more with four others, each calling down curses on themselves, and in the case of an apetairos with two others, and in the case of a serf the master and one other, that he captured him in adultery and not by deceit.

Divorce

If a husband and wife should be divorced, she is to keep whatever property she came to her husband with and half of the produce, if there is any, from her own property, (50) and half of whatever she has woven within the house, and if her husband is the cause of the divorce she is to have five staters; but if the husband should proclaim that he is not the cause, the judge shall decide on oath. (col. III) If the wife carries away anything else belonging to the husband, she shall pay five staters and whatever she may carry away; and let her restore whatever she may have stolen ....

Widowhood

(17) If a man dies leaving children, if the wife so wishes she may marry, keeping her own property and whatever her husband may have given her according to what is prescribed, in the presence of three adult free witnesses; but if she takes away anything belonging to the children, that is grounds for a trial. And if he leaves her childless, she is to have her own property and half of whatever she has woven within the house and is to obtain her portion of the produce in the house along with the lawful heirs as well as whatever her husband may have given her as is prescribed; (30) but if she takes away anything else, that is grounds for a trial. And if the wife dies childless, he is to return her property to the rightful heirs and half whatever she has woven in the house and half of the produce, if it is from her own property ....

Provisions for children

(44) If a woman who is divorced should bear a child, it is to be brought to the husband in his house in the presence of three witnesses. And if he does not accept it, the child shall be in the mother's power either to rear or to expose; and (50) the oaths of the relatives and witnesses shall have precedence .... (col. IV.8) If a woman who is divorced should expose her child before presenting it as is prescribed, she shall pay fifty staters for a free child, twenty-five for a slave. And if the man has no house to which she can bring it or she does not see him, there is to be no penalty if she exposes the child .... (31) And if a person should die, the city houses and whatever there is inside the houses in which a serf does not reside, and the small and large cattle which do not belong to a serf, shall belong to the sons, but all the rest of the property is to be divided fairly, and the sons, (40) however many there are, shall each receive two parts, while the daughters, however many there are, shall each receive one part. If the mother dies, her property shall also be divided, in the same way as is prescribed for the father's. But if there is no property other than the house, the daughters shall receive their share as prescribed. And if the father, while alive, wishes to give to a married daughter, (50) let him give according to what is prescribed but not more. Any daughter to whom he gave or promised before is to have these things, but shall receive nothing else from her father's property .... (col. VI.31) And if a mother dies leaving children, the father is to have control over the mother's estate, but he may not sell or mortgage unless the children consent and are of age .... (44) And if he marries another woman, the children are to have control of their mother's property.

Heiresses

(col. VII.15) The heiress is to be married to the brother of her father, the oldest of those living. And if there are more heiresses and brothers of the father, (20) they are to be married to the next eldest. And if there should be no brothers of the father, but sons of the brothers, she is to be married to the one who is the son of the eldest. And if there are more heiresses and sons of brothers, they are to be married to the next after the son of the eldest. The groom-elect is to have one heiress and not more. (30) While the groom-elect or heiress is too young to marry, the heiress is to have the house, if there is one, and the groom-elect is to receive half the revenue from everything. But if the groom-elect does not wish to marry the heiress, though they are both old enough to marry, on the grounds that he is still a minor, all the property and produce shall be at the heiress' disposal until he marries her. (40) But if the groom-elect as an adult does not wish to marry the heiress who is old enough and willing to marry him, the relatives of the heiress are to take the matter to court and the judge is to order the marriage to take place within two months. And if he does not marry her as prescribed, the heiress is to have all the property and marry the next in succession, if there is one. (50) But if there is no groom-elect, she shall be married to whomever she wishes of those who ask from the tribe. And if the heiress, though old enough, does not wish to be married to the groom-elect, or the groom-elect is too young and the heiress is unwilling to wait, (col. VIII) the heiress is to have the house, if there is one in the city, and whatever is in the house, and she is to receive half of the rest and be married to whomsoever she wishes of those who ask from the tribe; but she is to give a share of the property to that man (whom she rejected). And if there are no kinsmen of the heiress as defined, (10) she is to have all the property and be married to whomever she wishes from the tribe. And if no one from the tribe should wish to marry her, the relatives of the heiress are to proclaim throughout the tribe, 'Does no one wish to marry her?' And if someone marries her it should be within thirty days from the time of the proclamation, but if not she can be married to another, whomever she can. (20) And if a woman becomes an heiress after her father or brother has given her in marriage, if she does not wish to remain married to the one to whom they gave her, even if he is willing, if she has born children, she may be married to another of the tribe dividing the property as prescribed. But if there are no children, she is to be married to the groom-elect, if there is one, and take all the property, and if there is not, as prescribed. (30) If a husband dies leaving children to an heiress, she may marry whomever in the tribe she can, if she so wishes, but there is no compulsion. But if the deceased has left no children behind, she is to be married to the groom-elect as prescribed .... (40) An heiress is someone who has no father or brother by the same father. And while she is not old enough to marry, her father's brothers are to be responsible for the administration of the property, while she receives a half share of the produce. But if there should be no groom-elect while she is not old enough to marry, the heiress is to have control of the property and the produce and (50) as long as she is not old enough to marry is to be brought up with her mother; and if she should have no mother, she is to be brought up with her mother's brothers .... (col. XII.9) And where the heiress, there being no groom-elect or judges in the affairs of orphans, is brought up with her mother, her relatives on both sides who have been nominated are to administer the property and the revenue to the best of their ability until she is married. And she is to be married when she is twelve or older.

13.48 Solon's Legislation on Marriage and Inheritance

Plutarch *Solon* 20.2–23.2

Solon introduced a law permitting a man who had no sons to adopt a son by will and make him his heir, rather than leaving his property to other members of his family; however, a daughter could not be deprived of her rights as epikleros (MacDowell (1978) 100); cf. *Ath. Pol.* 35.2. Under Solon's legislation an illegitimate son was not obliged to support his father, and according to Plutarch sons who had not been taught a trade were similarly freed from this obligation (see doc. 3.27). Some of Plutarch's statements here should be taken with caution: heiresses in Athens married into their own not into their husband's family, and it is also unlikely that dowries would have been completely abolished. 21.6 is aimed at the employment of hired mourners, as opposed to family members; cf. doc. 12.33. Note that an adulterer caught in the act could be killed (cf. doc. 13.51).

20.2 Another law which seems out of place and ridiculous is that which allows an heiress, in the case of her lawful husband being unable to have intercourse with her, to be married by one of his next of kin. But some say that this was a sensible move against those who were impotent, but married heiresses for the sake of their property and used the law to do violence to nature. .... **20.3** It was also a good idea that an heiress should not be allowed to choose anyone for a husband but whomever she wished of the relatives of her husband, so that her offspring might be of his household and family (genos) .... **20.6** In all other marriages he abolished dowries, ordering the bride to bring with her three changes of clothing and household possessions of small value, and nothing else, for he did not want marriage to be a matter of profit or purchase, but the dwelling together of man and wife for the purposes of child bearing and love and affection .... **21.3** Solon also was well thought of for his law concerning wills. For before his time they were not allowed, and the property and house of the deceased had to remain in the family; but he, by allowing anyone who had no children, to leave his property to whomever he wished, honoured friendship more than kinship and goodwill more than compulsion, and made property the possession of those who owned it. **21.4** On the other hand he did not allow bequests to be totally uncomplicated and without restraint, but only those not made under the influence of illness or drugs or imprisonment or compulsion or through a wife's persuasion .... **21.5** He also made a law concerning women's appearance outside their house, as well as their mourning and their festivals, to prevent disorder and licence: when they went out he laid down that they were not to have more than three garments, nor carry more than an obol's worth of food or drink, or a basket more than a cubit in size, nor to travel at night except in a wagon with a lamp in front. **21.6** He also forbade laceration by mourners at funerals and using set dirges and lamenting anyone at the funeral ceremonies of other people .... **22.4** Even harsher was his regulation that sons born from a hetaira were not compelled to maintain their father, as Herakleides of Pontos narrates (F146 Wehrli).

For he who neglects the honourable state of marriage is clearly having a relationship with a woman not for the sake of children, but for pleasure, and forfeits his reward and has lost the right of free speech towards his sons, since he has made their very birth a reproach to them. **23.1** In general, Solon's laws concerning women seem extremely incongruous. For he allowed anyone who caught an adulterer to kill him; but if anyone seized and raped a free woman, he laid down a penalty of one hundred drachmas, and, if he seduced her, twenty drachmas except for those women who openly sell themselves, meaning the hetairai; for they go openly to those who pay them. **23.2** He did not allow anyone to sell his daughters or sisters, unless he discovered that a virgin had consorted with a man.

13.49 A Second Clytemnestra

Antiphon I *Prosecution of the Stepmother for Poisoning* 14–20

Antiphon wrote this speech for the deceased's son who is prosecuting his stepmother for murdering her husband by poison. The wife is supposed to have secured the services of a concubine (pallake) belonging to Philoneos, a friend of her husband, persuading her to serve the poison to both men in the belief that it was a love potion. The case at this point, c. 420, is being revived after several years; the concubine was arrested at the time and executed for the crime (cf. doc. 11.17); for concubines (who could either be slaves, or, if kept 'with a view to free children', might be free women of non-citizen birth like Aspasia), see MacDowell (1978) 89–90. For Clytemnestra, see doc. 13.62.

14 There was an upper room in our house, which Philoneos used to occupy when he visited Athens. He was a gentleman and a friend of our father's. Philoneos had a concubine, whom he intended to place in a brothel. My brother's mother made this woman her friend. **15** On hearing of the wrong she was going to be done by Philoneos, she sent for her, and when she came told her that she too was being wronged by our father. If she chose to follow her instructions, she said, she would be able to restore Philoneos' love for her and my father's love for herself, saying that she would find a way to do it, while the concubine's role was to carry this out. **16** So she asked her if she were willing to serve as her assistant, and the concubine, as I imagine, readily promised. Later on Philoneos happened to be involved in a sacrifice to Zeus Ktesios in the Peiraieus, while my father was about to sail to Naxos. It seemed an excellent idea to Philoneos that in the same trip he should accompany my father, his friend, to the Peiraieus and at the same time perform his sacrifice and give him a feast. **17** Philoneos' concubine accompanied him to assist at the sacrifice. And when they were at the Peiraieus he of course performed the sacrifice. When the victims had been sacrificed, then the female began to deliberate how to give the drug, whether before dinner or after diner. As she considered, it seemed to her to be best to give it after dinner, thus carrying out the instructions of this Clytemnestra .... **19** Philoneos' concubine, while she poured out the wine for the libation to accompany their prayers, which were not to be fulfilled, jurors, poured in the poison. Thinking that she was doing something clever she gave more to Philoneos, probably so that if she gave him more, she would be more beloved by Philoneos; for she did not yet know that she had been deceived by my step-mother, until she was already involved in the mischief; and she poured in a smaller portion for my father. **20** So they poured their libation, grasped their own destroyer, and drank down their last drink. Philoneos expired on the spot, while our father was seized with an illness from which he died on the twentieth day. For this, the woman who was carrying out orders when she did the deed has got the punishment she deserved, even though she was not at all responsible — she was broken on the wheel and handed over to the public executioner — and as for the woman who was responsible and planned it all, she too will get her punishment, if you and the gods are willing.

13.50 A Widow Fights her Father for her Sons' Rights

Lysias XXXII *Against Diogeiton* 11–15

This speech, probably delivered in 400, concerns the widow of a rich merchant named Diodotos, who had been killed in battle in 409. Diogeiton, who was the guardian of the estate, her father, and her husband's brother, had mishandled the property during her sons' minority, and, represented by her son-in-law in court, she charges him with having cheated her sons. Presumably the prosecution is being brought now because her eldest son has come of age. See Just (1989) 130–31, who points out that in some individual cases a woman could have a good deal of *de facto* authority. The grain mentioned in 15 was presumably interest on the investment of the 2,000 drachmas made in the Chersonese.

11 It would take too long to tell how much grief there was in my house at that time. Finally their mother begged and beseeched me to bring together her father and friends, saying that, even though she had not formerly been accustomed to speak amongst men, the size of their misfortunes compelled her to reveal to us everything concerning their troubles .... **12** And when we assembled, the woman asked him (Diogeiton) how he could have the heart to think it right to treat the children in such a way: 'You are their father's brother, and my father, and their uncle and grandfather. **13** Even if you're not ashamed before any man, you ought,' she said, 'to fear the gods; for you received from him, when he went off to war, five talents as a deposit. And I am willing to swear to this on the lives of my children, both these here and my younger ones in any place you may name.' .... **14** In addition she convicted him of having recovered seven talents and four thousand drachmas from bottomry loans and produced the records of these; for in the removal, when he was moving from Kollytos to the house of Phaidros, her sons came upon the register which had been mislaid and brought it to her. **15** And she proved that he had recovered a hundred minas which had been lent at interest on a mortgage on land, and another two thousand drachmas and some very valuable furniture, and that grain had come to them every year from the Chersonese.

13.51 A Husband's Defence against Killing an Adulterer

Lysias I *On the Murder of Eratosthenes* 6–10

Euphiletos killed Eratosthenes after catching him in the act of adultery with his wife, in accordance with Solon's law (see doc. 13.48), but was then prosecuted by Eratosthenes' relatives for premeditated murder and entrapment. Euphiletos in this speech presents the argument that seduction is a worse crime against the oikos than rape: for his argument, see Cole (1984) 99–104; Harris (1990) 370–77; Cohen (1991) 101–32; cf. Cohen (1984) 152–65, (1990) 153; Gardner (1989) 52–53. Euphiletos' domestic arrangements (the women's quarters being upstairs, but with the wife moving downstairs to be with the baby), and his relationship with his wife, are supposed to sound normal and reasonable to an Athenian jury: see Gould (1980) 47–50. Walker (1983) 81–91 with fig. at 87 discusses the archaeological evidence for housing in ancient Greece. It is significant that it was at Euphiletos' mother's funeral that his wife was seen by Eratosthenes, implying that funerals were one of the few occasions on which a women could be seen by men outside her family. Both Pomeroy (1975) 81–83 and Just (1989) 136–37 see in the wife's sleeping downstairs with the baby evidence that the wife's sexual role was primarily procreative rather than erotic, but this conclusion is, perhaps, not entirely justified.

6 When I, Athenians, decided to marry and brought a wife into my household, for some time my attitude was that I did not wish to annoy her, but neither was she to be able to do exactly what she liked, and I watched her as much as possible, and kept an eye on her as was reasonable. But once my child had been born, I had confidence in her and handed over to her all my possessions, believing that this was the greatest sign of marital intimacy. **7** Well, in the beginning, Athenians, she was the best of wives; she was a clever, economical housewife, and precise in her management of everything; but when my mother died, her death was the cause of all my misfortunes. **8** For when my wife was attending the funeral she was seen by this man, who in time seduced her; for he kept a look-out for the maidservant going to market and paid addresses to my wife which were her ruin. **9** Firstly, jurors (for I have to tell you this), my house has two stories, the upper equal in space to the lower, divided into the women's quarters and the men's quarters. When our child was born, his mother nursed him; but so that when she had to bath him she did not run the risk of going down the stairs, I used to live upstairs, and the women down below. **10** And so by this point it had become quite customary for my wife often to go downstairs to sleep with the baby, so she could give him the breast and stop him crying. Things went on in this way for some time, and I suspected nothing, but was foolish enough to think that my wife was the most chaste woman in the whole city.

13.52 Homosexual Rivalry

Lysias III *Against Simon* 5–7

This speech, delivered for the defence before the Areiopagos at some time after 394, concerns the amorous rivalry of Simon and the defendant for the possession of a young Plataean, Theodotos. For homosexuality in Athens and the difficulties attached to the seduction of young Athenians of free birth (ie the stigma of anal penetration as opposed to intercrural intercourse), see Cohen (1987) 3–21, (1991) 171–202; for illustrations of homosexual relationships, see Dover (1978) plates between pp.118–19; Keuls (1985) 274–99; cf. Golden (1984) 308–24.

5 We felt desire, councillors, for Theodotos a lad from Plataea, and while I thought it right to make him my friend by being kind to him, this man by insulting and ill-using him thought to compel him to do what he wished. It would take a long time to tell you all that the boy has suffered from him; but I think that you ought to hear all the offences he has committed against me. **6** For when he learnt that the boy was at my house, he came to my house at night drunk, and broke down the doors and entered the women's quarters, inside of which were my sister and nieces, who have lived so decently that they are even ashamed to be seen by their male relatives.

13.53 Dowries for Daughters of Thasian Heroes

Pouilloux (1954) 371, no. 141, lines 7–11, 16–22

This inscription from Thasos concerning the children of those who have died in war dates to the late fifth or early fourth century; see Pomeroy (1982) 116–18; for similar provisions for the children of state heroes at Athens (403/2), see Stroud (1971) 280–301; cf. Thuc. II.46. For dowries, see Schaps (1979) 74–88, 99–107; Harris (1993) 73–95.

(7) The polemarchs and the secretary of the boule are to inscribe their names and fathers' names on the list of Heroes, and summon (10) their fathers and sons whenever the city sacrifices to the Heroes .... (16) All of them who leave behind children, when they come of age, the polemarchs are to give them each, if they are boys, greaves, a breastplate, dagger, helmet, shield and spear worth not less than (20) [t]hree minas, at the games at the He[r]akleia, and proc[l]aim [their names]; and if they are daughters, for a dowr[y .... when] they bec[ome fou]rteen years old [....]

THE WORKING WOMAN: AT HOME AND ABROAD

While little is known about working women in fifth century Attica, it is clear that most working women were concerned primarily with 'women's work', such as spinning and weaving. But there is evidence that women were also employed in the market, as sellers of bread or garlands, and could be found as innkeepers; Pomeroy (1975) 71–73; Powell (1988) 361–64; Cohen (1989) 7–9, (1990) 156–59, (1991), 150–54; Just (1989) 106–114; the Caputi Hydria may even show a woman vase painter, which might imply that this would be a trade women could practice; see Venit (1988) 265–72. For other depictions of women and their activities, see Williams (1983) 92–106; Keuls (1985) 98–128, 229–66, and, for prostitutes, 153–86.

13.54 A Myrtle-Wreath Seller

Aristophanes *Thesmophoriazousai* 443–58

The women of Athens are assembled to celebrate the festival of the Thesmophoria (cf. doc. 12.39). Aristophanes fantasizes that they are planning revenge on the poet Euripides for supposedly revealing on stage their secrets and behaviour (see esp. *Thesm.* 383–432). Here a second woman, a seller of myrtle-wreaths worn at sacrifices and drinking-parties, makes a speech at the women's 'assembly'. It's a standing joke in Aristophanes that Euripides' mother sold vegetables in the agora (cf. *Thesm.* 387). For Myrtia, a respectable woman bread-seller, see *Wasps* 1388–98.

I've only come forward to say a few words.
This lady's charges have covered just about everything;

I just want to tell you what I've been through myself.
My husband died in Cyprus,
Leaving me with five little children, and it's with difficulty
That I've fed them by making garlands in the myrtle-wreath market.
At least, before, I managed a pretty miserable existence,
And now he by putting on his tragedies
Has persuaded people that there aren't any gods;
As a result we don't sell even half what we used to.
I tell you all, on my advice,
Punish this man for many reasons;
For he treats us quite savagely, ladies,
Probably because he was brought up among those wild vegetables.
Well I must be off to the agora — I've got twenty wreaths
To plait which gentlemen have specially ordered.

13.55 Two Redoubtable Lady Innkeepers in the Underworld

Aristophanes *Frogs* 549–78

The god Dionysos in his journey to the underworld with his slave Xanthias has attempted to disguise himself as Herakles. While there he unfortunately meets two ladies whose bill Herakles had omitted to discharge. A female innkeeper is also mentioned in *Wealth* 435–36. Ehrenberg (1943) 151 and n.8 notes that these women are metics, as the prostates, mentioned in line 569, was the patron which every metic needed in court.

Lady Innkeeper: Plathane, Plathane, come here, here's the villain
Who came into our inn one day
And ate up sixteen of our loaves.
Plathane: By Zeus,
That's the man.
Xanthias: Evil's coming to somebody!
Lady Innkeeper: As well as twenty pieces of boiled meat
At half an obol each.
Xanthias: Someone's going to be for it!
Lady Innkeeper: And all that garlic.
Dionysos: Woman, you're talking nonsense,
You don't know what you're saying.
Lady Innkeeper: So you didn't expect me
To know you, wearing those buskins?
Well then? I haven't even mentioned all that dried fish.
Plathane: Too true!, nor all that fresh cheese, you rogue,
Which you gulped down baskets and all.
Lady Innkeeper: And when I asked him for the money,
He gave me this sour look and bellowed.
Xanthias: His conduct exactly! He's always like that.
Lady Innkeeper: And he drew his sword, as if he'd gone mad.
Plathane: Yes, you poor woman.
Lady Innkeeper: And the two of us were so scared
That we had to run straight upstairs;
And then he rushed off taking the sleeping-mats with him.

Xanthias: That's just like him as well!
Plathane: We ought to do something!
Lady Innkeeper: You go and call Kleon, my champion (prostates).
Plathane: And you get Hyperbolos for me, if you meet him,
So we can crush this chap.
Lady Innkeeper: You horrible throat,
How I'd enjoy knocking out with a stone
Those molars of yours, which you used to devour my merchandise.
Plathane: And I'd like to throw you into a pit.
Lady Innkeeper: I'd like to get a sickle and cut out that windpipe
Which swallowed down that tripe.
Plathane: I'm off to get Kleon, he'll summons him today
And wind all this out of him.

13.56 The Alternative Profession

Aristophanes *Wasps* 500–02

Cf. *Wealth* 149–52, for the amenability of Corinthian courtesans to rich customers; for prostitution in Corinth, see doc. 2.12; Salmon (1984) 398–400; Powell (1988) 367–69. For prostitutes and commercial sex, see Dover (1973) 63–64; Pomeroy (1975) 88–92; Just (1989) 137–51.

Xanthias: Like that prostitute I visited yesterday at midday,
When I told her to get on top, she got mad at me
And asked if I wanted to set up a tyranny like Hippias.

13.57 Isomachos Teaches his Young Wife her Duties

Xenophon *Oeconomicus* 7.35–37, 10.10–13

For other advice by Isomachos to his wife, see doc. 11.9; for a housewife's duties (with husband, servants and baby), cf. Ar. *Lys.* 16–19. For this 'typical' Greek bride, married at fourteen, see Xen. *Oec.* 7.4–6, 7.42; note the privacy and self-contained nature of the upper-class oikos: Shaw (1975) 256; Powell (1988) 341–50, 359; Just (1989) 114–18, 151–52, 164; cf. Cohen (1991) 159–62 for the autonomy of the women's sphere.

7.35 'It will be your duty,' I said, 'to stay indoors and to send outside those of the servants whose work is outside, **7.36** and to superintend those whose work is inside and receive what is brought in, and to distribute what of this has to be expended, and to take thought for and watch over what has to be stored, so that the sum laid by for the year is not expended in a month. And whenever wool is brought in to you, you must see that there are cloaks made for those who need them. And you must take care that the dry provisions are properly edible. **7.37** However, one of the duties that will fall to you,' I said, 'may perhaps seem thankless, as you will have to see that any of the servants who is sick is cared for.' 'Not at all,' said my wife, 'it will be most pleasing, if those who have been well looked after will be grateful and even more well-intentioned than before.' .... **10.10** And I advised her, Socrates, not to be always sitting down like a slave, but with the help of the gods to try to stand before the loom like a mistress to teach what she might know better than another, and if she knows less, to learn, and to keep an eye on the baking-woman, and to stand by the housekeeper when she is measuring out, and to go round and see if everything is in its right place. I thought that this would give her a walk as well as occupation. **10.11** And I said that it was good exercise to mix and knead and to shake and fold cloaks and bedding. I said that with this exercise she would eat better and be healthier, and have a better natural colour .... **10.13** On the other hand those (wives) who spend all their time sitting about in a haughty manner expose themselves to comparison with decorated and fraudulent women.

13.58 Socrates' Advice Starts a Home Industry

Xenophon *Memorabilia* II.7.6–12

Aristarchos, a once-wealthy Athenian, has lost his farm and his town properties have been abandoned by his tenants because of the disorders of 404/3; a number of female relatives have come to live with him, and he is unable to feed all his household. Socrates ascertains that the female relatives are able to cook and make clothing and proceeds to give good advice. Wood (1983) 22–23 notes that Socrates refers to specific cases in which wealthy men have used the domestic skills of their slaves to make saleable domestic items. Certainly here Socrates, despite his general contempt for manual labour, sees no stigma in Aristarchos putting his womenfolk to work to produce marketable goods. Millett (1991) 73–74 points out that, rather than being evidence for the existence of 'productive credit', Socrates' solution is here in fact seen as a novelty.

II.7.6 'Don't you know that from one of these occupations, making barley-groats, Nausikydes maintains not only himself and his household but in addition lots of pigs and cattle and has enough left over to undertake liturgies for the city, that Kyrebos from baking keeps his whole household and lives in luxury, as does Demeas of Kollytos from making capes, and Menon by making cloaks, while most of the Megarians make a living out of tunic-making?' 'That's true,' replied Aristarchos, 'but they possess barbarian slaves they have bought and compel them to make whatever is convenient, whereas mine are free and relatives.' **II.7.7** 'Well, because they are free and relatives of yours, do you think they should do nothing else but eat and sleep? .... **II.7.10** If they were going to do something disgraceful, death would be better than that; but, as it appears, what they understand is thought the finest and most suitable occupation for women. And everyone does what he understands with the greatest ease and speed and pleasure and the finest result. So do not shrink from suggesting this to them, as it will be profitable both to you and them and which, very probably, they will willingly undertake.' **II.7.11** 'Indeed,' said Aristarchos,' your advice seems so good, Socrates, that I think I can now bear to borrow capital to make a start on this, whereas before I couldn't allow myself to borrow, knowing that when I had spent it I would not be able to pay the loan back.' **II.7.12** As a result the capital was provided, wool was bought, and the women worked through their midday meal and dined when they'd finished working. They were cheerful instead of gloomy and looked pleasantly at each other instead of with jealousy and loved him as a guardian, while he was fond of them because they were productive. Finally he came to Socrates and cheerfully told him this, as well as that they now criticized him because he was the only one in the household who ate without working.

WOMEN IN GREEK DRAMA

For an overview of women in Greek drama, see Gomme (1925) 1–25; Shaw (1975) 255–66; Pomeroy (1975) 93–119; Gould (1980) 52–55; Foley (1981) 127–68; Cohen (1989) 3–15. Conflicts which involve women frequently feature in Greek tragedy, which 'exploits the opposition between the sexes in order to dramatize larger issues': Katz (1994) 100. It would be rash to assume that the tragedians directly portrayed women of their own time on stage, but it could be argued that, while the Athenians would not normally expect their womenfolk to act so forcefully or articulately, they could envisage their doing so, *if* they were placed in situations of similar dramatic conflict. While the evidence of tragedy regarding the seclusion of women is ambivalent (see Gould (1980) 40), clearly women in comedy could go out of the house, and their husbands knew they did, even if they were not supposed to: Cohen (1989) 6–7, 12; cf. Gardner (1989) 51–61.

13.59 An Ill-Matched Couple

Aristophanes *Clouds* 39–55, 60–74

Strepsiades is a die-hard countryman, married (perhaps somewhat improbably) to an aristocratic wife from the Alkmeonid family and afflicted with a spendthrift son, who is encouraged in his expensive habits by his mother. This son is asleep near him dreaming of chariot-racing; '(h)ippos' means horse, whereas 'pheidon' means parsimonious. Koisyra is a female name in the Alkmeonid family (cf. Ar. *Ach.* 614; Davies *APF* Table I), and the name Megakles has obviously become a byword for aristocratic breeding; Pheidippides may be a portrait of Alkibiades (cf. doc. 9.35).

Strepsiades (to his son):
You just carry on asleep. But remember that these debts
Will one day fall on your own head.
Oh dear!
I wish that match-maker would die a miserable death,
Who persuaded me to marry your mother;
My lifestyle in the country was delightful —
Unwashed, no bugs, lying around at my ease,
With my fill of bees and sheep and pressed olives.
Then I married Megakles' son of Megakles
Niece — her a city girl and me from the country,
Ladylike and used to luxurious living just like a Koisyra.
When I married her I went to bed with her
Smelling of unfermented wine, dried figs, wool and profit,
While she smelt of perfume and saffron and sexy kisses,
Expense and gluttony and Aphrodite Genetyllis.
I don't say that she was lazy, she wove alright.
But I used to show her this cloak and
Take occasion to say, wife, you're weaving us out of house and home ....
Later on, when this son here was born to the two of us,

To me and my good wife,
From then on we quarrelled about what to call him;
She wanted to add something horsey to his name —
Xanthippos or Charippos or Kallippides,
While I wanted to name him Pheidonides after his grandfather.
So we kept arguing about it; and then in time
We compromised and called him Pheidippides.
She used to take the boy and caress him, saying
'When you're grown up and drive your chariot to the city,
Just like Megakles, wearing your lovely robe.' And I'd say,
'When you drive the goats from Phelleus,
Just like your father, wearing your leather jerkin.'
But he never listened to anything I said,
He just infected all my affairs with this equine disease.

13.60 The Women's Solution

Aristophanes *Lysistrata* 507–20, 565–97

The *Lysistrata*, like the *Thesmophoriazousai*, both of which were produced in 411, is full of jokes against women's predilection for drink and sex. Yet in her argument with the magistrate (proboulos), as elsewhere when she speaks of the war, Lysistrata is meant to be taken seriously: even though her final lines reflect the way women in particular have suffered from the war, obviously her remarks also struck home to a primarily male audience (cf. doc. 12.38). See Shaw (1975) 264–65 for Lysistrata's principles of oikos management; Henderson (1980) 153–218; Westlake (1980) 43–54.

Lysistrata: In the last war †we bore with† you men
Because of our modesty, whatever you did.
Nor did you allow us to complain. Yet we didn't approve.
But we kept a close eye on you, and often when we were indoors
We'd hear that you'd made a bad decision on some important matter;
Then we'd be upset inside, but would ask you with a smile,
'What have you decided to inscribe on the stele about the peace treaty
In the assembly today?' 'What's that to you?' my husband would say.
'Won't you shut up?' And I did.
Woman: I wouldn't have kept quiet!
Magistrate: And you'd have howled if you hadn't!
Lysistrata: Accordingly I kept quiet at home.
And then we'd hear of some even more worthless decree you'd passed;
So we'd ask, 'How is it, husband, that you manage things so foolishly?'
And he'd glare at me and say that, if I didn't weave my web,
I'd really have a headache to complain about: 'For war should be men's concern!' ....

Magistrate: So how would you be able to end so many muddled affairs
566 In the different countries and resolve them?
Lysistrata: Quite easily.
Magistrate: How? Show us.

Lysistrata: Just as we take our thread, like this, when it is tangled,
And draw it out with our spindles, this way and that,
That's how we'll put a stop to this war, if we're allowed to,
After sending our embassies, this way and that.
Magistrate: Do you think that with wool, threads and spindles you can end
Such a dreadful problem, you foolish women?
Lysistrata: Yes, and if you had any sense,
You'd manage the whole city on the principle of our wool.
Magistrate: How? Let me see.
Lysistrata: You ought first, just as in a bathtub
You wash away the dirt of a fleece, to beat out from the city
All the knaves and pick out the burrs,
And all those who form associations and stick close together
To get the magistracies you should pull them out and pluck their heads;
Then you should card all public good-will into a basket, mixing up
All the metics, and any other foreigner who's your friend,[1]
And anyone who's indebted to the state, and stir these all in together;
All the cities that are colonies of this country
You must certainly see that these are lying like flocks of wool
All separate; you should take the wool from all of these
Bring it here and gather it into one, and then make
A huge ball, and then out of it weave a cloak for the people.
Magistrate: Isn't it dreadful that these women should 'beat out' and 'make balls'
Who've had no share in the war at all!
Lysistrata: What! you accursed fool,
We bear more than twice as much of it as you do: first we've born sons
And sent them off as hoplites.
Magistrate: Silence! don't remind us of our miseries.
Lysistrata: And then when we ought to be having fun and enjoying our youth,
We've got to sleep alone because of the expeditions; and even if you leave us aside,
I grieve for the young girls who grow old in their bedchambers.
Magistrate: Don't men grow old as well?
Lysistrata: By heaven, that's not the same at all!
For when a man returns home, even if he's grey, he soon marries a young girl;
But a woman's time is short, and if she doesn't take advantage of it,
No one wants to marry her, and she sits at home looking for omens.

[1] Here reading ῇ 'is' with Coulon (Budé, 1967) not ἤ 'or' as in Hall & Geldart.

13.61 Could Athenian Women Attend the Theatre?

Aristophanes *Birds* 785–96

The *Birds* was produced at the Dionysia in 414. In this passage the chorus addresses the audience on the advantages of possessing wings. See Podlecki (1990) 27–43 for a collection of testimonia on whether women attended the theatre, noting that he does not (35–36) take this passage as conclusive evidence that they did not attend. On the whole it seems most likely that some women could and did attend, but these may primarily have been hetairai like Aspasia, while 'respectable' women of the middle-classes, like the councillor's wife below, would almost certainly have stayed home.

There's nothing better or nicer than to grow wings.
For as soon as any of you spectators acquired wings,
When he was hungry and tired of the tragic choruses,
He could fly off home and have lunch,
And once he was full up he could fly back again to watch us.
And if some Patrokleides amongst you wanted to shit,
He wouldn't have to soil his cloak, but just fly away,
Fart, get his breath again and fly back.
And if one of you who happened to be having an affair
Spotted the lady's husband in the councillors' seats,
He could fly away from you, wings flapping,
Have his screw and then fly back here again.

13.62 Clytemnestra Murders Agamemnon

Aeschylus *Agamemnon* 1377–98

After ten years of war against Troy, Agamemnon has returned home triumphant. Before sailing to Troy he had sacrificed his daughter Iphigeneia to obtain favourable winds: Clytemnestra's fury and frustration over this have long festered, and she has planned her revenge, taking as her lover Aegisthus, Agamemnon's cousin. On Agamemnon's arrival, she enticed him to display hybris by walking into the house over purple carpets, and while in the bath she threw a net-like garment she had woven over him and killed him, according to tradition with an axe, but apparently in the *Agamemnon* with a sword: Sommerstein (1989) 296–301. The doors of the house have now been thrown open and the chorus and audience see the evidence of her crime. For Clytemnestra's independence of thought and desire to rule, see Winnington-Ingram (1948) 130–47; Zeitlin (1981) 163–66; cf. MacLeod (1982) 141–44; Fisher (1992) 289–91. Yet she is still female: one of the principle issues of the *Agamemnon* is 'the inflection of sexuality with power': Katz (1994) 88–91; cf. Tyrrell (1984) 97–99, 93–100 for the fertility imagery in this episode.

Clytemnestra (to the chorus of elders of Argos):
For me this contest, long pondered from time past,
Came from an ancient quarrel, but in time it came;
There where I struck I stand with the deed accomplished.
Thus I acted, nor do I deny it,
So he could neither flee nor ward off fate;
An inextricable casting-net, just as for fish,
I threw round him, an evil wealth of garment;
And then I struck him twice, and after uttering two cries
His limbs went limp, and as he lay
I gave him a third stroke, to Zeus below the earth,
Saviour of the dead, in thanks for prayers accomplished.
So falling he gasped out his life
And, spouting forth a swift gush of blood,
He struck me with a dark shower of bloody dew,
And I rejoiced no less than, at the heaven-sent moisture,

The sown field exalts in the bursting of the bud.
So things stand, elders of Argos:
You may rejoice, if you choose, but I am exultant;
And if it were fitting over a dead man to pour libation,
It would be just, and more than just;
For in the house this man filled a mixing-bowl of evil
Curses, which he has returned and drained himself.

13.63 Medea Speaks her Mind to Jason

Euripides *Medea* 465–95

The *Medea* was performed in 431. Medea who left her home for Jason has been deserted by him, as he has arranged to marry the daughter of the king of Corinth, to find stability and security for his family by this alliance. Medea is clearly a barbarian and a witch: she betrayed her family for Jason, helping him to steal the Golden Fleece, and killing her younger brother to hinder pursuit; she persuaded the daughters of Pelias, Jason's enemy, to kill their father, by pretending that by chopping him up and boiling him they would renew his youth; at the play's denouement she sends the princess Glauke (her rival) a robe dipped in poison which kills both her and her father; see Shaw (1975) 258–64; des Bouvrie (1990) 214–39. Medea clearly (in Athenian terms) has the status of a metic, not a citizen: she has no rights, and no family to defend her; see Katz (1994) 96–100 for Medea's isolation, confined to an 'eccentric, off-center existence on the fringes of society'; unlike Clytemnestra, who has a masculine role and status, Medea insists on her womanhood, and complains about its disadvantages; cf. lines 230–66, where she speaks to the women of Corinth of women's problems: the lack of choice in marriage, the advantages a man has in an unhappy relationship, and the pain of childbirth: 'I would rather stand three times by my shield than once give birth' (250–51).

Medea to Jason:
You utter scoundrel! For that's the greatest insult
I can put into words regarding your cowardice;
Have you come to me, have you really come, you, who've become
The gods' worst enemy, and mine, and that of all the human race?
This is not courage, nor is it daring
To look friends whom you have wronged in the face,
But the greatest of all diseases amongst men —
Shamelessness! But you did well to come;
For my heart will be relieved by speaking
Ill of you and you will be grieved at hearing it.
I'll begin right at the beginning:
I saved you, as all the Greeks know
Who embarked on that same ship, the Argo, with you,
When you were sent to master the fire-breathing bulls
With yokes and sow the deadly field;
And the dragon, which encircled the golden fleece
With twisted coils and sleeplessly guarded it,
I slew, and raised for you the light of deliverance.
And I betrayed my father and my home
Coming to Iolkos under Mount Pelion
With you, showing more eagerness than wisdom;

And I killed Pelias, by a most distressing death,
At the hands of his own children, and wiped out the entire house.
And though you were treated like this by me, basest of men,
You betrayed me, and found yourself a new marriage-bed,
Even though we had children — for if I were still childless,
Your lusting after this marriage would be pardonable.
But respect for oaths is forgotten! nor do I know
If you think the gods of old no longer reign
Or that new customs apply nowadays to mankind,
Since you know well you have not kept the oath you swore to me.

13.64 Alcestis Dies for her Husband

Euripides *Alcestis* 152–84, 189–98

The *Alcestis* is Euripides' earliest surviving work, produced in 438. Its theme is the self-sacrificing love of a wife for an unworthy husband, for when Admetos was doomed to die, Alcestis volunteered to die for him, when even his elderly parents refused to take his place; at the end of the play she is rescued from the underworld by Herakles. While she is a worthy wife, the real tragedy of the play is that, to the spectators at least, he is obviously not a husband worth dying for. See Lefkowitz (1983) 34–36, (1986) 65–67; for Alcestis as a heroic 'male' figure, see Humphreys (1983) 41–42; des Bouvrie (1990) 193–213. A maid-servant here reports Alcestis' actions as she prepares for death.

Chorus: Let her know this, that in dying she will at least be renowned
As the best of wives by far beneath the sun.
Servant: How could she not be the best? Who could contradict it?
What would the woman have to be who could surpass her?
How could any wife more clearly show
That she honours her husband than by being willing to die for him?
The whole city knows that!
You will be amazed when you hear what she did in the house.
For when she learned that her appointed day
Had come, she washed her white skin with water
From the stream, and taking from the cedar chests
Clothes and adornments she dressed herself fittingly.
Standing before the altar of Hestia she prayed:
'Mistress, since I am going beneath the earth,
In this the last time that I will worship you I beg you
Take care of my orphaned children; wed my son
To a loving wife, and my daughter to a noble husband;
Let not my children die before their time,
As I who bore them perish, but be fortunate
And live out a long and happy life in their native land.'
All the altars, throughout Admetos' palace,
She visited and garlanded and prayed,
Stripping foliage from myrtle branches,
Without tears or lamentation, nor did the approaching evil
Change the lovely colour of her complexion.
And then in her bedroom, throwing herself on the bed,

There she indeed wept and spoke these words:
'O bed, where I lost my maidenhood
To this husband, for whom I die,
Farewell; I do not hate you; you alone have destroyed me;
For it is in dread of betraying you and my husband
That I die. Some other woman will possess you,
Not more faithful than I, though perhaps more fortunate.'
She fell on the bed and kissed it, and all the bedding
Grew wet with the tears flooding from her eyes ....
Her children, clinging to their mother's dress,
Wept; and she, taking them in her arms,
Embraced them first one and then the other, like one about to die.
All the servants were crying throughout the house
Pitying their mistress; and she stretched
Her right hand to each, nor was there any so base
That she did not speak to him and he again to her.
Such are the miseries in the house of Admetos.
If he had died, he would have perished, but by escaping death
He has acquired a grief that he will never forget.

EPILOGUE

13.65 The Ten Ages of Man

Solon 27

For the elderly in Greek society, see Finley (1981) 156–71, who does not discuss this passage; Garland (1990) 242–87.

The youthful boy loses the first row of teeth
He grew while a baby in seven years;
When god has completed the next seven years for him
He †shows† the signs that his youthful prime is on its way;
In the third seven, while his limbs are still growing
His chin grows downy with the bloom of changing skin.
In the fourth seven every man is at his best
In strength, when men give proof of valour.
In the fifth it is time for a man to think of marriage,
And seek a family of children to come after him.
In the sixth a man's mind is now disciplined in everything,
And he no longer wishes to do reckless deeds.
In the seventh he is now at his best in mind and tongue,
And in the eighth, that is fourteen years in total.
In the ninth he is still able, but less powerful than before
In both his speech and wisdom in matters of great prowess.
And if anyone comes to complete the tenth in full measure,
He will not meet the fate of death unseasonably.

Chronological Table

c. 1250	The 'Trojan War'
1200–1125	Destruction of Mycenaean centres in Greece
c. 1200–1000	Greek colonisation of Asia Minor coast
c. 825	Establishment of emporion at Al Mina
776	Traditional date for first Olympic Games
c. 750–25	Foundation of Pithekoussai
740–720	Spartan conquest of Messenia: 'First Messenian War'
734	Foundation of Sicilian Naxos
669/8	Argive defeat of the Spartans at Hysiai
c. 680–40	Reign of Gyges of Lydia
c. 650	Second Messenian War
664–10	Reign of Psammetichos I; establishment of Naukratis
c. 658 – c. 585	Kypselid tyranny at Corinth
656/5?– 556/5?	Orthagorid tyranny at Sicyon
c. 640	Theagenes becomes tyrant of Megara
?632	Attempted tyranny of Kylon at Athens
631	Foundation of Cyrene
621/0	Drakon lawgiver at Athens
607/6	Athenian and Mytilenaean dispute over Sigeion
594/3	Solon's archonship and nomothesia
590–80	Pittakos aisymnetes, elected tyrant, of Mytilene
c. 575	Marriage of Kleisthenes' daughter to Megakles of Athens
570–26	Amasis king of Egypt
561/0?	Peisistratos' first tyranny at Athens and expulsion
560–546	Croesus king of Lydia
559–556	Miltiades the elder becomes tyrant of the Chersonese
556/5?	Peisistratos' second tyranny at Athens and expulsion
546/5	Peisistratos' third tyranny at Athens; Cyrus defeats Croesus
c. 537	Battle of Alalia
532–22	Polykrates tyrant of Samos
c. 531	Pythagoras leaves Samos for Italy
530	Accession of Cambyses
528/7	Death of Peisistratos; rule of the Peisistratidai at Athens
525/4	Kleisthenes' archonship at Athens
521	Darius seizes power in Persia
521 or 520	Kleomenes king of Sparta
514/3	Harmodios and Aristogeiton assassinate Hipparchos at Athens
c. 513	Darius' Scythian expedition

CHRONOLOGICAL TABLE

511/0	Expulsion of the Peisistratidai from Athens
508/7	Isagoras' archonship at Athens; reforms of Kleisthenes
505	Beginning of tyranny at Gela
499	Ionian revolt
494	Battle of Lade and sack of Miletos
493/2	Themistokles' archonship at Athens
c. 491	Gelon becomes tyrant of Gela
491 or 490	Death of Kleomenes of Sparta
490	First Persian expedition; battle of Marathon
488/7	First ostracism at Athens (Hipparchos, ?grandson of Hippias)
486	Death of Darius; accession of Xerxes
485	Gelon becomes tyrant of Syracuse
483	Discovery of new vein of silver at Laureion
480	Second Persian invasion; the Carthaginians invade Sicily. Battles of Thermopylai, Artemision, Salamis and Himera
479	Battles of Plataea and Mykale
478/7	Delian League founded under Athens' leadership
c. 469–60	Persians defeated at the Eurymedon River
466	End of the Deinomenid tyranny at Syracuse
?465/4	Revolt of Thasos; helot revolt in Messenia
462/1	Reforms of Ephialtes at Athens
c. 460	Start of First Peloponnesian War
c. 460	Athenian expedition to Egypt
458/7	Battles of Tanagra and Oinophyta
454/3	First tribute quota lists; league treasury moved to Athens
451	Five Years' Peace
447	Building of the Parthenon begun in Athens
446	Revolts of Euboea and Megara; Thirty Years' Peace
440–439	Revolt of Samos
437/6	Foundation of Amphipolis with Hagnon as oikistes
435–433	War between Corinth and Corcyra
431	Second Peloponnesian War begins with the 'Archidamian War'
429	Death of Perikles from the plague
428-427	Revolt of Lesbos; the 'Mytilene debate'
426	Spartan foundation of Herakleia in Trachis
425	Athenian success at Pylos
422	Death of Kleon and Brasidas at Amphipolis
421	Peace of Nikias between Athens and Sparta
415–413	Sicilian Expedition
413	Spartan Fortification of Dekeleia
411	The Four Hundred take power at Athens
405	Athenian fleet defeated at Aigospotamoi; Athens besieged
404	Capitulation of Athens; the Thirty come to power
403	Restoration of the democracy
399	Death of Socrates

Bibliography

Journal Abbreviations

The abbreviations for journals are as in *L'Année Philologique.* New series are not indicated in the bibliography.

ABSA	Annual of the British School at Athens
AC	L'antiquité classique
AClass	Acta Classica
AD	'Αρχαιολογικὸν Δελτίον
AE	'Αρχαιολογικὴ 'Εφημερίς
AHB	The Ancient History Bulletin
AHR	American Historical Review
AJA	American Journal of Archaeology
AJAH	American Journal of Ancient History
AJPh	American Journal of Philology
AncSoc	Ancient Society
AncW	The Ancient World
ANSMusN	American Numismatic Society Museum Notes
APhs	American Philosophical Society
BICS	Bulletin of the Institute of Classical Studies of the University of London
CJ	The Classical Journal
ClAnt	Californian Studies in Classical Antiquity
C&M	Classica et Mediaevalia
CPh	Classical Philology
CQ	Classical Quarterly
CRDAC	Atti del centro ricerche e documentazione sull'antichità classica
EMC	Échos du monde classique (Classical Views)
G&R	Greece and Rome
GRBS	Greek, Roman and Byzantine Studies
HSPh	Harvard Studies in Classical Philology
HThR	Harvard Theological Review
ICS	Illinois Classical Studies
JHS	Journal of Hellenic Studies
JRS	Journal of Roman Studies
LCM	Liverpool Classical Monthly
MH	Museum Helveticum
MPhL	Museum Philologum Londiniense
NC	Numismatic Chronicle
OJA	Oxford Journal of Archaeology
P&P	Past and Present
PACA	Proceedings of the African Classical Association
PAPhS	Proceedings of the American Philosophical Society
PCPhS	Proceedings of the Cambridge Philological Society
PP	La Parola del Passato
QUCC	Quaderni Urbinati di Cultura classica

RA	Revue Archéologique
RBN	Revue Belge de Numismatique et de Sigillographie
REA	Revue des Études Anciennes
REG	Revue des Études Grecques
RhM	Rheinisches Museum
RIDA	Revue Internationale des Droits de l'Antiquité
RSA	Rivista storica dell'Antichità
SO	Symbolae Osloenses
TAPhA	Transactions and Proceedings of the American Philological Association
YClS	Yale Classical Studies
ZPE	Zeitschrift für Papyrologie und Epigraphik

Abbreviations of Editions of Inscriptions, Literary Sources, Commentaries and Frequently Cited Works

Agora XV — Meritt, B.D. and Traill J.S. (1974) *The Athenian Agora XV. Inscriptions: The Athenian Councillors*, Princeton.

Agora XIX — Lalonde, G.V., Langdon, M.K. and Walbank, M.B. (1991) *The Athenian Agora XIX. Inscriptions: Horoi, Poletai Records, Leases of Public Lands*, Princeton.

Andrewes (1956) — Andrewes, A. (1956) *The Greek Tyrants*, London.

ATL — Meritt, B.D., Wade-Gery, H.T., and McGregor, M.F. (1939–53) *The Athenian Tribute Lists I–IV*, Cambridge, Massachusetts.

Bogaert — Bogaert, R. (1976) *Epigraphica III: Texts on Bankers, Banking and Credit in the Greek World*, Leiden.

Buck — Buck, C.D. (1955) *The Greek Dialects*, Chicago, second edition.

Cadoux (1948) — Cadoux, T.J. (1948) 'The Athenian Archons from Kreon to Hypsichides' *JHS* 68: 70–123.

CAH — *Cambridge Ancient History*.

CAH III.3[2] — Boardman, J. and Hammond, N.G.L. (eds.) (1982) *The Expansion of the Greek World, Eighth to Sixth Centuries B.C., CAH* III.3, second edition: Cambridge.

CAH IV[2] — Boardman, J., Hammond, N.G.L., Lewis, D.M., Ostwald, M. (eds.) (1988) *Persia, Greece and the Western Mediterranean, c. 525 to 479 B.C. CAH* IV, second edition: Cambridge.

CAH V[2] — Lewis, D.M., Boardman, J., Davies, J.K., and Ostwald, M. (eds.) (1992) *The Fifth Century B.C., CAH* V, second edition: Cambridge.

Classical Contributions — Shrimpton, G.S. and McCargar, D.J. (eds.) (1981) *Classical Contributions: Studies in Honour of Malcolm Francis McGregor*, New York.

Classical Sparta — Powell, A. (ed.) (1989) *Classical Sparta: Techniques Behind her Success*, London.

Crux — Cartledge, P.A. and Harvey, F.D. (eds.) (1985) *Crux: Essays in Greek History Presented to G.E.M. de Ste Croix = History of Greek Political Thought* 6.

DAA — Raubitschek, A.E. (1949) *Dedications from the Athenian Akropolis*, Cambridge.

Davies (1971) — Davies, J.K. (1971) *Athenian Propertied Families 600–300 B.C.*, Oxford.

Develin (1989) — Develin, R. (1989) *Athenian Officials 684–321 B.C.*, Cambridge.

Diels — Diels, H. (1952–54) *Fragmente der Vorsokratiker*, I–III, Berlin.

FGH Jacoby, F. (1954–64) *Die Fragmente der griechischen Historiker*, Leiden, with *Supplements*.

Fontenrose (1978) Fontenrose, J. (1978) *The Delphic Oracle*, Berkeley.

Fornara & Samons (1991) Fornara, C.W. and Samons, L.J. (1991) *Athens from Cleisthenes to Pericles*, Berkeley.

Friedländer Friedländer, P. (1948) with the collaboration of H.B. Hoffleit *Epigrammata: Greek Inscriptions in Verse. From the Beginnings to the Persian Wars*, London.

Gomme *HCT*: Gomme, A.W. (1939–81) *A Historical Commentary on Thucydides*, vols. I–V, Oxford; IV–V with A. Andrewes and K.J. Dover.

Graham (1983) Graham, A.J. (1983) *Colony and Mother City in Ancient Greece*, Chicago, second edition.

Hansen Hansen, P.A. (1983) *Carmina Epigraphica Graeca Saeculorum VIII–V A. Chr. N.*, Berlin.

Hignett (1952) Hignett, C. (1952) *A History of the Athenian Constitution to the End of the Fifth Century B.C.*, Oxford.

Hornblower (1991) Hornblower, S. (1991) *A Commentary on Thucydides, vol. I, Books I–III*, Oxford.

How & Wells (1912) How, W.W. and Wells, J. (1912) *A Commentary on Herodotus*, vols. I–II, Oxford.

IG I² de Gaertringen, F.H. (1924) *Inscriptiones Graecae. Inscriptiones Atticae Euclidis anno anteriores*, Berlin, second edition.

IG I³ Lewis, D. (1981) *Inscriptiones Graecae. Inscriptiones Atticae Euclidis anno anteriores*, Berlin, third edition.

IG II² Kirchner, J. (1913–40) *Inscriptiones Graecae. Inscriptiones Atticae Euclidis anno posteriores*, fasc. 1, Berlin, second edition.

IG IV² von Gaertringen, F.H. (1929) *Inscriptiones Graecae. Inscriptiones Argolidis*, Berlin, second edition.

IG V Kolbe, G. (1913) *Inscriptiones Graecae. Inscriptiones Laconiae Messeniae Arcadiae*, Berlin.

Kassel & Austin Kassel, R. and Austin, C. (1983, 1984) *Poetae Comici Graeci*, IV: *Aristophon-Crobylus*, III.2: *Aristophanes*, Berlin.

Kock Kock, T. (1880–88) *Comicorum Atticorum Fragmenta* I–III, Leipzig.

Lang Lang, M.L. (1990) *The Athenian Agora XXV: Ostraka*, Princeton.

LSAG Jeffery, L.H. (1961) *The Local Scripts of Archaic Greece*, Oxford.

LSAM Sokolowski, F. (1955) *Lois sacrées de l'Asie mineure*, Paris.

LSCG Sokolowski, F. (1969) *Lois sacrées des cités grecques*, Paris.

LSCG Suppl. Sokolowski, F. (1962) *Lois sacrées des cités grecques: Supplément*, Paris.

*LSJ*⁹ Liddell, H.G., Scott, R., and Jones, H.S. *A Greek-English Lexicon*, Oxford, ninth edition 1940, with 1965 supplement.

ML Meiggs, R. and Lewis, D.M. (1988) *A Selection of Greek Historical Inscriptions: To the End of the Fifth Century BC*, Oxford, second edition.

Moretti Moretti, L. (1953) *Iscrizioni agonistische greche*, Rome.

NOMOS Cartledge, P., Millett, P. and Todd, S. (eds.) (1990) *NOMOS: Essays in Athenian Law, Society and Politics*, Cambridge.

Ober (1989) Ober, J. (1989) *Mass and Elite in Democratic Athens: Rhetoric, Ideology, and the Power of the People*, Princeton.

Osborne (1981–82) Osborne, M.J. (1981–82) *Naturalization in Athens* I–II, Brussels.

Ostwald (1969)	Ostwald, M. (1969) *Nomos and the Beginnings of the Athenian Democracy*, Oxford.
Ostwald (1986)	Ostwald, M. (1986) *From Popular Sovereignty to the Sovereignty of Law: Law, Society and Politics in Fifth-Century Athens*, Berkeley.
Page	Page, D.L. (1981) *Further Greek Epigrams*, Cambridge.
Page *EG*	Page, D.L. (1975) *Epigrammata Graeca*, Oxford.
Page *LGS*	Page, D.L. (1973) *Lyrica Graeca Selecta*, Oxford.
Parke & Wormell (1956)	Parke, H.W. and Wormell, D.E.W. (1956) *The Delphic Oracle* I & II, Oxford.
Pleket	Pleket, H.W. (1964) *Epigraphica I: Texts on the Economic History of the Greek World*, Leiden.
Rhodes (1972)	Rhodes, P.J. (1972) *The Athenian Boule*, Oxford.
Rhodes	Rhodes, P.J. (1981) *A Commentary on the Aristotelian Athenaion Politeia*, Oxford.
Salmon (1984)	Salmon, J.B. (1984) *Wealthy Corinth: A History of the City to 338 BC*, Oxford.
Sealey (1987)	Sealey, R. (1987) *The Athenian Republic: Democracy or the Rule of Law?*, Pennsylvania.
SEG	*Supplementum Epigraphicum Graecum.*
SIG^3	Dittenberger, W. (1915–24) *Sylloge Inscriptionum Graecarum* I–IV, Leipzig.
Starr (1990)	Starr, C.G. (1990) *The Birth of Athenian Democracy*, New York.
Tod	Tod, M.N. *A Selection of Greek Historical Inscriptions* I^2 (1946) II (1948), Oxford.
Travlos (1971)	Travlos, J. (1971) *Pictorial Dictionary of Ancient Athens*, London.
Wehrli	Wehrli, F. (1969) *Die Schule des Aristoteles VII: Herakleides Pontikos*, Stuttgart.
West	West, M.L. (1971–72) *Iambi et Elegi Graeci ante Alexandrum Cantati*, I–II, Oxford.

General Bibliography

The chapter bibliographies are not intended to be exhaustive but primarily list those works cited in the comments. Listed immediately below are works which serve as a useful introduction to Greek history. These do not re-appear in the subject bibliographies which follow.

Burn, A.R. (1960) *The Lyric Age of Greece*, London.

Bury, J.B. and Meiggs, R. (1975) *A History of Greece: To the Death of Alexander the Great*, Hampshire, fourth edition.

Cartledge, P. (1993) *The Greeks: A Portrait of Self and Others*, Oxford.

Ehrenberg, V. (1960) *The Greek State*, Oxford.

— (1973) *From Solon to Socrates*, London, second edition.

Fine, J.V.A. (1983) *The Ancient Greeks: A Critical History*, Cambridge Mass.

Finley, M.I. (1963) *The Ancient Greeks*, London.

Forrest, W.G. (1966) *The Emergence of Greek Democracy: the Character of Greek Politics, 800–400 B.C.*, London.

Hammond, N.G.L. (1986) *A History of Greece to 322 B.C.*, Oxford, third edition.

Jeffery, L.H. (1976) *Archaic Greece: The City-States c. 700–500 B.C.*, New York.

Jones, A.H.M. (1957) *Athenian Democracy*, Oxford.

Kitto, H.D.F. (1957) *The Greeks*, Harmondsworth, second edition.

Levi, P. (1984) *Atlas of the Greek World*, Oxford.

Powell, A. (1988) *Athens and Sparta: Constructing Greek Political and Social History from 478 BC*, London.
Roberts, J.W. (1984) *City of Sokrates: An Introduction to Classical Athens*, London.
Sealey, R. (1976) *A History of the Greek City States ca. 700–338 B.C.*, Berkeley.
Starr, C.G. (1977) *The Economic and Social Growth of Early Greece*, New York.

Chapter One

Adamesteanu, D. (1967) 'Problèmes de la zone archéologique de Métaponte' *RA* 1: 3–38.
Asheri, D. (1988) 'Carthaginians and Greeks' in *CAH* IV^2: 739–780.
Austin, M.M. (1970) *Greece and Egypt in the Archaic Age*, Cambridge.
— and Vidal-Naquet, P. (1977) *Economic and Social History of Ancient Greece: an Introduction*, tr. M.M. Austin, Berkeley.
Beaumont, R.C. (1936) 'Greek Influence in the Adriatic Sea before the Fourth Century B.C.' *JHS* 56: 159–204.
Bérard, J. (1957) *La colonisation grecque. De l'Italie méridionale et de la Sicile dans l'antiquité: l'histoire et la légend*, Paris, second edition.
Best, J.G.P. (1969) *Thracian Peltasts and their Influence on Greek Warfare*, Groningen.
Boardman, J. (1965) 'Tarsus, Al Mina and Greek Chronology' *JHS* 85: 5–15.
— (1966) 'Evidence for the Dating of Greek Settlements in Cyrenaica' *ABSA* 61: 149–156.
— (1980) *The Greeks Overseas: Their Early Colonies and Trade*, London, second edition.
— (1982) 'An Inscribed Sherd from Al Mina' *OJA* 1: 365–67.
— (1990) 'Al Mina and History' *OJA* 9: 169–90.
Bradeen, D.W. (1952) 'The Chalcidians in Thrace' *AJPh* 73: 356–80.
Brauer, G.C. (1986) *Taras: Its History and Coinage*, New York.
Braun, T.F.G.R. (1982a) 'The Greeks in the Near East' in *CAH* III.3^2: 1–31.
— (1982b) 'The Greeks in Egypt' in *CAH* III.3^2: 32–56.
Brinkman, J.A. (1989) 'The Akkadian Words for "Ionia" and "Ionian"' in R.F. Sutton (ed.) *Daidalikon: Studies in Memory of R.V. Schoder*, Wauconda: 53–71.
Buck, R.J. (1959) 'Communalism on the Lipari Islands (Diod. 5.9.4)' *CPh* 54: 35–39.
Burnett, A.P. (1983) *Three Archaic Poets: Archilochus, Alcaeus, Sappho*, London.
Calame, C. (1990) 'Narrating the Foundation of a City: the Symbolic Birth of Cyrene' in L. Edmunds (ed.) *Approaches to Greek Myth*, Baltimore: 277–341.
Carawan, E.M. (1987) '*Eisangelia* and *Euthyna*: the Trials of Miltiades, Themistokles, and Cimon' *GRBS* 28: 167–208.
Cartledge, P. (1979) *Sparta and Lakonia: a Regional History 1300–362 BC*, London.
— (1987) *Agesilaos and the Crisis of Sparta*, London.
Cawkwell, G.L. (1992) 'Early Colonisation' *CQ* 42: 289–303.
Coja, M. (1990) 'Greek Colonists and Native Populations in Dobruja (Moesia Inferior): the Archaeological Evidence' in J.-P. Descoeudres (ed.) *Greek Colonists and Native Populations*, Oxford: 157–68.
Cook, J.M. (1982) 'The Eastern Greeks' in *CAH* III.3^2: 196–221.
Cook, R.M. (1937) 'Amasis and the Greeks in Egypt' *JHS* 57: 227–37.
— (1946) 'Ionia and Greece in the Eighth and Seventh Centuries B.C.' *JHS* 66: 67–98.
— (1962) 'Reasons for the Foundation of Ischia and Cumae' *Historia* 11: 113–14.
Cunliffe, B. (1988) *Greeks, Romans and Barbarians: Spheres of Interaction*, London.
Danov, C.M. (1990) 'Greek Colonization in Thrace' in J.-P. Descoeudres (ed.) *Greek Colonists and Native Populations*, Oxford: 151–55.

BIBLIOGRAPHY

Demand, N.H. (1990) *Urban Relocation in Archaic and Classical Greece: Flight and Consolidation*, Norman.

Drews, R. (1976) 'The Earliest Greek Settlements on the Black Sea' *JHS* 96: 18–31.

Dunbabin, T.J. (1948) *The Western Greeks: The History of Sicily and South Italy from the Foundation of the Greek Colonies to 480 B.C.*, Oxford.

Dušanić, A. (1978) 'The ὅρκιον τῶν οἰκιστήρων and Fourth-Century Cyrene' *Chiron* 8: 55–76.

Ehrenberg, V. (1948) 'The Foundation of Thurii' *AJPh* 69: 149–70.

Edmonds, J.M. (1931) *Elegy and Iambus* II: *Anacreonta*, London.

Faraone, C.A. (1993) 'Molten Wax, Spilt Wine and Mutilated Animals: Sympathetic Magic in Near Eastern and Early Greek Oath Ceremonies' *JHS* 113: 60–80.

Finley, M.I. (1979) *Ancient Sicily*, London, second edition.

Forrest, W.G. (1957) 'Colonisation and the Rise of Delphi' *Historia* 6: 160–75.

— (1982) 'Euboia and the Islands' in *CAH* III.3²: 249–60.

Freeman, K. (1950) *Greek City-States*, London.

Gardiner, A. (1961) *Egypt of the Pharaohs*, Oxford.

Graham, A.J. (1958) 'The Date of the Greek Penetration of the Black Sea' *BICS* 5: 25–39.

— (1960) 'The Authenticity of the ΟΡΚΙΟΝ ΤΩΝ ΟΙΚΙΣΤΗΡΩΝ of Cyrene' *JHS* 80: 94–111.

— (1962) 'Corinthian Colonies and Thucydides' Terminology' *Historia* 11: 246–52.

— (1971) 'Patterns in Early Greek Colonization' *JHS* 91: 35–47.

— (1978) 'The Foundation of Thasos' *ABSA* 73: 61–98.

— (1980–81) 'Religion, Women and Greek Colonization' *CRDAC* 11: 293–314.

— (1982a) 'The Colonial Expansion of Greece' in *CAH* III.3²: 83–162.

— (1982b) 'The Western Greeks' in *CAH* III.3²: 163–195.

— (1984) 'Commercial Interchanges between Greeks and Natives' *AncW* 10: 3–10.

— (1992) 'Abdera and Teos' *JHS* 112: 44–73.

Gwynn, A. (1918) 'The Character of Greek Colonisation' *JHS* 38: 88–123.

Huxley, G. (1962) *Early Sparta*, London.

Jameson, M.H. (1983) 'Famine in the Greek World' in P. Garnsey and C.R. Whittaker (eds.) *Trade and Famine in Classical Antiquity*, Cambridge: 6–16.

Jeffery, L.H. (1961) 'The Pact of the First Settlers at Cyrene' *JHS* 10: 139–47.

Jones, A.H.M. (1967) *Sparta*, Oxford.

Labaree, B.W. (1957) 'How the Greeks Sailed into the Black Sea' *AJA* 61: 29–33.

Legon, R.P. (1981) *Megara: The Political History of a Greek City-State to 336 B.C.*, Ithaca.

Lewis, D.M. (1992) 'Sources, Chronology, Method' and 'The Thirty Years' Peace' in *CAH* V²: 1–14, 121–46.

Lewis, N. (1986) *Greeks in Ptolemaic Egypt*, Oxford.

Laronde, A. (1990) 'Greeks and Libyans in Cyrenaica' in J.-P. Descoeudres (ed.) *Greek Colonists and Native Populations*, Oxford: 169–80.

Londey, P. (1990) 'Greek Colonists and Delphi' in J.-P. Descoeudres (ed.) *Greek Colonists and Native Populations*, Oxford: 117–27.

Malkin, I. (1985) 'What's in a Name? The Eponymous Founders of Greek Colonies' *Athenaeum* 63: 114–30.

— (1987) *Religion and Colonization in Ancient Greece*, Leiden.

Meiggs, R. (1972) *The Athenian Empire*, Oxford.

Michell, H. (1952) *Sparta*, Cambridge.

Millar, F. (1983) 'Epigraphy' in M. Crawford (ed.) *Sources for Ancient History*, Cambridge: 80–136.

Miller, M. (1970) *The Sicilian Colony Dates: Studies in Chronography* I, Albany.

Mitchell, B.M. (1966) 'Cyrene and Persia' *JHS* 86: 99–113.

Morgan, C. (1990) *Athletes and Oracles: the Transformation of Olympia and Delphi in the Eighth Century BC*, Cambridge.
Noonan, T.S. (1973) 'The Grain Trade of the Northern Black Sea in Antiquity' *AJPh* 94: 231–42.
Oliver, J.H. (1966) 'Herodotus 4.153 and *SEG* IX 3' *GRBS* 7: 25–29.
Page, D. (1955) *Sappho and Alcaeus: An Introduction to the Study of Ancient Lesbian Poetry*, Oxford.
Paget, R.F. (1968) 'The Ancient Ports of Cumae' *JRS* 58: 151–69.
Parke, H.W. (1933) *Greek Mercenary Soldiers*, Oxford.
Parker, R. (1985) 'Greek States and Greek Oracles' in *Crux*: 298–326.
Parker, V. (1991) 'The Dates of the Messenian Wars' *Chiron* 21: 25–47.
Pease, A.S. (1917) 'Notes on the Delphic Oracle and Greek Colonization' *CPh* 12: 1–20.
Pesely, G.E. (1989) 'Hagnon' *Athenaeum* 67: 191–209.
Ridgway, D. (1973) 'The First Western Greeks: Campanian Coasts and Southern Etruria' in C. and S. Hawkes (eds.) *Greeks, Celts and Romans*, London: 5–38.
— (1992) *The First Western Greeks*, Cambridge.
Rihll, T. (1993) 'War, Slavery and Settlement in Early Greece' in J. Rich and G. Shipley (eds.) *War and Society in the Greek World*, London: 77–107.
Roebuck, C. (1951) 'The Organization of Naucratis' *CPh* 46: 212–20.
— (1959) *Ionian Trade and Colonization*, New York.
Rougé, J. (1970) 'La colonisation grecque et les femmes' *Cahiers d'Histoire* 15: 307–17.
Snodgrass, A. (1983) 'Archaeology' in M. Crawford (ed.) *Sources for Ancient History*, Cambridge: 137–84.
Vidal-Nacquet, P. (1986) *The Black Hunter: Forms of Thought and Forms of Society in the Greek World*, tr. A. Szegedy-Maszak, Baltimore.
Wilson, R.J.A. (1988) *Sicily Under the Roman Empire*, Warminster.
Woodhead, A.G. (1952) 'The Site of Brea: Thucydides 1.61.4' *CQ* 2: 57–62.
— (1962) *The Greeks in the West*, London.
Woolley, C.L. (1938) 'Excavations at Al Mina, Sueidia' *JHS* 58: 1–30.

Chapter Two

Andrewes, A. (1949) 'The Corinthian Actaeon and Pheidon of Argos' *CQ* 43: 70–78.
Asheri, D. (1988) 'Carthaginians and Greeks' in *CAH* IV^2: 739–780.
— (1992) 'Sicily, 478–431 B.C.' in *CAH* V^2: 147–170.
Austin, M.M. (1990) 'Greek Tyrants and the Persians, 546–479 B.C.' *CQ* 40: 289–306.
Barron, J.P. (1964) 'The Sixth-Century Tyranny at Samos' *CQ* 14: 210–29.
— (1969) 'Ibycus: To Polycrates' *BICS* 16: 119–49.
Beloch, K. (1913) *Griechische Geschichte* I.2, Strassburg.
Berger, S. (1992) *Revolution and Society in Greek Sicily and Southern Italy*, *Historia* Einzelschrift 71, Stuttgart.
Berve, H. (1967) *Die Tyrannis bei den Griechen*, I–II, Munich.
Billigmeier J.-C. and Dusing, A.S. (1981) 'The Origin and Function of the Naukraroi at Athens: an Etymological and Historical Explanation' *TAPhA* 111: 11–16.
Boardman, J. (1982) 'The Material Culture of Archaic Greece' in *CAH* III.3^2: 442–62.
Bowen, A. (1992) *Plutarch: The Malice of Herodotus*, Warminster.
Burnett, A.P. (1983) *Three Archaic Poets: Archilochus, Alcaeus, Sappho*, London.
Campbell, D.A. (1982–91) *Greek Lyric* I–III, London.
Caven, B. (1990) *Dionysius I: Warlord of Sicily*, New Haven.
Cook, J.M. (1982) 'The Eastern Greeks' in *CAH* III.3^2: 196–221.

Cook, R.M. (1979) 'Archaic Greek Trade: Three Conjectures' *JHS* 99: 152–55.
Davison, J.A. (1947) 'The First Greek Triremes' *CQ* 41: 18–24.
de Ste. Croix, G.E.M. (1981) *The Class Struggle in the Ancient World*, London.
Demand, N.H. (1990) *Urban Relocation in Archaic and Classical Greece: Flight and Consolidation*, Norman.
Drews, R. (1972) 'The First Tyrants in Greece' *Historia* 21: 127–44.
Drijvers, J.W. (1992) 'Strabo VIII 2,1 (C335): ΠΟΡΘΜΕΙΑ and the Diolkos' *Mnemosyne* 45: 75–78.
Dunbabin, T.J. (1948) *The Western Greeks: The History of Sicily and South Italy from the Foundation of the Greek Colonies to 480 B.C.*, Oxford.
Ellis, J. and Stanton, G.R. (1968) 'Factional Conflict and Solon's Reforms' *Phoenix* 22: 95–110.
Ferril, A. (1978) 'Herodotus on Tyranny' *Historia* 27: 385–98.
Figueira, T.J. (1985) 'A Chronological Table of Archaic Megara, 800–500 BC' in T.J. Figueira and G. Nagy (eds.), *Theognis of Megara. Poetry and the Polis*, Baltimore: 261–303.
Finley, M.I. (1979) *Ancient Sicily*, London.
Fisher, N.R.E. (1992) *Hybris: A Study in the Values of Honour and Shame in Ancient Greece*, Warminster.
Fol, A. and Hammond, N.G.L. (1988) 'Persia in Europe, Apart from Greece' in *CAH* IV^2: 234–53.
Graf, D. (1985) 'Greek Tyrants and Achaemenid Politics' in J.W. Eadie and J. Ober (eds.) *The Craft of the Ancient Historian. Essays in Honor of Chester G. Starr*, Lanham: 79–124.
Graham, A.J. (1982) 'The Western Greeks' in *CAH* III.3^2: 163–195.
Griffin, A. (1982) *Sikyon*, Oxford.
Hammond, N.G.L. (1956) 'The Family of Orthagoras' *CQ* 6: 45–53.
— (1982) 'The Peloponnese' in *CAH* III.3^2: 321–359.
Herington, C.J. (1967) 'Aeschylus in Sicily' *JHS* 87: 74–85.
Hershbell, J.P. (1993) 'Plutarch and Herodotus — The Beetle in the Rose' *RhM* 136: 143–63.
Hornblower, S. (1992) 'The Religious Dimension to the Peloponnesian War, or, What Thucydides does not tell us' *HSPh* 94: 169–97.
Huxley, G. (1958) 'Argos et les derniers Tèménides' *BCH* 82: 588–601.
— (1962) *Early Sparta*, London.
Jameson, M. (1965) 'Notes on the Sacrificial Calendar from Erchia' *BCH* 89: 154–72.
Jones, N.F. (1980) 'The Civic Organisation of Corinth' *TAPhA* 110: 161–93.
Jordan, B. (1970) 'Herodotos 5.71.2 and the Naukraroi of Athens' *ClAnt* 3: 153–75.
Kelly, T. (1976) *A History of Argos to 500 B.C.*, Minneapolis.
Lambert, S.D. (1986) 'Herodotus, the Cylonian Conspiracy and the ΠΡΥΤΑΝΙΕΣ ΤΩΝ ΝΑΥΚΡΑΡΩΝ' *Historia* 35: 105–12.
Lang, M.L. (1967) 'The Kylonian Conspiracy' *CPh* 62: 243–49.
Legon, R.P. (1981) *Megara: The Political History of a Greek City-State to 336 B.C.*, Ithaca.
Leahy, D.M. (1956) 'Chilon and Aeschines: A Further Consideration of the Rylands Greek Papyrus fr. 18' *Bulletin of the John Rylands Library* 38: 406–35.
— (1957) 'The Spartan Embassy to Lygdamis' *JHS* 77: 272–75.
— (1959) 'Chilon and Aeschines Again' *Phoenix* 13: 31–37.
— (1968) 'The Dating of the Orthagorid Dynasty' *Historia* 17: 1–23.
Lehmann, G.A. (1980) 'Der 'Erste Heilige Krieg' Ein Fiktion?' *Historia* 29: 242–46.
Lévy, E. (1978) 'Notes sur la chronologie athénienne au vi^{e} siècle' *Historia* 27: 513–21.
Marinatos, N. (1981) 'Thucydides and Oracles' *JHS* 101: 138–40.
Mitchell, B.M. (1975) 'Herodotus and Samos' *JHS* 95: 75–91.

Morgan, C. (1990) *Athletes and Oracles: the Transformation of Olympia and Delphi in the Eighth Century BC*, Cambridge.
Mossé, C. (1969) *La tyrannie dans la Grèce antique*, Paris.
Nagy, G. (1985) 'Theognis and Megara: A Poet's Vision of his City' in T.J. Figueira and G. Nagy (eds.), *Theognis of Megara. Poetry and the Polis*, Baltimore: 22–81.
Oost, S.I. (1972) 'Cypselus the Bacchiad' *CPh* 67: 10–30.
— (1974) 'Two Notes on the Orthagorids of Sicyon' *CPh* 69: 118–120.
Page, D. (1955) *Sappho and Alcaeus: An Introduction to the Study of Ancient Lesbian Poetry*, Oxford.
Parke, H.W. (1946) 'Polycrates and Delos' *CQ* 40: 105–08.
Parker, V. (1992) 'The Dates of the Orthagorids of Sicyon' *Tyche* 7: 165–75.
Robertson, N. (1978) 'The Myth of the First Sacred War' *CQ* 28: 38–73.
Scanlon, T.F. (1987) 'Thucydides and Tyranny' *ClAnt* 6: 286–301.
Sealey, R. (1960) 'Regionalism in Archaic Athens' *Historia* 9: 155–80.
Shipley, G. (1987) *A History of Samos 800–188 BC*, Oxford.
Snodgrass, A.M. (1965) 'The Hoplite Reform and History' *JHS* 85: 110–22.
Tausend, K. (1986) 'Die Koalition im 1 Heiligen Krieg' *RSA* 16: 49–66.
Toher, M. (1989) 'On the Use of Nicolaus' Historical Fragments' *ClAnt* 8: 159–72.
Walcot, P. (1978) *Envy and the Greeks: A Study of Human Behaviour*, Warminster.
van der Veen, J.E. (1993) 'The Lord of the Ring: Narrative Technique in Herodotus' Story on Polycrates' Ring' *Mnemosyne* 46: 433–57.
Wade-Gery, H.T. (1925) 'The Growth of the Dorian States' in J.B. Bury, S.A. Cook, and F.E. Adcock (eds.) *CAH* III: *The Assyrian Empire*: 527–570.
West, M.L. (1970) 'Melica' *CQ* 20: 205–15.
White, M. (1954) 'The Duration of the Samian Tyranny' *JHS* 74: 36–43.
— (1955) 'Greek Tyranny' *Phoenix* 9: 1–18.
— (1958) 'The Dates of the Orthagorids' *Phoenix* 12: 2–14.
Ure, P.N. (1922) *The Origin of Tyranny*, New York.

Chapter Three

Adkins, A.W.H. (1972) *Moral Values and Political Behaviour in Ancient Greece*, New York.
Andrewes, A. (1974) 'The Survival of Solon's *Axones*' in D.W. Bradeen and M.F. McGregor (eds.) *ΦΟΡΟΣ: Tribute to Benjamin Dean Meritt*, New York: 21–28.
— (1982) 'The Growth of the Athenian State' in *CAH* III.3²: 360–391.
Bailey, B.L. (1940) 'The Export of Attic Black-Figure Ware' *JHS* 60: 60–70.
Bérard, C. et al. (1989) *A City of Images: Iconography and Society in Ancient Greece*, tr. D. Lyons, Princeton.
Bers, V. (1975) 'Solon's Law Forbidding Neutrality and Lysias 31' *Historia* 24: 493–98.
Camp, J.M. (1979) 'A Drought in the Late Eighth Century B.C.' *Hesperia* 48: 397–411.
— (1986) *The Athenian Agora: Excavations in the Heart of Classical Athens*, London.
Chambers, M. (1973) 'Aristotle on Solon's Reform of Coinage and Weights' *ClAnt* 6: 1–16.
Chiasson, C.C. (1986) 'The Herodotean Solon' *GRBS* 27: 249–62.
Cook, R.M. (1958) 'Speculations on the Origins of Coinage' *Historia* 7: 257–62.
David, E. (1984) 'Solon, Neutrality and Partisan Literature of Late Fifth-Century Athens' *MH* 41: 129–38.
Day, J. and Chambers, M. (1962) *Aristotle's History of Athenian Democracy*, Berkeley.

de Ste. Croix, G.E.M. (1981) *The Class Struggle in the Ancient Greek World: From the Archaic Age to the Arab Conquests*, London.

Develin, R. (1977) 'Solon's Law on Stasis' *Historia* 26: 507–08.

— (1979) 'The Election of Archons From Solon to Telesinos' *AC* 48: 455–68.

Ducrey, P. (1986) *Warfare in Ancient Greece*, New York.

Dunbabin, T.J. (1948) *The Western Greeks: The History of Sicily and South Italy from the Foundation of the Greek Colonies to 480 B.C.*, Oxford.

Eliot, C.W.H. (1967) 'Where did the Alkmaionidai Live?' *Historia* 16: 279–86.

Ellis, J. and Stanton, G.R. (1968) 'Factional Conflict and Solon's Reforms' *Phoenix* 22: 95–110.

Figueira, T.J. (1984) 'The Ten Archontes of 579/78 at Athens' *Hesperia* 53: 447–73.

Fine, J.V.A. (1951) *Horoi: Studies in Mortgage, Real Security, and Land Tenure in Ancient Athens*, Princeton.

Finley, M.I. (1951) *Studies in Land and Credit in Ancient Athens 500–200 B.C.: the Horos-Inscriptions*, New Brunswick.

— (1968) 'The Alienability of Land in Ancient Greece: A Point of View' *Eirene* 7: 25–32.

— (1971) 'The Ancestral Constitution' in M.I. Finley (ed.) *The Use and Abuse of History*, London: 34–59.

— (1985) *The Ancient Economy*, London, second edition.

Forrest, W.G. and Stockton, D.L. (1987) 'The Athenian Archons: A Note' *Historia* 36: 235–40.

Freeman, K. (1926) *The Work and Life of Solon*, Cardiff.

French, A. (1956) 'The Economic Background to Solon's Reforms' *CQ* 6: 11–25.

— (1957) 'Solon and the Megarian Question' *JHS* 77: 238–46.

— (1963) 'Land Tenure and the Solon Question' *Historia* 12: 242–47.

— (1964) *The Growth of the Athenian Economy*, London.

Frost, F.J. (1981) 'Politics in Early Athens' in *Classical Contributions:* 33–39.

Fuks, A. (1953) *The Ancestral Constitution: Four Studies in Athenian Party Politics at the End of the Fifth Century B.C.*, London.

Gagarin, M. (1981) *Drakon and Early Athenian Homicide Law*, New Haven.

— (1986) *Early Greek Law*, Berkeley.

Gallant, T.W. (1982) 'Agricultural Systems, Land Tenure, and the Reforms of Solon' *ABSA* 77: 111–24.

Garland, R.S.J. (1989) 'The Well-Ordered Corpse: An Investigation into the Motives behind Greek Funerary Legislation' *BICS* 36: 1–15.

Garnsey, P. (1988) *Famine and Food Supply in the Graeco-Roman World: Responses to Risk and Crisis*, Cambridge.

Gill, D.W.J. (1991) 'Pots and Trade: Spacefillers or Objets d'Art?' *JHS* 111: 29–47.

Goldstein, J.A. (1972) 'Solon's Law for an Activist Citizenry' *Historia* 21: 538–45.

Hammond, N.G.L. (1940) 'The Seisachtheia and the Nomothesia of Solon' *JHS* 60: 71–83.

— (1961) 'Land Tenure in Athens and Solon's Seisachtheia' *JHS* 81: 76–98.

Hansen, M.H. (1975) *Eisangelia: The Sovereignty of the People's Court in Athens in the Fourth Century BC and the Impeachment of the Generals and Politicians*, Odense.

— (1978) '*Demos, Ecclesia* and *Dicasterion* in Classical Athens' *GRBS* 19: 127–46.

— (1981–82) 'The Athenian Heliaia from Solon to Aristotle' *C&M* 33: 9–47 = Hansen, M.H. (1989) *The Athenian Ecclesia II. A Collection of Articles 1983–89*, Copenhagen: 219–57.

— (1989) 'Solonian Democracy in Fourth-Century Athens' in W.R. Connor et al. (eds.) *Aspects of Athenian Democracy* (*Classica et Medievalia Dissertationes* XI), Copenhagen: 71–99.

— (1991) *The Athenian Democracy in the Age of Demosthenes: Structure, Principles and Ideology*, Oxford.

Harding, P. (1974) 'Androtion's View of Solon's Seisachtheia' *Phoenix* 28: 282–89.

Hölkeskamp, K.-J (1992) 'Written Law in Archaic Greece' *PCPhS* 38: 87–117.

Holloway, R. (1984) 'The Date of the First Greek Coins: Some Arguments from Style and Hoards' *RBN* 130: 5–18.

Hopper, R.J. (1968) 'Observations on the *Wappenmünzen*' in C.M. Kraay and G.K. Jenkins (eds.) *Essays in Greek Coinage Presented to S. Robinson*, Oxford 1968: 16–39.

Isager, S. and Skydsgaard, J.E. (1992) *Ancient Greek Agriculture: An Introduction*, London.

Jacoby, F. (1949) *Atthis: the Local Chronicles of Ancient Athens*, Oxford.

Jameson, M. (1983) 'Famine in the Greek World' in P. Garnsey and C.R. Whittaker (eds.) *Trade and Famine in Classical Antiquity*, Cambridge: 6–16.

Kagan, D. (1960) 'Pheidon's Aeginetan Coinage' *TAPhA* 91: 121–36.

— (1982) 'The Dates of the Earliest Coins' *AJA* 88: 343–60.

Knox, B.M.W. (1978) 'Literature' in W.A.P. Childs (ed.) *Athens Comes of Age: From Solon to Salamis*, Princeton: 43–52.

Kroll, J.H. (1981) 'From *Wappenmünzen* to Gorgoneia to Owls' *ANSMusN* 26: 1–32.

Kraay, C.M. (1964) 'Hoards, Small Change and the Origin of Coinage' *JHS* 84: 76–91.

— (1968) 'An Interpretation of *Ath. Pol.*, Ch. 10' in C.M. Kraay and G.K. Jenkins (eds.) *Essays in Greek Coinage Presented to S. Robinson*, Oxford 1968: 1–9.

— (1976) *Archaic and Classical Greek Coins*, Berkeley.

— (1988) 'Coinage' in *CAH* IV^2: 431–45.

Kroll, J.K. and Waggoner, N.M. (1984) 'Dating the Earliest Coins of Athens, Corinth and Aegina' *AJA* 88: 325–40.

Laix, de R.A. (1973) *Probouleusis at Athens: A Study of Political Decision-Making*, Berkeley.

Legon, R.P. (1981) *Megara: The Political History of a Greek City-State to 336 B.C.*, London.

Lewis, D.M. (1963) 'Cleisthenes and Attica' *Historia* 12: 22–40.

Linforth, I.M. (1919) *Solon the Athenian*, Berkeley.

MacDowell, D.M. (1978) *The Law in Classical Athens*, London.

Manville, B. (1980) 'Solon's Law of Stasis and *Atimia* in Archaic Athens' *TAPhA* 110: 213–21.

Markianos, S.S. (1974) 'The Chronology of the Herodotean Solon' *Historia* 23: 1–20.

Miller, M. (1969) 'The Accepted Date for Solon: Precise, but Wrong?' *Arethusa* 2: 62–86.

Millett, P. (1989) 'Patronage and its Avoidance in Classical Athens' in A. Wallace-Hadrill (ed.) *Patronage in Ancient Society*, London: 1–47.

Moore, J.M. (1983) *Aristotle and Xenophon on Democracy and Oligarchy*, London, second edition.

Morris, I. (1991) 'The Early Polis as City and State' in J. Rich and A. Wallace-Hadrill (eds.) *City and Country in the Ancient World*, London: 25–58.

Murray, O. (1990) 'The Solonian Law of *hubris*' in P. Cartledge, P. Millett and S. Todd (eds.) *Nomos: Essays in Athenian Law, Politics and Society*, Cambridge: 139–146.

Rhodes, P.J. (1979) 'Εἰσαγγελία in Athens' *JHS* 99: 103–14.

— (1984) *Aristotle: The Athenian Constitution*, Harmondsworth.

— (1991) 'The Athenian Code of Laws, 410–399 B.C.' *JHS* 111: 87–100.

Rihll, T.E. (1989) 'Lawgivers and Tyrants (Solon, FRR. 9–11 West)' *CQ* 39: 277–86.

— (1991) 'EKTHMOPOI: Partners in Crime?' *JHS* 111: 101–27.

Robertson, N. (1986) 'Solon's Axones and Kyrbeis, and the Sixth-Century Background' *Historia* 35: 147–76.

— (1990) 'The Laws of Athens, 410–399 BC: The Evidence for Review and Publication' *JHS* 110: 43–75.
Rosivach, V.J. (1992) 'Redistribution of Land in Solon, fragment 34 West' *JHS* 112: 153–57.
Ruschenbusch, E. (1958) 'Πάτριος πολιτεία' *Historia* 7: 398–424.
— (1966) ΣΟΛΩΝΟΣ ΝΟΜΟΙ: *Die Fragmente des Solonischen Gesetzwerkes, Historia* Einzelschrift 9, Wiesbaden.
Sallares, R. (1991) *The Ecology of the Ancient Greek World*, London.
Samuel, A.E. (1972) *Greek and Roman Chronology: Calendars and Years in Classical Antiquity*, Munich.
Sealey, R. (1960) 'Regionalism in Archaic Athens' *Historia* 9: 155–80.
— (1983) 'How Citizenship and the City Began in Athens' *AJAH* 8: 97–129.
Snodgrass, A. (1980) *Archaic Greece: The Age of Experiment*, London.
Starr, C.G. (1982) 'Economic and Social Conditions in the Greek World' in *CAH* III.3²: 417–41.
— (1990) *The Birth of Athenian Democracy: The Assembly in the Fifth Century B.C.*, Oxford.
Staveley, E.S. (1972) *Greek and Roman Voting and Elections*, London.
Stroud, R. (1968) *Drakon's Law on Homicide*, Berkeley.
— (1978) 'State Documents in Archaic Athens' in W.A.P. Childs (ed.) *Athens Comes of Age: From Solon to Salamis*, Princeton: 20–42.
— (1979) *The Axones and Kyrbeis of Drakon and Solon*, Berkeley.
Sumner, G.V. (1961) 'Notes on Chronological Problems in the Aristotelian 'ΑΘΗΝΑΙΩΝ ΠΟΛΙΤΕΙΑ' *CQ* 11: 31–54.
Thompson, H.A. (1976) *The Athenian Agora*, Athens, third edition.
— and Wycherley, R.E. (1972) *The Athenian Agora* XIV. *The Agora of Athens: the History, Shape and Uses of an Ancient City Centre*, Princeton.
Vickers, M. (1985) 'Early Greek Coinage, a Reassessment' *NC* 145: 1–44.
Vlastos, G. (1946) 'Solonian Justice' *CPh* 41: 65–83.
von Fritz, K. (1954) 'The Composition of Aristotle's *Constitution of Athens* and the So-called Dracontian Constitution' *CPh* 49: 74–93.
Wallace, R.W. (1985) *The Areopagos Council, to 307 B.C.*, Baltimore.
Wallace, W.W. (1983) 'The Date of Solon's Reforms' *AJAH* 8: 81–95.
Waters, K.H. (1960) 'Solon's Price "Equalisation"' *JHS* 80: 181–90.
Woodhouse, W.J. (1938) *Solon the Liberator*, Oxford.
Wycherley, R.E. (1957) *The Athenian Agora* III: *Literary and Epigraphical Testimonia*, Princeton.
— (1978) *The Stones of Athens*, Princeton.

Chapter Four

Andrewes, A. (1982) 'The Tyranny of Peisistratus' in *CAH* III.3²: 392–416.
Berve, H. (1967) *Die Tyrannis bei den Griechen*, I–II, Munich.
Boardman, J. (1972) 'Herakles, Peisistratos and Sons' *RA*: 57–72.
— (1975) 'Herakles, Peisisitratos and Eleusis' *JHS* 95: 1–12.
Bowra, C. M. (1961) *Greek Lyric Poetry From Alcman to Simonides*, Oxford, second edition.
Boersma, J.S. (1970) *Athenian Building Policy from 561/0–405/4 B.C.*, Groningen.
Brunnsåker, S. (1971) *The Tyrant Slayers of Kritios and Nesiotes*, Stockholm, second edition.
Camp, J.M. (1986) *The Athenian Agora: Excavations in the Heart of Classical Athens*, London.
Cole, J.W. (1975) 'Peisistratus on the Strymon' *G&R* 22: 42–44.

Connor, W.R. (1987) 'Tribes, Festivals, and Processions; Civil Ceremonial and Political Manipulation in Archaic Greece' *JHS* 107: 40–47.
— (1990) 'City Dionysia and Athenian Democracy' in W.R. Connor et al. (eds.) *Aspects of Athenian Democracy* (*Classica et Medievalia Dissertationes* XI), Copenhagen: 7–32.
Cook, R.M. (1987) 'Pots and Pisistratan Propaganda' *JHS* 107: 167–69.
Crosby, M. (1949) 'The Altar of the Twelve Gods in Athens' in *Commemorative Studies in Honor of T.L. Shear*, *Hesperia* Suppl. VIII, Princeton: 82–103.
Davison, J.A. (1955) 'Peisistratos and Homer' *TAPhA* 86: 1–21.
Day, J. (1985) 'Epigrams and History: The Athenian Tyrannicides, A Case in Point' in *The Greek Historians: Literature and History. Papers Presented to A.E. Raubitschek*, Stanford: 25–46.
Dover, K.J. (1978) *Greek Homosexuality*, London.
Dunkley, B. (1935–36) 'Greek Fountain-Buildings before 300 B.C.' *ABSA* 36: 142–204.
Ehrenberg, V. (1950) 'Origins of Democracy' *Historia* 1: 515–48.
Finley, M.I. (1981) *Economy and Society in Ancient Greece*, London.
Fitzgerald, T.R. (1957) 'The Murder of Hipparchus: a Reply' *Historia* 6: 275–86.
Fornara, C.W. (1970) 'The Cult of Harmodius and Aristogeiton' *Philologus* 114: 155–80.
Forrest, W.G. (1969) 'The Tradition of Hippias' Expulsion from Athens' *GRBS* 10: 277–86.
French, A. (1957) 'Solon and the Megarian Question' *JHS* 77: 238–46.
— (1959) 'The Party of Peisistratos' *G&R* 6: 46–57.
Frost, F.J. (1990) 'Peisistratos, the Cults, and the Unification of Attica' *AncW* 21: 3–9.
Garland, R.S.J. (1985) *The Greek Way of Death*, London.
— (1987) *The Piraeus, From the Fifth to the First Century B.C.*, London.
Harvey, D. (1985) 'Women in Thucydides' *Arethusa* 18: 67–90.
Hind, J.G.F. (1974) 'The 'Tyrannis' and the Exiles of Pisistratus' *CQ* 24: 1–18.
Holladay, J. (1977) 'The Followers of Peisistratus' *G&R* 24: 40–56.
Hopper, R.J. (1961) '"Plain", "Shore", and "Hill" in Early Athens' *ABSA* 56: 189–219.
Jacoby, F. (1949) *Atthis: The Local Chronicles of Ancient Athens*, Oxford.
Jordan, B. (1975) *The Athenian Navy in the Classical Period: A Study of Athenian Naval Administration and Military Organization in the Fifth and Fourth Centuries B.C.*, Berkeley.
Keuls, E.C. (1985) *The Reign of the Phallus: Sexual Politics in Ancient Athens*, Berkeley.
Kinzl, K.H. (1989) 'Regionalism in Classical Athens? (Or: An Anachronism in Herodotos 1.59.3?)' *AHB* 3: 5–9.
Knox, B.M.W. (1978) 'Literature' in W.A.P. Childs (ed.) *Athens Comes of Age: From Solon to Salamis*, Princeton: 43–52.
Lang, M.L. (1968) *Waterworks in the Athenian Agora*, Princeton.
Lavelle, B.M. (1984) 'Thucydides 6.55.1 and *Adikia*' *ZPE* 54: 17–19.
— (1986) 'Herodotus on Argive Misthotoi' *LCM* 11: 150.
— (1989) 'Thucydides and *IG* I^3 948: ἀμυδροῖς γράμμασι' in R.F. Sutton (ed.) *Daidalikon: Studies in Memory of Raymond V. Schoder*, Wauconda: 207–12.
— (1991) 'The Compleat Angler: Observations on the Rise of Peisistratos in Herodotos (1.59–64)' *CQ* 41: 317–24.
— (1992) 'Herodotos, Skythian Archers, and the *doryphoroi* of the Peisistratids' *Klio* 74: 78–97.
— (1992) 'The Pisistratids and the Mines of Thrace' *GRBS* 33: 5–23.

Legon, R.P. (1981) *Megara: The Political History of a Greek City-State to 336 B.C.*, London.
Lewis, D. (1963) 'Cleisthenes and Attica' *Historia* 12: 22–40.
— (1988) 'The Tyranny of the Peisistratidai' in *CAH* IV²: 287–302.
Lintott, A. (1982) *Violence, Civil Strife and Revolution in the Classical City: 750–330 BC*, London.
Millett, P. (1989) 'Patronage and its Avoidance in Classical Athens' in A. Wallace-Hadrill (ed.) *Patronage in Ancient Society*, London: 1–47.
Moretti, L. (1953) *Iscrizioni Agonistische Greche*, Rome.
Morgan, C. (1990) *Athletes and Oracles: the Transformation of Olympia and Delphi in the Eighth Century BC*, Cambridge.
Mossé, C. (1969) *La tyrannie dans la Grèce antique*, Paris.
Mylonas, G. (1961) *Eleusis and the Eleusinian Mysteries*, Princeton.
Nock, A.D. (1944) 'The Cult of Heroes' *HThR* 37: 141–74 = (1972) Z. Stewart (ed.) *A.D. Nock: Essays on Religion and the Ancient World I–II*, Oxford: 575–602.
Ostwald, M. (1991) 'Herodotus and Athens' *ICS* 11: 137–48.
Owens, E.J. (1982) 'The Enneakrounos Fountain-house' *JHS* 102: 222–25.
Parke, H.W. (1946) 'Polycrates and Delos' *CQ* 40: 105–08.
Podlecki, A.J. (1966) 'The Political Significance of the Athenian "Tyrannicide-Cult"' *Historia* 15: 129–41.
Pritchett, W.K. (1980) *Studies in Ancient Greek Topography* III: *Roads*, Berkeley.
Rhodes, P.J. (1976) 'Pisistratid Chronology Again' *Phoenix* 30: 219–33.
Richter, G.M.A. (1961) *Archaic Gravestones of Attica*, London.
Ruebel, J.S. (1973) 'The Tyrannies of Peisistratos' *GRBS* 14: 125–36.
Sealey, R. (1960) 'Regionalism in Archaic Athens' *Historia* 9: 155–80.
Shapiro, H.A. (1989) *Art and Cult under the Tyrants in Athens*, Mainz.
— (1990) 'Oracle-Mongers in Peisistratid Athens' *Kernos* 3: 335–45.
Shear, T.L. (1978) 'Tyrants and Buildings in Archaic Athens' in W.A.P. Childs (ed.) *Athens Comes of Age: From Solon to Salamis*, Princeton: 1–19.
Smith, J.A. (1989) *Athens under the Tyrants*, Bristol.
Stahl, M. (1987) *Aristokraten und Tyrannen im Archaischen Athen*, Stuttgart.
Stockton, D. (1990) *The Classical Athenian Democracy*, Oxford.
Stroud, R.S. (1971) 'Greek Inscriptions: Theozotides and the Athenian Orphans' *Hesperia* 40: 280–301.
Sumner, G.V. (1961) 'Notes on Chronological Problems in the Aristotelian 'ΑΘΗΝΑΙΩΝ ΠΟΛΙΤΕΙΑ' *CQ* 11: 31–54.
Taylor, M.W. (1991) *The Tyrant Slayers: the Heroic Image in Fifth Century B.C. Athenian Art and Politics*, Salem, second edition.
Thompson, H.A. (1976) *The Athenian Agora*, Athens, third edition.
— (1978) 'Some Hero Shrines in Early Athens' in W.A.P. Childs (ed.) *Athens Comes of Age: From Solon to Salamis*, Princeton: 96–108.
Thompson, H.A. and Wycherley, R.E. (1972) *The Athenian Agora* XIV. *The Agora of Athens: the History, Shape and Uses of an Ancient City Centre*, Princeton.
Thompson, W.E. (1971) 'The Prytaneion Decree' *AJPh* 92: 226–37.
Viviers, D. (1987) 'Pisistratus' Settlement on the Thermaic Gulf: a connection with Eretrian Colonization' *JHS* 107: 193–95.
Ure, P.N. (1922) *The Origin of Tyranny*, New York.
Wade-Gery, H.T. (1958) 'Miltiades' in *Essays in Greek History*, London: 155–70 = (1951) *JHS* 71: 212–21.
White, M.E. (1974) 'Hippias and the Athenian Archon List' in J.A.S. Evans (ed.) *Polis and Imperium: Studies in Honour of Edward Togo Salmon*, Toronto: 81–95.
Whitehead, D. (1986) *The Demes of Attica 508/7–ca. 250 B.C.: A Political and Social Study*, Princeton.
Wright, J.H. (1892) 'The Date of Cylon' *HSPh* 3: 1–74.

Wycherley, R.E. (1957) *The Athenian Agora* III: *Literary and Epigraphical Testimonia*, Princeton.
— (1964) 'The Olympieion at Athens' *GRBS* 5: 161–79.
— (1978) *The Stones of Athens*, Princeton.

Chapter Five

Andrewes, A. (1977) 'Kleisthenes' Reform Bill' *CQ* 21: 241–48.
Bicknell, P.J. (1969) 'Whom Did Kleisthenes Enfranchise?' *PP* 24: 34–37.
— (1972) *Studies in Athenian Politics and Genealogy*, *Historia* Einzelschrift 19, Wiesbaden.
— (1974) 'Athenian Politics and Genealogy; Some Pendants' *Historia* 23: 146–63.
— (1975) 'Was Megakles Hippokratous Alopekethen Ostracised Twice?' *AC*: 172–75.
— (1989) 'Athenians Politically Active in Pynx II' *GRBS* 30: 83–100.
Bowra, C. M. (1961) *Greek Lyric Poetry From Alcman to Simonides*, Oxford, second edition.
Broneer, O. (1938) 'Excavations on the North Slope of the Acropolis' *Hesperia* 7: 161–263.
Carawan, E.M. (1987) 'Eisangelia and Euthyna: the Trials of Miltiades, Themistocles and Cimon' *GRBS* 28: 167–208.
Connor, W.R. and Keaney, J.J. (1969) 'Theophrastus on the End of Ostracism' *AJPh* 90: 313–19.
Cromey, R.D. (1979) 'Kleisthenes' Fate' *Historia* 28: 129–47.
Develin, R. (1977) 'Cleisthenes and Ostracism: Precedents and Intentions' *Antichthon* 11: 10–21.
— (1985) 'Bouleutic Ostracism Again' *Antichthon* 19: 7–15.
Dover, K.J. (1960) 'ΔΕΚΑΤΟΣ ΑΥΤΟΣ' *JHS* 80: 61–77.
Ehrenberg, V. (1945) 'Pericles and His Colleagues between 441 and 429 B.C.' *AJPh* 66: 113–34.
— (1950) 'Origins of Democracy' *Historia* 1: 515–48.
Eliot, C.W.J. (1962) *Coastal Demes of Attika: A Study of the Policy of Kleisthenes*, Toronto.
— (1968) 'Kleisthenes and the Creation of the Ten Phylai' *Phoenix* 22: 1–17.
Figueira, T.J. (1987) 'Residential Restrictions on the Athenian Ostracized' *GRBS* 28: 281–305.
Finley, M.I. (1952) *Studies in Land and Credit in Ancient Athents 500–200 B.C.: the Horos-Inscriptions*, New Brunswick.
Fornara, C.W. (1971) *The Athenian Board of Generals From 501 to 404*, *Historia* Einzelschrift 16, Wiesbaden.
Forsén, B. (1993) 'The Sanctuary of Zeus Hypsistos and the Assembly Place on the Pnyx' *Hesperia* 62: 507–21.
Golden, M. (1990) *Children and Childhood in Classical Athens*, Baltimore.
Grace, E. (1974) 'Aristotle on the "Enfranchisement of Aliens" by Cleisthenes (a Note)' *Klio* 56: 353–68.
Hands, A.R. (1959) 'Ostraka and the Law of Ostracism — Some Possibilities and Assumptions' *JHS* 79: 69–79.
Hansen, M.H. (1982) 'The Athenian *Ecclesia* and the Assembly Place on the Pynx' *GRBS* 23: 241–49 = Hansen, M.H. (1983) *The Athenian Ecclesia: A Collection of Articles 1976–1983*: 25–34.
— (1987) *The Athenian Assembly in the Age of Demosthenes*, Oxford.
— (1988) 'The Organization of the Athenian Assembly: A Reply' *GRBS* 29: 51–58 = (1989): 155–62.

— (1989) 'The Organization of the Athenian Assembly: A Reply. Addenda' in Hansen, M.H. *The Athenian Ecclesia II. A Collection of Articles 1983–89*, Copenhagen: 163–65.

— (1991) *The Athenian Democracy in the Age of Demosthenes: Structure, Principles and Ideology*, Oxford.

Horsley, G.H.R. (1986) 'Kleisthenes and the Abortive Athenian Embassy to Sardis' *MPhL* 7: 99–107.

Jameson, M.H. (1955) 'Seniority in the *Strategia*' *TAPhA* 86: 63–87.

Kagan, D. (1961) 'The Origin and Purposes of Ostracism' *Hesperia* 30: 393–401.

— (1963) 'The Enfranchisement of Aliens by Cleisthenes' *Historia* 12: 41–46.

Karavites, P. (1974) 'Cleisthenes and Ostracism Again' *Athenaeum* 52: 326–35.

Keaney, J.J. (1970) 'The Text of Androtion F 6 and the Origin of Ostracism' *Historia* 19: 1–11.

— and Raubitschek, A.E. (1972) 'A Late Byzantine Account of Ostracism' *AJPh* 93: 87–91.

Kearns, E. (1985) 'Change and Continuity in Religious Structures After Cleisthenes' in *Crux*: 189–207.

— (1989) *The Heroes of Attica, BICS* Suppl. 57, London.

Kinzl, K.H. (1987) 'On the Consequences of Following *AP* 21.4 (on the Trittyes of Attika)' *AHB* 1: 25–33.

Kron, U. (1976) *Die zehn attischen Phylenheroen: Geschichte, Mythos, Kult und Darstellungen*, Berlin.

Lang, M.L. (1982) 'Writing and Spelling on Ostraka' in *Studies in Attic Epigraphy, History and Topography Presented to E. Vanderpool, Hesperia* Supplement 19, Princeton: 75–87.

Langdon, M.K. (1985) 'The Territorial Basis of the Attic Demes' *SO* 60: 5–15.

Lavelle, B.M. (1988) 'A Note on the First Three Victims of Ostracism ('Αθηναίων Πολιτεία 22.4)' *CPh* 83: 131–35.

— (1992) 'Herodotos, Skythian Archers, and the *doryphoroi* of the Peisistratids' *Klio* 74: 78–97.

Lewis, D.M. (1961) 'Double Representation in the Strategia' *JHS* 81: 118–23.

— (1963) 'Cleisthenes and Attica' *Historia* 12: 22–40.

— (1974) 'The Kerameikos Ostraka' *ZPE* 14: 1–4.

Longo, C.P. (1980) 'La Bulé e la Procedura dell' Ostracismo: Considerazioni su *Vat. Gr.* 1144' *Historia* 29: 257–81.

Martin, A. (1989) 'L'ostracisme Athénien: Un demi-siècle de découvertes et de recherches' *REG* 102: 124–45.

Mattingly, H.B. (1971) 'Facts and Artifacts: the Researcher and His Tools' *Leeds University Review* 14: 277–97.

— (1991) 'The Practice of Ostracism at Athens' *Antichthon* 25: 1–26.

Mikalson, J.D. (1975) *The Sacred and Civil Calendar of the Athenian Year*, Princeton.

— (1977) 'Religion in the Attic Demes' *AJPh* 98: 424–35.

Osborne, R. (1985) *Demos: The Discovery of Classical Attika*, Cambridge.

Oliver, J.H. (1960) 'Reforms of Cleisthenes' *Historia* 9: 503–07.

Ostwald, M. (1986a) 'New Ostraka From the Athenian Agora' *Hesperia* 37: 117–20.

— (1988) 'The Reform of the Athenian State by Cleisthenes' in *CAH* IV²: 303–46.

Parke, H.W. (1977) *Festivals of the Athenians*, London.

Parker, R. (1987) 'Festivals of the Attic Demes' in T. Linders and G. Norquist (eds.) *Gifts to the Gods. Boreas: Uppsala Studies in Ancient Mediterranean and Near Eastern Civilizations* 15, Stockholm: 137–47.

Patterson, C.B. (1981) *Perikles' Citizenship Law of 451/50 BC*, New York.

Phillips, D.J. (1982) 'Athenian Ostracism' in G.H.R. Horsley (ed.) *Hellenika: Essays on Greek Politics and History*, North Ryde.

— (1990) 'Some Ostraka from the Athenian Agora' *ZPE* 83: 123–48.

Rapke, T.T. (1989) 'Cleisthenes the Tyrant Manqué' *AHB* 3: 47–51.
Raubitschek, A.E. (1947) 'The Ostracism of Xanthippos' *AJA* 51: 257–62.
— (1953) 'Athenian Ostracism' *CJ* 48: 113–22.
Rhodes, P.J. (1986) 'Political Activity in Classical Athens' *JHS* 106: 132–44.
Rocchi, G.R. (1972) 'Politica di familia e politica di tribu' nella polis ateniese (V secolo)' *Acme* 24: 13–44.
Sealey, R. (1960) 'Regionalism in Archaic Athens' *Historia* 9: 155–80.
Siewert, P. (1982) *Die Trittyen Attikas und die Heeresreform des Kleisthenes*, Munich.
Sinclair, R.K. (1988) *Democracy and Participation in Athens*, Cambridge.
Stanton, G.R. (1970) 'The Introduction of Ostracism and Alcmeonid Propaganda' *JHS* 90: 180–83.
— (1984) 'The Tribal Reform of Kleisthenes the Alkmeonid' *Chiron* 14: 1–41.
— and Bicknell, P.J. (1987) 'Voting in Tribal Groups in the Athenian Assembly' *GRBS* 28: 51–92.
Staveley, E.S. (1966) 'Voting Procedure at the Election of Strategoi' in E. Badian (ed.) *Ancient Society and Institutxions: Studies Presented to V. Ehrenberg*, Oxford: 275–88.
— (1972) *Greek and Roman Voting and Elections*, London.
Stockton, D. (1990) *The Classical Athenian Democracy*, Oxford.
Thompson, W.E. (1971) 'The Deme in Kleisthenes' Reforms' *SO* 46: 72–79.
Thomsen, R. (1972) *The Origin of Ostracism: A Synthesis*, Copenhagen.
Traill, J.S. (1975) *The Political Organization of Attica: A Study of the Demes, Trittyes, and Phylai, and their Representation in the Athenian Council*, Princeton.
— (1982) 'An Interpretation of Six Rock-cut Inscriptions in the Attic Demes of Lamptrai' in *Studies in Attic Epigraphy, History and Topography Presented to E. Vanderpool*, Princeton: 162–71.
— (1986) *Demos and Trittys: Epigraphical and Topographical Studies in the Organization of Attica*, Toronto.
Vanderpool, E. (1968) 'New Ostraka from the Athenian Agora' *Hesperia* 37: 117–20.
— (1970) *Ostracism at Athens*, Lectures in Memory of Louise Taft Semple, Cincinnati.
— (1974) 'Ostraka From the Athenian Agora, 1970–1972' *Hesperia* 43: 189–93.
Wade-Gery, H.T. (1958) 'The Laws of Kleisthenes' in *Essays in Greek History*, Oxford: 135–54 = (1933) *CQ* 27: 17–29.
West, A.B. (1924) 'Notes on Certain Athenian Generals of the Year 424–3 B.C.' *AJPh* 45: 141–60.
Whitehead, D. (1977) *The Ideology of the Athenian Metic*, Cambridge.
— (1986) *The Demes of Attica 508/7–ca. 250 B.C.: A Political and Social Study*, Princeton.
Williams, G.M.E. (1978) 'The Kerameikos Ostraka' *ZPE* 31: 103–13.
Willemsen, F. (1968) 'Die Ausgraben im Kerameikos 1966' *AD* 23 *Chronika* B ': 24–32.
Winters, T.F. (1993) 'Kleisthenes and Athenian Nomenclature' *JHS* 113: 162–65.
Woodhead, A.G. (1949) 'I.G., I^2, 95, and the Ostracism of Hyperbolus' *Hesperia* 18: 78–83.
Young, R.S. (1951) 'An Industrial District of Ancient Athens' *Hesperia* 20: 125–288.
Zaidman, L.B. and Pantel, P.S. (1992) *Religion in the Ancient Greek City*, tr. P. Cartledge, Cambridge.

Chapter Six

Adkins, A.W.H. (1960) *Merit and Responsibility: A Study in Greek Values*, Oxford.
— (1972) *Moral Values and Political Behaviour in Ancient Greece: From Homer to the End of the Fifth Century*, New York.
Allison, J.W. (1984) 'Sthenelaidas' Speech: Thucydides 1.86' *Hermes* 112: 9–16.
Anderson, J.K. (1970) *Military Theory and Practice in the Age of Xenophon*, Berkeley.
— (1974) *Xenophon*, London.
Andrewes, A. (1978) 'Spartan Imperialism' in P.D.A. Garnsey and C.R. Whittaker (eds.) *Imperialism in the Ancient World*, Cambridge: 91–102.
Bloedow, E.F. (1987) 'Sthenelaidas the Persuasive Spartan' *Hermes* 115: 60–66.
Bonner, R.J. and Smith, G. (1943) 'Administration of Justice in the Delphic Amphictyony' *CPh* 38: 1–12.
Boring, T.A. (1979) *Literacy in Ancient Sparta*, Leiden.
Burkert, W. (1983) *Homo Necans: The Anthropology of Ancient Greek Sacrificial Ritual and Myth*, tr. P. Bing, Berkeley.
Burn, A.R. (1962) *Persia and the Greeks*, with postscript by D.M. Lewis (1984), London.
Butler, D. (1962) 'Competence of the Demos in the Spartan Rhetra' *Historia* 11: 385–96.
Cartledge, P. (1976) 'A New 5th-Century Spartan Treaty' *LCM* 1: 87–92.
— (1977) 'Hoplites and Heroes: Sparta's Contribution to the Technique of Ancient Warfare' *JHS* 97: 11–27.
— (1978) 'Literacy in the Spartan Oligarchy' *JHS* 98: 25–37.
— (1979) *Sparta and Lakonia: A Regional History 1300–362 BC*, London.
— (1981) 'Spartan Wives: Liberation or Licence?' *CQ* 31: 84–105.
— (1987) *Agesilaos and the Crisis of Sparta*, London.
— (1993) 'Like a Worm I' the Bud? A Heterology of Classical Greek Slavery' *G&R* 40: 163–80.
Cawkwell, G.L. (1983) 'The Decline of Sparta' *CQ* 33: 385–400.
— (1989) 'Orthodoxy and Hoplites' *CQ* 39: 375–89.
— (1993) 'Cleomenes' *Mnemosyne* 46: 506–27.
Chrimes, K.M.T. (1949) *Ancient Sparta: A Re-examination of the Evidence*, Manchester.
Connor, W.R. (1988) 'Early Greek Land Warfare as Symbolic Expression' *P&P* 119: 3–29.
David, E. (1984) 'The Trial of Spartan Kings' *RIDA* 32: 131–40.
— (1989a) 'Dress in Spartan Society' *AncW* 19: 3–13.
— (1989b) 'Laughter in Spartan Society' in *Classical Sparta:* 1–25.
den Boer, W. (1954) *Laconian Studies*, Amsterdam.
— (1956) 'Political Propaganda in Greek Chronology' *Historia* 5: 162–77.
de Ste. Croix, G.E.M. (1972) *The Origins of the Peloponnesian War*, London.
Ducrey, P. (1986) *Warfare in Ancient Greece*, New York.
Ehrenberg, V. (1960) *The Greek State*, Oxford.
Figueira, T.J. (1984) 'Mess Contributions and Subsistence at Sparta' *TAPhA* 114: 87–109.
— (1986) 'Population Patterns in Late Archaic and Classical Sparta' *TAPhA* 116: 165–213.
Finley, M.I. (1975) 'Sparta' in *The Use and Abuse of History*, London: 161–77 = (1968) in P. Vernant (ed.) *Problèmes de la guerre en Grèce ancienne*, Paris: 143–60.
Fitzhardinge, L.F. (1980) *The Spartans*, London.
Fornara, C.W. (1966) 'Some Aspects of the Career of Pausanias of Sparta' *Historia* 15: 257–71.

— (1967) 'Two Notes on Thucydides' *Philologus* 111: 291–95.
Forrest, W.G. (1963) 'The Date of the Lykourgan Reforms in Sparta' *Phoenix* 17: 157–79.
— (1980) *A History of Sparta*, London, second edition.
Golden, M. (1990) *Children and Childhood in Classical Athens*, Baltimore.
Griffiths, A. (1989) 'Was Kleomenes Mad?' in *Classical Sparta:* 51–78.
Hammond, N.G.L. (1950) 'The Lycurgean Reform at Sparta' *JHS* 70: 42–64.
— (1982) 'The Peloponnese' in *CAH* III.3^2: 321–359.
— (1992) 'Plataea's Relations with Thebes, Sparta and Athens' *JHS* 112: 143–50.
Hansen, O. (1990) 'The Date of the Archaic Dedication of the Lacedaemonians to Olympian Zeus' *Kadmos* 29: 170.
Hodkinson, S. (1983) 'Social Order and the Conflict of Values in Classical Sparta' *Chiron* 13: 239–81.
— (1986) 'Land Tenure and Inheritance in Classical Sparta' *CQ* 36: 378–406.
— (1989) 'Inheritance, Marriage and Demography: Perspectives upon the Success and Decline of Classical Sparta' in *Classical Sparta:* 79–121.
— (1993) 'Warfare, Wealth, and the Crisis of Spartiate Society' in J. Rich and G. Shipley (eds.) *War and Society in the Greek World*, London: 146–76.
Holladay, A.J. (1977) 'Spartan Austerity' *CQ* 27: 111–26.
— (1982) 'Hoplites and Heresies' *JHS* 102: 94–97.
Hooker, J.T. (1980) *The Ancient Spartans*, London.
— (1988) 'The Life and Times of Lycurgus the Lawgiver' *Klio* 70: 340–45.
Huxley, G.L. (1962) *Early Sparta*, London.
Jameson, M.H. (1991) 'Sacrifice Before Battle' in V.D. Hanson (ed.) *Hoplites: The Classical Greek Battle Experience*, London: 197–227.
Jacoby, F. (1944) 'ΧΡΗΣΤΟΥΣ ΠΟΙΕΙΝ (Aristotle fr. 592 R.)' *CQ* 38: 15–16.
Jeffery, L.H. (1988) 'Greece Before the Persian Invasion' in *CAH* IV^2: 347–67.
Jones, A.H.M. (1967) *Sparta*, Oxford.
Kagan, D. (1969) *The Outbreak of the Peloponnesian War*, Ithaca.
Kelly, D. (1978) 'The New Spartan Treaty' *LCM* 3: 133–41.
Kelly, T. (1985) 'The Spartan Scytale' in J.W. Eadie and J. Ober (eds.) *The Craft of the Ancient Historian. Essays in Honor of Chester G. Starr*, Lanham: 141–69.
Larsen, J.A.O. (1932) 'Sparta and the Ionian Revolt: A Study of Spartan Foreign Policy and the Genesis of the Peloponnesian League' *CPh* 27: 136–50.
— (1933) 'The Constitution of the Peloponnesian League' *CPh* 28: 257–76.
— (1934) 'The Constitution of the Peloponnesian League, II' *CPh* 29: 1–19.
Lateiner, D. (1982) 'The Failure of the Ionian Revolt' *Historia* 31: 129–60.
Lazenby, J.F. (1985) *The Spartan Army*, Warminster.
Lewis, D.M. (1977) *Sparta and Persia*, Leiden.
— (1992) 'Mainland Greece, 479–451 B.C.' in *CAH* V^2: 96–120.
MacDowell, D.M. (1986) *Spartan Law*, Edinburgh.
Michell, H. (1952) *Sparta*, Cambridge.
Munro, J.A.R. (1926) 'Marathon' in J.B. Bury, S.A. Cook and F.E. Adcock (eds.) *CAH* IV: *The Persian Empire and the West*: 229–67.
Oliva, P. (1971) *Sparta and Her Social Problems*, Amsterdam.
Parke, H.W. (1945) 'The Deposing of Spartan Kings' *CQ* 39: 106–12.
Parker, R. (1983) *Miasma: Pollution and Purification in Early Greek Religion*, Oxford.
— (1988) 'Were Spartan Kings Heroized?' *LCM* 13.1: 9–10.
— (1989) 'Spartan Religion' in *Classical Sparta:* 142–72.
Parker, V. (1991) 'The Dates of the Messenian Wars' *Chiron* 21: 25–47.
— (1993) 'Some Dates in Early Spartan History' *Klio* 75: 45–60.
Pearson, L. (1962) 'The Pseudo-History of Messenia and its Authors' *Historia* 11: 397–426.

Peek, W. (1974) 'Ein neuer Spartanischer Staatsvertrag' *ASAW, Philos. Hist. Klasse* 65.3: 3–15.

Pritchett, W.K. (1985) *The Greek State at War. Part* IV, Berkeley.

Proietti, G. (1987) *Xenophon's Sparta: An Introduction*, Leiden.

Rawson, E. (1969) *The Spartan Tradition in European Thought*, Oxford.

Redfield, J. (1977–78) 'The Women of Sparta' *CJ* 73: 146–61.

Roisman, J. (1984–86) 'The Image of the Political Exile in Archaic Greece' *AncSoc* 15–17: 23–32.

Ryder, T.T.B. (1965) *Koine Eirene*, Oxford.

Scanlon, T.F. (1988) '*Virgineum Gymnasium*: Spartan Females and Early Greek Athletics' in W.J. Raschke (ed.) *The Archaeology of the Olympics: the Olympics and Other Festivals in Antiquity*, Wisconsin: 185–216.

Snodgrass, A.M. (1964) *Early Greek Armour and Weapons from the End of the Bronze Age to 600 B.C.*, Edinburgh.

— (1965) 'The Hoplite Reform and History' *JHS* 85: 110–22.

— (1967) *Arms and Armour of the Greeks*, London.

Staveley, E.S. (1972) *Greek and Roman Voting and Elections*, London.

Talbert, R.J.A. (1989) 'The Role of the Helots in the Class Struggle at Sparta' *Historia* 38: 22–40.

Thomas, C.G. (1974) 'On the Role of the Spartan Kings' *Historia* 23: 257–70.

Trevett, J. (1990) 'History in [Demosthenes] 59' *CQ* 40: 407–20.

Toynbee, A. (1969) *Some Problems of Greek History*, London.

Tritle, L.A. (1988) 'Kleomenes at Eleusis' *Historia* 37: 457–60.

Usher, S. (1979) '"This to the Fair Critias"' *Eranos* 77: 39–42.

Wade-Gery, H.T. (1958) 'The Spartan Rhetra in Plutarch, *Lycurgus* VI' *Essays in Greek History*, Oxford: 37–85 = *CQ* 38 (1944) 1–9, 115–26.

Walcot, P. (1987) 'Plato's Mother and Other Terrible Women' *G&R* 34: 12–31.

Walker, E.M. (1926) 'Athens: The Reforms of Kleisthenes' in J.B. Bury, S.A. Cook and F.E. Adcock (eds.) *CAH* IV: 137–172.

Wallace, W.P. (1954) 'Kleomenes, Marathon, the Helots, and Arkadia' *JHS* 74: 32–35.

West, S. (1988) 'Archilochus' Message-Stick' *CQ* 38: 42–48.

Westlake, H.D. (1980) 'The *Lysistrata* and the War' *Phoenix* 34: 38–54.

Wheeler, E.L. (1982) '*Hoplomachia* and Greek Dances in Arms' *GRBS* 23: 223–33.

Whitehead, D. (1982/83) 'Sparta and the Thirty Tyrants' *Anc. Soc.* 13/14: 105–130.

— (1990) 'The Lakonian Key' *CQ* 40: 267–68.

Chapter Seven

Austin, M.M. (1990) 'Greek Tyrants and the Persians, 546–479 B.C.' *CQ* 40: 289–306.

Avery, H.C. (1972) 'Herodotus 6.112.2' *TAPhA* 103: 15–22.

— (1973) 'The Number of Persian Dead at Marathon' *Historia* 22: 757.

Armayor, O.K. (1978) 'Herodotus' Catalogues of the Persian Empire in the Light of the Monuments and the Greek Literary Tradition' *TAPhA* 108: 1–9.

Balcer, J.M. (1989) 'The Persian Wars Against Greece: A Reassessment' *Historia* 38: 127–43.

Bengtson, H. et al. (1968) *The Greeks and the Persians: From the Sixth to the Fourth Centuries*, London.

Bicknell, P. (1970) 'The Command Structure and Generals of the Marathon Campaign' *AC* 39: 427–442.

Bonner, C. (1906) 'The Omen in Herodotus VI.107' *CPh* 1: 235–38.

Borgeaud, P. (1988) *The Cult of Pan in Ancient Greece*, tr. K. Atlass and J. Redfield, Chicago.
Bowden, H. (1993) 'Hoplites and Homer: Warfare, Hero Cult, and the Ideology of the Polis' in J. Rich and G. Shipley (eds.) *War and Society in the Greek World*, London: 45–63.
Bradford, A.S. (1992) 'Plataea and the Soothsayer' *AncW* 23: 27–33.
Brown, T.S. (1981) 'Aeneas Tacticus, Herodotus and the Ionian Revolt' *Historia* 30: 385–93.
Brunt, P.A. (1953–54) 'The Hellenic League Against Persia' *Historia* 2: 135–63.
Buck, R.J. (1987) 'Boiotians at Thermopylae' *AHB* 1: 54–60.
Burn, A.R. (1962) *Persia and the Greeks*, with postscript by D.M. Lewis (1984), London.
— (1969) 'Hammond on Marathon: a Few Notes' *JHS* 89: 118–20.
Burstein, S.M. (1971) 'The Recall of the Ostracized and the Themistocles Decree' *ClAnt* 4: 94–110.
Bury, J.B. (1896) 'Aristides at Salamis' *CR* 10: 414–18.
Camp, J.M. (1986) *The Athenian Agora: Excavations in the Heart of Classical Athens*, London.
Caspari, M.O.B. (1915) 'The Ionian Confederacy' *JHS* 35: 173–88.
Castriota, D. (1992) *Myth, Ethos and Actuality: Official Art in Fifth-Century B.C. Athens*, Wisconsin.
Chambers, M. (1961–62) 'The Authenticity of the Themistocles Decree' *AHR* 67: 306–16.
— (1967) 'The Significance of the Themistocles Decree' *Philologus* 111: 157–67.
Chapman, G.A.H. (1972) 'Herodotus and Histiaeus' Role in the Ionian Revolt' *Historia* 21: 546–68.
Clairmont, C.W. (1983) *Patrios Nomos: Public Burial in Athens During the Fifth and Fourth Centuries B.C. Parts* I–II, Oxford.
Connor, W.R. (1993) 'The Ionian Era of Athenian Civic Identity' *PAPhS* 194–206.
Detienne M. and Vernant, J.-P. (1978) *Cunning Intelligence in Greek Culture and Society*, tr. J. Lloyd, Sussex.
Dodds, E. R. (1959) *The Greeks and the Irrational*, Berkeley.
Dow, S. (1962) 'The Purported Decree of Themistokles: Stele and Inscription' *AJA* 66: 353–68.
Evans, J.A.S. (1963) 'Histiaeus and Aristagoras: Notes on the Ionian Revolt' *AJPh* 84: 113–28.
— (1976) 'Herodotus and the Ionian Revolt' *Historia* 25: 31–37.
— (1982) 'The Oracle of the "Wooden Wall"' *CJ* 78: 24–29.
— (1984) 'Herodotus and Marathon' *Florilegium* 6: 1–27.
— (1988) 'The "Wooden Wall" Again' *AHB* 2: 25–30.
— (1993) 'Herodotus and the Battle of Marathon' *Historia* 42: 279–307.
Fornara, C.W. (1966) 'The Hoplite Achivement at Psyttaleia' *JHS* 86: 51–54.
— (1971) *The Athenian Board of Generals from 501 to 404, Historia* Einzelschrift 16, Wiesbaden.
Forrest, W.G. (1984) 'Herodotus and Athens' *Phoenix* 38: 1–11.
Francis, E.D. and Vickers, M. (1985) 'The Oenoe Painting in the Stoa Poikile, and Herodotus' Account of Marathon' *ABSA* 80: 99–113.
Frost, F.J. (1973) 'A Note on Xerxes at Salamis' *Historia* 22: 118–19.
— (1980) *Plutarch's Themistokles: A Historical Commentary*, Princeton.
Garland, R.S.J. (1985) *The Greek Way of Death*, London.
— (1992) *Introducing New Gods*, London.
Gillis, D. (1969) 'Marathon and the Alkmeonids' *GRBS* 10: 133–45.
Georges, P.B. (1986) 'Saving Herodotus' Phenomena: The Oracles and Events of 480 B.C.' *ClAnt* 5: 14–59.

Goldhill, S. (1988) 'Battle Narrative and Politics in Aeschylus' *Persai*' *JHS* 108: 189–93.

Gomme, A.W. (1952) 'Herodotos and Marathon' *Phoenix* 6: 77–83.

Graf, D.F. (1984) 'Medism: The Origin and Significance of the Term' *JHS* 104: 15–30.

Grant, J.R. (1961) 'Leonidas' Last Stand' *Phoenix* 15: 14–27.

Green, P. (1970) *The Year of Salamis, 480–479 BC*, London.

Hall, E. (1993) 'Asia Unmanned: Images of Victory in Classical Athens' in J. Rich and G. Shipley (eds.) *War and Society in the Greek World*, London: 108–33.

Hammond, N.G.L. (1968) 'The Campaign and the Battle of Marathon' *JHS* 88: 13–57.

— (1982) 'The Narrative of Herodotus VII and the Decree of Themistocles at Troezen' *JHS* 102: 75–93.

— (1986) 'The Manning of the Fleet in the Decree of Themistokles' *Phoenix* 40: 143–48.

— (1988) 'The Expedition of Datis and Artaphernes' in *CAH* IV^2: 491–517.

Harrison, E.B. (1972) 'The South Frieze of the Nike Temple and the Marathon Painting in the Painted Stoa' *AJA* 76: 353–78.

Herington, C.J. (1967) 'Aeschylus in Sicily' *JHS* 87: 74–85.

Hignett, C. (1963) *Xerxes' Invasion of Greece*, Oxford.

Hillard, T.W. (1991) 'Persians in the *Persae*' *Ancient History* 21: 132–51.

Hodge, A.T. and Losada, L.A. (1970) 'The Time of the Shield Signal at Marathon' *AJA* 74: 31–36.

Hodge, A.T. (1975a) 'Marathon: The Persians' Voyage' *TAPhA* 105: 155–73.

— (1975b) 'Marathon to Phaleron' *JHS* 95: 169–71.

Holladay, A.J. and Goodman, M.D. (1986) 'Religious Scruples in Ancient Warfare' *CQ* 36: 151–71.

Hudson, H.G. (1936–37) 'The Shield Signal at Marathon' *AHR* 12: 443–59.

Hughes, D.D. (1991) *Human Sacrifice in Ancient Greece*, London.

Jameson, M.H. (1960) 'A Decree of Themistokles from Troizen' *Hesperia* 29: 198–223.

— (1962) 'A Revised Text of the Decree of Themistokles from Troizen' *Hesperia* 31: 310–315.

— (1963) 'The Provisions for Mobilization in the Decree of Themistokles' *Historia* 12: 384–404.

— (1991) 'Sacrifice Before Battle' in V.D. Hanson (ed.) *Hoplites: The Classical Greek Battle Experience*, London: 197–227.

Isserlin, B.S.J. (1991) 'The Canal of Xerxes: Facts and Problems' *ABSA* 86: 83–91.

Jordan, B. (1979) *Servants of the Gods: A Study in the Religion, History and Literature of Fifth-Century Athens*, Göttingen.

— (1988) 'The Honors for Themistocles After Salamis' *AJPh* 109: 547–71.

Keaveney, A. (1988) 'The Attack on Naxos: A 'Forgotten Cause' of the Ionian Revolt' *CQ* 38: 76–81.

Knight, D.W. (1970) *Some Studies in Athenian Politics in the Fifth Century B.C.*, *Historia* Einzelschrift 13, Wiesbaden.

Lang, M.L. (1968) 'Herodotus and the Ionian Revolt' *Historia* 17: 24–36.

Lateiner, D. (1982) 'The Failure of the Ionian Revolt' *Historia* 31: 129–60.

— (1974) 'Again the Marathon Epigram' in D.W. Bradeen and M.F. McGregor (eds.) *ΦΟΡΟΣ: Tribute to B.D. Meritt*, Locust Valley: 80.

Larsen, J.A.O. (1932) 'Sparta and the Ionian Revolt: A Study of Spartan Foreign Policy and the Genesis of the Peloponnesian League' *CPh* 27: 136–50.

— (1944) 'Federation for Peace in Ancient Greece' *CPh* 39: 145–62.

— (1955) *Representative Government in Greek and Roman History*, Berkeley.

Lenardon, R.J. (1978) *The Saga of Themistocles*, London.

Lewis, D.M. (1980) 'Datis the Mede' *JHS* 100: 194–95.

— (1985) 'Persians in Herodotus' in *The Greek Historians: Literature and History. Papers Presented to A.E. Raubitschek*, Stanford: 101–17.
Lloyd-Jones, H. (1976) 'The Delphic Oracle' *G&R* 23: 60–73.
Loraux, N. (1986) *The Invention of Athens: The Funeral Oration in the Classical City*, Cambridge, Mass.
Manville, P.B. (1977) 'Aristagoras and Histiaios' *CQ* 27: 80–91.
Mattingly, H.B. (1981) 'The Themistokles Decree from Troizen: Transmission and Status' in *Classical Contributions*: 79–87.
Mitchell, B.M. (1975) 'Herodotus and Samos' *JHS* 95: 75–91.
Mosley, D.J. (1973) *Envoys and Diplomacy*, Weisbaden.
Murray, O. (1988) 'The Ionian Revolt' in *CAH* IV^2: 461–90.
Notopoulos, J.A. (1941) 'The Slaves at the Battle of Marathon' *AJPh* 62: 352–54.
Nyland, R. (1992) 'Herodotos' Sources For the Plataiai Campaign' *AC* 61: 80–97.
Parker, R. (1989) 'Spartan Religion' in *Classical Sparta:* 142–72.
Pemberton, E.G. (1972) 'The East and West Friezes of the Temple of Athena Nike' *AJA* 76: 303–10.
Podlecki, A.J. (1968) 'Simonides: 480' *Historia* 17: 257–75.
Pritchett, W.K. (1962) 'Herodotos and the Themistokles Decree' *AJA* 66: 43–47.
— (1974) *The Greek State at War. Part* II, Berkeley.
— (1979) *The Greek State at War. Part* III: *Religion*, Berkeley.
— (1985) *The Greek State at War. Part* IV, Berkeley.
Raubitschek, A.E. (1940) 'Two Monuments Erected after the Victory of Marathon' *AJA* 44: 53–59.
— (1960) 'The Covenant of Plataea' *TAPhA* 91: 178–83.
Robertson, N. (1976) 'The Thessalian Expedition of 480 BC' *JHS* 96: 100–120.
— (1982) 'The Decree of Themistocles in its Contemporary Setting' *Phoenix* 36: 1–44.
— (1987) 'The True Meaning of the "Wooden Wall"' *CPh* 82: 1–20.
Roebuck, C. (1955) 'The Early Ionian League' *CPh* 50: 26–40.
Rosenbloom, D. (1993) 'Shouting "Fire" in a Crowded Theatre: Phrynichos's *Capture of Miletos* and the Politics of Fear in Early Attic Tragedy' *Philologus* 137: 159–96.
Rosivach, V.J. (1987) 'Execution by Stoning in Athens' *ClAnt* 6: 232–48.
Sacks, K.S. (1976) 'Herodotus and the Dating of the Battle of Thermopylai' *CQ* 26: 232–48.
Sargent, R.L. (1927) 'The Use of Slaves by the Athenians in Warfare' *CPh* 22: 201–12, 264–79.
Schreiner, J.H. (1970) 'The Battles of 490 BC' *PCPhS* 16: 97–112.
Sealey, R. (1972) 'Again the Siege of the Acropolis' *ClAnt* 5: 183–94.
Shapiro, H.A. (1990) 'Oracle-Mongers in Peisistratid Athens' *Kernos* 3: 335–45.
Shipley, G. (1987) *A History of Samos 800–188 BC*, Oxford.
Simpson, R.H. (1972) 'Leonidas' Decision' *Phoenix* 26: 1–11.
Shrimpton, G. (1980) 'The Persian Cavalry at Marathon' *Phoenix* 34: 20–37.
Thompson, H.A. (1976) *The Athenian Agora*, Athens, third edition.
Tronson, A. (1991) 'The Hellenic League of 480 BC — Fact or Ideological Fiction?' *AClass* 34: 93–110.
Vanderpool, E. (1966) 'A Monument to the Battle of Marathon' *Hesperia* 35: 93–106.
van der Veer, J.A.G. (1982) 'The Battle of Marathon: A Topographical Survey' *Mnemosyne* 35: 290–321.
Vidal-Nacquet, P. (1986) *The Black Hunter: Forms of Thought and Forms of Society in the Greek World*, tr. A. Szegedy-Maszak, Baltimore.
Wade-Gery, H.T. (1933) 'Classical Epigrams and Epitaphs' *JHS* 53: 71–104.
Wallace, P.W. (1969) 'Psyttaleia and the Trophies of the Battle of Salamis' *AJA* 73: 293–303.

Walters, K.R. (1981a) 'Four Hundred Athenian Ships at Salamis?' *RhM* 124: 199–203.
— (1981b) '"We Fought Alone at Marathon": Historical Falsification in the Attic Funeral Oration' *RhM* 124: 204–11.
Wardman, A.E. (1959) 'Tactics and the Tradition of the Persian Wars' *Historia* 8: 49–60.
Waters, K.H. (1970) 'Herodotus and the Ionian Revolt' *Historia* 19: 504–08.
Wéry, L. (1966) 'Le meurtre des hérauts de Darius en 491 et l'inviolabilité du héraut' *AC* 35: 468–86.
West, S. (1991) 'Herodotus' Portrait of Hecataeus' *JHS* 111: 144–60.
West, W.C. (1969) 'The Trophies of the Persian Wars' *CPh* 64: 7–19.
— (1970) 'Saviors of Greece' *GRBS* 11: 271–82.
Wycherley, R.E. (1957) *The Athenian Agora* III: *Literary and Epigraphical Testimonia*, Princeton.

Chapters Eight and Nine

Adkins, A.W.H. (1960) *Merit and Responsibility. A Study in Greek Values*, Oxford.
Adshead, K. (1986) *Politics of the Archaic Peloponnese*, Hampshire.
Allison, J.W. (1983) 'Pericles' Policy and the Plague' *Historia* 32: 14–23.
Anderson, J. K. (1965) 'Cleon's Orders at Amphipolis' *JHS* 85: 1–4.
— (1974) *Xenophon*, London.
Andrewes, A. (1959) 'Thucydides on the Causes of the War' *CQ* 9: 223–39.
— (1962) 'The Mytilene Debate: Thucydides 3.36–49' *Phoenix* 16: 64–85.
— (1978) 'The Opposition to Perikles' *JHS* 98: 1–8.
— (1992) 'The Peace of Nikias and the Sicilian Expedition' in *CAH* V^2: 433–63.
Armstrong, A.H. (1949) *An Introduction to Ancient Philosophy*, London, second edition.
Asheri, D. (1969) 'Note on the Site of Brea: Theopompus, F 145' *AJPh* 90: 337–40.
Badian, E. (1987) 'The Peace of Kallias' *JHS* 107: 1–39.
— (1988) 'Towards a Chronology of the Pentekontaetia Down to the Renewal of the Peace of Callias' *EMC* 7: 289–310.
— (1990) 'Athens, the Locrians and Naupactus' *CQ* 40: 364–69.
Balcer, J.M. (1974) 'Separatism and Anti-Separatism in the Athenian Empire (478–433 B.C.)' *Historia* 23: 21–39.
— (1978) *The Athenian Regulations for Chalkis: Studies in Athenian Imperial Law*, *Historia* Einzelschrift 33, Wiesbaden.
Barron, J.P. (1964) 'Religious Propaganda of the Delian League' *JHS* 84: 35–48.
Bauer, A. and Frost, F.J. (1967) *Themistokles: Literary, Epigraphical and Archaeological Testimonia*, Chicago, second edition.
Bauman, R.A. (1990) *Political Trials in Ancient Greece*, London.
Bauslaugh, R.A. (1990) 'Messenian Dialect and Dedications of the "Methanioi"' *Hesperia* 59: 661–68.
Bicknell, P.J. (1974) 'Athenian Politics and Genealogy: Some Pendants' *Historia* 23: 146–63.
Bloedow, E.F. (1987) 'Pericles' Powers in the Counter-Strategy of 431' *Historia* 36: 9–27.
— (1990) '"Not the Son of Achilles, but Achilles Himself": Alcibiades' Entry on the Political Stage at Athens II' *Historia* 39: 1–19.
— (1992a) 'The Peaces of Kallias' *SO* 67: 41–68.
— (1992b) 'Alcibiades 'Brilliant' or 'Intelligent'?' *Historia* 41: 139–57.
Blum, A.F. (1978) *Socrates: the Original and its Images*, London.
Boersma, J.S. (1970) *Athenian Building Policy from 561/0–405/4 B.C.*, Groningen.

Bosworth, A.B. (1990) 'Plutarch, Callisthenes and the Peace of Callias' *JHS* 110: 1–13.
Bowra, C.M. (1971) *Periclean Athens*, London.
Bradeen, D.W. (1960) 'The Popularity of the Athenian Empire' *Historia* 9: 257–69.
Brickhouse T.C. and Smith, N.D. (1989) *Socrates on Trial*, Princeton.
— (1992) 'The Formal Charges against Socrates' in H.H. Benson (ed.) *Essays on the Philosophy of Socrates*, Oxford: 14–34.
Bridges, A.P. (1980) 'The Athenian Treaty with Samos, ML 56' *JHS* 100: 185–88.
Brunt, P.A. (1953–54) 'The Hellenic League Against Persia' *Historia* 2: 135–63.
— (1966) 'Athenian Settlements Abroad in the Fifth Century B.C.' in E. Badian (ed.) *Ancient Society and Institutions: Studies Presented to V. Ehrenberg*, Oxford: 71–92.
Buck, R.J. (1970) 'The Athenian Domination of Boeotia' *CPh* 65: 217–27.
— (1988) 'The Sicilian Expedition' *AHB* 2: 73–79.
Bugh, G.R. (1988) *The Horsemen of Athens*, Princeton.
Burke, E.M. (1992) 'The Economy of Athens in the Classical Era: Some Adjustments to the Primitivist Model' *TAPhA* 122: 199–226.
Cairns, F. (1982) 'Cleon and Pericles: A Suggestion' *JHS* 102: 203–04.
Camp, J.M. (1986) *The Athenian Agora: Excavations in the Heart of Classical Athens*, London.
Carawan, E.M. (1985) 'Apophasis and Eisangelia: the Role of the Areopagus in Athenian Political Trials' *GRBS* 26: 115–39.
— (1987) 'Eisangelia and Euthyna: the Trials of Miltiades, Themistocles and Cimon' *GRBS* 28: 167–208.
— (1990) 'The Five Talents Cleon Coughed up (schol. Ar. *Ach.* 6)' *CQ* 40: 137–47.
Cargill, J. (1981) *The Second Athenian League*, Berkeley.
Carter, L.B. (1986) *The Quiet Athenian*, Oxford.
Cartledge, P. (1979) *Sparta and Lakonia: A Regional History 1300–362 BC*, London.
Castriota, D. (1992) *Myth, Ethos and Actuality: Official Art in Fifth-Century B.C. Athens*, Wisconsin.
Cawkwell, G.L. (1970) 'The Fall of Themistokles' in B.F. Harris (ed.) *Auckland Classical Essays Presented to E.M. Blaiklock*, Auckland: 39–58.
— (1981) 'Notes on the Failure of the Second Athenian Confederacy' *JHS* 101: 40–55.
— (1988) 'Nomophulakia and the Areopagus' *JHS* 108: 1–12.
Chambers, M. (1992) 'Photographic Enhancement and a Greek Inscription' *CJ* 88: 25–31.
— (1993) 'The Archon's Name in the Athens-Egesta Alliance (*IG* I^3 11)' *ZPE* 98: 171–74.
—, Gallucci, R. and Spanos, P. (1990) 'Athens' Alliance with Egesta' *ZPE* 83: 38–63.
Christ, M.R. (1990) 'Liturgy Avoidance and *Antidosis* in Classical Athens' *TAPhA* 120: 147–69.
Christensen, J. & Hansen, M.H. (1983) 'What is *Syllogos* at Thukydides 2.22.1?' *C&M* 34: 17–31.
— (1989) 'What is *Syllogos* at Thukydides 2.22.1? Addenda' in M.H. Hansen *The Athenian Ecclesia II. A Collection of Articles 1983–89*, Copenhagen: 210–11.
Cohen, E.E. (1973) *Ancient Athenian Maritime Courts*, Princeton.
Connor, W.R. (1968) *Theopompos and Fifth Century Athens*, Washington.
— (1971) *The New Politicians of Fifth-Century Athens*, Princeton.
— (1984) *Thucydides*, Princeton.
Cornford, F.M. (1907) *Thucydides Mythistoricus*, London.
Crane, G. (1992) 'The Fear and Pursuit of Risk: Corinth on Athens, Sparta and the Peloponnesians (Thucydides 1.68–71, 120–121)' *TAPhA* 122: 227–56.
Culham, P. (1978) 'The Delian League: Bicameral or Unicameral?' *AJAH* 3: 27–31.
Daniel, J. and Polansky, R. (1979) 'The Tale of the Delphic Oracle in Plato's Apology' *AncW* 2: 83–85.

Davison, J.A. (1953) 'Protagoras, Democritus, and Anaxagoras' *CQ* 3: 33–45.
— (1966) 'Aeschylus and Athenian Politics, 472–456 B.C.' in E. Badian (ed.) *Ancient Society and Institutions: Studies Presented to V. Ehrenberg*, Oxford: 93–107.
de Romilly, J. (1963) *Thucydides and Athenian Imperialism*, tr. P. Thody, Oxford.
— (1992) *The Great Sophists in Periclean Athens*, tr. J. Lloyd, Oxford.
de Ste. Croix, G.E.M. (1954–55) 'The Character of the Athenian Empire' *Historia* 3: 1–41.
— (1956) 'The Constitution of the Five Thousand' *Historia* 5: 1–23.
— (1961) 'Notes on Jurisdiction in the Athenian Empire' *CQ* 55: 94–112, 268–80.
— (1972) *The Origins of the Peloponnesian War*, London.
Detienne M. and Vernant, J.-P. (1978) *Cunning Intelligence in Greek Culture and Society*, tr. J. Lloyd, Sussex.
Dorey, T.A. (1956) 'Aristophanes and Cleon' *G&R* 3: 132–39.
Dover, K.J. (1971) 'Socrates in the Clouds' in G. Vlastos (ed.) *The Philosophy of Socrates: A Collection of Critical Essays*, New York: 50–77.
Due, B. (1987) 'Lysander in Xenophon's Hellenica' *C&M* 38: 53–62.
Edmunds, L. (1975) *Chance and Intelligence in Thucydides*, Cambridge, Massachusetts.
Ehrenberg, V. (1948) 'The Foundation of Thurii' *AJPh* 69: 149–70.
— (1952) 'Thucydides on Athenian Colonization' *CPh* 47: 143–49.
Ellis, W.M. (1989) *Alcibiades*, London.
Evans, J.A.S. (1976) 'The Settlement of Artaphrenes' *CPh* 71: 344–48.
Ferguson, J. (1970) *Socrates: a Source Book*, London.
Figueira, T. J. (1991) *Athens and Aigina in the Age of Imperial Colonization*, Baltimore.
Finley, M.I. (1965) 'Trade and Politics in the Ancient World' in *Second International Congress of Economic History* I, Paris: 11–35.
— (1974) 'Athenian Demagogues' in M.I. Finley (ed.) *Studies in Ancient Society*, London: 1–25.
— (1977) *Aspects of Antiquity: Discoveries and Controversies*, Harmondsworth, second edition.
Flower, H.I. (1992) 'Thucydides and the Pylos Debate (4.27–29)' *Historia* 41: 40–57.
Forde, S. (1989) *The Ambition to Rule: Alcibiades and the Politics of Imperialism in Thucydides*, Ithaca.
Fornara, C.W. (1971) *The Athenian Board of Generals from 501 to 404, Historia* Einzelschrift 16, Wiesbaden.
— (1977) *Archaic Times to the End of the Peloponnesian War*, Baltimore.
— (1979) 'On the Chronology of the Samian War' *JHS* 99: 7–19.
Forrest, W.G. (1960) 'Themistokles and Argos' *CQ* 10: 221–41.
French, A. (1979) 'Athenian Ambitions and the Delian Alliance' *Phoenix* 33: 134–41.
— (1988) 'The Guidelines of the Delian Alliance' *Antichthon* 22: 12–25.
Frost, F.J. (1968) 'Themistocles' Place in Athenian Politics' *ClAnt* 1: 105–24.
— (1980) *Plutarch's Themistocles: A Historical Commentary*, Princeton.
Garland, R.S.J. (1987) *The Piraeus: From the Fifth to the First Century B.C.*, London.
Gomme, A.W. (1962) 'Thucydides and Kleon' *More Essays in Greek History and Literature*, Oxford: 112–21.
Gray, V.J. (1989) 'Xenophon's *Defence of Socrates*: The Rhetorical Background to the Socratic Problem' *CQ* 39: 136–40.
Green, P. (1989) *Classical Bearings: Interpreting Ancient History and Culture*, London.
Guthrie, W.K.C. (1967) *The Greek Philosophers from Thales to Aristotle*, London.
— (1971a) *Socrates*, Cambridge = (1969) *A History of Greek Philosophy* III: *The Fifth Century Enlightenment*, Cambridge: 323–507.

– (1971b) *The Sophists*, Cambridge = (1969) *A History of Greek Philosophy* III: *The Fifth Century Enlightenment*, Cambridge: 3–319.

Hall, L.G.H. (1990) 'Ephialtes, the Areopagus and the Thirty' *CQ* 40: 319–28.

Hamilton, C.D. (1979) 'On the Perils of Extraordinary Honors: the Case of Lysander and Conon' *AncW* 2: 87–90.

Hammond, N.G.L. (1955) 'Studies in Greek Chronology of the Sixth and Fifth Centuries B.C.' *Historia* 4: 371–411.

– (1967) 'The Origins and the Nature of the Athenian Alliance of 478/7 B.C.' *JHS* 87: 41–61.

Hansen, M.H. (1975) *Eisangelia: the Sovereignty of the People's Court in Athens in the Fourth Century BC and the Impeachment of Generals and Politicians*, Odense University Classical Studies 6, Odense.

– (1987) *The Athenian Assembly in the Age of Demosthenes*, Oxford.

– (1991) *The Athenian Democracy in the Age of Demosthenes: Structure, Principles and Ideology*, Oxford.

Harding, P. (1988) 'King Pausanias and the Restoration of Democracy at Athens' *Hermes* 116: 186–93.

Harris, E.M. (1993) 'The Constitution of the Five Thousand' *HSPh* 93: 243–80.

Henry, A. S. (1978) 'The Dating of Fifth-Century Attic Inscriptions' *ClAnt* 11: 75–108.

– (1992) 'Through a Laser Beam Darkly: Space-age Technology and the Egesta Decree (*IG* I^3 11)' *ZPE* 91: 137–45.

– (1993) 'Athens and Egesta (*IG* I^3 11)' *AHB* 7: 49–53.

Herman, G. (1990) 'Treaties and Alliances in the World of Thucydides' *PCPhS* 36: 83–102.

Higgins, W.E. (1977) *Xenophon the Athenian: the Problem of the Individual and the Society of the Polis*, Albany.

Holladay, A.J. (1977) 'Sparta's Role in the First Peloponnesian War' *JHS* 97: 54–63.

– (1985) 'Sparta and the First Peloponnesian War' *JHS* 105: 161–62.

– (1986) 'The Détente of Kallias?' *Historia* 35: 503–07.

– (1989) 'The Hellenic Disaster in Egypt' *JHS*: 176–82.

Hornblower, S. (1987) *Thucydides*, Baltimore.

– (1991a) *The Greek World 479–323 BC*, London, second edition.

– (1992) 'The Religious Dimension to the Peloponnesian War, or, What Thucydides does not tell us' *HSPh* 94: 169–97.

Hunter, V.J. (1973) *Thucydides the Artful Reporter*, Toronto.

Hussey, E. (1985) 'Thucydidean History' in *Crux*: 118–38.

Immerwahr, H.R. (1973) 'Pathology of Power and the Speches in Thucydides' in P.A. Stadter (ed.) *The Speeches in Thucydides*, Chapel Hill: 16–31.

Irwin, T.H. (1985–86) 'Socratic Inquiry and Politics' *Ethics* 96: 400–15.

Jackson, A.H. (1969) 'The Original Purpose of the Delian League' *Historia* 18: 12–16.

Jacobsen, H. (1975) 'The Oath of the Delian League' *Philologus* 119: 256–58.

Jones, L.A. (1987) 'The Role of Ephialtes in the Rise of Athenian Democracy' *ClAnt* 6: 53–76.

Jordan, B. (1986) 'Religion in Thucydides' *TAPhA* 116: 119–47.

Kagan, D. (1969) *The Outbreak of the Peloponnesian War*, Ithaca.

– (1974) *The Archidamian War*, Cornell.

– (1981) *The Peace of Nicias and the Sicilian Expedition*, Cornell.

– (1987) *The Fall of the Athenian Empire*, Cornell.

– (1991) *Pericles of Athens and the Birth of Democracy*, New York.

Kallet-Marx, L. (1989a) 'The Kallias Decree, Thucydides, and the Outbreak of the Peloponnesian War' *CQ* 39: 94–113.

– (1989b) 'Did Tribute Fund the Parthenon?' *ClAnt* 8: 252–66.

Kearns, E. (1989) *The Heroes of Attica*, *BICS* Suppl. 57, London.

Kirk, G.S. and Raven, J.E. (1960) *The Presocratic Philosophers: A Critical History with a Selection of Texts*, Cambridge.
Kraut, R. (1984) *Socrates and the State*, Princeton.
Krentz, P. (1982) *The Thirty at Athens*, Ithaca.
— (1984) 'The Ostracism of Thoukydides, son of Melesias' *Historia* 33: 499–504.
— (1993) 'Athens' Allies and the Phallophoria' *AHB* 7: 12–16.
Lactor[3]: Hornblower, S. & Greenstock, M.C. (1984) *The Athenian Empire: Sources Translated from Index III of Hill's Sources for Greek History*, London.
Lang, M.L. (1990) 'Illegal Execution in Ancient Athens' *PAPhS* 134: 24–29.
Lateiner, D. (1977) 'Heralds and Corpses in Thucydides' *CW* 71: 97–106.
Lenardon, R.J. (1956) 'The Archonship of Themistokles, 493/2' *Historia* 5: 401–19.
— (1959) 'The Chronology of Themistokles' Ostracism and Exile' *Historia* 8: 23–48.
— (1961) 'Charon, Thucydides, and "Themistokles"' *Phoenix* 15: 28–40.
— (1978) *The Saga of Themistocles*, London.
— (1981) 'Thucydides and Hellanikos' in *Classical Contributions:* 59–70.
Lewis, D.M. (1961) 'Double Representation in the Strategia' *JHS* 81: 118–23.
— (1966) 'After the Profanation of the Mysteries' in E. Badian (ed.) *Ancient Society and Institutions: Studies Presented to V. Ehrenberg*, Oxford: 177–91.
— (1977) *Sparta and Persia*, Leiden.
— (1981) 'The Origins of the First Peloponnesian War' in *Classical Contributions:* 71–78.
— (1989) 'Persian Gold in Greek International Relations' *REA* 91.1–2: 227–235.
— (1992) 'Mainland Greece, 479–451 B.C.' in *CAH* V[2]: 96–120.
Libourel, J.M. (1971) 'The Athenian Disaster in Egypt' *AJPh* 92: 605–15.
Lintott, A. (1982) *Violence, Civil Strife and Revolution in the Classical City, 750–330 BC*, London.
Loening, T.C. (1987) *The* Reconciliation *Agreement of 403/402 B.C. in Athens, Historia* Einzelschrift 53, Stuttgart.
Loomis, W.T. (1990) 'Pausanias, Byzantion and the Formation of the Delian League: A Chronological Note' *Historia* 39: 487–92.
— (1992) *The Spartan War Fund. IG V 1, 1 and a New Fragment* (*Historia* Einzelschrift 74), Stuttgart.
MacDonald, B.R. (1983) 'The Megarian Decree' *Historia* 32: 385–410.
MacDowell, D.M. (1962) *Andokides: On the Mysteries*, Oxford.
Macleod, C.W. (1978) 'Reason and Necessity: Thucydides III.9–14, 37–48' *JHS* 98: 64–78.
Mansfeld, J. (1979) 'The Chronology of Anaxagoras' Athenian Period and the Date of his Trial, I' *Mnemosyne* 32: 39–69.
— (1980) 'The Chronology of Anaxagoras' Athenian Period and the Date of his Trial, II' *Mnemosyne* 33: 17–95.
Marinatos, J. (1981) 'Thucydides and Oracles' *JHS* 101: 138–40.
Marr, J.L. (1993) 'Ephialtes the Moderate?' *G&R* 40: 11–19.
Marshall, F.H. (1905) *The Second Athenian Confederacy*, Cambridge.
Marshall, M.H.B. (1984) 'Cleon and Pericles: Sphacteria' *G&R* 31: 19–36.
Marshall, M. (1990) 'Pericles and the Plague' in E.M. Craik (ed.) *'Owls to Athens': Essays on Classical Subjects Presented to Sir Kenneth Dover*, Oxford: 163–70.
Mattingly, H.B. (1961a) 'Athens and Euboea' *JHS* 81: 124–32.
— (1961b) 'The Athenian Coinage Decree' *Historia* 10: 148–88.
— (1963) 'The Growth of Athenian Imperialism' *Historia* 12: 257–73.
— (1964) 'The Financial Decrees of Kallias (*IG* I[2] 91/2)' *PACA* 7: 35–55.
— (1966a) 'Periclean Imperialism' in E. Badian (ed.) *Ancient Society and Institutions: Studies Presented to V. Ehrenberg*, Oxford: 193–223.
— (1966b) 'Athenian Imperialism and the Foundation of Brea' *CQ* 16: 172–92.
— (1968) 'Athenian Finance in the Peloponnesian War' *BCH* 92: 450–85.

— (1970) '"Epigraphically the Twenties are too Late ..."' *ABSA* 65: 124–49.
— (1971) 'Facts and Artifacts: the Researcher and his Tools' *Leeds University Review* 14: 277–97.
— (1975) 'The Mysterious 3000 Talents of the First Kallias Decree' *GRBS* 16: 15–22.
— (1976) 'Three Attic Decrees' *Historia* 25: 38–44.
— (1981a) 'The Athenian Decree for Miletos (*IG* I^2, 22 + = *ATL* II, D 11): A Postscript' *Historia* 30: 113–17.
— (1981b) 'Coins and Amphoras — Chios, Samos and Thasos in the Fifth Century B.C' *JHS* 101: 78–86.
— (1984a) 'The Tribute Districts of the Athenian Empire' *Historia* 33: 498–99.
— (1984b) 'Review Article: D. Lewis, Editor. *Inscriptiones Graecae* I^3' *AJPh* 105: 340–57.
— (1986) 'The Alliance of Athens with Egesta' *Chiron* 16: 167–70.
— (1987) 'The Athenian Coinage Decree and the Assertion of Empire' in I. Carradice (ed.) *Coinage and Administration in the Athenian and Persian Empires*, Oxford: 65–71.
— (1992) 'Epigraphy and the Athenian Empire' *Historia* 41: 129–38.
— (1993) 'New Light on the Athenian Standards Decree (ATL II, D 14)' *Klio* 75: 99–102.
McGregor, M.F. (1987) *The Athenians and their Empire*, Vancouver.
McNeal, R.A. (1970) 'Historical Methods and Thucydides I.103.1' *Historia* 19: 306–25.
Meiggs, R. (1963) 'The Crisis of Athenian Imperialism' *HSPh* 67: 1–36.
— (1966) 'The Dating of Fifth-Century Attic Inscriptions' *JHS* 86: 86–98.
— (1972) *The Athenian Empire*, Oxford.
Meritt, B.D. (1984) 'The Samian Revolt from Athens in 440–439 B.C.' *PAPhS* 128: 123–33.
Mikalson, J.D. (1984) 'Religion and the Plague in Athens, 431–423 B.C.' in K.J. Rigsby (ed.) *Studies Presented to Sterling Dow*, *GRBS* Mono. 10: 217–25.
Milton, M.P. (1979) 'The Date of Thucydides' Synchronism of the Siege of Naxos with Themistokles' Flight' *Historia* 28: 257–75.
Missiou-Ladi, A. (1987) 'Coercive Diplomacy in Greek Interstate Relations' *CQ* 37: 336–45.
Mitchell, B. (1991) 'Kleon's Amphipolitan Campaign: Aims and Results' *Historia* 40: 170–92.
Momigliano, A. (1978) 'Freedom of Speech and Religious Tolerance in the Ancient World' in S.C. Humphreys (ed.) *Anthropology and the Greeks*, London: 179–93.
Montuori, M. (1981) *Socrates: Physiology of a Myth*, Amsterdam.
— (1990) 'The Oracle Given to Chaerephon on the Wisdom of Socrates. An Invention by Plato' *Kernos* 3: 251–59.
Morens, D.M. and Littman, R.J. (1992) 'Epidemiology of the Plague of Athens' *TAPhA* 122: 271–304.
Morgan, M.L. (1992) 'Plato and Greek Religion' in R. Kraut (ed.) *The Cambridge Companion to Plato*, Cambridge: 227–47.
Most, G.W. (1993) '"A Cock for Asclepius"' *CQ* 43: 96–111.
Nichols, M.P. (1987) *Socrates and the Political Community*, New York.
Nussbaum, M. (1980) 'Aristophanes and Socrates on Learning Practical Wisdom' in J. Henderson (ed.) *Aristophanes: Essays in Interpretation*, *YClS* 26: 43–97.
O'Brien, D. (1968) 'The Relation of Anaxagoras and Empedocles' *JHS* 88: 93–113.
O'Neil, J.L. (1981) 'The Exile of Themistokles and Democracy in the Peloponnese' *CQ* 31: 335–46.
Oost, S.I. 'Thucydides and the Irrational: Sundry Passages' *CPh* 70: 186–96.
Osborne, M. (1981–82) *Naturalization in Athens* I–II, Brussels.
Osborne, R. (1985) 'The Erection and Mutilation of the Hermai' *PCPhS* 31: 47–73.

Ostwald, M. (1979) 'Diodotus, Son of Eucrates' *GRBS* 20: 5–13.
— (1982) *Autonomia: Its Genesis and Early History*, USA.
Page, D.L. (1953) 'Thucydides' Description of the Great Plague at Athens' *CQ* 3: 97–119.
Parker, R. (1983) *Miasma: Pollution and Purification in Early Greek Religion*, Oxford.
Philippides, M. (1985) 'King Pleistoanax and the Spartan Invasion of Attica in 446' *AncW* 11: 33–41.
Pleket, H.W. (1963) 'Thasos and the Popularity of the Athenian Empire' *Historia* 12: 70–77.
Podlecki, A.J. (1966) *The Political Background of Aeschylean Tragedy*, Michigan.
— (1975) *The Life of Themistocles: A Critical Survey of the Literary and Archaeological Evidence*, Montreal.
Poole, J.C.F. and Holladay, A.J. (1979) 'Thucydides and the Plague of Athens' *CQ* 29: 282–300.
— (1984) 'Thucydides and the Plague' *CQ* 34: 483–85.
Pope, M. (1988) 'Thucydides and Democracy' *Historia* 37: 276–96.
Powell, C.A. (1979a) 'Religion and the Sicilian Expedition' *Historia* 28: 15–31.
— (1979b) 'Thucydides and Divination' *BICS* 26: 45–50.
Pritchett, W.K. (1985) *The Greek State at War* IV, Princeton.
Proietti, G. (1987) *Xenophon's Sparta: An Introduction*, Leiden.
Quinn, T.J. (1964) 'Thucydides and the Unpopularity of the Athenian Empire' *Historia* 13: 257–66.
— (1981) *Athens, and Samos, Lesbos and Chios: 478–404 B.C.*, Manchester.
Rankin, D.I. (1987) 'Sokrates, an Oligarch?' *AC* 56: 68–87.
Rankin, H.D. (1983) *Sophists, Socratics and Cynics*, London.
Rawlings, H.R. (1977) 'Thucydides on the Purpose of the Delian League' *Phoenix* 31: 1–8.
Rhodes, P.J. (1970) 'Thucydides on Pausanias and Themistocles' *Historia* 19: 387–400.
— (1985) *The Athenian Empire*, Oxford.
— (1987) 'Thucydides on the Causes of the Peloponnesian War' *Hermes* 115: 154–65.
Richardson, J. (1990) 'Thucydides I.23.6 and the Debate about the Peloponnesian War' in E.M. Craik (ed.) *'Owls to Athens': Essays on Classical Subjects Presented to Sir Kenneth Dover*, Oxford: 155–61.
Richardson, W.F. (1970) 'Δίκη in Aristophanes' Clouds' in B.F. Harris (ed.) *Auckland Classical Essays Presented to E.M. Blaiklock*, Auckland: 59–75.
Roberts, J.T. (1988) 'The Teflon Empire? Chester Starr and the Invulnerability of the Delian League' *AHB* 2: 49–53.
Robertson, N. (1980) 'The True Nature of the "Delian League" 478–61 BC' *AJAH* 5: 64–96.
Roller, D. W. (1989) 'Who Murdered Ephialtes?' *Historia* 38: 257–66.
Rusten, J.S. (1983) 'ΓΕΙΤΩΝ ΗΡΩΣ: Pindar's Prayer to Heracles (N. 7.86–101) and Greek Popular Religion' *HSPh* 87: 289–97.
Rutter, N.K. (1973) 'Diodorus and the Foundation of Thurii' *Historia* 22: 155–76.
Ryder, T.T.B. (1965) *Koine Eirene*, Oxford.
Santas, G.X. (1979) *Socrates: Philosophy in Plato's Early Dialogues*, London.
Scarrow, G.D. (1988) 'The Athenian Plague: a Possible Diagnosis' *AHB* 2: 4–8.
Seager, R. (1967) 'Alcibiades and the Charge of Aiming at Tyranny' *Historia* 16: 6–18.
Sealey, R. (1964) 'Ephialtes' *CPh* 59: 11–22 = (1968) *Essays in Greek Politics*, New York: 42–58.
— (1966) 'The Origin of the Delian League' in E. Badian (ed.) *Ancient Society and Institutions: Studies Presented to V. Ehrenberg*, Oxford: 235–55.
— (1975) 'The Causes of the Peloponnesian War' *CPh* 70: 89–109.

– (1981) 'Ephialtes, *Eisangelia*, and the Council' in *Classical Contributions:* 125–34.
Shipley, G. (1987) *A History of Samos 800–188 BC*, Oxford.
Sinclair, R.K. (1988) *Democracy and Participation in Athens*, Cambridge.
Smart, J.D. (1967) 'Kimon's Capture of Eion' *JHS* 87: 136–38.
Sommerstein, A.H. (1989) *Aeschylus, Eumenides*, Cambridge.
Stadter, P.A. (1989) *A Commentary on Plutarch's Pericles*, Chapel Hill.
– (1991) 'Pericles Among the Intellectuals' *ICS* 16: 111–24.
Starr, C.G. (1988) 'Athens and its Empire' *CJ* 83: 114–23.
– (1990) *The Birth of Athenian Democracy: The Assembly in the Fifth Century B.C.*, Oxford.
Staveley, E.S. (1972) *Greek and Roman Voting and Elections*, London.
Stockton, D. (1982) 'The Death of Ephialtes' *CQ* 32: 227–28.
– (1990) *The Classical Athenian Democracy*, Oxford.
Stone, I.F. (1988) *The Trial of Socrates*, London.
Strassler, R.B. (1988) 'The Harbor at Pylos' *JHS* 108: 198–203.
– (1990) 'The Opening of the Pylos Campaign' *JHS* 110: 110–25.
Strauss, B.S. (1983) 'Aegospotami Reexamined' *AJPh* 104: 24–35.
– (1986) *Athens after the Peloponnesian War: Class, Faction and Policy 403–386 BC*, London.
Strauss, L. (1966) *Socrates and Aristophanes*, Chicago.
Talbert, R.J.A. (1989) 'The Role of the Helots in the Class Struggle at Sparta' *Historia* 38: 22–40.
Tarrant, H. (1988) 'Midwifery and the *Clouds' CQ* 38: 116–22.
Thompson, W.E. (1981) 'The Peace of Kallias in the Fourth Century' *Historia* 30: 164–77.
Tréheux, J. (1991) 'Bulletin Épigraphique' *REG* 104: 469.
Unz, R.K. (1986) 'The Chronology of the Pentekontaetia' *CQ* 36: 68–85.
Usher, S. (1979) '"This to the Fair Critias"' *Eranos* 77: 39–42.
Vanderpool, E. (1974) 'The Date of the Pre-Persian Wall of Athens' in D.W. Bradeen and M.F. McGregor (eds.) *ΦΟΡΟΣ: Tribute to B.D. Meritt*, Locust Valley: 156–60.
Vickers, M. (1989) 'Alcibiades on Stage: Aristophanes' Birds' *Historia* 38: 267–99.
Vlastos, G. (1991) *Socrates. Ironist and Moral Philosopher*, Cambridge.
Wade-Gery, H.T. (1933) 'Classical Epigrams and Epitaphs' *JHS* 53: 71–104.
– (1958) 'Thucydides the Son of Melesias' in H.T. Wade-Gery (ed.) *Essays in Greek History*, Oxford: 239–70 = (1932) *JHS* 52: 205–27.
– (1958a) 'The Peace of Kallias' in H.T. Wade-Gery (ed.) *Essays in Greek History*, Oxford: 201–33 = (1940) *Athenian Studies Presented to W.S. Ferguson*: *HSPh* Suppl. 1: 121–56.
– (1958b) 'The Judicial Treaty with Phaselis and the History of the Athenian Courts' in H.T. Wade-Gery (ed.) *Essays in Greek History*, Oxford: 180–200.
Walbank, M.B. (1982) 'The Confiscation and Sale by the Poletai in 402/1 of the Property of the Thirty Tyrants' *Hesperia* 51: 74–98.
Walcot, P. (1987) 'Plato's Mother and Other Terrible Women' *G&R* 34: 12–31.
Wallace, R.W. (1974) 'Ephialtes and the Areopagos' *GRBS* 15: 259–69.
– (1985) *The Areopagos Council, to 307 B.C.*, Baltimore.
Walsh, J. (1981) 'The Authenticity and the Dates of the Peace of Callias and the Congress Decree' *Chiron* 11: 31–63.
Warner, R. (1958) *The Greek Philosophers*, New York.
Westlake, H.D. (1950) 'Thucydides and the Athenian Disaster in Egypt' *CPh* 45: 209–16.
– (1962) 'Thucydides and the Fall of Amphipolis' *Hermes* 90: 276–87.
– (1968) *Individuals in Thucydides*, Cambridge.
Whitehead, D. (1982/83) 'Sparta and the Thirty Tyrants' *AncSoc* 13/14: 105–30.

Wilson, J.B. (1979) *Pylos 425 BC*, Warminster.
Winnington-Ingram, R.P. (1965) 'TA ΔEONTA EIΠEIN: Cleon and Diodotos' *BICS* 12: 70–82.
Winton, R.I. (1981) 'Thucydides 1, 97, 2: The "Arche of the Athenians" and the "Athenian Empire"' *MH* 38: 147–52.
Woodhead, A.G. (1952) 'The Site of Brea: Thucydides I.61.4' *CQ* 2: 57–62.
— (1960) 'Thucydides' Portrait of Cleon' *Mnemosyne* 13: 289–317.
Woozley, A.D. (1971) 'Socrates on Disobeying the Law' in G. Vlastos (ed.) *The Philosophy of Socrates: A Collection of Critical Essays*, New York: 299–318.
Wycherley, R.E. (1978) *The Stones of Athens*, Princeton.
Wylie, J.A.H. and Stubbs, J. (1983) 'The Plague of Athens: 430–428 B.C.: Epidemic and Epizoötic' *CQ* 33: 6–11.

Chapters Ten and Eleven

Adeleye, G. (1983) 'The Purpose of the *Dokimasia*' *GRBS* 24: 295–306.
Andrewes, A. (1961) 'Philochorus on Phratries' *JHS* 81: 1–15.
— (1971) *Greek Society*, Harmondsworth.
— (1974) 'The Arginousai Trial' *Phoenix* 28: 112–22.
— (1978a) 'The Opposition to Perikles' *JHS* 98: 1–8.
— (1978b) 'Spartan Imperialism' in P.D.A. Garnsey and C.R. Whittaker (eds.) *Imperialism in the Ancient World*, Cambridge: 91–102.
Arnott, W.G. (1991) 'A Lesson from the *Frogs*' *G&R* 38: 18–23.
Austin, M.M. and Vidal-Nacquet, P. (1977) *Economic and Social History of Ancient Greece: An Introduction*, tr. M.M. Austin, Berkeley.
Balme, M. (1984) 'Attitudes to Work and Leisure in Ancient Greece' *G&R* 31: 140–52.
Bauman, R.A. (1990) *Political Trials in Ancient Greece*, London.
Beringer, W. (1982) '"Servile Status" in the Sources for Early Greek History' *Historia* 31: 13–32.
Bicknell, P.J. (1968) 'Demosthenes 24, 197 and the Domestic Slaves of Athens' *Mnemosyne* 21: 74.
Borza, E.N. (1987) 'Timber and Politics in the Ancient World: Macedon and the Greeks' *PAPhS* 131: 32–52.
Bravo, B. (1974) 'Une lettre sur plomb de Berezan: colonisation et modes de contact dans le Pont' in *Dialogues d'histoire ancienne* I, Centre de recherches d'histoire ancienne vol. 12, Paris: 111–87.
Burford, A. (1963) 'The Builders of the Parthenon' in G.T.W. Hooker (ed.) *Parthenos and Parthenon*, Oxford: 23–45.
Burke, E.M. (1990) 'Athens after the Peloponnesian War: Restoration Efforts and the Role of Maritime Commerce' *ClAnt* 9: 1–13.
— (1992) 'The Economy of Athens in the Classical Era: Some Adjustments to the Primitivist Model' *TAPhA* 122: 199–226.
Carey, C. (1991) 'Apollodoros' Mother: the Wives of Enfranchised Aliens in Athens' *CQ* 41: 84–89.
Carter, L.B. (1986) *The Quiet Athenian*, Oxford.
Cartledge, P. (1976) 'Did Spartan Citizens Ever Practise a Manual Techne?' *LCM* 1: 115–19.
— (1979) *Sparta and Lakonia; a Regional History 1300–362 BC*, London.
— (1993) 'Like a Worm I' the Bud? A Heterology of Classical Greek Slavery' *G&R* 40: 163–80.
Caspari, M.O.B. (1915) 'The Ionian Confederacy' *JHS* 35: 173–88.

Castriota, D. (1992) *Myth, Ethos and Actuality: Official Art in Fifth-Century B.C. Athens*, Wisconsin.

Cavanagh, W.G. (1991) 'Surveys, Cities and Synoecism' in J. Rich and A. Wallace-Hadrill (eds.) *City and Country in the Ancient World*, London: 97–118.

Chadwick, J. (1973) 'The Berezan Lead Letter' *PCPhS* 19: 35–37.

Christensen, K.A. (1984) 'The Theseion: a Slave Refuge at Athens' *AJAH* 9: 23–32.

Cole, S.G. (1984) 'Greek Sanctions against Sexual Assault' *CPh* 79: 97–113.

Cooper, A.B. (1977–78) 'The Family Farm in Ancient Greece' *CJ* 73: 162–75.

Crane, G. (1992) 'The Fear and Pursuit of Risk: Corinth on Athens, Sparta and the Peloponnesians (Thucydides 1.68–71, 120–121)' *TAPhA* 122: 227–56.

David, E. (1989) 'Dress in Spartan Society' *AncW* 19: 3–13.

Davies, J.K. (1967) 'Demosthenes on Liturgies: a Note' *JHS* 87: 33–40.

— (1977–78) 'Athenian Citizenship: the Descent Group and the Alternatives' *CJ* 73: 105–21.

— (1981) *Wealth and the Power of Wealth in Classical Athens*, Salem.

de Ste. Croix, G.E.M. (1954–55) 'The Character of the Athenian Empire' *Historia* 3: 1–41.

— (1957) Review of W.L. Westermann, *Slave Systems of Greek and Roman Antiquity*, *CR* 7: 54–59.

— (1972) *The Origins of the Peloponnesian War*, London.

— (1981) *The Class Struggle in the Ancient World*, London.

Dover, K.J. (1973) *Thucydides*, Oxford.

Duncan-Jones, R.P. (1980) 'Metic Numbers in Periclean Athens' *Chiron* 10: 101–09.

Ehrenberg, V. (1943) *The People of Aristophanes: A Sociology of Old Attic Comedy*, London.

— (1960) *The Greek State*, Oxford.

Emlyn-Jones C.J. (1980) *The Ionians and Hellenism: a Study of the Cultural Achievements of the Early Greek Inhabitants of Asia Minor*, London.

Figueira, T.J. (1984) 'Mess Contributions and Subsistence at Sparta' *TAPhA* 114: 87–109.

— (1986) 'Population Patterns in Late Archaic and Classical Sparta' *TAPhA* 116: 165–213.

Finley, M.I. (1951) *Studies in Land and Credit in Ancient Athens 500–200 B.C.: the Horos-Inscriptions*, New Brunswick.

— (1959) 'Was Greek Civilization Based on Slave Labour?' *Historia* 8: 145–64.

— (ed.) (1960) *Slavery in Classical Athens*, Cambridge.

— (1962) 'The Black Sea and Danubian Regions and Slave Trade in Antiquity' *Klio* 40: 51–59.

— (1973) *The Ancient Economy*, Berkeley.

— (1980) *Ancient Slavery and Modern Ideology*, Harmondsworth.

— (1981) *Economy and Society in Ancient Greece*, London.

— (1983) *Politics in the Ancient World*, Cambridge.

— (1985) *The Ancient Economy*, London, second edition.

Fisher, N.R.E. (1990) 'The Law of *Hubris* in Athens' in *NOMOS*: 123–38.

— (1992) *Hybris: a Study in the Values of Honour and Shame in Ancient Greece*, Warminster.

Flower, M.A. (1985) '*IG* II^{2}.2344 and the Size of Phratries in Classical Athens' *CQ* 35: 232–35.

Foxhall, L. (1993) 'Farming and Fighting in Ancient Greece' in J. Rich and G. Shipley (eds.) *War and Society in the Greek World*, London: 134–45.

Freeman, K. (1950) *Greek City-States*, London.

French, A. (1956) 'The Economic Background to Solon's Reforms' *CQ* 6: 11–25.

— (1964) *The Growth of the Athenian Economy*, London.

Frost F.J. (1976) 'Tribal Politics and the Civic State' *AJAH* 1: 66–75.

Gabrielsen, V. (1987) 'The *Antidosis* Procedure in Classical Athens' *C&M* 38: 7–38.
Garlan, Y. (1980) 'Le travail libre en Grèce ancienne' in P. Garnsey (ed.) *Non-Slave Labour in the Greco-Roman World,* Cambridge: 6–22.
– (1988) *Slavery in Ancient Greece,* tr. J. Lloyd, Ithaca.
Garland, R. (1990) *The Greek Way of Life: From Conception to Old Age,* Ithaca.
Garnsey, P. (1988) *Famine and Food Supply in the Graeco-Roman World: Responses to Risk and Crisis,* Cambridge.
Glass, S.L. (1988) 'The Greek Gymnasium' in W.J. Raschke (ed.) *The Archaeology of the Olympics: The Olympics and Other Festivals in Antiquity,* Wisconsin: 155–73.
Glotz, G. (1929) *The Greek City and its Institutions,* tr. N. Mallinson, London.
Golden, M. (1984) 'Slavery and Homosexuality at Athens' *Phoenix* 38: 308–24.
– (1985) '"Donatus" and Athenian Phratries' *CQ* 35: 9–13.
– (1990) *Children and Childhood in Classical Athens,* Baltimore.
Gomme, A. (1933) *The Population of Athens in the Fifth and Fourth Centuries B.C.,* Oxford.
Gould, J. (1980) 'Law, Custom and Myth: Aspects of the Social Position of Women in Classical Athens' *JHS* 100: 38–59.
Graham, A.J. (1984) 'Commercial Interchanges between Greeks and Natives' *AncW* 10: 3–10.
Hahn, I. (1983) 'Foreign Trade and Foreign Policy in Archaic Greece' in P. Garnsey and C.R. Whittaker (eds.) *Trade and Famine in Classical Antiquity,* Cambridge: 31–36.
Halliwell, S. (1991) 'Comic Satire and Freedom of Speech in Classical Athens' *JHS* 111: 48–70.
Hansen, M.H. (1976) 'How Many Athenians Attended the Ecclesia?' *GRBS* 17: 115–34.
– (1979a) 'Misthos for Magistrates in Classical Athens' *SO* 54: 5–22.
– (1979b) 'The Duration of a Meeting of the Athenian Ecclesia' *CPh* 74: 43–49.
– (1980) 'Seven Hundred Archai in Classical Athens' *GRBS* 21: 151–73.
– (1983) *The Athenian Ecclesia: a Collection of Articles: 1976–83,* Copenhagen.
– (1987) *The Athenian Assembly in the Age of Demosthenes,* Oxford.
– (1990) 'The Political Powers of the People's Court in Fourth-Century Athens' in O. Murray and S. Price (eds.) *The Greek City from Homer to Alexander,* Oxford: 215–43.
– (1991) *The Athenian Democracy in the Age of Demosthenes: Structure, Principles and Ideology,* Oxford.
Hanson, V.D. (1983) *Warfare and Agriculture in Classical Greece,* Pisa.
– (1992) 'Thucydides and the Desertion of Attic Slaves during the Decelean War' *ClAnt* 11: 210–28.
Harris, E.M. (1992) 'Perikles' Praise of Athenian Democracy: Thucydides 2.37.1' *HSPh* 94: 157–67.
Hedrick, C.W. (1989) 'The Phratry from Paiania' *CQ* 39: 126–35.
Hellenica Oxyrynchia (1988) ed. P.R. McKechnie and S.J. Kern, Warminster.
Hodkinson, S. (1983) 'Social Order and the Conflict of Values in Classical Sparta' *Chiron* 13: 239–81.
– (1988) 'Animal Husbandry in the Greek Polis' in C.R. Whittaker (ed.) *Pastoral Economies in Classical Antiquity,* Cambridge Philological Society Suppl. 14, Cambridge: 35–74.
Hornblower, S. (1982) 'Thucydides, the Panionian Festival, and the Ephesia (III.104)' *Historia* 31: 241–45.
– (1987) *Thucydides,* Baltimore.
Humphreys, S.C. (1974) 'The Nothoi of Kynosarges' *JHS* 94: 88–95.
– (1978) *Anthropology and the Greeks,* London.

Isager, S. and Hansen, M.H. (1975) *Aspects of Athenian Society in the Fourth Century B.C.*, tr. J.H. Rosenmeier, Odense.

Jameson, M.H. (1977–78) 'Agriculture and Slavery in Classical Athens' *CJ* 73: 122–45.

— (1983) 'Famine in the Greek World' in P. Garnsey and C.R. Whittaker (eds.) *Trade and Famine in Classical Antiquity*, Cambridge: 6–16.

— (1990) 'Private Space and the Greek City' in O. Murray and S. Price (eds.) *The Greek City from Homer to Alexander*, Oxford: 171–95.

Jocelyn, H.D. (1980) 'A Greek Indecency and its Students: Λαικάζειν' *PCPhS* 26: 12–66.

Jordan, B. (1975) *The Athenian Navy in the Classical Period*, Berkeley.

— (1990) 'The Ceremony of the Helots in Thucydides, IV, 80' *AC* 59: 37–69.

Just, R. (1989) *Women in Athenian Life and Law*, London.

Kagan, D. (1963) 'The Enfranchisement of Aliens by Cleisthenes' *Historia* 12: 41–46.

—(1991) *Pericles of Athens and the Birth of Democracy*, New York.

Kallet-Marx, L. (1989) 'Did Tribute Fund the Parthenon?' *ClAnt* 8: 252–66.

Krentz, P. (1980) 'Foreigners against the Thirty: *IG* II^2 10 again' *Phoenix* 34: 298–306.

Lacey, W.K. (1968) *The Family in Classical Greece*, London.

Laix, de R.A. (1973) *Probouleusis at Athens: A Study of Political Decision-Making*, Berkeley.

Lang, M.L. (1990) 'Illegal Execution in Athens' *PAPhS* 36: 24–29.

Larsen, J.A.O. (1955) *Representative Government in Greek and Roman History*, Berkeley.

— (1968) *Greek Federal States*, Oxford.

Lauffer, S. (1955–56) *Die Bergwerkssklaven von Laureion* I–II, Mainz.

Lavelle, B.M. (1992) 'Herodotos, Skythian Archers, and the *doryphoroi* of the Peisistratids' *Klio* 74: 78–97.

Lazenby, J.F. (1985) *The Spartan Army*, Warminster.

Lee, H.M. (1988) 'The "First" Olympic Games of 776 BC' in W.J. Raschke (ed.) *The Archaeology of the Olympics: the Olympics and Other Festivals in Antiquity*, Winsconsin.

Lewis, D. (1990) 'Public Property in the City' in O. Murray and S. Price (eds.) *The Greek City from Homer to Alexander*, Oxford: 245–63.

Loraux, N. (1986) *The Invention of Athens: the Funeral Oration in the Classical City*, Cambridge, Mass.

MacDowell, D.M. (1976) 'Bastards as Athenian Citizens' *CQ* 26: 88–91.

— (1978) *The Law in Classical Athens*, London.

Magie, D. (1950) *Roman Rule in Asia Minor to the End of the Third Century After Christ* I–II, Princeton.

Markle, M.M. (1985) 'Jury Pay and Assembly Pay at Athens' in *Crux*: 265–97.

Mattingly, H.B. (1961) 'The Athenian Coinage Decree' *Historia* 10: 148–88.

Meiggs, R. (1982) *Trees and Timber in the Ancient Mediterranean World*, Oxford.

Meritt, B.D. (1976) 'Normal Lengths of Prytany in the Athenian Year' *GRBS* 17: 147–52.

— and Wade-Gery, H.T. (1963) 'Dating of Documents to the Mid-Fifth Century' *JHS* 83: 100–17.

Merkelbach, R. (1975) 'Nochmals die Bleitafel von Berezan' *ZPE* 17: 161–62.

Merrill, W.P. (1991) 'Τὸ Πλῆθος in a Treaty concerning the Affairs of Argos, Knossos and Tylissos' *CQ* 41: 16–25.

Mikalson, J.D. (1977) 'Religion in the Attic Demes' *AJPh* 98: 424–35.

Miller, A.P. (1975) 'Notes on the Berezan Lead Letter' *ZPE* 17: 157–60.

Miller, S.G. (1978) *The Prytaneion: its Function and Architectural Form*, Berkeley.

Millett, P. (1989) 'Patronage and its Avoidance in Classical Athens' in A. Wallace-Hadrill (ed.) *Patronage in Ancient Society*, London: 1–47.
— (1991) *Lending and Borrowing in Ancient Athens*, Cambridge.
Morris, I. (1991) 'The Early Polis as City and State' in J. Rich and A. Wallace-Hadrill (eds.) *City and Country in the Ancient World*, London: 25–57.
Murray, O. (1990) 'The Solonian Law of *Hybris*' in *NOMOS:* 139–45.
Nixon, L. and Price, S. (1990) 'The Size and Resources of Greek Cities' in O. Murray and S. Price (eds.) *The Greek City from Homer to Alexander*, Oxford: 137–70.
Nussbaum, G. (1960) 'Labour and Status in the *Works and Days*' *CQ* 54: 213–20.
Osborne, M.J. (1981–82) *Naturalization in Athens* I–II, Brussels.
Osborne, R. (1985) *Demos: the Discovery of Classical Attika*, Cambridge.
— (1990) 'The Demos and its Divisions in Clasical Athens' in O. Murray and S. Price (eds.) *The Greek City from Homer to Alexander*, Oxford: 265–93.
— (1991) 'Pride and Prejudice, Sense and Subsistence: Exchange and Society in the Greek City', in J. Rich and A. Wallace-Hadrill (eds.) *City and Country in the Ancient World*, London: 119–45.
Parke, H.W. (1977) *Festivals of the Athenians*, London.
Parker, R. (1983) *Miasma: Pollution and Purification in Early Greek Religion*, Oxford.
Patterson, C.B. (1981) *Perikles' Citizenship Law of 451/50 B.C.*, New York.
— (1990) 'Those Athenian Bastards' *ClAnt* 9: 40–73.
Pomeroy, S.B. (1975) *Goddesses, Whores, Wives and Slaves*, New York.
Powell, A. (1989) 'Mendacity and Sparta's Use of the Visual' in *Classical Sparta:* 173–92.
Pritchett, W.K. (1956) 'The Attic Stelai: Part II' *Hesperia* 25: 178–317.
Raaflaub, K.A. (1990) 'Contemporary Perceptions of Democracy in Fifth-Century Athens' in W.R. Connor et al. (eds.) *Aspects of Athenian Democracy* (*Classica et Medievalia Dissertationes* XI), Copenhagen: 33–70.
Randall, R.H. (1953) 'The Erechtheum Workmen' *AJA* 57: 199–210.
Rhodes, P.J. (1982) 'Problems in Athenian *Eisphora* and Liturgies' *AJAH* 7: 1–19.
— (1986a) *The Greek City States: A Source Book*, London.
— (1986b) 'Political Activity in Classical Athens' *JHS* 106: 132–44.
Ridley, R.T. (1974) 'The Economic Activities of the Perioikoi' *Mnemosyne* 27: 281–92.
Rihll, T. (1993) 'War, Slavery and Settlement in Early Greece' in J. Rich and G. Shipley (eds.) *War and Society in the Greek World*, London: 77–107.
Roebuck, C. (1955) 'The Early Ionian League' *CPh* 50: 26–40.
Ruschbusch, E. (1985) 'Die Zahl der griechischen Staaten und Arealgrösse und Bürgerzahl der "Normalpolis"' *ZPE* 59: 253–63.
Sargent, R.L. (1927) 'The Use of Slaves by the Athenians in Warfare' *CPh* 22: 201–12, 264–79.
Schaps, D. (1982) 'The Women of Greece in Wartime' *CPh* 77: 193–213.
Schmitt-Pantel, P. (1990) 'Collective Activities and the Political in the Greek City' in O. Murray and S. Price (eds.) *The Greek City from Homer to Alexander*, Oxford: 199–213.
Sealey, R. (1983) 'How Citizenship and the City Began in Athens' *AJAH* 8: 97–129.
— (1984) 'On Lawful Concubinage in Athens' *ClAnt* 3: 111–33.
Sinclair, R.K. (1988) *Democracy and Participation in Athens*, Cambridge.
Sinn, U. (1993) 'Greek Sanctuaries as Places of Refuge' in N. Marinatos and R. Hägg (eds.) *Greek Sanctuaries: New Approaches*, London: 88–109.
Snodgrass, A. (1980) *Archaic Greece: The Age of Experiment*, London.
Sourvinou-Inwood, C. (1990) 'What is Polis Religion?' in O. Murray and S. Price (eds.) *The Greek City from Homer to Alexander*, Oxford: 295–322.
Stanier, R.S. (1953) 'The Cost of the Parthenon' *JHS* 73: 68–76.
Starr, C.G. (1987) 'Athens and its Empire' *CJ* 83: 114–23.

Stockton, D. (1990) *The Classical Athenian Democracy*, Oxford.
Strubbe, J.H.M. (1991) '"Cursed be He that Moves my Bones"' in C.A. Faraone and D. Obbink (eds.) *Magika Hiera: Ancient Greek Magic and Religion*, New York: 33–59.
Talbert, R.J.A. (1989) 'The Role of the Helots in the Class Struggle at Sparta' *Historia* 38: 22–40.
Thompson, W.E. (1968) 'An Interpretation of the "Demotionid" Decrees' *SO* 62: 51–68.
— (1971) 'Leagros' *Athenaeum* 49: 328–35.
Todd, S. (1990) 'The Purpose of Evidence in Athenian Courts' in *NOMOS:* 19–39.
Tyrrell, W.B. (1984) *Amazons: a Study in Athenian Mythmaking*, Baltimore.
Vidal-Naquet, P. (1986) *The Black Hunter: Forms of Thought and Forms of Society in the Greek World*, tr. A. Szegedy-Maszak, Baltimore.
Vogt, J. (1975) *Ancient Slavery and the Ideal of Man*, tr. T. Wiedemann, Cambridge.
Walker, S. (1983) 'Women and Housing in Classical Greece: the Archaeological Evidence' in A. Cameron and A. Kurht (eds.) *Images of Women in Antiquity*, London: 81–91.
Walters, K.R. (1983) 'Perikles' Citizenship Law' *ClAnt* 2: 314–36.
Webster, T.B.L. (1969) *Everyday Life in Classical Athens*, London.
— (1973) *Athenian Culture and Society*, Berkeley.
Welskopf, E.C. (1980) 'Free Labour in the City of Athens' in P. Garnsey (ed.) *Non-Slave Labour in the Greco-Roman World*, Cambridge Philological Society Suppl. 6, Cambridge: 23–25.
Westermann, W.L. (1955) *Slave Systems of Greek and Roman Antiquity*, Philadelphia.
Whitehead, D. (1977) *The Ideology of the Athenian Metic*, Cambridge.
— (1984) 'A Thousand New Athenians: *IG* II^2.10+' *LCM* 9: 8–10.
— (1986) *The Demes of Attica: 508/7 - ca. 250 B.C.*, Princeton.
Wiedemann, T.E.J. (1987) *Slavery*, Oxford.
Willetts, R.F. (1967) *The Law Code of Gortyn*, Berlin.
— (1977) *The Civilization of Ancient Crete*, London.
Wood, E.M. (1983) 'Agricultural Slavery in Classical Athens' *AJAH* 8: 1–47.
— (1988) *Peasant-Citizen and Slave: the Foundations of Athenian Democracy*, London.
Zaidman, L.B. and Pantel, P.S. (1992) *Religion in the Ancient Greek City*, tr. P. Cartledge, Cambridge.
Zimmern, A. (1931) *The Greek Commonwealth: Politics and Economics in Fifth-Century Athens*, Oxford, fifth edition.

Chapter Twelve

Aleshire, S.B. (1989) *The Athenian Asklepieion: the People, their Dedications, and the Inventories*, Amsterdam.
— (1991) *Asklepios at Athens: Epigraphic and Prosopographic Essays on the Athenian Healing Cults*, Amsterdam.
Behr, C.A. (1968) *Aelius Aristides and the Sacred Tales*, Amsterdam.
Benson, E.F. (1928) *The Life of Alcibiades*, London.
Bloch, R. (1963) *Les Prodiges dans l'antiquité classique (Grèce, Étrurie et Rome)*, Paris.
Bouché-Leclercq, A. (1879–1882) *Histoire de la divination dans l'antiquité* I–IV, Paris.
Brumfield, A.C. (1981) *The Attic Festivals of Demeter and Their Relationship to the Agricultural Year*, Salem.

Burford, A. (1969) *The Greek Temples at Epidauros: A Social and Economic Study of Building in the Asklepian Sanctuary*, Liverpool.

Burkert, W. (1979) *Structure and History in Greek Mythology and Ritual*, Berkeley.

— (1983) *Homo Necans: The Anthropology of Ancient Greek Sacrificial Ritual and Myth*, tr. P. Bing, Berkeley.

— (1985) *Greek Religion: Archaic and Classical*, tr. J. Raffan, Oxford.

— (1987) *Ancient Mystery Cults*, Harvard.

— (1992) 'Athenian Cults and Festivals' in *CAH* V^2: 245–67.

Caldwell, R. (1989) *The Origin of the Gods: a Psychoanalytic Study of Greek Theogenic Myth*, New York.

Castriota, D. (1992) *Myth, Ethos and Actuality: Official Art in Fifth-Century B.C. Athens*, Wisconsin.

Clairmont, C.W. (1979) 'The Lekythos of Myrrhine' in G. Kopcke and M.B. Moore (eds.) *Studies in Classical Art and Archaeology: A Tribute to Peter Heinrich von Blanckenhagen*, New York: 103–10.

Clark, R.J. (1968) 'Trophonios: the Manner of his Revelation' *TAPhA* 99: 63–75.

Clinton, K. (1971) 'Inscriptions From Eleusis' *AE*: 81–136.

— (1974) *The Sacred Officials of the Eleusinian Mysteries*, Philadelphia.

— (1993) 'The Sanctuary of Demeter and Kore at Eleusis' in N. Marinatos and R. Hägg (eds.) *Greek Sanctuaries: New Approaches*, London: 110–24.

Coldstream, J.N. (1985) 'Greek Temples: Why and Where?' in P.E. Easterling and J.V. Muir (eds.) *Greek Religion and Society*, Cambridge: 67–97.

Connor, W.R. (1988) 'Seized by the Nymphs: Nympholepsy and Symbolic Expression in Classical Greece' *ClAnt* 7: 155–89.

Culham, P. (1986) 'Again, What Meaning Lies in Colour!' *ZPE* 64: 235–45.

Daux, G. (1949) 'Un règlement cultuel d'Andros (Vème siècle avant J.-C.)' *Hesperia* 18: 59–72.

Davies, J.K. (1967) 'Demosthenes on Liturgies: a Note' *JHS* 87: 33–40.

de Romilly, J. (1992) *The Great Sophists in Periclean Athens*, tr. J. Lloyd, Oxford.

den Adel, R. (1983) 'Apollo's Prophecies at Delos' *CW* 76: 288–90.

Detienne, M., Vernant, J.P., et al. (1989) *The Cuisine of Sacrifice among the Greeks*, tr. P. Wissing, Chicago.

Dillon, M.P.J. (1990) ''The House of the Thebans' (*FD* iii.1 357–58) and Accommodation for Greek Pilgrims' *ZPE* 83: 64–88.

— (1994) 'The Didactic Nature of the Epidaurian Iamata' *ZPE*, forthcoming.

— (1995) 'Oionomanteia: Divination by the Birds in Ancient Greece' in M.P.J. Dillon (ed.) *Religion in the Ancient World*, Amsterdam: forthcoming.

Dodds, E.R. (1956) *The Greeks and the Irrational*, Berkeley.

— (1971) *The Ancient Concept of Progress and Other Essays on Greek Literature and Belief*, Oxford.

Ducrey, P. (1986) *Warfare in Ancient Greece*, tr. J. Lloyd, New York.

Edelstein, E.J. and L. (1945) *Asclepius: A Collection and Interpretation of the Testimonies* I–II, Baltimore.

Ellis, W.M. (1989) *Alcibiades*, London.

Emlyn-Jones, C.J. (1980) *The Ionians and Hellenism: A Study of the Cultural Achievement of the Early Greek Inhabitants of Asia Minor*, London.

Farnell, L.R. (1896–1909) *The Cults of the Greek States* I–V, Oxford.

— (1921) *Greek Hero Cults and Ideas of Immortality*, Oxford.

Ferguson, J. (1989) *Among the Gods: an Archaeological Exploration of Ancient Greek Religion*, London.

Festugière, A.J. (1954) *Personal Religion among the Greeks*, California.

Finley, M. (1985) 'Foreward' in P.E. Easterling and J.V. Muir (eds.) *Greek Religion and Society*, Cambridge: xiii–xx.

Fisher, N.R.E. (1992) *Hybris: A Study in the Values of Honour and Shame in Ancient Greece*, Warminster.

Flacelière, R. (1965) *Greek Oracles*, tr. D. Garman, London.

Fontenrose, J. (1968) 'The Hero as Athlete' *ClAnt* 1: 73–104.

— (1988a) *Didyma: Apollo's Oracle, Cult and Companions*, Berkeley.

— (1988b) 'The Cult of Apollo and the Games at Delphi' in W. J. Raschke (ed.) *The Archaeology of the Olympics. The Olympics and Other Festivals in Antiquity*, Wisconsin: 121–40.

Freeman, K. (1971) *Ancilla to the Pre-Socratic Philosophers*, Oxford.

Garland, R.S.J. (1984) 'Religious Authority in Archaic and Classical Athens' *BSA* 79: 75–123.

— (1989) 'The Well-Ordered Corpse: An Investigation into the Motives behind Greek Funerary Legislation' *BICS* 36: 1–15.

— (1990a) *The Greek Way of Life*, London.

— (1990b) 'Priests and Power in Classical Athens' in M. Beard and J. North (eds.) *Pagan Priests: Religion and Power in the Ancient World*, London: 75–91.

— (1992) *Introducing New Gods*, London.

Golden, M. (1990) *Children and Childhood in Classical Athens*, Baltimore.

Green, P. (1989) *Classical Bearings: Interpreting Ancient History and Culture*, London.

Guthrie, W.K.C. (1950) *The Greeks and their Gods*, Boston.

— (1967) *The Greek Philosophers from Thales to Aristotle*, London.

— (1971) *The Sophists*, Cambridge = (1969) *A History of Greek Philosophy* III: *The Fifth Century Enlightenment*, Cambridge: 3–319.

Halliday, W.R. (1913) *Greek Divination*, London.

Hamilton, M. (1906) *Incubation, or the Cure of Disease in Pagan Temples and Christian Churches*, London.

Harrison, J. (1922) *Prolegomena to the Study of Greek Religion*, Cambridge, third edition.

— (1925) *Themis: a Study of the Social Origins of Greek Religion*, London, second edition.

Hewitt, J.W. (1909) 'The Major Restrictions on Access to Greek Temples' *TAPhA* 40: 83–91.

Hodkinson, S. (1983) 'Social Order and the Conflict of Values in Classical Sparta' *Chiron* 13: 239–81.

Hornblower, S. (1982) 'Thucydides, the Panionian Festival, and the Ephesia (III.104)' *Historia* 31: 241–45.

Hughes, J.D. (1980) 'Early Greek and Roman Environmentalists' in L.J. Bilsky (ed.) *Historical Ecology: Essays on Environment and Social Change*, New York: 45–59.

Humphreys, S.C. (1980) 'Family Tombs and Tomb Cult in Ancient Athens: Tradition or Traditionalism?' *JHS* 100: 96–126.

Huxley, G. (1979) 'Bones for Orestes' *GRBS* 2: 145–48.

Jameson, M. (1983) 'Famine in the Greek World' in P. Garnsey and C.R. Whittaker (eds.) *Trade and Famine in Classical Antiquity*, Cambridge: 6–16.

Jordon, B. (1979) *Servants of the Gods: A Study in the Religion, History and Literature of Fifth-Century Athens*, Hypomnemata 55, Göttingen.

— (1986) 'Religion in Thucydides' *TAPhA* 116: 119–47.

— and Perlin, J. (1984) 'On the Protection of Sacred Groves' in K.J. Rigsby (ed.) *Studies Presented to Sterling Dow*, *GRBS* Mono. 10: 153–59.

Kagan, D. (1987) *The Fall of the Athenian Empire*, Ithaca.

Kearns, E. (1989) *The Heroes of Attica*, *BICS* Suppl. 57, London.

Kerényi, C. (1960) *Asklepios: Archetypal Image of the Physician's Existence*, tr. R. Manheim, London.

— (1967) *Eleusis: Archetypal Image of Mother and Daughter*, tr. R. Manheim, New York.
Kirk, G.S. and Raven, J.E.. (1960) *The Presocratic Philosophers: A Critical History with a Selection of Texts*, Cambridge.
Krug, A. (1984) *Heilkunst und Heilkult: Medizin in der Antike*, Munich.
Kurtz, D.C. and Boardman, J. (1971) *Greek Burial Customs*, London.
Lambridis, H. (1976) *Empedocles: a Philosophical Investigation*, Albama.
Lauenstein, D. (1989) *Die Mysterien von Eleusis*, Stuttgart.
Lefkowitz, M.R. (1986) *Women in Greek Myth*, Baltimore.
Lloyd-Jones, H. (1976) 'The Delphic Oracle' *G&R* 23: 60–73.
Luck, G. (1985) *Arcana Mundi: Magic and the Occult in the Greek and Roman Worlds*, Baltimore.
Martin, L.H. (1987) *Hellenistic Religions: An Introduction*, Oxford.
Mattingly, H.B. (1961) 'The Athenian Coinage Decree' *Historia* 10: 148–88.
— (1974) 'Athens and Eleusis: Some New Ideas' in D.W. Bradeen and M.F. McGregor (eds.) *ΦΟΡΟΣ: Tribute to Benjamin Dean Meritt*, Locust Valley: 90–103.
— (1982) 'The Athenian Nike Temple Reconsidered' *AJA* 86: 381–85.
Meritt, B.D. (1945) 'Attic Inscriptions of the Fifth Century' *Hesperia* 14: 61–133.
— (1946) 'Greek Inscriptions' *Hesperia* 15: 138–53.
Meritt, B.D. and Wade-Gery, H.T. (1963) 'Dating of Documents to the Mid-Fifth Century' *JHS* 83: 100–17.
Meyer, E. (1993) 'Epitaphs and Citizenship in Classical Athens' *JHS* 113: 99–121.
Mikalson, J. (1975) *The Sacred and Civil Calendar of the Athenian Year*, Princeton.
— (1983) *Athenian Popular Religion*, Chapel Hill.
— (1991) *Honor Thy Gods: Popular Religion in Greek Tragedy*, Chapel Hill.
Mills, H. (1984) 'Greek Clothing Regulations: Sacred and Profane' *ZPE* 55: 255–65.
Momigliano, A. (1978) 'Freedom of Speech and Religious Tolerance in the Ancient World' in S.C. Humphreys (ed.) *Anthropology and the Greeks*, London: 179–93.
Morgan, C. (1990) *Athletes and Oracles: the Transformation of Olympia and Delphi in the Eighth Century BC*, Cambridge.
Morgan, M.L. (1992) 'Plato and Greek Religion' in R. Kraut (ed.) *The Cambridge Companion to Plato*, Cambridge: 227–47.
Morris, I. (1992) *Death-Ritual and Social Structure in Classical Antiquity*, Cambridge.
Moyer, E.A. (1993) 'Epitaphs and Citizenship in Classical Athens' *JHS* 113: 99–121.
Muir, J.V. (1985) 'Religion and the New Education' in P.E. Easterling & J.V. Muir (eds.) *Greek Religion and Society*, Cambridge: 191–218.
Mylonas, G.E. (1961) *Eleusis and the Eleusinian Mysteries*, Princeton.
Nilsson, M.P. (1925) *Greek Religion*, Oxford.
— (1961) *Greek Folk Religion*, New York = (1940) *Greek Popular Religion*, Columbia.
Nock, A.D. (1942) 'Religious Attitudes of the Ancient Greeks' *APhS* 85: 472–82 = (1972) Z. Stewart (ed.) *A.D. Nock: Essays on Religion and the Ancient World* I–II, Oxford: 534–50.
— (1944) 'The Cult of Heroes' *HThR* 37: 141–74 = (1972) Z. Stewart (ed.) *A.D. Nock: Essays on Religion and the Ancient World* I–II, Oxford: 575–602.
Osborne, R. (1985) *Demos: the Discovery of Classical Attika*, Cambridge.
Parke, H.W. (1939) 'Notes on Some Delphic Charges' *Hermathena* 28: 59–65.
— (1967) *Greek Oracles*, London.
— (1977) *Festivals of the Athenians*, London.
— (1984) 'Croesus and Delphi' *GRBS* 25: 209–32.
Parker, R. (1983) *Miasma: Pollution and Purification in Early Greek Religion*, Oxford.
— (1985) 'Greek States and Greek Oracles' in *Crux*: 298–326.
— (1989) 'Spartan Religion' in *Classical Sparta:* 142–72.

Peppa-Delmousou, D. (1988) 'The Theoria of Brauron' in R. Hagg et. al (eds.) *Early Greek Cult Practice*, Stockholm.
Petropoulou, A. (1981) 'The *Eparche* Documents and the Early Oracle at Oropus' *GRBS* 22: 39–63.
Podlecki, A. (1971) 'Cimon, Skyros and Theseus' Bones' *JHS* 91: 141–43.
Pollard, J. (1965) *Seers, Shrines and Sirens*, London.
— (1977) *Birds in Greek Life and Myth*, London.
Pomeroy, S. (1975) *Goddesses, Whores, Wives and Slaves*, New York.
Popp, H. (1957) *Die Einwirkung von Vorzeichen, Opfern und Festen auf die Kriegführung der Griechen im 5. und 4. Jahrhundert v. Chr.*, Würzburg.
Powell, C.A. (1979) 'Religion and the Sicilian Expedition' *Historia* 28: 15–31.
Price, S. (1985) 'Delphi and Divination' in P.E. Easterling and J.V. Muir (eds.) *Greek Religion and Society*, Cambridge: 128–54.
Pritchett, W.K. (1971) *The Greek State at War*, Berkeley.
— (1979) *The Greek State at War, Part* III: *Religion*, Berkeley.
Rankin, H.D. (1983) *Sophists, Socratics and Cynics*, London.
Richardson, N.J. (1974) *The Homeric Hymn to Demeter*, Oxford.
— (1992) 'Panhellenic Cults and Panhellenic Poets' in *CAH* V^{2}: 223–44.
Richter, G.M.A. (1961) *Archaic Gravestones of Attica*, London.
Robinson, T.M. (1987) *Heraclitus: Fragments*, Toronto.
Roebuck, C. (1941) *Corinth* XIV: *The Asklepieion and Lerna*, Princeton
Rosen, R.M. (1987) 'Hipponax fr. 48 Dg. and the Eleusinian *Kykeon*' *AJPh* 108: 416–26.
Rougement, G. (1973) 'La hiéroménie des Pythia et les <trêves sacrées> d'Éleusis, de Delphes et d'Olympie' *BCH* 97: 75–106.
Schachter, A. (1981) *Cults of Boiotia* I: *Acheloos to Hera*, London.
Simms, R.M. (1990) 'Myesis, Telete, and Mysteria' *GRBS* 31: 183–95.
Simon, E. (1983) *Festivals of Attika: An Archaeological Commentary*, Wisconsin.
Smart, J.D. (1967) 'Kimon's Capture of Eion' *JHS* 87: 136–38.
Sokolowski, F. (1954) 'Fees and Taxes in the Greek Cults' *HThR* 47: 153–64.
— (1959) 'On the Rules Regulating the Celebration of the Eleusinian Mysteries' *HTR* 52: 1–4.
— (1960) 'On the Episode of Onchestus in the Homeric Hymn to Apollo' *TAPhA* 91: 376–80.
— (1973) 'On the Pergamene Lex Sacra' *GRBS* 14: 407–13.
Sordi, M. (1984) 'Il Santuario di Olimpia e la Guerra d'Elide' in M. Sordi (ed.) *I Santuari la Guerra nel Mondo classico*, Milan: 20–30
Sourvinou-Inwood, C. (1990) 'What is Polis Religion?' in O. Murray and S. Price (eds.) *The Greek City from Homer to Alexander*, Oxford: 295–322.
Symeonoglou, S. (1985) 'The Oracles of Thebes' in *La Béotie Antique: Lyon-St. Étienne 16–20 mai 1983 (Colloques Internationaux du Centre National de la Recherche Scientifique)*, Paris: 155–58.
Tomlinson, R.A. (1976) *Greek Sanctuaries*, London.
— (1983) *Epidauros*, London.
Tyrrell, W.B. (1984) *Amazons: A Study in Athenian Mythmaking*, Baltimore.
van Straten, F.T. (1981) 'Gifts for the Gods' in H.S. Versnel (ed.) *Faith, Hope and Worship: Aspects of Religious Mentality in the Ancient World*, Leiden: 65–193.
Walcot, P. (1978) *Envy and the Greeks: A Study of Human Behaviour*, Warminster.
Warner, R. (1958) *The Greek Philosophers*, New York.
Wasson, R.G., A. Hoffman and C.A.P. Ruck (1978) *The Road to Eleusis: Unveiling the Secret of their Mysteries*, New York.
— Kramrisch, S., Ott, J. and Ruck, C.A.P. (1986) *Persephone's Quest: Entheogens and the Origins of Religion*, New Haven.
Watkins, C. (1978) 'Let us Now Praise Famous Grains' *PAPhS* 122: 7–17.

West, M.L. (1978) *Hesiod: Works and Days*, Oxford.
Willetts, R.F. (1962) *Cretan Cults and Festivals*, London.
Winkler, J. (1990) *The Constraints of Desire: The Anthropology of Sex and Gender in Ancient Greece*, New York.
Woodbury, L. (1965) 'The Date and Atheism of Diagoras of Melos' *Phoenix* 19: 178–211.
Woodward, A.M. (1962) 'Athens and the Oracle of Ammon' *ABSA* 57: 5–13.
Zaidman, L.B. and Pantel, P.S. (1992) *Religion in the Ancient Greek City*, tr. P. Cartledge, Cambridge.

Chapter Thirteen

Andersen, Ø. (1987) 'The Widows, the City and Thucydides (II,45,2)' *SO* 62: 33–49.
Arthur, M.B. (1973) 'Origins of the Western Attitude towards Women' *Arethusa* 6: 7–58.
Blok, J. and Mason, P. (1987) *Sexual Asymmetry: Studies in Ancient Society*, Amsterdam.
Burnett, A.P. (1983) *Three Archaic Poets: Archilochus, Alcaeus, Sappho*, London.
Cameron, A. (1932) 'The Exposure of Children and Greek Ethics' *CR* 46: 105–14.
Cantarella, E. (1987) *Pandora's Daughters: The Role and Status of Women in Greek and Roman Antiquity*, tr. M. Fant, Baltimore.
Cartledge, P.A. (1978) 'Literacy in the Spartan Oligarchy' *JHS*: 25–37.
— (1981a) 'The Politics of Spartan Pederasty' *PCPhS* 27: 17–36.
— (1981b) 'Spartan Wives: Liberation or Licence?' *CQ* 31: 84–105.
Clark, G. (1989) *Women in the Ancient World*, Oxford.
Cohen, D. (1984) 'The Athenian Law of Adultery' *RIDA* 31: 147–65.
— (1987) 'Law, Society and Homosexuality in Classical Athens' *P&P* 117: 3–21.
— (1989) 'Seclusion, Separation, and the Status of Women in Classical Athens' *G&R* 36: 3–15.
— (1990) 'The Social Context of Adultery at Athens' in *NOMOS:* 147–65.
— (1991) *Law, Sexuality, and Society: the Enforcement of Morals in Classical Athens*, Cambridge.
Cole, S.G. (1984) 'Greek Sanctions against Sexual Assault' *CPh* 79: 97–113.
Cox, C.A. (1988) 'Sisters, Daughters and the Deme of Marriage: a Note' *JHS* 108: 185–88.
Davies, J.K. (1977–78) 'Athenian Citizenship: the Descent Group and the Alternatives' *CJ* 73: 105–21.
des Bouvrie, S. (1990) *Women in Greek Tragedy*, Norwegian University Press (*SO* Suppl. 27).
de Ste. Croix, G.E.M. (1981) *The Class Struggle in the Ancient World*, London.
Dewald, C. (1981) 'Women and Culture in Herodotus' Histories' in H.P. Foley (ed.) *Reflections of Women in Antiquity*, New York: 91–125.
Dover, K.J. (1973) 'Classical Greek Attitudes to Sexual Behaviour' *Arethusa* 6: 59–73.
— (1978) *Greek Homosexuality*, London.
duBois, P. (1984) 'Sappho and Helen' in J. Peradotto and J.P. Sullivan (eds.) *Women in the Ancient World: the Arethusa Papers*, Albany: 95–105.
De Quesne, T. (1989) *Sappho of Lesbos: the Poems*, Thame.
Ehrenberg, V. (1943) *The People of Aristophanes: a Sociology of Old Attic Comedy*, London.
Engels, D. (1980) 'The Problem of Female Infanticide in the Greco-Roman World' *CPh* 75: 112–20.
— (1984) 'The Use of Historical Demography in Ancient History' *CQ* 34: 386–93.

Finley, M.I. (1981) 'The Elderly in Classical Antiquity' *G&R* 28: 156–71.

Fisher, N.R.E. (1992) *Hybris: A Study in the Values of Honour and Shame in Ancient Greece*, Warminster.

Fitton, J.W. (1970) 'That Was No Lady, That Was ...' *CQ* 20: 56–66.

Foley, H.P. (1981) 'The Concept of Women in Athenian Drama' in H.P. Foley (ed.) *Reflections of Women in Antiquity*, New York: 127–68.

Fowler, R.L. (1987) *The Nature of Early Greek Lyric: Three Preliminary Studies*, Toronto.

Gardner, J.F. (1989) 'Aristophanes and Male Anxiety — the Defence of the Oikos' *G&R* 36: 51–62.

Garland, R.S.J. (1990) *The Greek Way of Life: From Conception to Old Age*, Ithaca.

Geddes, A. (1975) 'The Philosophic Notion of Women in Antiquity' *Antichthon* 9: 35–40.

Golden, M. (1981) 'Demography and the Exposure of Girls at Athens' *Phoenix* 35: 316–31.

— (1984) 'Slavery and Homosexuality at Athens' *Phoenix* 38: 308–24.

— (1988) 'Did the Ancients Care When Their Children Died?' *G&R* 35: 152–63.

Gomme, A.W. (1925) 'The Position of Women in Athens in the Fifth and Fourth Centuries BC' *CPh* 20: 1–25 = (1937) *Essays in Greek History and Literature* 89–115.

Gould, J. (1980) 'Law, Custom and Myth: Aspects of the Social Position of Women in Classical Athens' *JHS* 100: 38–59.

Harris, E.M. (1990) 'Did the Athenians Regard Seduction as a Worse Crime than Rape?' *CQ* 40: 370–77.

— (1993) 'Apotimema: Athenian Terminology for Real Security in Leases and Dowry Agreements' *CQ* 43: 73–95.

Harris, W.V. (1982) 'The Theoretical Possibility of Extensive Infanticide in the Graeco-Roman World' *CQ* 32: 114–16.

Harvey, D. (1985) 'Women in Thucydides' *Arethusa* 18: 67–90.

Henderson, J. (1980) 'Lysistrate: the Play and its Themes' in J. Henderson (ed.) *Aristophanes: Essays in Interpretation*, *YClS* 26: 153–218.

Hodkinson, S. (1986) 'Land Tenure and Inheritance in Classical Sparta' *CQ* 36: 378–406.

Humphreys, S.C. (1974) 'The Nothoi of Kynosarges' *JHS* 94: 88–95.

— (1983) *The Family, Women and Death: Comparative Studies*, London.

Just, R. (1989) *Women in Athenian Life and Law*, London.

Katz, M.A. (1994) 'The Character of Tragedy: Women and the Greek Imagination' *Arethusa* 27: 81–103.

Keuls, E.C. (1985) *The Reign of the Phallus: Sexual Politics in Ancient Athens*, Berkeley.

Kunstler, B. (1987) 'Family Dynamics and Female Power in Ancient Sparta' in M. Skinner (ed.) *Rescuing Creusa: New Methodological Approaches to Women in Antiquity*: 31–48 (= *Helios* n.s. 13) Texas University Press.

Lacey, W.K. (1964) 'Thucydides II, 45, 2' *PCPhS* 10: 47–49.

— (1968) *The Family in Classical Greece*, London.

Lateiner, D. (1985) 'Limit, Propriety, and Transgression in the *Histories* of Herodotus' in *The Greek Historians: Literature and History. Papers Presented to A.E. Raubitschek*, Stanford: 87–100.

Lee, H.M. (1988) '*SIG*^{3} 802: Did Women Compete Against Men in Greek Athletic Festivals?' *Nikephoros: Zeitschrift für Sport und Kultur in Altertum* 1: 103–17.

Lefkowitz, M.R. (1983) 'Wives and Husbands' *G&R* 30: 31–47.

— (1986) *Women in Greek Myth*, Baltimore.

— and Fant, M.B. (1992) *Women's Life in Greece and Rome*, Baltimore, second edition.

Lloyd, G.E.R. (1983) *Science, Folklore and Ideology: Studies in the Life Sciences in Ancient Greece*, Cambridge.

Lloyd-Jones, H. (1975) *Females of the Species: Semonides on Women*, London.

MacDowell, M.D. (1976) 'Bastards as Athenian Citizens' *CQ* 26: 88–91.

— (1978) *The Law in Classical Athens*, London.

— (1989) 'The *Oikos* in Athenian Law' *CQ* 39: 10–21.

Macleod, C.W. (1982) 'Politics and the *Oresteia*' *JHS* 102: 124–44.

Millett, P. (1991) *Lending and Borrowing in Ancient Athens*, Cambridge.

Mulroy, D. (1992) *Early Greek Lyric Poetry, Translated with an Introduction and Commentary*, Ann Arbor.

Munson, R.V. (1988) 'Artemisia in Herodotos' *ClAnt* 7: 91–106.

Nielsen, T.N. et al (1989) 'Athenian Grave Monuments and Social Class' *GRBS* 30: 411–20.

Padel, R. (1983) 'Women: Model for Possession by Greek Daemons' in A. Cameron and A. Kurht (eds.) *Images of Women in Antiquity*, London: 3–19.

Page, D. (1955) *Sappho and Alcaeus: An Introduction to the Study of Ancient Lesbian Poetry*, Oxford.

Parker, H.N. (1993) 'Sappho Schoolmistress' *TAPhA* 123: 309–51.

Patterson, C.B. (1985) '"Not Worth the Rearing": The Causes of Infant Exposure in Ancient Greece' *TAPhA* 115: 103–23.

— (1987) '*Hai Attikai*: the Other Athenians' in M. Skinner (ed.) *Rescuing Creusa: New Methodological Approaches to Women in Antiquity*, Texas: 49–67.

— (1990) 'Those Athenian Bastards' *ClAnt* 9: 40–73.

— (1991) 'Marriage and the Married Woman in Athenian Law' in S.B. Pomeroy (ed.) *Women's History and Ancient History*, Chapel Hill: 48–72.

Podlecki, A.J. (1990) 'Could Women Attend the Theater in Ancient Athens? A Collection of Testimonia' *AncW* 21: 27–43.

Pomeroy, S. B. (1974) 'Feminism in Book V of Plato's Republic' *Apeiron* 8: 33–35.

— (1975) *Goddesses, Whores, Wives and Slaves*, New York.

— (1982) 'Charities for Greek Women' *Mnemosyne* 35: 115–35.

Pouilloux, J. (1954) *Recherches sur l'histoire et les cultes de Thasos*, Études Thasiennes III, Paris.

Redfield, J. (1977–78) 'The Women of Sparta' *CJ* 73: 146–61.

Richter, D.C. (1971) 'The Position of Women in Classical Athens' *CJ* 67: 1–8.

Robbins, E. (1980) '"Every Time I Look at You ...": Sappho Thirty-One' *TAPhA* 110: 255–61.

Rosivach, V.J. (1987) 'Execution by Stoning in Athens' *ClAnt* 6: 232–48.

Scanlon, T.F. (1988) '*Virgineum Gymnasium: Spartan Females and Early Greek Athletics*' in W.J. Raschke (ed.) *The Archaeology of the Olympics: The Olympics and Other Festivals in Antiquity*, Wisconsin: 185–216.

Schaps, D. (1975) 'Women in Greek Inheritance Law' *CQ* 25: 53–57.

— (1977) 'The Women Least Mentioned' *CQ* 27: 323–30.

— (1979) *Economic Rights of Women in Ancient Greece*, Edinburgh.

— (1982) 'The Women of Greece in Wartime' *CPh* 77: 193–213.

Seaford, R. (1990) 'The Imprisonment of Women in Greek Tragedy' *JHS* 110: 76–90.

Sealey, R. (1984) 'On Lawful Concubinage in Athens' *ClAnt* 3: 111–33.

Seltman, C. (1955) 'The Status of Women in Athens' *G&R* 2: 119–24.

— (1957) *Women in Antiquity*, London.

Shaw, M. (1975) 'The Female Intruder: Women in Fifth Century Drama' *CPh* 70: 255–68.

Snyder, J.M. (1989) *The Woman and the Lyre: Women Writers in Classical Greece and Rome*, Illinois.

— (1991) 'Public Occasion and Private Passion in the Lyrics of Sappho of Lesbos' in S.B. Pomeroy (ed.) *Women's History and Ancient History*, Chapel Hill: 1–19.

Sommerstein, A.H. (1989) 'Again Klytaimestra's Weapon' *CQ* 39: 296–301.
Stigers, E.S. (1981) 'Sappho's Private World' in H.P. Foley (ed.) *Reflections of Women in Antiquity*, New York: 45–61.
Strauss, B.S. (1990) '*Oikos/Polis*: Towards a Theory of Athenian Paternal Ideology 450–399 B.C.' in W.R. Connor et al. (eds.) *Aspects of Athenian Democracy* (*Classica et Medievalia Dissertationes* XI), Copenhagen: 101–27.
Stroud, R.S. (1971) 'Greek Inscriptions: Theozotides and the Athenian Orphans' *Hesperia* 40: 280–301.
Strubbe, J.H.M. (1991) '"Cursed be He that Moves my Bones"' in C.A. Faraone and D. Obbink (eds.) *Magika Hiera: Ancient Greek Magic and Religion*, New York: 33–59.
Sussman, L.S. (1984) 'Workers and Crones: Labor, Idleness and Gender Definition in Hesiod's Beehive' in J. Peradotto and J.P. Sullivan (eds.) *Women in the Ancient World: the Arethusa Papers*, Albany: 79–93.
Svenbro, J. (1993) *Phrasikleia: an Anthropology of Reading in Ancient Greece*, Cornell.
Thompson, W.E. (1967) 'The Marriage of First Cousins in Athenian Society' *Phoenix* 21: 273–82.
— (1972) 'Athenian Marriage Patterns: Remarriage' *ClAnt* 5: 211–25.
Tyrrell, W.B. (1984) *Amazons: a Study in Athenian Mythmaking*, Baltimore.
Venit, S.M. (1988) 'The Caput Hydria and Working Women in Classical Athens' *CW* 81: 265–72.
Walcot, P. (1984) 'Greek Attitudes Towards Women: the Mythological Evidence' *G&R* 31: 37–47.
— (1987) 'Plato's Mother and Other Terrible Women' *G&R* 34: 12–31.
Walker, S. (1983) 'Women and Housing in Classical Greece: the Archaeological Evidence' in A. Cameron and A. Kurht (eds.) *Images of Women in Antiquity*, London: 81–91.
Webster, T.B.L. (1969) *Everyday Life in Classical Athens*, London.
— (1973) *Athenian Culture and Society*, Berkeley.
Wender, D. (1973) 'Plato: Misogynist, Paedophile, and Feminist' *Arethusa* 6: 75–90.
Westlake, H.D. (1980) 'The *Lysistrata* and the War' *Phoenix* 34: 38–54.
Whitehead, D. (1990) 'The Lakonian Key' *CQ* 40: 267–68.
Wiedermann, T. (1983) 'Thucydides, Women and the Limits of Rational Analysis' *G&R* 30: 163–70.
Williams, D. (1983) 'Women on Athenian Vases: Problems of Interpretation' in A. Cameron and A. Kurht (eds.) *Images of Women in Antiquity*, London: 92–106.
Willetts, R.F. (1967) *The Law Code of Gortyn*, Berlin.
— (1977) *The Civilization of Ancient Crete*, London.
Winkler, J. (1981) 'Gardens of Nymphs: Public and Private in Sappho's Lyrics' in H.P. Foley (ed.) *Reflections of Women in Antiquity*, New York: 63–89.
— (1990) *The Constraints of Desire: the Anthropology of Sex and Gender in Ancient Greece*, New York.
Winnington-Ingram, R.P. (1948) 'Clytemnestra and the Vote of Athena' *JHS* 68: 130–47.
Wood, E.M. (1983) 'Agricultural Slavery in Classical Athens' *AJAH* 8: 1–47.
Zeitlin, F.I. (1981) 'Travesties of Gender and Genre in Aristophanes' Thesmophoriazousae' in H.P. Foley (ed.) *Reflections of Women in Antiquity*, New York: 169–217.
— (1984) 'The Dynamics of Misogyny: Myth and Mythmaking in the *Oresteia*' in J. Peradotto and J.P. Sullivan (eds.) *Women in the Ancient World: the Arethusa Papers*, Albany: 159–94.

Index of Ancient Sources

Numbers here refer to documents. The texts used in translations are given in brackets after each author (editor(s), publisher, date). Abbreviations used for authors and titles are given in square brackets [Aeschyl.], [*Agam.*].

General Index

Numbers refer to documents and their introductions. For ancient authors, see also the index of ancient sources.

TABLE I

The Alkmeonidai

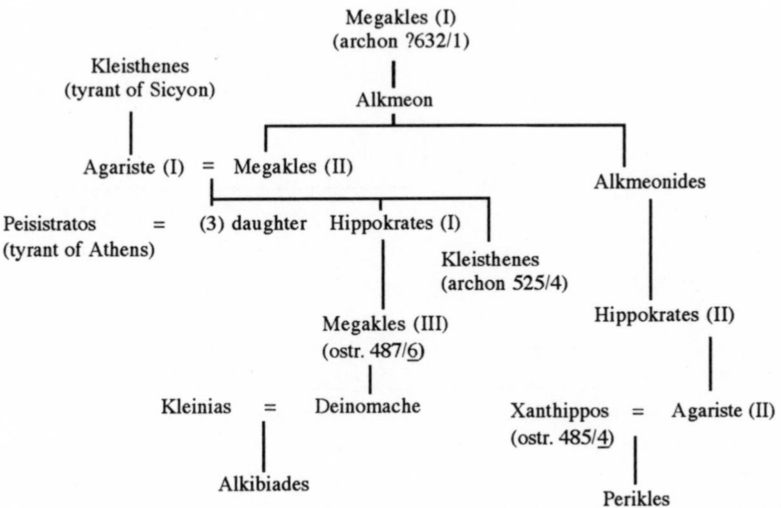

Adapted from Davies (1971) Table I

TABLE II

The Family of Peisistratos

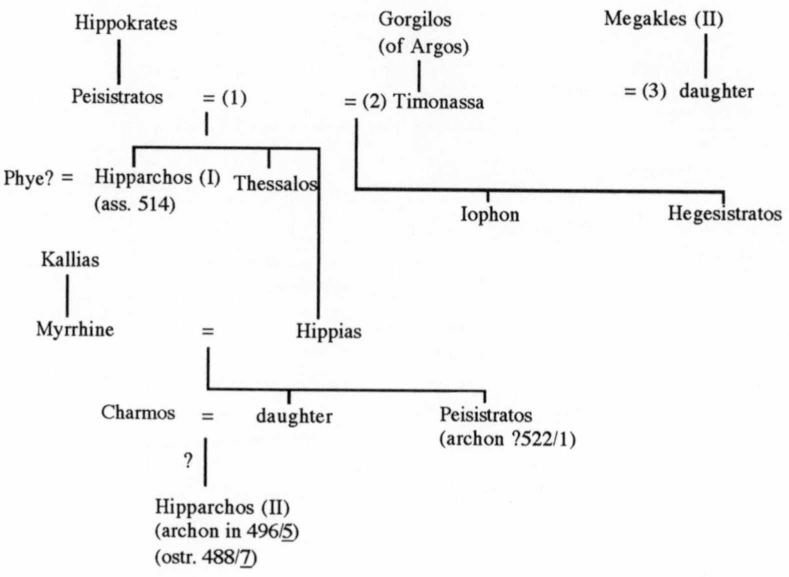

Adapted from Davis (1971) Table I

TABLE III

The Philaidai

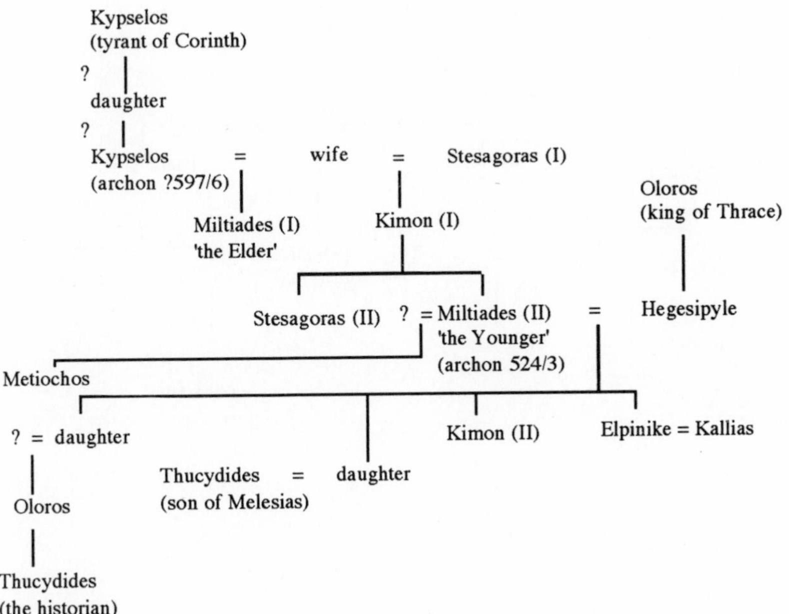

Adapted from Davies (1971) Table I

TABLE IV

The Family of Kleomenes

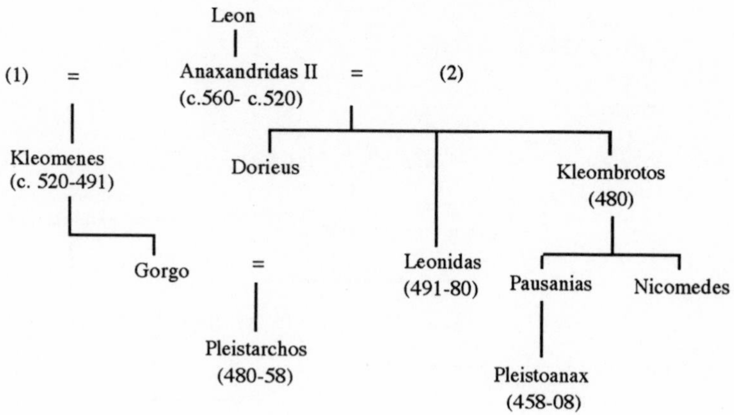

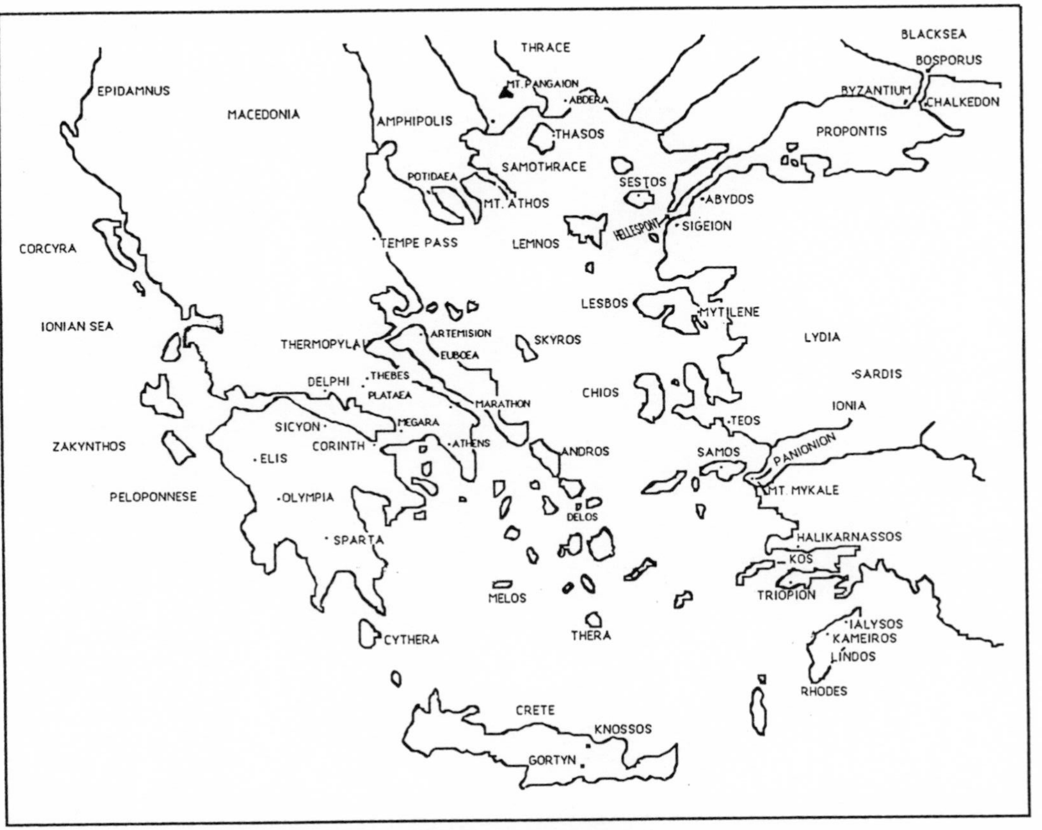

Map I The Greek World

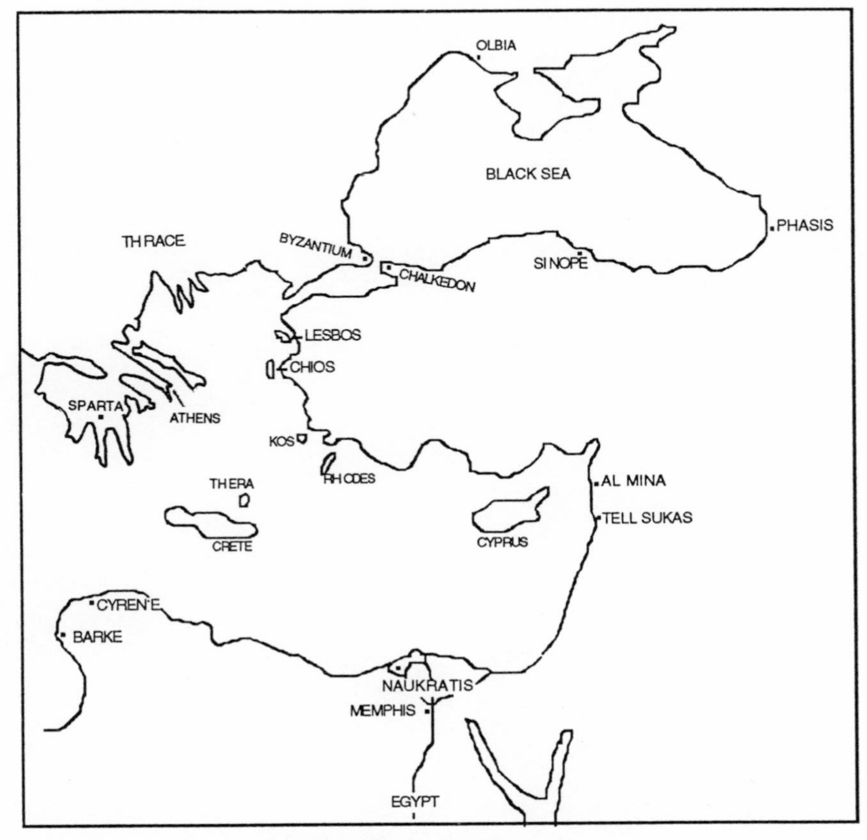

Map II The Greeks in the East

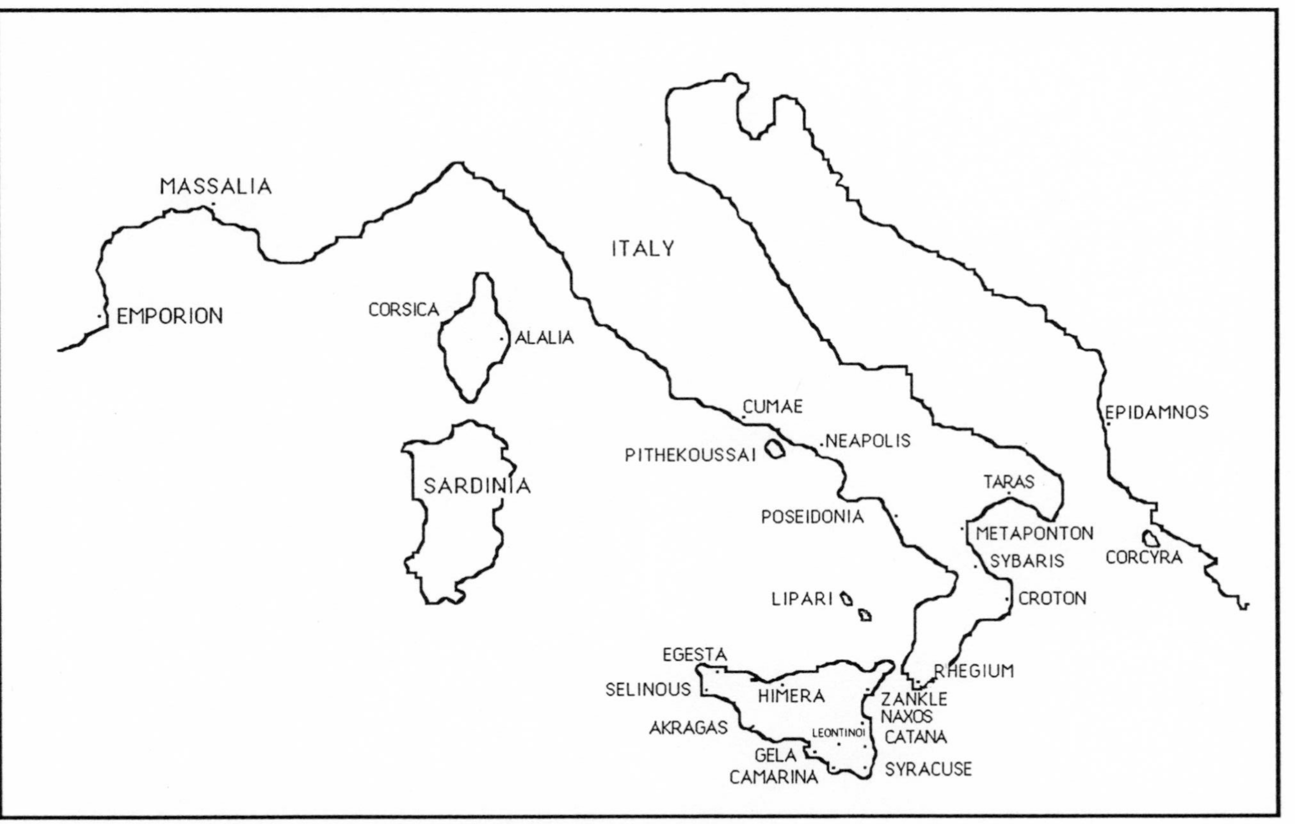

Map III The Greeks in the West

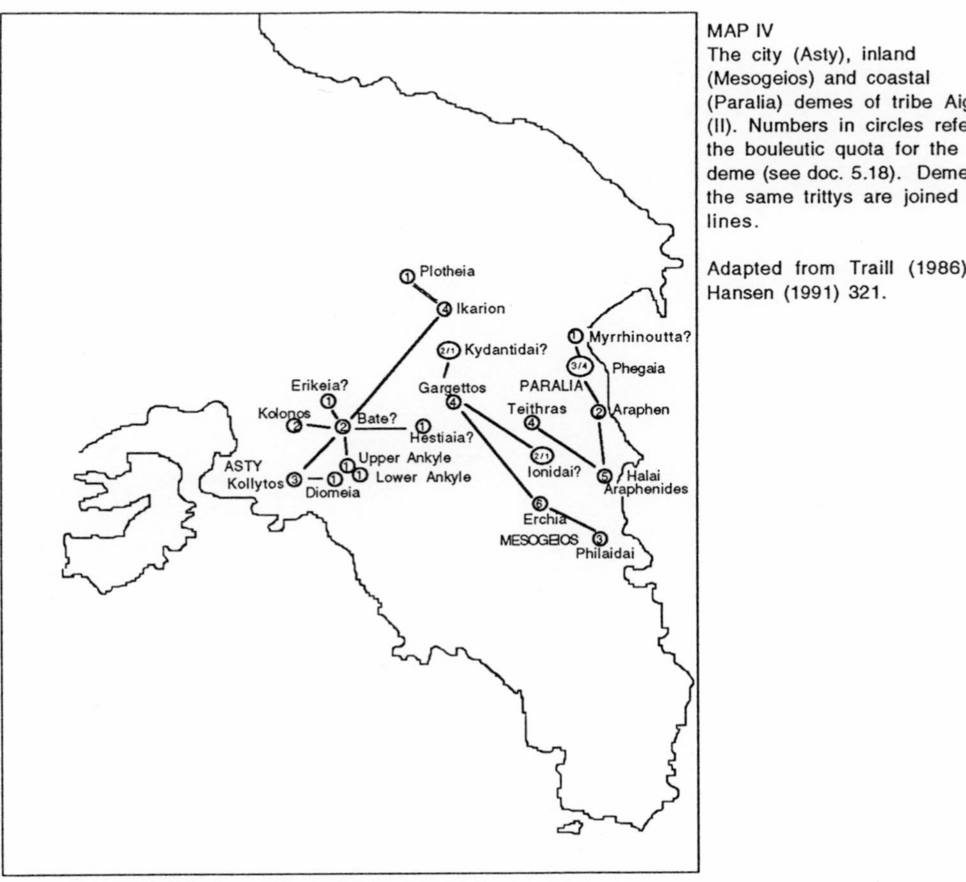

MAP IV
The city (Asty), inland (Mesogeios) and coastal (Paralia) demes of tribe Aigeis (II). Numbers in circles refer to the bouleutic quota for the deme (see doc. 5.18). Demes of the same trittys are joined by lines.

Adapted from Traill (1986), Hansen (1991) 321.

Map IV Attica and the Demes of Aigeis (II)